Real Estate Economics

Real Estate Economics: A point-to-point handbook introduces the main tools and concepts of real estate (RE) economics. It covers areas such as the relation between RE and the macro-economy, RE finance, investment appraisal, taxation, demand and supply, development, market dynamics and price bubbles, and price estimation. It balances housing economics with commercial property economics, and pays particular attention to the issue of property dynamics and bubbles – something very topical in the aftermath of the US house-price collapse that precipitated the global crisis of 2008.

This textbook takes an international approach and introduces the student to the necessary 'toolbox' of models required in order to properly understand the mechanics of real estate. It combines theory, technique, real-life cases, and practical examples, so that in the end the student is able to:

- read and understand most RE papers published in peer-reviewed journals;
- make sense of the RE market (or markets); and
- contribute positively to the preparation of economic analyses of RE assets and markets soon after joining any company or other organization involved in RE investing, appraisal, management, policy, or research.

The book should be particularly useful to third-year students of economics who may take up RE or urban economics as an optional course, to postgraduate economics students who want to specialize in RE economics, to graduates in management, business administration, civil engineering, planning, and law who are interested in RE, as well as to RE practitioners and to students reading for RE-related professional qualifications.

Nicholas G. Pirounakis is Professor of Economics at the American College of Greece (Deree College). He also works as an economic analyst/consultant, and economic writer and journalist.

Routledge Advanced Texts in Economics and Finance

1. **Financial Econometrics**
   Peijie Wang

2. **Macroeconomics for Developing Countries 2nd edition**
   Raghbendra Jha

3. **Advanced Mathematical Economics**
   Rakesh Vohra

4. **Advanced Econometric Theory**
   John S. Chipman

5. **Understanding Macroeconomic Theory**
   John M. Barron, Bradley T. Ewing and Gerald J. Lynch

6. **Regional Economics**
   Roberta Capello

7. **Mathematical Finance: Core Theory, Problems and Statistical Algorithms**
   Nikolai Dokuchaev

8. **Applied Health Economics**
   Andrew M. Jones, Nigel Rice, Teresa Bago d'Uva and Silvia Balia

9. **Information Economics**
   Urs Birchler and Monika Bütler

10. **Financial Econometrics (Second Edition)**
    Peijie Wang

11. **Development Finance**
    Debates, dogmas and new directions
    Stephen Spratt

12. **Culture and Economics**
    On values, economics and international business
    Eelke de Jong

13. **Modern Public Economics Second Edition**
    Raghbendra Jha

14. **Introduction to Estimating Economic Models**
    Atsushi Maki

15. **Advanced Econometric Theory**
    John Chipman

16. **Behavioral Economics**
    Edward Cartwright

17. **Essentials of Advanced Macroeconomic Theory**
    Ola Olsson

18. **Behavioural Economics and Finance**
    Michelle Baddeley

19. **Applied Health Economics (Second Edition)**
    Andrew M. Jones, Nigel Rice, Teresa Bago d'Uva and Silvia Balia

20. **Real Estate Economics**
    A point-to-point handbook
    Nicholas G. Pirounakis

Real Estate Economics

A point-to-point handbook

Nicholas G. Pirounakis

Routledge
Taylor & Francis Group
LONDON AND NEW YORK

First published 2013
by Routledge
2 Park Square, Milton Park, Abingdon, Oxon OX14 4RN

Simultaneously published in the USA and Canada
by Routledge
711 Third Avenue, New York, NY 10017

Routledge is an imprint of the Taylor & Francis Group, an informa business

British Library Cataloguing in Publication Data
A catalogue record for this book is available from the British Library

Library of Congress Cataloging-in-Publication Data
Pirounakis, Nicholas G., 1955–
Real estate economics : a point-to-point handbook / by Nicholas G. Pirounakis.
p. cm. – (Routledge advanced texts in economics and finance)
Includes bibliographical references and index.
1. Real estate business. 2. Real estate investment. 3. Urban economics.
4. Commercial real estate. 5. Residential real estate. I. Title.
HD1375.P656 2012
333.33–dc23 2012012458

ISBN: 978-0-415-67634-2 (hbk)
ISBN: 978-0-415-67635-9 (pbk)
ISBN: 978-0-203-09464-8 (ebk)

Typeset in Times New Roman
by Cenveo Publisher Services

MIX
Paper from responsible sources
FSC® C004839

Printed and bound by CPI Group (UK) Ltd, Croydon, CR0 4YY

In memory of my parents,
George and Anastasia,
who taught me to love book-reading.

To my economist wife, Maria,
and my son, George.

My thanks to
Odysseus Katsaitis and Annie Triantafyllou,
colleagues at the Economics Department of
the American College of Greece,
for their helpful comments
on parts of the manuscript.

My thanks to
David Donnison and Duncan Maclennan,
for their support and guidance
during my PhD studies
at the University of Glasgow.

Contents

Figures

Tables

Boxes

Abbreviations

A-REIT	Australian REIT
ARM	adjustable-rate mortgage
AVM	automated valuation model
BC	budget constraint
BL	budget line
BPF	British Property Federation
CBD	central business district
CDO	collateralized debt obligation
CDS	credit-default swap
CES	constant elasticity of substitution
CFA	Chartered Financial Analyst
CG	capital gain
CGRR	capital gain rate of return
CGT	capital-gains tax
CML	Council of Mortgage Lenders
CMO	collateralized mortgage obligation
CP	commercial property
CPPI	commercial property price index
CRRA	constant relative risk aversion
CSAM	capital stock adjustment model
DCF	discounted cash flow
DCLG	Department for Communities and Local Government
DiPW	DiPasquale–Wheaton (model)
DSE	debt service expense
DWL	deadweight loss
EC	European Commission
ECB	European Central Bank
ECR	equity cap rate
EDHEC	École de Hautes Études Commerciales du Nord
EHP	entire holding period
ER	economic rent
EtY	equated yield
EvY	equivalent yield
FBI	Fiscale Beleggingsinstelling
FCEH	final consumption expenditure by households
FHA	Federal Housing Administration

FHFA	Federal Housing Finance Agency
FHLB	Federal Home Loan Bank(s)
FHLMC	Federal Home Loan Mortgage Corporation (Freddie Mac)
FI	financial institution(s)
FNMA	Federal National Mortgage Association (Fannie Mae)
FRB	Federal Reserve Bank
FRB IMO	Federal Reserve Board Index of Manufacturing Output
FSA	Financial Services Authority
FTA	Financial Times Actuaries
FTSE	Financial Times Stock Exchange Group
FV	future value
FX	foreign exchange
GDP	gross domestic product
GFCF	gross fixed capital formation
GIS	geographical information system
GIPS	global investment performance standards
GNMA	Government National Mortgage Association (Ginnie Mae)
GSE	government-sponsored enterprise
GVA	gross value added
HECM	home equity conversion mortgage
HELOAN	home equity loan
HELOC	home equity line of credit
HI	Herfindahl Index
HPF	hedonic price function
HPI	house price index
HPRR	holding period rate of return
HUD	(Department of) Housing and Urban Development
HWE	housing wealth effect
IAI	industrial absorption indicator
IC	indifference curve
IMF	International Monetary Fund
IPD	Investment Property Databank
IRR	internal rate of return
ISM PMI	Institute for Supply Management Purchasing Managers' Index
IVG	International Valuation Guidance
JCHS	Joint Center of Housing Studies (of Harvard University)
k	capitalization rate
LIFT	Low-cost Initiative for First-Time buyers
LP	Limited Partnership
LTV	loan-to-value
LVT	land-value tax
M	multiplier
MBS	mortgage-backed security
MC	marginal cost
MID	mortgage interest deductibility
MIG	mortgage indemnity guarantee
MIP	mortgage insurance premium
MIRAS	mortgage-interest relief at source

Mo.C	mortgage constant
MPC	marginal propensity to consume
MPP	marginal physical product
MR	marginal revenue
MRA	multiple regression analysis
MRS	marginal rate of substitution
MRT	marginal rate of transformation
MRTS	marginal rate of technical substitution
MS	mortgage securitization
MSA	metropolitan statistical area
MWRR	money-weighted rate of return
NAV	net asset value
NPI	NCREIF Property Index
NAIOP	National Association of Industrial and Office Properties
NAREIT	National Association of REITs
NBER	National Bureau of Economic Research
NCREIF	National Council of Real Estate Investment Fiduciaries
NERA	National Economic Research Associates
NNEG	No Negative Equity Guarantee
NOI	net operating income
NPV	net present value
NRMLA	National Reverse Mortgage Lenders Association
NVR	natural vacancy rate
ODPM	Office of the Deputy Prime Minister
OECD	Organisation for Economic Co-operation and Development
OEIC	open-ended investment company
OFHEO	Office of Federal Housing Enterprise Oversight
OHW	out of housing wealth
PI	price index
PIA	Property Industry Alliance
PILC	permanent income–life cycle
plc	Public Limited Company
PPP	Purchasing Power Party
PR	planning restriction(s)
PREA	Pension Real Estate Association
PrERE	Private Equity Real Estate
PRUPIM	Prudential Property Investment Managers Ltd
PSID	panel study of income dynamics
PUT	property unit trust
PV	present value
RCG	rate of capital gain
RD	research and development
RE	real estate
R_e	expected return
REIT	real estate investment trust
RIRR	rental income rate of return
RMBS	residential mortgage-backed security
RMD	residential mortgage debt

RMMI	reverse mortgage market index
RPI	retail price index
RPPI	residential property price index
RREEF	Rosenberg Real Estate Equity Funds
RRR	required rate of return
RTR	rate of total return
SDLT	Stamp Duty Land Tax
SEC	Securities and Exchange Commission
SHIP	Safe Home Income Plan
SIIC	Sociétés d'Investissement Immobilier Cotées
SPAR	sale price appraisal ratio
SPN	Scottish Property Network
SPV	special purpose vehicle
TE	transfer earnings
TEGoVA	The European Group of Valuers' Association
TPC	total production cost
TR	total revenue
TRR	total rate of return
UC	user-cost
TWRR	time-weighted rate of return
UCIT	Undertaking for Collective Investment in Transferable Securities
UN	United Nations
VAT	value-added tax
VR	vacancy rate
WFA	Wells Fargo Associates
W-I-R-I-S	work–innovate–risk–invest–save
ε_p	price elasticity
ε_s	elasticity of substitution

Preface

This textbook introduces students to the main tools and concepts of real estate (RE) economics. It covers areas such as the relation between RE and the macro-economy, RE finance, investment appraisal, taxation, demand and supply, development, market dynamics and price bubbles, and price indices. It deals with both residential and commercial RE. It does not discuss the whole sweep of urban economics, except in relation to certain aspects (e.g., the land-use pattern; the bid-rent, or bid-price, curve) that impinge directly on RE assets and markets. Nor does it discuss housing policy or social housing. It focuses, that is, on market-related processes.

Being an introductory book under a length constraint, it does not even cover all topics relevant to RE economics. As a result, it does not do justice to all issues discussed or pursued in the context of ongoing (and exciting) RE economics research. Interesting areas have been left out, like household inter-temporal choice between housing and non-housing consumption, tenure choice, search theories, RE derivatives and options, the econometrics of building cycles, or what the Basle II and Solvency II frameworks mean for RE investments by banks and insurance companies, respectively.

But it does attempt to offer a useful introduction to the main areas of RE economics, and does so in a way that bridges a perceived gap between elementary introductions to the subject and more demanding treatises. To provide a background to the discussion in many parts of the book, a refresher chapter is included on the mathematical and statistical techniques and economic concepts that are utilized in RE research. In the same vein, wherever in the text some new or extra bit of mathematics is introduced, this is done with a lot of attention to detail – a kind of 'spoon-feeding', if one may excuse the term. Crucially, the book tries to balance housing economics with commercial property economics, and pays particular attention to the issue of property dynamics and bubbles – something very topical in the aftermath of the US house-price collapse that precipitated the global crisis of 2008 onwards.

The intended readership is third-year undergraduate students of economics who may take up RE economics as an elective course, postgraduate economics students who want to specialize in RE or urban economics, graduates in management, business administration, civil engineering, planning, or law who wish to look at RE from an economist's perspective; and also students reading for RE-related professional qualifications. Non-economics majors, however, need to have a good grasp of basic economics and of finite mathematics (the latter requirement is obviously met in the case of civil engineers at least!), while knowledge of differential calculus and intermediate statistics (up to the level of multiple regression) would help. Nevertheless, this is not an econometrics text, and, while it presents the conclusions of many econometric applications, it does not analyse the methodologies involved. The idea is to make most of this book accessible even to those who have a weak (although not *very* weak!) background in mathematics or even economics, while retaining its usefulness for more advanced students.

Consequently the book tries to be more like a handbook than a reader; to allow conclusions to be drawn, wherever possible; to avoid being unnecessarily theoretical or long-winded but also to indicate contentious points or areas where further research is underway or needed; to cater both to economists and RE practitioners; to answer questions like ‘how or why is this done?’, ‘what is it I should know?’; to stimulate critical thinking; and to combine theory, technique, real-life case-studies, and practical examples (many of which can be replicated in a spreadsheet program) – all of this so that, in the end, a student will be able to

- read and understand a majority of RE papers published in peer-reviewed journals;
- make sense of the RE market (or markets); and
- contribute positively to the preparation of economic analyses of RE assets and markets soon after joining any company or other organization (including government agencies or departments) involved in RE investing, appraisal, management, policy, or research.

It is up to the reader to judge whether the book succeeds as intended.

1 Real estate (RE)

An overview of the sector

Main sections

Having gone through this chapter, a student should be able to

1 Define RE and list its main components.
2 Distinguish between 'derived' and 'authentic' demand for RE.
3 Explain how RE subsectors (or submarkets) are created.
4 List and discuss RE's main characteristics.
5 Discuss the main implications of those characteristics for (a) a cityscape, (b) financial markets and rates, and (c) the GDP.
6 Advance reasons for studying RE economics.

1.1 Definition of real estate (RE)

What is real estate (RE)? It is a name given to land, buildings, and legal rights over immovable property,[1] especially when they can be priced for possible sale in an actual or potential market.[2] Usually such a price reflects *derived demand*. The latter originates from demand for the physical good or service that is or can be produced, or sold, on a piece of land or in buildings. For example, residential land is demanded for the dwellings it can support; the dwellings, in turn, are usually demanded for the flow of 'housing services' (including access to work or amenities) they can generate. Agrarian land is demanded for the crop one can grow on it. Retailers demand sites as gateways to customers (see Chapter 6).

In some cases (e.g., landscapes of pristine beauty, conservation land, or monuments), land is demanded as is, i.e., for itself rather than as a means to an end. This type of land, however, is often subject to protection (meaning that its current use becomes legally exclusive of all others), and can easily become priceless too, even though one can still evaluate it in terms of opportunity cost. Of course, any such evaluation would almost certainly result in lower opportunity cost estimates than the value of land in its current state: that of an exceptionally beautiful landscape or as location of a monument, like the Acropolis of Athens, England's Stonehenge, the Taj Mahal in India, or – maybe! – Elvis Presley's Graceland mansion in Memphis, Tennessee.

1.2 RE subsectors (or submarkets)

Derived demand for RE is the rule rather than the exception. Its existence is one way whereby RE *subsectors* or *submarkets* are created.[3] As an example, agrarian land competes with residential land, and the latter with commercial (offices, hotels, retail outlets) and industrial (including warehousing), since all these different land uses are defined by different goods or services, which, moreover, sell at different prices. A structure of land prices is thus created that is very much determined by the highest price that can be paid for the 'best' land use.

A second way whereby subsectors or submarkets come about involves the specific characteristics of land (its location, its features and properties, and its relative scarcity) and of the general environment – which means that even within the same broad land use (e.g., residential), different prices and different subsectors or submarkets will emerge (e.g., 'good' versus 'bad' neighbourhoods). A third way relates to the characteristics of buildings, giving rise, for example, to the markets for new versus old buildings. A fourth way is generated by the diversity of legally recognized property rights pertaining to RE assets. Examples of such rights are ownership versus renting versus in-between[4] tenures or *freehold* versus *leasehold* (see Box 1.1). All four ways interact, creating a fluid plethora of RE subsectors or submarkets.

In this universe, the broadest possible distinction is between housing and non-housing RE. Both are extremely important. Both interact. But of course the largest part of the so-called urban environment is made up of housing, whether rented or owner-occupied. The sum of housing-related transactions constitutes the housing market.[5]

Box 1.1 Freehold versus leasehold

Freehold (or *fee simple* or *fee simple absolute*) is the right to own land in perpetuity (IVG, 2003).

Leasehold is the right to hold or use property for a fixed period of time at a given price, without transfer of ownership, on the basis of a *lease* contract (www.investorwords.com).

A *lease* is a contract arrangement in which rights of use and possession are conveyed from a property's title owner (called the landlord, or *lessor*) in return for a promise by another (called a tenant, or *lessee*) to pay rents as prescribed by the lease (IVG, 2003).

> In the UK residential sector, a lessee who buys the freehold of the house he/she has been renting from a lessor achieves *enfranchisement.* So do lessees of flats who collectively buy the freehold of their building. The process creates a *marriage value* (an increase in the value of the property resulting from the joining of the freehold and leasehold interests), which under law is split between landlord and (enfranchised) tenant(s). Marriage value is also created from the granting of a lease extension. (For details and analysis, see www.lease-advice.org.)

Because housing submarkets obviously exist, some authors have gone as far as to ask whether it is legitimate or meaningful to speak of a single, homogenized market in housing at all (Alhashimi and Dwyer, 2004). This is perhaps too extreme; by analogy, one shouldn't speak of the market for chocolate, because there are different brands and kinds of chocolate. It is more fruitful, and also more helpful to policy makers, to determine why and how housing submarkets arise in the first place, or whether they persist over time. To this end, an interesting question is whether the definition of a housing submarket should be limited to instances where obviously different dwellings (in terms of location, the physical and socio-economic environment, and/or structural attributes) have different prices, or should be extended to instances where the same, or a 'standardized', dwelling, or an attribute of a dwelling, is found at different prices (see Robinson, 1979: 33–7; Jones et al., 2002; Pryce and Evans, 2007).[6]

Not only do housing submarkets exist (see Munro and Maclennan, 1987), but, moreover, they persist over time (Jones et al., 2002). This is not a trivial conclusion. For, in theory, price differences could be eliminated, and submarkets vanish, if developers built in high-price areas and households relocated to low-price ones (Jones et al., 2002: 3). Since this is not happening, housing submarkets can be interpreted as a measure of housing market imperfections, relating to things such as search and transaction costs, moving inertia, insufficient information, and inelastic supply, to name but some of standard economic theory's culprits. Such 'imperfections', however, may be inevitable, impossible to remove, and even desirable: for example, households of a certain social class may be more than willing to pay a premium for a 'standardized' dwelling in order to congregate away from other groups (see Kain and Quigley, 1970; Maclennan and Tu, 1996).

1.3 The location factor

The defining characteristic of RE is that it is *specific to location.* Again, location is usually demanded as a means to an end, but very often it is also demanded for its own sake – without in fact becoming priceless. For example, when one says, 'I like this neighbourhood because I grew up here', how can one separate location from what location gives one in terms of feelings or social contacts? Is this a case of demand for the item or of derived demand for what the item is associated with? In truth, the one is subsumed under the other, and an attempt at separation would be tantamount to hair-splitting, with little, if any, practical significance or implications.

What is more important is that location imparts a monopoly element, i.e., an element of 'uniqueness' or 'exclusiveness', to any particular piece of RE. The monopoly element can be weak, as when many different locations convey fundamentally the same cost (or revenue, or utility)[7] advantage of access to work, amenities, feelings and social contacts, markets, suppliers, or clienteles; or, alternatively, it can be strong, as when a small number of locations (or one, at the limit) confer such an advantage.

Still, in the vast majority of cases, a RE market cannot be truly monopolized, even though any particular location can be or is so. The reason is that there usually are substitute locations to choose from; possibly at a lower land cost to the interested user, but at a higher transport cost or at a higher opportunity cost of foregone revenue or utility. Thus, *the RE market is a typical example of monopolistic competition* (many buyers and sellers, each seller offering more-or-less different versions of fundamentally the same good, and, therefore, extensive – even though not perfect – *substitutability* between RE assets).

Whether weak or strong, the monopoly element exists, and is the decisive factor making the supply of land inelastic. In turn, inelastic land supply implies that increases in demand for RE will result in higher than otherwise RE prices (see Box 1.2, Figure 1.1, and Box 1.3). It also implies that price rises in RE are, most of the time, demand-, rather than supply-, driven.

Box 1.2 The supply of land is inelastic

Land's inelasticity of supply means that on any given geographical area the percentage change in the quantity of land supplied is smaller than the percentage change in land price; if no amount of change in price causes the quantity of land supplied to change, then inelasticity is perfect, and the supply of land in a typical price–quantity diagram graphs as a vertical line (see Figure 1.1).

Perfect inelasticity of land supply would occur only in two cases: (a) over land as a whole, i.e., all the land in a country or even on the planet; (b) over land at a specific location. However, the supply of land in a given area or for a specific use will usually be imperfectly inelastic, since, given the 'right' price, more land can be attracted away from other areas or uses. As a special case, improvements in high-rise building technology may increase the elasticity of land supply even in a vacant plot, i.e., a specific location. ('Vacant' here also means a plot where a standing building has exhausted its economic value.)

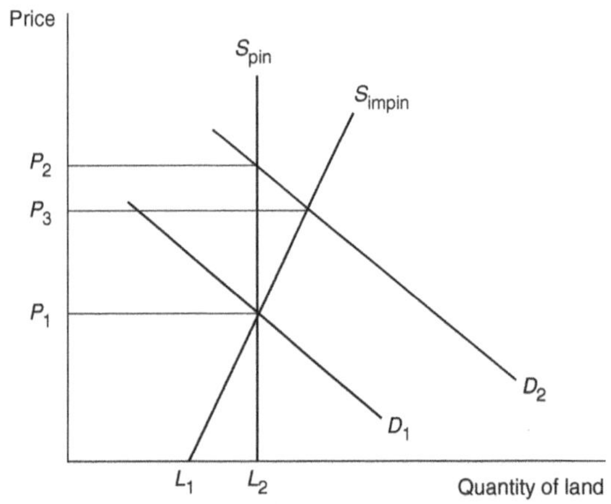

Figure 1.1 An increase in demand from D_1 to D_2 causes price to rise from P_1 to P_2 when supply is perfectly inelastic (S_{pin}), but only to P_3 if supply is imperfectly inelastic (S_{impin}).

In Figure 1.1, the horizontal intercepts L_1 and L_2 mean that in a certain area or location, some 'land' (in the form of one or more plots, or one or more buildings) will still exist even at a zero price. In the case of imperfectly inelastic land supply (S_{impin}, with a horizontal intercept L_1), subsequent increases in quantity supplied as price rises come about through more land being attracted away from other uses, or through existing land being more intensively utilized. In the case of perfectly inelastic land supply (S_{pin}, with a horizontal intercept L_2), no rise in price can create (or make available) more land.

Box 1.3 The importance of land: an example

In the USA '[b]etween 1975 and 2006 [land accounted], on average, for 36 percent of the value of the aggregate housing stock. Over the same period, the inflation-adjusted price of residential land nearly quadrupled, while the real price of structures increased cumulatively by only 33 percent. At business cycle frequencies the price of land is more than three times as volatile as the price of structures.'

(Davis and Heathcote, 2007: 3)

1.4 Location and 'authentic' versus 'derived' demand for RE

Because of the location factor, it would be hasty to assume that all demand for RE is fully derived; instead, it is quite likely that in many pieces of RE total demand for the item includes a non-derived (i.e., authentic) element, for example when the built structure and/or the location in question have emotional, social, or 'brand' value. Residential RE is the strongest example. On occasion, some types of commercial RE, mainly offices, may also give rise to 'authentic' demand, for example if having an office in a certain location and/or at a certain building adds to a firm's reputation.

In fact, the relatively large extent of authenticity in residential RE demand is one factor that sets this kind of RE apart from other kinds (e.g., commercial, industrial, and agrarian), even though standard economic models of residential RE demand relate the latter to distance from work or amenities (see Chapters 7 and 10); any authentic element in this demand (for the item itself rather than for any economic benefits with which the item may be associated) is usually subsumed under the notion of utility. In fairness to the economic profession though, it must be stressed that the necessities of practical life do tend to make most households choose where to live on the basis of mostly 'mundane' considerations, like house price in relation to income, proximity to employment, transport costs, and suchlike.

In the case of owner-occupation, another 'mundane' consideration is the relationship between a homeowner's outstanding mortgage debt and the market price of the property. A large debt relative to price may actually 'pin' a homeowner down when, perhaps, he or she might be better off moving. Hence an important issue that often arises in relation to owner-occupation in particular is whether, and to what extent, it affects the *mobility of labour* (see Chapter 3). This is an important consideration in its own right, as it impacts on the functioning of the labour market and, possibly, on the extent of unemployment. It may also be that residential owner-occupiers' 'authentic' demand for location is frequently stronger than residential renters' 'authentic' demand for location. If true, this would also reduce the mobility of owner-occupiers relative to that of renters.

Be that as it may, most human activities, particularly productive ones, take part on or in pieces of RE. This is what makes it important and worthwhile to study.

1.5 Other characteristics of RE – and wider interactions

In addition to a fixed location, there are other characteristics of RE that merit notice. One is *durability* – a long physical life span. Another is the *high construction cost* of buildings. Land as ground is 'there'; it is not destroyed easily, although soil erosion and pollution are problems in many parts of the world. Land can be upgraded or improved too – but then it is more proper to consider such improvements as capital additions to land, and separate from the latter. Buildings tend to last a long time (although not as long as the ground does). Their cost of construction (or renovation) is high relative to the prices of most other products – or to average income. Construction takes place on land, and land is in short supply at any given location – a fact that raises its price significantly once there is a demand, or demand increases, for the plot. High construction and land costs make for a rather expensive final product (the built structure), at least in relation to most incomes.

Yet another characteristic of RE is that it constitutes *wealth*: it is durable, expensive, relatively scarce (on any given location), and can function as an asset, i.e., it can command a relatively high price, often an income (e.g., an actual rent), and possibly a capital gain if it is sold. It thus tends to be readily comparable with other assets (stocks, bonds, money, and other physical capital) that are capable of commanding returns and/or a capital gain – and then its attractiveness goes beyond its use as a consumption item, and extends to its potential as investment (see Chapter 5).

Also, residential RE, being the most important asset that most people possess or go for, can be a key factor in determining a given generation's well-being, the life-chances of the next generation (who stand to inherit RE wealth), the degree of financial security for older persons (whose pensions may be insufficient), and people's willingness to save more in order to acquire RE. The last point – about saving – is important: a higher savings rate can lead to more investment – therefore greater prosperity in the future for society – and may help finance social security systems that are hit by adverse demographics.

The six facts mentioned about RE – location specificity, inelasticity of land supply, pivotal place in human activities, durability, high construction costs, and the wealth feature – have, alone or, usually, in combination, three wide-ranging implications:

1 Once a building is erected, it helps define the landscape, particularly a cityscape, for many a year; other construction must take its existence into account – and by that are meant questions like: What is the current use of the building? Is it wise (i.e., profitable, or maybe 'functional') for a new building near this one to be dedicated to the same use? How far away from, or how near to, this one must a new building be? This way, a chain reaction is created, with repercussions spreading all over an urban area. For instance, if the building is a shanty, the 'final' outcome of its existence may be the creation of a shanty town or a downgraded neighbourhood. Or, if the building is an expensive single house with garden, the area may in time grow or change into a luxury suburb; or if it is *already* a luxury suburb, its character as such will become more pronounced. Thus, *RE affects – indeed is the most important part of – urban structure and form.*
2 The time horizon for *investment* in buildings (or other land-bound construction) is long-term, and the investment itself is usually of substantial size. In shanty towns, such

'investment' betrays a commitment to gain a foothold in the city, with all sorts of social, political, environmental, and labour-market repercussions. In free-market developed countries, such investment (more properly called so in this context), whether in the form of new construction, or renovation, or in the form of purchase of second-hand buildings, and on account of its necessarily large size, typically requires substantial monetary outlays.

This means that, one way or another, sooner or later, long-term financial instruments like mortgage loans come into play, whose interest rates interact, however, with those of other long- and even short-term financial instruments (if the wider financial market is efficient enough). Thus, *RE affects – and is affected by – financial markets through interaction between mortgage and other interest rates and yields*, which then affect the entire economy. However, the interaction between mortgage rates and other rates is not the only interface between RE and financial markets. RE is itself an asset, and as a result *RE returns interact directly with returns on other assets* (see Chapter 5). For example, rents and the prospects of capital gains on a piece of RE compete with dividends and possible capital gains on a company's stock, or with the yield on a government bond.

3 Because mortgage interest rates affect the extent to which loans will be taken up in order to finance investment in RE (see Chapter 4), they affect the extent of such investment (see Chapter 3). The latter affects GDP directly and materially, while the ups and downs of (real) GDP (hence of real incomes) tend to affect investment in RE (whether physical investment – as in the case of new construction – or financial investment[8] – as in the case of buying existing properties). Also, the wealth aspect of RE, particularly residential RE, is thought to affect consumption spending – the biggest component of GDP: as house values appreciate, owner-occupying households are supposed to feel more confident about spending more on current consumption (see Chapter 3). This is called the *housing wealth effect*.

So, in addition to RE interacting with financial markets, RE and GDP also interact, first through RE investment flows, second through the asset, or wealth, feature of RE (see Figure 1.2).

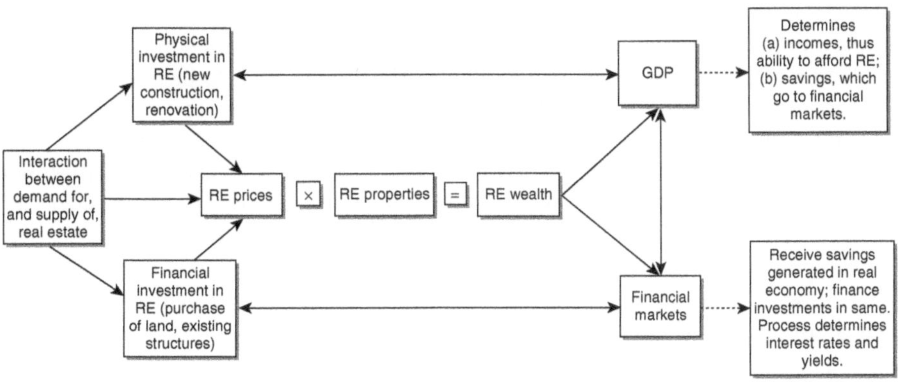

Figure 1.2 From RE demand and supply to GDP and financial markets.

The list of RE characteristics goes on:

- RE is not a homogeneous product: RE pieces differ from one another if for no other reason than location – and obvious additional differences abound of course. Nevertheless, any RE class can be treated at a general level, depending on the purpose of the analysis. Take *generic* housing, for example; if the purpose is to construct a demand model for housing in general, looking at those factors that *broadly* determine such demand, then the specific characteristics of each and every house – or household – can be ignored.
- The very heterogeneity of RE makes obtaining accurate information about different pieces of RE particularly difficult. Thus, pricing RE is partly guesswork and only partly science, especially where large databases on RE physical characteristics do not exist or are inadequate.
- Together, heterogeneity (due to location and other differentiating attributes), imperfect information, substitutability between RE assets, and (typically) large numbers of buyers and sellers define the nature of the RE market as a monopolistically competitive one.
- Because of RE's effect on urban structure and form, and also because of its wealth aspect, RE is heavily regulated by government, with zoning and building regulations, solvency and valuation rules involving the investment of financial institutions in RE,[9] inheritance laws and taxation, etc.
- As opposed to most other goods that are placed on a market, RE is associated with substantial indivisibilities. For example, it is usually neither sensible nor possible to buy half a single house,[10] and there may even be limits to subdividing land plots (limits set both by planning authorities and by economic necessity).
- Heterogeneity and imperfect information, the need to secure the legal rights that change hands in RE transactions, indivisibilities, and the obligation to conform to government regulations imply high transaction costs (including search costs) for RE (see Quigley, 2002).

Overall, RE is a key element of the macro-economy, including (local) government finances. RE's relationship to consumption, saving, and the GDP has already been mentioned. So has its investment aspect, and its link to the capital and the labour markets. Through all these channels, RE interacts with the wider economy. For instance, new construction and renovation contribute significantly to GDP. But consider the following example, which draws the capital market into the picture too. A drop in lending rates makes RE more affordable (a rise has the opposite effect). Greater affordability leads to increased demand; i.e., for a given RE price, the quantity demanded becomes larger. However, with the supply of RE being rather inelastic (especially in the short term), the price of RE rises too. There will probably be an increase in the availability of previously vacant properties, but eventually the rise in price will make new construction more profitable, so supply increases further. New construction augments GDP and (presumably) overall economic prosperity. Interestingly, the whole process may proceed relatively smoothly, or it may lead to a RE price bubble (see Chapters 8 and 11), whose eventual burst may have dramatic consequences for lending institutions and ultimately the whole economy – and thus for the lives of millions. Reasons for such a big effect involve the wealth aspect of RE, its investment aspect, and its relation to debt (i.e., the debt that many people incur in order to finance their purchase of RE).

Under a different scenario, stronger demand for RE (say, due to population pressures or to the establishment of foreign companies in a city) may lead to higher lending rates for the finance of RE. But in a modern financial market all rates interact, so, *ceteris paribus,*[11] *lending rates on industrial or retail finance will also go up. This will negatively affect the non-RE sector of the economy.*

Finally, changes in the value of RE affect the amount of RE-related tax revenue a central or local government will collect, while, on the other hand, increased taxation of RE will adversely affect both demand for and the supply of it (see Chapters 9 and 10).

Figure 1.3 presents a stylized picture of the position of RE in the wider economy, emphasizing many of the links presented above.

Box 1.4 sums up the attributes characterizing RE.

Box 1.4 Characteristics of real estate (RE)

1. Fixity of location
2. Price determined mostly by derived demand, subject to inelastic land supply
3. Use and availability defined by forms of legal (property) rights
4. Heterogeneity
5. Imperfect information
6. High transaction, search, management, and moving costs
7. Monopolistically competitive market organization
8. Indivisibility, in most cases, most of the time
9. Fragmentation into (interacting) subsectors or submarkets
10. Durability
11. High construction cost of buildings (in relation to most products and to most incomes)
12. Impact on urban structure and form
13. Interaction with financial markets
14. A strong wealth aspect
15. Multi-faceted interaction with the wider economy

1.6 Why study RE economics?

The preceding discussion helps advance reasons why a study of RE economics can be socially and professionally useful:

1. To assist in policy-making (see Chapters 3, 4, 7, and 9–11). If RE-related processes interact with the wider economy to the extent suggested, economists who understand the basics of this interaction can help central and local governments, and also monetary authorities, formulate appropriate economic, social and monetary policies – even when such policies are not intended to impact directly on the RE sector.
2. To learn how to price RE and make better RE investment decisions (see Chapters 5–7, 9, 11, and 12). All sorts of business investors and ordinary people are interested in buying, selling, exchanging, keeping, upgrading, demolishing, building, or renting RE. Many financial institutions in particular (banks, insurance companies, pension funds, and REITs)[12] are keen to invest other people's savings (which those institutions manage)

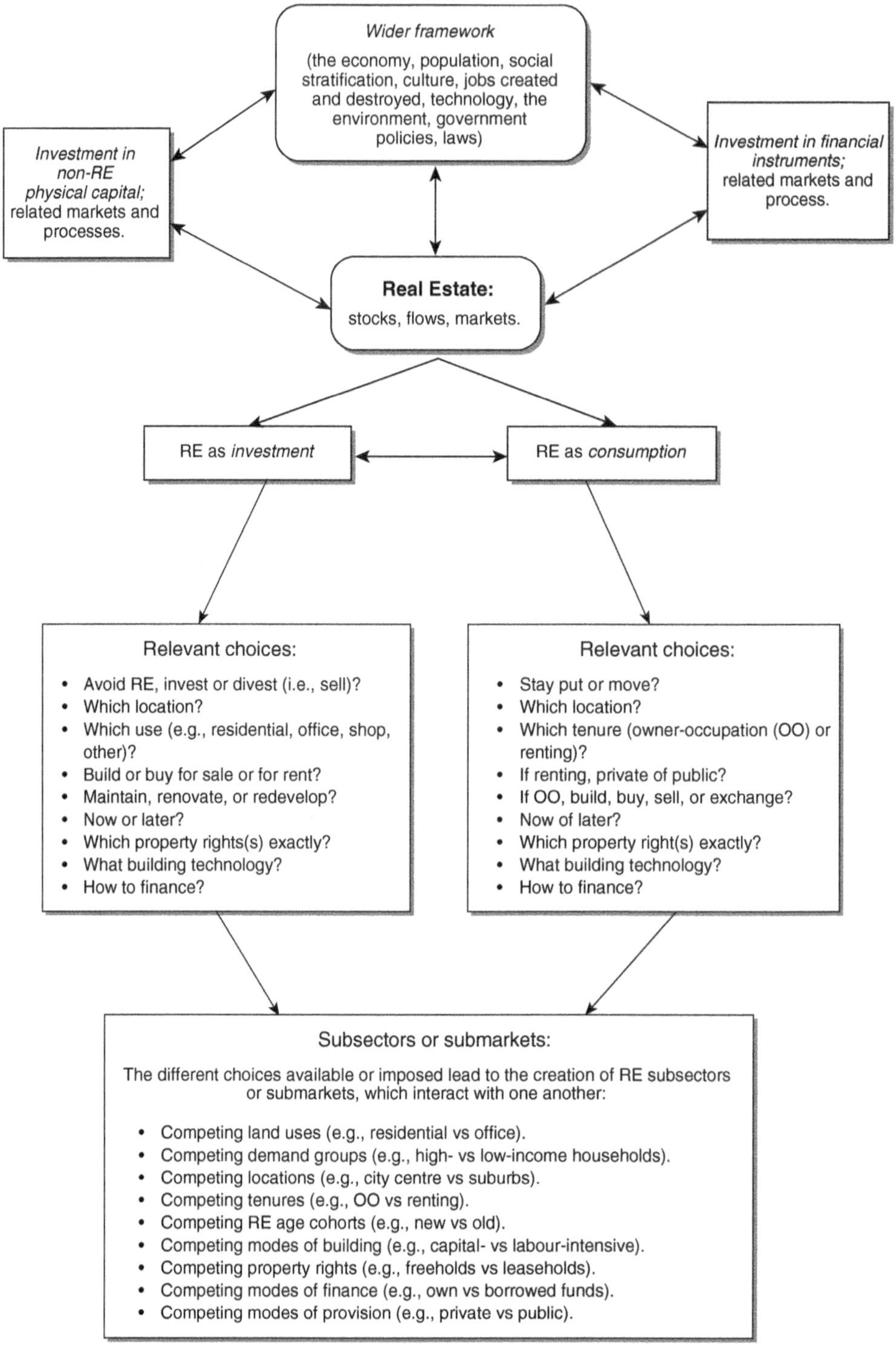

Figure 1.3 The position of RE in the wider scheme of things.

in RE, or divest themselves of particular properties, if the price and outlook are right. Other entities who get involved in those processes are estate agents, surveyors, valuers, builders, developers, and, importantly, tax authorities. All of the above want to know what affects the value of RE, and ultimately the value itself.

3 To find employment in one or other of the institutions and entities just mentioned.

4 To learn how the economic processes surrounding RE affect, or are likely to affect, cities and, generally, the landscape (see Chapters 6, 7, and 10). This is an area of great interest to city planners and central and local governments, one of whose typical responsibilities is the design and implementation of appropriate land and housing policies. It is also of interest to many private businesses (e.g., retail shops and chains) and ordinary people who happen to operate or live in cities and want to assess the merits and demerits of specific location decisions.

2 RE

Tools of analysis

Main sections

Having gone through this chapter, a student should be able to

1. Find the derivative of y with respect to x in $y = f(x)$.
2. Solve simple optimization, and constrained optimization, problems.
3. Differentiate an implicit function.
4. Calculate the elasticity of various demand functions.
5. Distinguish between price elasticity and elasticity of substitution.
6. Discuss the advantages and disadvantages of a Cobb–Douglas utility function.
7. Derive an expression for (housing) demand, given a Cobb–Douglas utility function and a budget constraint.
8. Distinguish between income and substitution effects of a price change, and calculate the tangency solutions.
9. Explain how different elasticities of substitution affect consumer budget shares between housing and non-housing consumption, and the significance of this.
10. Apply isoquant and isocost analysis to the problem of profit maximization.
11. Define and compare regression with co-integration using ordinary language.
12. Discuss briefly the problem of causality in both of the above, and define Granger causality.

Attention! This chapter is relatively difficult; the reader may skip it, and come back to it as needed later. Its purpose is to act as a refresher course on important economic concepts (e.g., own-price elasticity, indifference curves, utility and demand functions (particularly of the Cobb–Douglas variety), income and substitution effects, and elasticity of substitution) and on related mathematical and statistical techniques (such as derivatives, differentiation, optimization, regression, and co-integration).

Essentially the material in Chapter 2 should allow a student to follow the few mathematically demanding parts found in some of the subsequent chapters without recourse to specialized maths or stats books. Some other mathematical concepts or techniques are introduced in later chapters. It is assumed that the reader is familiar with basic economics and finite mathematics, and has had some exposure to differential calculus.

A very pertinent example for applying most of the mathematical techniques introduced here concerns the allocation of consumer budget shares between housing and non-housing consumption. To this end, the reader is taken from the concept of indifference curves to Cobb–Douglas utility, then to demand and the income and substitution effects, and finally to the concept of the elasticity of substitution ε_s.

2.1 Mathematical techniques

The mathematical techniques that interest us most are those centred on the concept of the derivative. This is akin to the concept of the *slope* of a line (whether straight or a curve) that describes the relationship between a dependent variable y and an independent variable x when their values are plotted on the axes of a Cartesian graph (i.e., in $x-y$ space). The slope is a number that shows what the change in y (the 'vertical' variable) is when there is a change in x (the 'horizontal' variable), and is given as

$$s = \frac{\Delta y}{\Delta x}.$$

If the relationship between the two variables is linear (i.e., if it graphs as a straight line), there is no problem: the line has the same slope throughout. If it is a curve, its slope at any particular point is the slope of a straight line that is tangent to the curve at that point. If the change in x is extremely small, i.e., point-like, the corresponding change in y is called the *derivative* of y with respect to x. So the derivative is really a slope measured at a point on a line. It is denoted by dy/dx.

We shall now present ways of finding the derivative of a function showing the relationship between y and any number of independent variables, $x_1, x_2, \ldots, x_n$, as well as finding the maximum or minimum values of a function.

2.1.1 Differentiation

Given a function $y = f(x)$, differentiation, or derivation, is the mathematical process of finding (deriving) the change in the value of the dependent variable y when there is an infinitesimal change in the value of the independent variable x – or in the value of any of a series of independent variables $x_1, x_2, \ldots, x_n$ if there are more than one of those in the function $f(x)$. The value sought is the *derivative* of y with respect to x, i.e., dy/dx. The technique is useful in all sorts of economic analyses. For example, it can be used to calculate the price elasticity of demand for, or supply of, a good at a point on the demand (or supply) curve. (See Section 2.2.1 for a definition of elasticity.) Some rules of differentiation are as follows:

(a) The constant-function rule

The derivative of a constant is zero. If $y = f(x) = k$, then $dy/dx = 0$.

EXAMPLE

If $y = f(x) = 3$, then $dy/dx = 0$, which stands to reason since, if a function equals a constant k for all values of x, there is never a change in $f(x)$ with respect to x.

(b) The power-function rule

The derivative of ax^n is nax^{n-1}.

EXAMPLE

If $y = 3x^5$, then $dy/dx = 15x^4$. Also, if $y = 9x^1$, then $dy/dx = (1)9x^{1-1} = 9x^0 = 9$.

(c) The product rule

The derivative of the product of two functions equals the first function times the derivative of the second plus the derivative of the first times the second function, i.e.,

$$\text{if } y = f(x)g(x), \quad \text{then } \frac{dy}{dx} = f(x)\frac{dg(x)}{dx} + \frac{df(x)}{dx}g(x).$$

EXAMPLE

If $f(x) = 2x$, $g(x) = 3x^2 + 5$, and $y = f(x)g(x) = 2x(3x^2 + 5)$, then

$$\frac{dy}{dx} = 2x(6x) + 2(3x^2 + 5) = 10 + 18x^2.$$

(d) The quotient rule

The derivative of the quotient of two functions is the derivative of the numerator times the denominator minus the derivative of the denominator times the numerator, the difference subsequently divided by the square of the denominator, i.e.,

$$\text{if } y = \frac{f(x)}{g(x)}, \quad \text{then } \frac{dy}{dx} = \frac{\frac{df(x)}{dx}g(x) - \frac{dg(x)}{dx}f(x)}{g^2(x)}$$

EXAMPLE

If $f(x) = 2x$, $g(x) = 3x^2 + 5$, and $y = \frac{f(x)}{g(x)} = \frac{2x}{3x^2+5}$, then

$$\frac{dy}{dx} = \frac{2(3x^2 + 5) - 6x(2x)}{(3x^2 + 5)^2}.$$

(e) The derivative of an exponential function

This is the function times the natural logarithm of the exponent, i.e., if $y = a^x$, then $dy/dx = a^x \ln x$. A natural logarithm is a logarithm to the base e. The latter is an irrational number approximately equal to 2.7182818.

EXAMPLE

If $y = 13^x$, then $dy/dx = 13^x \ln x$. If $x = 2.5$ in this case, then $dy/dx = 13^{2.5}(0.916291) = 558.33$, where 0.916291 is the number to which e would have to be raised to equal 2.5.

(d) The chain rule

The derivative of a function z of variable y, where y is a function of variable x, equals the derivative of z with respect to y times the derivative of y with respect to x, i.e.,

$$\text{if } z = f(y) \text{ and } y = f(x), \text{ then } \frac{dz}{dx} = \frac{dz}{dy}\ \frac{dy}{dx}.$$

EXAMPLE

If $y = 10 - x^5$ and $z = 4y^3 + 14 = 4(10 - x^5)^3 + 14$, then

$$\frac{dz}{dx} = 12y^2\left(-5x^4\right) = 12\left(10 - x^5\right)^2\left(-5x^4\right).$$

2.1.2 Partial and total differentiation

Often the dependent variable y is a function of more than one independent variable, say x and h. Even so, we may need to find what happens to y if there is an infinitesimal change in any one of those variables. This calls for *partially differentiating y* with respect first to x and then to h. We need, that is, to find the *partial derivatives*

$$\frac{\partial y}{\partial x} \text{ and } \frac{\partial y}{\partial h}$$

(or, in alternative notation, y_x and y_h).

EXAMPLE

If $y = 10 + 28x + 7x^2 - 14xh + 4h + 5h^2$, then

$$\frac{\partial y}{\partial x} = 28 + 14x - 14h \quad \text{and} \quad \frac{\partial y}{\partial h} = -14x + 4 + 10h.$$

If, however, there is an infinitesimal change in both x and h simultaneously, the combined effect on y is referred to as the *total differential*, dy, of the y function, found through *total differentiation*:

$$dy = \frac{\partial y}{\partial x}dx + \frac{\partial y}{\partial h}dh.$$

EXAMPLE

With y as in the preceding example, let $x=110$, $h=37.5$, $dx=0.02$, $dh=0.006$. Then

$$dy=\frac{\partial y}{\partial x}dx+\frac{\partial y}{\partial h}dh=(28+14x-14h)(0.02)+(-14x+4+10h)(0.006)=13.894.$$

Notice that the true change in y (found by working with the 'primitive', or original, function) is 13.8953, implying a 0.0013 discrepancy between the true value and dy.

2.1.3 Optimization

Optimization is the process of finding the extreme point(s) of a curve; or, generally, the maximum and/or minimum values of a function such as $y=f(x)$. To do that, we must recall from finite mathematics that a straight line of zero slope on an $x-y$ diagram implies that a given change in the variable plotted on the horizontal axis (the x axis) leads to no change in the variable plotted on the vertical axis (the y axis). On a curve, this can happen at a specific point only: in which case, $dy/dx=0$. Thus, to find the extreme point(s) on a curve, we must set the first derivative of $f(x)$ equal to zero (since dy/dx is indeed a description of the slope at a point), and solve the resulting equation.

EXAMPLE

Let $y=3+12x+3x^2$. Then $dy/dx=12+6x$, and setting $12+6x=0$ and solving gives $x=-2$.

So -2 is an extreme point on the curve described by $y=3+12x+3x^2$. But is it a maximum or a minimum point? To answer this, we need to find the second derivative of the function $y=3+12x+3x^2$, i.e., the derivative of $12+6x$. This is denoted by d^2y/dx^2 and is obviously

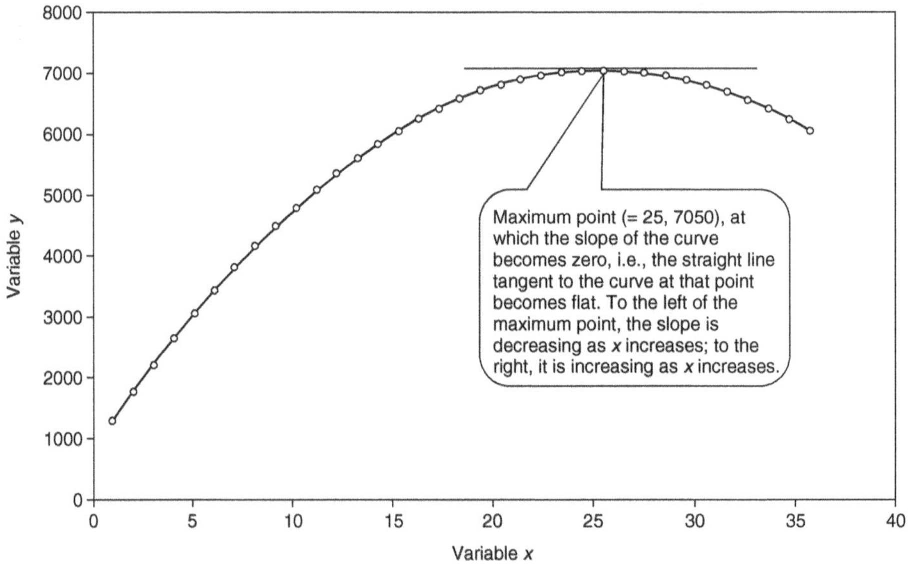

Figure 2.1 A curve with a maximum point.

equal to 6. It is positive, so $y = 3 + 12(-2) + 3(-2)^2 = -9$ must be the minimum value of the function $y = f(x)$. The rule is straightforward:

If the second derivative is positive, we have a minimum; if negative, a maximum.

> Incidentally, if dy/dx is a second-degree equation of the form ax^2+bx+c, then the value of x that sets it equal to zero is found as
>
> $$x = \frac{-b \pm \sqrt{b^2 - 4ac}}{2a}.$$
>
> This results in two values of x that satisfy $dy/dx = 0$. These must be substituted for x in d^2y/dx^2 in order to determine whether either value implies a maximum or a minimum $y = f(x)$.

Generally, the signs of the first and second derivatives determine whether the function $y = f(x)$ increases or decreases as x increases, and the rate at which it does so (see Table 2.1).

2.1.4 *Optimizing functions of more than one variable*

How would we go about finding the extreme point of a function made up of more than one independent variable (i.e., a *multivariate* function)? Well, the first task is to find the partial derivatives of the function, as shown above. Let's assume that we are dealing with two independent variables as in $y = f(x, h)$. Then, following the logic presented in Section 2.1.2, we set both partial derivatives equal to zero, obtaining a system of two equations in two unknowns. Solving this, we find the separate effects on the 'primitive' function of infinitesimal changes in x and h (i.e., one effect when x changes infinitesimally but h remains constant, and one effect when x remains constant but h changes infinitesimally). Substituting these values into the 'primitive' function, we get the extreme value of that function – the one that results when both x and h change infinitesimally.

Table 2.1 Behaviour of function $y = f(x)$ as x increases

If the first derivative is	*and the second derivative is*	*the function $y = f(x)$ is*	*the slope's sign is*	and, in relation to the origin, the curve is
> 0	> 0	rising at an increasing rate	positive	convex
> 0	< 0	rising at a decreasing rate	positive	concave
< 0	> 0	decreasing at a decreasing rate	negative	convex
< 0	< 0	decreasing at an increasing rate	negative	concave

Note: In a convex curve, a straight line connecting two points on it lies above it. In a concave curve, a line connecting two points on it lies below it.

EXAMPLE

From Section 2.1.2, we have $y = 10 + 28x + 7x^2 - 14xh + 4h + 5h^2$. Then

$$\frac{\partial y}{\partial x} = 28 + 14x - 14h \quad \text{and} \quad \frac{\partial y}{\partial h} = -14x + 4 + 10h.$$

Setting $28 + 14x - 14h = 0$ and $-14x + 4 + 10h = 0$, we get (by substitution) $h = 8$, $x = 6$. Substituting these values into $y = f(x, h)$, we find its extreme value to be 110. A second-derivative test, to ascertain whether the extreme value found is a maximum or a minimum, must also be used in this case, although we will not pursue the issue here. The interested reader is advised to consult any good mathematical economics textbook.

2.1.5 Constrained optimization

Sometimes optimizing a function is subject to a constraint. For example, maximizing consumer utility is invariably subject to a budget (or income) constraint; maximizing output can be subject to the amount of resources available and/or other things. Any constraint must therefore be taken into account, since it delineates the range of feasible values among those implied by a proposed relationship between two or more variables.

One method of optimizing a function subject to a constraint is to work with *Lagrange* multipliers. It goes like this:

Once again, we shall work with $y = 10 + 28x + 7x^2 - 14xh + 4h + 5h^2$ (our 'primitive' function). Only, this time, we shall assume that $x + h = 10$. This is the constraint.[1]

We set the constraint equal to zero: $x + h - 10 = 0$. After we multiply this by λ (Greek *lambda*), we add it to the 'primitive' function to form the *Lagrangian* function L:

$$L = 10 + 28x + 7x^2 - 14xh + 4h + 5h^2 + \lambda(x + h - 10).$$

Because $\lambda(x + h - 10) = 0$, it does not affect the value of the 'primitive' function $y = f(x, h)$. The great benefit of forming a Lagrangian function, however, is that now we have explicitly incorporated the constraint into the 'primitive' function. Basically what we have now is a function of three unknown independent variables (x, h, and λ), which we can try and optimize in the standard way (see Section 2.1.4 above). First we take the partial derivatives of the function L:

$$\frac{\partial L}{\partial x} = 28 + 14x - 14h + \lambda,$$

$$\frac{\partial L}{\partial h} = -14x + 4 + 10h + \lambda,$$

$$\frac{\partial L}{\partial \lambda} = x + h - 10.$$

Setting the three derivatives equal to zero (because these are the first-order conditions for optimization), and solving the resulting system of equations, we get $x = 4.15$, $h = 5.85$, $\lambda = -4.3$. Substituting the constrained values for x and h into the 'primitive' function, we find the extreme value of the latter to be 101.4 – whereas in the unconstrained case (see Section 2.1.4), we had found it to be 110.

2.1.6 Implicit differentiation

Certain functions of x and y are given implicitly, i.e., instead of y being on the left-hand side as the dependent variable and x on the right-hand side as the independent variable, they are both on one side, the whole expression being equal to some constant. It may of course be possible to transform an implicit function into an explicit one, and then the process of finding the rate of change of y with respect to x (i.e., dy/dx) involves straightforward differentiation. Then again, it may not be possible, or at least easy, to effect this transformation. For instance,

$$\text{if } 3x+4y=2, \text{ then } y=\frac{2-3x}{4}, \text{ in which case } \frac{dy}{dx}=-\frac{3}{4}.$$

But if $y^2+x^2+x^2y^3=k$, things become quite difficult. In such cases, implicit differentiation is called for, which means finding the implicit derivative of y with respect to x, or $\frac{d}{dx}$. Using the rules of differentiation, this works as follows:

$$\frac{d}{dx}y^2+\frac{d}{dx}x^2+\frac{d}{dx}x^2y^3=\frac{d}{dx}k$$

$$\Rightarrow 2y\frac{dy}{dx}+2x+\left[(x^2)\left(3y^2\frac{dy}{dx}\right)+(2x)(y^3)\right]=0$$

$$\Rightarrow \frac{dy}{dx}\left[2y+(x^2)(3y^2)\right]=-2x-(2x)(y^3)$$

$$\Rightarrow \frac{dy}{dx}=\frac{-2x-(2x)(y^3)}{2y+(x^2)(3y^2)}$$

$$=-\frac{F_x}{F_y}=-\frac{\text{derivative of implicit function } F \text{ with respect to } x}{\text{derivative of implicit function } F \text{ with respect to } y}.$$

Notice that the term

$$\left[(x^2)\left(3y^2\frac{dy}{dx}\right)+(2x)(y^3)\right]$$

comes from applying the product rule (see Section 2.1.1) to $(d/dx)(x^2y^3)$. The process described allows us, among other things, to derive the slope of a *Cobb–Douglas utility function* (a function often utilized in modelling housing consumption vis-à-vis non-housing consumption in a consumer preference framework). The slope is then used in deriving the demand curve for, say, housing from the given Cobb–Douglas utility function subject to a budget constraint (see Section 2.2.4).

2.1.7 The S curve

Some growth processes peter out (i.e., they gradually diminish over time). Examples are the share of insurance consumption, or of construction investment, into GDP. Such processes can be approximated by what are called S curves because of the latter's resemblance to the letter S (see Figure 2.2). The relevant equation is

$$y=b_1+\exp\left(b_2+\frac{b_3}{x}\right)=b_1+e^{b_2+b_3x^{-1}},$$

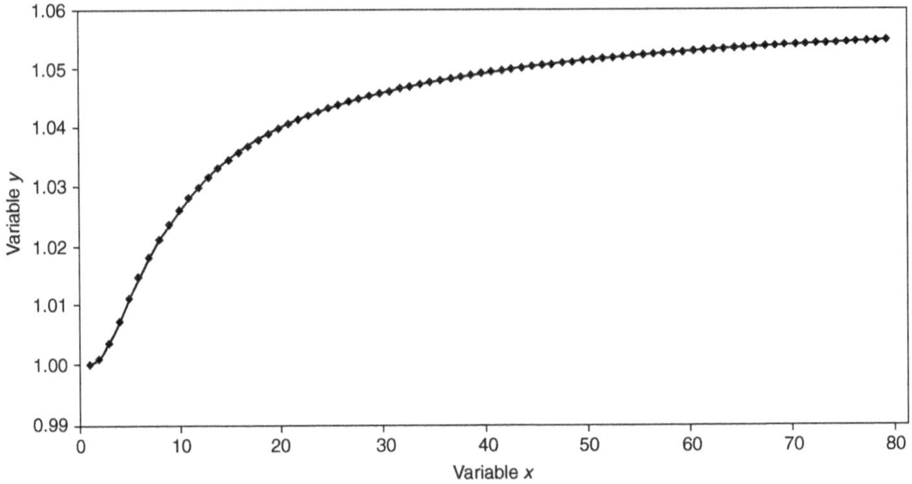

Figure 2.2 Example of an S curve.

and the values for the parameters b_1, b_2, and b_3 are easily supplied by statistical software packages which can fit an S curve onto data sets that behave as mentioned.

2.2 Economic concepts

2.2.1 Elasticity

Elasticity is a number showing the percentage change in the dependent variable in response to a percentage change in an independent variable. On a demand (or supply) diagram (with price plotted on the vertical axis and quantity on the horizontal), *price elasticity*, in particular, measures the sensitivity (or degree of responsiveness) of the quantity demanded (or supplied) to changes in the price of the product. Over a part (arc) of the demand (or supply) line, the price elasticity ε_p is defined as

$$\varepsilon_p = \frac{\%\Delta \mathrm{Q}}{\%\Delta P} = \frac{\frac{\Delta Q}{\mathrm{Av}Q}}{\frac{\Delta P}{\mathrm{Av}P}} = \frac{\Delta Q}{\Delta P}\frac{\mathrm{Av}P}{\mathrm{Av}Q} = \frac{1}{s}\frac{\mathrm{Av}P}{\mathrm{Av}Q},$$

where

ΔQ = change in quantity,
ΔP = change in price,
$\mathrm{Av}Q$ = average quantity (between start and finish),
$\mathrm{Av}P$ = average price (between start and finish),
s = slope of demand (or supply) line.

For a given demand (or supply) line of the form $P = a + bQ$ (with $b < 0$ for demand, $b > 0$ for supply), the above formula becomes

$$\varepsilon_p = \frac{1}{b}\frac{\mathrm{Av}P}{\mathrm{Av}Q}, \quad \text{since } b \text{ is the slope of the line.}$$

A variant of the price elasticity of demand defined above is the income elasticity of demand, ε_y, which measures the sensitivity of the quantity demanded to changes in consumers' income:

$$\varepsilon_y = \frac{\Delta Q}{\Delta Y}\frac{\text{Av}Y}{\text{Av}Q}, \quad \text{where } Y = \text{income.}$$

Using calculus, it is also possible to measure elasticity at a point on a demand (or supply) line, something that is particularly useful when dealing with a curve rather than a straight line:

$$\varepsilon_p = \frac{dQ}{dP}\frac{P}{Q} = \frac{dQ}{dP}\bigg/\frac{Q}{P}, \quad \text{where } \frac{dQ}{dP} \text{ is the derivative of } Q \text{ with respect to } P.$$

EXAMPLE

If $P = 14 - 1.1Q, dP/dQ = -1.1 \Rightarrow dQ/dP = 1/(-1.1)$. If we want to find the point elasticity when $Q = 6$, for example, we first calculate the corresponding P, which is 7.4. Then, $\varepsilon_p = (dQ/dP)/(Q/P) = [1/(-1.1)]/(6/7.4) = -1.12$ (which, being larger than $|1|$, suggests that demand is elastic at $Q = 6, P = 7.4$).

Remember that elasticity changes as we move up or down a non-flat straight demand (or supply) line. Some curvilinear demands, though, are characterized by constant elasticity.

2.2.2 *Indifference curves*

Indifference curves are plotted on $X - Y$ diagrams to show combinations of two goods (or classes of goods) that yield the same amount of *total utility* (i.e., satisfaction, or want-satisfying power) to the consumer. Consequently, the latter is indifferent between buying this or that, or any other, combination as long as all combinations lie on the same indifference curve.

It is possible to imagine a map of indifference curves for a consumer. On such a map, higher indifference curves (i.e., those are further away from the origin of the diagram) yield more total utility than lower ones, and represent superior choices for the consumer.

Indifference curves cannot intersect.[2]

An indifference curve is *convex* in relation to the origin, i.e., it bows towards it (see Figure 2.3). This shape represents an important property of an indifference curve, namely, that in order to keep the amount of utility constant, decreasing the quantity of one good – and therefore moving from one combination to another on the curve – must be accompanied by increases in the quantity of the other good. Assuming that good x is plotted on the horizontal axis, and good y on the vertical axis, the rate of change from one good to the other is called the *marginal rate of substitution* between the two goods. Thus,

$$\frac{\Delta Y}{\Delta X} = \text{MRS},$$

i.e., losing (gaining) ΔY is compensated by gaining (losing) ΔX. (Calculating the MRS at a point on the curve requires differentiation of course.)

Not only that: the MRS is diminishing too as the consumer goes down any particular indifference curve on his or her indifference curve map. It diminishes because obtaining

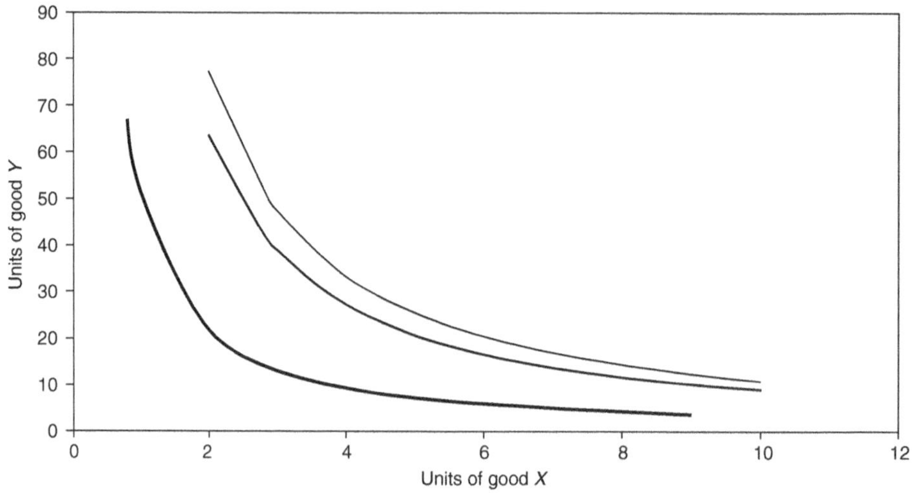

Figure 2.3 Indifference curves.

more of X is associated with less and less utility from additional units of X – which implies that the consumer is less and less prepared to give up additional units of Y to obtain one more unit of X. Nevertheless, the utility *gained* by getting one more unit of x must be exactly offset by the utility *lost* by getting less of Y (which has to happen in order to preserve a *constant total* utility along a given indifference curve). If, say, 7 units of Y have to be sacrificed in order to obtain *one* more unit of X (and keep the level of *total* utility constant), the *extra* (or additional or incremental) utility of more x must be seven times as great as the corresponding *reduction* in the utility of Y. This is *marginal utility*, MU. Hence,

$$\text{MRS} = \frac{-\Delta Y}{\Delta X} = \frac{\text{MU}_X}{-\text{MU}_Y} = -7.$$

For the consumer to exercise a choice, he or she will not only look at his or her preferences (as implied by the indifference curve map), but also at whether he or she can afford to buy whatever combination the consumer likes. This means that the consumer has to take into account his or her budget line. The latter shows combinations of two goods, priced P_X and P_Y, which the consumer can buy with a given budget (or income).

Consequently the consumer's rational choice of combination will be at the point of tangency between his or her budget line and the highest possible indifference curve on his or her indifference curve map.

The slope of the budget line is the ratio of a decrease (increase) in the quantity of good Y over a corresponding increase (decrease) in the quantity of good X. Since the budget is given, the expenditure on less (more) Y, i.e., ΔY, must be equal to the expenditure on more (less) X, i.e., ΔX. Therefore, and ignoring the negative sign of, say, a drop in Y:

$$P_X \Delta X = P_Y \Delta Y \Rightarrow \frac{P_X}{P_Y} = \frac{\Delta Y}{\Delta X} = \text{slope of budget line},$$

which *at equilibrium* (i.e., at the point of tangency between the budget line and the highest possible indifference curve) equals

$$\frac{MU_X}{MU_Y} = MRS.$$

Changes in income (i.e., in the consumer's budget) are tantamount to parallel shifts in the budget line, making the consumer buy more (or less) of both products, without changing the ratio of the product quantities he or she buys. The same thing happens if there is no change in nominal income but, instead, the prices of the two goods change the same way (say, 2 per cent each, so that the ratio of the two prices is unchanged).

On the other hand, a change in the price of one product implies a pivot-like shift of the budget line, making the consumer readjust his or her pattern of purchases (i.e., the ratio of the product quantities), substituting units of one product for units of the other. For example, on an $X - Y$ diagram, a reduction in P_X will result in more X being bought with a given budget, even though the consumer will be able to buy the same maximum number of units of Y as before.[3]

2.2.3 Useful demand and utility functions

Let us now look at two classes of demand functions, and calculate the elasticities.

(a) Demand function in the form of a straight line

Consider, for example,

$$P = 35 - 2.5Q.$$

Given a demand (or other *total*) function like this, the elasticity is

$$\varepsilon_p = \frac{dQ}{dP} \Big/ \frac{Q}{P},$$

which is the ratio of the *marginal* function to the *average* function. Therefore, since

$$Q = \frac{35 - P}{2.5},$$

it follows that the marginal function is

$$\frac{dQ}{dP} = -0.4,$$

the average function is

$$\frac{35 - P}{2.5} \Big/ P = \frac{35 - P}{2.5P},$$

and

$$\varepsilon_p = \frac{-0.4(2.5P)}{35-P} = \frac{-P}{35-P}.$$

Applying this formula to the example of Section 2.2.1, i.e., $P = 14 - 1.1Q$, the elasticity when $P = 7.4$ is

$$\varepsilon_p = \frac{-P}{14-P} = \frac{-7.4}{14-7.4} = -1.12, \text{ as in Section 2.2.1.}$$

(b) Demand function in the form of a curve

Two curves that can be useful in RE economics are

(i) a power function like $Q_h = aP_h^{b_1}Y^{b_2}$, where Q_h = housing consumption, P_h = price of housing, and Y = consumers' income; and
(ii) an isoelastic demand curve like $P = k/Q$ (characterized by constant elasticity).

Let us have a closer look.

(i) A function like $Q_h = aP_h^{b_1}Y^{b_2}$ offers an important advantage: direct knowledge of the elasticities involved, as the parameters b_1 and b_2 are the price elasticity and income elasticity of the demand for housing, respectively. The parameters still need to be estimated, however. Fortunately, this is the second advantage of the power function, as it can be easily transformed into a straight-line one by taking natural logarithms, ln, on both sides:

$$\ln Q_h = \ln a + b_1 \ln P_h + b_2 \ln Y.$$

Collecting data on housing consumption (maybe in the form of owner-occupied units purchased, if that is the researcher's interest), house prices, and consumers' incomes, and running a *regression analysis* (see Section 2.3.1) on the variables, is then required in order to arrive at the desired estimation.

(ii) A function like $P = k/Q$ has a constant elasticity equal to -1 (but, obviously, not a constant slope – see Figure 2.4). It suggests that revenue (i.e., income) is the same, no matter what the price. Consequently, the seller(s)' profit is derived from variations in costs as quantity adjusts so that $PQ = k$.

The usefulness of this functional form is that it links to the well-known (among economists, that is) *Cobb–Douglas utility function*, which has the form $U(X, Y) = X^aY^{1-a}$ (where $0 \leq a \leq 1$, and X and Y are quantities of commodities; in fact, X can be a specific commodity, e.g., housing, and Y a vector, or basket, of all others). For example, let $U(X, Y) = X^{0.2}Y^{0.8}$ and also assume a budget constraint $B = XP_X + YP_Y$ (where P_X and P_Y are the prices of X and Y, respectively). The demand equation for housing corresponding to the given utility function will then be $Q_X = \frac{0.2B}{P_X}$, i.e., a constant-elasticity (or *isoelastic*) demand curve.

An advantage of the Cobb–Douglas utility function is that it can easily be extended from the level of the individual consumer to the level of the market, thus 'solving' the *demand aggregation problem* – how to go from a single consumer's demand to demand by all consumers. Another advantage is its simplicity. A third is its ability to incorporate more than two goods (or classes of goods), as in $U(X, Y, h) = X^{a_1}Y^{a_2}h^{a_3}$, with $a_1 + a_2 + a_3 = 1$. A fourth is that, over the years, it has fitted many data sets rather well (Miller, 2008).

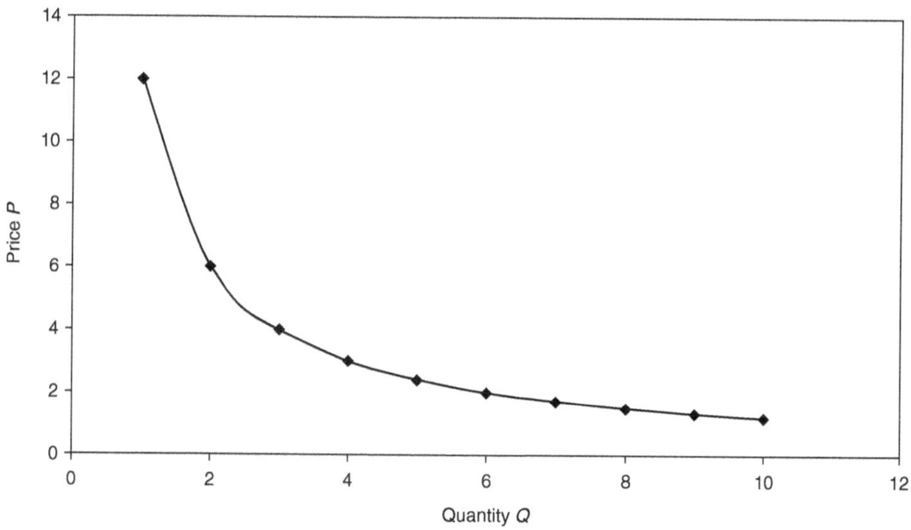

Figure 2.4 A constant-elasticity demand curve, $P = 12/Q$.

But a demand function that is based on a Cobb–Douglas utility function has disadvantages, too:

- The assumption of constant budget share parameters for all consumers, under which the demand aggregation problem is 'solved', is too restrictive. (See Box 2.1 for an elaboration.)
- Another disadvantage of the isoelastic demand curve is that it is very inappropriate for analysing monopoly – but this should not be a problem when dealing with RE markets, which are typically characterized by monopolistic competition among buyers and sellers, including constructors.

Box 2.1 Cobb–Douglas, CES, and budget shares

The Cobb–Douglas utility function (on which Cobb–Douglas demand is based) is a special case of a family of utility functions characterized by constant elasticity of substitution (CES).

An example of a more general CES utility function is

$$U(X, Y) = [aX^{\rho} + (1 - a)Y^{\rho}]^{1/\rho}.$$

What is special about the Cobb–Douglas function is that its CES is equal to 1. The practical implication of CES = 1 is this: in Cobb–Douglas utility, an increase in the price of X (say, housing) does not affect the quantity of Y (i.e., non-housing) bought; it only reduces the quantity of X bought, so that the consumer's budget share going to housing is the same as before.

This may not be the case in reality; an increase in the price of housing will indeed reduce the quantity of housing bought, but may also reduce the quantity of non-housing bought, as consumers may choose to buy a little less of non-housing in order to preserve, as much as possible, their consumption of housing. Or the rise in the price of housing may increase the quantity of non-housing bought, as consumers may be deterred from going for 'more' housing, and may decide to step up their consumption of non-housing instead. (The issue is discussed further in Section 2.2.8.)

2.2.4 From Cobb–Douglas utility to Cobb–Douglas demand

Let us see how the demand equation $Q_X = 0.2B/P_X$ in Section 2.2.3 was arrived at, given a utility function of the form $U(X, Y) = X^{0.2}Y^{0.8}$. To this effect, we shall work out a more general solution, namely, how to get to $X = aB/P_X$ from $U(X, Y) = X^aY^{1-a}$, where utility is constant (along any particular indifference curve). The problem is that in the utility function, X and Y are quantities, and in order to find demand (for product X or for product Y) we need to associate quantity and price. Prices, of course, are implicit in the budget line; moreover, at the point of tangency between the consumer's budget line and the highest possible indifference curve, the slopes of the budget line and of the indifference curve are equal to one another. Therefore, finding those slopes and solving for either X or Y will allow one to feed the resulting value into the budget line equation and find the desired demand equation.

Given a budget-line equation of the form $B = XP_X + YP_Y$, involving the quantities X and Y and their respective prices, the slope of the budget line is the rate of change of Y with respect to X, i.e., dY/dX. The budget line equation is an implicit function of X and Y – but fortunately it can be easily transformed into an explicit one:

$$Y = \frac{B - XP_X}{P_Y},$$

whose derivative with respect to X is

$$\frac{dY}{dX} = \frac{-P_X}{P_Y}.$$

The slope of the indifference curve given by $U(X, Y) = X^aY^{1-a}$ is more difficult to find because $U(X, Y)$ is an implicit function that is not easily transformed into an explicit one. The solution is to resort to implicit differentiation (see Section 2.1.6):

$$X^a(1-a)Y^{1-a-1}\frac{d}{dX} + aX^{a-1}Y^{1-a} = \frac{d}{dX}U(X, Y) = \frac{d}{dX}k$$

$$\Rightarrow X^a(1-a)Y^{-a}\frac{dY}{dX} + aX^{a-1}Y^{1-a} = 0$$

$$\Rightarrow \frac{dY}{dX} = \frac{-aX^{a-1}Y^{1-a}}{X^a(1-a)Y^{-a}} = \frac{-aX^{a-1}Y^{-(a-1)}}{\frac{Xa}{Ya}(1-a)} = \frac{-a\frac{X^{a-1}}{Y^{a-1}}}{\left(\frac{X}{Y}\right)^a(1-a)} = \frac{-a\left(\frac{X}{Y}\right)^{a-1}}{\left(\frac{X}{Y}\right)^a(1-a)}$$

$$= \frac{-a}{1-a}\left(\frac{X}{Y}\right)^{a-1}\left(\frac{X}{Y}\right)^{-a} = \frac{-a}{1-a}\left(\frac{X}{Y}\right)^{a-1-a} = \frac{-a}{1-a}\left(\frac{X}{Y}\right)^{-1} = \frac{-a}{1-a}\frac{Y}{X}.$$

Now setting the slope of the indifference curve equal to the slope of the budget line, we have

$$\frac{-a}{1-a}\frac{Y}{X} = \frac{-P_X}{P_Y} \Rightarrow aYP_Y = (1-a)XP_X \Rightarrow X = \frac{aYP_Y}{(1-a)P_X}.$$

Substituting $aYP_Y/(1-a)P_X$ for X in the budget line equation, we get

$$B = XP_X + YP_Y = \frac{aYP_Y}{(1-a)P_X}P_X + YP_Y = \frac{YP_Y}{1-a} \Rightarrow Y = \frac{B(1-a)}{P_Y},$$

which is the demand function for product Y. Following the same procedure, we obtain $X = Ba/P_X$, which is the demand equation for product X we associated with the Cobb–Douglas utility function in Section 2.2.3 (i.e., $X = 0.2B/P_X$). These results imply that if utility is of the Cobb–Douglas form, the budget shares going to the two goods remain constant. So if the price of X rises, consumers will buy less of it, but will spend as much as before.

2.2.5 Income and substitution effects

Given a budget constraint, a change in price has an income and a substitution effect on the quantity demanded. The *income effect* means that the consumer, after the increase (decrease) in price, will buy less (more) of a given *normal* good (e.g., owner-occupied housing). The *substitution effect* means that the consumer will, in addition, rearrange his or her purchases, substituting (certainly in a relative sense, but maybe also in an absolute sense) more of the relatively cheaper good for the relatively dearer one. This is illustrated graphically in Figure 2.5, which shows quantities of products X (on the horizontal axis) and Y (on the

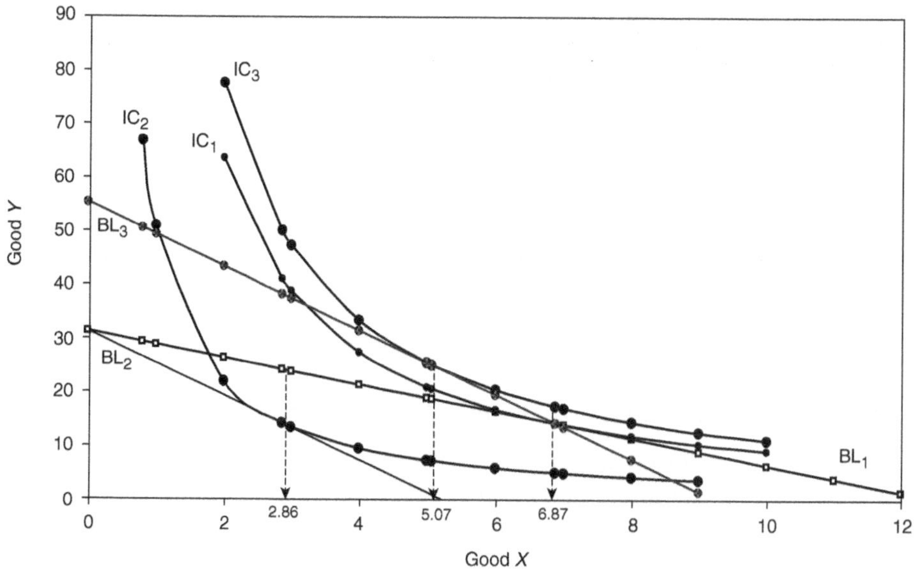

Figure 2.5 The income and substitution effects: a demonstration.

vertical axis) that a consumer contemplates. Initially, the consumer has a budget line BL_1. Given that $B = 125$, $P_x = 10$, and $P_y = 4$, the maximum quantity of X that can be bought is 12.5 units, and the maximum quantity of Y is 31.25 units. Equilibrium exists at the point of tangency with indifference curve 1 (IC_1), where 6.87 units of X and 14.06 units of Y are bought. After the price of X rises to 24, the budget line pivots to BL_2, and at equilibrium (point of tangency with IC_2), 2.86 units of X and 14.06 units of y are bought. Under the given budget of 125, the maximum quantities that can now be bought are $Y = 31.25$ and $X = 5.21$. Crossing through the initial equilibrium point is a hypothetical budget line, BL_3, parallel to BL_2, which is tangent to IC_3 at $X = 5.07$ and $Y = 4.89$. The distance from 6.87 to 2.86 is the total effect of the rise in the price of X. The distance, however, from 6.87 to 5.07 is the substitution effect, and the distance from 5.07 to 2.86 is the income effect.[4] (How we have arrived at the tangency solutions is explained in Section 2.2.6.)

The logic behind it is this: A hypothetical BL_3 goes through the initial equilibrium – this is a way to imagine that 'real' income has stayed constant. But even if the consumer has enough income to absorb the rise in the price of X so that he or she is able to buy the initial equilibrium combination of X and Y (6.87 and 14.06), he or she will still adjust his or her purchases on account of the different ratio of the two prices now that the price of X has risen (that is why BL_3 is drawn parallel to BL_2). At equilibrium (i.e., at the point of tangency between BL_3 and IC_3), he or she will buy a different quantity of X (and Y) from what he or she could buy at the initial equilibrium (before the rise in the price of X).

And why not? The combination $X = 5.07$, $Y = 24.89$ lies on a higher indifference curve than the combination $X = 6.87$, $Y = 14.06$, so the consumer gets more utility. This adjustment (buying less of X than before, holding 'real' income constant hypothetically) shows the extent to which the consumer adjusts his or her purchases merely on account of the change in relative prices rather than on account of the rise in the price of X (which actually implies a reduction in real income). So, going down from $X = 6.87$ to $X = 5.07$ must be the substitution effect. Anything beyond that (i.e., going from 5.07 units of X to 2.86) is then simply the income effect of the price change (consumers buying less of X than before simply because the rise in the price of X means less real income).

In this particular example, the total change in purchases of X is 4.01 units less than originally: $6.87 - 2.86 = 4.01$. In percentage terms, therefore, the substitution effect accounted for 45 per cent of the total change, i.e.,

$$\frac{6.87 - 5.07}{4.01},$$

and the income effect for 55 per cent, i.e.,

$$\frac{5.07 - 2.86}{4.01}.$$

2.2.6 Income and substitution effects: locating the tangency solutions

Let us acquire a 'feel' for the income and substitution effects by means of a numerical example. Our task is to calculate actual tangency solutions, given (i) a budget line equation and (ii) an indifference-curve-type utility equation, and (iii) assuming a change in the price of X. The initial budget line is

$$125 = 10X + 4Y,$$

where 10 = price of X (P_X) and 4 = price of Y (P_Y). The initial indifference curve is a typical Cobb–Douglas utility function:

$$U = X^a Y^{1-a} = X^{0.55} Y^{0.45}.$$

We know from Section 2.2.4 that the slope of such an indifference curve is

$$\frac{a}{1-a}\frac{Y}{X},$$

and that the slope of the budget line is

$$\frac{P_X}{P_Y} \text{ (we ignore the minus sign).}$$

At equilibrium, the two are equal to one another, so

$$\frac{a}{1-a}\frac{Y}{X} = \frac{P_X}{P_Y} = \frac{10}{4} = 2.5 = \frac{0.55}{0.45}\frac{Y}{X}$$

$$\Rightarrow 2.5 = 1.222\frac{Y}{X} \Rightarrow \frac{2.5}{1.222} = 2.0458 = \frac{Y}{X}.$$

Setting $Y = 2.0458X$ and substituting this for Y in the budget line expression, we get $B = 10X + 4(2.0458)X \Rightarrow X = 6.8745 \Rightarrow Y = 14.0638$. Their ratio is precisely 2.0458. Expectedly these are also the values that satisfy

$$\frac{a}{1-a}\frac{Y}{X} = 2.5.$$

But we also need to find a workable equation for the tangent indifference curve. Fortunately we know from theory that U is the same along all points on an indifference curve. Setting $U = 6.87^{0.55}14.06^{0.45}$, we find $U = 9.487$. Knowing, then, that $U = X^{0.55}Y^{0.45} = 9.487$,

$$Y = \left(\frac{9.487}{X^{0.55}}\right)^{1/0.45},$$

which is the equation we seek. Given, then, the initial budget line equation (BL_1), and the tangent indifference curve equation (IC_1), we are now able to calculate appropriate numerical values for X and Y (see Table 2.2), and draw the corresponding lines (see Figure 2.5).

Repeating the process after the rise in the price of X from 10 to 24 (which means that the slope of the new budget line, BL_2, is 6), we find

$$Y = \left(\frac{5.8615424}{X^{0.55}}\right)^{1/0.45}.$$

And, finally, the equation of the indifference curve IC_3 that is tangent to the hypothetical budget line BL_3 is

$$Y = \left(\frac{10.37446}{X^{0.55}}\right)^{1/0.45}.$$

Table 2.2 Budget line and indifference curve: finding the tangency point

Initial budget line BL_1: $125 = 10X + 4Y$, with $P_X = 10, P_Y = 4$
Slope of $BL_1 = -10/4 = -2.5$
Initial indifference curve IC_1: $U = X^{0.55}Y^{0.45}$
Slope of IC_1: $(0.55/0.45)\ (Y/X)$

Units of good X	*Corresponding units of Y along BL*$_1$	*Y/X*	*Corresponding units of Y along tangent IC*$_1$	*Slope of IC*$_1$
1	28.75	28.75		
2	26.25	13.13	63.60	38.87
3	23.75	7.92	38.75	15.79
4	21.25	5.31	27.26	8.33
5	18.75	3.75	20.75	5.07
6	16.25	2.71	16.61	3.38
6.87450	**14.0638**	**2.0458**	**14.0638**	**2.50**
7	13.75	1.96	13.76	2.40
8	11.25	1.41	11.68	1.79
9	8.75	0.97	10.12	1.37
10	6.25	0.63	8.90	1.09

(*Hint:* to calculate BL_3, we must recall that it is parallel to BL_2, and so $P_X = 24$ and $P_Y = 4$; only BL_3 also includes $X = 6.87$, $Y = 14.06$. As a result, the budget B is 221.24 rather than 125.)

2.2.7 Income and substitution effects in housing

The income and substitution effects are also observed in housing. A rise in the price of owner-occupied homes will mean, *ceteris paribus*, that *less* of this type of housing will be bought, perhaps through buying smaller owner-occupied homes (the income effect). It will also mean a substitution effect: a shift towards different forms of housing (say, from owner-occupation to renting), or a decision to stay with relatives rather than moving (if staying with relatives can be thought of as another form of housing).

A rise in the price of *generic* housing will also result in less *generic* housing being consumed. It may, in addition, result in an absolute increase in non-housing consumption if the share of consumers' budget spent on housing at the same time drops (cf. Section 2.2.8). 'Less' generic housing can mean a variety of things: buying or renting or living in a smaller property, or one with fewer amenities, or one in a 'worse' or 'inconvenient' area.

We must be careful here to distinguish between *normal* and *inferior* goods. Demand for the former rises when consumers' income does – and vice versa. Demand for the latter drops when incomes rise. Thus, if, say, rented housing is an inferior good, a rise in consumers' income will not increase demand for it, but will diminish it, as more people will turn towards owner-occupation, *ceteris paribus*. This was the case, for example, in the USA in 2005 (see Table 2.3): above a certain level of income (found in the third, or middle, quintile of income before taxes), absolute expenditure on rented accommodation began to diminish as incomes rose – while, in the case of owner-occupation, spending kept on increasing.

Table 2.3 Is rented housing an inferior good? The US case in 2005

Expenditure on owned and rented dwellings by quintile of income before taxes					
	Lowest 20%	*Second 20%*	*Third 20%*	*Fourth 20%*	*Highest 20%*
Average income before taxes in $	9,676	25,546	42,622	67,813	147,737
% of home-owning households	42	57	67	80	92
Expenditure on:					
Owned dwelling	1,628	2,600	4,573	7,203	13,771
Rented dwelling	2,718	2,985	2,809	2,033	1,181

Source: US Dept of Labor, US Bureau of Labor Statistics, Report 998, *Consumer Expenditures in 2005*, published in February 2007, p. 7. www.bls.gov/cex/csxanno5.pdf. Accessed on 28 December 2010.

2.2.8 Elasticity of substitution (ε_s)

The elasticity of substitution (ε_s) is a number that shows the sensitivity of the ratio of the units of two goods purchased *on the basis of a given budget* to changes in the ratio of the respective prices.[5] Thus, whereas the price elasticity of demand is the percentage change in quantity in response to a percentage change in price, ε_s relates to two products and two prices, and is the percentage change in the ratio of the two quantities in response to a percentage change in the ratio of the respective prices.

A Cobb–Douglas utility function has a constant, and in fact unitary, ε_s. Using a numerical example (see Section 2.2.5) we found those ratios to be as follows:

$$\text{for budget line BL}_1\text{, quantities ratio} = \frac{14.0638}{6.8745} = 2.04579\text{, prices ratio} = \frac{10}{4} = 2.5;$$

$$\text{for budget line BL}_2\text{, quantities ratio} = \frac{14.0638}{2.86436} = 4.9099\text{, prices ratio} = \frac{24}{4} = 6.$$

Therefore,

$$\text{elasticity of substitution, } \varepsilon_s = \frac{\text{percentage change in quantities ratio}}{\text{percentage change in prices ratio}}$$

$$= \frac{\dfrac{\text{change in quantities ratio}}{\text{average of quantities ratio}}}{\dfrac{\text{change in prices ratio}}{\text{average of prices ratio}}} = \frac{\dfrac{4.9099 - 2.04579}{(4.9099 + 2.04579)/2}}{\dfrac{6 - 2.5}{(6 + 2.5)/2}} = \frac{0.82353}{0.82353} = 1.$$

This result implies that a one per cent change in the ratio of prices leads to a one per cent change in the ratio of quantities (as the rise in the price of X is exactly offset by a proportional drop in the quantity of X). So if the price of housing increases and consumers have Cobb–Douglas utility, consumers will be spending *as much on it as before* – only they will be buying less housing, maybe in the form of smaller units, or by moving to less desirable areas. On the other hand, cheaper credit (i.e., lower interest rates) for house purchase is really tantamount to a drop in the price of housing, so consumers will be spending on housing *as much as before*, but they will be buying more 'units' of housing (say, in the form of bigger and/or generally 'better' houses).

However, a number of researchers (e.g., Piazzesi et al, 2007; Bajari et al., 2010a) have found that ε_s for housing is greater than one (meaning that, say, a drop in the price of housing changes the ratio of the quantities of housing versus non-housing bought, so that consumers spend a bigger budget share on housing than before). Other researchers (e.g., Kahn, 2008; Li et al., 2009) have found the opposite, namely that ε_s for housing is less than one (meaning that a drop in the price of housing makes consumers spend a smaller budget share on housing than before). Both results would suggest that Cobb–Douglas utility may not be appropriate for modelling housing demand. But others have found evidence in favour of Cobb–Douglas – for example, 'evidence from the 1980, 1990, and 2000 [US] Decennial Census of Housing that the expenditure share on housing is constant over time and across US metropolitan areas' (Davis and Ortalo-Magné, 2011). Research on the topic, therefore, continues.

In Table 2.4, we use data from the example in Section 2.2.5 to show what happens to quantities of housing versus non-housing consumption, and to consumer budget shares between the two, assuming that in response to a rise in the price of housing from \$10 to \$24, people begin to consume (a) 3 units of housing (thus $\varepsilon_s < 1$), or (b) 2.86 units (thus $\varepsilon_s = 1$, implying Cobb–Douglas utility), or (c) 2.5 units (thus $\varepsilon_s > 1$).

The practical importance of the size of ε_s is this: an $\varepsilon_s > 1$ would mean that in a business cycle expansion with rising house prices, people would, *ceteris paribus*, spend more of their income on non-housing, i.e., they would *substitute* non-housing for housing.

Table 2.4 Effects of a *rise* in the price of housing (from \$10 to \$24) on equilibrium quantities of housing and non-housing bought, and on allocation of consumer budget shares between housing and non-housing, given different ε_S between housing and non-housing consumption, a total budget of \$125, and price of non-housing of \$4

	Quantity consumed of housing	*Quantity consumed of non-housing*	*Budget share of housing*	*Budget share of non-housing*
Conclusions specific to example used above:				
Initial values, before housing price change	6.8745	14.0638	68.745	56.2552
Subsequent values assuming the following elasticities of substitution:				
$\varepsilon_S = 0.89$	3	13.25	72	53
$\varepsilon_S = 1$	2.86436	14.0638	68.745	56.2552
$\varepsilon_S = 1.27$	2.5	16.25	60	65
General conclusions:				
$\varepsilon_S < 1$	Drops from initial level, but less than in $\varepsilon_S = 1$ case	Drops from initial level	Rises from initial level	Drops from initial level
$\varepsilon_S = 1$	Drops from initial level, just enough to leave budget share of housing unchanged	Same as initially	Same as initially	Same as initially
$\varepsilon_S > 1$	Drops from initial level, but more than in $\varepsilon_S = 1$ case	Rises from initial level	Drops from initial level	Rises from initial level

But in a business cycle downturn with falling house prices, they would spend less of their income on non-housing, exacerbating the decline in economic activity. On the other hand, if $\varepsilon_s < 1$, people would do the opposite. Therefore the size of the elasticity of substitution between housing and non-housing consumption provides a microeconomic foundation for the behaviour of a macroeconomic magnitude, namely aggregate consumption. The issue is further explored in Chapter 3, through a discussion of the so-called housing wealth effect (HWE).

2.2.9 *Characteristics theory*

An important idea in housing economics is that dwellings are not wanted as lumps but for the sets of characteristics or attributes they possess. Hence, to consume, say, less of 'housing' is to opt for dwellings of fewer and/or less desirable characteristics. This approach is very handy when it comes to constructing house-price indices (see Chapter 12), as the dominant method for doing that – the hedonic method – is based on efforts to price dwelling attributes rather than 'total' houses. The characteristics approach was mainly developed by Kelvin Lancaster in 1966 (Lancaster, 1966),[6] its key tenets being that (i) consumers base their choices on price, income, and the characteristics of goods, and (ii) such characteristics are measurable.

A key potential weakness of the above approach is that on many occasions characteristics (not only of dwellings but of other goods too) may not be quantifiable, as already suggested in Chapter 1. Moreover, the 'totality' of a house may well be more than the sum of its parts – i.e., the identified and measurable attributes of a dwelling. The extent to which this is so is not, and probably cannot be, known with certainty. It is nevertheless a safe bet that visible and quantifiable characteristics (like dwelling type, location, tenure, size, number of rooms, existence of garden or garage, type of neighbourhood, etc.) are a very large part of the mechanism of dwelling selection (under given budget constraints) for most housing consumers most of the time.

2.2.10 *Isoquants, isocosts, MPP, MRP, and profit maximization*

Turning to the production, or supply, side of the economy, let us introduce a production function. This relates output to *quantities* of the factors of production used, whereas the functional form shows *how* the factors are used. Thus,

$$\text{TPP} = \text{total physical product} = f(T, L, K)$$

where T, L, and K represent land, labour, and capital, respectively.[7] In Cobb–Douglas form $f(T, L, K)$ might be $T^{\alpha}L^{1-\alpha}K^{1-\alpha-\beta}$, with the exponents summing to 1.

Anticipating our discussion of construction in Chapter 7, we need now to recall how a firm chooses its combination of inputs, and examine whether choice of a least-cost combination also implies profit maximization – and if that is not the case, determine the extra condition that would assure profit maximization.

It is well known that the concept of efficient production requires using the least-cost-combination of inputs, or factors of production. In turn, this requires that the extra, or marginal, output achieved per euro (or dollar, or pound) spent on an input is equal to the extra, or marginal, output achieved per euro spent on every other input employed. This extra output is called the marginal physical product of input x, MPP_x (where $x = T$, L, or K). The suggested condition for least-cost production is

$$\frac{\mathrm{MPP}_T}{P_T} = \frac{\mathrm{MPP}_L}{P_L} = \frac{\mathrm{MPP}_K}{P_K},$$

where P_T, P_L, and P_K are the prices of land, labour, and capital. It should also be noted that

$$\text{if } \frac{\mathrm{MPP}_L}{P_L} = \frac{\mathrm{MPP}_K}{P_K}, \text{ then } \frac{\mathrm{MPP}_L}{\mathrm{MPP}_K} = \frac{P_L}{P_K}.$$

The reason for this condition is simple: if, say, one more worker hired at P_L contributes more to output per euro spent to hire the worker than what one more piece of capital hired at P_K contributes to output per euro spent to hire that piece, the firm will hire more labour rather than more capital. The process will continue until there is no reason to adjust the combination of inputs, i.e., until the ratios of MPP to price are all equal.

This is one way to define the least-cost combination of inputs. There is another, involving isoquants and isocost lines. (The two methods will be shown to lead to the same result.) Considering a two-factor case, an *isoquant* is a curve made up of all possible combinations of inputs (say, labour and capital, to be applied on a given piece of land) that produce the same output – say, so many square metres of floor space (see Figure 2.6).

The ratio of one input to another, the marginal rate of technical substitution, MRTS, is the slope of the isoquant, and it shows the rate at which units of one input (say, capital) are substituted by units of the other input (say, labour), keeping total output constant. The MRTS (akin to the MRS related to indifference curves) is diminishing as one goes down the isoquant because less and less capital is discarded as labour increases by one unit every time; alternatively, for every one-unit drop in capital, the number of additional workers needed to

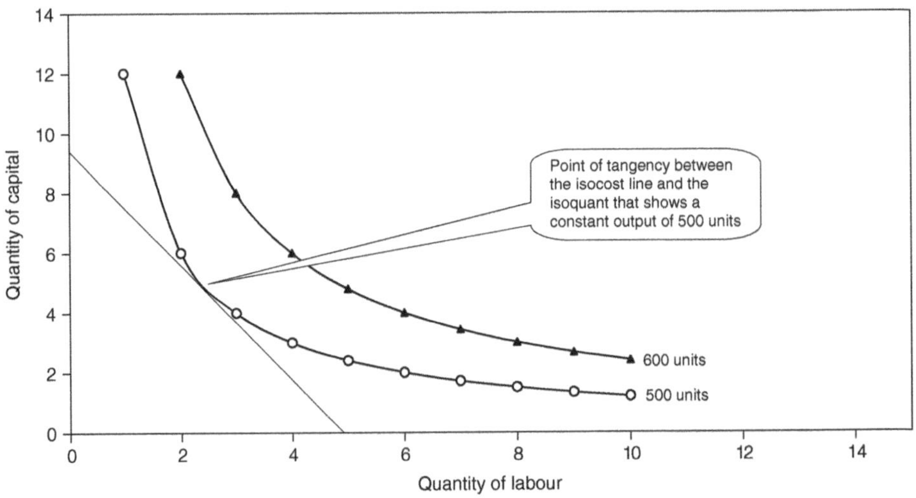

Figure 2.6 Isoquants and an isocost line.

achieve the same output as before increases. Either way,

$$\text{MRTS} = \frac{\Delta_K}{\Delta_L} \rightarrow \text{ a diminishing number.}$$

Now, the loss in output as capital is reduced along the isoquant must be exactly offset by the gain in output as labour increases, so that

$$\text{MPP}_K(\Delta_\text{K}) = \text{MPP}_L(\Delta_L) \Rightarrow \frac{\text{MPP}_L}{\text{MPP}_K} = \frac{\Delta_K}{\Delta_L} = \text{MRTS} = \frac{P_L}{P_K}.$$

This means that the ratio of the marginal physical products of the two inputs, $\text{MPP}_L/\text{MPP}_K$, is equal to the ratio of the two input prices, P_L/P_K, and both are equal to the inverse ratio of the two inputs, Δ_K/Δ_L.

Enter isocosts (see Figure 2.6). An *isocost* line shows combinations of units of two inputs (say, capital and labour) that cost the same to buy. It is akin to the budget line of consumer theory, which shows combinations of units of two goods that a consumer can buy with a given budget, or income. Because a firm faces a universe of isoquants (a higher one meaning more output than a lower one), exactly like a consumer facing a universe of indifference curves, the choice of input combination will have to be determined by cost considerations, i.e., a given isocost line. The optimal point, of course, is where the isocost just touches the highest possible isoquant.

Just as in consumer theory, the slope of the isocost line is the inverse ratio of the two factor prices. If, that is, labour is plotted on the horizontal axis, and capital on the vertical axis, the slope of the isocost line is P_L/P_K. At the point of tangency, this slope is equal to that of the isoquant, so

$$\frac{P_L}{P_K} = \frac{MPP_L}{MPP_K}.$$

But this is also exactly what satisfies the condition for least-cost production, as shown above. Therefore, whether the firm equates the ratios of marginal physical products to factor prices, or equates the slopes of an isocost line and an isoquant line, the result is the same: efficient production.

Now, having achieved least-cost production, the firm has gone a long way towards its ultimate goal: profit maximization. Not all the way, though, because the demand, or product price, side of the market must also be taken into account. The standard rule for profit maximization is that the firm needs to produce that output at which marginal revenue equals marginal cost, or MR = MC. This rule links the cost of producing one more unit of output to the extra revenue its sale brings in, and that in turn is a function of price. But it is also possible to link the use of production inputs to revenue, and develop a profit-maximizing condition. To do so, we need the concept of marginal revenue product, MRP, which is the change in total revenue, TR, that results from a one-unit change in resource quantity, RQ:

$$\text{marginal revenue product, MRP} = \frac{\Delta TR}{\Delta \text{RQ}}.$$

It stands to reason that the firm will be making a profit as long as the increase in total revenue brought about by hiring one more unit of a resource (which helps produce a certain output) is greater than the cost of that resource unit. The firm should therefore keep hiring resource units as long as this holds, and stop at the point where the marginal revenue product of the resource (say, labour or capital) equals the marginal resource cost, i.e., the resource price. So the condition for profit maximization is

$$\text{MRP}_L = P_L \text{ and also } \text{MRP}_K = P_K, \text{ and so on for all resources used.}$$

But that means that, at equilibrium,

$$\frac{\text{MRP}_L}{\text{MPP}_K} = \frac{P_L}{P_K},$$

and therefore also

$$\frac{\text{MPP}_L}{\text{MPP}_K} = \frac{\Delta_K}{\Delta_L} = \text{MRTS},$$

since, at equilibrium, i.e., at the point of tangency between an isocost and an isoquant,

$$\frac{\text{MPP}_L}{\text{MPP}_K} = \frac{P_L}{P_K}.$$

Notice that not each and every $\text{MRP}_L/\text{MPP}_K$ is equal to $\text{MPP}_L/\text{MPP}_K = \Delta_K/\Delta_L = \text{MRTS}$, but only that particular $\text{MRP}_L/\text{MPP}_K$ which has become equal to P_L/P_K, a condition that suggests achievement of equilibrium.

Box 2.2 A quick review of 'combination' curves relevant to consumer and producer choice

All of the curves below are defined for two items each; but they can all be extended, conceptually and mathematically, to *n* items.

An *indifference curve* shows combinations of two goods between which a consumer is indifferent because they all yield the same level of utility to him/her. It is convex to the origin.

A *budget line* shows combinations of two goods that can be bought for the same amount of money (or budget or income). It graphs as a straight line.

An *isoquant* shows all combinations of quantities of two factors of production that produce a given output. It is convex to the origin.

An *isocost line* shows combinations of quantities of two factors of production that can be bought for the same amount of money (or cost). It graphs as a straight line.

A *production-possibilities curve* (or *frontier*) shows all quantity combinations of two goods that can be had if all available resources are fully and efficiently employed. It is concave to the origin.

Box 2.3 A quick review of 'marginal rates'

The marginal rate of substitution (MRS) is the slope of an *indifference curve*. It shows the rate at which a consumer is willing to sacrifice units of one good in order to acquire one more unit of another good, keeping his or her level of utility constant.

The marginal rate of technical substitution (MRTS, also known as the marginal rate of factor substitution) is the slope of an *isoquant*. It shows the rate at which a producer gives up units of one resource in order to acquire one more unit of another resource, keeping his or her output constant.

The marginal rate of transformation (MRT) is the slope of a production-possibilities frontier. It shows the rate at which a producer or society as a whole sacrifices units of one *good* in order to have one more unit of another *good*, keeping the total cost of production constant, or keeping all available resources employed, respectively.

Under perfect competition, social efficiency requires that production takes place at the point where MRS = MRT.

2.3 Statistical primer: regression, co-integration, Granger causality

The purpose of this section is to refresh the concept of regression[8] in the minds of students who do not remember it well and introduce them to the more difficult (but, in a way, derivative) concepts of co-integration and Granger causality. The reason for this introduction is that (a) traditionally regression used to be the main method for searching for causal relationships between variables, particularly time-series ones; (b) there was growing understanding of the limits of this approach, as often correlation between the variables was erroneously interpreted as causation; and (c) co-integration analysis came into being as a way to search for causality on more robust grounds. This type of analysis is now applied in most economic studies, including RE ones, that involve time series. Examples of such studies are mentioned in a number of subsequent chapters, particularly Chapter 3.

2.3.1 Regression

Like all science, economics is about identifying, measuring, and explaining relationships between variables. One traditional way of doing some of this is *regression analysis*. In regression (which means 'going backwards'), the observed values of a so-called dependent (or response) variable are traced back (i.e., regressed) to values of one or more so-called independent (or explanatory) variables. The archetypal regression equation is

$$y_t = \alpha + \beta x_t + \varepsilon_t,$$

where

y = dependent variable at time t (or of order t),
x = independent variable at time t (or of order t),
ε = an error term at time t (or of order t); it registers the deviations of the actual values of y from the average (or predicted) values which the regression calculates.

In this formulation, the relationship between y and x is approached by means of a straight line that, on a Cartesian system of axes, passes through the scatter of points defined by pairs

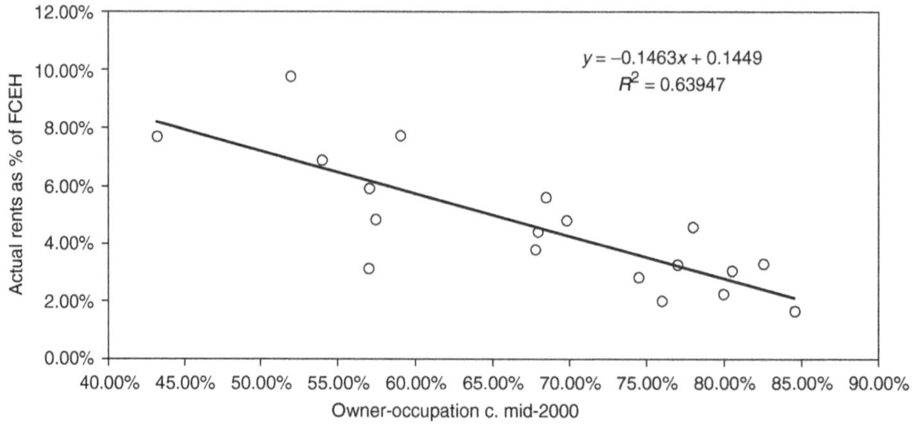

Figure 2.7 Linear regression example: 19 Western industrialized countries: household owner-occupation rate versus actual rents as a percentage of actual consumption expenditure (net of imputed rents) by households. (Source: Table 3.2.)

of x and y each. (Variable x is typically plotted on the horizontal axis, variable y on the vertical axis.) The vertical intercept of the line is α, the slope is β. The line passes through the scatter of points in such a way that the sum of the squared distances (or deviations) of the points from the line is the minimum possible. So the line essentially shows the average relationship between x and y – which can be interpreted as evidence of a trend (see Figure 2.7).

The vertical distances of the points from the trend line in Figure 2.7 are the error terms. Their sum is bound to be zero, since some of the points deviate positively in relation to the line (they lie above it), some deviate negatively (they lie below it), and the line itself is an average between all the points. (Technically, the sequence of errors is said to have a zero mean.) Therefore, the above equation suggests that the actual value of any particular y_t is equal to the right-hand side of the trend line equation, $\alpha + \beta x_t$, plus a (positive or negative) corresponding distance from the trend line, which is the error term ε_t.

A straight-line, or linear, regression equation like the one shown above is highly suitable when the original data points form a roughly straight path. If not, then nonlinear regression analysis may have to be used, involving what is known as curve-fitting, i.e., approximating the general shape of the scatter of data points by means of a curve rather than a straight line. There are many types of curves that may do the job: logarithmic, exponential, S, or polynomial.

Three important statistics related to regression analysis are the following:

(a) The correlation coefficient r. This measures the strength of the linear relationship between *two* variables. It takes values from -1 to $+1$. The closer it is to $+1$ or to -1, the stronger the linear relationship between x and y (i.e., the closer the data points are to the regression line), or, put differently, the more the two variables vary together. The negative sign means that the relationship between x and y is inverse, the positive sign that it is direct. Thus, the sign of r always matches the sign of the parameter β (i.e., the slope of the estimated regression line). The formula for r is

$$r_{xy} = \frac{\sum_{i=1}^{n} x_i y_i - n\bar{x}\bar{y}}{\sqrt{\left(\sum_{i=1}^{n} x_i^2 - n\bar{x}^2\right)\left(\sum_{i=1}^{n} y_i^2 - n\bar{y}^2\right)}}.$$

(b) The co-efficient of determination R^2. This is related to the correlation co-efficient (in fact, $r = \sqrt{R^2}$, i.e., $r^2 = R^2$). It shows the proportion of the total variation in the dependent variable (say, y) that is 'explained' by the variation in one *or more* independent variables (x_1, x_2, etc.). R^2 is therefore defined as 'explained variation in y' divided by 'total variation in y'. Being a proportion, it can only take values from 0 to 1. As an example (taken from Fig. 2.7), if $r = -0.7997$, then $R^2 = 0.6395$.

(c) The covariance s_{xy} (or Cov_{xy}). In a sample of paired observations between x and y, this shows the tendency for x and y to increase or decrease together. The concept is akin to the correlation coefficient r, except that the covariance depends on the units in which x and y are measured; moreover, r is always bounded by $-1 \leq r \leq 1$. The covariance formula is $\mathrm{Cov}_{xy} = r_{xy}\sigma_x\sigma_y$, i.e., the covariance between x and y equals the correlation between x and y times the product of the two standard deviations.

2.3.2 Regression and causality

Regression is a very useful tool in that it allows one to describe in shorthand a trend relationship between variables – a shorthand that may subsequently be used for prediction (i.e., coming up with a future value of y from a given or assumed future value of x). More specifically, a forecaster may use regression for purposes of prediction provided he or she has taken into account a number of potential problems, such as *multicollinearity*, *heteroscedasticity*, *autocorrelation*,[9] *endogeneity*.[10] Descriptions of these are found in any good statistics or econometrics book.

The main danger with regression, however, is that, although it does not prove *causality* between the variables (i.e., it does not prove that changes in the independent variable(s) *cause(s)* changes in the dependent one), it may be tempting to interpret regression this way, even though in reality there may be no causal relationship between the variables. If that is the case, then regression is *spurious*. The temptation to interpret mere correlation as causality is stronger of course if a high correlation coefficient (positive or negative) is involved, and one cannot be too careful about this matter.

The general rule about how to overcome the above danger is that, if regression throws up a strong linear relationship between the variables, such a relationship may be interpreted as evidence (or, rather, confirmation) of causation if the researcher has *a priori* (i.e., logical or theory-based) reasons to believe that the independent variable indeed causes the dependent one.[11] For example, if the researcher feels it is logical to expect that changes in household wealth cause consumption changes, and a regression between the two variables shows a strong linear relationship between them, then this may be accepted as an empirical validation of the *a priori* expectation.

The reverse danger also exists. This is where any two variables, for example in the form of time series, appear not to be moving together. As a result, a researcher may rush to conclude that there is no causal relationship between them – when in fact there is! A way to solve the causality problem when time series are involved, both in cases of spurious regression and in cases of apparent lack of common movement between the variables, is provided by *co-integration analysis*, pioneered by Clive Granger and Robert Engle. They deservedly got the Nobel prize for their work in 2003.

2.3.3 Co-integration

Strictly speaking, co-integration is not a technique in the way that regression analysis is a technique. Rather, it is a property of some (but not all) time series of data (or of *panel* data, which are a combination of *cross-sectional* and time-series data). One does not co-integrate time series – one checks for the existence of co-integration between them, even though this is often referred to as co-integration.[12]

Let us see what co-integration is about. Imagine two time series, say, one for GDP and one for construction investment. It stands to reason that if at least one of the variables affects (causes) the other, then some kind of equilibrium is likely to exist between them, in the sense of a tendency for any (temporary) deviations between them to be ironed out over time – if not in the short-term, then maybe in the long-term. Therefore, the two time series cannot move too far apart and remain there; they may do so for a while, but eventually they will come together again. If that is the case, the variables are said to be co-integrated.

Moreover, the presence of co-integration necessitates the existence of a causal relationship between the two variables; for, roughly speaking, why else would the two series re-approach one another after some deviation? Thus, co-integration is the tendency of time series that share a causal relationship to drift back towards each other even if they drift away from each other for a time, thus maintaining a certain average distance over time.

However, two series simply moving closely together for ever is not necessarily evidence of a causal relationship. Car sales and toothpaste sales (both expressed in real prices) in a developing country may well have moved together for three of four decades, but one cannot be causing the other! Rather, both result from a third factor at work – namely, overall economic development, which on the one hand raises incomes, and on the other makes people more conscious of the need for personal hygiene.

This, of course, is a simple example. Other cases are more difficult to judge on merely logical grounds. This is where co-integration comes into play. If two or more time series do not merely move together, but exhibit a measured tendency to re-establish some kind of equilibrium (a certain mean distance between them) even after a shock, then (a) they are co-integrated and (b) causality must be involved. This kind of causality is usually referred to as Granger causality, after Clive Granger, and we say that GDP Granger-causes construction investment, or construction investment Granger-causes GDP, or they cause one another, in the short run or in the long run or both, depending on the results of relevant econometric tests.

2.3.4 More on time series

That should be enough for starters. For a slightly more detailed analysis, continue reading. First, let us make the observation that many real-life processes (and the series of data points generated by those processes) have a constant mean. For example, take the height of men of a certain age.[13] The population of these men will be characterized by a certain average height. This implies that on taking a random sequence of such men, a particularly tall one (in relation to the average) will be countered, sooner or later, by a particularly short one (again, in relation to the average). Therefore, as more men are (randomly) added to the sequence, the mean height of the counted men will tend towards the population average height, no matter which man we pick up first.

Now, a time series that has

- a constant mean, but also has
- constant variance, and for which
- the value of the covariance between any two time periods depends only on the distance between the two periods, rather than on the actual time at which the covariance is computed (cf. Gujarati, 2003: 797)

is called 'weakly stationary'. If mean and/or variance are not constant, the underlying time series is called 'non-stationary'. The distinction[14] is important for three reasons:

1. Stationary time series tend to return to their mean – that is, they exhibit *mean reversion* (cf. Section 8.6) – and fluctuations around this mean, measured by its variance, will have a broadly constant amplitude (Gujarati, 2003: 798).

   As a counter-example, historic experience (so far) has revealed that GDP tends to grow with time, despite business-cycle fluctuations, so its time series cannot have a constant mean, and must be non-stationary. Actually, GDP may be *trend-stationary*, i.e., exhibit a trend as well as fluctuations around the trend, which themselves may well be stationary. There is, however, some debate among economists as to whether GDP returns to a long-run trend after a shock – a so-called structural break – or not.
2. If a time series is stationary or trend-stationary, it can be used in forecasting. If it is not, prediction using ordinary regression has a much higher chance of being incorrect than in the case of stationary series (Gujarati, 2003: 798).
3. The distinction has also a lot to do with establishing the existence or otherwise of causality between time series. Two (or more) non-stationary time series may run relatively smoothly together, which will involve a high correlation (not necessarily causation) between them (which is when both series exhibit similar trends), or may appear to bear no relationship to one another (which is when the series appear to run stochastically, i.e., go here and there, seemingly at random).

It is possible, though that the two (or more) time series manage to maintain a certain stable relationship (e.g., a certain average distance) between them (or among them, if there are more than two). This can happen, for example, because even if they do not appear to run smoothly together, they approach each other at points. If they do this, it is because there is a causal relationship with one another, and the implied reason for this causality is that the series share some kind of long-run equilibrium. If they have this property, they are said to be *co-integrated.*

Take the example of a drunken man's random walk. His walk is probably random, but if a friend follows that man to see that he comes to no harm, then each person's individual walk may appear random (i.e., be non-stationary), but the distance between them never gets too large or too small for ever. Their distance, that is, tends to fluctuate around a constant mean – so it is stationary. Then the two walks are co-integrated.

Consider now construction investment and real GDP. If the percentage of the former into the latter tends to constancy, it is likely that the percentage and real GDP are co-integrated.

Another example might be offered by a time series of real house prices (see Figures 2.8 and 2.9 below). Such a series usually appears non-stationary, since real house prices (as measured by some house price index) tend to increase over time (thus exhibiting a trend).

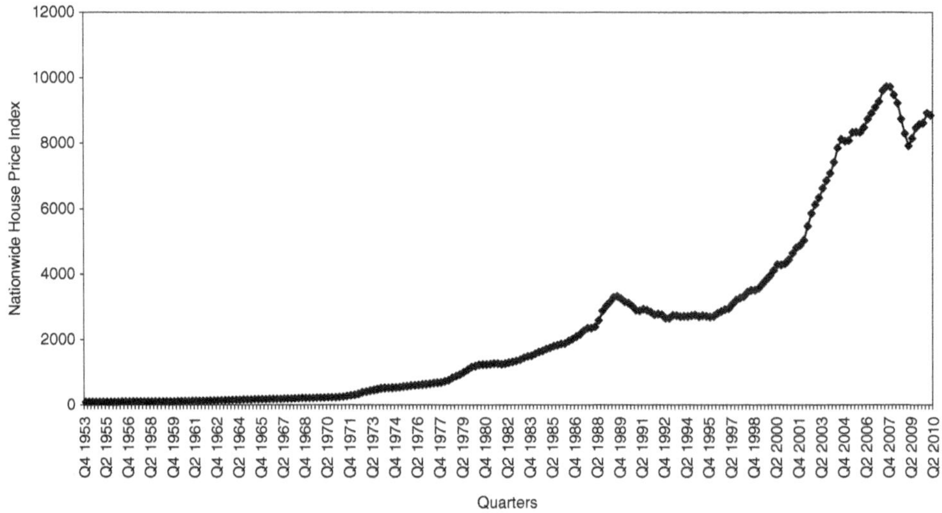

Figure 2.8 Non-stationary time series: real house prices in the UK, 1953 Q4 to 2010 Q3 (1952 Q4 = 100).

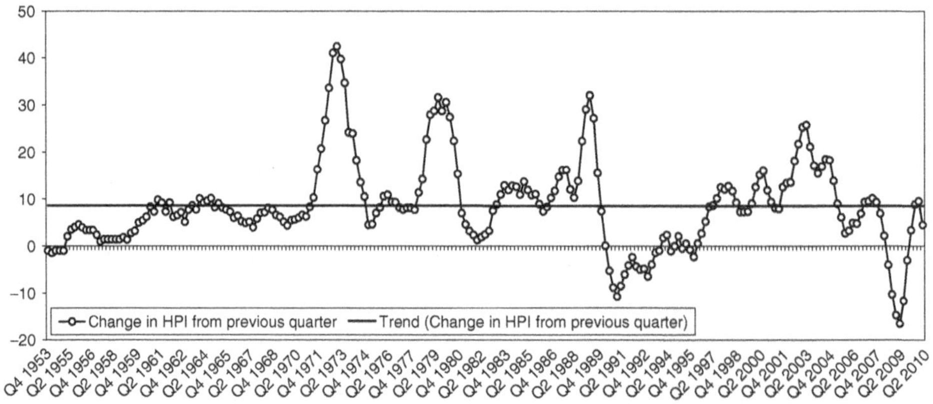

Figure 2.9 Stationary time series: annual percentage change in Nationwide UK House Price Index by quarter, 1953 Q4 to 2010 Q3, with trend line.

But if the percentage differences between pairs of those prices form a stationary series, then the house-price time series should be more appropriately viewed as *trend-stationary* – and would also exhibit reversion to the trend. (The trend would be the mean, in this case.) It is also more likely that house-price differences would co-integrate with other relevant variables, like income or interest rates.

2.3.5 A graphical example

Figures 2.8 and 2.9 show how a time series of quarterly house prices can be non-stationary, yet the (percentage) differences between them can be stationary. The data in the two graphs come from Nationwide's House Price Index, and concern real house prices in the UK from 1953 Q4 to 2010 Q3, the base period being 1952 Q4.

Interestingly, the trend line in Figure 2.9 seems completely horizontal. This is just the way things turned out over the given time frame. On other time frames, the trend line goes up or down.

As can be seen in Figure 2.9, a stationary time series tends to return to its average value over time, i.e., to exhibit *mean reversion*. It is also possible that the series may return to its long-term *trend* over time rather than to a specific mean – after all, a trend line is in the nature of a mean – provided that the trend itself does not change with time. However, a series that does have this property is not necessarily stationary, because stationarity requires three conditions to be met: constant mean, constant variance, and constant covariance between values in the series, irrespective of the size of those values or of the time period in which the covariance is measured.

2.3.6 Granger causality

The causality implicit in co-integration is best understood as 'Granger causality'. This has a very specific meaning, notwithstanding the fact that the concept of causality has bedevilled philosophers for many centuries now. A good example is David Hume (1711–76), who, among other contributions, reduced causal connections to experiences of frequent conjunctions (B happening after A, rather than A, somehow, causing B). Later, Bertrand Russell (1872–1970), in his *History of Western Philosophy* (1946), wrote that the principle of induction (i.e., generalizations based on specific facts) could serve as an approach to establishing causality if instances of A followed by B happened frequently enough so as to give 'a sufficient probability for practical purposes' (Russell, 1946: 699). (We must interpret this correctly: in no way did Russell confuse causality with correlation. Rather, the importance of Hume's – and Russell's – contributions was that even where we expect A to be causing B on logical grounds, at the end of the day we have nothing concrete but conjunctions or, at most, a high expected probability of occurrence.)

Against this background, Clive Granger (1934–2009) suggested that a pragmatic way of defining causality would be linked to prediction: if X at time t happens before Y at time $t+1$, and X_t contains information about Y_{t+1} that makes X_t more successful in forecasting Y_{t+1} than is information found in any other appropriate variable (including past values of Y), then X is said to 'Granger-cause' Y. Thus, if, over a certain time frame and in a certain country, construction investment seems to affect GDP more than past values of GDP do (and both construction investment and GDP are found to be co-integrated), then construction investment is said to Granger-cause GDP.

What is the connection between Granger causality and co-integration? In his Nobel lecture, Granger himself had this to say: 'When the idea of cointegration was developed [over a decade after Granger causation was], it became clear immediately that if a pair of series was cointegrated then at least one of them must cause the other. There seems to be no special reason why these two quite different concepts [co-integration and Granger causation] should be related; it is just the way that the mathematics turned out' (Granger, 2003: 366).

Which means that co-integration has not solved the problem of causality fully. But it has supplied a far more robust interpretation of causality than mere regression ever could. That is not to say that regression is an old and flawed technique, whereas co-integration is the new thing now. The two complement one another in the sense that where two or more time series are found to be co-integrated, interpreting the results of regression analysis as evidence of causality is justified.

2.3.7 Further reading

Granger, C. W. J. (2003) *Time Series Analysis, Cointegration, and Applications.* Nobel Lecture, Stockholm, Sweden, December. http://nobelprize.org/nobel_prizes/economics/laureates/2003/granger-lecture.pdf (accessed 30 November 2010).

Gujarati, D. N. (2003) *Basic Econometrics*, 4th edn. New York: McGraw-Hill.

Royal Swedish Academy of Sciences (2003) *Time-Series Econometrics: Cointegration and Autoregressive Conditional Heteroscedasticity.* Advanced information on the Bank of Sweden Prize in Economic Sciences in Memory of Alfred Nobel, 8 October. www-stat.wharton.upenn.edu/~steele/HoldingPen/NobelPrizeInfo.pdf (accessed 30 November 2010).

Seddighi, H. (2011) *Introductory Econometrics: A Practical Approach*, 2nd edn. London: Routledge.

Summary of main points

1 Definitions of various mathematical, economic, and statistical concepts.
2 Differentiation, optimization.
3 Budget shares of consumption between housing and non-housing depend on the size of the *elasticity of substitution* ε_s between the two goods.
4 If $\varepsilon_s > 1$, then, *ceteris paribus*, changes in the price of housing have a same-sign effect on non-housing consumption (i.e., a rise in the price of housing will increase non-housing consumption, and a drop will reduce it). If $\varepsilon_s < 1$, then the opposite occurs.
5 A Cobb–Douglas utility function is a convenient way of modelling housing demand, but is associated with $\varepsilon_s = 1$; this is a contentious assumption, which is still under empirical investigation.
6 In a two-good consumption framework, the following is true at equilibrium:

$$MRS = \frac{\Delta Y}{\Delta X} = \frac{\mathrm{MU}_x}{\mathrm{MU}_y} = \frac{P_x}{P_y}.$$

7 In a two-factor production framework, the following is true at equilibrium:

$$\mathrm{MRTS} = \frac{\Delta_K}{\Delta_L} = \frac{MPP_L}{MPP_K} = \frac{P_L}{P_K}.$$

Review questions and exercises

1 Define the following:

- own-price elasticity and elasticity of substitution
- utility
- indifference curve
- marginal rate of substitution
- marginal rate of technical substitution
- income effect, substitution effect

- isocost and isoquant
- marginal physical product, marginal revenue product.

2 'A demand curve that has constant elasticity also has constant elasticity of substitution.' Discuss the validity of this statement.
3 How is a constant price elasticity of demand different from a constant elasticity of substitution?
4 Given the function $x+2y^2+xy+x^3y-xy^2=35$, find the derivative of y with respect to x.
5 Consider the function $y=10+28x+7x^2-14xh+4h+5h^2$ from Section 2.1.5. Using the constraint $x+h=10$, we found the extreme value of the function to be 101.4. Without a constraint, we had found the extreme value of the function to be 110 (see Section 2.1.4) for $h=8$ and $x=6$. Would we, therefore, find the same result (i.e., 110) if we set a constraint $x+h=14$? If not, why not?
6 List and briefly discuss advantages and disadvantages of a Cobb–Douglas utility function.
7 Look at Table 2.4. Following the procedure suggested at the beginning of Section 2.2.8, verify the values supplied. Prepare a similar table on the assumption that there is a drop in the price of housing.
8 Given a utility function $U(x,y)=x^{0.25}y^{0.75}$ and a budget constraint $B=xP_x+yP_y$, state AND derive the corresponding demand function for x.
9 Using ordinary English, briefly define regression analysis, co-integration analysis, and Granger causality.
10 Prove that the marginal rate of (technical) substitution between, say, capital K and labour L, i.e., Δ_K/Δ_L, is equal to the inverse ratio of the two input prices, P_L/P_K, and to the inverse ratio of the marginal physical products, MPP_L/MPP_K, of the two factors.
11 'Rented housing is an inferior good.' Discuss.
12 Look at Figure 2.9. The period covered is from 1953 Q4 to 2010 Q3. Notice that the trend line seems completely horizontal. Now access the Nationwide HPI on the Internet at www.nationwide.co.uk/hpi/downloads/UK_house_price_since_1952.xls and recreate the diagram, choosing other time frames. Is the trend line still horizontal? If it is not, does this necessarily mean that the time series of house-price changes is not stationary in such a case?

3 RE in the wider economy

Main sections

Having gone through this chapter, a student should be able to

1. Understand the treatment of RE items in National Accounts, and collect relevant data.
2. Discuss the dynamic contribution of construction investment to GDP, utilizing the concept of partial multipliers as derived from input–output tables, the extent to which such contribution is uni- or bi-directional, and how it is likely to vary depending on the level of (real) GDP (as shown in a comparison between developed versus developing countries).
3. Explain the determinants of construction investment, emphasizing the influence of Tobin's *q* ratio, but also drivers such as viewing RE as a store of value, incomes and demographics.
4. Reconcile Tobin's *q* ratio to the observation that new properties usually sell for more than (roughly similar) older properties.
5. Describe and analyse the channels through which the RE market affects the wider economy.
6. In particular, define, and evaluate the strength of, the so-called housing wealth effect (HWE) as a threefold mechanism through which changes in house prices affect consumption.

7 Analyse the three possible components of an HWE mechanism: a home-equity adjustment, a permanent income–life cycle (PILC) adjustment, a consumer credit adjustment.
8 Critically assess Oswald's thesis that there is a positive relationship between homeownership and unemployment.

3.1 RE in the National Accounts

RE-related activities contribute to both GDP and employment. Prime examples of such activities are construction (residential and non-residential), the generation of 'shelter' services by dwellings and other buildings, and services by estate agents, factors, and others. However, the word 'contribution' is a bit ambiguous. It can mean 'percentage share' (a static, additive contribution) or an actual process whereby a total becomes greater than its initial parts (a dynamic, multiplicative contribution). The latter interpretation is based on the fact that any kind of spending (typically, investment – including, of course, RE investment) tends to expand GDP by more than the value of the initial expenditure (at least in most cases).[1] In other words, $1 of investment augments national output by more than $1.

There is a difference, however, between investment spending (which is defined as an addition to the stock of capital) and, say, the generation of service flows by dwellings. Such flows can command actual rents (paid by renting households) or may be treated as *imputed rents* (which owner-occupying households would in theory pay if they rented their homes from others). Those incomes (because rents *are* incomes) augment GDP in a mostly additive way but do not directly set in motion productive processes (like construction) that interconnect with other productive processes (like building materials industries, and so on down the line), which augment GDP in a strongly multiplicative way. That is why the link of construction to GDP is stronger, and therefore worthy of more attention, than the link of rental incomes to GDP.

Having made this point, we must be careful not to diminish the indirect importance of rents in helping or retarding construction activity. The reason is that in a free-market economy it is precisely the promise of high rents, or of high RE prices, that encourages constructors to build more – and *vice versa*.

A number of questions follow:

(a) How strong is the effect of construction investment on GDP?
(b) How does the effect of construction compare with the effect of other kinds of investment (say, in manufacturing)?
(c) Is there a difference in the strength of the effect of construction between developed and developing countries? Or over time in a given country?

In the same vein, one could ask: How much employment does a euro spent in some RE-related activity create in comparison to what other activities achieve? But an answer to this question is meaningful only if one has controlled for the possibility that spending of that euro may have coincided with a change in the ratio of capital to labour involved in the given RE-related activity.

Here is an example of the problem. In period A, spending of €100,000 is required to build a house with the application of 20 workers and 8 units of capital (on a given-size plot). In period B, the same amount of money may not translate in employment for 20 workers, because a change in building technology, or in the relative prices of capital and labour, or both, may result in only 17 workers and 9 units of capital being used. So the employment effect of any kind of spending is likely to be modified by changes in the ratio of labour resources to total resources involved.

Obviously attempts to answer questions (a), (b), and (c) above require National Accounts data. In Table 3.1, we show how to make sense of such data, using Australia as an example. The source is the OECD National Accounts.[2] OECD is chosen because its data cover all developed countries that are broadly referred to as traditional market economies, the data are of high quality (even if not extremely detailed), and comparisons between the OECD member countries are a usual and meaningful research procedure.

In general, the contribution of RE to employment and GDP takes the following forms:

(i) Value added by new construction and renovation (including demolitions and disposal of waste material). Relevant occupations are workers, operators, civil engineers, surveyors, architects, planners, accountants, economists, managers, and assorted clerical staff.

(ii) Value added by industries and firms (including outsourced ones) supplying building and renovating materials and equipment. Relevant occupations are their workforces and special, managerial, and clerical staff.

(iii) Value added by facilitating transactions in RE, resolving disputes, and managing properties. Relevant occupations are brokers, estate agents, advertisers, valuers, surveyors, notaries and solicitors, factors, staff of financial institutions, economists; and assorted clerical staff.

(iv) Value added through the generation of 'shelter' services by dwellings (which in the National Accounts take the forms of actual and imputed rents).[3] The actual value added, of course, is the gross income generated (or, from another point of view, rental expenditure by households) minus the *user cost* of the property (cf. Section 7.1).

OECD's National Accounts, however, supply actual value-added data on (i), and only expenditure data on (iv). They do not supply data on value added by, say, building materials industries or estate agents. With this in mind, let us look at Table 3.1.

There are three relevant National Account tables in the OECD: on GDP, on value added and its components by activity, and on final consumption expenditure by households (FCEH). In the GDP table, GDP is measured in the three standard ways: as output, as expenditure, and as income. In all cases, the figure for GDP naturally comes up the same. The main difference between gross value added (GVA) and GDP is net taxes on products.[4]

The main items in the National Accounts that are obviously related to RE are construction and rental payments for housing (actual and imputed). Rents earned for making RE available for business purposes are not shown separately; they are part of 'gross operating surplus and gross mixed income', calculated in the context of the income approach to GDP. Other items where RE shows up are 'financial intermediation, real estate, renting and business activities', and 'housing, water, electricity, gas and other fuels', only this comes under FCEH rather than under GDP or Value Added. Also, the rental payments accounts come under the FCEH account. The reader should notice that the figure for FCEH ($690,695 million) in Part C of Table 3.1 is the same as in Part A (GDP, expenditure approach).

Table 3.1 How to make sense of OECD National Account statistics as regards RE

Example: Australia (national currency, current prices, millions, 2008)						
Part A: Gross domestic product (GDP)						
GDP, output approach						1,253,121
Gross value added (GVA) at basic prices, excluding FISIM*					1,156,900	
Of which:	Construction			85,789		
	Financial intermediation, real estate, renting, and business activities			353,011		
* FISIM = financial intermediation services indirectly measured						
GDP, expenditure approach						1,253,121
Of which:	Final consumption expenditure by households (FCEH)			690,695		
	Gross fixed capital formation (GFCF)			363,719		
	Of which:	Dwellings	71,039			
		Other buildings and structures (OBS)	128,778			
GDP, income approach						1,253,121
Of which:	Compensation of employees			607,511		
	Of which:	Construction		47,478		
		Financial intermediation, real estate, renting, and business activities		157,150		
	Gross operating surplus and gross mixed income			517,207		

Table 3.1 Cont'd

Part B: Value added and its components by activity						
Total Activity						1,156,900
	Of which:	Construction		85,789		
		Financial intermediation	124,615			
		Real estate, renting, business activities	228,396			
		Subtotal =		353,011		
	How is the difference between total activity and GDP accounted for?					
		Total Activity		1,156,900		
		+ Taxes less subsidies on products		88,581		
		+ Statistical discrepancy		7,640		
		= GDP		1,253,121		
Part C: Final consumption expenditures by households (FCEH)						
FCEH						690,695
Of which:	Housing, water, electricity, gas, and other fuels				141,410	
	Of which:	Actual rentals for housing		29,032		
		Imputed rentals for housing		91,037		
		Maintenance and repair of the dwelling		NA		
		Water supply and miscellaneous services related to the dwelling		6,531		
		Electricity, gas, and other fuels		14,810		
		Subtotal =		141,410		

Under the income approach to GDP construction appears to be $47,478 million, whereas under the output approach it is $85,789 million. Look more carefully, though: under the income approach, those $47,478 million are only compensation of employees working in construction – hence the difference (which is made up of earned rent, interest, and mostly profit).

Finally, under the expenditure approach to GDP, the sum of gross fixed capital formation in dwellings and other buildings and structures (i.e., the whole of construction) is $199,817 million (= 71,039 + 128,778 million), whereas under the output approach to GDP, construction is $85,789 million. The difference is due to the following three factors:[5]

1. Net (indirect) taxes.
2. In compiling GDP under the output approach, GVA for each industry is compiled as the sum of gross output (measured at basic, i.e., after-tax, prices) less the sum of intermediate consumption (measured at purchasers' prices). But investment activity, under the expenditure approach to GDP, is recorded on a gross output basis. Hence GVA for the construction industry is smaller than GFCF in construction because intermediate consumption has been deducted from gross output.
3. Under the output approach to GDP each unit – like 'construction' – is classified to the industry reflecting its primary productive activity. Units contributing to the 'construction' industry are those engaged primarily in construction. Construction activity undertaken by a mining company, for instance, would be reflected in industry GVA for mining, not construction, since mining is its primary activity. Thus GFCF is recorded as a total irrespective of originating industry under the expenditure approach to GDP, whereas not all GFCF relates to the construction industry under the output approach to GDP.

Table 3.2 gives an idea of the contribution of dwelling rents to the GDP of a sample of developed countries. Table 3.2 allows one to conclude the following as regards the contribution of residential rents to consumption and GDP in the given sample of developed countries for the period 1998–2009:

(a) Actual and imputed rents contributed about 8.5 per cent to the GDP of those countries over the period.
(b) Actual rents corresponded to about 4.6 per cent of the final consumption expenditure of households (net of imputed rents, since they do not represent actual outlays). The figure provides no indication on the burden of rent expenditure for actually renting households; it only shows how much of total consumption expenditure (net of imputed rents) is accounted for by actual rents.
(c) Actual rents were about 25 per cent of all rents, which is roughly in line with the proportion of actually renting households to all households (32.28 per cent), especially if the latter proportion is qualified by taking out households which occupy rent-free.

Table 3.3 shows the contribution of construction to GDP, and of construction employment to total employment. A number of conclusions follow from Table 3.3:

(a) Gross fixed capital formation (GFCF) in dwellings and other buildings and structures (D&OBS) was nearly 12 per cent of GDP (expenditure approach).
(b) GFCF in D&OBS was nearly 55 per cent of all physical investment.

Table 3.2 Shares of household rents in consumption and GDP in sample of developed countries, 1998–2009 period averages; owner-occupation rates, c. mid-2000s

	Sum of actual and imputed rents as % of GDP	*Actual rents as % of final consumption expenditure by households, net of imputed rents (i.e., AR/(FCEH-IR)*	*Actual rents as % of all rents (i.e., actual and imputed)*	*Owner-occupation c. mid-2000s*
Australia	9.47%	4.78%	25.45%	69.80%
Canada	10.55%	5.56%	24.84%	68.40%
USA	10.56%	3.83%	21.66%	67.80%
Austria	6.73%	3.10%	22.11%	57.00%
Belgium	8.37%	4.56%	24.57%	78.00%
Denmark	8.73%	6.89%	32.96%	54.00%
Finland	10.88%	7.68%	29.09%	59.00%
France	9.78%	4.78%	23.24%	57.40%
Germany	9.18%	7.66%	43.10%	43.20%
Greece	9.16%	3.03%	21.25%	80.60%
Iceland	8.37%	3.31%	19.03%	82.50%
Ireland	7.24%	2.81%	15.35%	74.50%
Italy	8.00%	2.21%	14.41%	80.00%
Netherlands	6.89%	5.86%	37.11%	57.00%
Norway	6.21%	3.27%	19.97%	77.00%
Portugal	5.98%	1.97%	18.91%	76.00%
Spain	7.04%	1.66%	11.95%	84.50%
Sweden	10.04%	9.73%	39.41%	52.00%
UK	8.49%	4.42%	29.39%	68.00%
Average	8.51%	4.58%	24.94%	67.72%
StDev	1.52%	2.19%	8.47%	11.96%
CV	17.82%	47.71%	33.98%	17.66%

Explanations: The percentages in Table 3.2 are derived from OECD data (OECD.stat, National Accounts) from 1998 to 2008 or 2009, with some exceptions (say, 2000–7 or later), except for data on owner-occupation, which are from the mid-2000s, and come from EMF Hypostat 2008, except for Australia, Canada, and the UK, data for which come from HFN. Table 3.2 contains the 16 biggest countries in Western Europe, and 3 advanced English-speaking countries outside Europe. New Zealand and Switzerland are not included because OECD had no original data on rents for them (which is unfortunate as Switzerland in particular has the lowest rate of owner-occupation in Western Europe). Greece is included because traditionally it has belonged to the Western European group, although geographically it is in Eastern Europe.

(AR+IR)/GDP = ratio of the sum of actual and imputed rentals to GDP.

AR/(FCEH-IR) = ratio of actual rentals (AR) to final consumption expenditure by households (FCEH) net of imputed rents (IR).

AR/TR = ratio of actual to total rentals.

CV = coefficient of variation = StDev/Average, a metric that shows how large the standard deviation is in relation to the corresponding average.

(c) GFCF in dwellings only was about 26 per cent of all physical investment – and therefore approximately half of all construction.
(d) Gross value added (GVA) by construction was about 6 per cent of GDP (output approach).
(e) Employment in construction was nearly 8 per cent of total employment.

Combining information from Tables 3.2 and 3.3, it would appear that slightly more than 20 per cent of GDP (expenditure approach) was accounted for by residential rents (actual and imputed) and total construction. Adding the output of other RE-related services

Table 3.3 Investment in construction as percentage of GDP and of GFCF; GVA by construction as percentage of GDP; construction employment as percentage of total employment, in sample of developed countries, 1998–2009 period averages

	GFCF in dwellings and OBS as % of GDP (expenditure approach)	*GFCF in dwellings and OBS as % of all GFCF*	*GFCF in dwellings as % of all GFCF*	*GVA by construction as % of GDP (output approach)*	*Employment in construction as % of total employment*
Australia	13.52%	50.99%	22.89%	6.93%	8.22%
Canada	12.75%	61.28%	28.35%	5.49%	6.02%
NZ	11.56%	52.82%	26.38%	4.72%	7.34%
USA	9.69%	51.87%	24.87%	4.68%	7.06%
Austria	11.84%	52.90%	21.48%	7.33%	8.52%
Belgium				4.96%	6.67%
Denmark	10.21%	50.97%	25.68%	5.42%	6.89%
Finland	12.74%	63.94%	30.83%	6.33%	6.53%
France	11.86%	59.93%	30.17%	5.69%	5.77%
Germany	10.36%	54.34%	31.32%	4.58%	7.50%
Greece	12.17%	58.38%	33.53%	6.45%	7.80%
Iceland	15.84%	67.84%	20.57%	8.13%	7.75%
Ireland	16.52%	71.23%	41.68%	8.27%	10.91%
Italy	10.12%	49.78%	22.55%	5.57%	8.18%
Netherlands	11.50%	56.57%	29.63%	5.55%	5.92%
Norway	13.05%			4.62%	6.92%
Portugal	15.02%				11.17%
Spain	15.15%	55.89%	26.75%	9.94%	11.91%
Sweden	7.24%	40.24%	15.07%	4.73%	5.83%
Switzerland	7.86%	36.56%	20.55%	5.54%	7.03%
UK	9.05%	53.90%	19.59%		7.75%
Average	11.90%	54.97%	26.22%	6.05%	7.70%
StDev	2.54%	8.49%	6.20%	1.48%	1.72%
CV	21.31%	15.44%	23.64%	24.46%	22.35%

Sources: (a) For National Accounts data, OECD.stat; (b) For employment data, OECD.stat (employment construction as % of total employment), except for France (employees in construction as % of employees in all activities), and the US, where the source was www.economagic.com (employment level 16 yrs+ in construction as % of civilian labour force). Coverage: 1998–2009, but in some cases (countries) some years were missing from the OECD tables.

GFCF = gross fixed capital formation.

OBS = Other buildings and structures.

GVA = Gross value added (GDP net of intermediate consumption).

(e.g., facilitating transactions in RE, etc.) and of business rents – which is not done here – would push this figure higher still.

3.2 RE investment and economic growth

3.2.1 Multiplier effects

The dynamic contribution of RE investment to GDP and employment comes through multiplier effects. But we need to clarify something: there is a difference between the aggregate investment spending multiplier, on the one hand, and so-called partial multipliers, on the other. Partial multipliers aim at capturing the impact of particular sectors of the economy on other sectors, or on the whole economy.

The macroeconomic multiplier M is a number that shows by how much GDP changes given an initial change in aggregate spending (usually investment). This multiplier is a function of[6] (i) the marginal propensity to consume, c, (ii) the marginal propensity to import, m, (iii) the marginal propensity to tax, t, and (iv) inflation. The simplest way to measure the size of M is through an *ex post*[7] calculation,i.e., dividing a measured final change in real GDP by an initial measured change in spending, the quotient being the multiplier, all on the assumption of a given aggregate supply (AS) curve. Subsequently a forecast can be made on the effect on real GDP of a given change in spending, assuming the same AS curve. So, although inflation is known to reduce the size of the multiplier, the *ex post* approach on the basis of real, rather than nominal, figures is a good enough way to assess the multiplier strength of investment spending.

Partial multipliers[8] are derived from input–output tables, the basic tool of an economic technique called input–output analysis (see Box 3.1).

Box 3.1 Input – output analysis

This is a method for analysing linkages between sectors (or geographical regions) in an economy. Imagine a grid with rows and columns, very much like a MS Excel worksheet. Each row and each column represents an industry in the economy. A cell entry shows the output of the industry specified by the row – an output that at the same time is delivered as input to the industry specified by the column, like this:

Industry	A	B	C	Total output
A	20	30	30	80
B	35	15	5	55
C	25	10	40	75
Total input	80	55	75	**210**

In the above table, industry A has produced a sum-total of 80 units of output value, which have been used as inputs by industry A itself (20 units), industry B (30 units), and industry C (30 units). Turning to inputs, industry A has used 20 units of inputs (produced by itself), 35 units of inputs produced by industry B, and 25 units of inputs produced by industry C, giving a total of 80 units of inputs. It may seem strange to see industries producing as much output as their inputs, but if one thinks of profit as the price of the input called 'entrepreneurial ability', then the mystery is solved. In this form the table's function is to show the interdependencies between industries.

Further reading

Leontief, W. (1986) *Input–Output Economics*, 2nd edn. Cambridge: Cambridge University Press.

ten Raa, T. (2006) *The Economics of Input–Output Analysis*. Cambridge: Cambridge University Press.

http://mailer.fsu.edu/~tchapin/garnet-tchapin/urp5261/lectures/Input-Output%20Overview.ppt.

Table 3.4 Partial multipliers for construction and RE-related, as well as other, industries in Scotland in 2004

	Type I multiplier			*Type II multiplier*		
	Output multiplier	*Employment multiplier*	*GVA multiplier*	*Output multiplier*	*Employment multiplier*	*GVA multiplier*
Housing-related industries:						
Construction	1.59	1.58	1.62	1.88	1.93	1.95
Owning and dealing in RE	1.39	2.55	1.27	1.59	3.65	1.43
Letting of dwellings	1.37	2.85	1.27	1.46	3.38	1.34
Estate agent activities	1.4	1.2	1.34	1.72	1.37	1.61
Non-housing-related industries:						
Motor vehicles	1.2	1.19	1.33	1.4	1.45	1.71
Retail distribution	1.4	1.16	1.34	1.73	1.33	1.63
Hotels, catering, pubs, etc.	1.2	1.07	1.13	1.53	1.2	1.39
Banking and finance	1.38	1.54	1.34	1.63	1.93	1.57
Education	1.22	1.14	1.16	1.74	1.42	1.54
Health and veterinary services	1.16	1.1	1.12	1.62	1.36	1.46

Adapted from Monk et al. (2010: 9).

Table 3.4 presents some RE-related partial multipliers for Scotland, and compares them with those of other industries.

Explanations

Economic activity has direct, indirect, and induced effects. A *direct effect* is the change in output as producers react to a change in the final demand for a product. An *indirect effect* is the result of a change in demand on those producers' suppliers, and so on down the supply chain. An *induced effect* is the amount of income spent on final goods and services as a result of the initial change in income that was brought about by the direct and indirect effects. *Type I multipliers* capture the combined impact of direct and indirect effects. *Type II multipliers* capture also the induced effects. There are four kinds of Type I multipliers commonly used[9] (Type II multipliers are derived the same way, with induced effects added to the numerator):

$$\text{output multiplier} = \frac{\text{direct and indirect output changes}}{\text{direct output change}},$$

$$\text{employment multiplier} = \frac{\text{direct and indirect changes in employment}}{\text{direct employment change}},$$

$$\text{income multiplier (not shown)} = \frac{\text{direct and indirect changes in income}}{\text{direct income change}},$$

$$\text{GVA multiplier} = \frac{\text{direct and indirect GVA changes}}{\text{direct GVA change}}.$$

These multipliers show the effects on output, employment, income, and GVA of a direct output change due to a unit change in final demand. For example, for every £1 increase in final demand for construction, there was generated an extra £0.59 of output through direct and indirect effects, or an extra £0.88 if induced effects are also taken into account. For every 100 jobs generated directly in construction, there were generated another 58 jobs (Type I multiplier), or another 93 jobs (Type II multiplier, i.e., including induced effects). And so on. Interesting conclusions follow from Table 3.4. Scottish construction had the strongest Type I and Type II output and GVA multipliers among all industries in the table. It also had a stronger Type I employment multiplier than all non-housing-related industries in the table, and again a stronger Type II employment multiplier than those industries, with the exception of banking and finance, whose multiplier, at 1.93, just matched the one for the construction sector. 'Owning and dealing in RE' as well as 'letting of dwellings' also showed stronger Type I and Type II employment multipliers than any other industry.

The reader must be warned that an employment multiplier of, say, 2.85 for the 'letting of dwellings' does not mean that this activity employs more people than, say, the construction sector: it only means that it creates more new jobs indirectly per additional person employed directly than construction does. Also, these multipliers are not given for all time or for all places: earlier data from 2001 suggested an employment multiplier for construction that was smaller than those for various financial sectors (Munro and Karley, 2005). And a Philippines study using I–O tables from 2000 (Dumaua, 2010) found that, among the 11 most important industries in the country, the manufacturing industry showed the highest output multiplier, the construction industry the highest GVA multiplier, and the private services industry the highest income and employment multipliers. Such differences between times or countries are due to national variations in interdependencies between industries, which in turn result from differences in technology, in the mix of resources used (e.g., capital versus labour), and in the social and institutional framework.

But the most important point brought up by the two national experiences cited (Scotland and the Philippines) is that construction and/or other RE-related activities tend to be associated with strong multiplier performance (although not always the strongest). Corroborating evidence abounds:

- *USA:* Evaluating President Obama's American Recovery and Reinvestment Plan (which was supposed to save or create at least three million jobs by end-2010), Romer and Bernstein (2009) utilized a simulation that suggested that 18.4 per cent of all jobs created would be in construction – a higher percentage than any other industry.
- *Minnesota:* The Minnesota Housing Finance Agency (2009) calculated that 'between 2Q 2005 and 2Q 2008 the number of employees in Minnesota's residential construction industry dropped by 27.8 per cent [...]. The largest decline in all the other industries was only 2.7 per cent.' This goes to show that a large multiplier performance is bound to cut both ways: a strong positive effect in good times, but also a strong negative effect in bad times.
- *UK:* A study using 2002 data calculated that the construction industry's Type I multiplier was 2.09, and the total output multiplier 2.84 (LEK Consulting, 2009). The Type I result placed construction above such sectors as agriculture, motor vehicles, shipbuilding and repair, and banking and finance.
- *Australia:* On the basis of 1996–97 data, for every \$1 million spent on construction, a total of \$2.9 million would be generated, as well as 37 new jobs (including 9 jobs in construction directly). In value-added terms, the industry was described as one of the five largest in the economy (ABS, 2002).

If construction, in comparison with other sectors, has such strong multiplier effects, one would expect that construction investment, and residential investment in particular (being about half of all construction, at least in the sample of developed countries of Table 3.3), is a major contributor to economic growth. But how much does it actually help economic growth? Or is it helped by it instead? The evidence is not clear-cut, for a number of reasons:

One way to measure the macroeconomic contribution of construction to economic growth is by associating (i) value added by construction (CVA) as a proportion of GDP to (ii) real GDP (or real GDP per capita) over many years, or across many countries, or both. If a high positive correlation is the result, then one might conclude, tentatively, that a lot of construction is good for growth. But there are two concerns:

1 There must surely be a limit to the rise in the CVA/GDP ratio as real GDP (or real GDP per capita) rises. That is, the share of any ascendant industry (not just construction) into GDP cannot keep rising indefinitely, but, after a point, will tend to flatten out, or even decline. That is because a growing GDP usually allows and even encourages the introduction and/or rise of other industries, which sooner or later will command expanding shares of their own. Thus, the time path of CVA/GDP might conceivably be better represented by an S curve,[10] rather than an upward-sloping straight line – and so might the relationship between real GDP (on the horizontal axis) and CVA/GDP (on the vertical axis).
2 Is it construction that pulls GDP, or the other way around?

3.2.2 A limit to the share of construction in GDP?

The first concern is the behaviour of the ratio CVA/GDP as real GDP (per capita) increases. Does it reach a plateau – as it must – and how soon? To answer the question, we shall look into (i) a group of underdeveloped countries from 1970 to 1994, (ii) the US experience from 1969 to 2009, and (iii) the related pattern shown by 173 countries from 1970 to 2008.

(i) Studying 15 developing countries of sub-Saharan Africa from 1970 to approximately 1994, Lopes et al. (2002) concluded that, roughly, where GDP per capita increased, the ratio CVA/GDP tended to remain practically constant; where GDP per capita decreased, the ratio declined too. They interpreted this as evidence that 'the construction sector pursues the economic lead of the manufacturing industry, its main partner in economic growth and development' rather than the other way around – so, in effect, Lopes et al. addressed the issue of the ratio CVA/GDP by going over to the issue of who pulls whom.
(ii) The share of (private) construction in the US GDP from 1969 to 2009 has not changed much over 41 years. It has moved roughly between 6 and 10 per cent (with an average of 8.12 per cent and a standard deviation of 1.01 per cent; the corresponding figures for residential investment are 4.52 per cent and 0.76 per cent). If anything, the overall trend is a declining one (see Figure 3.1).
(iii) Our own survey of UN panel data covering 173 countries from 1970 to 2008 has also provided useful insights. The design of the study was as follows. The UN has National Accounts data for 216 countries, covering the years from 1970 to 2008. On the basis of those National Accounts, time series were constructed on real GDP per capita per country and on the ratio of construction investment to GDP (i.e., C/GDP) per country for the entire period 1970–2008. Then period average values for those two variables were calculated for each country. Of those countries, 36 were rejected because the time series on them were not continuous (e.g., USSR, Russia). Of the remaining 180, seven

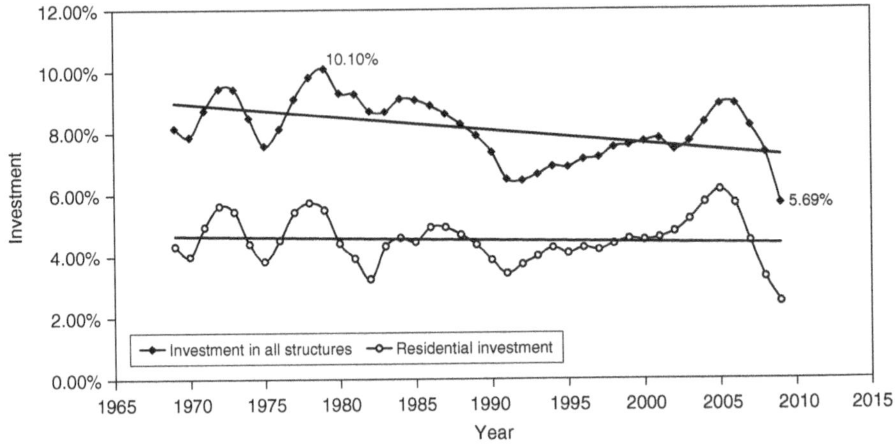

Figure 3.1 USA, 1969–2009: Gross private domestic investment in residential and non-residential structures as a percentage of GDP.

more were rejected because they involved extreme C/GDP values; they were, that is, 'outliers'. ('Extreme' was defined as any national C/GDP average value lying outside two standard deviations from the corresponding total average for all 180 countries.) Those seven countries were Trinidad and Tobago, Guinea-Bissau, Montserrat, Poland, Anguilla, Myanmar, and Bhutan. In their cases, the average C/GDP ranged from 11.57 per cent (Trinidad and Tobago) to 19.30 per cent (Bhutan).

The remaining 173 countries were split between 5 cohorts, ranked by real GDP per capita. The first cohort (lowest) contained 34 countries, the next three 35 countries each, and the last cohort (highest) 34 again. Then, the average real GDP per capita, the corresponding standard deviation, the average C/GDP, and the corresponding standard deviation were calculated. Another metric that was calculated was the ratio of standard deviation to the average value for each variable (the so-called coefficient of variation, which shows how much a sequence of values fluctuates in relation to its mean). The results are shown in Table 3.5.

1. Overall, C/GDP for the given sample of countries over the period of study was 5.68 per cent, with a standard deviation of 2.14 percentage points around it.
2. It would appear that (a) the ratio of construction investment to GDP tends to grow with real GDP per capita, and stabilize once a certain level of economic development is reached; and (b) as shown by the CV, fluctuations around the average C/GDP tend to become smaller as a proportion of the mean, as that mean becomes larger and at the same time real incomes grow (the second factor seems the more important).
3. These two points, 1 and 2, give rise to graphs that can actually be approximated by S curves as suggested above (see Figures 3.2 and 3.3).[11]

3.2.3 Who pulls whom – GDP or construction?

The second concern is about which variable pulls the other more strongly – is it GDP growth that augments construction investment or the opposite? A number of studies have tried to

Table 3.5 Economic growth and proportion of construction investment into GDP

Effective sample: 173 countries, 1970–2008

Cohort	*Average GDP per capita (AvGDPpc) in constant 1990 $US*	*Average ratio of construction/ GDP (AvC/GDP)*	*Standard deviation of AvGDPpc in constant 1990 $US*	*Standard deviation of AvC/GDP*	*AvGDPpc: coefficient of variation (CV)*	*AvC/GDP: coefficient of variation (CV)*
34 countries	335.66	4.41%	117.62	2.15%	35.04%	48.69%
35 countries	827.03	5.01%	170.84	1.96%	20.66%	39.14%
35 countries	1,815.16	6.28%	472.81	2.15%	26.05%	34.23%
35 countries	6,835.57	6.43%	3,116.88	2.00%	45.60%	31.11%
34 countries	22,351.78	6.24%	7,773.26	1.73%	34.78%	27.75%
173 countries	6,376.29	5.68%	9,042.74	2.14%	141.82%	37.71%

Source of primary data: UNO.

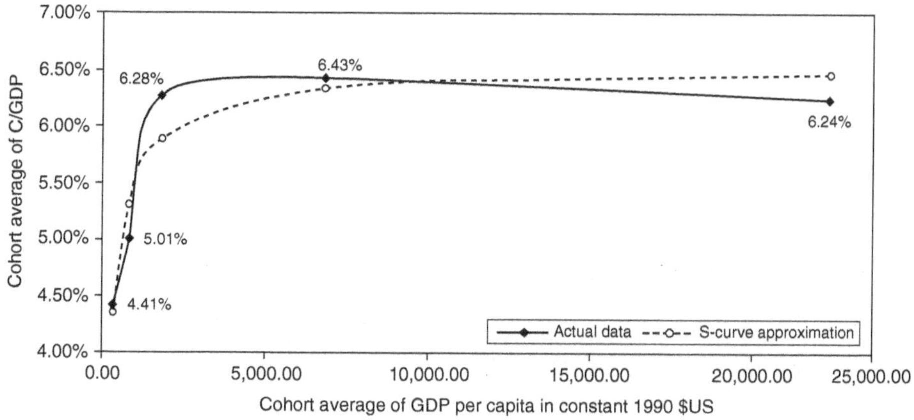

Figure 3.2 Economic growth and ratio of construction investment to GDP (C/GDP): 173 countries, distributed in five cohorts (from lowest to highest average GDP per capita), 1970–2008.

answer this question. Some of these are presented below, but the reader would do well to refer to Chapter 2 before proceeding, as most of them involve advanced econometric techniques that are explained in that chapter:

- Using Granger-causality methodology on Hong Kong data from 1983 Q1 to 1995 Q1, Tse and Ganesan (1997) found that GDP tended to lead the construction sector flow and not the other way around.
- Studying the pattern of housing investment in advanced economies from the nineteenth century to 1992, Ball and Wood (1999) concluded that housing investment is subject to long cycles, the most pronounced of which happened after the Second World War. They also concluded that in the 1950s and 1960s, housing investment contributed to economic stability (i.e., it helped economies come out of recessions by positively affecting GDP growth), but as of the 1970s it had become a destabilizing force in the world economy

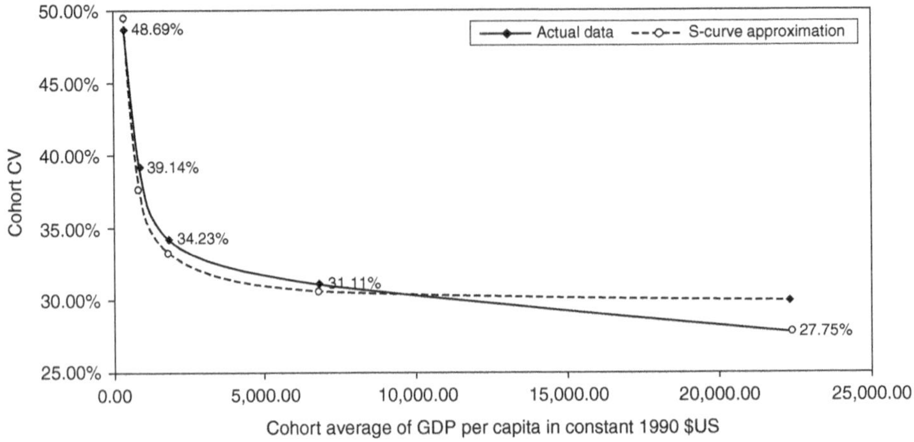

Figure 3.3 Economic growth and coefficient of variation (CV) of construction investment to GDP: 173 countries, distributed in five cohorts, 1970–2008 (CV = StDev of construction investment to GDP as a proportion of average construction investment to GDP).

(a point made well before the 2008 global crisis, which came to a head with the collapse of house prices in the USA).

- Using Granger-causality analysis, Hongyu et al. (2002) found evidence that over the period 1981–2000 housing investment in China had a stronger short-run effect on economic growth than non-housing investment. They also found that housing investment had a long-run effect on economic growth while economic growth had a long-run effect on both housing and non-housing investment.
- Wigren and Wilhelmsson (2007) addressed the issue of the link between building investment and economic development in 14 Western European countries (12 in the EU), with data from 1980 to 2004. They concluded that GDP Granger-caused total construction in the short run, but not vice versa, that particularly infrastructure investment Granger-caused GDP in the short run, and that residential construction had a long-run effect on economic growth.
- Using the statistical techniques of co-integration and the Granger-causality test, in a study that covered the period 1950–2005, Ali Khan (2008) showed that there was a causal relationship between the economy and the construction sector in Pakistan. Moreover, the relationship was unidirectional in that it was construction that affected GDP (with a one-year lag), rather than the opposite.
- Using panel co-integration analysis and quarterly province-level data from 1999 Q1 to 2007 Q4 from China, Chen and Zhu (2008) identified a bidirectional Granger causality between housing investment and GDP in both the short run and the long run for the whole of China. Their paper is particularly interesting because it documents a remarkable divergence in the Granger-causality relationship between housing investment and GDP across the three regions of China particularly studied. Citing Quigley (2008), who has found evidence for strong links between urbanization and economic development, they concluded that 'housing investment will Granger-cause GDP only at regions that have reached a high level of economic development often characterized by a high level of urbanization' (p. 24).

- Mallick and Mahalik (2008) studied Indian data from 1961–62 to 2005–06 in a co-integration time-series framework. They concluded that the Indian construction sector was a major contributor to economic growth, especially if the influence of the existing stock of capital were dropped from their model. In addition, they drew attention to the possibility that construction investment has a stronger short-run impact on the economy in developed countries than in developing countries. They made this observation citing Leamer (2007), who, on the basis of post-Second World War data, had concluded that housing construction *is* (sic) the business cycle in the USA, i.e., housing construction is the decisive factor causing the ups and downs of total economic activity in the country.

It seems that there is no clear-cut, or law-like, answer to the question of who pulls whom. Sometimes it is GDP that pulls construction investment (in the short run or in the long run, or both), sometimes it is the opposite, and sometimes the pull is mutual. And the pull may well vary depending on the component of total construction that is being studied (housing versus other buildings versus infrastructure).

The reason for the fluidity of the results of those studies can probably be attributed to construction activity depending not simply on the level of real economic growth, but on (a) the level of economic development (a broader concept than growth, that involves the overall structure and dynamics of an economy), (b) the frequency and amplitude of business cycles, which in turn tend to characterize advanced free-market economies more than less developed or statist ones, and (c) the institutional framework (laws, regulations, bureaucracy, strength and nature of land and property rights) of the country concerned.

3.3 Determinants of RE investment; Tobin's *q*

So far, we have looked into the possible macroeconomic relationship between construction investment and GDP. But what determines construction investment at the micro-level – the level of consumers, suppliers, and their motives? The question cannot be answered in a blanket way, as construction is made up of three broad components: housing, other buildings (e.g., offices), and other structures (e.g., roads). In this section, we shall examine a number of, not mutually exclusive, possibilities (using housing as example), whose underlying and unifying theme is that construction is basically demand-driven:

3.3.1 Utility-driven investment

One idea is that housing consumers will go on demanding (and buying) 'housing services' (in the general forms of owner-occupation or of private renting) to the point where the utility they derive from one last unit of housing is equal to its price. As long as the marginal utility MU of housing is greater than the price P of housing, there will be demand for housing services, and therefore new construction or renovation of dwellings will be occurring (usually after a number of previously vacant properties have been put on the market and taken).

For example, if there is a population increase (and/or a rise in the rate of household formation), the MU of the existing stock of dwellings will rise higher than the (equilibrium) market price P_e of housing that existed just before the demographic change; alternatively, households will be demanding a greater quantity of housing services at the old equilibrium price. In other words, the market demand curve (which is supposed to be the horizontal sum of all individual demand curves and hence of MU curves) will shift to the right. But a higher MU implies a greater willingness on the part of (income-constrained) households to pay more

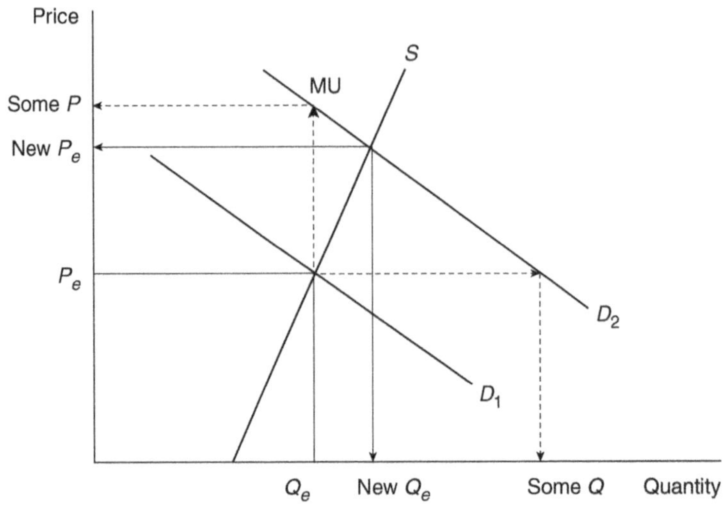

Figure 3.4 Changes in marginal utility cause the equilibrium price to change. A rise in demand from D_1 to D_2 increases the MU of the original equilibrium quantity Q_e. As a result, the price P increases from P_e to some P – or, alternatively, at the original P_e a bigger Q is demanded. The rise in P induces suppliers to supply more, causing MU to drop. The drop in MU continues until MU is equal to a new P_e.

for their housing, i.e., a higher market price (although not an equilibrium one at this point). Suppliers will respond to the higher price of the existing dwelling stock by building more. As additional units are added to the stock, its MU drops (law of diminishing MU), until MU (measured in money) is equated to the price at which suppliers are willing and able to create more dwellings. At that point, a new (higher than before) equilibrium market price will have been established, at which MU $= P_e$ rather than MU $> P_e$ (see Figure 3.4).

3.3.2 *Tobin's q*

A variant of the previous idea is that investment will take place if the ratio of house prices to the cost of construction is larger than 1. This is, roughly, a real estate application of Tobin's q ratio.[12] Tobin's q was originally developed for firms and capital assets in general (including, therefore, non-residential RE). In a typical formulation, the numerator is the market value of a firm and the denominator is the replacement cost of the firm's capital assets. More precisely (Tobin and Brainard, 1976: 238),

$$\text{Tobin's } q = \frac{\text{market valuation of reproducible real capital assets}}{\text{current replacement cost of those assets}}.$$

In the case of housing, this is transformed into (Jud and Winkler, 2003)

$$\text{Tobin's } q = \frac{\text{price of existing housing}}{\text{price of new homes}}.$$

In another formulation, the cost of building new homes includes the price of land (which can be very substantial), so the q ratio becomes (Deichmann Haagerup, 2009)

$$q = \frac{\text{market price of existing houses}}{\text{construction cost plus land cost for new housing}}.$$

Better still, as Schulz and Werwatz (2004), and also Corgel (1997), have pointed out, the numerator should explicitly be a hedonic price index,[13] and the denominator a replacement cost index[14] that includes both construction and land costs:

$$q = \frac{\text{a hedonic price index}}{\text{a replacement cost index (for construction and land costs)}}.$$

In fact, the previous, demand-oriented, explanation of housing investment and this one, which is supply-oriented, join very nicely together, in the sense that an imbalance between (a rising) MU and original equilibrium price P_e pushes up the average price of existing homes. If the increase is sufficiently large, developers will build new ones. Jud and Winkler (2003) provided empirical evidence in favour of Tobin's q in their study of housing investment in the USA from 1979 to 2000. The Tobin's q they used in order to conduct their study was defined in the following way:

$$q = \frac{\text{OFHEO price index for existing homes}}{\text{Census Bureau's quality-adjusted series for new home prices}},$$

where OFHEO is the Office of Federal Housing Enterprise Oversight.[15] The ratio was then compared with building permits, housing starts, and housing investment expenditures over the period of study. Using co-integration analysis, the authors concluded that 'the housing market indeed functions as Tobin has theorized. Housing suppliers appear to respond to the demands of housing consumers, building more new homes when existing home prices are high relative to new home prices' (Jud and Winkler, 2002: 2). A strong link between Tobin's q and housing investment was also identified by Deichmann Haagerup (2009) in his study of Danish single-family houses from 1968 to 2008.

If properly calculated, a $q > 1$ is supposed to encourage property investment, for it means that there are profits to be had, as cost of construction and land, i.e., the replacement cost of real estate, is less than the price at which property will expectedly sell. Tobin's q, however, seems to conflict with the empirical observation that new properties often sell for more than older properties (Corgel, 1997). An explanation for this is as follows:

1. A $q > 1$ acts as a signal to show developers that there are profits to be had from supplying more RE (because at this point the average price of old properties is higher than the cost of replacement, i.e., the cost of supplying new ones).
2. Once a new property is built, a direct comparison between it and a (roughly similar) old one will almost certainly mean that the new one will sell at a premium over the price of the old property, if for no other reason than that the new building has a longer time horizon in which to bring in rents.
3. But when, with time, a large enough number of new properties has been supplied, causing the total RE stock to increase, the average market price will drop, depressing Tobin's q in turn.

The mechanism described should work more conspicuously where most transactions in the housing market involve older (i.e., secondhand) properties (which implies a planning constraint on land availability for building, and a greater willingness on the part of households to move home, as is the case, for example, in the UK). If, on the other hand, most transactions involve new-built properties (in the context of, say, an urbanization phase and, consequently, of laxer planning constraints), Tobin's q reaches a kind of limit: in essence, Tobin's q compares replacement cost to market value, but that presupposes that there is something to replace.

In the case of an urbanizing country, or expanding city, or maybe even of an effective constraint (perhaps an institutional or behavioural one) on selling or renting out one's property, there are not enough houses to start with, so new construction is not about 'replacing' but about augmenting the capital stock. The same thing – i.e., to augment rather than 'replace' – is likely to happen where (e.g., in Greece) the population, due to historic experiences of galloping inflation and/or for other reasons, has a particularly strong tendency (and the opportunity) to amass real estate wealth, i.e., direct their savings into real estate rather than stocks or business ventures.

In the UK, for example, there were 21,830,000 dwellings in 2007 (18,527,000 owner-occupied and 3,303,000 rented privately).[16] In the same year, the number of private dwellings completed by private enterprise was 197,460.[17] According to Nationwide,[18] the housing market turnover (i.e., the percentage of the private sector housing stock changing hands on an annualized basis) was about 7.2 per cent (it fell significantly the next year as the housing market got into a downturn, and recovered a bit in 2009). This means that, in 2007, about 1,572,000 dwellings were traded – nearly eight times the number of those completed.

In Greece,[19] by contrast, in 1998 (a not particularly special year, but the last one on which there are relevant data on property transfers), the number of transferred apartments (most of which were dwellings, but the figure also includes bequests in addition to sold properties) and the number of buildings transferred (a large number of which were dwellings) were 64,232 and 18,715, respectively – a total of 82,947 properties. In the same year 97,306 permits for the construction of new dwellings were issued by planning offices, while the housing stock was about 5,476,000. That means a ratio of transferred dwellings to construction activity of about 85 per cent. So in the UK it was the secondary housing market that carried the most weight in house price determination (that it was, in other words, the focus of housing demand), while in Greece it was the opposite.

In conclusion, if empirical data suggest that $q < 1$, we should normally expect a decrease in housing investment; if $q > 1$, we should expect an increase. But if $q < 1$ and there is a rise in investment, or $q > 1$ and there is a drop in investment, maybe we should check for time lags between the signal given by q and the investment response (and also make sure that we are comparing like with like, e.g., single houses in q's numerator with single houses in q's denominator).

3.3.3 RE investment as inflation hedge

A third idea about what determines construction investment, especially in the housing sphere, is that, in addition to 'mundane' demand-side drivers (like shelter, conspicuous consumption, and access to work and amenities), housing investment is also, under certain conditions, driven by store-of-value considerations on the part of households. This, however, really boils down to a rather ad hoc notion of utility. An example already mentioned is Greece, where most households' historic experiences of inflation have traditionally led them to view real estate as a safe haven for their savings. This attitude became laxer in 1998–99 (partly because of a significant drop in the rate of inflation in the preceding years), but the collapse of the Athens Stock Exchange in 2000 reawakened old sentiments – until, that is, the Greek economic crisis that started in 2009 began to depress property prices too.

In the same vein, the post-war growth of the British property market was once explained as 'the response of a financially sophisticated, land-locked, exchange-controlled people to inflation' (*The Economist*, 1978: 3). But large-scale investment in RE as a store of value is only possible if the tax regime does not discourage the possession of real estate wealth (which in Greece it unfortunately does as of 2010), and inevitable if other investment outlets are either absent or discredited or mistrusted. Importantly, store-of-value investment in RE is not only undertaken by households, but by financial institutions too (e.g., insurance companies and pension funds) with an interest in long-term capital maintenance and/or growth.

3.3.4 The role of 'fundamentals'

A fourth idea is that housing investment is determined by long-run 'fundamentals' like economic growth (and the way it is manifested in incomes), interest rates, demographics, and the institutional environment. That is true, but at the end of the day such factors in a free market shape individual and aggregate utilities which in turn shape private housing demand (whereas social housing, in the days when it was fashionable, was mostly affected by political considerations).

The precise modelling of the interaction between macro- and micro-factors is still an open research question. One reason is lack of data, particularly as regards utilities. Another is the aggregation problem: how to go from individual utility preferences to aggregate ones for communities, or for an entire country. Without solving this problem, linking the micro- and the macro-dimensions becomes virtually impossible (cf. Hildenbrand, 2008). Thus, whether a researcher should place more emphasis on 'fundamentals' or on utility modelling as (demand-side) explanations for housing investment depends a lot on which approach has better access to empirical data (of significance to the particular question asked), on the chosen time frame for research, and on the researcher's personal interests.

3.3.5 What about non-residential property?

Leaving private housing aside, two other kinds of construction merit notice. One is public works (including public housing), which are usually undertaken in response to perceived needs to facilitate development, but also as part of counter-cyclical policies on the part of governments – ostensibly at least (cf. Burns and Grebler, 1984). This kind of construction investment therefore depends a lot on government tax revenue and/or a government's ability to borrow. Another kind of construction is industrial premises (including warehousing), retail outlets, and offices. These are usually undertaken by the private sector, and are a response to the need to shelter presumably profitable activities. Developers may of course anticipate such demand (usually on the basis of current market rents) and rush ahead to build (McGough and Tsolacos, 1999). To a certain extent, developers may this way create a self-fulfilling prophecy: for example, the existence of modern office space in a city may actually attract customers who are searching nationally or globally for appropriate office locations.

3.4 The effect of RE prices on the economy

Changes in RE prices affect the wider economy through a number of channels (see HKMA (2001) and Figure 3.5). These are:

- consumption
- investment
- the financial sector
- inflation
- the government's fiscal position.

Let us have a closer look.

3.4.1 The consumption channel

This works primarily through the so-called 'housing wealth effect'.[20] ('Primarily' because housing wealth, in developed countries at least, tends to be the largest part of households' total wealth – and certainly the largest part of non-financial wealth (see Table 3.6).) The housing wealth effect is the idea that changes in house prices affect the housing wealth of households, who then respond by adjusting their non-housing consumption. This simple schema[21] raises at least two issues:

1 How exactly do house price changes lead to changes in consumption? Do they change the proportion of households' income going to consumption, or do they affect the willingness and ability of households to liquidate (some of) their home equity by taking a mortgage loan? Or both? Or something else? The answer to this involves, among others, the PILC (permanent income–life cycle)[22] hypothesis.
2 How strong is the housing wealth effect? And is it stronger or weaker than changes in consumption brought about by changes in households' financial wealth (e.g., stocks or shares)?

This is an important issue not just in theory, but also in practice, because if the housing wealth effect is strong, then a fall in house prices stands to reduce consumption spending, and this in turn will cause a sizable decline in the rate of real GDP growth (Bostic et al., 2008) – as it indeed happened in the USA following the collapse of house prices in 2008 and after.

A detailed discussion of the housing wealth effect is pursued in Section 3.5.

3.4.2 The investment channel

Changes in property prices (and not just housing) can affect investment via two channels:

1 A rise in property prices may make new construction more economical than buying existing properties. However, this can happen if the investor already owns the building land. If not, the rise in property prices will pull up the price of building lots (assuming an efficient land market) and may well erase the advantage of building vis-à-vis buying.
2 Rising property prices tend to improve firms' and banks' balance sheets, resulting in more bank lending to the business sector. Assuming that at least part of the increased lending is for fixed capital formation, investment should increase.

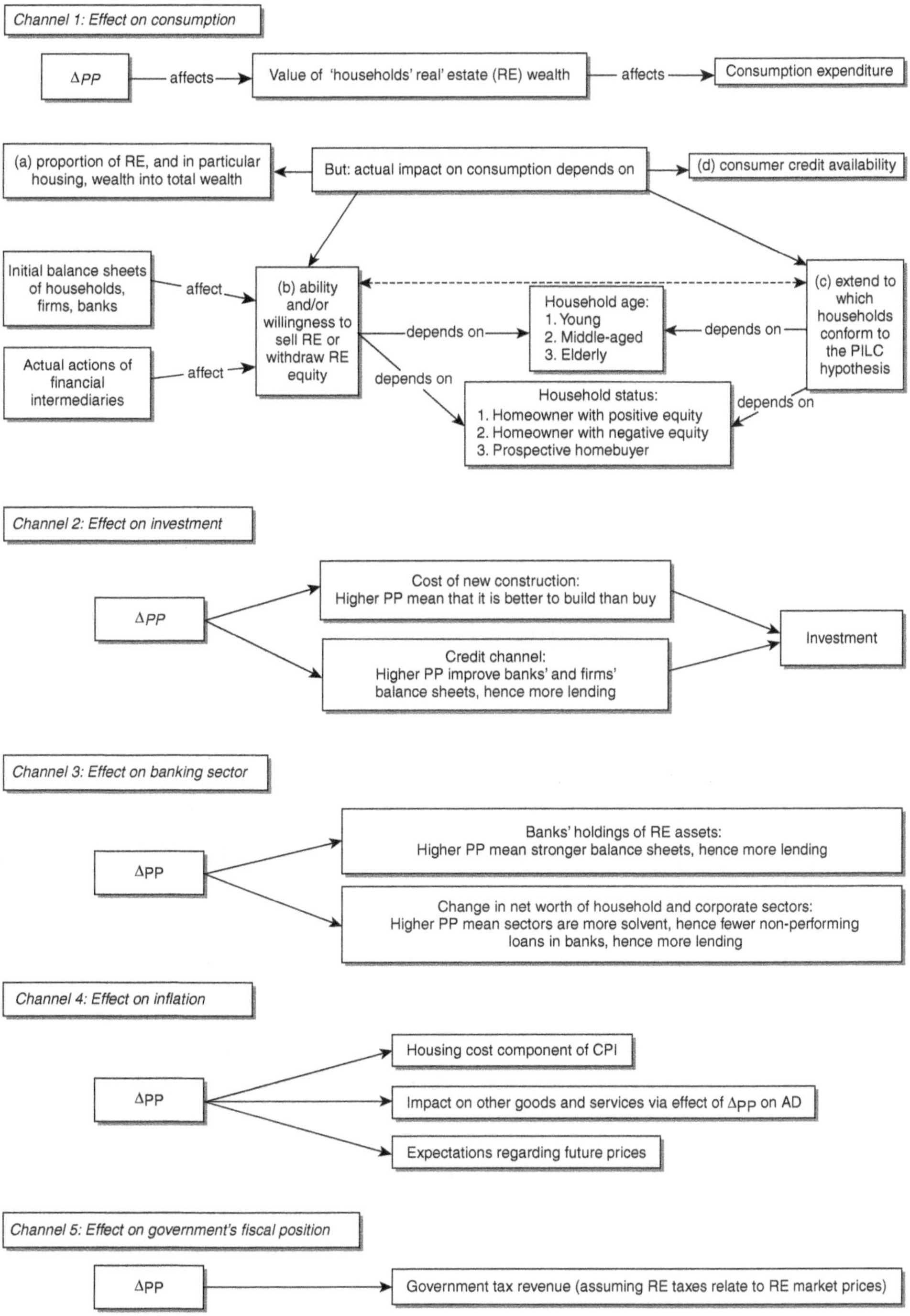

Figure 3.5 How changes in property prices (Δ_{PP}) affect the wider economy. (Adapted from HKMA (2001).)

Table 3.6 Household wealth and debt c. 2000 in 14 countries (percentage analysis)

	Canada	*Finland*	*Germany*	*Italy*	*Sweden*	*UK*	*US*	*US*
Source:	*Statistics Canada*	*Statistics Finland*	*DIW, Berlin*	*Bank of Italy*	*Statistics Sweden*	*BHPS*[1] *(ESRC)*	*PSID*[2]	*SCF*[3]
Year:	*1999*	*1998*	*2002*	*2002*	*2002*	*2000*	*2001*	*2001*
Non-financial assets	78	84	87	85	72	83	67	62
Of which:								
Principal residence[4]	64	64	64	68	61	74	52	45
Other real estate[4]	13	20	23	17	11	9	14	17
Financial assets	22	16	13	15	28	17	33	38
Total (%)	100	100	100	100	100	100	100	100
Debt[4]	26	16	18	4	35	21	22	21
Of which:								
Home-secured[4]	22	11		2		18		18
	Australia	*China*	*India*	*Japan*	*Netherlands*	*New Zealand*	*Spain*	
Non-financial assets	68	78	95	70	80	72	87	
Of which:								
Housing assets[4]	53.7	56.9	28.5	53.9	70.4	36.7	58.3	
Financial assets	32	22	5	30	20	28	13	
Total (%)	100	100	100	100	100	100	100	
Debt[4]	14	1	3	10	27	16	9	

[1] BHPS = British Household Panel Survey.
[2] PSID = Panel Study of Income Dynamics (Survey Research Centre of the University of Michigan).
[3] SCF = Survey of Consumer Finances (FRB and US Treasury Department).
[4] As percentage of total assets.
Source: Top row of countries: Sierminska et al. (2006). Bottom row of countries: Davies et al. (2006), based on 2000 survey data.

3.4.3 The financial sector channel

Again, there are two channels through which changes in property prices can affect the financial sector:

1 Directly, by affecting the value of real estate holdings on the part of financial institutions (banks and insurance companies). If property prices rise, this should allow institutions to meet capital adequacy requirements[23] more easily. In turn, this means greater ability to take on more business.
2 Indirectly, by affecting the solvency of households and corporate borrowers. If property prices rise, the extent of non-performing loans in banks' balance sheets, and of contract cancellations in the case of insurers, should diminish (enhancing their capital position and ability to lend or write more business), and vice versa.

3.4.4 The inflation channel

Changes in property prices affect inflation through three routes: (a) by affecting the housing cost component of the Consumer Price Index (CPI); (b) by first affecting consumption and investment, thereby affecting aggregate demand (AD) and ultimately the prices of other goods and services; (c) by affecting expectations of future prices on most any good or service.

3.4.5 The government's fiscal position channel

Changes in property prices have an impact on the amount of property tax revenue central or local governments can collect. *Ceteris paribus*, a rise would increase tax revenue, reducing a budget deficit (or increasing a budget surplus). A drop would have the opposite effect. This of course assumes that calculated taxes depend on actual market prices, which is not always the case: for example, in Greece, property taxes are calculated on the basis of imputed or 'objective' property prices, which, being arbitrary, can be quite removed from reality (even though they are occasionally updated).

3.5 The housing wealth effect (HWE)

Recall from Section 3.4.1 that the HWE is a change in consumption that happens or may happen as a result of a change in house prices. Of course a (housing) wealth effect and a (housing) collateral effect (i.e., cashing in on the value of one's home through borrowing) are not the only forces that impact on consumption: there is also the impact of financial wealth to consider, and, in addition, there may well be common causes that affect both house prices and consumption simultaneously – causes such as changes in expected income growth, tax changes or changes in credit market conditions (Attanasio et al., 2010).

For the HWE to take place (and be statistically significant), housing wealth must be a large part of households' total wealth – a requirement that is broadly met in developed countries (see Table 3.6). Given this premise, the mechanism whereby the effect on consumption of, say, a rise in house prices may materialize is threefold:

1 Some households sell their dwellings; or take a mortgage loan on the strength of the value of their home, thereby turning (part of) their home equity into cash. A house sale or a home-equity withdrawal (HEW) is a more frequent response in case of house

price rises than in case of house price falls – hence the possibility that the response of consumption to house price changes is asymmetrical: it depends on the direction of house price change. In addition, the form of the response (a house sale or a HEW) may be an important determinant of the final effect on consumption.

2 A large number of home-owning households simply adjust the proportion of their income they spend on non-housing consumption: a higher proportion if there is a rise, a smaller one if there is a fall. They would do this if they thought, for example, that greater housing wealth reduces the need to save for old age.

3 Many homeowners incur debt in the form of consumer credit, expecting higher house prices in the future – which, they think, will cushion them from any risks involved in a larger debt burden. (This is the stuff price bubbles are made of.) They then go on to debt-finance their current non-housing (and even housing) consumption.

Let us investigate these three mechanisms in greater detail.

3.5.1 The HWE as a home-equity adjustment

A home-equity adjustment (in response to a change in house prices) can happen through a homeowner either selling their home, or borrowing using their home as collateral (i.e., mortgaging a home they already own).

Home-equity adjustment through selling

In the case of selling, the immediate effect on consumption may depend on whether the seller manages to earmark all or part of the cash received from the sale for non-housing consumption (rather than buying another, equally priced or higher-priced, property). For most sellers to be able to do that, they must move downmarket after the sale of their original property. The frequency with which this happens is an open question, but it is more likely to involve owners of high-priced properties on the brink of retirement. Then again, such owners might not wish to move at all. If in need of extra cash, they would either use up their accumulated financial wealth, or, in a flexible mortgage market, would probably consider some form of equity withdrawal through borrowing (see Chapter 4).

There is another problem. To sell, someone must buy. The buyer may be a renter who wants to enter owner-occupation, or another homeowner who is moving upmarket (or across the market). If the proceeds from the sale of a property somehow allow the seller to increase their non-housing consumption now, wouldn't the typical buyer have to curtail their non-housing consumption in order to afford servicing the mortgage loan on the property? And wouldn't then one's increase in non-housing consumption be 'neutralized' by the other's decrease in non-housing consumption?

The answer to this depends, to a large extent, on the applicable interest rate and the other terms of financing. Broadly, the ability to borrow hinges on (a) the initial balance sheets (i.e., possessions of assets versus liabilities) of households, firms, and, of course, lenders (usually banks) and (b) the actual actions of financial intermediaries. For example, if households and firms are in broad financial health (i.e., they are not heavily into debt already), they will find it easier to borrow if property prices increase. Moreover, a rise in property prices tends to improve the financial health of households and firms by raising the value of their property assets. Banks, on their part, can extend credit more easily if they have strong balance sheets and, moreover, the structure of their asset holdings is such that it allows expansion of mortgage lending in particular. Deregulated credit will further enhance such expansion, while restricted credit will hamper it.

So it may be that a renter who is house-buying has secured such advantageous mortgage terms that his or her monthly mortgage payment is actually less, or only slightly higher, than what he or she had been paying by way of rent. It may also be that the buyer had been saving for years in order to accumulate the down-payment for the property, so here is another reason why his or her consumption pattern after the purchase will not be much different from what it had been before the purchase.

On the other hand, the seller's windfall gain (if that is the case), may constitute exactly the down payment required for him/her to move upmarket. As a result his or her mortgage payments may be more-or-less the same as before. This way, the seller, who has moved upmarket, may not increase his or her non-housing consumption, but will certainly experience an increase in welfare.[24] And if the fact that he or she now lives in a higher-priced property makes them feel less of a need to save for the future, the effect on their consumption will be positive too.

Against this possibility, a prospective homebuyer (with no other assets) typically needs to save in order to afford the down-payment that will allow them to borrow towards house purchase, so a rise in property prices will increase the need to save and reduce their consumption (and that of all others in similar circumstances). If borrowing is not practicable, the need to save towards house purchase becomes all the greater. A renter's consumption with no particular wish to become an owner-occupier may not be affected at all by a rise in house prices (Cambell and Cocco, 2005).

Thus, the cumulative effect of the rented sector on consumption depends on how big it is in relation to the owner-occupied sector (in numbers of households), and also on how many renting households actually wish to become homeowners. Certainly in most developed countries, owner-occupation is now the norm rather than the exception.

On balance, therefore, we can say that in an environment of rising house prices, there will be a wealth effect from home sales, especially if favourable credit terms (interest rates, loan maturity, size of down-payment, and rating criteria) are a powerful influence behind those rises. But the size of the wealth effect from this channel may not be particularly strong.

Home-equity adjustment through borrowing

An HWE can also happen through borrowing on the strength of one's property equity in order to finance current spending – a so-called 'collateral' effect[25] (Miller et al., 2009). However, the probability of tapping into one's home equity in response to, say, a rise in property prices is not the same for all households. It varies, depending on whether a home-owning household have negative or positive equity in the property (i.e., whether they have an ownership share that has a value respectively greater or less than what they owe on the property). Rising prices may increase the consumption of homeowners with 'positive equity' through a PILC adjustment (see below) or through greater ability to borrow against the value of their home – but that response may depend on the householder(s)' age (Skinner, 1993). Notably, the same result obtains in the case of owner-occupiers with 'negative equity' initially, as rising house prices may reduce their negative equity or even bring them into positive equity (Disney et al., 2010).

Overall, borrowing against the value of one's home is an important avenue whereby an HWE may materialize (and most probably has a stronger effect on consumption than selling one's home does), but going down this road requires an environment of rising house prices.

This road may become increasingly popular (or necessary) among elderly households in developed countries, due to weaknesses in the social security systems of those countries. (Elderly households typically enjoy positive home equity too.)

How symmetrical is the HWE?

It is not certain that a drop in house prices has an effect on the consumption of homeowners that is the symmetrical opposite of a rise in house prices. Apparently there is no symmetry. For example, at least in the 1990s, house price rises in the UK impacted more strongly on consumption than house price drops did, yet the reverse was true in the USA (Disney et al., 2010). Nevertheless, it is a safe bet that a price drop leads to less non-housing consumption on the part of young, first-time house buyers on a mortgage. Such persons typically have 'negative equity', and need to restrain their current consumption anyway in order to service the mortgage loan, and perhaps even curtail it (i.e., increase their saving) in order to achieve other long-term goals (e.g., a better pension later on). The need to curtail is probably much stronger when house prices are falling (a situation that increases negative equity) than when the housing market is on an upswing (cf. Barker, 2005: 10). We must also bear in mind that, whereas a buoyant housing market probably encourages home-equity withdrawal, a suppressed one does not raise the value of home equity (so, again, there is no symmetry).

3.5.2 The HWE as a PILC adjustment

In addition to an HWE possibly working through home-equity adjustments (involving selling or borrowing – both more likely during house price rises than during house price drops), there is also the possibility that an HWE will work through adjustments in the relative proportions of consumption and saving into one's income, in response to changes in property values. This brings us to PILC territory. Both the permanent income (PI) and the life cycle (LC) hypothesis of consumption attempt to explain the way people consume. The PI hypothesis suggests that people adjust their consumption spending on the basis of their permanent, rather than current, income. PI is what they expect their income will be, in real terms and on average, over a long time ahead, maybe their entire expected life spans. Their consumption will thus be relatively stable, and will not respond significantly to 'erratic' changes in income, unless people are convinced that a change in the latter is likely to last for a considerable time.

The LC hypothesis brings assets into the picture, on the assumption that accumulation of assets allows individuals to smooth out their consumption pattern over their entire lives, including retirement (when people do not earn income, but normally receive transfer payments in the form of pensions). Assets can have this effect to the extent they can be sold, or allow borrowing against them, in order to generate cash, which is then spent on consumption.

So, obviously, there is overlap, and interaction, between home-equity adjustments and PILC adjustments. The difference is that a PILC adjustment can change the proportion of consumption into disposable income for a long time ahead, without requiring an actual property sale or a new mortgage loan. The knowledge that the value of the property has risen, and especially the expectation that the rise is permanent, or part of a rising trend, is usually enough. A home equity adjustment, on the other hand, presupposes the sale of a property or a new mortgage loan on it, and, by its one-off nature, is likely to have a transitory impact (even if a positive one) on non-housing consumption.

The age factor

In the PILC framework, the utilization of assets combines with estimations of PI to suggest pathways whereby individuals maintain or adjust their level of consumption. A related proposition of the PILC hypothesis is that 'the marginal propensity to consume out of wealth increases with the age of the consumer' (Sierminska and Tachtamanova, 2007: 3). That is because, according to the LC part of the PILC hypothesis, people go through phases in life: the young earn little or no income; the middle-aged earn most of their life-long income; and the retirees live off their accumulated savings (which are part of their total wealth, along with housing wealth) and social security.

Different studies, however, have documented that this relationship is not straightforward (Skinner, 1993; Li and Yao, 2007; Sierminska and Tachtamanova, 2007; Disney et al., 2010). The reason is that different forms of wealth have different characteristics – for example financial wealth more liquid, housing wealth usually viewed as more permanent – and are therefore likely to affect the marginal propensity to consume (MPC) out of 'wealth' differently. Thus, Skinner (1993) found that in the US, house price rises tended to increase the consumption/decrease the saving of younger, rather than elderly, households. He explained this by means of the precautionary saving effect, i.e., the proposition that rises in (housing) wealth make homeowners require less insurance against future contingencies. (But, remember, his study was conducted at a time when most young households probably still trusted the ability of the social security system to deliver.) Disney et al. (2010) cast doubt on the strength of this finding, suggesting instead that, at least in the UK, the owner–renter dichotomy is a more important determinant of the extent to which changes in housing wealth affect consumption. Also diverging from Skinner (1993) and in closer accordance with the standard PILC hypothesis, Sierminska and Takhtamanova (2007) found the housing wealth effect to be significantly lower for younger households in Canada, Italy, and Finland (with data from 1999, 2002, and 1998, respectively).

Such a diversity of results implies that the PILC hypothesis may need to be qualified accordingly. For example:

- Young households may consume more (as a proportion of PI) than elderly households in response to a rise in house prices (or to inheritance of property, and also expected inheritance) if they feel that the property price rise mitigates the need to save for old age, or offers a chance for a capital gain on the sale of one's property, which will augment one's financial wealth and again reduce the need to save. (This is a response predicted by the PI model because it amounts to an upward adjustment of PI; i.e., more consumption out of current income happens because households are now counting on a higher PI.) The effect may well be a rise in aggregate consumption in the economy.
- Elderly households may consume more than their *pension* income (which can be estimated quite accurately), either by effecting a home-equity withdrawal (something more easily done when house prices rise) or by using up their financial wealth (i.e., their lifetime's savings). Either response is predicted by the LC model because it amounts to *dissaving*. Dissaving can cause a rise in aggregate consumption in the economy – only, if the number of elderly households liquidating their home equity (or using up their savings) becomes quite large, younger households may respond by adjusting upwards the proportion of saving in *their* income, either because they will interpret the elderly households' actions as evidence that future pensions will not be enough or because those actions imply smaller bequests for the younger generation.

In turn, the latter's extra saving will neutralize, in whole or in part, the increase in aggregate consumption associated with elderly households. (Such an increase in consumption, coming from elderly households, also implies a change in the structure of consumption: probably less for cars, appliances, and entertainment, and more for health and care services.)

There may be reasons, however, why elderly households will *not* increase their consumption as a result of a rise in house prices. Such reasons can include the following:

- They judge their financial wealth enough (along with their pension income) to cover their needs. Put differently, they are more likely to dissave out of financial wealth first, and only later out of non-financial wealth.
- Barring dire contingencies, elderly households may be disinclined to readjust their consumption pattern anyway, precisely because they are old and have secured a smooth and predictable way of life, i.e., their PI adjustments are already completed. In normal circumstance, therefore, they would not want to move home, so a change in house prices might well leave them uninterested.
- They may be averse to selling, or borrowing against, their housing wealth, because they wish to leave a large bequest to their children, in order to support or stabilize at an accustomed level the standard of living – and income pattern – of those children. (A strong inter-generational PI effect has certainly existed in some countries, e.g., Greece.)

It is thus obvious that the nature of the social security system, as well as cultural and behavioural factors, affect the 'final' effect on consumption of, say, a rise in house prices. The households' age factor behind the housing wealth effect is particularly important in Western societies because of their increasing numbers of aging homeowners, while their social security systems are under mounting financial pressure. The situation had probably not been factored into the PI calculations of today's elderly households when they were young (i.e., they had probably overestimated their pension income, or underestimated their future needs). A logical response to insufficient pensions, or financial wealth, on the part of a growing number of elderly households may well be to sell, or borrow against, their housing wealth in order to finance their current consumption (of anything, from food and heating to long-term care). This would probably dampen housing markets in the future. In the face of social security systems' problems, though, the issue of the extent to which a rise in house prices may induce elderly households to spend a bit more on non-housing consumption appears the lesser worry.

3.5.3 The HWE as a consumer-credit adjustment

As already suggested, a third channel whereby an HWE may happen is through households incurring more consumer credit in response to higher house prices, irrespective of, or in addition to, any home-equity withdrawal (HEW), or a possible upward adjustment to their PI. Households would do that in order to boost their non-housing (and even housing) consumption, and without regard to debt servicing considerations, as long as they expected house prices to go on increasing. This appears to have been the case mostly in Anglo-Saxon countries, where

> growth in consumer credit regularly outstripped growth in GDP [...] and saving ratios fell to historic lows. At the end of the second world war in 1945 consumer credit in

> America totalled just under $5.7 billion; ten years later it had already grown to nearly $43 billion [...] The peak, so far, was almost $2.6 trillion in July 2008. Household debt approached 100% of GDP in 2007, a level seen only once before, rather ominously in 1929. [...] In Britain household debt rose from 105% of disposable income in 2000 to 160% in 2008 [...] and in Spain the ratio rose from 69% to 130% over the same period.
>
> (*The Economist*, 2010: 7)

Although statistically it is difficult to separate the consumer-credit effect from the PI effect, growth in consumer credit in many developed countries prior to 2008 had been so large that the effect must have existed – and was probably the 'truest' HWE from among the three mentioned (one coming from a home-equity adjustment, one coming from a PILC adjustment, and one coming from a consumer credit adjustment).

3.5.4 How strong is the HWE, then?

The strength of the housing wealth effect would obviously depend, first and foremost, on the extent of such wealth, and only secondarily on (mostly unanticipated)[26] changes in it. For instance, Dvornak and Kohler (2003) in their study of this effect in Australia over the period 1984 Q4 to 2001 Q4, concluded that

> a permanent increase in households' stock market wealth of one dollar increases annual consumption by 6 to 9 cents in the long run while a permanent increase in housing wealth of one dollar is estimated to increase annual consumption by around 3 cents. However, given that households' housing assets are more than three times as large as stock market assets, our estimates imply that a one per cent increase in housing wealth has an effect on aggregate consumption that is at least as large as that of a one per cent increase in stock market wealth
>
> (p. i)

Table 3.6 presents the percentage distribution of household wealth (and of debt) in 14 countries from around 2000. According to Table 3.6, non-financial assets, and particularly a household's primary residence, constitute most of household wealth in 12 out of 14. Only in India and New Zealand, and perhaps in the USA, was housing wealth less than 50 per cent of a household's total assets, but even there non-financial assets (like agrarian land in India) comprised most of a household's wealth, as in all countries. (There is no reason to think that the pattern has changed materially as a result, say, of the 2008–09 global crisis.)

As already mentioned, financial wealth is more liquid, but non-financial wealth, and changes in it, may be customarily viewed by households as more permanent (Sierminska and Takhtamanova, 2007). Perhaps this is one reason why studies of the comparative strength of those two forms of wealth yield sometimes contradictory results (see Carroll et al., 2010: 16–18; Slacalek, 2009: 9–10; and, for a literature review, Sousa, 2009: 12–13). For example, in their 2001 seminal paper on the wealth effects of the stock versus the housing market (covering a panel of 24 developed countries from 1975 to 1999, and a panel of US states from 1982 to 1999), Case et al. (2005) recorded a statistically significant and rather large effect of housing wealth upon household consumption, and 'at best weak evidence of a stock market wealth effect' (p. 26). Using data from 10 OECD countries over the period 1970Q1 to 2005 Q4, Demary (2009) found that 'increasing house prices lead to an increase in households' net worth which leads to increasing consumption'. Carroll et al. (2010), studying the USA from 1960 Q1 to 2007 Q4, concluded that 'the immediate (next quarter) MPC from a $1 change in housing wealth is about 2 cents, with a final eventual effect around 9 cents, substantially larger than the effect of shocks to financial wealth' (p. 4).

On the other hand, Slacalek (2009), studying 16 industrial countries from 1965 Q1 to 2003 Q4 (with variations from country to country), concluded that 'the effect of housing wealth is somewhat smaller than that of financial wealth for most countries, but not for the US and the UK. The housing wealth effect has risen substantially after 1988 as it has become easier to borrow against housing wealth' (p. 4). More strongly, Sousa (2009), studying the Euro area (11 countries) from 1980 Q1 to 2007 Q4, concluded that 'financial wealth effects are relatively large and statistically significant; housing wealth effects are virtually nil and not significant' (p. 4). A suggested explanation for this finding is that an increase in house prices forces young renters, who wish to become owner-occupiers, to save more in order to afford the higher down-payment required. As a result, their reduced consumption offsets the allegedly increased consumption of current homeowners (Sousa, 2009: 12–13). In the same vein, Bajari et al. (2005) and Buiter (2010) have suggested that the property-price-induced wealth effect is less strong than previously thought, as rising house prices may simply be redistributing wealth, favouring those who own and disfavouring those who are about to buy residential properties.[27]

Calomiris et al. (2009) have also pointed out that an identified strong HWE may have been due to a certain error in methodology, i.e., failing to realize that changes in housing wealth may be correlated with changes in expected PI. Such a correlation can easily be the result of incomes and house prices rising together – but the observed increase in consumption is (mainly) the result of the former rather than of the latter.

Apart from that, why do some studies turn in results that imply a weak HWE? There are four reasons:

1 The 'wealth' effect may actually require a 'collateral' effect (i.e., borrowing on the strength of one's home equity) in order to 'kick off'. A 'collateral' effect reinforces, and may in fact be stronger than, the 'wealth' effect (Miller et al., 2009). The reason is that the 'wealth' effect impacts on households' desired consumption (out of permanent income), while the 'collateral' effect impacts on households' actual consumption, and is therefore more predictable (by households) than the 'wealth' effect – unless, of course, 'desired consumption' is realized through consumer credit, discussed in Section 3.5.3.

   In addition, the collateral effect tends to predominate precisely where/when households are under credit constraints (i.e., find it difficult to borrow on the strength of their home equity). For instance, Muellbauer (2008) has suggested that there was no housing wealth effect before credit market liberalization in the USA and the UK. In such an environment, rising house prices can ease credit constraints, this being, perhaps, one reason for the mentioned asymmetry in the response of consumption to rises versus drops in house prices. The importance of the credit system as a factor behind the collateral-cum-wealth effect has also been identified by Catte et al. (2004), who, in their study of 10 OECD countries, found that the strongest marginal propensity to consume out of housing wealth (MPC OHW) was registered in countries that had 'large, efficient and responsive mortgage markets'. More specifically,

   (a) Using the 2002 mortgage debt-to-GDP ratio as an indicator of mortgage market efficiency, they found an R^2 of 53.4 per cent[28] between that indicator and the MPC

OHW. The countries that had the highest MPC OHW were Netherlands, the UK, Australia, Canada, and the USA, with values ranging from 8 per cent for Netherlands to 5 per cent for the USA. In this comparison, Germany turned out to be an 'outlier' (probably because of its large rented sector), because although it had a ratio of mortgage debt to GDP of 54 per cent (versus 58 per cent for the USA, 43.1 per cent for Canada, and 50.8 per cent for Australia), it had a statistically insignificant MPC OHW.

(b) Using the average level of housing equity withdrawal (HEW) in 1990–2002 (as a proportion of disposable income) as an indicator of mortgage market efficiency, they found an R^2 of 84.8 per cent between that indicator and the MPC OHW.

The 'collateral' effect is therefore a reason why a markedly stronger housing 'wealth' effect has been found in the USA and the UK than in other countries (do not forget that the UK is not part of the Euro area, and was therefore outside the scope of Sousa's study). These two countries have for some time now been characterized by relatively unconstrained credit systems that facilitate borrowing against one's housing wealth.

2 A second reason for a weak HWE in some countries is that a strong one requires an active, lively, and efficient housing market, a situation helped by (a) low transaction costs, (b) easy credit, and (c) greater readiness on the part of households to move home (and city) in search of employment opportunities – all three factors rather strongly associated with English-speaking countries. Table 3.7 provides some cursory evidence for this by presenting the ratio of the number of transactions in dwellings to the total dwelling stock around the mid-2000s in 14 countries. Notice that the three English-speaking countries have ratios in excess of 5.5 per cent, and so does Norway (which, however, was also outside the scope of Sousa's study as it is not in the Euro area).

3 A third reason for a weak HWE is that in some countries households may not define their PI in ways that would make their consumption respond positively to house price changes (even if the changes were rises). They might, that is, define PI not in an individualistic, but in an inter-generational, manner. To the extent that this happened, households would

Table 3.7 Dwelling transactions and total stock in various countries, c. mid-2000s

	Number of transactions in dwellings	*Total dwelling stock*	*Transactions/stock*
Belgium	121,043	4,903,000	2.47%
Denmark	71,905	2,645,000	2.72%
Finland	77,121	2,700,000	2.86%
France	804,000	30,425,000	2.64%
Germany	442,000	39,753,000	1.11%
Ireland	110,790	1,804,000	6.14%
Italy	807,157	26,700,000	3.02%
Portugal	285,483	5,520,000	5.17%
Spain	955,186	24,626,000	3.88%
Sweden	58,751	4,436,000	1.32%
Netherlands	209,767	6,912,000	3.03%
Norway	177,094	2,055,000	8.62%
UK	1,670,000	26,418,000	6.32%
USA	7,529,000	126,198,000	5.97%

Source: EMF Hypostat (2010). Data are from 2006, except for France (2004), Italy (2003), and Norway (2005).

not increase their consumption in response to a higher PI due to house price rises, but would keep it roughly the same (as a proportion of current income) in order to ensure that the process of wealth accumulation for the next generation would not be interrupted.

4 A fourth reason for a weak HWE may relate to the nature of the social security system, as a generous one may mitigate the need to liquidate property. Because an HWE is often expressed most visibly through a 'collateral' effect, not liquidating property reduces the collateral effect and thus the HWE.

In conclusion, there is probably an HWE in most countries and most of the time (especially if house prices are rising), but its strength depends on particular circumstances and factors (related to culture, social behaviour, household age, the numbers of renters wanting to become homeowners versus the numbers of homeowners, the housing and the mortgage market, the proportion of non-financial wealth into households' total wealth, the social security system, and the laxity of consumer credit). Its *measured* strength, moreover, depends on how well one can meaningfully separate it from (a) a 'collateral' effect and (b) changes in expected PI – and also on how well one can separate the consumer credit effect from the PI effect.

Ignoring the consumer credit effect for the moment, the probability of all those factors being present and working together in the direction of creating and augmenting an HWE is not large. Thus a statistically significant HWE is more likely to be the exception than the rule – but it happens. Turning to the consumer credit effect (i.e., high house prices causing more consumption spending by first encouraging the assumption of more consumer credit), this seems perfectly capable of creating an HWE on its own, if large enough. But, judging by what happened in the US economy when house prices collapsed in 2007–08, it is doubtful whether the positive impact of an HWE on consumption during good times is enough compensation for its negative impact during bad times.

3.6 Homeownership and the labour market

The last link between the RE sector and the wider economy that we shall investigate in this chapter concerns the impact of homeownership on labour mobility and, ultimately, unemployment. An intuitive thought is that extensive homeownership in a country reduces the ability and/or the incentive to move to another city or region in search of employment, and is therefore an impediment to labour market adjustment. This was the gist of *Oswald's thesis* (see Oswald, 1997; 1999), namely that (Leuvensteijn, 2000)

1 homeowners move less than renters;
2 unemployed homeowners move less than unemployed renters;
3 homeowners are less willing than renters to find another job; and
4 homeowners are more likely to become unemployed than renters are.

Intuition, however, is not always a good counsellor. Correlating high rates of owner-occupation with high unemployment rates is a statistical minefield, as both rates may be the result of other factors, working independently of each other, and only happening to coincide at times. Extensive homeownership in developed countries is the result of economic growth, of easy credit, and, often, of government policy (not to mention household preferences), whereas surges in unemployment typically result from faltering economic growth, sometimes in conjunction with over-generous unemployment benefits, trade-union practices, and rigid hire/fire labour laws.

Thus, associating a high rate of owner-occupation – which has been achieved after decades of economic growth – with a high (and persistent) unemployment rate that has occurred because the economy has entered the downward phase of some kind of business cycle (maybe a relatively short one, or maybe a long, Kondratiev-type,[29] one) is likely to be spurious. At the very least, it stands a good chance of failing Occam's razor test:[30] 'It is vain to do with more what can be done with fewer' (cited in Russell, 1946: 494–5), meaning that it is not very fruitful to keep finding reasons for something when its most important determinants have already been identified.

Another problem is the selectivity bias in this type of study when it is done at an aggregate level (Green and Hendershott, 1999: 11–12, who otherwise found support for Oswald's thesis in their study of the USA for 1970–90). This involves the possibility that those who become homeowners may be those who plan to be less mobile than others anyway. So, for example, a renter moves not because the renting tenure makes it easier for him, but because he is more reconciled to the idea of moving than an owner-occupier is.

A way to tackle this problem is by using household level, rather than aggregate, data. This was attempted by Green and Hendershott (2001) for the USA, using PSID[31] data from 1988 to 1991. They concluded that unemployed persons in home-owning households find work less quickly than unemployed persons in renting households but that 'the impact is only an eighth of that reported by Oswald and others using aggregate data' (p. 2).

There may be some restriction on labour mobility as a result of owner-occupation in certain cases, but one doubts whether the restrictive effect is strong enough to justify a policy about-turn in favour of the rented sector – or that less labour mobility between cities or regions automatically or necessarily implies more unemployment. One reason is that in a business cycle downturn, when unemployment increases, moving to another city or region is not likely to raise one's employment prospects significantly, as the economic slump affects, more or less, the entire country rather than only parts of it. True, some areas are more affected than others, but in such an environment will the less affected areas offer enough employment opportunities to warrant moving to them – whether one is an owner-occupier or a renter (even though renters face lower moving costs than homeowners)? More to the point, will there be a match of vacancies and skills – an issue which is present in both good and bad economic times? For instance, how easily can unemployed financial sector workers from New York become car factory workers in Detroit – or vice versa?

A second reason is that, rather than encouraging a return to renting, a more plausible way to encourage homeowners to move in search of work might be to reduce the transaction costs involved in moving home, primarily taxes (Ewijk and Leuvensteijn, 2010).

A third reason is that the argument about the facilitating impact on labour mobility that a large rented sector may have ignores other advantages of owner-occupation, namely its crucial role in creating and reproducing a developed country's middle class. In turn, a strong middle class is very important for other reasons (e.g., social cohesion, support for democracy, and law-and-order) that go beyond a narrowly focused economic analysis.

Empirical findings

In addition to Oswald's own research (Oswald, 1997), other studies have found supporting evidence for his thesis. Green and Hendershott's (1999) has already been mentioned. Cochrane and Poot (2007) found in favour of Oswald's thesis too, in their study of New Zealand (where, interestingly, since the early 1990s, the percentage of owner-occupation had declined along with the long-run unemployment rate).

Yet other studies have found only partial support for the thesis, or no support. For example, Leuvensteijn (2000), in a study of the Netherlands in the 1990s, found that

1 homeowners *do* move less than renters;
2 unemployed homeowners move *(slightly) more* than unemployed renters (because this way they adjust their cost of living; they would move less than unemployed renters only during an economic downturn, due to the potential for a capital loss;
3 homeowners are *indeed* less willing than renters to find another job; and
4 homeowners are *less, not more*, likely to become unemployed than renters are – for three reasons: (a) homeowners may have 'hidden characteristics' that are valued by employers; (b) mortgage obligations may motivate homeowners to stay employed; (c) banks typically give mortgage loans to those likely to be employed for a long time.

The last result – namely that homeownership does not necessarily increase the chances of becoming or staying unemployed – is also confirmed in Graaf and Leuvensteijn (2007) and in Rouwendal and Nijkamp's (2007) literature review. However, in their multi-city model of the USA c. 2000, Head and Lloyd-Ellis (2010) concluded that 'the likelihood of unemployment for home-owners exceeds that for otherwise identical renters', but that 'unemployment is negatively related to ownership rates across cities because unemployed renters tend to live disproportionately in low rent (low wage) cities, where home ownership is also lower' (p. 39). They also identified a small effect of homeownership on aggregate unemployment because 'the rate at which households receive offers from other cities is small' and 'the majority of the difference in mobility between renters and owners comes from the difference for employed rather than unemployed households' (pp. 39–40).

The point about the low frequency of job offers coming from other cities echoes our point about New York office workers and Detroit car workers made above. And, testing Oswald's thesis, Lerbs (2010) concluded that (rather than homeownership) 'factors like average labour productivity, [labour market] participation, export orientation, and human capital endowment seem to dominate the impact of home ownership' in German regions in 1998–2006. Non-confirmation of Oswald's thesis (that home ownership raises the 'natural rate of unemployment'),[32] as well as non-confirmation of the alternative hypothesis (that home ownership is associated with lower rates of unemployment), was also the case in Flatau et al.'s (2002) study of Australian regions in 1986–2001.

The Australian study probably sums up a reserved assessment of the Oswald thesis: there is no inevitable positive or negative link between homeownership and unemployment (even though there does seem to be a positive link between homeownership and labour mobility); the two variables are largely unrelated causally, but they happen to move together occasionally.

Summary of main points

1 In the OECD National Accounts, the most important and individually accessible accounts that relate to RE are gross value added (GVA) by construction, gross fixed capital formation (with separate mention of (i) dwellings and (ii) other buildings and structures), and final consumption expenditures by households (with separate mention of actual and imputed rentals for housing).
2 Input–output tables are used to calculate partial multipliers for various industries, i.e., the extent to which the latter contribute to an economy's output, to total employment, and

to total GVA. Evidence suggests that construction multipliers are particularly strong – in other words, construction industry changes in output, employment, or GVA impact significantly upon changes in the corresponding aggregate variables.

3 There tends to be a limit in the proportion of construction investment to GDP as an economy grows. This limit depends on the level of (real) GDP, or, more broadly, on a country's development level. It would appear that the limit is between 6 and 6.5 per cent, but the proportion for the lowest-income countries is not much smaller, averaging about 4.4 per cent.
4 Statistical evidence suggests that construction investment and GDP affect one another. Sometimes it is construction that affects GDP the most, sometimes it is the opposite. The strength and direction of the 'pull' depend on the component of construction studied, on a country's level of development, on a country's business cycle phase at the time of study, and on a country's institutional framework.
5 Determinants of construction investment are Tobin's q (the ratio of existing asset market value to cost of replacement), store of value considerations, and fundamentals like incomes and demographics. A $q > 1$ normally encourages property investment, a $q < 1$ the opposite.
6 Changes in property prices affect the wider economy through a number of channels: consumption, investment, the financial sector, inflation, and the government's fiscal position.
7 The consumption channel works through the housing wealth effect (HWE), which in turn involves any of three types of adjustment: a home-equity one, a permanent income–life cycle (PILC) one, and a consumer credit one.
8 Homeownership may reduce labour mobility. Nevertheless, it probably contributes less to unemployment than suggested in Oswald's thesis. To the extent it does, maybe the proper response is to reduce transaction costs on moving home rather than augmenting the rented sector.

Review questions and exercises

1 Define the following terms:

GFCF–GVA–FCEH
Input–output analysis
Type I and Type II multipliers
S-curve
Housing wealth effect (HWE)
Permanent income–life cycle (PILC) hypothesis
Home equity adjustment
PILC adjustment
Consumer-credit adjustment
Selectivity bias

2 Go to OECD → Statistics → OECD.Stat → National Accounts, at www.oecd.org; choose a country, and prepare a table like Table 3.1 of this chapter using the latest available data.
3 In National Accounts, what is the difference between gross value added (GVA) and GDP?

4 Why do you think the ratio of construction investment to GDP does not keep rising, the larger (real) GDP becomes?
5 Go to UNO National Accounts Main Aggregates Database at http://unstats.un.org/unsd/snaama/dnlList.asp; go to the section 'GDP and its breakdown at constant 2005 prices in US dollars'; choose 10 countries, and prepare a table showing the ratio of construction to GDP from 1970 to 2009. What conclusions can you draw? How can you manipulate your data in order, perhaps, to draw more meaningful conclusions?
6 'Construction investment enhances GDP growth.' Discuss.
7 Accepting the validity of the proposition that investment in fixed capital is a function of Tobin's q, how do you account for the phenomenon that, typically, new houses sell for more than comparable older houses?
8 Briefly discuss how changes in property prices may affect the wider economy.
9 List and evaluate the three channels through which a housing wealth effect (HWE) may materialize. In your opinion (to the extent that this is a matter of opinion rather than of econometric research), which channel is the strongest? Why?
10 'If homeownership restricts labour mobility, it must surely lead to more unemployment.' Discuss.
11 'If homeownership leads to more unemployment, governments must start encouraging growth of the rented sector.' Discuss.

4 RE finance

Loans, equity withdrawal, and MBSs

Main sections

Having gone through this chapter, a student should be able to

1. Calculate an interest-and-capital loan repayment instalment.
2. Calculate the interest part and the principal part in a given instalment.
3. Develop a repayment schedule for a number of mortgage loan types, including endowment and low-start.
4. Explain the peril that loan prepayment represents to a mortgage lender, and under what conditions a borrower might want to remortgage.
5. Define all main categories of mortgage loans: forward (including remortgages and equity withdrawal) and reverse (or equity release) ones (including HECM, lifetime mortgages, and home reversion plans). Then explain their mechanics.
6. Describe the kind of challenge (i.e., the social need) that reverse mortgages are supposed to meet.
7. Determine an appropriate range of interest rates to be used on a reverse mortgage, given a rate of house price growth.
8. Assess the link between housing finance and owner-occupation, and analyse possible determinants of mortgage finance.

9 Distinguish between the primary and the secondary mortgage market, and describe the mechanics of mortgage-backed securities (MBSs).
10 Suggest reasons why a mortgage lender would go for mortgage securitization, and discuss its significance for housing finance and the housing market.

4.1 Loans, mortgages, and maths

In developed countries, most individuals get indebted as a matter of course, and the largest single amount they will borrow will usually be for house purchase. Credit enables them to consume more of housing services now at the expense of consumption of other goods or services, now or in the future. In this shift in the pattern of consumption, crucial determinants are (a) an individual's income and preferences, and (b) the interest rate and how it is applied, i.e., what the loan mechanics is.

Example 1

Take an individual who earns €35,000 in each of two years. Say that the individual feels they can set aside €12,000 each year for house purchase. Assuming no inflation, how much 'house' (i.e., what price house) could they *presently* buy, maximum, on the basis of a bank loan? Let us look at the problem assuming, first, a one-year time horizon and, second, a two-year time horizon.

(a) *One-year time horizon.* A hasty answer might be €12,000 worth of a house. A loan, however, is repaid with interest. So, for the individual to be able to spend no more than €12,000 of their income on repaying the loan, they will need to make sure that the loan (call it K) must satisfy the following equation:

$$K + iK = 12{,}000 \Rightarrow K = \frac{12{,}000}{1+i}, \text{ where } i = \text{the interest rate.}$$

If $i = 4$ per cent, $K = 11{,}538.46$. Therefore, the individual can only buy a house = get a loan worth €11,538.5 rather than €12,000. This is less than the amount the individual had earmarked for house purchase out of their current annual income, but, because income is earned monthly, borrowing will allow purchase now than a year later.

(b) *Two-year time horizon.* The individual will repay the loan by making a €12,000 payment at the end of this year, and another €12,000 payment at the end of next year. The discounted value of those two payments is

$$K = \frac{12{,}000}{1+i} + \frac{12{,}000}{(1+i)^2} \quad \Rightarrow 11{,}538.46 + 11{,}094.67 = 22{,}633.13$$

The house value bought with this amount is less than the earmarked €24,000, but more than current annual income, and much more than a month's income.

In what follows, we shall study a number of mortgage loans. The purpose of such a loan is to enable a borrower to buy property using the latter as collateral, i.e., mortgaging the property. The mortgage itself is a conveyance of property in security of a loan, or (another definition) a *lien*[1] on a property to secure loan repayment. A mortgage means that in the event of the borrower *defaulting* (or *falling in arrears*, or *becoming delinquent*) on his or her payments the lender has the right to *repossess* the property (or *foreclose* on the loan).[2] In legalese, the borrower is called a *mortgager* and the lender a *mortgagee.*

Most mortgage loans are taken for the purpose of buying property. Others aim at replacing an existing mortgage loan by a new, cheaper, one. This is called remortgaging. And still others – called equity withdrawal loans – are taken in order to enhance the non-housing consumption possibilities of someone who is already a homeowner but who will use their equity in the property (i.e., their ownership share of the value of the property) as security for the loan. All three varieties are 'forward' mortgages because they require active repayment by the borrower, typically over a number of years. During this period, the borrower's debt decreases (through the repayment process), and his or her home equity increases.

On the other hand, a 'reverse' mortgage involves getting a loan now, secured on the borrower's home, then repaying it only after the borrower dies (or permanently moves out of the property). In this arrangement, the borrower retains the right to continue using the property for life rent-free, and the bank gets the right to sell the property after the homeowner's death (or after they have permanently moved out), hoping that the proceeds from the sale will be enough to cover the value of the loan at that point in time. Thus, during the life of a reverse mortgage, the borrower's debt increases, and his or her home equity decreases.

Reverse mortgages are fast becoming an important way of financing retirement in a number of countries, chiefly advanced English-speaking ones. They therefore merit special consideration. We shall also discuss the extent to which housing finance is used internationally, and what its determinants are. We shall finish with a look on mortgage securitization (which for a number of years now has been the new, elevated, phase of real estate finance – and not just for housing).

All loan business is based on the mathematics of compound interest. This calculates the future value of a sum of money that earns interest at so much per cent per period, over a number of periods. At the end of each period, the earned interest is capitalized, and the new sum continues to earn interest until maturity (the end of the number of agreed upon periods). By the same token, it is possible to find the present value of a future sum. The process is the opposite of compounding and is called discounting. So the fundamental formulas are as follows:

for compounding,

$$\text{future value, FV} = K\left(1+\frac{i}{m}\right)^{mt}, \tag{4.1}$$

where

K = initial sum, also called capital or principal,
i = interest rate,
t = number of years the sum will be earning interest,
m = number of periods within a year (say, every month, quarter, or semester) in which interest is capitalized;

for discounting,

$$\text{present value, PV} = K = \frac{\text{FV}}{\left(1+\frac{i}{m}\right)^{mt}}. \tag{4.2}$$

Example 2

Let $K = 1000$, $i = 4\%$, $t = 10$ years, $m = 12$ (if interest is calculated monthly; if it were calculated quarterly, m would be 4). Then

$$\text{FV} = 1000\left(1+\frac{0.04}{12}\right)^{12\times 10} = 1000 \times 1.49083 = 1490.83,$$

and

$$\text{PV} = \frac{1490.83}{\left(1+\frac{0.04}{12}\right)^{12\times 10}} = \frac{1490.83}{1.49083} = 1000.$$

Bear in mind that the smaller (higher) the number of periods in a year in which interest is capitalized, the smaller (higher) the future value, *ceteris paribus*. For instance, in the above example if $m = 1$ (i.e., interest is capitalized annually), FV = 1480.24. If interest were capitalized continuously, then FV $= Ke^{it}$, where $e =$ an irrational constant approximately equal to 2.71828. Using values from Example 4.2, we would thus have in the continuous case

$$\text{FV} = 1000e^{0.04\times 10} = 1491.82,$$

which is higher than in the discrete-period case.

4.2 Forward mortgages: basic loan types

The result 1490.83 that we found in Example 4.2 means that in 10 years time a person who has just borrowed €1000 (or dollars or pounds) will have to return to the lender the principal of 1000 plus interest of 490.83. That is a long time for a lender to wait. So ways have been found to speed up repayment of a loan in cases of long maturities, which are a typical characteristic of mortgage loans. Some of these ways are examined below.

4.2.1 The interest-and-capital-repayment loan

Two standard ways of repaying any loan exist: (a) by paying interest and capital over the life of the loan and (b) by paying interest only over the life of the loan, and then paying the capital at maturity. Any other way is really a variant of the one or the other. The first way – interest-and-capital repayment – involves repayment by means of equal instalments, given at equal intervals until maturity, each instalment containing part interest and part capital. Since the instalments are equal (which, incidentally, will be the case only if the interest rate on the loan is not allowed to fluctuate), the proportions of capital and interest in each instalment will have to vary from one instalment to the next: initially, the interest part is much larger than it is at the end, and it gradually diminishes. The instalment formula is derived from the one for the present value of a deferred annuity, which in turn is derived from the fundamental formula for interest compounding presented in Section 4.1.

A *deferred annuity* is a series of equal payments a made at the end of each of a series of periods, for the purpose of accumulating a sum at maturity. If, instead, the payments are made at the beginning of each period, this is called an *annuity due*. (In what follows, interest i is supposed to be capitalized annually for simplicity's sake. However, it is a small matter to extend this to cases where interest is capitalized in m periods within a year.)

$$\text{future value of a deferred annuity: } \mathrm{FV}_{\mathrm{da}} = \frac{a}{i}\left[(1+i)^t - 1\right], \tag{4.3}$$

$$\text{present value of a deferred annuity: } \mathrm{PV}_{\mathrm{da}} = \frac{a}{i}\left[1 - \frac{1}{(1+i)^t}\right], \tag{4.4}$$

$$\text{future value of an annuity due: } \mathrm{FV}_{\mathrm{ad}} = \frac{a(1+i)}{i}\left[(1+i)^t - 1\right], \tag{4.5}$$

$$\text{present value of an annuity due: } \mathrm{PV}_{\mathrm{ad}} = \frac{a}{i}\left[(1+i) - \frac{1}{(1+i)^{t-1}}\right]. \tag{4.6}$$

The formula that gives the amount of an interest-and-capital loan repayment instalment is derived from the one for the present value of a deferred annuity simply because in the loan case the present value K is known (it is the amount of the loan, also called *principal*) and what is sought is the periodic equal payment a that is made at the end of each period. Thus,

$$a = \frac{Ki}{1 - \frac{1}{(1+i)^t}} \tag{4.7}$$

It is often desirable to know the amount of interest contained in any particular instalment, as, for example, in many countries interest payments towards buying a house are income-tax deductible, in whole or in part.[3] Using T to denote interest (from *tokos*, the Greek word for interest), we have

$$T = a - \frac{a}{(1+i)^N} = a\left[1 - \frac{1}{(1+i)^N}\right], \tag{4.8}$$

with N indicating the particular period in which an instalment is paid. Notice that the higher N is, the nearer to the present we are.

Example 3

Let $K = 1000$, $i = 4\%$, $t = 10$ years, and $m = 12$. This gives

$$a = \frac{1000(0.04/12)}{1 - \frac{1}{(1+0.04/12)^{12\times 10}}} = 10.12.$$

Now, if we want to find the amount of interest contained in the first (or last) instalment, we set $N = 120$ (or $N = 1$) and use the T formula introduced above:

$$\text{interest in 1st instalment: } T = 10.12 - \frac{10.12}{(1+0.04/12)^{120}} = 3.33,$$

$$\text{Interest in 120th instalment: } T = 10.12 - \frac{10.12}{(1+0.04/12)^{1}} = 0.03.$$

As a fuller example, Table 4.1 shows the repayment schedule for a 10-year interest-and-capital repayment loan of $200,000. For simplicity, a fixed interest rate is used, but going on to variable rates presents no conceptual difficulties. If, for instance, at the end of the 4th year the interest rate changed to 3 per cent, remaining instalments to maturity would be calculated at that rate rather than 4 per cent (and on the basis of the remaining principal). In the particular example of Table 4.1, the remaining principal at the end of the 4th year is $129,261.60. The number of remaining periods is 6, so at a new interest rate of 3 per cent, the new annual instalment to repay the loan would be $23,861.37.

4.2.2 The interest-only loan

This is the second standard way of repaying loans. An interest-only loan (e.g., an endowment mortgage loan in the UK) typically entails the borrower paying only interest to the bank[4] at

Table 4.1 Interest-and-capital repayment loan

Principal = 200,000 Interest rate = 4.00% Maturity = 10

Period	*Periods to maturity*	*Repayment instalment*	*Interest part*	*Principal part*	*Cumulative principal paid*	*Principal remaining*
1	10	24,658.19	8,000.00	16,658.19	16,658.19	183,341.81
2	9	24,658.19	7,333.67	17,324.52	33,982.71	166,017.29
3	8	24,658.19	6,640.69	18,017.50	52,000.20	147,999.80
4	7	24,658.19	5,919.99	18,738.20	70,738.40	129,261.60
5	6	24,658.19	5,170.46	19,487.72	90,226.12	109,773.88
6	5	24,658.19	4,390.96	20,267.23	110,493.36	89,506.64
7	4	24,658.19	3,580.27	21,077.92	131,571.28	68,428.72
8	3	24,658.19	2,737.15	21,921.04	153,492.32	46,507.68
9	2	24,658.19	1,860.31	22,797.88	176,290.20	23,709.80
10	1	24,658.19	948.39	23,709.80	200,000.00	0.00
Total		246,581.89	46,581.89	200,000.00		

the end of each agreed upon period (the interest calculated on the amount of loan outstanding, which in this case means the entire principal).

At the same time, the borrower makes periodic payments to an insurance company (usually) for the purpose of accumulating an amount which at maturity is supposed to equal the principal – a typical case of setting up a *sinking fund* – so that the bank can get its money (the value of the loan) back (remember that up to then the bank will be earning interest on the entire principal).

This investment plan is typically combined with the purchase of a life insurance policy, whose purpose is to safeguard the borrower or their family in the event of the borrower suffering permanent disability or death.

One can make the following remarks:

1 The stream of periodic payments made to the insurance company for the purpose of retiring the loan at maturity is an annuity due (since equal payments are made at the beginning of each period, as with all insurance contracts).
2 A life policy can easily be – and usually is – a characteristic of interest-and-capital repayment mortgage loans. Conversely, it is not an obligatory additional feature of an annuity programme like the one just described.
3 Disregarding the life policy momentarily, the cost to the borrower of an interest-only loan is a bit higher than the cost of an interest-and-capital repayment loan simply because the investment vehicle (typically, an insurance company) will charge expenses for investing the annuity payments and generally managing the programme.
4 On the other hand, in some countries such annuity payments (whose purpose is to accumulate enough capital to retire the loan at maturity) may be income-tax-deductible[5] – a situation that may actually compensate the borrower for the slightly higher cost of an endowment mortgage over the interest-and-capital repayment one.
5 In some countries, too, life premiums are income-tax-deductible.
6 Whether life premiums are income-tax-deductible or not, a mortgager will not necessarily face the same life insurance cost, irrespective of whether they get an interest-and-capital repayment loan or an interest-only loan. The reason is that when a life policy is combined with an annuity programme, the life policy cost may actually drop due to cross-subsidisation between the two products.
7 The amount that must be paid an insurance company for the purpose of accumulating the value of the mortgage loan is derived from the formula for an annuity due, only the latter is solved for a (the periodic payment) since the future value is known in advance:

$$\mathrm{FV}_{\mathrm{ad}} = \frac{a(1+i)}{i}\left[(1+i)^t - 1\right] \Rightarrow a = \frac{\mathrm{FV}_{\mathrm{ad}}(i)}{(1+i)[(1+i)^t - 1]}. \tag{4.9}$$

Using values from Table 4.1, and ignoring commissions and other expenses, the above formula gives

$$a = \frac{200,000(4\%)}{(1+4\%)[(1+4\%)^{10} - 1]} = 16,017.49.$$

Table 4.2 shows the relevant pattern of payments.

8 In Table 4.2, the opportunity cost to the borrower of the interest income foregone due to each annuity payment is 640.70 (= 16,017.59 × 0.04). It has been calculated at 4 per cent,

Table 4.2 Endowment mortgage loan (without taking a life insurance premium into account)

Principal = 200,000 Interest rate = 4.00% Maturity = 10

Period	*Periods to maturity*	*Interest on principal (= 4% × 200,000)*	*Periodic payment to insurer calculated as annuity due*	*Future value of each annuity payment (i.e., $a(1+i)^t$)*	*Cost to borrower-cum-insured*	*Opportunity cost to the borrower of interest income foregone on annuity payment*
a	*b*	*c*	*d*	*e*	$f=c+d$	*g*
1	10	8,000.00	16,017.49	23,709.80	24,017.49	640.70
2	9	8,000.00	16,017.49	22,797.88	24,017.49	640.70
3	8	8,000.00	16,017.49	21,921.04	24,017.49	640.70
4	7	8,000.00	16,017.49	21,077.92	24,017.49	640.70
5	6	8,000.00	16,017.49	20,267.23	24,017.49	640.70
6	5	8,000.00	16,017.49	19,487.72	24,017.49	640.70
7	4	8,000.00	16,017.49	18,738.20	24,017.49	640.70
8	3	8,000.00	16,017.49	18,017.50	24,017.49	640.70
9	2	8,000.00	16,017.49	17,324.52	24,017.49	640.70
10	1	8,000.00	16,017.49	16,658.19	24,017.49	640.70
Total		80,000.00	160,174.89	200,000.00	240,174.89	6,407.00
$g+f=$					246,581.89	

i.e., the same as the mortgage rate. In real life, this is extremely unlikely to be the case. If a bank or building society can lend at 4 per cent, its deposit rate will be less than that – so the effective opportunity cost to the borrower will be less than \$640.70. In theory, this opportunity cost can be 'recovered' through the annuity payments made to the sinking fund programme. This is easy to prove: adding together the interest payments made to the bank, the annuity payments made to the insurer, and the opportunity cost gives 246,581.89, exactly equal to the total cost to the borrower under the interest-and-capital repayment case (Table 4.1). In practice, it is also very unlikely that an insurance company will be able to reinvest the annuity payments at a rate as high as the mortgage rate – which implies that the mortgager will have to contribute slightly higher annuity payments towards the sinking fund programme than the payments suggested in Table 4.2 in order to make up for the shortfall.

4.2.3 The low-start loan

In this type of mortgage loan, the borrower initially repays the loan at an interest rate that is lower than the 'standard' or 'reference' rate. The difference between what he or she would have paid under the high rate and what he or she pays under the low rate is capitalized and brought forward (at the high rate). At the end of the low-rate period, the borrower begins to repay the sum of the capitalized deferred payments (a sum which amounts to a new loan) at the high rate till maturity, while he or she continues repaying the original principal that still remains outstanding. The calculations are shown in Table 4.3, for a principal of \$200,000 with the interest rate being 2 per cent during the first four years and 4 per cent during the next six.

Table 4.3 Low-start mortgage loan

Principal = 200,000
Reference, or high, interest rate = 4.00%
Maturity (in years) = 10
Reduced, or low, interest rate = 2.00%
Low rate period (in years) = 4
High rate period (in years) = 6

Period	*Periods to maturity*	*Repayment instalment (incl. capital and interest) at high rate*	*Repayment instalment (incl. capital and interest) at low rate*	*Interest part of repayment at high rate*	*Interest part of repayment at low rate*	*Interest income the bank sacrifices over first 4 years*	*Future (i.e., capitalized) value of interest foregone (calculated at high rate)*
1	10	24,658.19	22,265.31	8,000.00	4,000.00	4,000.00	4,499.46
2	9	24,658.19	22,265.31	7,333.67	3,634.69	3,698.98	4,000.82
3	8	24,658.19	22,265.31	6,640.69	3,262.08	3,378.61	3,513.75
4	7	24,658.19	22,265.31	5,919.99	2,882.02	3,037.97	3,037.97
5	6	23,791.36					
6	5	23,791.36					
7	4	23,791.36					
8	3	23,791.36					
9	2	23,791.36					
10	1	23,791.36					
Total			89,061.22			14,115.56	**15,052.00**

Period	*Periods to maturity*	*Principal that would have been amortized if repayment during first 4 years had been at high rate*	*Principal actually amortized during repayment at low rate*	*Principal actually amortized during repayment at high rate*	*Repayment instalment for capitalized interest at end of 4th year, calc. at high rate*	*Amortization of capitalized interest*	*Total repayment schedule*
1	10	16,658.19	18,265.31				22,265.31
2	9	17,324.52	18,630.61				22,265.31
3	8	18,017.50	19,003.22				22,265.31
4	7	18,738.20	19,383.29				22,265.31
5	6			18,802.66	2,871.35	2,269.27	26,662.71
6	5			19,554.76	2,871.35	2,360.04	26,662.71
7	4			20,336.96	2,871.35	2,454.44	26,662.71
8	3			21,150.43	2,871.35	2,552.62	26,662.71
9	2			21,996.45	2,871.35	2,654.72	26,662.71
10	1			22,876.31	2,871.35	2,760.91	26,662.71
Total		70,738.40	**75,282.43**	**124,717.57**	17,228.09	**15,052.00**	249,037.48
Original principal =			**200,000.00**				

Explanations

1 We calculate an interest-and-capital repayment schedule for the low-rate period of 4 years, but using the high rate (the rate that the borrower would have paid if this had been a normal interest-and-capital repayment loan, i.e., without a 'low-start' period). Each payment is $24,658.19.
2 We similarly calculate an interest-and-capital repayment schedule for the low-rate period of 4 years, but using the low rate (the rate that the borrower actually pays over that period). Each payment is $22,265.31.
3 Using the formula for interest calculation introduced in Section 4.2.1, we derive the interest part of the two kinds of payments for each year, we find the difference between them (which amounts to interest income the bank sacrifices during the first 4 years because of the low rate), and we bring each difference forward in time (at the high rate) using $K(1+i)^t$, with $t = 3$ for the first-year difference, $t = 2$ for the second-year difference, and so on. Capitalized interest is thus $15,052.
4 We calculate an interest-and-capital repayment schedule for repayment of the capitalized interest from the first 4 years, which really is in the nature of another loan given the borrower at the end of the 4th year. Each instalment is equal to $2871.35.
5 We also calculate the amount of original principal paid during the low-rate period (i.e., $75,282.43), and subtract it from the original principal ($200,000) to find the principal the borrower still owes the bank at the end of the 4th year, i.e., $124,717.57. Repayment of this amount (with interest) over the next 6 years involves six instalments equal to $23,791.36. (We use the formula for interest-and-capital repayment to find this.)

So the borrower pays $22,265.31 in each of the first 4 years and $23,791.36 plus $2871.35 (i.e., $26,662.71) in each of the last 6 years. The sum-total of those payments amounts to $249,037.48 compared with the $246,581.89 that is the case under a normal interest-and-capital repayment loan (see Section 4.2.1). The difference is due to the fact that part of the interest income was not earned by the bank in time, but capitalized at the end of the 4th year. As a check on the calculations, we can add the principal actually amortized during the low-rate period and the principal actually amortized during the high-rate period: the sum is indeed $200,000. And of course the amortization part of the payments made towards servicing the capitalized interest which had formed at the end of the 4th year is $15,052, i.e., equal to the capitalized interest.

4.2.4 The stabilized loan

A borrower services this loan through constant interest-and-capital repayment instalments calculated at an interest rate that may be either lower than the market interest rate at inception of the loan or equal to it. If it is lower, the mechanics described in Section 4.2.3 (case of low-start mortgage) apply, in combination with the mechanics involved even if the loan interest rate is initially equal to the market interest rate. If it is equal, and subsequently the market interest rate rises, the borrower will be charged an interest difference that will be carried forward at the risen rate and the borrower will have to make good (i.e., pay it to the bank) eventually.

Payment of this additional interest can be in the form of a lump sum at maturity or through extending the maturity of the original loan. If, on the other hand, the market interest rate drops, the borrower will be credited the interest difference between his or her stable rate and the market rate. In this case, the borrower will either receive the difference at maturity (with interest, since this difference will also be carried forward at the market rate) or will have the chance to repay the original loan before maturity.

4.2.5 The select-payment loan

This loan resembles both the stabilized mortgage loan (see Section 4.2.4) and the low-start mortgage loan (see Section 4.2.3), with some interesting twists. The borrower has the freedom (usually within limits) to choose the amount of a particular loan repayment instalment, so that sometimes he or she will be paying more than his or her regular (or 'reference') instalment, and sometimes less. Negative differences will be cancelled out by positive differences over the life of the loan, either in whole or in part. At maturity, there will usually be a remainder that, if positive, will be received by the borrower; if it is negative, it will be paid to the bank by the borrower.

This feature may make the select-payment mortgage loan even more convenient to repay than either the stabilized or the low-start mortgage. For instance, the borrower may see to it that his or her payments more closely reflect his or her current financial situation. If the borrower is in difficulties, he or she will be paying less than what he or she should, and if the borrower comes to better times, he or she will be paying more, the 'surplus' payments compensating for the 'deficit' payments. Notice that in the select-payment mortgage, there is not a defined period of low payments (as is the case with the low-start mortgage); all that is required is that, roughly, over the life of the loan, the 'surplus' payments make good the 'deficit' ones.

4.2.6 The cap-and-collar loan

This loan has some similarity to the stabilized mortgage, but does not involve capitalization of part of the interest payments like the stabilized mortgage and the low-start mortgage do. Essentially, it offers an interest rate that is halfway between a fixed and a fluctuating one. The interest rate can change within a margin defined by an upper limit (the cap) and a lower one (the collar). This gives the borrower some protection against sudden or large increases in market interest rates, whereas it allows him or her to benefit should interest rates drop. The benefit is greater if the loan is offered only with a cap but no collar, or if the latter is set at a very low level. If the loan has a cap but no collar, then it is called a 'capped-rate' mortgage.

4.2.7 The index-linked loan

Such mortgages have been around for some time (Statman, 1982; Lunde, 1997; Miles and Pillonca, 2008). In one variant, a relatively low interest rate is used at the beginning, to which subsequently the rate of consumer price inflation is added. This way, the lender preserves the 'real' value of the repayments of principal plus interest. The borrower, however, will benefit only if, over the life of the loan, (a) the inflation rate plus the 'real' rate of interest charged is less than a fixed nominal interest rate that could have been applied at inception, or less than the series of adjustable nominal interest rates that could have been applied, and (b) his or her income grows in tandem with, or more than, the inflation rate. If not, such a loan may prove worse for the borrower than a normal, nominal-rate, mortgage loan.

In another variant, the index to which the mortgage loan is linked is not the CPI but a house-price one. This, in effect, turns the mortgage loan into a house-price financial derivative.

If the market value of the property drops, either the borrower will pay less by way of interest payments or the drop in value will be subtracted from the outstanding debt. This would reduce both the mortgager's house price risk (i.e., making payments on a loan for a house whose value is now less than the value for which the loan was calculated) and the mortgagee's credit risk (i.e., the possibility of default, or of late payment, on the mortgager's part) (Syz et al., 2006).

4.3 Remortgaging and equity withdrawal

Remortgaging occurs when a mortgager who is in the process of repaying a prior mortgage on his or her property chooses to substitute a new, presumably cheaper, mortgage loan for the existing, dearer, one. *Equity withdrawal* occurs when a person already owns fully (or mostly) a property (usually their home), and wants to obtain refinancing, i.e., some cash, on the strength of the property's value. To this purpose, the person mortgages the property anew, or gets a second or third mortgage on it.

Because remortgaging is typically justified on the basis of a comparison between fixed and variable interest rates, it is perhaps best to introduce such loans through a discussion of how the interest rate regime affects the incidence of early repayment (or *prepayment*, or early redemption) of an existing loan.

4.3.1 Variable versus fixed interest rates

For many years after the Second World War, almost all mortgage loans were made available at fixed rates. Since then, things have changed all over the world. For example, following regulation changes, *adjustable rate mortgages* (ARMs) were introduced in 1981 in the USA, and by 1984 they accounted for two-thirds of mortgage originations (Boleat, 1988: 11–12). Nowadays, adjustable-rate mortgages (and adjustable rates on many other kinds of loans) are the rule rather than the exception, although fixed-rate loans are also used. Such rates are usually pegged to the London Interbank Offer Rate (LIBOR) in the UK, the European Central Bank (ECB) tender rate for main refinancing operations in the Eurozone, the Constant Maturity Treasury rate as calculated by the Federal Reserve Board in the USA, or (again in the USA) a Cost of Funds Index (COFI) calculated by one or other Federal Home Loan Bank,[6] plus a margin expressed in basis points.[7]

Adjustable rates offer two distinct advantages to financial institutions. They help reduce *interest rate risk* and *prepayment risk*. More specifically,

1 ARMs allow much better matching of balance sheet assets and liabilities. Take a bank whose liabilities are mostly in the form of savings deposits and that continuously adjusts its interest rate(s) on those deposits according to movements in current market rates. The same bank has most of its assets in the form of (long-term) mortgage loans. It will then suffer a drop in profitability if interest rates on those loans are fixed, and market interest rates rise. It *may* even register a loss if the weighted average of the loan rates gets to be lower than the weighted average of deposit rates.[8] Both possibilities form *interest rate risk*. But if the bank can adjust its loan rates in accordance with changes in deposit rates, thus preserving a desirable spread between them, it can make this particular danger go away.

   Of course if the (fixed) loan rates are higher than (variable) deposit rates to start with, the bank may profit further if deposit rates drop. Also, if a bank expects short-term rates (the ones typically applied on savings deposits) to be lower over the life of a prospective mortgage loan than the fixed rate it can currently charge on that loan, it may well choose to propose the fixed-rate loan to the prospective borrower. This, however, brings up the issue of *prepayment risk*.

2 ARMs reduce the possibility of prepayment and thus the *reinvestment risk* inherent in that possibility. *Prepayment* (or *early redemption*) is the act of retiring part or all of a debt earlier than maturity. Because mortgage loans typically have long lives, prepayment risk is particularly pronounced in their case. A risk exists in that a bank (or other financial institution) might plan on receiving interest calculated at, say, 8 per cent on the loan that was retired early, and to do so for, say, 10 more years till maturity. Assuming that interest rates on similar debt instruments are presently 5 per cent, the bank can now reinvest the principal received through early repayment at 5 per cent (rather than continuing to earn interest on it at 8 per cent). Therefore, over the next 10 years, it stands to lose planned interest income to the tune of 3 percentage points. ARMs mitigate the prepayment risk two ways: (a) by enabling more orderly cash-flow planning on the part of the financial institution and (b) by reducing the incentive for borrowers to retire their (high-rate) loans earlier than maturity (an important consideration in the case of mortgage-backed securities too – see Section 4.7).

Institutions with (fixed-rate) mortgage loan portfolios can go some way towards reducing prepayment risk by calculating expected prepayment rates on pools of mortgage loans, and compensating for expected losses through their pricing policies. Thus, prepayment risk becomes a problem to the extent that expected prepayment rates on particular pools of mortgages prove lower than actual prepayment rates. It becomes a problem not only because of prospective interest income foregone, but also because, *ceteris paribus*, the borrowers who are likelier to repay early are those whose incomes and/or house prices have risen. The result is that, this way, the overall creditworthiness of the particular pool of mortgages is reduced, increasing the average risk of default on loan payments.

To minimize the incidence of prepayment, banks often impose prepayment penalties on borrowers, especially if prepayment takes place early in the loan repayment schedule. (The exact definition of 'early' varies between lenders.) These penalties are usually equivalent to so many months of interest[9] (usually 3–6), and come in two forms: a *soft prepayment penalty* that is only imposed if the borrower refinances his or her mortgage (but not if they just sell their home) and a *hard prepayment penalty* that is imposed whether they refinance or sell.

4.3.2 From prepayment to refinancing

The preceding discussion inevitably begs the question: When is a borrower likelier to repay a loan early? There are three possibilities:

1 When house prices go up, as more borrowers than usual will attempt to realize capital gains by selling their properties. If those houses are mortgaged, selling them implies prepayment of existing mortgages. To the extent that house price appreciation has happened *because* of lower loan rates than in the past (a situation that usually fuels housing demand), early repayment (of fixed-rate loans) will not of course make banks happy, but, on the other hand, banks will probably be compensated by a growth in mortgage business as well as the fact that mortgaged properties will now be higher-priced (implying more readily acceptable loan-to-value (LTV) ratios[10] on the part of banks).

2 When, irrespective of house price appreciation, borrowers are paying relatively high fixed rates, and (a) fixed interest rates on new loans drop materially below the level of fixed interest rates on outstanding loans or (b) adjustable interest rates on new loans drop materially below the level of fixed interest rates on outstanding loans,[11] and simultaneously borrowers expect the level difference to persist. In such a situation, borrowers may well want to 'remortgage' because this way they will be able to substitute a new, lower-priced, mortgage loan for an existing, higher-priced, one.

3 When borrowers with variable-rate mortgage loans think that variable mortgage rates will in the future exceed current fixed mortgage rates on new loans. However, it is unlikely that the average borrower will outsmart a financial institution in this regard: according to the liquidity premium theory of the term structure of interest rates, long-term rates are an average of the short-term rates that are expected to occur over the life of a long-term debt instrument (like a mortgage loan) plus a liquidity premium, which reflects supply and demand conditions for the particular instrument involved (Mishkin, 2010: 136). If so, a financial institution's expectation of future short-term rates – and thus of future long-term rates – (a) will most probably be better informed than that of the average borrower and (b) will already be reflected in the fixed long-term rate charged on a new loan.

A decision to prepay one's mortgage loan in order to replace it by a cheaper one (i.e., to refinance an existing mortgage or, simply, to remortgage) has to take into account (in addition to the prepayment penalty) transaction costs on the new deal and how far into the existing loan repayment schedule the borrower is. It may be that the transaction (or closing) costs of a new deal will outweigh the benefits of a lower interest rate on the new loan.

For example, in 2010 in the UK, such costs[12] would typically include the following:[13]

- An arrangement fee of about £500 (with much higher fees also possible, as well as lower ones – only in their case the mortgage loans offered might have been uncompetitive in other ways).
- A mortgage indemnity guarantee (MIG) insurance premium, to protect the lender in case of borrower's default. (Basically, this is the lender's way of making the borrower pay for the lender's risk – implying that in the event of default it would be the insurance company coming after the borrower's property rather than the bank.) A MIG would be demanded by most lenders if the borrower's initial deposit, or down-payment, were less than 10 per cent of the property's value (but sometimes even if it were as high as 25 per cent), and it would cost about £1500 per £100,000 of property price.
- Valuation fees.[14]
- Conveyancing (i.e., legal) fees.

A numerical example is constructed in Table 4.4. Let us assume (a) an original mortgage of £200,000 at 4 per cent, repaid annually over 25 years, (b) a prepayment penalty of £2000 (imposed whenever prepayment takes place) and transaction costs of £1500, and (c) a maturity of any remortgage deal equal to the number of years remaining for repayment of the original loan. Under these assumptions, Table 4.4 shows that remortgaging at the end of the 7th year makes economic sense if the interest rate on a remortgage loan (for the remaining principal) is less than 3.81 per cent, and at the end of the 17th year it makes sense if the rate is less than 3.17 per cent.

Table 4.4 When is remortgaging worthwhile?

Original mortgage:	
Principal	200,000
Interest rate (fixed)	4.00%
Maturity	25
Annual repayment instalment (interest-and-capital) on existing loan	12,802.39
Prepayment penalty in case of redemption (3-month interest, calculated as [(interest rate × original principal)/12](3))	2,000
Total transaction costs on possible remortgage deal	1,500
(A) Refinancing at end of 17th year:	
Principal remaining at end of 17th year	86,195.24
Annual allocation of prepayment penalty (2,000/8)	250
Annual allocation of transaction costs (i.e., 1,500/8)	187.5
Refinancing is sensible only if the annual repayment instalment on the new deal, plus the above allocations, is less than the annual repayment instalment on the existing loan. For this to happen, the annual repayment instalment on the new loan must be less than	12,364.89
Which implies an interest rate on the new deal not greater than, approximately,	3.17%
(B) Refinancing at end of 7th year:	
Principal remaining at end of 7th year	162,069.29
Annual allocation of prepayment penalty (2,000/18)	111.11
Annual allocation of transaction costs on new deal (1,500/18)	83.33
Refinancing is sensible only if the annual repayment instalment on the new deal, plus the above allocations, is less than the annual repayment instalment on the existing loan. For this to happen, the annual repayment instalment on the new loan must be less than	12,607.95
Which implies an interest rate on the new deal not greater than, approximately,	3.81%

4.3.3 Cash-out refinancing

A variant of remortgaging is 'cash-out refinancing' (a mostly US term), which involves both substituting a new for an existing mortgage loan *and* getting some extra cash (on the strength of one's remaining equity in the property) to spend as one pleases. This makes cash-out refinancing a hybrid category between remortgaging and equity withdrawal.

Take a mortgager who still owes $50,000 on a $150,000 property. In a remortgage, he or she would substitute a new loan equal to $50,000 for the balance owed. In cash-out refinancing, he or she might go for an $80,000 loan. The $80,000 loan would repay the old balance outstanding, and the remainder would accrue to the mortgager (minus any closing expenses over the deal, paid to the originator of the new loan – either the same bank that owned the old loan or a new lender).

Notice that if the property had been originally bought with a $90,000 loan at a time when it was worth, say, $105,000, the loan-to-value (LTV) ratio would have been about 86 per cent. The new $80,000 loan results in an LTV of about 53%, so it is an almost safe deal for the bank.

4.3.4 Tapping into one's home equity

Remortgaging must not be confused with a second (or third) mortgage, a *home equity loan* (HELOAN), or a *home equity line of credit* (HELOC). These are all examples of a class of forward loans enabling *equity withdrawal* from one's home. Let us have a look.

One step up from 'cash-out refinancing' is a home equity loan (HELOAN). The property owner borrows against the equity he or she has in the property. Any existing mortgage loan is not replaced; a new mortgage loan is added on the existing one, secured on the owner's equity and, of course, the actual market value of the property. Such an additional (second or even third) loan, however, will almost certainly be granted at a higher interest rate since it will have second priority over the property against the first priority enjoyed by the existing mortgage loan. That is, in the event of the property owner's default on payments, the owner of the first mortgage will be compensated first out of the proceeds from the sale of the property, and the owner of the second mortgage will be compensated second. This reduces the chances of the second mortgagee getting fully compensated – hence the higher interest rate on the second mortgage. If the mortgager subsequently refinances his or her first mortgage (i.e., remortgages), the refinanced mortgage will usually retain its first-priority status, but not necessarily.

A *home equity loan* (HELOAN) means that the mortgager gets a lump sum from the lender (minus expenses). A variant is a *home equity line of credit* (HELOC), in which the mortgager can draw funds from a credit line as needed, rather than being given a whole lump sum up front. This way, the interest cost to the mortgager is reduced. On the other hand, a HELOC carries an adjustable rate rather than a fixed rate (which is the usual case with a HELOAN). A typical HELOC, moreover, is broken down into two periods:[15] the draw period, in which monies are drawn from the credit line and the borrower makes interest-only payments on the amount drawn upon; and a repayment period, in which interest-and-capital are repaid. (In a variant of this, interest-only continues being paid in the repayment period, with a *balloon payment* at the end to repay the principal owed.)

Bear in mind that the mechanics of all forward loans are basically the same, involving variants of interest-and-capital repayment or interest-only repayment and fixed rates or variable rates. They may or may not be accompanied by tax breaks as far as the interest payments are concerned, depending on the tax legislation applicable in a specific country at a specific time.

4.4 Reverse (or equity release) mortgages

Although reverse mortgages are still a small part of the overall primary mortgage market, they merit particular attention because they may well prove to be the most important way of financing retirement in countries where the social security system and/or the government budget are facing mounting funding problems. The list includes almost all advanced countries, which are presently in the grip of gaping public deficits and galloping sovereign debts, while for a number of years now those countries have been increasingly burdened with ageing populations and suffering from low or declining personal saving rates.

In such countries, a major challenge is for retirees not to outlive their wealth. Three devices have been found for the purpose (Swiss Re, 2008): life annuities, long-term care insurance (LTCI), and *reverse mortgages* (known in the UK as *equity release mortgages*). The first two are offered by insurance companies, the third by both insurance companies and banks (and companies specializing in home reversion plans – a form of equity release mortgage – in the UK). Life annuities typically guarantee a regular stream of fixed payments over a person's lifetime. That is, a person first makes annuity payments to an insurance company over a number of years, and when the person retires the insurance company uses the accumulated capital in order to make annuity payments back to the person, usually for life. LTCI is an insurance policy aiming at safeguarding against the unexpected costs of caring for an elderly person.

Reverse mortgages release the equity in an elderly person's home, allowing them at the same time to stay there until death (or until they permanently move). In different ways, all three devices try to address the problem of retired households with insufficient liquid savings or incomes – but with a valuable physical asset like one's home. In so doing, reverse mortgages link the housing market to the social security system.

Reverse mortgages first appeared in the USA in 1989,[16] and spread to the UK, Canada, Australia, New Zealand, and elsewhere (e.g., India).[17] European countries other than the UK where such products have been relatively significant are the Netherlands, Spain, and Sweden (DEMHOW, 2010).

An interesting study of the economic and social significance of reverse mortgages in Europe has been undertaken in the context of DEMHOW (Demographic Change and Housing Wealth), involving researchers from 10 member states of the European Union and funded under its 7th Framework Programme. Some of the DEMHOW conclusions are worth mentioning:

1 Equity withdrawal loans differ from reverse mortgage loans in terms of their effect on the business cycle. Demand for equity withdrawal loans picks up when the economy is booming (and house prices rise), and drops when it is on a downturn (and house prices are stable or falling). So they are typically pro-cyclical products. Reverse mortgages, on the other hand, are considered to have little, if any, effect on the business cycle.
2 Reverse mortgages are still a small part of the overall primary mortgage market, in countries where they exist at all.
3 They are more prevalent in countries where the mortgage market is highly developed anyway.
4 Their greatest potential exists in countries where (a) the social security system is not very generous (i.e., where pensions and other forms of support for senior citizens are small or insufficient), or is likely to stop being as generous as in the past, (b) retirees are asset-rich even if income-poor, and (c) mortgage markets are developed and sophisticated enough to enable potential demand stemming from (a) and (b) to be realized.
5 Reverse mortgages are products that crucially depend on the future course of house prices. Following the burst of the house price boom in the USA and the UK in 2007–09, financial institutions are likely to weigh the risks of such products far more than in the past.

Knowing, however, that the social security systems of all advanced countries will be facing difficulties in the years ahead, and that these are the very countries with the most developed mortgage markets, the growth prospects of a market for reverse mortgage loans in particular look reasonably good,[18] especially when housing markets recover.

In this respect, we should note that, in addition to figures about the number and value of reverse mortgage loans outstanding in a country, or about the rates of growth of these magnitudes, there are two other important metrics to use in order to gauge the market potential for such loans in a country with a well-functioning and unfettered mortgage market:

1 The value of the equity locked into senior householders' homes over an extended time horizon, say, 20 years ahead.

2 The penetration level, which is the ratio of existing reverse mortgage loans to all senior homeowning households.

Thus,

1 In the UK, the Equity Release Report 2005, prepared by the Equity Release Working Party (ERWP, 2005), estimated that the unmortgaged equity of the over-65s was at least £1.1 trillion (p. 1). The report predicted an increase of equity release sales from £1 billion (or 20,000 sales) in 2005 to £4 billion a year (or 80,000 sales) by 2031 (p. 15).
2 In the USA in 2007, the National Reverse Mortgage Lenders Association (NRMLA) and The Hollister Group (which together launched the first Reverse Mortgage Market Index, or RMMI) calculated that Americans aged 62 or older held $4.3 trillion of home equity, but that the market penetration of this type of product was less than 1 per cent.[19] By January 2010, however, the market had crossed the 2 per cent mark.[20]

4.4.1 Mechanics of a reverse mortgage

A typical reverse, or equity release, mortgage (of the type that in the UK is called a *lifetime, roll-up*, mortgage) involves the homeowner (who must be a relatively elderly person – over 62 in the USA, over 55 in the UK, depending on the financial institution and the kind of loan sought) getting a lump sum (or a stream of regular payments, or a combination of both) from a financial institution (say, a bank), secured on the value of the home. The homeowner pays nothing in return, but when he or she dies (or permanently moves out), the bank has the right to sell the property and get as much as is required to cover the principal plus capitalized interest (plus expenses, of course). That is, precisely because the homeowner pays nothing to service the loan while he or she lives, all interest due is brought forward (i.e., rolled up) and capitalized.

Eventually, a hefty sum is created, which will be subtracted from the value of the property when the bank sells it. Fortunately for the owner (or his or her estate), the bank's claim stops there: if the sale price is not enough to cover the bank's claim, tough (for the bank)! In other words, this kind of reverse mortgage (which is the typical, and also most popular, kind) has a *non-recourse limit*, the limit being the value of the mortgage property. Unfortunately for the homeowner's inheritor(s), on the other hand, the reverse mortgage deal 'eats up' rather quickly the value of the property, so there is usually little left to inherit anyway.

Figure 4.1 displays the mortgage history of such a homeowner. Initially, at the age of 30, he or she bought a home with a typical forward mortgage (say, an interest-and-capital repayment one). The amount borrowed was, for example, £200,000, corresponding to a 100 per cent LTV, with a 25-year maturity and an interest rate of 4 per cent. The rate of house price growth was 2 per cent per annum, on average.

Figure 4.1 shows that as the loan was being repaid, the owner's equity in the home kept on increasing at an increasing rate even while the bank's interest (i.e., share of the property's ownership) was coming down at an increasing rate. The reason for the owner's accelerating equity is twofold: (a) the mathematics of interest-rate compounding and (b) the fact that the value of the property was going up throughout the period, which served to reduce the bank's percentage share in the property faster than the extent to which the repayment of the loan alone was reducing it. At the end of the 25th year, the bank's share had become nil, and the owner's share (his or her equity) 100 per cent – and was exactly equal in value to the price of the property then. Subsequently, the owner's equity share remained constant, but in absolute terms its value moved along with the property price, to which it was identical.

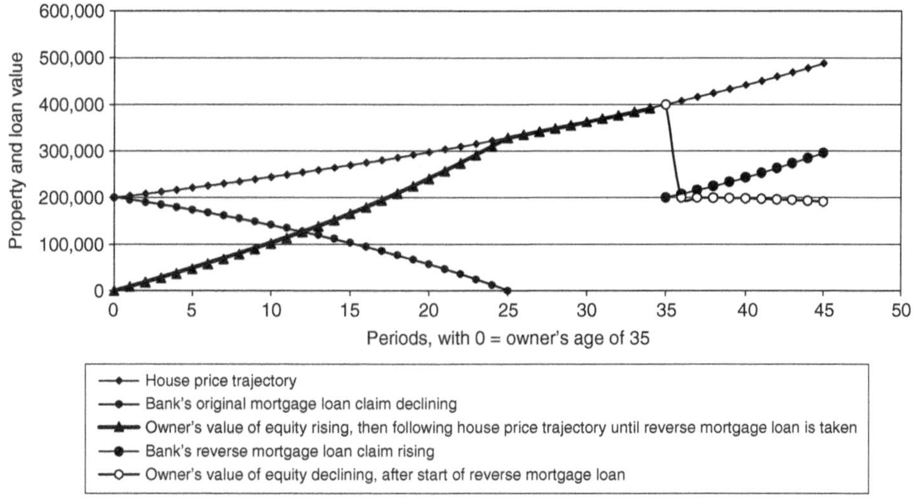

Figure 4.1 A homeowner's mortgage history, assuming that after a reverse mortgage loan is taken, the house price goes on rising.

Ten years later, when the owner was 65, he or she decided to take a reverse mortgage loan to increase his or her liquidity (see Table 4.5). At that time, and assuming that the rate of house price growth was still 2 per cent per annum, the value of the property had become £399,978. Following usual procedure, the bank decided to extend a reverse mortgage loan to the homeowner to the tune of half that amount (i.e., £199,989), at 4 per cent again. Eventually the homeowner died 10 years later. The value of the loan had become £296,033, but the value of the property (assuming that growth had continued at 2 per cent) was now £487,571. Ignoring expenses, the bank sold the property, satisfied its claim, and gave the balance (£191,538) to the homeowner's inheritor(s). That balance was 39.28 per cent of the property's sale price of £487,571.

Figure 4.2 tells a different tale. Everything is the same, except that, following the reverse mortgage deal, house prices began a long descent to the tune of 2 per cent per annum; alternatively, in the very year when the homeowner died, house prices dropped down to £326,811 (equivalent to an annual rate of growth of -2 per cent). The inheritors' share of the price was now 9.42 per cent of the property's sale price of £326,811, or £30,779 (in contrast to £191,538 under the previous scenario). In either case, though, the bank got its due, i.e., £296,033 (ignoring expenses).

Finally Table 4.6 shows what the owner's (rather, the inheritor(s)') share would have been under different house price growth rates and interest rates.

A number of conclusions can be drawn:

1 No matter what the house price growth, the bank's formal claim depends only on the interest rate charged, the initial principal, and the amount of time till the homeowner's death (or their moving out permanently).
2 The fulfilment of the claim, however, does depend on the rate of house price growth over the duration of the reverse mortgage. On the other hand, it does not depend on the initial house price.

Table 4.5 A homeowner's mortgage history, assuming that after a reverse mortgage loan is taken, the house price declines

Period	*Homeowner's age*		*Bank's claim (4% interest rate)*	*Owner's equity*	*House price (2% growth rate)*
					0
0	30	Initial mortgage loan to buy house	200,000	0	200,000
1	31		195,198	8,802	204,000
2	32		190,203	17,877	208,080
25	55	Repayment of loan	0	328,121	328,121
26	56			334,684	334,684
34	64			392,135	392,135
35	65	Reverse mortgage loan taken, equal to 1/2 of 399,978	199,989	399,978	399,978
36	66		207,989	199,989	407,977
37	67		216,308	199,829	416,137
44	74		284,647	193,364	478,011
45	75	Homeowner dies	296,033	191,538	487,571

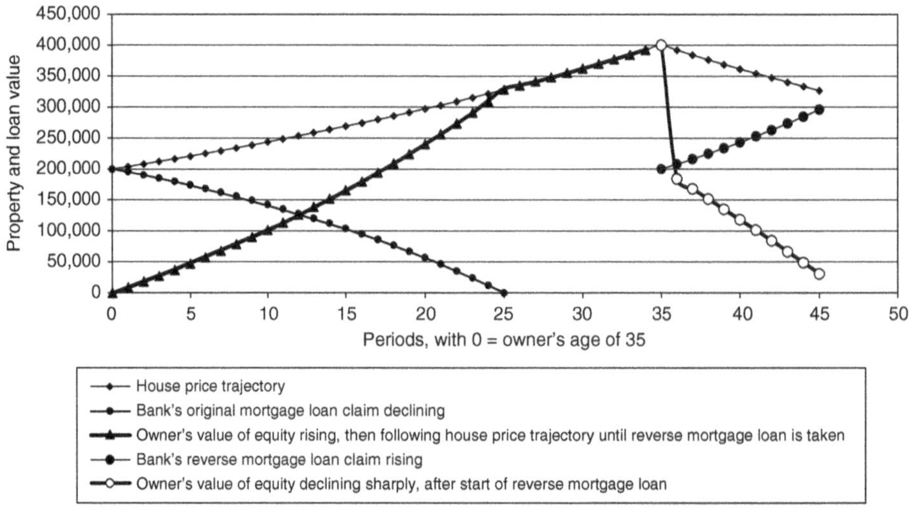

Figure 4.2 A homeowner's mortgage history, assuming that after a reverse mortgage loan is taken, the house price declines.

3 The rate of house price growth is also crucial to the inheritor(s) as it determines how much they stand to get following the homeowner's death (i.e., after repayment of the reverse mortgage loan).

4 The bank may be getting a larger share of the value of the property at lower rates of house price growth, but in absolute terms it only gets the compounded value of the principal it gave the homeowner when the reverse mortgage deal was made.

Table 4.6 Percentage of property value left to inheritor(s), if homeowner dies 10 years into the reverse mortgage, under different assumptions about house price growth and interest rates

	Interest rate on reverse mortgage				
Rate of house price growth	1.00%	2.00%	3.00%	4.00%	5.00%
2.00%	54.69%	50.00%	44.88%	39.28%	33.19%
1.00%	50.00%	44.82%	39.17%	33.00%	26.27%
0.00%	44.77%	39.05%	32.80%	25.99%	18.56%
−1%	38.93%	32.61%	25.70%	18.16%	9.94%
−2%	32.40%	25.40%	17.77%	9.42%	0.32%

5 Even if the bank charges a high interest rate, this will not increase its chances of getting its money back with interest; it all depends on what the house price is at the time of the homeowner's death, in relation to the bank's accumulated claim. It may in fact be in the bank's interest to charge a rate as low as capital market conditions permit. (Technically, the opportunity cost of alternative investments must be higher than or equal to the opportunity cost of investing in reverse mortgages.)

The last point describes one important kind of financial institution risk related to reverse mortgages: the risk that within an expected time horizon, house prices will not be high enough to allow the institution to recover its capital with interest. There is also another risk: that the homeowner will live 'too long' (longer than an expected time horizon). In the example of Figure 4.2, if the homeowner does not die at 75, but at 77, the bank will start losing money on this investment; even if the annual decrease in house prices is not 2 per cent, but 1 per cent, the bank will again start losing money if the homeowner dies at 80 (rather than 77). This possibility suggests that proper pricing of reverse mortgages must make use of the concept of life expectancy; ideally, too, a financial institution granting such products must try and create a large enough pool of loan accounts so that the law of large numbers can safeguard the institution from cases of mortgagers living 'too long'.

4.4.2 *A right interest rate for a reverse mortgage?*

It is actually possible to calculate what the interest rate in a reverse mortgage loan should be in order for a bank to receive the full value of the loan at maturity, which is when the homeowner dies. Assuming that the time of death has been forecast correctly (which is not very difficult if we are talking about a large group rather than an individual), knowing that the owner's (or inheritor(s)') share of the property will be zero at maturity only if the accumulated debt equals the market value of the property, we have

$$kP_0(1+i)^t = P_0(1+g)^t, \tag{4.10}$$

where

P_0 = market value of property at loan inception,
i = bank interest rate,
k = proportion of market value of property that determines the initial value of the loan,
g = annual house price growth,
t = expected time horizon (i.e., expected number of years till homeowner's death).

The inheritor(s)' share will then be zero, and the bank will be fully repaid for the loan, which will just equal the market value of the property, if

$$g = k^{1/t}(1+i) - 1 = \sqrt[t]{k}(1+i) - 1, \tag{4.11}$$

or

$$i = \left(\frac{1}{k}\right)^{1/t}(1+g) - 1 = \sqrt[t]{\frac{1}{k}}(1+g) - 1. \tag{4.12}$$

By extension, any i that satisfies $g > k^{1/t}(1+i) - 1$ should guarantee that the bank will get its money back with interest. This formula suggests that it is not always necessary for the house price growth to be greater than the interest rate; the time to maturity and the proportion of the initial value of the property given as loan have also to be taken into account (whereas the absolute initial value of the property plays no role in the calculation).

Example 4

Given $k = ½$, $i = 4$ per cent, and $t = 10$, the inheritor(s)' share will be zero, and the market value of the property will be just enough to allow the bank to receive full compensation for the loan, if $g = -0.0296$. Anything above that, say, $g = -0.028$ (a negative rate!), will also allow the bank to be fully repaid (i.e., make a profit on the deal, as implied by the interest rate applied). Since i is largely under the control of the bank, the main challenge here is to predict correctly the rate of house price growth in order to set i at an appropriate level.

Example 5

Find a range of acceptable interest rates that would allow a bank to be fully repaid (i.e., make a profit) on a reverse mortgage deal with a homeowner aged 70 whose life expectancy is 10 years, given that the bank's policy is $k = ½$ and its estimates of average annual house price growth over that period, along with respective probabilities of occurrence, are as shown in Table 4.7. Assume also that the bank attracts deposits at an average rate of 2 per cent (determined by capital market conditions), and that it requires at least a 3 percentage point spread between its rate on deposits and its average loan rate. Provide answers both for each separate house price growth rate scenario, and for all the scenarios combined.

Answer: Combining the different scenarios requires of course finding the expected value of the house price growth rates over the given period. Finding the interest rates that are profitable and acceptable requires two things: (a) For each house price growth scenario, to find the interest rate (the cut-off rate) at which the loan value equals the house price at maturity. The interest rate found, as well as any interest rate smaller than this, is profitable, i.e., it guarantees realization of the value of the loan. Any higher interest rate is not profitable, because it implies a loan value higher than the house price, i.e., a loan value that cannot be realized fully. (b) From the set of profitable interest rates, to choose those rates that are larger than, or equal to, the minimum acceptable rate (MAR), which in this case is 5 per cent.

Eventually the bank will define a range of potentially profitable rates bracketed, on the one hand, by the cut-off rate (8.57 per cent), which corresponds to the expected rate of house price growth (1.3 per cent), and, on the other, by the MAR.

Table 4.7 Range of profit-generating, and of acceptable, interest rates on the reverse mortgage loan of Example 5

Probability of occurrence	*House price growth rate*	*Cut-off interest rate (equating the bank's claim to the value of the property)*	*Property value at maturity (given an initial value of £399,978)*	*Range of interest rates that guarantee realization of the loan value (i.e., a loan value ≤ value of house) and a positive return*	*Range of acceptable interest rates, given a reference rate of 5%*
35.00%	3.00%	10.39%	537,537	$0 < i \leq 10.39\%$	$5\% \leq i \leq 10.39\%$
25.00%	2.00%	9.32%	487,571	$0 < i \leq 9.32\%$	$5\% \leq i \leq 9.32\%$
10.00%	1.00%	8.25%	441,824	$0 < i \leq 8.25\%$	$5\% \leq i \leq 8.25\%$
10.00%	0.00%	7.18%	399,978	$0 < i \leq 7.18\%$	$5\% \leq i \leq 7.18\%$
10.00%	−1%	6.11%	361,733	$0 < i \leq 6.11\%$	$5\% \leq i \leq 6.11\%$
5.00%	−2%	5.03%	326,811	$0 < i \leq 5.03\%$	$5\% \leq i \leq 5.03\%$
5.00%	−3%	3.96%	294,953	$0 < i \leq 3.96\%$	None
Expected values:	1.30%	8.57%	455,125	$0 < i \leq 8.57\%$	$5\% \leq i \leq 8.57\%$

On their part, mortgagers face a different kind of risk to that of mortgagees: that, if they take a reverse mortgage loan too soon, they may use up the proceeds from it, and then have no liquid or other assets to fall back on (other than a pension). At that point, pressures on them may stem from two sources in particular: (a) special care needs, which usually manifest themselves later rather than earlier in one's life, and (b) having to pay property taxes they will no longer be able to afford. If (b), they will have to move (this is also a clause in many reverse mortgage contracts) at a time when they will be most fragile, physically and emotionally. (This is one more reason why the whole system of property taxation may have to be reviewed radically – see Chapter 12.)

4.5 Reverse mortgages in the USA and the UK

There are similarities as well as differences in reverse mortgages between the USA and the UK, notwithstanding the fact that they are called 'equity release' mortgages in the UK. Broadly speaking, these are as follows:

In the USA

The most widely available reverse mortgage loan in the USA is the Home Equity Conversion Mortgage (HECM), which is insured (not given!) by the Federal Housing Administration

(FHA), a part of the Department of Housing and Urban Development (HUD). The insurance charge is called a Mortgage Insurance Premium (MIP), and is made up of two parts (AARP, 2008):

1 2 per cent of the value of the borrower's home (or 2 per cent of the HUD's home value limit, whichever is less). This is charged up-front at 'closing' (i.e., time of signing the contract).
2 0.5 per cent added to the interest rate applied on the loan.

The MIP guarantees that the borrower gets what is promised them (e.g., monthly advances) no matter how long they live, or what happens to the lender, or to the value of the property. It also guarantees that they do not have to repay the loan as long as they live (or until they permanently move out), and, most importantly, that the total debt can never be more than the value of the borrower's home (if the latter is sold to repay the loan).

The borrower must be at least 62 years old. Because reverse mortgages are complex financial arrangements, involving risks for both the borrower and their estate (i.e., their inheritors), and because prospective borrowers are senior citizens, HUD has made it compulsory for them, prior to applying for a HECM, to consult with a counsellor employed by a non-profit or public agency approved by HUD. A US reverse mortgage pays cash as a lump sum, as a regular monthly advance, as a credit line allowing irregular withdrawals, or as a combination of these. Repayment becomes due when the last surviving borrower dies (or moves out permanently). A lender, however, may require repayment any time if borrower fails to pay property taxes, maintain or repair the property, or buy hazard insurance.

In the UK

There are two equity release products in the UK: Lifetime mortgages and home reversion plans. In a lifetime mortgage the homeowner retains ownership of the property, and they or their estate (i.e., their inheritors) can lift the mortgage on the property simply by repaying the loan in full. A lifetime mortgage can involve either a lump sum given the homeowner at inception of the loan, or a credit line facility, which allows the homeowner to draw money on an 'as needed' basis (a *drawdown* mortgage).

As the second choice actually allows interest to be calculated on smaller amounts of principal, taken at different times, it helps keep the loan costs down. In a home reversion plan, the homeowner sells all or part of the property to a reversion company, in exchange for money now plus the right to stay in the property rent-free until death. Because the exact time of the homeowner's death is unknown, the amount of money given them is less than the value of the property, and depends on their life expectancy. (The amount is usually about a third of the property value for a woman aged 65.)[21]

Since 2004, the equity release business in the UK has been supervised by the Financial Services Authority (FSA). Before that time, many lenders adopted a voluntary code of conduct called SHIP (Safe Home Income Plans),[22] which, among other things, required the lender to give a No Negative Equity Guarantee (NNEG) to the homeowner. The guarantee meant that the bank's claim would never exceed the value of the property. An NNEG is still offered by a number of financial institutions, but, although it is good precaution for a prospective borrower to seek out one that offers this, he or she should also be aware that the sum they can borrow under a NNEG is smaller than what they can borrow without one. But, contrary to US HECM loans, equity release loans in the UK are not government-insured, nor is proof of consultation with a government-approved source required prior to applying for one (Sinclair, 2010). Nonetheless, mortgage brokers who offer advice on equity release products in the UK must be FSA-approved (FSA, 2010).

A UK lifetime mortgage comes under four variants (FSA, 2005):

1 A home income plan: the borrower receives a lump sum that buys an annuity that gives them a monthly income. Part of the income pays interest on the loan (the lump sum borrowed). The principal is repaid when the borrower's home is sold. The borrower must be aware that the earlier in life they buy a home income plan, the smaller the 'free' income available to them will be.
2 An interest-only mortgage: the borrower takes a lump sum, and pays interest on it. The principal is repaid when the borrower's home is sold. The borrower must make sure that their income from other sources (e.g., a pension) is enough to enable payment of interest.
3 A roll-up mortgage (studied in Section 4.4.1). This is the one leading to the fastest-growing bank's claim on the borrower's property.
4 A fixed repayment mortgage. The borrower receives a lump sum and agrees to let the bank have a higher sum, out of the market price of the property, when the latter is sold. How much higher depends on the borrower's life expectancy.

4.6 Housing finance and homeownership

The mortgage business worldwide is made up of the primary and the secondary market. The primary market involves financial institutions granting loans for the purchase of property (or granting loans on the strength of the value of one's property). Mortgage loans on non-income residential properties are of course the bulk of this market, the rest comprising commercial mortgages (for the purpose of buying business premises or income real estate).[23] The secondary market, on the other hand, involves either the purchase of existing mortgages or – and much more usually – the issue of mortgage-backed securities (see Section 4.7). Here we shall look into the residential mortgage primary market in particular.

Housing credit is in many countries the only way for most households to become owner-occupiers, and its importance is on the increase in many more. Would therefore large ratios of mortgage debt to GDP correlate with high rates of owner-occupation? The metrics in Table 4.8 show that this not necessarily so.

Table 4.8 Housing debt to GDP ratio versus owner-occupation; 49 countries c. mid-2000s

		GDP per capita, 2008, based on PPP (current international $)	*Residential mortgage debt/GDP ratio (%); data from c. 2005*	*Residential mortgage debt/GDP ratio (%); data from 2009 or slightly earlier*	*Proportion of households owner-occupying (%); data from c. 2005*
25 high- to middle- : income countries	Average	35,730	54	65	67
	StDev	7,141	24	25	12
13 transitional Eastern European countries:	Average	17,965	8	18	84
	StDev	5,872	7	12	15
11 developing countries:	Average	8,327	9	11	78
	StDev	4,659	11	12	13

Source: Table 4.9

The reason is that, in addition to using credit, there have been three other ways to become an owner-occupier, all involving mainly a social and political answer to the question of 'who owns the land'.

1 In many of the poorest countries of the world, one way to own your home in a city has been to build it yourself on public or disputed land, particularly peripheral urban land. It goes without saying that this mode has been associated with tremendous negative externalities, especially in an urban context of rapid population growth. Moreover, it has been a mode that intrinsically discourages the use of credit (which could promote better building quality and improvements as well as more investment) because the lack of legal titles on the plots makes mortgage finance near impossible.[24]

   In 1990, for example, the ratio of informal housing[25] to all housing in Cairo, Egypt, was 65 per cent, the ratio of housing loans to all loans 7 per cent, and the rate of owner-occupation 32 per cent. Turning to Constantinople, Turkey, the ratio of informal housing to all housing was 51 per cent, and the other two percentages were 3 and 60, respectively.[26] Notice, though, that the percentages refer to a city in each country; the extent of owner-occupation and informal housing nationally must have been much higher. In Turkey, for instance, in 2003 the rate of owner-occupation was 72 per cent and the ratio of mortgage debt to GDP was 4.5 per cent, much lower than in all advanced countries (see Table 4.9).
2 The second way to acquire your dwelling without the use of credit has been through a combination of high rates of economic growth and the use of already owned assets, chiefly other land assets. For example, rapid economic growth from the late 1950s to the late 1970s plus the very wide distribution of landed ownership in Greece allowed many Greeks to settle in cities during the decades after the Second World War through selling first some of their rural land assets. In Greece, this practice allowed most households to achieve relatively quickly high standards of housing quality and wealth, as well as the reproduction in an urban context of the wide distribution of real estate property that originally characterized the Greek countryside. As a result, by 2009, the rate of owner-occupation was 80.0 per cent and the ratio of mortgage debt to GDP 33.9 per cent, whereas the corresponding figures for, say, the USA were 67.2 per cent and 81.4 per cent (Table 4.9).

   An interesting characteristic of the Greek experience has been the wide incidence of unauthorized building (usually on publicly owned land). As in many less developed but more populous countries, this has contributed to urban problems like congestion. On the other hand, Greek housing has broadly been of good quality (as opposed to the shanties of many of those countries). The practice of unauthorized building also implies a state unwilling and/or unable to enforce its property rights, which is another feature that Greece has had in common with poorer countries.
3 The third way to owner-occupation without the use of credit (or of *much* credit) has been through privatization of public housing, which the UK pioneered under Margaret Thatcher, and reached its greatest possible extent in Eastern European countries following the collapse of communism.

All three ways, therefore, hinge crucially on the land question: a lack of legal titles on the land (or the weak enforcement of a state's claims on public land in particular) has helped owner-occupation based on one's own means (rather than on credit) no less than a very wide distribution of such titles, in a historic tradition of rural smallholderism – and no less than the one-off revolutionary change that happened in Eastern Europe. Conversely, where land and property rights (the state's or individuals') were strongly upheld, whether in town or in country, most households have had difficulty achieving urban owner-occupation in any way other than relying on credit – especially in countries where (a) there was no tradition, or only a weak tradition, of rural smallholderism, or (b) rural assets, for whatever reason, could not be utilized to enable large numbers of households to become urban homeowners.

This does not mean that anarchic land ownership patterns are a good alternative to housing finance if one's goal is owner-occupation: lack of titles, or their weak enforcement, is typically associated with negative externalities, low investment levels, and anaemic wealth creation. But as countries modernize, a number of things usually happen: the links with the countryside weaken, property rights become better defined, land markets become both more efficient and expensive, quality standards increase[27] – and, as a result, the use of credit rises. There should therefore exist a rough correlation between high real personal incomes (as an indicator of development) and high ratios of both mortgage debt to GDP and of owner-occupation. This is indeed so (see Table 4.9), as long as one takes certain qualifications into account. These are the following:

1 First of all, income is not the only thing that affects the extent to which credit is utilized in order to finance owner-occupation; nor is housing finance the only determinant of owner-occupation levels anyway. Additional relevant variables are philosophy and effectiveness of the planning function, land ownership patterns, government policies as regards taxes on, and subsidies to, owner-occupation, household preferences, cost of renting compared to cost of owning, rates of economic growth, level of real mortgage rates, and a political decision to roll-back the size of the 'social-rented', or public-housing, sector. The most famous of such a decision was Margaret Thatcher's 'right-to-buy' policy of the 1980s, but the process was taken to extremes in most Eastern European countries following the 1989 revolutions. Turning to EU-15 in particular, Wolswijk (2006) showed that real mortgage debt in 1982–2003 was affected significantly by after-tax mortgage interest costs, house prices, financial deregulation, and stock markets, while the impact of household disposable income and of inflation was weaker (which is not surprising, given that the sample was made of high-income countries anyway).
2 In Eastern Europe, the percentages of owner-occupation are today very high, while incomes and the ratios of mortgage debt to GDP are low – but the combination is due to the one-off historic experience of the region after the collapse of communism (see Scanlon and Whitehead, 2004: 3, 11, 15). Interestingly, the ratios of residential mortgage debt to GDP in these countries appear to be rising faster than in the sample of developing countries with which those countries are compared in 2005 and again in 2009 (see Table 4.9).
3 In most developing countries 'owner-occupation' overlaps with informal housing, so income is definitely not a factor behind high levels of owner-occupation. By contrast, informal housing has not been associated with Eastern European transitional economies, which perhaps explains the faster growth in the rate of residential mortgage debt to GDP in the latter, as opposed to developing countries.
4 In many developing countries as well as Greece (discussed on p. 108), it is the very laxity with which the state enforces its (often vague) property rights over land that allows squatting and the achievement of 'owner-occupation' during urbanization. This kind of 'owner-occupation' usually involves substandard dwellings, but not necessarily so – cf. Greece. In such a context, housing finance plays, at least initially, a small role – and it seems to be affected by the issue of property rights over land more decisively than by people's incomes (even though these two factors – rights and incomes – affect one another also).

Table 4.9 Residential mortgage debt (RMD) to GDP versus owner-occupation, c. mid-2000s

	GDP per capita, 2008, based on PPP (current international $)	*Source and data year →*	*RMD/ GDP c. 2005*	*Source and data year →*	*Owner-occupation c. 2005*	*Source and data year →*	*RMD/ GDP c. 2009*
High- to middle-income countries:							
Australia	38,356	HFN, 2005	77.8%	HFN, 2006	69.8%	HFN, 2008	84.2%
Canada	39,080	HFN, 2005	45.7%	HFN, 2006	68.4%	HFN, 2008	53.9%
NZ	27,106	HFN, 2007	87.0%	HFN, 2006	66.9%	HFN, 2009	89.9%
USA	47,393	H, 2005	88.8%	H, 2009	67.2%	H, 2009	81.4%
Austria	39,887	H, 2005	22.1%	H, 2009	56.2%	H, 2009	26.2%
Belgium	36,345	H, 2005	33.4%	H, 2007	78.0%	H, 2009	43.3%
Cyprus	28,986	H, 2005	30.3%	H, 2006	68.0%	H, 2009	61.3%
Denmark	37,465	H, 2005	84.9%	H, 2009	54.0%	H, 2009	103.8%
Finland	36,128	H, 2005	41.9%	H, 2008	59.0%	H, 2009	58.0%
France	34,204	H, 2005	29.2%	H, 2007	57.4%	H, 2009	38.0%
Germany	35,539	H, 2005	51.9%	H, 2002	43.2%	H, 2009	47.6%
Greece	30,189	H, 2005	23.2%	H, 2009	80.0%	H, 2009	33.9%
Iceland	40,576	H, 2005	80.4%	H, 2008	82.5%	H, 2009	
Ireland	42,110	H, 2005	61.0%	H, 2009	74.5%	H, 2009	90.3%
Italy	30,520	H, 2005	17.0%	H, 2002	80.0%	H, 2009	21.7%
Malta	23,971	H, 2005	31.8%	H, 2006	75.0%	H, 2009	43.0%
Netherlands	40,558	H, 2005	93.5%	H, 2008	57.2%	H, 2009	105.6%
Norway	53,361	H, 2005	56.5%	H, 2001	76.7%	H, 2009	70.8%
Portugal	22,251	H, 2005	53.3%	H, 2006	76.0%	H, 2009	67.5%
Spain	30,815	H, 2005	52.3%	H, 2008	85.0%	H, 2009	64.6%
Sweden	37,334	H, 2005	59.4%	H, 2008	66.3%	H, 2009	82.0%
Switzerland	43,196	H, 2005	88.9%	H, 2000	34.6%	H, 2009	
UK	36,233	H, 2005	77.5%	H, 2007	69.5%	H, 2009	87.6%
Japan	33,957	HFN, 2005	36.7%	HFN, 2000	60.0%	H, 2009	
Korea	27,681	K&R, 2006	35.7%			H, 2009	
	35,730		54.41%		66.89%		64.50%
	7,141		24.34%		12.40%		24.91%
Transitional Eastern European countries:							
Bulgaria	12,322	H, 2005	4.6%	H, 2002	96.5%	H, 2009	12.6%
Czech Republic	25,061	H, 2005	6.0%	H, 2001	47.0%	H, 2009	19.4%
Estonia	20,561	H, 2005	23.4%	H, 2008	96.0%	H, 2009	44.5%
Hungary	19,522	H, 2005	10.5%	H, 2003	92.0%	H, 2009	16.7%
Latvia	17,111	H, 2005	19.1%	H, 2007	87.0%	H, 2009	36.6%
Lithuania	19,090	H, 2005	10.9%	H, 2008	97.0%	H, 2009	22.6%
Poland	17,556	H, 2005	6.0%	H, 2004	75.0%	H, 2009	18.2%
Romania	16,638	H, 2005	1.8%	H, 2009	95.7%	H, 2009	4.9%
Slovakia	22,044	H, 2005	8.0%	H, 2008	88.0%	H, 2009	14.6%
Slovenia	29,537	H, 2005	4.8%	H, 2006	82.0%	H, 2009	11.4%
Russia	15,941	H, 2005	0.2%	H, 2003	63.8%	H, 2009	2.1%
Serbia	10,822	H, 2005	1.5%	H, 2002	89.0%	H, 2009	
Ukraine	7,342	H, 2005	2.6%			H, 2009	11.0%
	17,965		7.65%		84.08%		17.88%
	5,872		6.92%		15.32%		12.18%

(*Continued*)

Table 4.9 Cont'd

	GDP per capita, 2008, based on PPP (current international $)	*Source and data year →*	*RMD/ GDP c. 2005*	*Source and data year →*	*Owner-occupation c. 2005*	*Source and data year →*	*RMD/ GDP c. 2009*
Developing countries:							
Brazil	10,512	HFN, 2005	1.4%	HFN, 2004	74.0%	HFN, 2008	2.2%
Chile	14,592	HFN, 2005	14.0%	HFN, 2002	73.0%		18.5%
China	5,999	HFN, 2005	9.0%	HFN, 2005	93.0%	HFN, 2007	10.9%
Indonesia	3,980	HFN, 2005	2.0%	HFN, 2001	96.0%	HFN, 2007	2.4%
India	2,790					HFN, 2008	6.0%
Mexico	14,528	HFN, 2005	8.7%	HFN, 2000	75.0%	HFN, 2008	8.1%
South Africa	10,442	HFN, 2005	34.1%	HFN, 2001	56.0%	HFN, 2008	42.3%
Thailand	8,232	HFN, 2005	17.1%	HFN, 2000	81.2%	HFN, 2007	18.3%
Turkey	13,107	H, 2005	2.1%	S, 2003	72.0%	H, 2009	4.6%
Egypt	5,897	HFN, 2005	0.1%			HFN, 2008	0.4%
Ghana	1,518	HFN, 2004	2.5%			HFN, 2006	3.9%
	8,327		9.10%		77.53%		10.69%
	4,659		10.52%		12.69%		12.15%

Sources: For GDP per capita: IMF World Economic Outlook Database, April 2010.
H: EMF Hypostat 2005, 2008, 2009, at www.hypo.org/
HFN: Housing Finance Network, at www.housing-finance-network.org/
K&R: Kim and Renaud (2009), p. 15.
S: Sarioglu et al. (2007), p. 2.

The issue was brought very much to the fore in the 2008 IBRD/World Bank document 'Financing Homes', which stressed that the low level of mortgage market development in poorer countries stems to a large extent from two kinds of difficulty: that which buyers face in registering a mortgage and effecting the title transfer, and another which creditors face in foreclosing a property when a borrower defaults. In a similar vein, Warnock and Warnock (2008) concluded in their seminal study of the housing finance systems of a sample of 62 developed and emerging economies that, among other factors, stronger legal rights for both borrowers and lenders contributed to 'deeper'[28] housing finance systems.

5 Even as regards developed countries, there are instances where the expected correlation between high personal incomes and owner-occupation (and/or high mortgage debt to GDP ratios) breaks down severely. Notable examples are Germany and Switzerland (see Table 4.9).

In Germany, the residential mortgage debt (RMD) to GDP ratio in 2005 was 51.9 per cent; the rate of owner-occupation was 43.2 per cent in 2002. So Germany's RMD/GDP ratio was less than the average for the 25 advanced countries of Table 4.9, and close to her (rather low) owner-occupation rate. The latter was comparatively low for three reasons: (a) Up to the end of 1986 (and for over 100 years), owner-occupied dwellings had been subject to (imputed) income tax. The tax was then abolished, but so was the possibility of deducting mortgage interest from tax (Degner, 1987). Taxation of imputed income from owner-occupation has been the case in other countries too, for example, Luxembourg and the Netherlands, but in the latter the tax deductibility of mortgage interest payments was (at least until 2007) almost unrestricted (Hoek and Radloff, 2007). (b) Germany has traditionally extended considerable protection to tenants through the Tenancy Law and the Law on Rent Levels (Busch-Geertsema, 2000). (c) Contrary to what happened in other Eastern European countries after 1989, East German public housing was not transformed overnight into owner-occupied housing, and has been transforming only slowly. For example, in 1993, the rate of owner-occupation in Easter Germany was 26.4 per cent; 10 years later, it had climbed just to 35.4 per cent (Schlatterer and Linsin, 2008).

The case of Switzerland requires a bit more explanation. To start with, available data are inconsistent. According to Hypostat (2005), the RMD/GDP ratios in 2003, 2004, and 2005 were 82.7, 86.1, and 88.9 per cent, respectively; according to Hypostat (2006), the ratio in 2003 was indeed 82.7 per cent, but over the next three years it went to 97.2, 101, and 101.9 per cent. On their part, Miles and Pillonca (2008) quoted 112.6, 115.5, 119, and 132.3 per cent for the period 2003–06 . As regards owner-occupation, a 2010 publication of the Swiss Federal Statistical Office still quoted a 2000 figure, namely 34.6 per cent. Be that as it may, Switzerland seems to have a comparatively high (actually very high!) RMD/GDP ratio, as well as a relatively low rate of owner-occupation.

This is a starker discrepancy than one finds in Germany. The reasons are also threefold: (a) very high house prices in Switzerland (due to high land prices, which are in turn due to there being very little developable land);[29] (b) generally unfavourable tax treatment of owner-occupation – for example, there is both a wealth tax and a tax on imputed rent from owner-occupation (but mortgage interest is deducted from income for tax purposes) (Bourassa and Hoesli, 2010; Brown, 2004); (c) remortgaging and equity withdrawal – for example, in 2005 remortgaging accounted for 8 per cent of new loans in France and 80 per cent in Switzerland (Scanlon and Lunde, 2007).

Korea is also an interesting case. It is the only country in the list of the 25 advanced countries in Table 4.9 for which no figure for owner-occupation is given. Part of the reason is that in Korea there is what is called *jonsei* housing, which is a tenure halfway between owning and renting privately. *Jonsei* households pay a lump-sum deposit, between 30 and 70 per cent of the value of the property, to the landlord in lieu of rent, with the entire sum returned to them if and when they move out (Ronald, 2006). Halfway tenures are also found elsewhere (e.g., equity-sharing or shared-ownership schemes, or, in the USA, housing equity partnerships). These are usually meant for lower-income households. They basically allow a person to buy a share in a house when they cannot afford to buy all of it. Alternatively, such a scheme may restrict a homeowner's rights to the full value of the home's equity. In the UK, shared-equity schemes come under the HomeBuy banner in England and the LIFT (= Low-cost Initiative for First-Time buyers) banner in Scotland. Both are government-supported. In some variants of the schemes (e.g., HomeBuy Direct), financial institutions participate by extending shared-equity mortgage loans to prospective home-buyers.[30]

Table 4.10 sums up our above discussion of various mortgage loan types for easy reference.

4.7 Mortgage securitization (MS)

One of the most significant developments in real estate finance in advanced countries over the last 40 years has been the rise of mortgage securitization (MS), i.e., turning mortgage loans into securities, and selling them to investors. Such securities are then called mortgage-backed securities (MBSs), and can be either residential MBSs or commercial MBSs. The USA is the largest MBS market in the world, having started in 1970, when the Government National Mortgage Association (GNMA) sold securities backed by a pool of mortgage loans,[31] and

Table 4.10 Types of mortgage loans

A. Forward mortgages
  A.1 Basic types
  - Interest-and-capital repayment
  - Interest-only (e.g., the endowment mortgage)
  - Low-start
  - Stabilized
  - Select-payment
  - Cap-and-collar
  - Capped-rate (if loan has a cap, but no collar)
  - Index-linked (e.g., linked to CPI or to house price index)
  - Shared-equity (in the UK)

  A.2 Remortgaging and cash-out refinancing
  A.3 Equity withdrawal loans
  - An additional (2nd, 3rd) mortgage
  - HELOAN (= Housing Equity LOAN), in the USA
  - HELOC (= Housing Equity Line of Credit), in the USA

B. Reverse (or equity release) mortgages
  B.1 Reverse mortgages in the USA
  - HECM (= Home Equity Conversion Mortgage)

  B.2 Equity release mortgages in the UK
    B.2.1 Lifetime mortgage (homeowner retains ownership)
    - Home Income Plan (a cash lump sum buys homeowner an annuity)
    - Interest-only
    - Roll-up (interest on loan is capitalized)
      - Loan taken as regular income or cash lump sum, or
      - Loan taken on a drawdown basis
    - Fixed-repayment (lender gets pre-fixed sum of value of sold home)

    B.2.2 Home Reversion Plan (homeowner cedes ownership)

registering impressive growth in the 1998–2008 decade. The concept, however, was born at the end of the 18th century in Denmark, where mortgage lending has traditionally been financed through the issuing of bonds listed on the Copenhagen Stock Exchange (ADMB, 1998; Danske Research, 2008).

Mortgage securitization held many advantages for the financial institutions that practised it, but the way it was carried out proved to be one of the main reasons behind the global economic crisis that exploded in 2008 (see Chapter 9). First developed in the context of residential finance, the practice was eventually carried over to the field of commercial real estate (i.e., any real estate that is not single-family homes or residential apartments – but 'multi-family buildings' are considered commercial real estate too).

In what follows we shall study the basics of mortgage securitization (MS). Our main interest, however, is not the intricate mechanics of various types of MS.[32] It is, rather, the impact of the practice on real estate, particularly housing, markets.

4.7.1 How MS works

Turning mortgages into securities (bonds) is a rather complex process that requires a number of steps (see Figure 4.3):

1 A mortgage lender must first decide to repackage some of its mortgages into securities. The mortgages chosen form a pool, usually with common interest rate, maturity, and

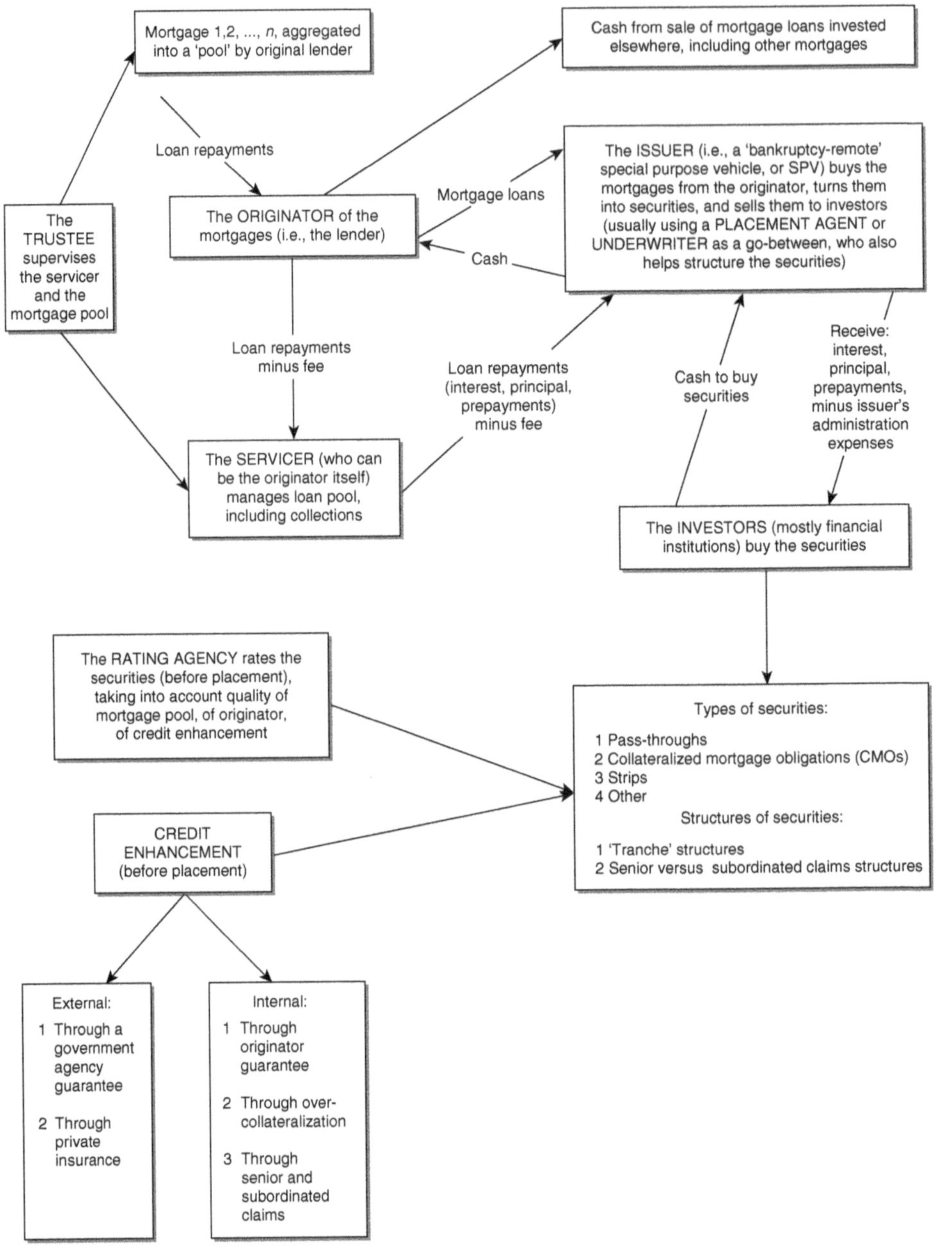

Figure 4.3 Mortgage securitization.

risk characteristics – although diversification of the mortgages in the pool may have benefits of its own, for example in the case of surplus cash flow overcollateralization (see below). The lender then becomes the *originator*.

2. The originator sets up a company (a special purpose vehicle, SPV) which buys the pool of mortgages from the originator with cash supplied by investors who, in turn, buy the mortgage-backed securities issued by the SPV. The issuer is *bankruptcy-remote*, meaning that, should the originator go bankrupt, the mortgage assets controlled by the SPV will be unaffected, and therefore an investor into the related MBSs will not lose their money. (That is one reason why a SPV needs to be set up.) The issuer may actually use a placement agent, or underwriter, to act as a middleman between itself and prospective investors, and will also help with the structuring of the securities so that they be attractive to investors.
3. In the meantime, the originator will continue managing the pool of mortgage loans it had originally created (e.g., collecting payments from mortgagers). Or it may use a servicer for the purpose, who will perform this service for a fee.
4. Those payments (interest, principal, and prepayments) will then be diverted to the issuer (for a fee), who will subsequently channel them (minus administrative expenses) to the owners of the mortgage-backed securities – the investors.
5. A *trustee* may also get involved in the process, whose job will be to supervise the servicer and the mortgage pool (e.g., to execute the mortgage in case of repossession).
6. Prior to being offered to investors, MBSs must receive a good rating by one or other rating agency (e.g., Standard and Poor's, Moody's Investors Service, Fitch Ratings). MBSs traditionally attracted AAA ratings, although, following the onset of the 2008 global crisis, doubts have been raised as to the actual quality of many of those ratings.[33]
7. *Credit enhancement* involves ways of making MBSs look safer and more desirable to investors. There are two broad ways to do that: *external enhancement* and *internal enhancement*:

   (a) External credit enhancement:
      (i) A government agency, like GNMA (Ginnie Mae), which is a US-government-owned enterprise, or FNMA (Fannie Mae) or FHLMC (Freddie Mac), both US-*government-sponsored enterprises* (GSEs), may offer, or be assumed to offer, guarantees on the MBSs they handle. The guarantee is real enough in the case of GNMA (which guarantees the timely repayment of principal and interest on residential MBSs insured by US government agencies). It was widely assumed in the case of the two GSEs mentioned – an assumption that was nevertheless not far from the truth in that in the wake of the 2008 crisis the US government bailed those two GSEs out by placing them in *conservatorship* (i.e., under direct government control). Until then, Fannie Mae and Freddie Mac had been involved in buying *conforming* residential mortgage loans from lenders (i.e., loans that conformed to their guidelines) and selling them in the secondary mortgage market (broadly, the market for MBSs).
      (ii) Private insurance.
   (b) Internal credit enhancement:
      (i) The originator itself may provide investors with *full* or *partial recourse* to itself, i.e., the originator will pay if a mortgager will not.
      (ii) *Overcollateralization*. This can take a number of forms (Books and Najafi, 1989). In the *surplus equity value* form, the value of the property asset that is

higher than the value of the loan provides a cushion against the mortgager's default. In the *surplus cash flow* form (appropriate for commercial MBSs), it is the diversification of the loan portfolio that is supposed to provide a cushion in cases of individual mortgagers defaulting.

(iii) The structure of an issue of MBSs may involve segments, or *tranches*, each with different rights on the cash flows from the mortgages. That is, *senior claims* will have first call on incoming cash flows, and *subordinated claims* will be satisfied only to the extent that the claims of tranches above them have been satisfied. On the other hand, of course, subordinated claims, being riskier, will enjoy higher yields than senior claims.

4.7.2 *Types of MBSs*

There are many types of MBSs. Here we shall look at just a few:

- *Pass-through securities*. These are the most common type of MBS. Mortgagers' payments are made to the lender (or servicer), and end in the MBS-buyers' pockets (minus administrative expenses), passing through the issuer.
- *Collateralized mortgage obligations* (CMOs). These are derivative MBSs (derived, that is, from mortgage pass-through securities or mortgage loans). Each CMO issue is made up of *tranches*, each with particular characteristics (chiefly, different maturities or cash-flow patterns) designed to meet particular investor preferences. As mortgagers' payments come through, the issuer will typically first pay the interest part to all holders of MBSs. Payments of principal as well as prepayments will then go to owners of early-maturing tranches, with later tranches receiving such payments only after prior tranches have been paid off. This is a *sequential pay* or *plain vanilla* CMO.
- *Strips*. These are also derivative MBSs. The cash flow from a pool of mortgage loans is broken down into two derivative securities, each with a different proportion of the interest payment and of the principal payment in the cash flow. At the extreme, each security may be stripped down, so that it contains only interest payments (an interest-only, IO, strip) or only principal payments (a principal-only, PO, strip). The rationale is that different investors may want either the interest stream or the principal stream (or a particular combination of the two). For example, PO strips increase in value as interest rates drop (and prepayments of mortgage loans increase), and vice versa.

  IO strips, on the other hand, increase in value as interest rates rise, and vice versa. At the same time, rising interest rates decrease prepayments (for two reasons: no incentive to refinance and higher prepayment penalty), and declining interest rates increase prepayments. A decrease in prepayments is of course beneficial to IO strips (because this way interest will be collected longer). So, depending on an investor's forecast of interest rates over the long term, different preferences form.

4.7.3 *Reasons for MS*

Outside (i.e., loan) financing of the housing market has historically taken many forms (Boleat, 1988: 6):

1 Direct lending to house buyers.
2 Direct lending to housing finance institutions.

3 Purchasing marketable securities issued by housing finance institutions.
4 Purchasing loans from housing finance lenders.
5 Purchasing MBSs from housing finance lenders.

The so-called secondary mortgage market is made up of (4) and (5) – and, of these, only (5) counts as securitization. In some cases (e.g., Fannie Mae and Freddie Mac in the USA), activities (4) and (5) have been undertaken by the same institution. Still, the MBS market has registered impressive growth in a number of countries (which already had well-developed mortgage markets). In the USA, for instance, the MBS market in 1999 accounted for about 47 per cent of total mortgage debt outstanding, rising to about 53 per cent in 2009 (Table 4.11).

Turning to commercial MBSs (Table 4.12) we notice that the USA is the world leader, with about 74 per cent of total issuance by 2010-end. Annual issues, however, appear quite erratic. For example, from 2000 to 2007, US issues registered a strongly rising trend (CRE, 2011: 6), reaching more than $230 billion in 2007; thereafter, they suddenly dropped to less than $13 billion, thanks to the onset of the global crisis. A similar pattern characterized the UK.

Finally, an inter-country comparison of residential MBSs between 2003 and 2009 (Table 4.13)[34] shows particularly strong growth in the ratio of RMBS issues to gross residential loans. However, this was only partly due to the admittedly significant rise in the amounts of RMBS issues between the two years, as at the same time the amounts of gross residential loans dropped markedly too, in the aftermath of the 2008 crisis. Still, the ratio of RMBS to total outstanding residential loans clearly rose.

Table 4.11 The US mortgage market, 1999 and 2007–09

	1999	*2007*	*2008*	*2009*
Mortgage debt outstanding, $million, end of period →	6,315,131	14,524,581	14,618,475	14,325,968
Of which, held by:				
Major financial institutions*	2,394,271	5,064,584	5,044,409	4,778,095
Federal and related agencies**	319,738	725,455	797,268	816,071
Mortgage pools or trusts***	2,946,546	7,406,954	7,553,058	7,581,568
Individuals and others	654,576	1,327,588	1,223,740	1,150,234
Pools or trusts in total	46.7%	51.0%	51.7%	52.9%
Mortgage debt held by three agencies, whether directly, or in the form of MBS insured or guaranteed:				
GNMA (Ginnie Mae)	582,270	443,483	636,653	880,422
FNMA (Fannie Mae)	1,109,989	2,702,649	2,947,901	3,069,263
FHLMC (Freddie Mac)	805,757	1,797,118	1,909,326	1,977,735
% of three agencies into total mortgage debt outstanding	39.6%	34.0%	37.6%	41.4%

* Commercial banks, savings institutions, life insurance companies.
** Including Ginnie Mae, Fannie Mae, Freddie Mac, and others.
*** Outstanding principal balances of MBSs insured or guaranteed by an agency.
Category includes the three agencies mentioned above, other government agencies, and private mortgage conduits.
Source: Federal Reserve Board, www.federalreserve.gov/econresdata/releases/mortoutstand/

Table 4.12 Commercial MBSs: Issuance by selected countries, $million

	2000	*2007*	*2008*	*2009*	*2010*	*Total issuance, including years not shown*	*% of country total issuance in global total*
USA	46,894.4	230,193.0	12,145.9	3,073.6	12,311.9	1,242,442.9	73.7%
UK	4,701.3	19,187.8	1,177.8	3,630.9	1,434.5	150,505.6	8.9%
Japan	4,009.0	14,806.8	3,348.6	1,259.6	229.4	59,687.4	3.5%
Germany	0.0	14,662.5	2,145.3	7,346.2	0.0	53,726.5	3.2%
Italy	385.5	0.0	0.0	0.0	2,013.0	24,964.7	1.5%
Canada	886.4	3,235.2	0.0	670.0	0.0	20,089.4	1.2%
France	0.0	2,081.6	0.0	0.0	0.0	13,177.1	0.8%
Netherlands	0.0	5,358.7	238.6	0.0	470.2	12,923.5	0.8%
Australia	283.0	1,173.6	0.0	222.9	567.9	12,763.2	0.8%
Non-US	12,116.4	85,306.6	17,177.8	23,843.0	6,714.2	442,640.4	26.3%
Europe	6,785.5	64,063.3	9,567.7	21,491.3	5,572.5	325,335.0	19.3%
Total	59,010.8	315,499.6	29,323.7	26,916.6	19,026.1	1,685,083.3	100.0%

Source: CRE (Commercial Real Estate) Finance Council, Compendium of Statistics, 14 January 2011. www.crefc.org/uploadedFiles/CMSA_Site_Home/Industry_Resources/Research/Industry_Statistics/CMSA_Compendium.pdf

Given those rising trends or high volumes of MBS business, it is obvious that securitization must have meant significant benefits to mortgage lenders and other financial institutions – at least while the securitization party was in full swing (i.e., prior to 2008). These are as follows:

1 Financial institutions are usually subjected to 'capital adequacy' requirements. This means that they have to have prescribed amounts of own capital, or net worth, in relation to the amount (and kind) of assets (like loans) they create. To the extent, therefore, that a financial institution can originate more loans than its capacity to hold them (i.e., its availability of required capital), securitization makes sense. Basically, it allows a financial institution to remove such assets from its balance sheet, and substitute cash for them. (This is called *true-sale* securitization (TEGoVA, 2002).) Even if the assets remain on the balance sheet (*synthetic* securitization), they can be treated as off-balance-sheet items (i.e., they can still free capital for the institution), depending on prevailing accountancy or central bank rules (Peston, 1991).
2 The cash 'windfall' (from the sale of the mortgage loans) can then be used to generate more (loan) business. The sale price of the mortgages is also often slightly higher than the principal tied in them (because of the interest factor).
3 In the process, the institution passes to someone else (the investors buying the MBSs) at least part of the risk the mortgage loans represent (which prior to 2008 was not considered much, anyway, at least as far as default, or credit, risk was concerned).
4 The institution can also earn a fee from the SPV (the issuer) for servicing the securitized mortgage pool.
5 True, the lending institution (the originator) loses the interest income from the pool of mortgages it sells. But through securitization it reduces its risk, frees capital, and acquires cash to expand its business.

Table 4.13 Residential MBSs in sample of countries, 2003 and 2009, € million

	2003					2009				
	Total outstanding residential loans	*Gross residential loans**	*Total RMBS issues*	*c/a*	*c/b*	*Total outstanding residential loans*	*Gross residential loans**	*Total RMBS issues*	*c/a*	*c/b*
	a	*b*	*c*			*a*	*b*	*c*		
Ireland	59,362	13,524	1,820	3.1%	13.5%	147,654	8,076	13,757	9.3%	170.3%
Italy	173,357	59,850	8,871	5.1%	14.8%	330,585	75,292	53,166	16.1%	70.6%
Netherlands	400,153	95,996	17,900	4.5%	18.6%	602,192	61,824	40,894	6.8%	66.1%
Spain	312,916	91,387	15,867	5.1%	17.4%	678,872	68,918	26,621	3.9%	38.6%
UK	1,110,477	401,945	55,460	5.0%	13.8%	1,372,659	161,087	70,534	5.1%	43.8%
US	6,336,643	3,491,150	2,213,156	34.9%	63.4%	7,994,457	1,305,755	3,731,529	46.7%	285.8%

* Total amount of residential loans advanced during period (without subtracting repayments).

Source: Hypostat (2009), pp. 82, 83, 92.

4.7.4 Effect on real estate market

The advantages of securitization mentioned above are from the 'narrow' point of view of an originator. But what is the impact of securitization on the wider real estate, particularly housing, market?

One impact is on the amount of funding available for house, and other real estate, purchase. By allowing originators to acquire more cash easily, and to shed some of the credit risk inherent in the mortgage assets, originators are in a position to expand their loan business, and, *ceteris paribus*, the larger amounts of available funds exercise downward pressure on interest rates. This increases affordability on the part of real estate consumers and investors, causing the real estate, and particularly the housing, market to expand further.

The downside is that, if the real estate market is on the road to forming a price bubble, the whole process of securitization accelerates movement to that direction, while making the eventual bubble larger than otherwise. In effect securitization tends to increase real estate prices more than what they would have been in its absence. At the same time, and precisely because securitization facilitates a widening spread of the ownership of the MBSs (across institutions and across countries), the ripple effects of a real estate bubble bursting are likely to cause systemic, rather than individual institution, problems (Brunnermeier, 2009).

Recent evidence corroborates this analysis. A NERA (2009) study of the effects of securitization in the USA in various periods from 1985 to 2006 concluded that

1 As regards the effect of securitization on the cost of credit, a negative relationship was identified between the rate of mortgage securitization and mortgage yield spreads (i.e., the difference between mortgage rates and comparable government securities). Thus, more securitization was related with lower mortgage interest rates.
2 As regards the effect of securitization on the availability of credit, the study found a 'positive and significant' impact of secondary market purchases on mortgage credit per capita – so more securitization was related with more mortgage credit.
3 As regards the effect of securitization on the quality of mortgage loans, it was unclear whether securitized loans performed consistently worse than all loans.

On their part, Hoffmann and Nitschka (2010) studied pairwise correlations of quarterly housing and equity (i.e., share) returns for 16 industrialized countries from 1985Q1 to 2008Q1. They found that in all cases house prices had much lower inter-country correlations than stock markets. They interpreted this as evidence that fluctuations in the value of residential real estate (or of RMBSs) were significantly affected by country-specific characteristics, and therefore represented a (non-insurable) country-specific risk. Securitization helped diversify such risks by making mortgage-related debt internationally tradable. In turn, this allowed banks in countries with well-developed MBS markets to keep on lending even in recessions (when credit is normally tight), thus enabling households largely to maintain their consumption level. Hence, such countries registered smaller fluctuations in consumption in response to 'typical' business-cycle shocks than countries without such markets. But in exceptional circumstances, like the 2008 crisis when credit dried up, MS and the international risk sharing it made possible failed to have this positive effect, and may have even had a negative effect (p. 3).

Summary of main points

1 Mathematical formulae:

Future value of a compounded sum: $\mathrm{FV} = K\left(1+\frac{i}{m}\right)^{mt}$.

Present value of a compounded sum: $\mathrm{PV} = K = \frac{\mathrm{FV}}{\left(1+\frac{i}{m}\right)^{mt}}$.

Future value of a deferred annuity: $\mathrm{FV}_{\mathrm{da}} = \frac{a}{i}\left[(1+i)^t - 1\right]$.

Present value of a deferred annuity: $\mathrm{PV}_{\mathrm{da}} = \frac{a}{i}\left[1 - \frac{1}{(1+i)^t}\right]$.

Future value of an annuity due: $\mathrm{FV}_{\mathrm{ad}} = \frac{a(1+i)}{i}\left[(1+i)^t - 1\right]$.

Present value of an annuity due: $\mathrm{PV}_{\mathrm{ad}} = \frac{a}{i}\left[(1+i) - \frac{1}{(1+i)^{t-1}}\right]$.

Amount a of an interest-and-capital loan repayment instalment: $a = \frac{Ki}{1-\frac{1}{(1+i)^t}}$.

Amount of interest T contained in a given instalment:

$$T = a - \frac{a}{(1+i)^N} = a\left[1 - \frac{1}{(1+i)^N}\right],$$

where N = number of instalment period (the higher N is, the earlier the period).

In the case of a reverse (or equity release) mortgage, the interest rate i at which the value of the loan at maturity (time of mortgager's death) equals the house price:

$$i = \left(\frac{1}{k}\right)^{1/t}(1+g) - 1 = \sqrt[t]{\frac{1}{k}}(1+g) - 1,$$

where

k = proportion of market value of property that determines the initial value of the loan,
g = annual house price growth,
t = expected time horizon (i.e., expected number of years till mortgager's death).

2 In a *forward mortgage*, the borrower's debt decreases during repayment, and their home equity increases. In a *reverse* (or *equity release*) *mortgage*, the borrower's debt increases till maturity (time of borrower's death), and their home equity decreases.

3 *Remortgaging* occurs when a mortgager who is in the process of repaying a prior mortgage on his or her property chooses to substitute a new, presumably cheaper, mortgage loan for the existing, dearer, one. *Equity withdrawal* occurs when a person already owns fully (or mostly) a property (usually their home), and wants to obtain refinancing, i.e., some cash, on the strength of the property's value. To this purpose, the person mortgages the property anew, or gets a second or third mortgage on it.

4 *Prepayment* most commonly occurs when mortgagers wish to remortgage in order to take advantage of a lower mortgage rate than the one at which their existing mortgages are

currently priced. Adjustable rate mortgages (ARM) reduce both a lender's *reinvestment risk*, which prepayment creates, and *interest rate risk*, which involves a mismatch between the lender's assets and liabilities.

5 Reverse (or equity release) mortgages are one way for retirees in developed countries with strained social security systems to try and ensure that they will not outlive their wealth. They are likely to grow in importance in the future, but their success depends on house prices showing an upward trend.

6 Housing finance is not the only way to achieve (urban) homeownership. Three other ways have been (a) squatting on public land, (b) utilizing own assets (e.g., rural land or country properties), and (c) privatizing public housing. But housing finance is bound to increase in importance everywhere as societies develop, incomes grow, financial systems become more sophisticated, and legal titles over land and property become better defined and protected.

7 Mortgage securitization offers advantages to mortgage institutions, particularly as regards conformity to capital adequacy requirements. It also increases the amount of funding available for the purchase of houses and other RE. But it can exacerbate a property price bubble, and can spread systemic risk throughout the financial system.

Review questions and exercises

1 Define the following terms:

interest-only/low-start/index-linked loan
mortgager–mortgagee
adjustable-rate mortgage (ARM)
lifetime mortgage–home reversion plan
a lifetime, roll-up, draw-down mortgage
HECM–HELOAN–HELOC
mortgage securitization–MBSs
credit enhancement (in relation to MBSs)
pass-through securities–CMOs–strips
overcollateralization
tranches–senior claims–subordinated claims
GNMA–FNMA–FHLMC
FSA

2 Find the amounts of principal and interest included in the 17th instalment of a 6%, 25-year, €120,000 interest-and-capital repayment loan that is repaid annually.

3 Notice in Table 4.2 that the periodic interest on the loan plus the annuity payment, i.e., $24,017.49, is less than the repayment instalment, $24,658.19, of the interest-and-capital repayment loan of Table 4.1, although the principal, interest rate, and maturity are the same between the two loans. Can you tell why?

4 Assuming a €220,000 loan, to be repaid annually over 25 years at 7 per cent, calculate the annual interest-and-capital repayment instalment during the first 5 years if the applicable interest rate during that period is 3 per cent; then calculate the annual interest-and-capital repayment instalment during the rest of the life of the loan. Check your answers by making sure that the principal amortized during the low-rate period and the principal amortized

during the standard-rate period together amount to the total value of the principal. Use a spreadsheet program for your calculations.

5 Distinguish between 'interest rate risk', 'reinvestment risk', and 'prepayment risk'. Give two reasons why prepayment is a problem for banks, and explain how banks normally try to counter this threat.
6 Distinguish between 'remortgaging', 'equity withdrawal', 'cash-out refinancing', and a 'reverse' (or 'equity release') mortgage.
7 Describe three scenarios under which a homeowner with a mortgage might consider remortgaging.
8 What's the impact of 'equity withdrawal' and 'reverse mortgage' loans on the business cycle?
9 'It is better to remortgage earlier than later in the life of a mortgage loan.' Discuss.
10 Assess the prospects for a growing market in reverse mortgages in your country's future.
11 Explain Germany's and Switzerland's relatively low rates of owner-occupation c. 2005. In view of this, how do you account for Switzerland's very high ratio of residential mortgage debt to GDP?
12 List ways, other than using credit, in which owner-occupation can be/has been enhanced.
13 List and explain five advantages of mortgage securitization to mortgage lenders.
14 Is mortgage securitization invariably good for the housing market? Discuss.
15 Utilizing the data source for Table 4.12, try to find out what the relationship was (if any) between a country's total issuance of commercial MBSs outstanding in 2007 and the size of the subsequent drop in new issues due to the global crisis, both for 2008 and for 2008–10. You can extend your analysis to countries not shown in Table 4.12. How do you explain your results?

5 RE as an investment decision

Main sections

Having gone through this chapter, a student should be able to

1. Define commercial property (CP) and recognize and define a number of CP-related terms: core, non-core, invested versus investible, private versus public equity RE, staggered leases, listed versus unlisted RE, NAV, REIT, etc.
2. List and explain the dominant RE investment styles.
3. Compare the investment characteristics of RE with those of stocks and bonds.
4. Justify a portfolio approach to investment.
5. Discuss how RE returns correlate with returns on other assets, and whether it makes sense to include RE in a portfolio.
6. Assess the efficacy of constructing an 'efficient frontier' of portfolios that contain RE.
7. Given historic returns for various asset classes, construct an 'efficient frontier' between RE and a portfolio of other assets by varying the proportion of investor funds between RE and that portfolio.
8. Define NPV, IRR, equated and equivalent yield, and explain and compare them.
9. Discuss problems involved in, and ways of calculating, a required rate of return (RRR), or capitalization rate, for RE.
10. Distinguish between the physical life and economic life of RE assets.

5.1 Definition of commercial RE

Commercial RE refers to all properties (including land plots) meant either to generate an actual (rather than imputed) rental income (the standard case) or to be sold for profit or capital gain, now or, potentially, in the future. Residential properties fall loosely (and elusively) into this category when they are built by developers for sale to the general public – but fall out of this category when they are actually bought by occupiers (even if many of those subsequently sell the residence and realize a capital gain). The reason is that in the vast majority of cases residential properties are bought mostly for consumption rather than investment purposes (although both motives are certainly present). *Reita*, an initiative run by the British Property Federation (www.bpf.org.uk/en/reita/index.php), defines commercial property as 'property that's intended to produce a financial return for its owner by being used or occupied by businesses', but this definition ignores, for example, what is referred to as 'multi-family' commercial property in the USA.

Commercial RE typically comprises offices, retail outlets (e.g., stores, shopping centres, and malls), industrial premises, warehouses, hotels, apartment (also called 'multi-family') buildings, garages, petrol stations, other specialized buildings (e.g., hospitals and cinemas), farmland, etc. (A usual categorization is 'retail–offices–warehousing–factories–other commercial'.) Yet apartment buildings do not count as commercial property if the apartments are owner-occupied, but may do so if the building is owned by an investor who rents out the apartments; or may be treated as commercial property for tax purposes (in the USA) even if the apartments are owner-occupied. Certainly the scope of the definition of 'commercial property' includes many grey areas, but, in short, it is RE speculatively built and speculatively managed.[1]

Further, commercial property is split into 'core' and 'non-core', 'rented' and 'owner-occupied', and 'total', 'invested', and 'investible'. For example,

- *Total stock* refers to the overall stock of commercial RE.
- *Investible stock* means investment-grade properties. This stock may currently be owned by institutions (e.g., insurance companies and pension funds) or be owner-occupied but, in time, it should all become 'institutional'. Investible stock is smaller than total stock as much commercial RE is of too poor a quality to become institutional, or will always remain owner-occupied.
- *Invested stock* (i.e., the current stock) refers to those properties that are currently owned by professional RE investors for investment purposes.

On the basis of these definitions,[2] Table 5.1 presents the global commercial RE market, broken down by region.

Another distinction associates 'core' and 'non-core' with particular investment styles. Thus, we have 'core' and 'core+' styles (focused on 'core' properties, involving a low-return–low-risk approach), while 'non-core' is associated with 'value-added' and 'opportunistic' styles (progressively higher-return–higher-risk approaches, centred on properties that do have these attributes). Finally, investment in commercial property can be either direct (as when a person or company owns a property directly) or indirect (as when a person or company buys shares of or into property companies, which come in quite a few shapes and forms). By way of illustration, Table 5.2 presents a categorization of commercial property assets and investment styles, and Figure 5.1 presents a panorama of UK commercial property in 2009.

Table 5.1 The global commercial RE market, 2006 and 2009 (US $trillion)

	Stock at end-2006			*Stock at end-2009*		
	Invested	*Investible*	*Total*	*Invested*	*Investible*	*Total*
Americas	4.7	6.6	9.5	4.3	6.4	9.2
Asia–Pacific	1.9	3.5	5.9	1.4	3.3	6.1
Europe	3.2	6.1	9.2	3.3	6.6	9.3
Total	9.8	16.2	24.6	9	16.3	24.7

Sources: RREEF (2007: 2); RREEF (2010a: 33). (Some rounding has taken place.)

Note: 'Total' does not necessarily equal the sum of 'invested' and 'investible'.

Table 5.2 Categorization of commercial property assets and investment styles

Core	*Non-core*
Core	Value-Added
Low-risk, low-return	Moderate- to high-risk and return
Zero or low leverage	Leverage between core+ and opportunistic
Main (rather than 'niche') property types	Mix of main and 'niche' property types
Typically A-class properties*	Need to enhance to upgrade to A-class properties
Well-maintained properties	Lower quality buildings
Primary locations and markets	Primary and secondary markets
Substantial income, modest value appreciation	Less income, more value appreciation
Strong tenant quality	Weaker tenants
Staggered/long leases	Weaker lease structure
Market rents	Sub-market rents frequent
Low vacancy	Higher vacancy
Core+	Opportunistic
Moderate risk, moderate return	High-risk, high-return
Low to moderate leverage	High leverage
	Focus on volatile or emerging markets
Substantial income, modest value appreciation	Return mostly from value growth
Some extra capital expenditure for property upgrading may be required	Substantial capital expenditure required to redevelop or reposition** properties

Selected sources: RREEF (2010a); GMAC (2005); Briddell (2010).
* See Chapter 6 for a definition of property classes.
** Repositioning: bringing a distressed (i.e., problematic) asset to market as a viable investment. See Altoon (2010).

5.2 The language of the marketplace

5.2.1 Some definitions

According to RREEF (2010b),

> Core real estate investments include high-quality, multi-tenant properties located in major metropolitan areas. The credit quality of such tenants is high and the lease expirations are staggered over the hold period. These are unleveraged or low-leveraged investments in income-producing office, apartment, industrial or retail properties. Investments may be individual buildings in portfolios or portfolios of properties

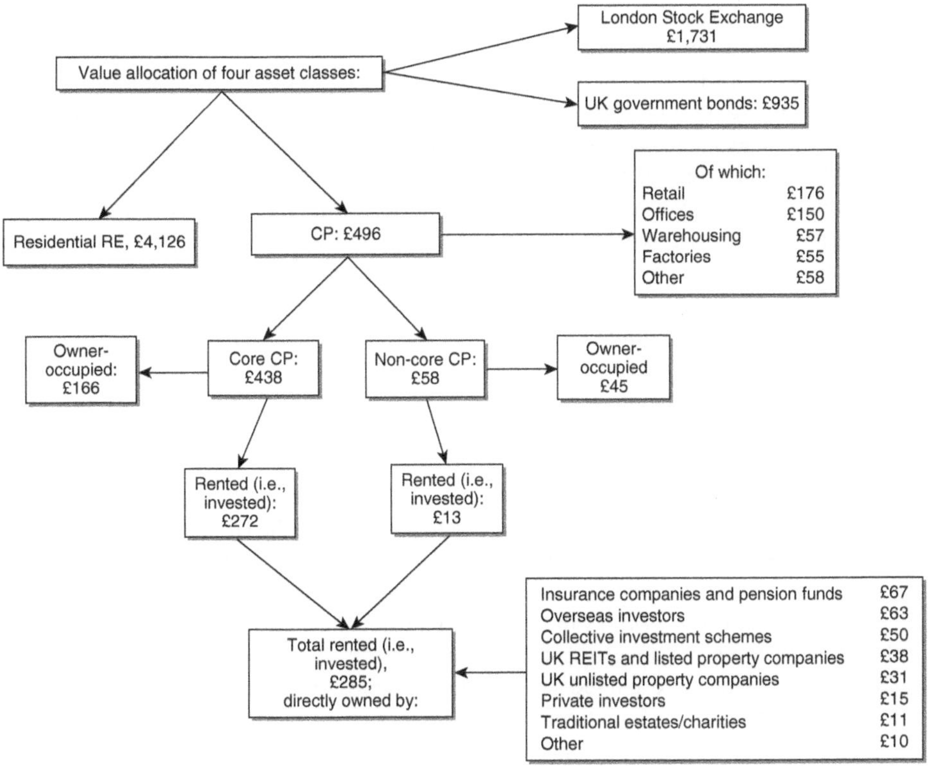

Figure 5.1 UK Commercial Property (CP), end 2009 (figures in £billion). (Adapted from PIA, 2010.)

diversified by building type, investment size and geographic location. Finally, unlike non-core investments, private equity core real estate has a well-established benchmark, which in the US is the NCREIF Property Index (NPI).

There are some terms in this definition that need explaining.

- *Staggered leases* are tenants' leases in (parts of) a building that expire on different dates. This reduces the volatility associated with future cash flows from the building, so it becomes a more attractive investment.

  Explanation: Say you own an office building with 20 business tenants in it. If the leases of all expire at the same time and they leave, your income from the property will drop to zero. If, however, their leases are staggered, some tenants stand to leave at time X, others later, and others still later. This means that the property will always earn *some* income, while you also have the time to find new tenants for the one or two that vacate when their leases expire. As a result your property has a higher value than otherwise, and can be sold more easily.
- An *unleveraged* (or *low-leveraged*) property is free (or largely free) from an obligation to repay debt secured on the property. Debt-financing of an investment (also called 'leveraging' the investment) increases the return on the investor's equity (i.e., own capital

invested) if things go as expected, but decreases it if they do not. Debt financing is thus a strategy whose risk increases along with the extent of leverage. An unleveraged (or low-leveraged) property is a more secure (yet lower-return) investment than otherwise, so its 'core' character is strengthened.

- *Private equity real estate* (PrERE) means commercial RE that has been acquired either directly for investment purposes (rather than for owner-occupation) or indirectly through privately traded vehicles that in turn invest in RE. It can be contrasted to public equity RE, which is property assets acquired by REITs and other publicly traded RE vehicles. More narrowly, PrERE is capital raised in the context of a dedicated programme of direct investment into property, usually through a 'limited partnership'.

The following are other important terms:

- *Listed (unlisted) real estate* refers to property companies whose shares are (are not) traded on a stock exchange. For example, listed real estate investment trusts (REITs) are publicly traded; limited partnerships are not.
- *Collective investment vehicles* are many and varied. Perhaps the most familiar forms are the 'mutual fund' and the 'unit trust', but there are more. In the UK, the label 'collective investment scheme' is applied to 'authorized' and 'unauthorized' unit trusts, 'open-ended investment companies', 'investment trust companies', 'limited partnerships', and 'venture capital trusts'. REITs in the UK are also a 'collective investment scheme' as they are constituted as 'investment trust companies'.
- *Open-ended* funds issue and redeem (buy back) shares (or *units*, in the UK) in response to investor demand. Redemption takes place according to predetermined procedures (e.g., *authorized* funds are normally open for dealing every day; *unauthorized* funds may do dealing every month or quarter); sometimes, in the case of property funds, redemption that may require the sale of a property in adverse market conditions may be deferred for a more opportune time. *Closed-ended* funds issue a certain number of shares at inception, and usually have a fixed life span. Investors do not have the right to redeem shares with the fund, but it may be possible to sell shares on a secondary market (in the case of an unlisted fund), and certainly it is possible to trade shares on a stock exchange (in the case of a listed fund). An example is a UK REIT, which is both listed and closed-ended.
- *Authorized* (*unauthorized*) funds are those that have (have not) obtained authorization from a supervisory body to market to the general public. In the UK, that body is the FSA (Financial Services Authority). In the USA it is the SEC (Securities and Exchange Commission). An example of an authorized fund in the UK is a UCIT (undertaking for collective investment in transferable securities), a form of unit trust. An example of an unauthorized fund in the UK is an 'exempt' unauthorized property unit trust (i.e., exempt from capital gains tax, which happens when all investors in the fund are tax-exempt).

The usual way to evaluate a fund is by calculating the NAV (net asset value) per share. The NAV is an estimate of the market value of the fund's holdings (of, say, real estate) minus debt (e.g., mortgage debt outstanding). This then is divided by the number of the fund shares (or units) outstanding to give the NAV/share. However, the market price of those shares (which, in a listed closed-ended fund, are publicly traded) may differ from the NAV/share, being at a premium or at a discount in comparison to it.

5.2.2 Investment vehicles

In most advanced countries, there is a plethora of vehicles or schemes providing opportunities for third parties to invest (indirectly) in RE. Important questions to ask in relation to such vehicles or schemes are whether they are

- Listed or unlisted.
- Open-ended or closed-ended.
- Tax-transparent, semi-tax-transparent, or non-tax-transparent (i.e., whether they pay corporation or income tax, or capital gains tax, or not; if not, the tax may simply be passed on to the investors – if they are not tax-exempt themselves – who will thus avoid being taxed twice).
- Authorized versus unauthorized (by a supervisory body like the FSA in the UK). It is important to note that lack of authorization does not necessarily imply absence of regulation: for example, the manager of an unauthorized property unit trust in the UK will be regulated by the FSA just like the manager of an authorized trust, but the (unauthorized) trust itself may be free from regulation to a certain extent.

Of increasing importance among the universe of RE-investing conduits are real estate investment trusts (REITs). They were launched in the USA in 1960 'as a way to make investment in large-scale, income-producing real estate accessible to all investors in the same way they typically invest otherwise – through the purchase and sale of liquid securities. Prior to the creation of listed real estate equities, access to the investment returns of commercial real estate equity as a core asset was available only to institutions and wealthy individuals having the financial wherewithal to undertake direct real estate investment.'[3]

In order for a company to qualify as a REIT in the USA, it must invest at least 75 per cent of its total assets in real estate; derive at least 75 per cent of gross income as rents from real property or interest from mortgages on real property; and distribute annually at least 90 per cent of their (net) income to shareholders in the form of dividends.

In addition to the liquidity they offer investors (i.e., the ability to turn their shares into cash easily and at any time), REITs also offer a crucial tax advantage: the cash flow they distribute to their shareholders is not taxed at the level of the REIT, thus allowing investors to avoid being taxed twice – first at the level of the REIT, then personally.

US REITs have been very successful, having by end-2007 reached about '10 per cent of the financial sector and nearly one-quarter of the domestic equity sector' (Cussen, 2008). Because of their advantages, REITs began to appear in the rest of the world, including, among others, Australia, the UK (in 2007), France (in 2003, known as SIICs), the Netherlands (in 1969, known as FBI), Japan (in 2001), and Turkey (in 1996). In Australia, REITs were introduced in 1971. They were of two forms: listed and unlisted property trusts. Since 2008, the former have been renamed A-REITs.

Figure 5.2 shows some of the most important commercial RE vehicles,[4] focusing mainly on the UK and distinguishing between private and public equity RE.

5.3 Characteristics of investment in RE

Although publicly traded shares of property companies behave much the same as other stocks, such companies still have to invest in RE directly one way or another, to some extent at least.

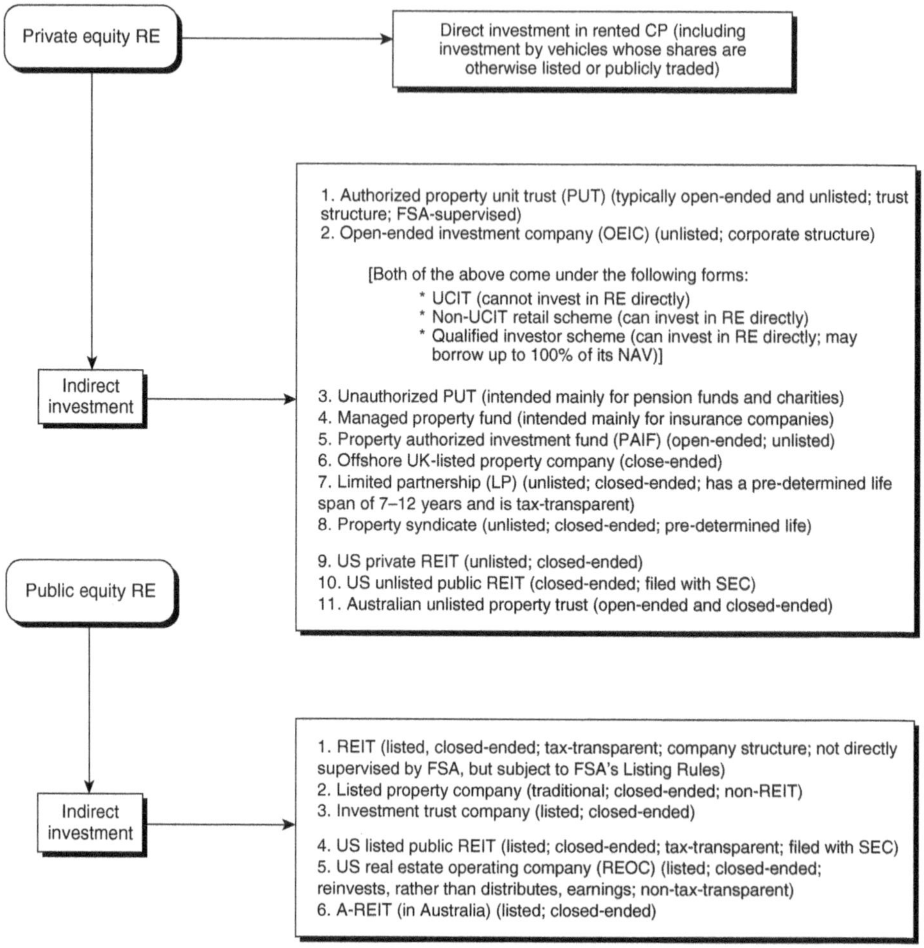

Figure 5.2 Main methods and vehicles for investing in commercial property (CP) in the UK, the USA, and Australia (UK implied, unless otherwise stated).

They thus have to take the particular investment characteristics of RE into account, no less than all other direct investors in RE. Table 5.3 presents a comparison of those characteristics across RE, stocks, and bonds.

A cursory look at Table 5.3 shows that RE has many characteristics that set it apart from other main asset classes, so it is reasonable to expect that returns on RE move up when returns on other assets move down, and vice versa. Because of this, direct RE may be a welcome addition in many an asset portfolio. Even if someone wants to avoid the hassle of direct investment in RE, the existence of vehicles offering the opportunity to invest in RE indirectly could perhaps go some way towards allowing one to combine the advantages of RE assets and stock or bond assets. It is thus likely that 'low correlations with stocks and bonds make real estate a diversification opportunity for traditional portfolio managers' (Ibbotson and Siegel, 1984). To this, we now turn.

Table 5.3 Comparison of RE, stocks, and bonds as investments

	Real estate	*Stocks and bonds*
1	Immobility	Portability
2	Heterogeneity; not two pieces of RE are identical	Homogeneity; units of any given stock or bond are identical. Less trivially, there is usually more similarity between stocks (or bonds) than between RE pieces
3	Requires continuous management (from maintenance and insurance to leasing, collecting rents, resolving disputes)	Do not require management, other than reshuffling them in a portfolio of assets
4	Even small investors can improve properties they've bought	Small investors cannot affect the quality of these assets
5	Durability	Durability of stocks and long-term bonds (especially perpetuities) comparable to that of RE; not so with short-term bonds
6	Price discovery for any piece of RE, a costly and uncertain process	Price discovery very easy for listed stocks and for bonds; more difficult for unlisted stocks
7	Difficult to acquire accurate and full info on most any piece of RE; on the other hand, certain kinds of crucial info (like location) are readily available and interpretable	Same information applies on units of any particular stock or bond; basic information on a stock or bond easily obtained; still, crucial information that could allow estimation of, say, default risk is hard to find or validate
8	Given price, low to very low liquidity (usually)	Given price, high liquidity (usually), especially for short-term government bonds
9	High transaction costs	Low transaction costs
10	High capital requirements due to indivisibility of direct RE investments	Low capital requirements in most cases
11	Subject to building, zoning, and planning laws and regulations	Free of burdensome special legislation
12	Subject to special taxation, often quite burdensome	Much less burdensome or complicated taxation
13	It is still physically 'there' even in situations of systemic economic adversity or if owner defaults; therefore likely to recover its value (it has, that is, strong hedging potential)	Almost certain to become worthless if issuer defaults; situations of systemic economic adversity can debilitate particular stocks or bonds permanently

5.4 A portfolio approach to RE investment

5.4.1 Portfolio basics

The justification for a portfolio approach to investment in general is risk reduction – which happens if there is no perfect positive correlation[5] between the expected returns of the assets in the portfolio, i.e., if $r < +1$. The greatest reduction of risk is achieved when there is perfect negative correlation, i.e., if $r = -1$ (in fact, in such a case, a combination of the proportions of the assets in the portfolio can be found that results in zero risk for the portfolio). Significant risk reduction takes place also if correlation between expected returns is zero. If the correlation between asset returns is positive but less than one, i.e., if $0 < r < +1$, a portfolio combining a higher-risk and a lower-risk asset will have less risk than the high-risk asset alone does.

However, true elimination of all risk is practically impossible. One reason is that total asset (or portfolio) risk is the sum of *diversifiable risk* (which can be taken care of through forming and managing a portfolio of appropriately correlated assets) and *systematic risk*. The latter is the risk that results from developments that adversely affect all assets in a relevant asset market. By definition, this kind of risk cannot be fully diversified away, except to the extent that a portfolio is broadened to include assets from a greater variety of markets and/or asset classes. It is not a bad strategy, but it does require (a) investors with more and better information (and probably more money) than usually and (b) that different asset classes and/or asset markets have negative, or low positive, correlation between them. However, as the 2008–09 global crisis showed, the latter requirement may be getting harder to satisfy in an increasingly globalized economy (with gold and fully owned RE being perhaps the assets of last resort if a crisis becomes uncontrollable).

Another reason why true elimination of all risk is practically impossible is that expected returns – and hence the expected volatility, or risk, of those returns – are ultimately based on historic returns. Unfortunately, historic returns are not at all a safe pointer to future returns, although historic volatility may be more enduring and therefore predictable. Still, a well-formed portfolio *will* reduce risk in relation to a given target return – and that is good enough for most investors.

The usual measure of portfolio risk is the standard deviation of the portfolio expected returns around their mean. The expected return on, and the risk of, a two-security portfolio are:

$$E(R_p) = w_1 R_1 + w_2 R_2, \tag{5.1}$$

$$\sigma_p = \left(w_1^2\sigma_1^2 + w_2^2\sigma_2^2 + 2w_1 w_2 r_{1,2}\sigma_1\sigma_2\right)^{1/2}, \tag{5.2}$$

where

$E(R_p)$	=	expected return on portfolio
σ_p	=	standard deviation of portfolio returns (a measure of the portfolio risk),
w_1	=	proportion of asset 1 in the portfolio,
w_2	=	proportion of asset 2 in the portfolio,
R_1	=	expected return on asset 1,
R_2	=	expected return on asset 2,
σ_1	=	standard deviation of returns on asset 1,
σ_2	=	standard deviation of returns on asset 2,
$r_{1,2}$	=	correlation coefficient of returns between assets 1 and 2.

Notice that σ_p is not a weighted average of σ_1 and σ_2, because account must be taken of the fact that the riskiness of the separate assets changes when held in a portfolio. The impact of this is captured by the *covariance* term in the σ_p formula, i.e., by $r_{1,2}\sigma_1\sigma_2$.

More generally, for an n-asset portfolio, the return and risk are:

$$E(R_p) = \sum_{i=1}^{n} w_i R_i, \tag{5.3}$$

$$\sigma_p = \left(\sum_{i=1}^{n} w_i^2 \sigma_i^2 + \sum_{i=1}^{n} \sum_{j=1}^{n} w_i w_j \sigma_i \sigma_j r_{i,j} \right)^{1/2} \quad (with i \neq j). \tag{5.4}$$

A risk–return space is composed of various portfolios, each with its own risk–return characteristics. Two portfolios are particularly important: the global minimum-risk portfolio and the global maximum-return portfolio. Between them, they define the *efficient frontier*, which is made up of portfolios that dominate all others by offering either the highest expected return for a given level of risk or the lowest risk for a given expected return. The efficient frontier can only be concave or a straight line. The reason why the efficient frontier cannot be convex is that in such a case the combined assets would have more risk *than the highest-risk asset alone*. At most, an efficient frontier will be a straight line (if the risk–return trade-offs of the portfolios comprising the frontier are proportionate), and that would happen only if the assets in the portfolios showed perfect positive correlation between them (see Figure 5.3).

The effective *opportunity set*, on the other hand, is composed of all portfolios that are characterized by both an expected return that is higher than, or equal to, the expected return associated with the global minimum-risk portfolio and a level of risk that is lower than, or equal to, the risk associated with the global maximum-return portfolio.

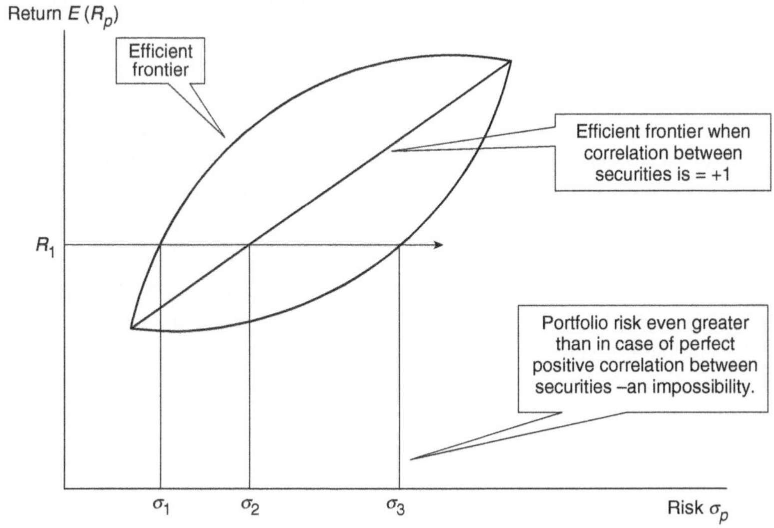

Figure 5.3 Risk–return space for portfolio selection: the efficient frontier can only be concave or straight. $E(R_p)$ = expected return on portfolio, σ_p = standard deviation of portfolio.

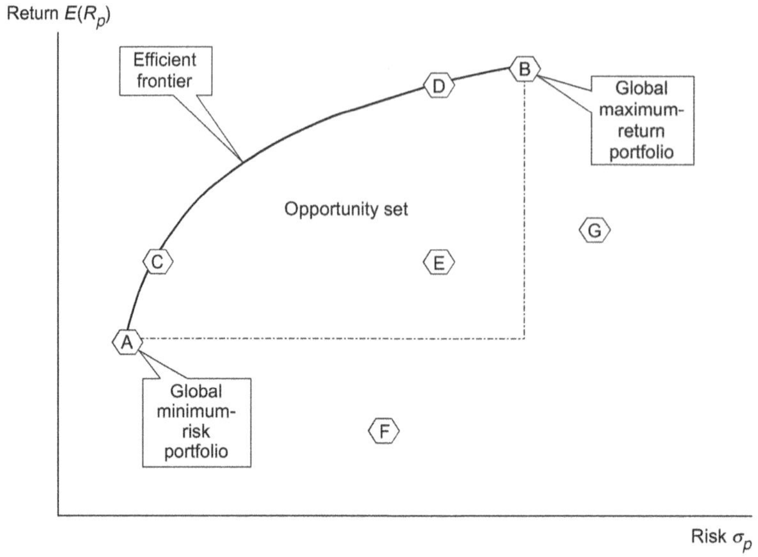

Figure 5.4 Risk–return space for portfolio selection: efficient frontier portfolios dominate all others. $E(R_p)$ = expected return on portfolio, σ_p = standard deviation of portfolio.

Thus, in Figure 5.4, the global minimum-risk portfolio is A, the global maximum-return portfolio is B. Portfolio D dominates E because it offers a higher return for the same risk, and C also dominates E because it offers the same return for less risk. Portfolio G is outside the effective opportunity set because it offers more risk than B, and so is F as it offers a lower return than A.

A risk-averse investor who considers risk–return combinations is characterized by the kind of indifference curves shown in Figure 5.5. These plot differently from those depicted in Chapter 2 because risk is not a 'good' but a 'bad'. Otherwise, the idea behind them is the same – that of a trade-off: for the investor to take up more risk, he or she must be compensated by a higher return, if the level of utility is to be kept constant. Since higher indifference curves represent more utility, the investor will eventually choose that portfolio on the efficient frontier which is at the point of tangency between the frontier and the highest possible indifference curve (i.e., IC_1) from the investor's indifference curve map.

In Figure 5.6, we get more realistic. We are considering office properties in five European cities. (This is just an example – we could have considered different property types in a given country instead.) The data, taken from SWIP (2010), are presented in stylized form. For the purposes of Figure 5.6, we have proclaimed Helsinki to be the minimum-risk portfolio, and London to be the maximum-return portfolio. Dublin and Athens are outside the effective opportunity set, Athens being the worst of the two at the time (April 2010).

Figure 5.6 suggests three possibilities for a frontier:

1 *No frontier.* 'Helsinki' is made up of office properties in Helsinki only, 'London' is made up of office properties in London only, and inter-city portfolios are not

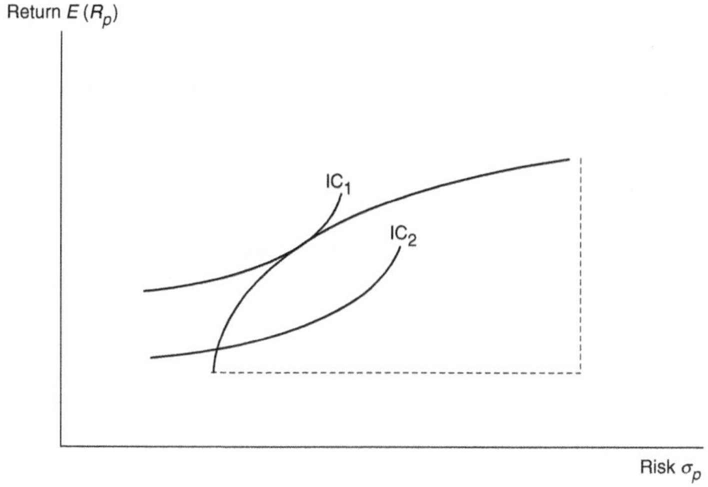

Figure 5.5 Choice of portfolio at the point of tangency between the efficient frontier and a (risk-averse) investor's highest possible indifference curve between risk and return. $E(R_p)$ = expected return on portfolio, σ_p = standard deviation of portfolio.

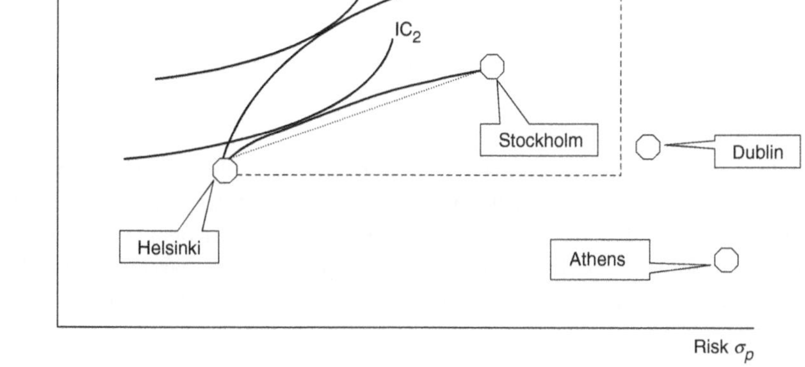

Figure 5.6 An inefficient frontier for office space across Europe? A stylized adaptation based on SWIP Real Estate Research, June 2010.

allowed – a metaphor for a presumed inability to move capital freely across jurisdictions. Thus, office markets are perfectly segmented, and no 'frontier' between them is possible.

2 *Weakly concave frontier.* This happens between 'Helsinki' and 'Stockholm'. Inter-city investment in office property is possible, but tends to go to city-markets that are similar to one another: maybe because they are part of the same region (if the 'region' shows a high degree of economic integration and/or cultural similarity), or because they are characterized by similar investment vehicles and styles, or both. Inter-city portfolios contain varying proportions of representative samples of office properties from each city, but the efficient frontier is weakly concave as the similarity between city-markets leads to relatively high inter-city correlations. For example, Table 5.4 below shows that from 2001 to 2010 property returns between Finland and Sweden had a correlation of 85 per cent, whereas between the UK and Sweden the correlation was 52 per cent, and between the UK and Finland it was just 15 per cent. An investor whose risk–return profile is as shown in Figure 5.4 would choose to hold that portfolio on the frontier which is at the point of tangency between the frontier and indifference curve IC_2.

   Historic data (RREEF, 2010) lend support to the regional character of cross-border RE investment. For example, in 2005, funds worth $155 billion were invested in European commercial property, but of these only $56 billion were cross-border investments (i.e., 36 per cent). Most of the cross-border activity was in office space and concentrated in just three countries (the UK, France, and Germany). More to the point, 63 per cent of the $56 billion activity came from Europe, 23 per cent from the USA, and 6 per cent from the Middle East. All in all, 87 per cent of European investment in commercial property in 2005 came from within Europe itself.

3 *Strongly concave frontier.* This happens between 'Helsinki' and 'London', the reason being the low correlation (15 per cent) between Finland and the UK. In addition, 'London' dominates 'Stockholm' return-wise. An investor whose risk-return profile is as shown in Figure 5.6 would choose to hold that portfolio on the frontier which is at the point of tangency between the frontier and indifference curve IC_1.

In theory, it may be possible to form a frontier from combinations of (representative) properties coming only from the global minimum-risk portfolio and the global maximum-return portfolio, but:

- If we talk about *direct property investment* (rather than investment in shares representing property), it is very unlikely that there would be enough 'representative' properties in either market (remember, pieces of RE are invariably heterogeneous) to allow formation of enough portfolios to exhaust the risk–return possibilities making up an efficient frontier. Adding specific properties from other city-markets would go some way towards solving the problem.
- Direct property comes in lumps rather than fractions (i.e., it is indivisible), so there are bound to be *discontinuities* along a notional efficient frontier anyway. The number of discontinuities will be smaller (but still significant) if specific properties from other city-markets (even from Dublin and Athens, in Figure 5.6) are included in the efficient frontier portfolios.

Table 5.4 Property returns in sample of countries, 2001–10

	Australia	*Canada*	*Finland*	*Ireland*	*Sweden*	*UK*	*USA*
2001	10.30%	9.20%	7.40%	8.10%	4.60%	6.80%	6.30%
2002	9.50%	8.80%	5.80%	2.40%	2.40%	9.60%	6.10%
2003	12.00%	8.30%	5.90%	12.40%	0.90%	10.90%	9.90%
2004	13.10%	12.90%	5.60%	11.40%	5.80%	18.30%	13.10%
2005	13.80%	18.70%	7.50%	24.40%	12.70%	19.10%	19.10%
2006	17.30%	18.30%	10.00%	27.20%	16.10%	18.10%	14.90%
2007	18.40%	15.80%	11.30%	9.80%	14.70%	−3.4%	14.30%
2008	−0.3%	3.70%	5.10%	−34.5%	−3.3%	−22.1%	−7.4%
2009	−2.2%	−0.3%	3.80%	−23.3%	1.40%	3.50%	−17.1%
2010	9.50%	11.10%	7.00%	−1.1%	10.40%	15.10%	14.20%
Mean	10.14%	10.65%	6.94%	3.68%	6.57%	7.59%	7.34%
StDev	6.73%	6.10%	2.27%	19.39%	6.56%	12.69%	11.29%

Correlation matrix

	Australia	*Canada*	*Finland*	*Ireland*	*Sweden*	*UK*	*USA*
Australia	100.00%						
Canada	91.44%	100.00%					
Finland	82.12%	79.10%	100.00%				
Ireland	91.13%	87.39%	62.88%	100.00%			
Sweden	78.50%	87.04%	84.69%	73.37%	100.00%		
UK	54.51%	55.28%	14.73%	78.21%	52.13%	100.00%	
USA	91.88%	92.37%	67.17%	87.11%	73.05%	61.72%	100.00%

Four two-country portfolios, with RE from each country making up 50% of portfolio value:

	Sweden and Finland	*UK and Finland*	*UK and Sweden*	*UK and Ireland*
Mean	6.76%	7.27%	7.08%	5.64%
StDev	4.28%	6.61%	8.53%	15.18%

Source of primary data: PREA (2011: 7), based on IPD index.

- *Information*, *management*, and *transaction costs* (including taxes) are likely to be different across cities; so are RE market *liquidity* (how easy it is to sell a property), RE market *transparency* (ability and opportunity to estimate local prices correctly and generally gather reliable market data), and the degree of *FX risk*.[6] Such (differentiated) factors increase the complexity of forming inter-city portfolios of direct property, and render city-wide property markets imperfectly segmented. As a market practitioner once put it, 'Real estate is, ultimately, a local business' (Briddell, 2010).
- All of the above strengthen the idea that forming a portfolio of properties alone is necessarily (and particularly) *sub-optimal* – 'sub-optimal', that is, not in the sense that buying offices only in London is a better strategy than buying offices in a variety of cities because clearly there will be reduction of risk (including systematic risk) in the latter case anyway; but in the sense that an 'efficient' frontier involving direct property is almost certain to be fragmented rather than smooth and continuous; as a result, locating

tangency solutions (between the frontier and some indifference curve) becomes very difficult, if not impossible.

- 'Sub-optimality' holds not only in regard to direct property investment across different cities (as in the example pursued above), but across property types too. By extension, some degree of 'sub-optimality' should remain even in portfolios made up of direct RE and other asset classes. 'Sub-optimality' should also be reduced in case of *indirect property investment* – which is one reason why so many types of financial institutions that invest in property and issue property shares have become increasingly popular.

5.4.2 RE and correlations between assets

'Sub-optimal' or not, RE shows significantly less than perfect positive correlation with other asset classes. For example, in the USA from 1970 to 2004, the correlations between RE returns (with REITs used as a proxy for RE) and S&P 500, international stocks, emerging markets, US bonds, and global bonds were 52, 36, 31, 14, and 3 per cent, respectively (Coaker, 2007). Because of this, a portfolio combining RE and non-RE should reduce investors' risk. However, indirect investment in property may not necessarily impart the same risk-reducing advantage as direct investment (in a portfolio context), as property shares may often be influenced more by what happens to the overall stock market than by what happens to the value of the underlying properties.

There is also evidence (Coaker, 2007; Krishnan et al., 2009) that correlations between asset returns change over time (even though the historic pattern of volatility is more resilient than the pattern of historic returns). Moreover, they tend to 'increase during financial crises, and [...] in bear markets' (Krishnan et al., 2009). In the same vein, Ang and Chen (2002) had found that correlations of returns between stocks and the market are not the same when markets are booming and when they are falling (i.e., they identified *correlation asymmetries* between asset returns). This result was reiterated in Yang et al. (2011), who identified correlation asymmetries between REIT and stock returns in the USA from 1999 to 2008. They felt that this suggested 'reduced hedging potential of REITs against the stock market downturn during the sample period' (i.e., investment in REITs would not reduce much – *hedge against* – the risk represented by investment in the stock market as a whole). On the other hand, turning to direct RE, Lee (2003) found that, although its inclusion in a portfolio of RE, equities, and bonds would have improved portfolio returns only about 30 per cent of the time (over the 1977 Q4–2002 Q3 period; FTA[7] index for equities, gilts for bonds), the increase in performance happened when the alternative asset showed negative returns, i.e., adding RE in a portfolio helps an investor avoid large losses but also makes for lower returns.

Investment returns bear some relationship to the length of the holding period. Investigating the investment performance of major UK asset classes in relation to holding periods from 1963 to 2005, Alles and Murray (2009) found that 'the probability of ending with a shortfall in end-of-period wealth decreases as the holding period lengthens. [...] higher risk asset classes outperform lower risk asset classes and have higher end-of-period wealth for longer holding periods.' Also, Gardner and Matysiak (2005), analysing UK office returns from 1983 to 2003, found that 'over the longer term there is a reversion towards performance in line with market averages. The lesson here is that, investors who hold properties which have recorded a strong performance over the first five years, may consider the possibility to take profits, as they are unlikely to sustain out-performance over the longer term.' However, a serious methodological problem when investigating returns and holding period length is how to disentangle 'length' from the economic history characteristics of the given holding period. Thus, Ciochetti and Fisher (2002), in their study of a sample of 3444 NCREIF properties in the USA from 1980 to 2001, discovered that 'properties acquired and/or sold early or late in the study period outperform those acquired and/or sold in the interim period' but this result may have been due to the particular economic climate during the 'early' or 'late' period.

5.4.3 RE across countries: correlations (A)

Correlations of RE returns across countries show a strong tendency to be in the region $0 < r < +1$. Confirming this, Table 5.4 presents property returns from 2001 to 2010 in a sample of seven countries.

In the four two-country portfolios shown in Table 5.4, an investor holding initially Swedish property only would reduce his or her risk if they invested 50 per cent of their wealth in Finnish property; an investor holding initially UK property only would also enjoy less risk if they invested 50 per cent of their wealth in either Finnish or Swedish property. But the combination of UK with Irish property would have in fact made a UK investor worse off (in both risk and return terms) than if the investor had only held UK property over the sample period. An Irish investor, however, would have benefited.

5.4.4 RE and other asset classes: correlations (B)

What is the picture if one looks at correlations between RE and other asset classes? Relevant data from the UK are shown in Table 5.5.

It is evident from Table 5.5 that commercial property has significantly less than perfect positive correlation with five of the other six asset classes included in Table 5.5 (the highest correlation being with UK equity), and in addition correlates negatively with 'cash'.[8] Expanding the time scale does not change this result, as Table 5.6 makes clear. In fact, commercial property in the UK has shown better (real) return than either gilts or cash, and lower return than UK equities (and actually better return than UK equities over the 1998–2007 period). On the other hand, it has shown more risk than cash (rather expectedly!), less risk than gilts, and considerably less risk than UK equities.

As already mentioned, commercial property is hardly homogeneous. It is made up of various sub-markets. Table 5.7 shows decade-related yields for three such sub-sectors in the UK (based on quarterly averaged data), comparing them with those of three other asset classes and the Retail Price Index (RPI).[9]

5.4.5 An application

In this section, we shall construct an efficient frontier between commercial property and a portfolio of the six other asset classes presented in Table 5.5. To this end, the first task is to construct the six-asset portfolio.

We assume that someone (say, a mutual fund investment manager) wants to invest equally into the six other asset classes. This means that each of those will have 16.667 per cent of the sum-total of funds earmarked for the six-asset portfolio. The return on the six-asset portfolio is then 6.74 per cent, i.e., the average of the (historic) returns on each of the asset classes.

Table 5.5 Returns on various asset classes in the UK, 1998–2007

Year	*UK equities*	*Overseas equities*	*Commercial property (CP)*	*Fixed-interest gilts*	*Index-linked gilts*	*Corporate bonds*	*Cash*
1998	13.80%	22.00%	11.80%	29.60%	19.90%	14.80%	7.20%
1999	24.20%	31.00%	14.50%	−0.4%	4.40%	−0.2%	5.20%
2000	−5.9%	−4.1%	10.50%	8.00%	4.20%	10.20%	5.70%
2001	−13.3%	−14.2%	6.80%	−0.9%	−0.5%	6.90%	4.80%
2002	−22.7%	−27.5%	9.60%	9.90%	8.20%	9.50%	3.70%
2003	20.90%	20.30%	10.90%	1.20%	6.60%	5.70%	3.50%
2004	12.80%	7.50%	18.30%	8.40%	8.50%	6.70%	4.30%
2005	22.00%	24.60%	19.10%	11.00%	9.00%	9.00%	4.60%
2006	16.80%	5.50%	18.10%	0.00%	2.90%	0.80%	4.60%
2007	5.30%	9.70%	−3.4%	2.70%	8.50%	1.80%	5.60%
Mean	7.39%	7.48%	11.62%	6.95%	7.17%	6.52%	4.92%
StDev	16.17%	18.43%	6.71%	9.17%	5.41%	4.69%	1.08%

Correlation matrix

	UK equities	*Overseas equities*	*Commercial property (CP)*	*Fixed-interest gilts*	*Index-linked gilts*	*Corporate bonds*	*Cash*
UK equities	100.00%						
Overseas equities	94.85%	100.00%					
Commercial property (CP)	46.38%	29.75%	100.00%				
Fixed-interest gilts	1.06%	13.86%	13.82%	100.00%			
Index-linked gilts	23.54%	35.60%	2.40%	90.76%	100.00%		
Corporate bonds	−32.84%	−20.57%	8.58%	83.03%	59.76%	100.00%	
Cash	10.52%	30.41%	−22.13%	59.65%	51.91%	33.10%	100.00%

Source of primary data: BBS (2008: 6). 'Gilts' are UK government bonds, the equivalent of US Treasury securities.

Table 5.6 How UK commercial property compares with other asset classes

	1970–2006			*1998–2007*		
	Return	*Risk*	*Correlation*	*Return*	*Risk*	*Correlation*
CP	5.10%	10.30%	100.00%	11.62%	6.71%	100.00%
UK equities	6.40%	25.20%	19.00%	7.39%	16.17%	46.38%
Gilts	3.60%	14.40%	4.00%	7.17%	5.41%	2.40%
Cash	1.90%	4.20%	−27%	4.92%	1.08%	−22.13%

Source: For 1970–2006, IPF (2007: 9). For 1998–2009, Table 5.3.

Table 5.7 Historic yields in the UK from various asset classes

	Shops	*London offices*	*Industrial*	*All three*	*15-year gilts*	*Base rates*	*Equities*	*RPI*
1950s	5.5%	7.0%	10.0%	7.5%	4.5%	4.0%	6.5%	4.2%
1960s	6.0%	6.6%	9.5%	7.3%	6.7%	6.3%	4.5%	3.7%
1970s	5.6%	5.9%	7.7%	6.4%	12.0%	9.6%	5.3%	12.7%
1980s	3.9%	5.1%	7.1%	5.3%	11.1%	11.7%	4.8%	7.4%
1990s	4.7%	5.5%	7.4%	5.8%	7.9%	7.8%	3.9%	3.7%
2000s	4.9%	5.3%	5.9%	5.4%	4.6%	4.3%	3.2%	2.6%
Mean	5.1%	5.9%	7.9%	6.3%	7.8%	7.3%	4.7%	5.7%
StDev	0.8%	0.8%	1.5%	1.0%	3.2%	3.0%	1.1%	3.8%

Source: Cushman & Wakefield, Business Briefing: The UK Property Investment Market, February 2011.

Table 5.8 Seven asset classes of Table 5.5 reduced to just two

	Commercial property (CP)	*Six other asset classes*
	11.80%	17.88%
	14.50%	10.70%
	10.50%	3.02%
	6.80%	−2.87%
	9.60%	−3.15%
	10.90%	9.70%
	18.30%	8.03%
	19.10%	13.37%
	18.10%	5.10%
	−3.40%	5.60%
Mean	11.62%	6.74%
StDev	6.71%	6.68%

Note: Mean and StDev of six-asset portfolio computed by use of Equations (5.3) and (5.4).

However, the risk of the six-asset portfolio cannot be the simple average of the standard deviations of the returns on the asset classes because the correlations between the latter must also be taken into account. Applying Equation (5.4), we find the standard deviation of the six-asset portfolio to be 6.68 per cent (rather than 9.16 per cent) – an example of how diversification reduces risk.

Now we are ready to consider combining the six-asset portfolio with commercial property (see Table 5.8).

The correlation between the two asset classes (or portfolios) of Table 5.8 is 36.26 per cent. Our problem is to find that proportion of the investor's total funds invested in commercial property that minimizes the total risk of the combined portfolio. We work as follows.

Given that

$$\sigma_p = \left(w_1^2\sigma_1^2 + w_2^2\sigma_2^2 + 2w_1w_2r_{1,2}\sigma_1\sigma_2\right)^{1/2},$$

we take the derivative of σ_p with respect to w_1 (= weight of funds invested in commercial property), set $\partial\sigma_p/\partial w_1 = 0$, and solve for w_1, so that

$$w_1 = \frac{\sigma_2^2 - \sigma_1\sigma_2(r_{1,2})}{\sigma_1^2 + \sigma_2^2 - 2\sigma_1\sigma_2(r_{1,2})}. \tag{5.5}$$

In the case under consideration, the proportion of funds invested in commercial property that minimizes σ_p is 49.67 per cent, minimum σ_p = 5.529 per cent, and corresponding $E(R_p)$ = 9.16 per cent. But this does not mean that the investor will necessarily invest his or her funds in this portfolio, because he or she may want to go for a higher return (at more risk). The highest return they can go for is of course 11.62 per cent (the return on commercial property only). Given the minimum-risk, and the maximum-return, portfolios, we can plot an efficient frontier between them simply by varying the proportion of commercial property into the combined portfolio. (This efficient frontier, though, is not necessarily the global efficient frontier as we have not considered, for example, the country-related investments of Table 5.4, or weights for the six assets in the six-asset portfolio other than 16.667 per cent for each.)

The efficient frontier we have arrived at is shown in Figure 5.7. In the absence of an explicit utility function for our investor, the latter may choose to form a portfolio anywhere along the given efficient frontier just on a 'hunch' (which is another name for his or her implicit utility function) or on the basis of his or her fund's strategic guidelines on risk tolerance or target return.

5.5 Property valuation

It is all very well having a portfolio approach to investment. Before one adopts it, though, one must first have or calculate rates of return on the particular investments or assets that will go into the portfolio. Such *rates of total return* (RTR) are a function of both the income rate, or yield, and the rate of capital gain of an investment. To make this clear in a property

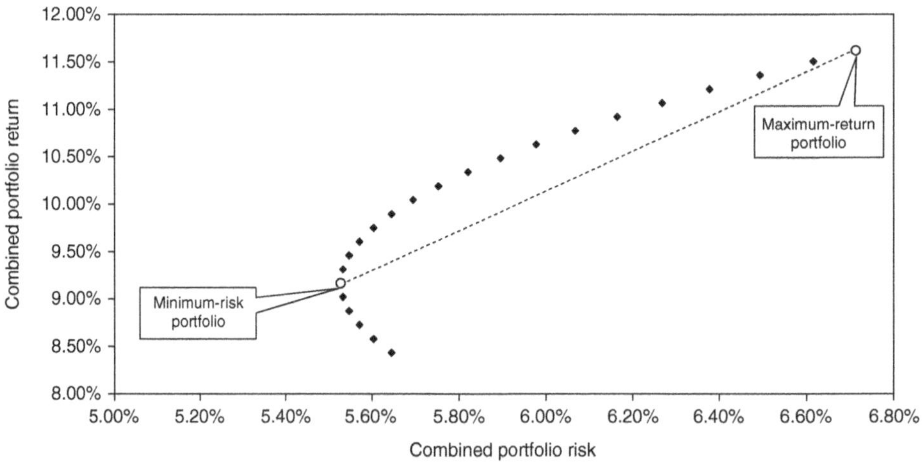

Figure 5.7 Efficient frontier between commercial property and a portfolio of other asset classes in the UK, based on historic returns from 1998 to 2007.

context, and assuming a one-year holding period without inflation or an adjustment for the time value of money, we have

$$\text{RTR} = \frac{\text{Rent} + P_1 - P_0}{P_0} = \frac{\text{Rent}}{P_0} + \frac{P_1 - P_0}{P_0} = \text{income rate} + \text{rate of capital gain}, \quad (5.6)$$

where

Rent = (net) rental (or operating) income within period,
P_1 = price at which property is sold at end of period,
P_0 = price at which property was bought (or capital outlay made towards the investment) at beginning of period.

RTRs are calculated at the end of the holding period, which can extend over many years. They are *ex-post* (i.e., after the fact) rates of return. Vendors of commercial RE performance measures (see Box 5.1) systematically calculate RTR for calendar years (although some performance measures are derived on a quarterly, monthly, or even daily basis), taking into account both the rental income that commercial properties have generated within the year and the change in property prices between the beginning and the end of the period. With this kind of information, vendors can easily calculate RTR for longer periods, say 5 or 10 years.[10]

It is obvious from Equation (5.6) that both the income rate and the rate of capital gain (RCG) involve estimates of the value of the asset or investment under consideration. This brings us to *valuation* or *appraisal* territory,[11] which is about two things: (a) finding out what the current or future value of an asset is or will be; (b) determining whether it is worthwhile to buy (or sell) the asset or embark on a particular investment venture or construction project, now.

Box 5.1 Some well-known vendors of commercial property performance measures

Organization	*Country*	*Explanation*
IPD, www.ipd.com	UK	IPD (Investment Property Databank) is a London-based independent organization specializing in performance analysis for the owners, investors, managers and occupiers of RE. It was established in the UK in 1985 by Rupert Nabarro and Ian Cullen. IPD's Annual Property Indices measure ungeared (i.e., unleveraged) total returns to directly held standing property investments from one open market valuation to the next in each of the most mature and transparent property markets around the world. They measure

Organization	*Country*	*Explanation*
IPD, www.ipd.com	UK	total returns for all directly held RE assets (All Property) and for the four main market sectors – retail, office, industrial, residential – wherever they are held in professionally managed portfolios. An important aspect of the IPD indices is that, following licensing by IPD, they can be linked to financial products like derivatives for the purpose of determining a product's capital value or income yield.
FTSE, www.ftse.com/ukcommercialproperty	UK	FTSE (Financial Times Stock Exchange Group) is an independent company jointly owned by the *Financial Times* and the London Stock Exchange. In addition to many other indices, they prepare the FTSE UK Commercial Property Index Series, which provides a daily measure of the performance of investable, institutional grade commercial property (retail, office, industrial, all RE) in the UK. Each of the four indices provides capital value and total returns performance data driven by the performance of the underlying property assets.
Moody's/REAL CPPI, http://mit.edu/cre/research/credl/rca.html	USA	Moody's/Real Estate Analytics LLC Commercial Property Price Index. The index has been developed by the MIT's Center for Real Estate based on data from Real Capital Analytics Inc. Its purpose is to support the trading of commercial property derivatives. It utilizes a repeat-sales regression suggested by Geltner and Pollakowski (2007). In addition to a national All-Property Index, there are also indices for the four major property sectors.
Moody's TBI, http://mit.edu/cre/research/credl/rca.html	USA	A transaction-based index (like the CPPI; also published on the MIT/CRE website), but, whereas CPPI utilizes RCA data, TBI utilizes NCREIF data. It is thus based on a smaller population of more purely institutionally held properties.

Organization	*Country*	*Explanation*
NCREIF, www.ncreif.org	USA	NCREIF (National Council of Real Estate Investment Fiduciaries) is a Chicago-based organization that serves the institutional RE investment community as a non-partisan collector, processor, validator and disseminator of real estate performance information. It publishes a series of property indices, like the NCREIF Property Index, the NFI-ODCE (short for NCREIF Fund Index–Open-End Diversified Core Equity), or the NCREIF Townsend Fund Index, which are considered benchmarks for US commercial real estate.

'Value' and 'market price' are not necessarily identical. Estimations of value are arrived at through some appropriate technique or procedure. Such estimations are crucial to both sides involved in a market transaction or bargaining process, but, ultimately, value will approach, or coincide with, market price only if the latter is determined 'fairly'. In turn, a transaction would be 'fair' if the two parties involved had access to, and made good use of, the same and sufficient pertinent information (e.g., overall market conditions and prospects; current vacancy rate; and natural vacancy rate – see Chapter 6), and either the need to sell or to buy were roughly equal to one another, or 'seller' and 'buyer' were roughly representative of 'sellers' and 'buyers' in the wider market. Again, 'good' use of pertinent information is not the same as 'identical' use. In the case of income properties, there are so many assumptions and inaccuracies, and also differences in perspective, involved in estimations of future cash flows or of required rates of return to be used in discounting those cash flows that buyer and seller hardly ever come up with identical valuations initially – even though, in the end, they may agree on a transaction price through bargaining.

There are three mainstream approaches to property valuation or appraisal, each utilizing specialized techniques and formulas:

1. The *sales comparison approach*, that bases valuation of a subject property on the (known) sale prices of similar properties (called 'comparables') sold at about the same time, in the same area.
2. The *cost approach*, which involves calculating how much it would cost to reproduce or replace the existing built structure of the subject property; subtracting any accrued depreciation; and adding the value of land. (Reproduction cost is about rebuilding the subject property as is; replacement cost is about rebuilding it using modern materials and methods.)
3. The *income approach*, which comprises discounted cash flow techniques (DCF). These make use of an appropriate discount or capitalization rate to discount, i.e., calculate the present value (PV) of any (net) incomes that the property is expected to generate in

the future. The PV thus calculated is taken as the current market value of the subject property.

The value thus found will be compared with an ask price (or estimated initial cost of an investment) in order to determine whether the ask price (or investment cost) is acceptable. In the case of commercial properties, an additional step might be to include this investment (if its expected return is found satisfactory) in a portfolio of assets and evaluate its contribution to a target risk-return combination for the portfolio.

Contrary to the *ex-post* RTR mentioned in Equation (5.6), the discount rate used in a DCF technique is an *ex-ante* (i.e., before the fact) rate. It represents an investor's required rate of return (RRR) from the investment under consideration, and is used just before the beginning of the investor's holding period. It is almost certain, therefore, to be different from the RTR, which is realized at the end of the holding period.

In what immediately follows we shall concentrate on the income approach because it is the most sound from a theoretical standpoint, and also because it is the most appropriate for commercial, or income-generating, properties. All three approaches, however, as well as a number of more advanced ones (cf. Pagourtzi et al., 1999; Baum and Crosby, 2007) can be useful, depending on context. For example, the sales comparison approach is perhaps best, and certainly very quick and economical, when the purpose is house-price appraisal. The cost approach may be best for property insurance purposes.

5.5.1 Investment appraisal: NPV and IRR

In Chapter 4, we saw that the present value (PV) of a future amount of money K received at time t is

$$\mathrm{PV} = \frac{K}{(1+i)^t}, \text{ with } t = \text{ number of years, } i = \text{ a discount rate} \tag{5.7}$$

We also saw that the PV of a series of equal payments a received at the end of each of a number of years into the future is

$$\mathrm{PV} = \frac{a}{i}\left[1 - \frac{1}{(1+i)^t}\right]. \tag{5.8}$$

To see the difference between (5.7) and (5.8) better, let us consider (a) the PV of €50 received 20 years from now, assuming a discount rate $i = 0.08$, and (b) the PV of a series of €50, each received at the end of each year over 20 years:

$$\text{(a)}\quad \mathrm{PV} = \frac{50}{(1+0.08)^{20}} = €10.73,$$

$$\text{(b)}\quad \mathrm{PV} = \frac{50}{0.08}\left[1 - \frac{1}{(1+0.08)^{20}}\right] = €490.91.$$

The PV of a series of, say, three unequal payments K_t received *at the end* of each of three years into the future is

$$PV = \frac{K_1}{(1+i)^1} + \frac{K_2}{(1+i)^2} + \frac{K_3}{(1+i)^3}, \text{ and, generally, } PV = \sum_{t=1}^{n} \frac{K_t}{(1+i)^t}. \tag{5.9}$$

If K_1 increases every year over n years by a certain growth factor g, the PV becomes

$$PV = \sum_{t=1}^{n} \frac{K_1(1+g)^{t-1}}{(1+i)^t}. \tag{5.10}$$

And the PV of a series of equal payments a received *at the end* of each year into the future *in perpetuity* is

$$PV = \sum_{t=1}^{\infty} \frac{a}{(1+i)^t} = \frac{a}{i}. \tag{5.11}$$

If, however, a increases *perpetually* by a growth rate g, the formula (5.10) has to be modified to

$$PV = \sum_{t=1}^{\infty} \frac{a(1+g)^{t-1}}{(1+i)^t}, \tag{5.12}$$

which can be transformed into Gordon's[12] model of the PV of a *perpetually* growing amount as[13]

$$PV = \frac{a}{i-g}. \tag{5.13}$$

The formulas (5.11)–(5.13) require some explanation. How logical is it to assume a *perpetually* received a (i.e., rent or net rent or net operating income) from a property? In other words, are these formulas sensible and of practical use? Well, there are two answers to that. First, the difference between the formulas (5.10) and (5.12) or (5.13) diminishes the larger the value of t is – and buildings tend to have a long physical life anyway; the difference becomes smaller too, the larger i is. Second, although it is true that an investor's holding period is not infinite, and often it is not inordinately long either, the investor has to consider as part of the PV of a property the PV of the price he or she will get when they sell the property; in turn, that price is the PV of an income stream further ahead. Therefore, using (5.12) or (5.13) is a good enough approximation to an income stream that in practice extends very long into the future.

Now that we have seen basic ways of calculating the current value (or PV) of a property (or most any investment for that matter), it is time we looked at ways of reaching an investment decision. The dominant and correct ways are just two: the net present value (NPV) method and the internal rate of return (IRR) method.

The NPV is found by subtracting from the PV any initial outlay towards the investment (e.g., money spent to buy the property, or to develop a building). If the NPV is positive, i.e., if PV > initial outlay, the investment is profitable; if the NPV is negative, the investment should not be undertaken (according to this method). If it is zero, the investment can still be undertaken provided the discount rate used is larger than, or equal to, the investor's RRR.

The main problem with finding the current value of a property this way is how to determine the discount factor i. We shall deal with it later. In the meantime let us introduce the IRR method of investment appraisal. The IRR is that discount rate which equates the PV of future (net) incomes from an investment to the initial outlay required to buy or undertake the investment; it is the rate that guarantees a zero NPV. The investment rule then becomes as follows: if the IRR is greater than some benchmark rate (say, the yield on 10-year government bonds), or greater than some other discount rate used in the PV calculation, the investment should be considered; if not, not. We are saying that the investment 'should be considered' rather than 'should be undertaken' because there are bound to be differences between the benchmark and the given investment in terms of risk or liquidity. Ultimately, the spread between the IRR and the benchmark is the factor that allows the investor to judge whether he or she is compensated enough in cases where the investment under consideration is perceived as having more risk and less liquidity than the benchmark investment. Points to stress are:

1 The IRR method is not about calculating the current value of an investment; the latter is already given, either because it is some 'ask' price or an estimate of the capital outlay required for a project or because it has been estimated through a PV formula. The IRR only allows assessment of the investment through a comparison between rates: the IRR versus some benchmark (or other discount) rate.
2 The current value of an investment is found by applying some PV formula, using an appropriate discount rate. But a seller's and a buyer's estimates may well differ from each other's as they may estimate both future net incomes and the 'appropriate' discount rate differently.
3 Like the IRR, the NPV method allows one to assess the worth of an investment. Unlike the IRR, it involves a comparison between values: the PV found by discounting future (net) incomes and the capital outlay required for the investment.
4 When comparing investments, the two appraisal methods – NPV and IRR – do not always agree on which is 'best'. One problem is that, between two investments characterized by different time schedules and amounts of (net) incomes generated, the NPV method 'penalizes' the one that generates incomes later – the more so, in fact, the higher the discount rate is. On the other hand, because the IRR method would select one of the two investments as the best once and for all, it is often the case that the chance of agreement between the two methods depends on the discount rate used to estimate the PV.
5 Usually the two methods correctly indicate an investment as worthwhile or as better than another, but when the two methods 'disagree', it is perhaps best to trust the NPV more. After all, the IRR method requires the IRR to be compared with an appropriate discount rate, but if such a rate can be identified, it makes sense to adjust it for risk and then use it in the PV calculation anyway. Then the IRR method becomes sort of superfluous, its main advantage being the ability to allow quick reappraisal of a given investment if the (exogenous) 'benchmark' rate changes.

To sum up:

PV = sum of discounted future (net) incomes from investment (including future sale price);
NPV = PV – initial outlay;
IRR = that discount rate used in PV calculation which makes NPV = 0.

- Advantages of NPV method: is more intuitive – forces estimation and use of 'correct' discount rate – provides room for assessing investor's risk margin in value terms.
- Advantages of IRR method: is in line with business practice of comparing yields – provides room for assessing investor's risk margin in percentage point terms – allows quick reappraisal.
- NPV rule: accept investment if NPV > 0 (or if NPV = 0, provided the PV has been estimated with a RRR) and rank investments from highest to lowest NPV
- IRR rule: accept investment if IRR > benchmark rate and rank investments from highest to lowest IRR

5.5.2 Special cases in property valuation

We shall consider two cases:

(A) Rent growth only once, at time of next rent review

PROBLEM

Calculate the value of a property under lease, given that the rent R will be reviewed in m years and assuming that presently R is below market rent MR, but upon review will equate (i.e., *revert*) to MR, the latter *staying constant thereafter*. This suggests two income streams: one starting at time of PV calculation, which is before the next rent review, one starting just after that review.

$$\mathrm{PV} = \frac{R_t}{i} + \frac{(\mathrm{MR}_t - R_t)/i}{(1+i)^m} = \frac{R_t}{i} + \frac{\mathrm{MR}_t - R_t}{i(1+i)^m}. \tag{5.14}$$

INTERPRETATION

The first term, R_t/i, assumes that the current rent received under the lease at time t will flow in forever – so it is akin to Equation (5.11). The second term assumes that after the review the investor will be receiving in perpetuity the *difference* between the current market rent and the current lease rent *in addition to the latter, which has already been taken care of in the first term.* The discounted value of this difference *at the time of the reversion* is of course $(\mathrm{MR}_t - R_t)/i$, but to bring this value down to the present time when the property value calculation is taking place we need also to discount $(\mathrm{MR}_t - R_t)/i$ by $(1+i)^m$, m being the number of remaining years between the time of the calculation and the next rent review (or *reversion*) date.[14] An added advantage of having $i(1+i)^m$ in the denominator of the second term is that this way some note of recognition is given to the extra risk inherent in the more distant cash flow (since $i(1+i)^m > i$).

There are thus two discount factors in the formula (5.14): i and $i(1+i)^m$. The first discount factor is the *initial yield* (or *all-risks yield*), and is simply the capitalization rate. The second discount factor is the *reversionary yield* because it takes into account the reversion of the lease rent to market rent. If, in both of those factors, an i can be found that equates the PV of the corresponding income streams to the current market price (or capital value) of the property, then that i is the *equivalent yield* (EvY). If no such market price or valuation is known, the EvY is simply that *single* discount factor that, given a required rate of return, $RRR = i$, on the basis of which Equation (5.14) is solved, allows R_t/EvY to equal the PV found.

EXAMPLE

Consider a 15-year lease contract with rent reviews every 5 years. PV calculation is taking place at the end of one year after the first review, so the next review will take place in four years (i.e., $m = 4$). The current (net) rental income is £75,000, but the current market rent that the property could have fetched if it were rented out now (and which is expected also at reversion time) is £85,000 (net of expenses). Assuming a required rate of return of 8 per cent, what is the PV of the property? What is the EvY? What is the EvY if the current market price is £950,000?

ANSWER

- Assuming no market price is known,

$$\mathrm{PV} = \frac{75{,}000}{0.08} + \frac{85{,}000 - 75{,}000}{0.08(1+0.08)^4} = 937{,}500 + \frac{10{,}000}{0.1088} = 1{,}029{,}379.$$

- EvY (found through trial and error) = 8.2574 per cent, since

$$\frac{75{,}000}{0.082574} + \frac{85{,}000 - 75{,}000}{0.082574} = 908{,}276 + 121{,}103 = 1{,}029{,}379.$$

  Because this EvY is greater than the RRR, the investment is profitable.
- Assuming a market price of £950,000,
  EvY (found through trial and error) = 8.65 per cent, since

$$\frac{75{,}000}{0.0865} + \frac{85{,}000 - 75{,}000}{0.0865(1+0.0865)^4} = 950{,}000.$$

- Because this EvY is greater than the RRR, the investment is profitable.

The formula (5.14) suffers, however, from a crucial weakness: it assumes a constant market rent every time. This is patently unrealistic, as shown by the fact that a different market rent will be used on any different year throughout the lease when the PV calculation takes place (unless, miraculously, market rents are indeed constant). But different market rents imply growth, which is precisely what (5.14) does not assume![15]

(B) Constant rent growth, rent reviews every m years

PROBLEM

Calculate the value of a property under a lease contract that has rent reviews every *m* years, assuming that with every rent review the current lease rent increases so that it equals market rent, the latter *growing by a constant rate g*. In other words, we are assuming an infinite series of rent reviews that happen every *m* years, the rent rising each time to equal the market rent, which has been increasing too. Under this assumption, the PV of the property is (Fraser, 1993; Brown and Matysiak, 2000; McGough and Tsolacos, 2001)

$$\mathrm{PV} = \sum_{m=1}^{T} \frac{R}{(1+i)^m} + \sum_{m=1}^{T} \frac{R(1+g)^T}{(1+i)^{T+m}} + \sum_{m=1}^{T} \frac{R(1+g)^{2T}}{(1+i)^{2T+m}} + \ldots, \tag{5.15}$$

which simplifies to

$$\mathrm{PV} = \frac{R}{i\left[1 - \frac{(1+g)^T - 1}{(1+i)^T - 1}\right]} = \frac{R}{i}\left[\frac{(1+i)^T - 1}{(1+i)^T - (1+g)^T}\right]. \tag{5.16}$$

INTERPRETATION OF EQUATION (5.15)

Until the first rent review, the rent under the lease is R. It is discounted by $(1+i)^m$, where $m =$ each successive year until the end of the lease term T. In the beginning, R was equal to the market rent, but the latter has been growing at an annual rate g ever since, while R will 'revert' to market rent at the first rent review. Thus, by the end of the first lease term T, the market rent has become $R(1+g)^T$. This, now, will be the lease rent until the next rent review – only it will have to be discounted by $(1+i)^{T+m}$, where $T+m =$ number of years elapsed by the end of the previous lease term plus each successive year until the end of the new lease term, which is also T.

Now, if the market price is known, the i that equates the expression (5.16) to that market price is the *equated yield*, EtY, which is therefore an IRR (different from equivalent yield EvY in that it assumes constant rental *growth*). If the market price is not known, the EtY is simply the RRR $= i$.

EXAMPLE

Presently a property earns a £75,000 (net) rent per annum. Rent reviews take place every 5 years, which is also when the next review will happen. Market rents grow in such a fashion that, after expenses are accounted for, they imply an annual growth of (net) rent for the property equal to 4 per cent. The RRR is 8 per cent. Calculate the PV of this property, and also the EtY if the current market price of the property is £2m.

ANSWER

- Assuming no market price is known:

$$\mathrm{PV} = \frac{75{,}000}{0.08\left[1 - \frac{(1+0.04)^5 - 1}{(1+0.08)^5 - 1}\right]} = \frac{75{,}000}{0.08}\left[\frac{(1+0.08)^5 - 1}{(1+0.08)^5 - (1+0.04)^5}\right] = 1{,}741{,}347$$

- Assuming a market price of £2 million, EtY (found through trial and error) = 7.4814 per cent. Because this IRR is less than the RRR, this is not a profitable investment at the moment. Notice that under the assumption of a £2 million market price, both the NPV method and the IRR method of investment valuation give the same indication as to this investment's worth.

5.5.3 The capitalization rate

It is apparent from Sections 5.5.1 and 5.5.2 that in PV calculations three factors are all-important, given the initial outlay for a RE investment: future (net) incomes, future price, and the capitalization rate (or required rate of return, RRR). Future (net) incomes are difficult to predict – which is the reason why recent or current net incomes from the given or from similar properties, adjusted for expected inflation, often serve as a proxy for future net incomes. Future price is crucial where the investor (e.g., developer or owner-occupier) goes for capital gain rather than income, as it typically happens in the residential owner-occupied market. In this case, a developer will base his or her decision to build on expected market price at time of completion rather than on estimates of future rents (in turn, expected prices are in practice projections of current prices – see Chapter 8). A cap rate and incomes from the property will not normally enter the calculation (at least not directly, since RE prices are supposed to be capitalizations of future net incomes). Instead, given the expected market price and the (inflation- and time-adjusted) cost of development,[16] project profitability is assessed through a comparison between the (expected) rate of capital gain (RCG) from the given project (which normally takes one to two years to complete; longer for commercial properties, especially office buildings) and the RCG that is typical for the particular construction industry sector at the time.

For example, if the market price of a house is £150,000 and the cost of development (with all adjustments made) is £100,000, the RCG is (price-cost)/cost = 50 per cent. More usually, a developer will mark up the cost of development by the current and locally relevant industry-standard RCG in order to arrive at the selling price, i.e., given a RCG of, say, 50 per cent, a development cost of £100,000 will be marked up to £150,000 to give the selling price, assuming a sale will take place just after completion. (It is also possible, as happens in some countries (e.g., Greece), when the RE market is booming, that sales will even take place before completion.)

But with income-earning properties, things are different. Current value very decisively hinges on future incomes which are generated over many years, and a cap rate has to be used in order to discount those flows. What, then, determines cap rate choice?

In theory, a cap rate has to include the following components:[17]

1. Expected inflation (to preserve the purchasing power of invested capital, as measured by a market basket).
2. Risk premium (to compensate the investor for the risk inherent in the given investment). This depends on estimates of future economic conditions both locally and nationally, on the quality of the tenants and their covenants, on the kind of property involved, on the property's location and liquidity, etc. It should also reflect the level of risk achieved when the given property is held in a properly diversified portfolio of assets rather than when it is held in isolation.
3. Recapture premium (to compensate the investor for the physical deterioration of the property over time – i.e., the reduction in the value of capital invested, which is typically captured by accounting depreciation procedures). Physical deterioration or accounting

depreciation, however, are not safe pointers to the loss in capital value over time, as, before a structure has reached the end of its physical life (and often far before that), it may well have exhausted its economic life (see Section 5.6).

Because of this, the recapture component of a cap rate should ideally secure not the recovery of the value of bricks and mortar, but the economic value of the invested capital at the end of the holding period, i.e., the ability to generate the kind of income that the present use of the capital was able to generate. In practice, this might mean having enough capital at the end of the holding period so as to demolish the existing structure and develop another, capable of earning an economic profit then. Unfortunately, such a calculation would be fraught with extreme uncertainty – hence, the recourse to some measure of accounting depreciation (say, dividing the capital outlay by an expected physical life of 50 or 75 years for the structure) as a second-best solution.

4 Real return (to reward the investor for committing his or her funds to the given investment). This should be over and above any expected inflation, and would be related to what is the norm for this type of investment (in the given location) at the time. In theory, the 'norm' is determined in the context of an economy-wide general equilibrium, in which rates of real return (not considering risk) across industries and sub-sectors are equalized for all sectors (in other words: they tend to adjust around the rate of growth of real potential GDP) after account is taken of differences in the amount and quality of human and non-human capital invested in each sector. In practice, though, the 'norm' is determined by information exchange among market participants at a time and place, and is subject to human error, misjudgement, and 'myopia'. (For convenience, the real return is sometimes taken to be the difference between the inflation rate and the rate on government bonds of equivalent maturity to the investment that is being appraised.)

Thus, if expected inflation is 3 per cent, the risk premium is 4 per cent, the recapture premium is 1.33 per cent (= 1/75), and the real required return is 3.5 per cent, the cap rate would be 11.83 per cent.

Notice, though, that the above components rely on estimates, so the problem of obtaining a fail-safe cap rate (i.e., one that is bound to be realized *ex-post*) is not solved. Indeed it cannot be solved, whether one 'builds' a cap rate by adding up components or uses a 'wholesale' rate taken from market practice. In general, adopting a cap rate boils down to a combination of guesswork, subjective attitude to risk, and the (only partly true) assumption that past values contain information useful for predicting the future. For example, future incomes from, and the future price of, a property are estimates. An investor will commit capital if the purchasing power of the latter is preserved over time – but expected inflation is also an estimate. Further, the expected return from the investment must be higher than the return on what is perceived as a reasonably risk-free alternative (e.g., government bonds of equivalent maturity) – otherwise the risk-free alternative would be chosen every time. (The word 'reasonably' is inserted to suggest that in the post-2008 world not even government bonds are truly risk-free.)

In turn, the acceptable level of risk cannot be considered separately from the level of expected return – and the choice of any particular risk–return combination is clearly subjective (cf. Figure 5.5). Finally, using market data, i.e., historic returns on similar property investments, simply reiterates the objective results of other economic agents' past subjective estimates, which is an unsafe procedure. There is also the problem of which historic returns to use – for example, last year's or an average of, say, the last five years? For these reasons, it is doubtful that an objectively 'correct' cap rate can exist irrespective of actual market practice, 'feeling', and experience, no matter how 'subjective' the latter is. As a result, the practical choices open to an investor are the, in increasing order of sophistication, the following:

1 Use a reasonably risk-free discount rate, like the coupon rate on currently issued government bonds of equivalent maturity, or maybe the interest rate that a prestigious bank offers on time deposits of comparable maturity. This could be adjusted upwards by the rate of expected inflation, a *recapture rate* (to account for building depreciation), and possibly a risk premium (determined either subjectively or on the basis of the volatility of historic returns in this market sector). It is likely, however, that the rate of expected inflation has already been incorporated in the coupon rate on new issues of such bonds. Then, after a PV has been calculated by a cap rate determined this way, use the NPV or the IRR method of investment appraisal to decide on whether either a positive NPV or a positive spread between the IRR and the applied discount rate allow enough room to cover any perceived risk (if not already factored into the discount rate) as well as a real return appropriate for the specific property sector.
2 Use a sector-specific rate of total return (RTR), derived either through informal processes of information dissemination among market participants or from specialized vendors like FT or IPD in the UK, or NCREIF in the USA. As an example, Table 5.5 shows IPD-derived data on UK commercial property returns from 1998 to 2007. Using the mean of those returns as the cap rate (which implies the questionable assumption that the 10-year period from 1998 to 2007 is a good frame of reference) will again allow the investor to decide on whether the NPV or the spread between the IRR and the applied discount rate are acceptable.
3 Construct a (partial) 'efficient frontier' like the one in Figure 5.7. (This obviously requires inputs of historic total returns, however obtained.) Settle on a particular risk–return combination that includes the investment under consideration. Use that return as the cap rate.

5.5.4 The cap rate cycle

Summing up the discussion so far, we can make five points regarding the cap rate:

1 It is a required rate of return (RRR), but not necessarily an expected RR, let alone an *ex-post*, i.e., realized, return.
2 It can be broken down into four components (expected inflation, risk premium, recapture premium, and real return).
3 Whether the components are calculated separately and then added up, or some kind of historic total return serves as the cap rate, it is market practice (rather than some 'objective' or 'abstract' calculation) that provides the necessary inputs.
4 The basic capitalization formula (price, or PV = income/cap rate) suggests that there is an inverse relationship between price and the cap rate.
5 If a rising cap rate coincides with a drop in rental income, property prices will be suppressed even more; if a dropping cap rate coincides with a rise in rental income, property prices will increase further.

An interesting question is, 'to what extent does such a coincidence (i.e., rises in the cap rate together with drops in rental income, and vice versa) occur?' There is evidence from the US market that this is indeed the case (Wheaton, 1987; Dokko et al., 1999; Sitivanides et al., 2003; Glass and Clayton, 2009), creating a so-called *cap rate cycle*, which moves against (rather than with) an observed *RE cycle* (the recurring ups and downs in rents in commercial

RE markets – see Chapter 6). Let us suggest a mechanism (see also Figure 5.8) that explains this result.

We can begin by assuming that there is a one-off increase in demand for, say, office space. This has three effects, realized over three different time frames:

1 Office rents (on expiring leases) rise almost instantaneously.
2 The vacancy rate in this locale's office sector begins to drop, as, with some delay, rising rents help various landlords decide to avail their (unoccupied) properties for letting.
3 Positive signals are sent over to developers, encouraging them to consider expanding their activities (which take quite longer to bear fruit, though) in the sector.

Rising rents also cause RE prices to increase because, at this stage, relevant calculations are done at the existing cap rate (call it k). This further encourages developers who compare prices to replacement (i.e., construction) costs (cf. Section 3.3.2, on Tobin's q).

Together, rising rents and RE prices create perceptions of reduced risk among investors. As a result, the risk premium component of k drops, causing k to drop, which pushes (calculated) RE prices up even more, which accelerates development projects or *repositioning* of physical assets. But the real return component of k does not rise yet (which could have countered the effect of a dropping risk component) because it reflects the 'normal' return for the sector and is in turn determined in a general equilibrium context; but, as yet, no (significant) inflows of capital from other sectors into this sector have occurred, so the general equilibrium in the economy is not upset.

Thus, we have the connection:

rising rents ↔ lower cap rate.

As time goes by, *ex-post* RE returns from the sector (information on which either becomes common knowledge among market participants or is supplied by specialized vendors) begin to increase because such returns are calculated with past rather than current prices in the denominator of the *rate of total return* (cf. Equation (5.6)). This creates higher *expected* returns, which in turn begin to attract capital from other sectors (or from other localities too – cf. Chichernea et al., 2008), causing a general equilibrium adjustment. Some investors go for capital gain rather than income, so this again pushes up prices in the sector.

Gradually, the cap rate begins to rise as the increase in RE *ex-post* returns raises the real return component of the cap rate. Simultaneously, reductions in the vacancy rate in the sector may absorb the initial increase in demand (depending on how strong that increase was in the first place), causing a mild drop in rents (but most likely to a level that is higher than what it was before the increase in demand).

Thus, we have a new connection:

dropping rents ↔ rising cap rate.

Over time, the effect of more development, which was decided upon when rents and prices had initially risen, begins to play itself out. At least some of those plans have been turned into actual buildings. This, depending on how strong the initial increase in demand was, will start raising the vacancy rate, suppressing rents even more.

The drop in rents, however, increases the risk premium component of the cap rate at a time when the real return component has also increased.

Thus, we have

even lower rents ↔ even higher cap rate.

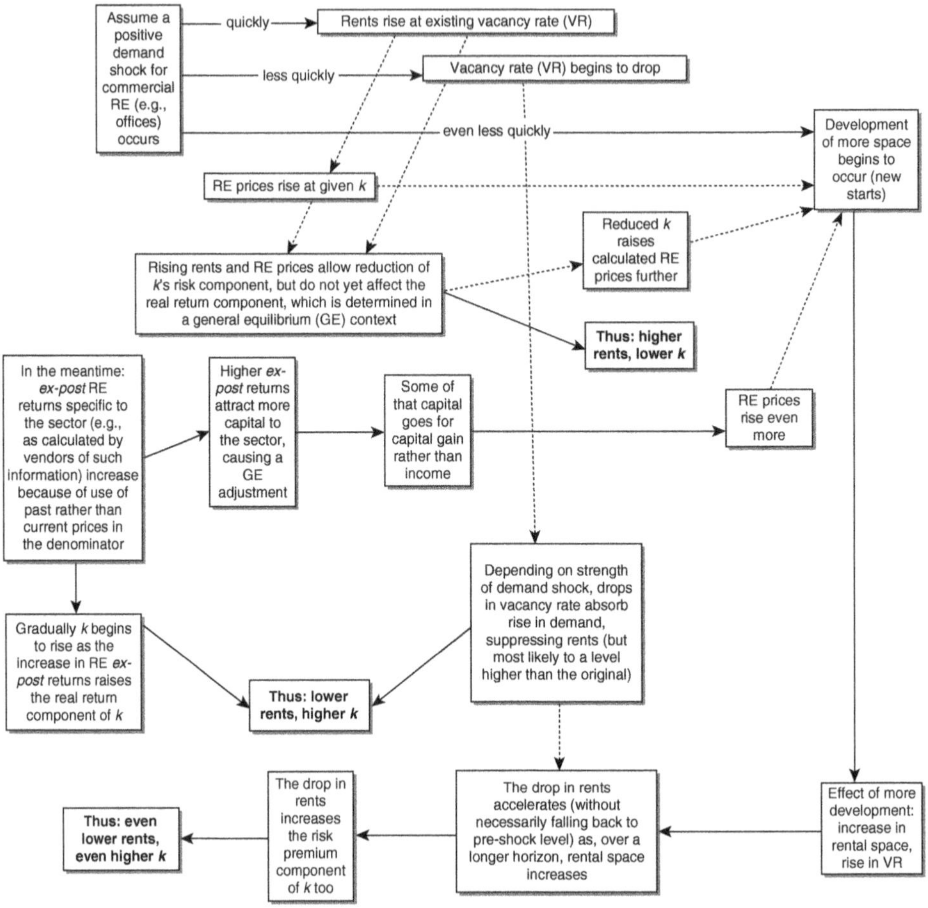

Figure 5.8 A model of the cap rate (k) cycle and the RE cycle.

This sequence of events may not, in practice, be particularly obvious, as: (a) demand shocks may follow one another before each has run its course, sometimes partly cancelling one another; (b) capital inflows from other sectors may be weaker or stronger, depending on what is happening elsewhere in the economy (and also on factors such as taxation); (c) the extent to which changes in the vacancy rate may or may not absorb a given demand shock is difficult to estimate (see Chapter 6 for more on office vacancy rates); (d) the suggested mechanism (see Figure 5.8) involves different time frames (shorter, intermediate, and longer), which sometimes may overlap; (e) the speed, timing, and extent of response of developers to initial signals may vary between times and across places, depending, among others, on supply constraints (cf. Chichernea et al., 2008).

5.5.5 The band-of-investment concept

This is a technique for breaking down an overall cap rate into an equity component (EC) and a debt component (DC), when part of the investment is debt-financed (cf. de Roos and

Rushmore, 2003). The technique can also show whether the required rate of return (RRR) on equity is achieved, given that the equity cap rate (ECR) appears as a residual once the debt cap rate has been calculated.

Suppose, for example, that the purchase price of an office property is £5 million. The investor may finance this with 25 per cent equity and 75 per cent debt. The ECR is the annual net operating income (NOI) from the property minus the annual debt service expense (DSE), divided by the equity capital invested:

$$\text{ECR} = \frac{\text{NOI} - \text{DSE}}{\text{equity capital invested}} = \frac{\text{NOI} - \text{DSE}}{0.25(5\text{ million})}. \tag{5.17}$$

Let us assume that estimated NOI is £420,000 per annum (for simplicity assumed to be constant until repayment of the loan), and the debt terms are 8 per cent interest rate, annual repayment, and a 20-year maturity. The DSE would then be £381,945.78 (i.e., the interest-and-capital repayment instalment of a fixed-rate loan; see Equation (4.7) in Section 4.2.1), which gives a *mortgage constant* (MoC) of DSE/principal = 381,945.78/3,750,000 = 0.10185. That is,

$$\text{MoC} = \frac{\text{debt service expense}}{\text{loan amount}} = \frac{\text{DSE}}{0.75(5\text{ million})}. \tag{5.18}$$

It follows that ECR = (420,000 − 381,945.78)/1,250,000 = 0.03044, and that the overall cap rate is (0.75)(0.10185) + (0.25)(0.03044) = 0.0764 + 0.0076 = 8.4 per cent. The formula is

$$\text{band-of-investment cap rate} = \text{DC} \cdot \text{MoC} + \text{EC} \cdot \text{ECR}. \tag{5.19}$$

Notice that 8.4 per cent is the quotient of 420,000/5 million. Alternatively, 8.4 per cent is the cap rate that equates the PV of 420,000 received in perpetuity to 5 million (after Equation (5.11)). It is *not* the investor's RRR, as it is simply the cap rate that links expected income and asset price once these two variables are *already* given. Thus, the band-of-investment concept is not about discovering the investor's RRR, but about allocating a given cap rate between debtor (the investor) and creditor (the lender).

Now, if this investor's RRR is higher than 3.04 per cent (and the holding period is 20 years, i.e., as long as the maturity of the loan), this investment may not sound as a good idea. The reason is that solving Equation (5.17) for the value of equity invested, with a RRR in the denominator higher than 3.04 per cent, will result in an equity value for the property less than £1,250,000. However, we have not yet factored in the price at which the property will be sold at the end of the 20-year period. Let us assume that by that time market rent will have increased enough to make a (nominal) NOI of £760,000 possible, expected to be received in perpetuity. (In reality, NOI is likely to be lower in real terms than £420,000 because the property will be nearer the end of its economic life – see Section 5.6.) Whatever this investor's *entry cap rate* (or RRR) was at the *start* of the holding period (say, 12 per cent), his or her *exit cap rate* (with which to calculate the resale price of the property at the *end* of the holding period) must be higher than that (say, 14 per cent, to reflect the greater uncertainty of a price expected to be realized so far into the future). This means that the (relevant to the investor) PV of this property will be $\text{PV} = \frac{a_1}{i_1}\left[1 - \frac{1}{(1+i_1)^t}\right] + \frac{a_2/i_2}{(1+i_1)^t}$ (after Equations (5.8), (5.11), and (5.14)).

Therefore,

$$\mathrm{PV} = \frac{420,000 - 381,945.78}{0.12}\left[1 - \frac{1}{(1+0.12)^{20}}\right] + \frac{760,000/0.14}{(1+0.12)^{20}} = 847,005.8.$$

Thus, the NPV will be 847,005.8 – 1,250,000 = −402,994.2, and this investment is a loss-maker under the assumptions used. For the investment to realize at least its RRR (12 per cent), a larger future NOI should have been predicted. For example, if, instead of 760,000, future NOI had been forecast at 1,304,000 (achievable if the initial NOI of 420,000 – presumably a function of the market rent at the time – had been growing at 5.83 per cent per annum over 20 years), the NPV would have been zero – and the IRR of the investment would equate to the RRR, so the investment would have been profitable (since the 12 per cent RRR includes, in theory, a real return over and above expected inflation as well as a risk and a recapture premium).

5.6 Physical life and economic life

A crucial investment decision for owners of commercial properties is when to redevelop an existing site, i.e., demolish an existing building and raise a new one. A rushed, but wrong, answer might be, 'at the end of the building's physical life'. The correct answer is, 'at the point in time when the PV of the existing building's future net incomes becomes equal to the PV of the future net incomes that a new building would bring (minus the cost of demolishing the existing building, clearing the site, and rebuilding)'. The point is that, at the beginning, when a building for a certain use is erected, it normally earns a higher income than any other use of the site would have earned – that is why the site was devoted to the given use rather than to an alternative use in the first place.

Soon after occupation, though, the PV of future net incomes from the given building begins to diminish for a number of reasons. First, the physical life of the building is finite, so with every passing year the time horizon in which the building is expected to generate incomes becomes smaller. Second, the building may begin to be less capable of satisfying the evolving needs of future occupiers (unless, as it happens sometimes, the traditional look of some old buildings is considered an attractive trait by some users). Third, maintenance and other costs increase with the age of a building.

On the other hand, in time, possible alternative uses begin to command higher incomes: they enjoy longer time horizons in which to bring in rents, increasing capability to satisfy occupier needs, and possibly lower maintenance costs.

At some point, therefore, the PV of net incomes from an alternative use (also taking into account the cost of demolition and reconstruction) will begin to exceed the PV of net incomes from the existing use. This 'break-even' point between the two competing uses would mark the end of the existing building's economic life, even though it might still have a number of years of physical life left (see Figure 5.9).

5.7 Property derivatives and options

Commercial property derivatives are financial instruments whose value depends on the value of underlying commercial property, as measured by a security or index, for example, the FTSE UK Commercial Property Index Series, the IPD, or, in the USA, the NCREIF. Examples of derivatives are swaps, *in-specie* swaps (or 'property repos'), forward contracts, and options.

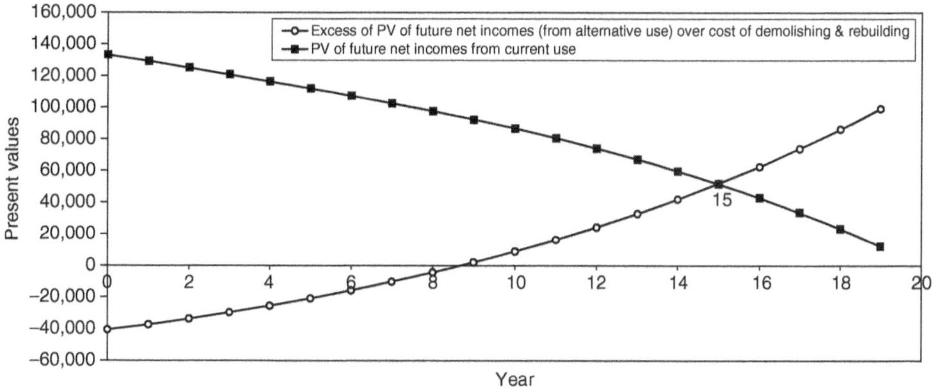

Figure 5.9 A property's economic life versus physical life. In this example, it makes economic sense to redevelop the site at the 15th year of the property's remaining lifespan of about 20 years.

The most common users of derivatives are financial institutions and property companies who wish for a way to protect (or 'hedge') themselves from the risk they are exposed to when they hold a non-derivative instrument, or who wish to achieve greater liquidity. As RE derivatives and options are beyond the scope of this book, interested readers should consult EDHEC (2007), FTSE (2008), and Mauboussin (1999), as well as any finance book that discusses such instruments.

Summary of main points

1 Commercial RE, or commercial property (CP), is primarily income-earning RE.
2 In terms of investment styles, CP is categorized into core, core+, value-added, and opportunistic (cf. Table 5.2).
3 Collective investment vehicles allow indirect investment in CP. Such vehicles can be listed or unlisted, open-ended or closed-ended, tax-transparent or not, authorized or unauthorized (cf. Figure 5.2).
4 CP can also be categorized into private equity RE (involving both direct and indirect investment in RE) and public equity RE (cf. Figure 5.2).
5 RE differs from investment in stocks or bonds along a number of dimensions (cf. Table 5.3).
6 A portfolio approach to RE (or any other investment) is best, as the risk of any individual asset can be reduced when that asset is held together with others. This is because returns on individual assets frequently have less than perfect positive correlation, or (less frequently) even have negative correlation, with returns on other assets.
7 As direct property investments come in lumps, and are impossible to subdivide, a truly efficient frontier (in a portfolio sense) that involves direct property may be difficult to construct. The problem is much mitigated if indirect property investments (like shares into property companies) are considered.
8 There is evidence that correlations between asset returns tend to change over time. There also seems to be correlation asymmetry between particular asset returns and the market (i.e., correlations are not the same when markets go up and when they go down).

9 The basic property valuation formula is value = income/cap rate. Especially for income properties, the dominant valuation method is the discounted cash flow (DCF) technique.
10 The NPV and the IRR are the dominant methods of investment appraisal. Appraisal is about deciding whether a particular investment should be undertaken or not.
11 Especially important for CP valuation are the concepts of equivalent yield and equated yield.
12 The capitalization rate (cap rate) used in the basic valuation formula is in the nature of a required rate of return (RRR). It is made up of expected inflation, a risk premium, a recapture premium, and a real return.
13 There is a cap rate cycle, which tends to run counter to the RE cycle (the recurrent ups and downs in the level of rents).
14 The physical life of a property differs from its economic life.
15 Yields:

- *Initial yield* (or *all-risks yield*) is the first discount factor, i.e., the capitalization rate, in the formula for the PV of a property, when the latter is subject to rent growth only once, at time of next rent review.
- *Reversionary yield* is the second discount factor in the above formula, which takes into account the reversion of the lease rent to market rent.
- *Equivalent yield* (EvY) is the discount rate i that equates the PV of the aforementioned income streams to the market price (if it is known) of the property.
- *Equated yield* (EtY) is the discount rate $i$that equates the PV of a property to the market price (if it is known) of it, when the latter is subject to constant rent growth, with rent reviews every m years.

Review questions and exercises

1 Be sure you understand the meaning of the following terms:

'Invested', 'investible', and 'total' commercial RE
'Core', 'core+', 'value-added', and 'opportunistic' RE
Staggered lease
Repositioning
Listed versus unlisted and authorized versus unauthorized collective investment schemes
PUT and REIT
Tax transparency versus RE market transparency
Liquidity of a RE asset
Correlation between assets
Discounted cash flow (DCF) valuation technique
NPV and IRR
Initial yield, all-risks yield, reversionary yield
Equivalent yield, equated yield
Lease rent versus market rent
Capitalization rate
The 'band-of-investment' method
Mortgage constant
Rent reversion

2 Use the Internet to find information that will allow you to run a full comparison of UK REITs, UK property unit trusts (authorized and unauthorized), and limited partnerships.

3 Prepare a report describing the extent to which UK property investment vehicles are or are not tax-transparent, and compare them in this regard with US listed public REITs, Australian A-REITs, and French SIICs.
4 Have a look at Table 5.7. Construct a correlation matrix between the asset classes (include RPI too). Discuss your results.
5 Suppose an investor wants to consider forming a portfolio consisting of the six UK asset classes epitomized in Table 5.8, and another set of assets consisting of equal shares in US and Finnish property, as shown in Table 5.4 (ignore the fact that the two tables show returns from slightly different time periods). Offer the investor an 'efficient' frontier delineating his or her choices between combinations of the 'six' and 'USA + Finland'.
6 In Table 5.8, we show the mean and standard deviation of the returns on a portfolio made of (equal weights of) the six asset classes of Table 5.5 to be 6.74 per cent and 6.68 per cent, respectively. Using Equations (5.3) and (5.4), confirm this.
7 Assume that the purchase price of a property is £6,500,000. An investor considers financing it with 30 per cent own funds and 70 per cent debt. The debt terms offered are 7 per cent interest rate (fixed), annual repayment, 25-year maturity. The investor's time horizon is also 25 years, and he or she calculates an annual NOI of £500,000 over that period, based on current market rent (for simplicity, assume no reversions). Calculate the mortgage constant and the equity cap rate, and then the overall cap rate for this investment. What is the technique used called?
8 (Continuing from 7.) Now assume that in 25 years the investor plans to sell the property, that the NOI, still a function of market rent, will have gone up to £1,500,000, and that this investor's RRR is 12 per cent over his or her given time horizon, and 14 per cent thereafter. Appraise this investment. If you do not assess it as profitable, (a) what should the (perpetual) NOI be after the 25th year for this investment to be profitable and (b) at what rate should the NOI of £500,000 be growing over 25 years in order to guarantee achievement of the profitable future NOI?
9 Using spreadsheet software, construct an analysis of physical versus economic life for a property that has an expected remaining lifespan of 20 years. Make your own assumptions regarding future NOI from this property as well as from an alternative property that could be erected in the site – but be sure to assume a declining PV of the future NOI stream from the existing property, and a rising PV (taking estimates of the future cost of demolition and rebuilding also into account) for NOIs from the alternative. Remember that the expected physical life of the alternative should be longer than 20 years. Come up with appropriate figures to justify a time to redevelop the site that is less than 20 years. Feel free to use any reasonable cap and inflation rate(s).

Hints:

- You do not have to assume a declining *nominal* NOI from the existing property to do the analysis; in fact, you could make this exercise more fruitful and realistic by assuming a *rising* nominal NOI.
- For simplicity, you could assume that on any particular year the NOI from the alternative is earned in perpetuity – but, of course, on any particular year the alternative is expected to command a higher *real* NOI than in the year before.

6 Demand for office–retail–industrial space

Main sections

Having gone through this chapter, a student should be able to

1 List and discuss the main drivers of demand for office, retail, and industrial space.
2 Illustrate McDonald's model of office space demand.
3 Define and contrast the concepts of natural and actual vacancy rates, and explain why a 'natural vacancy rate' (NVR) exists at all.
4 Explain the significance of situations when the actual vacancy rate deviates from the natural vacancy rate, and define 'net absorption'.
5 List factors that determine the NVR; define 'pre-letting' and list its benefits and drawbacks for both occupier and developer; define 'office class'.
6 Explain the significance for the office rental cycle of changes in the NVR, and, given appropriate data, calculate the time of adjustment in an office market for different NVRs.
7 Describe the steps involved in preparing a basic analysis of an office market.
8 Define the trade area concept, list methods for its determination, and explain how trade area determination affects demand for retail space.
9 Apply the checklist method and various gravity models on the problem of trade area determination.
10 Evaluate the pros and cons of Reilly's, the break-point, and Huff's models.
11 List factors that must be taken into account when selecting industrial space.
12 Explain why the industrial property sector is the least cyclical of all property sectors.
13 List important drivers of industrial RE demand, and justify the increasing popularity of manufacturing output as an explanatory variable in relevant models.

6.1 Demand for office space

Commercial RE demand has a certain peculiarity that distinguishes it from (non-commercial) residential RE demand: it is not only about space to occupy (so it does not come only from prospective users), but is also about vacant space, coming from landlords themselves.

6.1.1 Vacant space–occupied space

Landlords of commercial RE end up holding vacant space for a number of reasons (in practice this applies mostly to office or apartment property):

1 It usually takes time to find a new tenant, so stock will be vacant between lettings or until a first tenant (in the case of newly built properties) arrives. This is referred to as 'frictional vacancy' (McCartney, 2010: 2).
2 As a special case of 'frictional vacancy', the waiting may involve a search for appropriate tenants, for example reliable ones (McDonald, 2000: 57), and then it will be longer than if the search were for just any tenant.
3 Landlords may be waiting for better conditions (chiefly, higher rents) before they let out stock, even though they could secure tenants at the going rent if they so wished. McCartney (2010: 6) calls this the 'landlords' propensity to hold vacant space'.

The so-called 'natural vacancy rate' (NVR) expresses the proportion of vacant stock (due to the three factors mentioned) into total available stock (more on NVR below).

In what follows, we shall present and analyse McDonald's (2000) model of commercial RE demand that explicitly incorporates demand for vacant space, in addition to demand for occupied space. The focus is on office space.

Figure 6.1 is a typical demand–supply diagram, with net rent (i.e., gross rent minus operating expenses) on the vertical axis and occupied space in square units on the horizontal axis. The demand and supply lines intersect, indicating the equilibrium net rent that clears the market for occupied space. The numerical calculations are shown in Table 6.1, where $R_d = 110 - 4Q$ and $R_s = -40 + 7Q$.

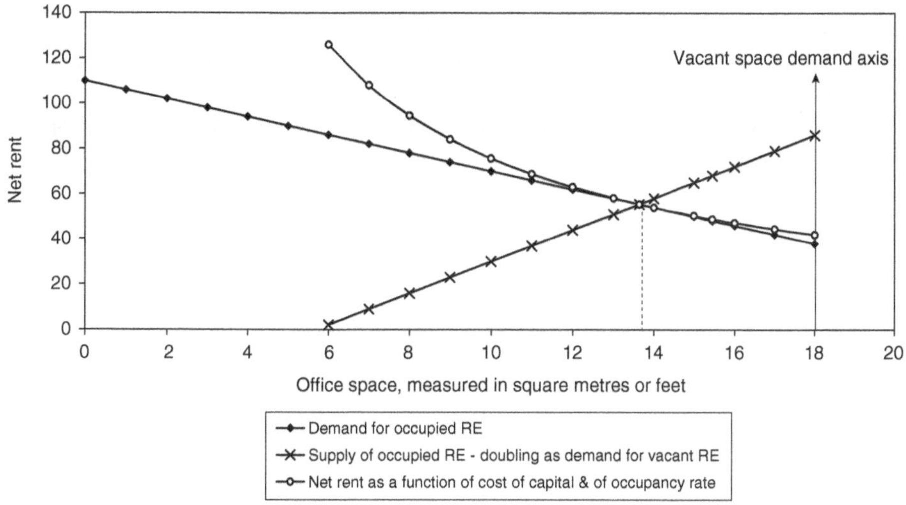

Figure 6.1 Commercial RE market in long-run equilibrium, showing demand for vacant space.

Table 6.1 Spreadsheet calculations related to Figure 6.1

Units of space	*Rent offered by tenants (i.e., demand line)*	*Rent asked by landlords (i.e., supply line)*	*Rent as a function of cost of capital and occupancy rate*
7	82	9	108
8	78	16	95
9	74	23	84
10	70	30	76
11	66	37	69
12	62	44	63
13	58	51	58
13.636	**55.455**	**55.455**	**55.455**
14	54	58	54
15	50	65	50
16	46	72	47
17	42	79	44
18	38	86	42
19	34	93	40
20	30	100	38

But there are two novelties in Figure 6.1. First, there is a vertical line set at 18 units of space. This is supposed to indicate the total amount of available space, occupied and vacant. It is a copy of the diagram's net rent axis on the left, only it is set at 18 units of space. Looked at this way, the supply line in the diagram doubles as the landlords' demand line for vacant space. This is easily seen if we consider the equilibrium quantity of occupied space. The difference between this quantity and total space, set at 18 units, is by definition vacant space. In Figure 6.1, this difference is the distance between the vertical line set at 18 units of space and the vertical broken line.

Then there is a curve, which in this instance is deliberately drawn so that it is tangent to the demand line at the equilibrium point. (It does not have to be a tangent to the demand line, though; the requirement for long-run equilibrium is that the curve must go through the intersection of the demand and supply lines. We shall see why in a moment.) This curve shows net rent as a function of the ratio of the cost of capital to the occupancy rate, which is the ratio of occupied space to all available space. Alternatively put, net rent equals the capital cost of all space divided by occupied space, i.e., the average cost of capital per unit of occupied space.

Thus, if R = net rent, C = cost of capital (per unit of floor space), S = all space, Q = occupied space, and V = vacant space, then

$$q = \text{occupancy rate} = \frac{Q}{S},$$

$$v = \text{vacancy rate} = \frac{V}{S},$$

$$q + v = 1,$$

and

$$R = \frac{C}{q} = \frac{CS}{Q}.$$

Explanation: C, the cost of capital, is a function of the cost of construction, a rate of return (which also serves as a discount rate), and the depreciation rate of the stock. Without going into details about the precise functional form,[1] suffice it to say that at long-run equilibrium, the rent R, adjusted for the actually occupied stock, must be equal to C.

What does 'adjusted for the actually occupied stock' mean? Suppose that there are 100 units of floor space and that only 80 are occupied. If the rent those 80 units yield is £12 per unit, then the *per unit* rent from all units is $(80/100)12 = £9.6$.

And why must R be equal to C at equilibrium? Because if $R > C$, there is an incentive to build more floor space, and if $R < C$, there is an incentive not to replace stock that wears out (i.e., depreciates).

Thus, at equilibrium, $qR = C$, or

$$R = \frac{C}{q} = \frac{CS}{Q},$$

as shown above, and for long-run equilibrium this must hold at the point of intersection of the demand and supply lines. The vacancy rate corresponding to that equilibrium is called the *natural vacancy rate* (NVR), i.e., the vacancy rate at which there is no incentive to change the stock of floor space. In Figure 6.1, the NVR is $(18 - 13.636)/18 = 24.2$ per cent (unrealistically high, but it helps make Figure 6.1 easier to see in detail).

Now, if there is a market disturbance – say, an upward shift in the demand for occupied space – there will be a new equilibrium between demand for, and supply of, occupied space, but because in this situation the new rent is higher than C/q, there will be an incentive to produce more floor space (see Figure 6.2).

Put differently, an incentive to change the quantity of space supplied exists whenever there is a gap between the natural and the actual vacancy rates (Crone, 1989). The 'rule' is simple:

1 If NVR > actual vacancy rate, rents rise and there is more net building. The mechanism involved works as follows. There is, say, a disequilibrating upward shift in demand for occupied space like the one shown in Figure 6.2. This in turn causes (a) the actual

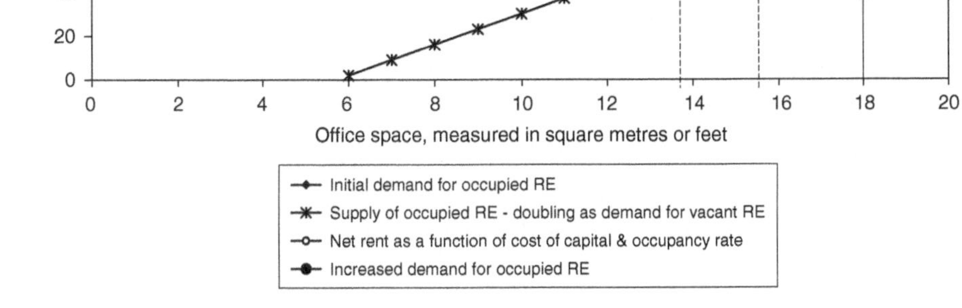

Figure 6.2 Commercial RE market after a deviation of the actual vacancy rate from the natural vacancy rate.

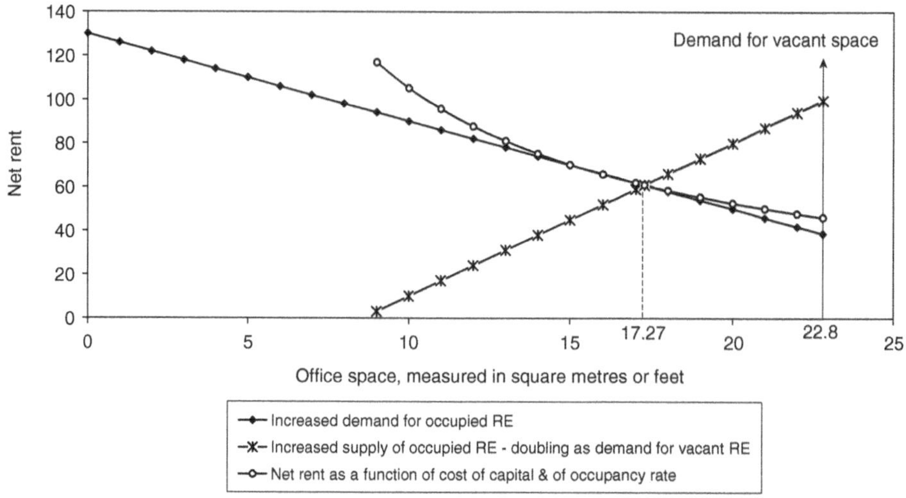

Figure 6.3 Commercial RE market after re-establishment of long-run equilibrium (where $R_d = R_s = CS/Q$, NVR = actual vacancy rate).

occupancy rate to rise – i.e., the actual vacancy rate to drop – and (b) rents to rise. Eventually, however, rents fall (precisely because the property stock has expanded through more net building), bringing the actual vacancy rate in line with NVR, and re-establishing equilibrium (see Figure 6.3) at the point where $R = CS/Q = R_d = R_s$. (Note that, at the new equilibrium, the absolute number of vacancies is not the same as before; rather, the natural vacancy *rate* coincides again with the actual vacancy *rate*.)

2 If NVR < actual vacancy rate, rents drop and there is less building. Rents eventually rise (through less building, thus allowing depreciation to take its toll of the available stock), again bringing the actual vacancy rate in line with NVR.

Figure 6.3 shows the 'final' long-run adjustment, as described above. In short, what has happened is this:

- Initial long-run equilibrium (Figure 6.1):

  space $S = 18$, $Q_d = Q_s = 13.6$ at a rent of 55.45 equal to SC/Q, and actual vacancy rate $= (18 - 13.6)/18 = 24.2$ per cent = NVR.

- Disequilibrium situation (Figure 6.2):

  space $S = 18$, demand increases, $Q_d = Q_s = 15.45$ at a rent of $68.18 \neq SC/Q$, and actual vacancy rate $= (18 - 15.45)/18 = 14.2$ per cent $\neq$ NVR.

- New long-run equilibrium (Figure 6.3):

  space $S = 22.8$, supply increases in response to drop in actual vacancy rate, $Q_d = Q_s = 17.27$ at a rent of $60.91 = SC/Q$, and actual vacancy rate $= (22.8 - 17.27)/22.8 = 24.2$ per cent = NVR.

Let us investigate mathematically the model just described.

Our task is to develop formulas that express rent, occupied space, and vacant space as functions of the demand for both occupied and vacant space; then extend the model to the long-run by bringing in the $R = C/q$ equilibrium condition.

6.1.2 Mathematical modelling of the short term

To avoid confusion, it is perhaps best to base our modelling on Figure 6.1. Let us consider the following equations:

$$\text{demand line:}\quad R_d = 110 - 4Q = a - bQ,$$

$$\text{supply line:}\quad R_s = -40 + 7Q = c + dQ.$$

Expressing Q as a function of R yields

$$\text{demand line:}\quad Q_d = 27.5 - \frac{1}{4}R = \frac{a}{b} - \frac{1}{b}R = \kappa - \lambda R,$$

$$\text{supply line:}\quad Q_s = 5.714 + \frac{1}{7}R = -\frac{c}{d} + \frac{1}{d}R = \theta + \eta R.$$

Now, the supply line of occupied space $R_s = f(Q) = -40 + 7\,(Q)$ doubles as the demand line for vacant space, but to express the latter mathematically we need its vertical intercept, treating the vertical line set at 18 units of space (i.e., all available space) as the rent axis for the vacant space demand line. (Its slope is the opposite of the slope of the corresponding supply line, i.e., -7.) To find the vertical intercept, we work as follows:

$$R_s = -40 + 7Q;\ \text{ if } Q = 18,\ \text{ then } R_s = -40 + 7(18) = 86 \Rightarrow R_v = 86 - 7V,$$

where R_v = rent for vacant space and V = quantity of vacant space; with a little rearrangement, this gives

$$V = 12.2857 - \frac{1}{7}R_v = V_o - \eta R_v.$$

We thus have two demand equations to work with:

$$Q_d = 27.5 - \frac{1}{4}R \quad\text{and}\quad V = 12.2857 - \frac{1}{7}R_v.$$

We also know that $S = Q + V \Rightarrow V = S - Q$. Substituting, we get

$$Q_d = 27.5 - \frac{1}{4}R \quad\text{and}\quad S - Q = 12.2857 - \frac{1}{7}R_v.$$

At equilibrium, $Q_d = Q$ and $R = R_v$. Solving the above two-equation system for R yields

$$R = \frac{18 - 12.2857 - 27.5}{-1/4 - 1/7} = 55.4545 = \frac{S - V_o - \kappa}{-\lambda - \eta} = \frac{V_o + \kappa - S}{\lambda + \eta}.$$

This says that rent is the ratio of the sum of the vertical intercepts of the demands for vacant space and for occupied space minus total space to the sum of the slopes of the two demand equations. Notice that the number found, 55.4545, is the equilibrium rent shown in Table 6.1.

Knowing R, it is a small matter to find expressions for Q and V:

$$Q = \kappa - \lambda R = \kappa - \lambda \frac{V_o + \kappa - S}{\lambda + \eta} = \frac{\kappa\eta + \lambda(S - V_o)}{\lambda + \eta},$$

i.e., the demand function for occupied space;

$$V = V_o - \eta R = V_o - \eta \frac{V_o + \kappa - S}{\lambda + \eta} = \frac{\lambda V_o + \eta(S - \kappa)}{\lambda + \eta},$$

i.e., the demand function for vacant space. Solving for Q, we get

$$Q = \frac{27.5(1/7) + (1/4)(18 - 12.2857)}{1/4 + 1/7} = 13.636,$$

which is exactly the equilibrium amount of occupied space shown in Table 6.1. Solving for V, we get

$$V = \frac{(1/4)(12.2857) + (1/7)(18 - 27.5)}{1/4 + 1/7} = 4.3636,$$

which if added to 13.636 gives 18, i.e., all available space.

A number of conclusions follow:

$$\frac{\partial R}{\partial S} = -\frac{1}{\lambda + \eta} = \text{the partial derivative of rent with respect to all space } S, \quad (6.1)$$

$$\frac{\partial Q}{\partial S} = \frac{\lambda}{\lambda + \eta} = \text{the partial derivative of occupied space with respect to } S, \quad (6.2)$$

$$\frac{\partial V}{\partial S} = \frac{\eta}{\lambda + \eta} = \text{the partial derivative of vacant space with respect to } S, \quad (6.3)$$

$$\frac{\partial Q}{\partial S} + \frac{\partial V}{\partial S} = 1 \text{ (to be expected, since } Q + V = S), \quad (6.4)$$

$$\frac{d(Q/S)}{dS} = \frac{(dQ/dS)S - Q}{S^2} = \frac{dQ/dS}{S} - \frac{Q}{S^2} = \frac{1}{S}\left(\frac{dQ}{dS} - \frac{Q}{S}\right) = \frac{1}{S}\left(\frac{dQ}{dS} - q\right)$$

$$= \text{the derivative of the occupancy rate with respect to } S. \quad (6.5)$$

And since

$$\frac{dQ}{dS} = \frac{\lambda}{\lambda + \eta},$$

it follows that

$$\frac{d(Q/S)}{dS} = \frac{1}{S}\left(\frac{\lambda}{\lambda + \eta} - q\right). \quad (6.6)$$

The result (6.6) means that a rise in S will cause the occupancy rate to fall only if the marginal change in occupied space is less than the initial occupancy rate.

6.1.3 Mathematical modelling of the long term

The difference between the short- and the long-term equilibrium is in the inclusion of the cost of capital in the mathematical expression for long-term equilibrium. The reason, as already said, is that in the long run there is no incentive to change the stock of capital (the amount of floor space), a situation that is secured if the cost of capital C is equal to net rent (adjusted for the occupancy rate). Thus, at equilibrium,

$$qR = C \Rightarrow \frac{Q}{S}R = C \Rightarrow S = \frac{QR}{C} \Rightarrow R = \frac{SC}{Q}$$

Our task is to find an expression for long-term R by incorporating C into the demand functions for occupied and for vacant space, as shown in 6.1.1 and Figure 6.1. This is done as follows:

$V = S - Q$, i.e., vacant space is the difference between all space and occupied space,

$V = V_o - \eta R$, i.e., the demand function for vacant space,

$Q = \kappa - \lambda R$, i.e., the demand function for occupied space.

Therefore,

$$S - Q = \frac{QR}{C} - Q = Q\left(\frac{R}{C} - 1\right) = V_o - \eta R \Rightarrow (\kappa - \lambda R)\left(\frac{R}{C} - 1\right) = V_o - \eta R \Rightarrow$$

$$\Rightarrow -\frac{\lambda R^2}{C} + R\left(\lambda + \eta + \frac{\kappa}{C}\right) - (\kappa + V_o) = 0$$

This is a quadratic equation (see Section 2.1.3), whose solution is

$$R = \frac{-\left(\lambda + \eta + \frac{\kappa}{C}\right) \pm \sqrt{\left(\lambda + \eta + \frac{\kappa}{C}\right)^2 - 4\left(-\frac{\lambda}{C}\right)[-(\kappa + V_o)]}}{2\left(-\frac{\lambda}{C}\right)}. \tag{6.7}$$

Application

We know the values of all the parameters in (6.7) but for C. However, we also know that in long-term equilibrium,

$$\frac{Q}{S}R = C \Rightarrow \frac{13.636}{18}(55.45) = C = 42.01.$$

Plugging this into (6.7) then gives

$$R = 55.45 \quad \text{or} \quad R = 120.6$$

But $R = 120.6$ is rejected because at this level of rent the quantity of occupied space demanded is not equal to the quantity of occupied space supplied (cf. Table 6.1).

6.1.4 A disturbance and re-establishment of equilibrium

Let us now build on the numerical example of Figure 6.1 and Table 6.1 to see what will happen if there is a disturbance in this market. Let us assume an increase in demand for occupied space Q (see Figure 6.2), so that the market is now described by the following equations:

$$R_d = 130 - 4Q \text{ (rather than } 110 - 4Q\text{)},$$

$$R_s = -40 + 7Q.$$

It follows that the equilibrium occupied space $Q_e = 15.45$ and the equilibrium rent $R_e = 68.18$. (Remember that total space S is still 18.)

This, however, is an unstable situation, for two reasons:

(a) The actual vacancy rate is now = (total space – occupied space)/total space = $(S - Q_e)/S = (18 - 15.45)/18 = 14.1$ per cent, i.e., less than the NVR of 24.2 per cent that was the case before the disturbance.
(b) The cost of capital C is not consistent with the new (short-run) equilibrium, as $C = 42.01 \neq (68.18)(15.45)/18$. (Remember that, at long-run equilibrium, $C = R_eQ_e/S$.)

The instability is resolved through an increase in supply (in response to the drop in the actual vacancy rate and the concomitant rise in expected rent), which causes the total space S to increase (see Figure 6.3). To cut a long story short, let us just say that the increase in supply is such that we now have

$$R_d = 130 - 4Q,$$

$$R_s = -60 + 7Q \text{ (rather than } -40 + 7Q\text{)}$$

As a result, $Q_e = 17.27$ and $R_e = 60.91$. For the actual vacancy rate to become equal again to the NVR, it must be equal to $(S - Q_e)/S = 24.2$ per cent; therefore total space S must be equal to $17.27/(1 - 0.242) = 22.8$.

At this level of total space, the cost of capital C is equal to $R_eQ_e/S = 46.14$, which is consistent with the new equilibrium. The economic rationale for the increase in C is that the increase in supply has raised the demand for funds on the part of developers. Notice that if S ends up being more than 22.8, the actual vacancy rate will be more than 24.2 per cent, causing expected rent to fall, and, ultimately, supply to shrink. The process is the basis for empirically observed office rental cycles centred around the NVR.

6.1.5 The office rental cycle and the NVR

Rents and prices (and building activity) in property markets move in 'cycles' (cf. Figure 2.8 and Figures 8.9 and 8.10) (Kummerow and Quaddus, 1998; Wheaton, 1999; Mueller, 1999; Hendershott et al., 2008; CBRE 2010Q3; JLL 2010Q4). In fact, Pyhrr et al. (1997: 17) have gone as far as to assert that 'the economic and real estate literature demonstrates that economic factors are cyclical, cash flow variables (rents, vacancies, capitalization rates) are cyclical and real estate performance (rates of return) is cyclical at the national and regional levels.' The 'cycles' differ in frequency and amplitude between property sectors, from one historic period to another, and across places. They may be visible in terms of levels (i.e., absolute

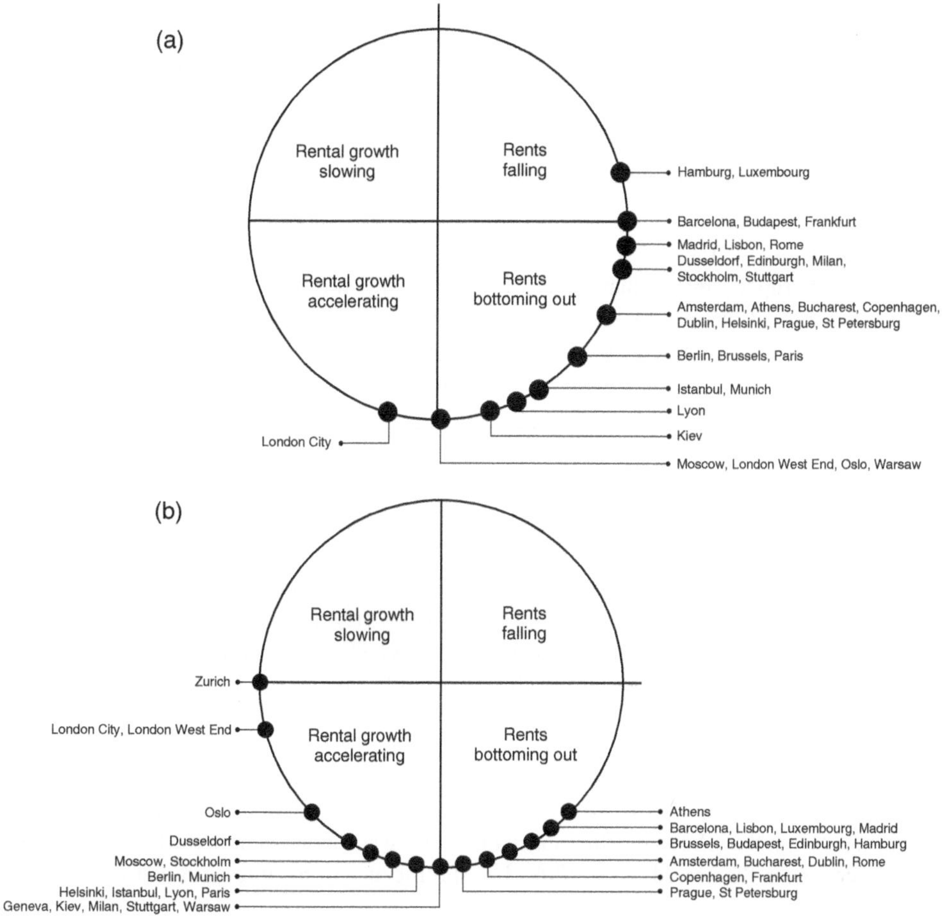

Figure 6.4 The European Office Property Clock (Source: Jones Lang LaSalle, with permission and thanks.) (A) First quarter of 2010 (B) Fourth quarter of 2010.

quantities expressed in real terms), but are usually more obvious in terms of differences (i.e., the percentage differences of the absolute quantities from one period to the next). Rental cycles should not come as a surprise, because the economy as a whole behaves 'cyclically' (i.e., it registers a so-called 'trade' or 'business' cycle pattern) – which is perhaps why Jones Lang LaSalle, a property firm, uses the clock metaphor to show the way office market rents in various European cities behave during the year (see Figure 6.4).

An interesting question for research is to what extent the 'cycles' in various property sectors lead or lag the overall 'trade' cycle. Most probably, there is no definitive answer to this question, as different places or times are characterized by different causalities, as, for example, between GDP and construction investment (cf. Chapter 3). Another question is the extent and ways in which a property cycle in one place and/or one property sector affects a property cycle elsewhere – hence the relatively recent interest in global RE cycles (Pyhrr et al., 1999), the mechanism for which is not yet clearly understood but is thought to relate to the emergence of closer links between capital and RE markets, and greater capital mobility, roughly since 1985 (Renaud, 1997; Hoffmann and Nitschka, 2010). A third question however, is about sector-specific factors that cause property 'cycles' endogenously, quite apart, that is, from any exogenous influences originating from a 'trade' cycle.

Box 6.1 presents the main classes of factors that can cause property cycles.

Box 6.1 General factors responsible for property rental and building cycles

1 The economy, through the 'trade' cycle.
2 Other property cycles that affect a given property sector.
3 Any and all factors that cause shifts in the demand for space of a particular kind and that are generated from within the sector itself, leading to rent adjustments and/or over-optimistic/over-pessimistic building activity.

In Chapter 8, we examine the issue of RE cycles in terms of a rather general model that attaches a lot of importance to private developers becoming overly optimistic or pessimistic on the basis of recent property price patterns. If optimistic, they build a lot; if pessimistic, the opposite. Either way, the general model presented in Chapter 8 shows the mathematical conditions for re-establishment of equilibrium in a property market after a price change in a real estate sector (due to a demand shift) causes deviation from an assumed initial equilibrium. In the case of commercial property markets, this equilibrium has a name: the natural vacancy rate (NVR).

But what if the NVR itself changes over time? Following McCartney (2010), we shall investigate this issue, taking office space as an example. The issue is important because if the NVR changes, the characteristics of the property cycle change also. For example, McCartney (2010) found that the NVR for office space in Dublin was 5.2 per cent in the period 1978–98 and 15 per cent in the period 1999–2009. The significance of his finding is as follows:

- Given the fundamental proposition that a market tends to return to equilibrium after a disturbance, the return to equilibrium will take longer, following a price shock, if the NVR is low (in comparison with the actual vacancy rate established after the price shock) than if the NVR is high and closer to the established actual vacancy rate. And if the NVR changes between two periods, the same price shock, resulting in the same post-shock actual vacancy rate, will take different amounts of time to unwind until NVR = actual vacancy rate. In other words, changes in the NVR do not cause property cycles, but can change the speed of adjustment implicit in a given cycle.

In the case of Dublin in 2010 (and abstracting from wider economy influences) the amount of time to adjustment would be 8 years if the NVR were still 7 per cent (as industry practitioners maintained, in contrast to McCartney's finding of 5.2 per cent for the 1978–98 period), and only 4 years if the NVR had actually jumped to 15 per cent in the 1999–2009 period.[2]

These figures were arrived at on the basis of the following calculation (McCartney, 2010: 15):

- Dublin office stock in 2010 = 3.5 million square metres;
- vacant space = 800 thousand square metres, or 23 per cent of stock;

- an NVR of 7 per cent means 245 thousand square metres (= 0.07 × 3.5 million);
- therefore, 'overhang' = 555 thousand square metres (= 800 – 245);
- net absorption of office space[3] (on the basis of long-term historic data) = 69 thousand square metres per annum;
- therefore, time (in years) in which the 'overhang' will be absorbed = 8;
- but if NVR = 15 per cent, absorption time = 4.

In this example, absorption (i.e., a reduction in the number of vacant properties) will take place because the relatively low rents (since NVR < actual vacancy rate) will cause less building, and ultimately net depreciation of the stock. The point is that the downward phase of the rental cycle should finish more quickly if NVR is 15 per cent than if it is 7 per cent.

So what could change the NVR? Table 6.2 presents a list of the factors that affect it.

Explanations

1 The length of the lease and break-options. Short leases imply higher tenant turnover, i.e., more tenants arrive – and go – in a given time span than otherwise. In turn, the prevalence of short leases means that the market has digested the possibility that the chances of a mismatch between property and tenant characteristics are high. A perennial mismatch of this type, however, increases the probability that, *ceteris paribus*, at any one time, the number of vacancies will be relatively large – hence the probability of a high NVR.

2 Break-options. These are clauses in lease contracts that allow for one or both of the parties involved (tenant and landlord) to terminate the lease before time, under certain conditions. If break-options are utilized infrequently and/or are costly to invoke, then both landlord and tenant have an incentive to search[4] for the right tenant or property more diligently than otherwise, before they commit themselves. Because of the longer search time and higher costs involved (in other words, because of the extra friction in the property market), the number of vacancies will be larger than otherwise. The result, again, is a high NVR.

3 Rate of new construction. High rates of (speculative) new construction tend to create more space than can be quickly sold or rented (especially if the price elasticity of supply is high and if prospective buyers or tenants are not too particular about the characteristics of the built properties). This amounts to a high NVR.

4 GNP (or GDP) growth. This factor works by first affecting positively speculative development (through the formation of positive rental growth expectations on the part of speculative developers).

5 Average lot size. A frequent activity in commercial RE markets is pre-letting. This is an agreement between a potential tenant and a developer to lease a building whose construction has not begun yet (Morley et al., 2007: 2). However, one of the advantages a prospective tenant has through pre-letting (see Table 6.3) is access to a building specifically designed to accommodate their needs (Morley et al., 2007: 2) – or a building over whose design the prospective tenant can at least exercise a lot of influence. Such buildings can be costly, and also riskier, to make, compared with generic buildings. They are better justified economically if they are built to a large scale – a typical prerequisite for which is a large lot. Therefore, where the average lot size is small, pre-lets are fewer than otherwise – which implies (a) that more buildings will be let *after* they are completed, (b) a longer average waiting period before newly constructed vacant buildings are taken, and (c) a higher NVR.

Table 6.2 Factors expected to influence the NVR

A. Factors influencing friction

	Variable	*Expected influence*	*Reason*
1	Lease length	Shorter leases → higher NVR	Higher tenant turnover
2	Break-options	Infrequent and/or costly → higher NVR	Higher frictional vacancies
3	Rate of new construction	More completions → higher NVR	More speculative development
4	GNP (or GDP) growth	Higher growth → higher NVR	Higher rent expectations, more speculative development
5	Average lot size	Smaller tenant requirements → higher NVR	Smaller lots difficult to pre-let; therefore low average lot size → more speculative development
6	Elasticity of supply	More elastic supply → higher NVR	More speculative development
7	Real interest rates	Lower rates → higher NVR	Low rates encourage speculative development

B. Factors influencing landlords' propensity to hold vacant space

	Variable	*Expected influence*	*Reason*
8	Heterogeneity of occupier and office stock	More heterogeneity → higher NVR	Higher expected returns to search activity
9	GNP (or GDP) growth	Higher growth → higher NVR	Positive rent expectations; therefore 'lock-in' imposes higher expected opportunity cost
10	Revisions mechanism	If indexation → higher NVR	'Lock-in' imposes higher expected opportunity cost where indexation is used
11	Revisions frequency	Lower frequency → higher NVR	'Lock-in' imposes higher expected opportunity cost where revisions are infrequent
12	Real interest rates	Lower rates → higher NVR	Low rates reduce cost of holding vacant space

Adapted from McCartney (2010), with permission and thanks.

6 Elasticity of supply. Again, this works by first affecting positively speculative development.
7 Real interest rates. Low rates mean that a developer can finance a project more cheaply, so more speculative development will be undertaken, leading to a relatively high NVR, as explained above.
8 Heterogeneity of occupier and office stock. If market agents perceive a high potential for a mismatch between tenant and property characteristics, the value of a longer search time to eliminate such a mismatch increases. Hence there will normally be more vacant

Table 6.3 Pre-letting: benefits and drawbacks

For occupiers	
Potential benefits	*Potential drawbacks*
1 It is a solution where an available and suitable (usually office) building has not been found in a desired area.	1 Risk that the building will not be delivered on time or meet expectations.
2 Better financial terms, like free-rent periods, deferred rents, or cover of fit-out costs.	2 Difficulty in sub-letting if the building is too bespoke.
3 Creation of a bespoke building, tailor-made to the prospective occupier's business requirements (e.g., regarding design, layout, size, facilities)	3 Longer lease.
For developers	
Potential benefits	*Potential drawbacks*
1 Risk reduction.	1 Profit may be less than in the absence of pre-letting.
2 Improved covenant strength. (Covenant means binding agreement or contract.)	2 Developer cannot take advantage of rising rental values during construction (if that is the case).
3 Better capital value (because a pre-let shows that the project in question has the capacity to generate demand even before completion).	
4 Quicker and cheaper bank finance.	
5 A pre-let helps kick-start large projects (because it allows better access to bank finance).	
6 A pre-let may facilitate forward sales to investors. (A forward sale involves getting paid now, but delivering the good(s) later.)	

(Adapted from Morley et al. (2007), with permission and thanks.)

properties around than otherwise, hence a higher NVR. (The value of search would increase further still if break-options are in addition infrequent and/or costly to invoke.) Longer search times can also stem from the physical geography of a city, with 'spread-out' cities (e.g., in North America as opposed to Europe) damping the need to occupy space at a specific location, and enabling search over a wider area – hence a higher NVR in the USA than in Europe (PRUPIM Research, 2010).

9 GNP (or GDP) growth. If such growth creates expectations of higher rents in the future, landlords will be averse to getting locked in a particular contract now. Vacancies will increase in expectation of more lucrative deals, and, if growth looks as if it is going to be long term, the NVR should rise.

10 Revisions mechanism. Office rents are subject to revision during an ongoing lease (the process is called 'rent escalation'). Revisions usually happen through market review or through indexation. (Table 6.5 shows 22 country examples from 2009.) A question arises as to which method allows real rents to increase the most during a lease. The answer hinges on a comparison of expected general with rent inflation. If expected rent inflation

Table 6.4 Office rent escalations in a sample of countries

Country	*Method of office rent escalation*
Australia	Rents usually reviewed every 2 years, or annually, as negotiated. They may increase by a fixed percentage, inflation rate (CPI), or a market review. Most rent reviews are 'upward only'.
Brazil	Usually, annually to a local price index known as IGPM.
Canada	Leases may include negotiated increases over the lease term.
China	Rent generally fixed during lease term for leases < 5 years. For longer-term leases, rent sometimes escalates at an agreed rate.
France	French commercial leases are for 3, 6, or 9 years, with the tenant having the right to renew. Rents indexed most commonly annually to the Cost of Construction Index, with a market review at the end of the 9th year.
Germany	The law allows landlords to escalate rent by indexation only for leases that allow a tenant to remain for 10 years or more, or for 5-year leases that include a tenant's option to renew for 5 more years.
Greece	Usually, annually to CPI plus 1%.
India	In most cases rent escalation is pre-fixed, typically 15–20% every 3 years.
Ireland	Rents usually reviewed every 5 years to the open market rental value and only upwards.
Israel	Rent normally indexed to CPI.
Japan	Rent escalation is negotiable. Typically, landlords attempt to raise rents to cover increases in the land tax, building tax or cost of living. Rent is not indexed.
New Zealand	Rent reviews every 2 or 3 years, depending on lease length.
Norway	Rent indexed annually to 100% or 80% of CPI.
Poland	Annual indexation to US or Euro-Zone CPI.
Portugal	Annually to 75–100% of CPI.
Spain	Annually to CPI, with open market review every 3-5 years.
Russia	Rents typically fixed for the lease term. Rent indexation applies from the 2nd or 3rd year of the lease to the US CPI or a fixed percentage (usually 5–10%).
Switzerland	Rent usually indexed in line with CPI.
Turkey	Rent either subject to an annual percentage increase, usually 3–5%, or adjusts to a variable such as the US CPI, subject to negotiation as specified in the agreement.
UK	Rent normally subject to review every 5 years to the open-market level, usually upward only. Between periods, the amount payable is fixed.
USA	Tenants pay gross or net rent. (i) If gross, they pay a proportionate share of increases in the landlord's cost in operating the building. Various methods of calculating operating cost increases are used, including indexation in line with a CPI. (ii) If net, tenants pay their full *pro-rata* share of the building operating costs.

(Source: CB Richard Ellis (2009), with permission and thanks.)

is higher than expected general inflation, then, under an indexation system, a landlord will get locked in a contract that involves a relatively high opportunity cost (in the sense of foregone real rental income). In such a situation, landlords will tend to hold more space vacant than otherwise, hence NVR will be high.

11 Revisions frequency. By the same token, a lower frequency of rent reviews will also imply higher opportunity costs to landlords (where indexation is used), leading to a high NVR.
12 Real interest rates. Carrying a vacant building in one's portfolio is costly, both in terms of maintenance costs and property taxes and, importantly, in terms of opportunity cost. A vacant building, that is, is a commitment of capital that would have yielded a certain return if alternatively invested. At the very least, that return is approximated by the real

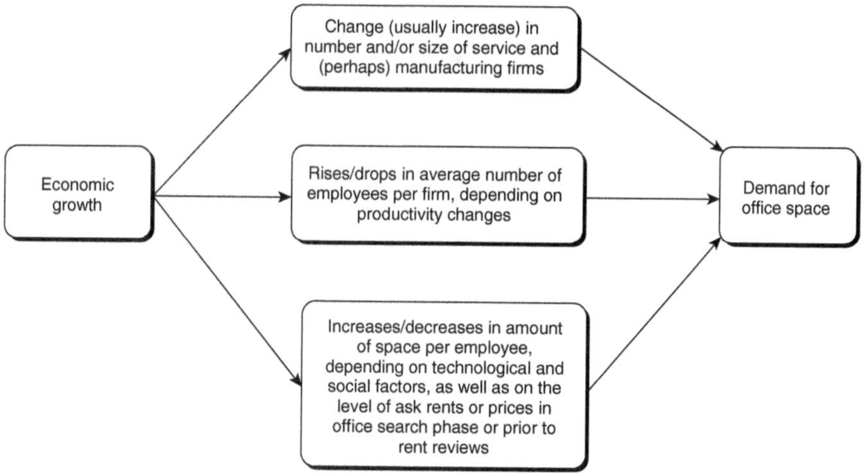

Figure 6.5 From economic growth to demand for office space.

interest rates associated with various financial instruments, including bank time deposits. Low rates therefore reduce that opportunity cost, increase the propensity to hold vacant space (for the reasons already stated above), and raise the NVR.

6.1.6 Determinants of office demand (and supply)

Intuitively, the most important determinants of office market demand must be office employment (Wheaton et al., 1997) and rent. The challenge is how to model this relationship mathematically so that it can be tested empirically. The main factors involved are shown in Figure 6.5. In what follows, we shall present a sample of such attempts.

(A) The Hendershott–Lizieri–MacGregor (HLM) model (Hendershott et al., 2008)

$$\ln D(R, E) = \lambda_o + \lambda_R \ln R + \lambda_E \ln E,$$

which says that (office) demand (i.e., the quantity demanded of office space), expressed as a natural logarithm (ln), is a (negative) function of (the natural logarithm of) the real rent R on new contracts and a (positive) function of (the natural logarithm of) the employment E that occupies office space. The authors note that actual occupancy may deviate from this model because of the additional factors of transaction costs (e.g., in searching, closing a deal, and moving) and tenants being locked into old contracts, but that in the long-run the actual vacancy rate equals the NVR, all leases carry the current rent, and all adjustments have been made (Hendershott et al., 2008: 3). In that case, the quantity demanded, D, must equal the quantity supplied, S, minus equilibrium vacancies, v:

$$D(R^*, E) = (1 - v^*)S,$$

where the asterisks indicate equilibrium values.

We then work as follows:

1 We take the logarithms of the terms in the second equation:

$$\ln D(R^*, E) = \ln(1 - v^*) + \ln S.$$

We set

$$\lambda_o + \lambda_R \ln R^* + \lambda_E \ln E = \ln(1 - v^*) + \ln S.$$

We solve for ln R^*, getting

$$\ln R^* = \frac{1}{\lambda_R}[\ln(1 - v^*) - \lambda_o] - \frac{\lambda_E}{\lambda_R}\ln E + \frac{1}{\lambda_R}\ln S.$$

Utilizing this formula in an econometric estimation of office market adjustment processes in the City of London for 1977–2006, the authors concluded, among other things, that office rent change in the City of London showed asymmetrical responses to outside shocks. The asymmetries observed related both to the nature of the shock (positive or negative) and to the state of the market when the shock occurs (Hendershott et al., 2008: 16). In particular, they discovered that increases in employment (a positive shock) had a significant (positive) effect on rents and that increases in the quantity supplied of office space (a positive shock) had a significant (negative) effect on rents.

On the other hand, decreases in employment or space did not have significant (even measurable!) effects on rents. The authors attributed this lack of significance to tenants being locked into long-term leases (as regards the effect of a decrease in employment) and to the temporary nature of space decreases as new developments appear. Turning to the state of the market, the authors discovered that increases in employment tended to cause rents to rise more quickly when rents were below equilibrium at the time of the shock than when rents were above equilibrium; equally, increases in space (which, remember, reduce rents, *ceteris paribus*) tended to cause rents to fall more rapidly when rents were above equilibrium than when they were below equilibrium.

(B) The Wheaton–Torto–Evans (WTE) model (Wheaton et al., 1997)

Actually this is a model of two basic equations, one for office space demanded, one for office construction. They are:

For office space demanded:

$$\mathrm{OS}_t^* = \alpha_o + E_t(\alpha_1 + \alpha_2 R_{t-1}),$$

where

OS_t^* = potentially demanded (hence the asterisk) office space at time t, in the absence of leases (which tend to bind tenants to space, thus restricting the adjustment of space consumption to changing demand conditions), moving, or adjustment costs (notice that potential demand OS_t^* does not necessarily equal the actual consumption of space, OS_t,

E_t = number of office workers at time t,

α_1 = a coefficient showing baseline square feet per worker,

α_2	=	a coefficient showing how much the use of space varies (negatively) with rent,
R_{t-1}	=	rent in previous period,
α_2	=	a coefficient showing how much space use varies with rent.

For office space construction:

$$C_t = \beta_0 + \beta_1 R_t + \beta_2 V_t + \beta_3 I_t + \beta_4 \mathrm{RC}_t,$$

where

C_t	=	new construction at time t,
R_t	=	office rents,
V_t	=	office vacancy,
I_t	=	an interest rate or any (more complicated) capitalization rate,
RC_t	=	a measure of replacement cost.

The fundamental idea here is that new construction depends on the ratio of the asset price of office space to its replacement cost, which should bring into the reader's mind Tobin's q ratio, first encountered in Chapter 3. In turn asset price depends on current net rental income (taking vacancy into account), and a capitalization rate.[5]

Subsequently subjecting the London office market to econometric analysis for 1970–95, the authors concluded that demand shocks closely replicated historic market changes (such as were caused by recessions and recoveries). Such changes, in turn, would bring about relatively small fluctuations in vacancy (4–13 per cent, smaller than those typical of US markets) which, however, would then 'generate major swings in rents and construction' (Wheaton et al., 1997: 90).

(C) The Brunes (2005) model

This makes use of Tobin's q in a more straightforward way than Wheaton et al. (1997), but the question it asks is about what determines investment in office buildings (i.e., new supply) rather than what determines demand for office space. The basic equation is

$$P_t = \alpha + \beta \mathrm{TQ}_{t-m} - \varepsilon_t,$$

where

P_t	=	production of office buildings completed at time t,
TQ_{t-m}	=	Tobin's q, i.e., ratio of price of building m years before completion to replacement cost m years before completion,
ε_t	=	the statistical error term (i.e., a term that captures deviations from the general, or expected, trend of the relationship between dependent and independent variables).

The author studied the office market of Kista, a suburb of Stockholm, for 1980–2002. He concluded that in this particular case the 'the explanatory power of the TQ model [was] quite good when a time lag of three to four [was] included in the model' (Brunes, 2005: 16). He attributed this to 'myopic' behaviour on the part of investors in office property – i.e., behaviour predicated on past or current prices rather than on expected or forecast prices of office buildings (cf. Section 8.5).

(D) The Fuerst (2006) model

There are two immediately interesting things about this model of office space demand: (i) in addition to office employment and (past) rents, it incorporates a measure of the intensity of space usage expressed as the average amount of square feet per office worker; (ii) it also incorporates an exceptional outside shock, namely, the 9/11 attack on the New York Twin Towers, in its investigation of the New York office market. This is it:

$$\mathrm{OS}_t^* = \alpha_0 + E_t\left(\alpha_1 + \varphi_1\frac{E_t - E_{t-1}}{E_t} - \varphi_2 R_{t-1}\right) + Z_1,$$

where

OS_t^*	=	total demand for office space – as in Wheaton et al. (1997), the hypothetical demand OS_t^* does not necessarily equal observed consumption OS_t,
α_1	=	basic square feet per worker (as in Wheaton et al., 1997),
E_t	=	current total number of office workers in a city,
$\frac{E_t - E_{t-1}}{E_t}$	=	change in office employment between current and previous period,
φ_1	=	a coefficient showing the degree to which dynamic growth in office employment translates into additional space consumption in excess of the space required to accommodate the employees of a firm,
R_{t-1}	=	rent level in previous period,
φ_2	=	price elasticity of demand, i.e., the proportionate change in office space per worker that occurs in response to changes in rents (it is expected to be positive, so that $-\varphi_2$ is negative, guaranteeing that quantity demanded of space varies inversely with level of rents),
Z_1	=	a 9/11 dummy variable that takes on the value of 1 in the period immediately following the 9/11 attack and 0 otherwise to account for the sharp decline in occupied space after 9/11 that would not be fully accounted for in an estimation of the standard model.

The model was used in an econometric estimation of the New York office market using two databases: one from 1979 to 2004, another from 1992 to 2004. Among other results, the author concluded that rents adapted to changes in vacancy rates with a significant lag – three quarters, to be exact. It took, that is, three quarters before landlords effectively lowered rents to a level that was in line with prevailing vacancy rates (Fuerst, 2006: 17–18). Contrary, therefore, to the efficient market hypothesis – that markets adjust very rapidly to new information – it seems this was not the case in the New York office sector, probably because 'market sentiment as established in the previous quarters prevails in the bargaining process and imperfect information is likely to contribute to persisting prices' (Fuerst, 2006: 18). McDonald (2000: 59) has also observed that rents adjust later than the occupancy rate, but has attributed this to 'the long-term nature of many existing leases'.

6.1.7 How is the NVR estimated?

It is frequent practice among market practitioners to estimate the NVR by means of the following simple equation (PRUPIM Research, 2010):

$$\Delta\mathrm{Rents} = \alpha - \beta VR_t \quad (\beta > 0),$$

where ΔRents is the change in rents, α is the change in rents when the vacancy rate is zero, β is the change in rents given a change in the vacancy rate (i.e., the slope of the line implicit in the above equation), and VR is the vacancy rate. In this formulation, a rise in VR reduces rents, and vice versa. If the VR is such that the change in rents is zero, then VR must be the NVR, in which case

$$\mathrm{VR}_t = \mathrm{NVR}_t = \alpha/\beta.$$

Therefore, if one runs a time-series regression of rent changes to vacancy rates over a long period, one can obtain values for α and β, which are supposed to be a good enough approximation to the 'true' NVR (on the assumption that in the long run the property market tends to return to equilibrium, around and near its NVR). However, if the NVR itself changes (as McCartney (2010) has suggested it may well do), then the above formula will not return valid results.

McCartney (2010) himself has approached the problem of NVR estimation starting from a more complex equation, in which the change in rents in a given period depends on more variables than just the vacancy rate. That is,

$$\Delta \mathrm{RR}_t = \alpha - \beta_1 \mathrm{VR}_{t-1} + \beta_2 \Delta \mathrm{GNP}_{t-1} - \beta_3 \Delta I_t - \beta_4 \Delta S_t + \varepsilon_t,$$

where

$\Delta \mathrm{RR}_t$	=	change in real office rents in period t,
VR_{t-1}	=	actual vacancy rate in previous period,
$\Delta \mathrm{GNP}_{t-1}$	=	change in GNP of previous period,
ΔI_t	=	change in real interest rates in period t,
ΔS_t	=	change in office stock in given city (e.g., Dublin) in period t,
ε_t	=	statistical error term.

On the basis of this equation, he estimated NVR figures for the Dublin office market, which were reported above.

6.1.8 Office market analysis[6]

An office market report has to say something about future office rental rates. This requires calculation of

1 existing office stock in chosen area of study;
2 new office building construction;
3 net absorption;
4 vacancy rates; and
5 asking rental rates.

In turn:

1 Calculation of existing stock really means making an availability and vacancy analysis. This can be done a number of ways: (i) by gathering figures on existing owner-occupied area, tenant-occupied area, and vacant area, in square metres or feet; (ii) by breaking down these figures by geographical sub-market (say, between the Central Business District,

if such is the case, and adjacent sub-markets) and/or by number of properties falling inside a given floor space rank (say, so many properties with a floor area from 100,001 to 150,000 square feet), and/or by office class (see Box 6.2); etc.

Box 6.2 What is office class?

Offices are usually classified as A, B, or C. These classifications have been developed by BOMA (Building Owners and Managers Association) International, a Washington-based professional body, and the ULI (Urban Land Institute), another Washington-based professional body. According to the BOMA definition,

- Class A properties are the most prestigious buildings competing for premier office users with rents above average for the area. Buildings have high-quality standard finishes, state-of-the art systems, exceptional accessibility, and a definite market presence.
- Class B properties are buildings competing for a wide range of users with rents in the average range for the area. Building finishes are fair to good for the area, and systems are adequate, but the buildings do not compete with Class A at the same price.
- Class C properties are buildings competing for tenants requiring functional space at rents below the average for the area.

Source: www.boma.org/Resources/classifications/Pages/default.aspx (accessed 20 February 2011).

2 New office building construction requires enumeration of underway and proposed projects, with account taken of the possibility that some will not materialize. A time frame must be decided upon, say 2–4 years in the future. A useful categorization here is 'properties under construction or just completed', 'properties that have been approved by the planning authorities', 'proposed properties'. The following is an example:

	2013	*2014*	*2015*	*2016*
Status of new projects:				
Properties under construction or just completed				
Properties approved by planning authorities				
Proposed properties				
Total new construction forecast =				

3 Net absorption (the annual increase or decrease of space occupied by tenants) depends on employment growth (or decline). A problem here is how to estimate the number of tenants who vacate a building in order to move into another. The researcher has to balance the marginal cost of finding accurate information of this type against the marginal benefit of doing so. Other than that, the office market literature accepts that there is a strong relationship between employment changes and demand for office space, with service industry employment (e.g., from the financial sector or the government)

being the heaviest user of such space. Of course, the analyst must also make estimates of future employment changes, perhaps by developing a low, an average, and a high scenario.

4 Together, the existing stock situation, new construction, and net absorption allow estimation of future vacancy rates. That is, knowing how much occupied stock there is, how much vacant stock there is, how much new (net) stock will be added over the report horizon, and what the absorption rate will be (based on the historic relationship between employment changes and net absorption), it is possible to calculate future vacancy rates. (Again, a low, an average, and a high scenario may be imperative here.)
5 Finally, the vacancy rate trend allows forecast of future rents. This should also be based on the historic relationship between (real) rents and vacancy rates.
6 This basic analysis can be improved in two ways: (i) by calculating a NVR for the area under study (see Section 6.1.7), and then incorporating this explicitly into the analysis; and (ii) by breaking down the analysis by sub-market and/or by office class and/or size category.

6.2 Demand for retail space

Demand for retail space is a derived demand for trade, or catchment, areas. Retailers demand a location, first and foremost (Pearson, 2007), not for its own sake, but as a gateway to sales. Next to the location factor, property rents or prices (together with property taxes) come second, and costs of establishment and maintenance come third. A serious location selection process involves much more than the standard tools of economics, as, in addition to the latter, it also utilizes inputs from economic geography, GIS (geographical information systems), and gravity modelling.

It is true, of course, that demand from retailers for retail space combines with demand for office, residential, or industrial space into total demand for space, thus affecting the level and structure of urban land prices and, ultimately, the level and structure of property rents and prices. In turn, such demands broadly depend on variables like population, real incomes, and interest rates – provided that the variables are correctly matched to the appropriate markets. For instance, an international financial centre does not cater only to its 'home' city, but to outside markets, many of which are abroad. A large proportion of the business enjoyed by financial institutions in this centre depends, therefore, on incomes generated elsewhere. A mail-order company may be in the same situation, getting perhaps most of its revenue from other cities or countries.

In Chapter 10 we shall have more to say about how demands for different land uses determine the level and structure of land rents/prices in a city. For now, we need to take rents and prices for granted, and discuss how individual retailers make location choices. It should be emphasized that the method(s) retailers use in order to do that is the basis of retail space demand, no less than actual sales estimates (as the latter depend on identifying appropriate locations and trade areas). Given the product(s) that a retailer promotes, there are three areas of decision-making that are important in the location selection process:

1 The geographical frame of reference.
Focus: strategy.
2 The identification of appropriate trade areas (which presupposes choosing a suitable estimation method, or combination of methods).
Focus: revenue.

3 The estimation of expenses involved in establishing oneself and operating in a particular area and site.
Focus: costs.

6.2.1 The geographical frame of reference

Relevant frames of reference involve the 'country' (the UK), the 'region' (Scotland), the 'trade area' (Glasgow or Greater Glasgow), the 'locality' (West End), and the 'site' (junction of Byres Road and Great Western Road). Of these, the trade area is perhaps the most important, because it is not merely a particular geographical unit, placed between the region and the locality as in the example just given, but a fluid concept-cum-area that can easily link to any of the other four units. There is thus bound to be some friction between the trade area concept and the geographical unit of analysis that the concept will actually be applied upon.

For instance, a firm located in country A may have as its trade area country A itself and other countries also – although not necessarily its immediate locality. An optician's or seamstress's shop may have as its trade area its immediate locality, but not the rest of the town, let alone adjacent towns. Or, an initial evaluation might suggest that, *ceteris paribus*, region A is preferable to region B, but subsequent analysis may demonstrate that catchment area Y in region B is preferable to catchment area X in region A (on the grounds that it is more likely to bring in a target level of revenue). Unless the retailer has other reasons to insist on Region A (e.g., specific long-term plans that are better served in region A, or materially higher rents, tax rates, labour and/or red-tape costs in B than in A, or maybe subjective reasons), they should choose catchment area Y in region B.

In all cases, the retailer's location criterion is simply this: which location promises the highest possible revenue at the lowest possible cost so that profit is maximized. In this context, a retailer with an established trade will assess a location for possible expansion (say, a locality or a region) depending on the product they sell, their available resources, and their overall strategy. But the reverse also happens: someone identifies potential demand for a product in an area, and supplies it, perhaps by establishing themselves there.

Area attributes that can inform location decisions are the following:

1 *For a country.* The relevant attributes are overall size of national market (itself a function of population and incomes), political (in)stability, economic growth prospects, clarity and predictability of the legal and taxation system, labour laws and costs, degree of social cohesion and law-enforcement, general infrastructure, business ethics and practice, and extent of competition.
2 *For a region.* There may be differences between regions within the same country as regards variables like population, purchasing power, labour laws and costs, economic growth prospects, applicable laws and tax rates, extent of competition, and proximity to suppliers.
3 *For a trade (or catchment) area.* For business purposes, this is defined as the geographical area where the actual and/or potential customers of a firm for a particular good or service can be found – but the concept can be extended to refer to 'free' public utilities, like a public library. A number of corollaries follow:

   (a) Trade areas must be places where actual and/or potential buyers' profiles (including incomes) are compatible with the given product and store profile.

(b) The nature of the product on offer and the way it is sold – through what type and size of store (e.g., convenience versus department store) and through what method (e.g., walk-in versus mail-order versus e-commerce) – dictate what may count as a trade area.
(c) Population size and structure, and income levels, are crucial 'raw' determinants of potential revenue, and, therefore, of trade areas.
(d) Given a suitable trade area in terms of population, incomes, other (taste-related) consumer characteristics, and transport network, the actual number of potential customers a newly arrived retailer will gain depends on the number, location, and comparative attractiveness of pre-existing retailers in the trade area, selling a similar good or service.
(e) A special case to consider in choosing a trade area, or a site within a trade area, is competition between retail outlets (e.g., franchisees) of the same firm (the phenomenon is referred to as 'cannibalization').

4 *For a locality.* This is a small area within a chosen trade area that can provide sites for the physical establishment of a vendor. The general level of property rents or prices, along with other locality attributes (e.g., zoning and safety regulations, traffic congestion, parking spaces), are important here.
5 *For a site.* Strictly speaking, this is where the actual physical premises of the retailing business are found. In addition to the level of rent or price for the property, what also matters at this level is the lease particulars (in case of renting), the general condition of the building, how accessible the building is, and how easily seen from the street the retailer's actual premises are.

To find, delineate, assess, and select a trade area, a retailer can employ a number of (not mutually exclusive) methods:[7]

1 the checklist method;
2 the analogue method;
3 multiple regression analysis;
4 gravity modelling; and
5 GIS.

The methods are complementary in the sense that methods 1–3 are mostly about assessing and comparing the sales potential of different areas once the latter have been identified (even provisionally or intuitively), and methods 4 and 5 are mostly about identifying and delineating promising trade areas. The two approaches clearly overlap.

6.2.2 Methods of finding trade areas: the checklist method

This is the simplest method possible (Koontz, 1994), and is perhaps the most appropriate for small businesses (Gattis, 2010) or those with limited funds. It works like this. A retailer first makes a list of sites that seem intuitively appropriate (on the basis of a target customer profile and a target site profile), usually (but not necessarily) in the same broad locality. For each site, the retailer does the following (Gattis, 2010):

1 Makes a list of specific locality and site characteristics, or attributes, and defines them in a positive way (see Table 6.5). That is because, for example, 'parking spaces' (the

Table 6.5 The checklist method for assessing a retail site

Site name: Elm Street

Possible positive attributes from prospective retailer's point of view	*Importance of attribute*	*Score of attribute in terms of presence or size (5 = very large or strongly present, 1 = very small or virtually absent)*	*Value of site*
A. Locality-related:			
A.1. Per-capita income	20%	4	0.8
A.2. Population	15%	3	0.45
A.3. Freedom from traffic congestion	5%	4	0.2
A.4. Parking spaces	10%	2	0.2
A.5. Freedom from competitors	8%	2	0.16
A.6. Neighbourhood safety	5%	5	0.25
A.7. Freedom from noise pollution	2%	2	0.04
B. Site-related:			
B.1. Attractive rent level	10%	3	0.3
B.2. Visibility	10%	3	0.3
B.3. Ingress and egress	15%	4	0.6
Total	100%		**3.30**

more, the better) cannot go together with 'extent of competition' (which is 'the less, the better'), but can go together with 'freedom from competition' (the more, the better). Numerical values for some of the attributes may be taken from census data, others from canvassing the area physically.

2 Assigns an importance value (a percentage) to each attribute, so that cumulative importance is 100 per cent.
3 Assigns a score to each attribute (say, from 0 or 1 to 5 or 10); the higher the score, the stronger the size, or the presence, of the attribute in the locality or site (and vice versa).
4 Multiplies importance by score to determine 'qualitative' value of attribute.
5 Adds attribute values to determine the 'qualitative' value of the site (see Table 6.6).
6 Chooses the highest-value sites to create a *pro forma* (i.e., a forecast) income statement and cash flow analysis for each, taking into account both expected revenues from area and expected costs related to establishment and operation; conducts a NPV analysis (cf. Chapter 5).
7 Selects the site with the highest NPV.

Because the method is to a large extent based on intuition and on assignment of subjective importance values and scores, it may not be advisable in cases of multi-million-dollar location decisions or in complex cases. For instance, localities with high per capita incomes are also likely to be relatively safe – and the people there want to keep them that way. A retailer who attaches an importance of, say, 50 per cent to per capita income, while at the same time attaching an importance of 5 per cent to neighbourhood safety, probably has a confused customer profile in his or her mind. The method's allure, therefore, lies in it being simple and cost-effective.

Of course if two prospective retailers choose the same site, they may push up the rent for the property. In such a case the winner, *ceteris paribus*, will be the one who, based on his or her site assessment and *pro forma* analyses, will come up with the highest NPV for the site (because he or she will be the one capable of bidding most for the site). But this shows that commercial RE demand is a function of subjective estimates as much as of objective data – and this is the case even when more sophisticated location analyses are undertaken.

6.2.3 Methods of finding trade areas: the analogue method

This is based on the assumption that the power of a site to attract patronage or custom (i.e., customers, especially on a regular basis) is analogous to what similar stores have achieved in comparable market conditions (Koontz, 1994). This power is usually measured by means of on-site surveys, and then the trading area is analogously determined. Interestingly, analogue methods of retail location tend to be the most popular among practitioners, and have been 'the foundation of retail sales forecasting since the 1930s' (Rogers, 2007: 74). Again, simplicity and cost-effectiveness are some of the method's strengths, along with adaptability, and the ability to quantify the unique image and performance of a retailer. On the other hand, it suffers from subjectivity when it comes to deciding which analogous data are appropriate for consideration, and what the combined effect of competition, demographics, and distance is likely to be in a new location (Rogers, 2007: 75).

6.2.4 Methods of finding trade areas: multiple regression analysis (MRA)

This is a statistical method that involves the probabilistic quantification of the impact of assorted independent variables on a single (dependent) variable of interest. In our case, the latter is location-related sales, and the question is how chosen variables (or their absence from, or weak presence in, a considered area or site), such as average income, population density, extent of competition, availability of parking space, and distance of store from various points on the map, determine sales. This is reminiscent of the checklist method (after all, all retail location methods have things in common, and to a large extent tend to use the same variables). A difference is that MRA is more precise, more robust, subject to rigorous statistical tests for errors (like testing for *multicollinearity*, i.e., roughly, using two or more explanatory variables when one will do), and better able to assess the importance of the variables used. A problem with MRA is that it requires 'a rare combination of statistical experience and practical retail experience' (Rogers, 2007: 76).

6.2.5 Methods of finding trade areas: gravity modelling

Gravity modelling implies a change of focus: the task is still to find trade areas, only the focus is not on listing, quantifying, and comparing assortments of area or site characteristics or attributes. Rather, it is on measuring or gauging the 'pulling' power, in marketing terms, of a city or town (or even a retail outlet) over its surrounding area; to define, that is, the trade, or catchment, area of a settlement (or retail outlet), relative to the attraction power of other settlements (or retail outlets).

The question gravity models try to answer is, what are the chances that, given distance or travel time, a consumer will do their shopping in a particular city or town (or retail outlet) rather than somewhere else? So retail sales gravity models are not about the chances of a consumer walking into one's shop as opposed to a competitor's shop across the street!

They are about the 'raw' pulling power of one location over that of another location. In comparison to the three retail location models discussed above, they tend to work at a broader geographical level, and to rely a lot on comparative population sizes and distance (or travel time) between locations, although sometimes other variables (like shopping space) are substituted for population.

Now, if we accept the premise that larger cities, towns or shopping centres exercise a marketing 'pull' on other cities, towns or shopping centres, and generally on their surrounding areas, the next question to ask is, how strong is that pull? A number of answers have been provided (for a review, see Babin et al., 1994; Anderson et al., 2010):

1 Reilly's model;
2 the break-point model;
3 Mason and Mayer's 'inverse' break-point model; and
4 Huff's model.

W. J. Reilly's model (1929–31)

Reilly's model proposes a way to estimate the relative ability of two cities, A and B, to attract trade from a location X between them. This relative, or proportional, ability is directly related to the ratio of the two populations and inversely related to the square of the ratio of the distances of the two cities to location X. (The physics-inclined will recognize this as inspired by Newton's law of universal gravitation, without the gravitational constant.) Thus, if

P_A, P_B = populations of city A and city B, respectively,
D_A, D_B = distances between city A and point X and between city B and point X, respectively,
T_A, T_B = amounts of trade originating from X that 'gravitate' towards city A and city B, respectively,

then

$$\frac{T_A}{T_B} = \frac{P_A}{P_B}\left(\frac{D_B}{D_A}\right)^2.$$

Accordingly, if $P_A = 62{,}000$; $P_B = 15{,}000$, $D_A = 24$ km, and $D_B = 6$ km, then $T_A/T_B =$ 25.83 per cent, i.e., for every \$100 of trade that will be going city B's way from location X, city A will be getting only \$25.83 of trade from location X.

The break-point model

P. D. Converse (1949) revised Reilly's model into what has come to be known as the break-point model.[8] This is supposed to determine the location between two cities, separated by a total distance *D*, at which a consumer is indifferent as to whether they will do their shopping in city A or city B. By extension, having found that point on the map, one has also identified the potential catching area for either city. The model calculates the distance of, say, city A from the break-point as follows:

$$D_A = \frac{D}{1+\sqrt{\frac{P_B}{P_A}}}.$$

Using numbers from the previous example, we get $D_A = 30/1.4919 = 20.11$ km = the break-point (from A) between A and B.

So city A, being bigger, has a larger catchment area than city B (whose catchment area is $30 - 20.11 = 9.89$ km). Notice, though, that in the example given of Reilly's model, the imaginary location X was 6 km away from city B, so it does not fall within the trading radius of city A, as defined by means of the break-point formula. In fact location X falls decisively within the trade area of city B. This is why in the previous example so little trade was found to be going A's way from location X, in relation to the amount going towards B (the ratio was 25.83 per cent). (Can you explain, however, why some trade from X is going towards A at all, since X is inside B's trade area?)

An illustration of the break-point model is shown in Figure 6.6, in which towns B, C, and D surround town A. Applying the break-point formula gives the break-points of town A relative to the other three at 3.14 miles (to B), 2.38 miles (to C), and 1.76 miles (to D). These points delineate the potential trade areas of A, in addition to its own. Actual estimation of each trade area's ability to supply customers to A rather than to B, C, or D would then require finding the size and shape of each trade area (probably a function of transport network), and the number of households within each (using census data). Subsequent calculation of potential spending going A's way would also require, at the very least, an estimate of average income in A itself as well as in the delineated trade areas around it.

A retailer considering which town to establish themselves in might have to compare a number of possible candidate towns (like A above), and see which generates an overall greater sales potential.

The model could also be applied within a town, as when a retailer might want to estimate how much trade they would attract from competing retail outlets in other intra-urban localities. In this case, the operative variable would not be population but shopping space. Since each outlet's trade area would not depend only on shopping space, but also on distance between

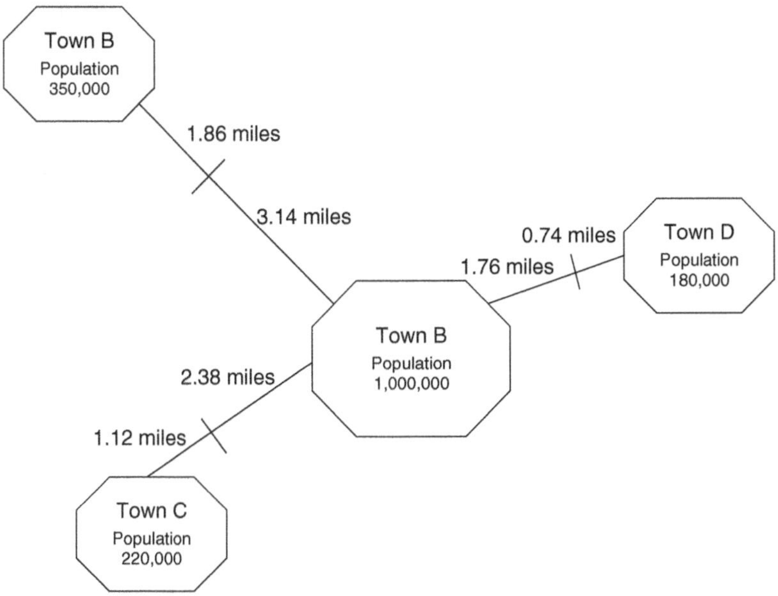

Figure 6.6 Illustration of Reilly's/Converse's model: trade area limits of town A.

a given outlet and competing ones, selection of any site for establishment would impact upon the sales potential (and therefore market share) of the prospective retailer (and upon the actual sales – and market shares – of pre-existing retailers). It would, in short, impact on competition between them. This requires further elaboration.

One way to gauge the extent of competition in a market is through the Herfindahl[9] Index (HI). This is the sum of the squared market shares of all firms in an industry (or of all competing firms in a location):

$$\mathrm{HI} = \sum_{i=1}^{n} \mathrm{MS}_i^2.$$

One interesting thing about HI is that as a new firm (an 'intruder') comes in a market characterized by static sales, the size of HI depends on the intruder's sales – but in a nonlinear way! That is, at low sales levels, HI drops as the biggest among the pre-existing firms lose(s) market share; after a point (the minimum point on the relevant bowl-shaped curve – see Figure 6.7), HI begins to rise as the intruder itself achieves 'critical mass'. Figure 6.7 shows the pattern by means of a numerical example (see Table 6.6), on the *ad hoc* assumption that the effect of an intruding retailer's rising sales (→ rising market share) falls on all pre-existing firms (which lose sales), in proportion to the original market share of each. In turn, the intruder's sales depend, *ceteris paribus*, on the site where it chooses to establish itself, as variations in the distance between the intruder's location and the locations of competitors affect the catchment area of each! In the end, as the set of suitable locations is not infinite, a retailer's final choice (among a limited set offered in the urban landscape) will dictate, *ceteris paribus*, both the extent of competition among retailers offering the same product (broadly defined) in the city, and a retailer's capacity to bid for a chosen site.

A weakness of the break-point model is that it tends to gloss over specific, and often important, factors that affect catchment areas, focusing on a location's 'raw' pulling power on the basis of a couple of variables only. Its strength lies precisely in quickly identifying

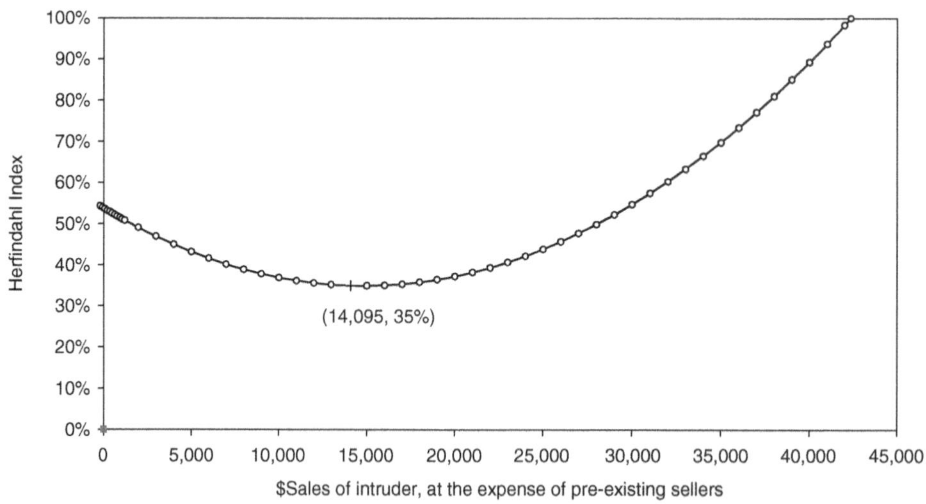

Figure 6.7 Behaviour of the Herfindahl Index as an intruder in a static sales market of size X (= \$42,360) acquires a market share, given an HI = 53.74 per cent before the intruder's entry.

Table 6.6 A stylized comparison of retailing competition situations to show the behaviour of the Herfindahl Index as market shares vary

	Initial situation			*Situation after intruder's arrival**			
Original retailers	*Sales ($)*	*Market share*	*Squared market share*	*Original retailers plus new-comer*	*Sales ($)*	*Market share*	*Squared market share*
R1	30,000	70.82%	50.16%	R1	20,018	47.26%	22.33%
R2	7,400	17.47%	3.05%	R2	4,938	11.66%	1.36%
R3	2,500	5.90%	0.35%	R3	1,668	3.94%	0.16%
R4	1,550	3.66%	0.13%	R4	1,034	2.44%	0.06%
R5	910	2.15%	0.05%	R5	607	1.43%	0.02%
				R6	14,095	33.27%	11.07%
Total	42,360	100.00%	53.74%	Total	42,360	100.00%	35.00%

* Assuming the intruder achieves sales of $14,095, which, due to the intruder's location, cause all pre-existing retailers to lose sales in proportion to the original market share of each. For example, 14,095(70.82%) = 9,982.1 and 30,000 – 9,982.1 = 20,017.9.

promising areas. This is a good reason to use gravity models to complement detail-seeking models, like MRA.

Mason and Mayer's 'inverse' break-point model

As noted by Anderson et al. (2010), B. J. Mason and M. L. Mayer (1990) suggested the following inversion of Reilly's/Converse's model:

$$D_A = \frac{D}{1 + \sqrt{\frac{P_A}{P_B}}}.$$

The difference between the 'inverted' and the original model is in the term under the radical. In Reilly's/Converse's original formula we have P_B/P_A; in Mason and Mayer's (MM's) revision, we have P_A/P_B. The result is an inversion of the trade area around each of the two settlements, with the larger settlement's trade area becoming smaller than the smaller settlement's trade area. For instance, applying MM's formula on the illustration in Figure 6.6 gives the trade area of A with respect to B as 1.86 miles rather than 3.14. The rationale for the inversion is that many modern cities tend to become metropolitan areas, with high population densities over very large areas, and plenty of shopping choices within convenient travelling distances open to consumers in those areas. Reilly's/Converse's model, on the other hand, would make more sense in the context of an older settlement pattern, with expansive rural areas around relatively small, or at least well-defined, cities or towns. In such a context a trade area would be expected to vary inversely with population density around the main settlement – a relation that is obfuscated in today's metropolitan areas. Therefore, the proposed inversion of the Reilly/Converse model may fit 'current shopping realities' better (Anderson et al., 2010: 8).

D. L. Huff's model (1964)

Huff's model – one of the most sophisticated, and the retail industry standard (Anderson et al., 2010) – centres around the probability that a consumer living in a given trade area will shop at a particular retail outlet. To estimate the outlet's sales in that trade area, what is then required is to multiply total consumer expenditure on the given product in the area by the estimated probability. A strength of Huff's model over, say, the break-point model, is that it takes explicit account of all competition in an area; also, that, through appropriate specification of exponents in the model, it can handle different products. So there are three steps involved in the process:

1 Calculate the total consumer expenditure in the area:

$$(\text{total consumer population}) \times (\text{average spending per consumer}) = \text{total expenditure}.$$

2 Calculate the probability of consumer shopping from a particular retail outlet (Huff, 2003):

$$P_{ij} = \frac{S_j^a / T_{ij}^b}{\sum_{j=1}^{n} S_j^a / T_{ij}^b},$$

where

S_j	=	size of retail outlet j in square metres or feet,
T_{ij}	=	travel time (or distance) from consumer's domicile i to outlet j,
a	=	parameter capturing the fact that store size is more important for some products than others ($\Rightarrow$ a higher a would be required),
b	=	parameter capturing the effect of travel time on different kinds of shopping trips, e.g., a trip to buy convenience goods as opposed to specialty goods ($\Rightarrow$ a higher b would be required for the first kind than for the second).

Notice that in Huff's formula, S^a is divided by T^b (or, alternatively, that S^a is multiplied by T^{-b}), meaning that the longer the trip, the smaller the probability of someone undertaking it for shopping purposes – hence the reason why convenience goods would have a higher b.

3 Calculate expected purchases E_{ij} from outlet j, originating from area i:

$$E_{ij} = P_{ij}(B_{ik}),$$

where B_{ik} = amount budgeted by consumers in area i from product k (Huff, 2003).

Figure 6.8 illustrates Huff's model by positing three shopping centres for specialty goods around a town without such a centre. Centre A has a shopping space of 60,000 square metres, B of 80,000 square metres, and C of 40,000 square metres. The parameter values are $a = 1.2$ and $b = 0.8$.

A problem with Huff's model is parameter estimation, as the probabilities obviously depend on the parameter (i.e., the exponent) values. Some practitioners attach arbitrary values, usually centred around 1, but this can easily lead to erroneous results. Solutions to the problem do exist (Nakanishi and Cooper, 1974, 1982; Huff, 2008), but require statistical expertise.

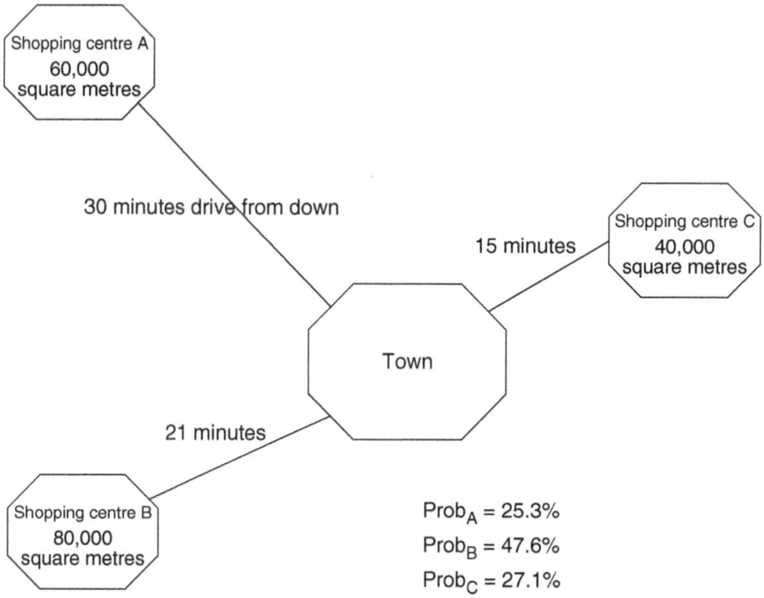

Figure 6.8 Application of Huff's model: probability of each shopping centre getting customers from town.

6.2.6 Methods of finding trade areas: use of GIS

A geographical information system (GIS) is a system that captures, stores, analyses, manages, and presents data that are linked to location(s). In assence, a GIS merges cartography, statistical analysis, and database technology. It is precisely because of these features and functionalities that GIS have been increasingly used since the early 1990s on a huge variety of problems, including retail trade area identification and analysis (Segal, 1998; Dramowicz, 2005; Pearson, 2007; Huff, 2008).

A typical GIS approach to trade area analysis involves delimiting a trade area via one of a number of methods (e.g., concentric rings or Thiessen/Voronoi polygons), and then preparing a market profile by extracting and aggregating area-related statistical data using GIS software (Dramowicz, 2005). This kind of functionality may be better appreciated through presenting one of the area-delimiting methods – namely, Thiessen[10]/Voronoi[11] polygons.

A Thiessen/Voronoi polygon is any of a set of polygons, each surrounding or enclosing a certain reference point (e.g., a location on a map) and having the property that any point inside such a polygon is closer to that polygon's reference point than to the reference point of any other polygon in the same cluster.

Figure 6.9 presents an example of Thiessen/Voronoi polygons. In this, the dots in the left frame can be taken to mean localities (e.g., towns), which subsequently are enclosed by Thiessen/Voronoi polygons in the right frame.[12] Notice that any point inside a polygon is closer to that polygon's dot than it is to the dot of any other polygon, as defined above. If these points are customers, then they are more likely to shop from the dot in 'their' polygon than from any other dot, since any other dot is further away from them. This way, a trade area can be delimited, which can then be further analysed for, say, marketing information and profiling. A retailer could choose the 'best' of these trade areas for setting up shop in the

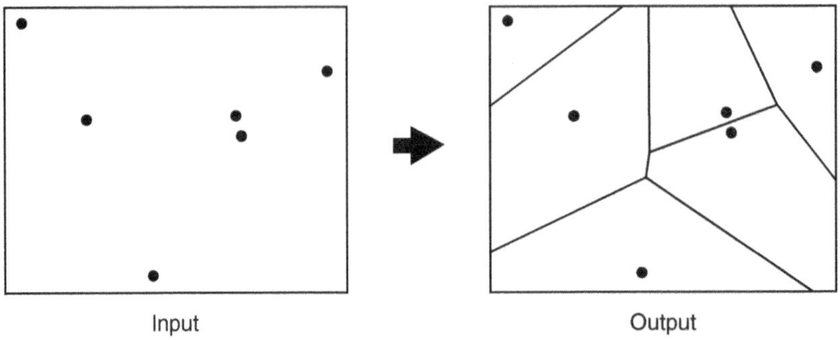

Figure 6.9 Example of Thiessen/Voronoi polygons.
(Source: ESRI, http://resources.esri.com/help/9.3/arcgisdesktop/com/gp_toolref/analysis_tools/create_thiessen_polygons_analysis_.htm.)

relevant dot – and his or her decision would add to demand for retail space in that particular trade area's 'dot' (whether the dot is a town or some other kind of place).

6.3 Demand for industrial space

Demand for industrial space is demand for factory, warehousing, and research and development (RD) space. Logically, therefore, industrial activity should be the primary determinant of this demand as well as of industrial rents (if the activity could be measured appropriately and accurately, e.g., as output, as manufacturing employment, as truck shipments, or another relevant variable). Empirical research has confirmed this intuition, even though different studies have used different proxies for industrial activity (Wheaton and Torto, 1990; Brown et al., 2000; AMB, 2002; Anderson and Guirguis, 2011).

Industrial site selection has to take into account a number of factors, the most important of which are the following:[13]

1 suitability of the geographical location (e.g., how near it is to sources of supplies and/or the firm's customers);
2 availability of transport links;
3 adequacy of space, including parking space;
4 room for expansion, in case it's needed later;
5 suitability of the building itself (in terms of, e.g., electrical, plumbing, heating, and ventilation systems);
6 existence of satisfactory loading and unloading facilities; and
7 adequacy of utility services (including sewerage) to the site.

This is a longer list than the one usually describing requirements for office or retail facilities. Other aspects to the industrial property sector that set it apart from other property types are the following:

1 Industrial RE is the least cyclical of all property sectors (AMB, 2002). There are three reasons for this:

   (a) The sector is characterized by owner-occupied, rather than rented, structures – and even most rented structures are single-tenant-occupied (Wheaton and Torto,

1990). At the same time ,industrial property typically is not the largest part of the wealth of an industrial firm in the way things are with most households. And, industrial mortgages are more difficult to obtain than other commercial mortgages because industrial properties (i) are usually under heavier scrutiny than others for environmental reasons and (ii) take longer to liquidate in case of default (due, among other things, to their highly specific descriptions).

(b) The capital-intensive and long-term nature of industrial activity discourages moving. This tendency to 'stay put' is reinforced by the need to control two critical factors in the supply chain of an industrial firm: speed and transportation costs. In turn, such control is better achieved when the industrial firm is established near densely populated areas (like big cities), which are a primary source of demand and also contain the infrastructure that supports global trade (AMB, 2009).

(c) Industrial property rents (a fixed cost) are usually a very small proportion of total value added.

2 The sector is diversified both in terms of property types (manufacturing, warehousing, R&D) and in terms of user variation within those types (AMB, 2002).

As a result, the industrial RE sector is perhaps both the least-studied and the most difficult to study of all property sectors, with office demand models being inappropriate for the purpose without at least significant modifications (Rabianski and Black, 1997).

Important variables that have been used or are used to forecast industrial RE demand, or which have been identified as significant determinants, include the following:

1 Industrial employment (along with after-tax cost of corporate capital) was used by Wheaton and Torto (1990) in a study of 52 US metropolitan areas.
2 Gross value added (see Chapter 2) was used in the Brown et al. (2000) study of the Scottish industrial RE market (referred to below as the Paisley model).
3 Industrial land prices were identified as a factor explaining industrial rents in six UK markets in Tsolacos et al. (2001).
4 The Federal Reserve Board's Index of Manufacturing Output (IMO) was used in AMB Property Corporation's Industrial Absorption Indicator (IAI) for predicting industrial RE demand (AMB, 2002).
5 Industrial firm sales, cash flow, and profitability were used (along with two output variables) in a study of nine English regions in Tsolacos et al. (2005).
6 Trade (i.e., imports and exports) was identified in AMB (2009) as capable of explaining 79 per cent of net absorption[14] in US industrial RE from 1990 to 2008.
7 In the USA, the Purchasing Managers' Index (PMI), issued by the Institute for Supply Management (ISM), was used, along with the Federal Reserve Board's IMO, as leading indicators of industrial RE demand in Anderson and Guirguis (2011) (also referred to as the NAIOP model).

Let us have a look at some of these studies.

The Wheaton and Torto (1990) model

Following their observation that most industrial buildings in their area of study were either owner-occupied or single-tenant-occupied, they felt that this warranted modelling the production (and demand) of industrial RE as a capital investment decision. To that effect, they advanced an 'accelerator-type' model, linking plant deliveries to industrial (i.e., manufacturing) employment and the after-tax cost of corporate capital. (An 'accelerator' model treats 'induced investment' as a function of the change in some other variable, typically national income or consumption.)

It is doubtful, however, whether manufacturing (and distribution) employment is a good predictor of industrial RE demand. First, because changes in the technology and structure of industrial production may well result in drops in industrial employment while, at the same time, demand for industrial RE may be rising. This happened, for instance, in the USA, when from 1990 Q1 to 2002 Q1 manufacturing employment fell by 13.7 per cent, while occupied industrial stock increased by 18.5 per cent (AMB, 2002). Second, because many employees who in the US are census-classified as manufacturing employees work in fact in offices rather than in industrial premises (Rabianski and Black, 1997) – so reliance on the 'manufacturing employment' classification may well yield erroneous results if attempted for the purpose of industrial RE demand forecasting.

The Paisley (2000) model

The Paisley University model was an attempt to explain rents in the Scottish industrial property market, developed by academics associated with the University of Paisley, and published in 2000 as a RICS (Royal Institute of Chartered Surveyors) paper[15] (Brown et al., 2000). The model took the following form:

$$R_t = \beta_0 + \beta_1 \mathrm{GVA}_{t-n} + \beta_2 \mathrm{VR}_{t-n} + \beta_3 \frac{\mathrm{TU}_{t-n}}{\mathrm{TS}_{t-n}} + \beta_4 R_{t-n} + \varepsilon,$$

where the terms have the following meanings:

R_t	=	average nominal rent in year t.
GVA_{t-n}	=	Scottish gross value added (see Chapter 2) at constant prices; this was a proxy for industrial activity, the idea being that rises in GVA increase the willingness and ability of industrial enterprises to bid for industrial space. (Notice the prefix t versus $t-n$: t is a given year; $t-n$ is some previous year. For example, if $t = 2011$ and $n = 1$, $t-n = 2010$. So GVA_{t-n} is the assumption that the GVA of year 2010 affects next year's rents.)
VR_{t-n}	=	actual vacancy rate (= available industrial space/total stock); again, the assumption is that previous period's VR affects this period's rent.
$\mathrm{TU}_{t-n}/\mathrm{TS}_{t-n}$	=	take-up over total stock. 'Take-up' is floor space let or sold for occupation within designated period. It is not total occupied space, as 'only market activity can be measured' (Brown et al., 2000: 4). Total stock, in this study, was defined as all industrial units within recognized industrial estates or areas, but excluding large, single-user facilities, and 'non-standard' premises. Premises identified as 'business units', yards, and open storage were also excluded (Brown et al., 2000: 1).
R_{t-n}	=	average rent in previous period.
ε	=	error term (see Section 6.1).

The model was applied to Central Scotland, utilizing data from May 1995 to May 2000. The data came from SPN, and included industrial stock in units greater than 999 square metres constructed since 1990. The researchers concluded that both take-up and the actual vacancy rate determined rental values for industrial property, but that the 'strength of the economy' (as measured by GVA) and rents paid in previous periods were more significant determinants.

The model did not try to calculate a NVR for industrial RE, or a total occupancy rate, the way that is usually done in office demand models. Instead, the authors assumed that as long as the take-up rate is less than the actual vacancy rate (both rates being possible to calculate from market data), it should be a good indicator of overall demand. (Otherwise 'latent' (i.e., unsatisfied) demand cannot be measured.) In the period of study, vacancy rates happened to be relatively high, so the model may have captured the 'true' demand for industrial RE in Central Scotland.

The AMB (2002) model

The AMB Property Corporation, a US owner, operator, and developer of industrial RE, advanced in 2002 an in-house predictor of industrial RE demand in the USA, which they called the AMB Industrial Absorption Indicator (IAI). In their model,

$$\text{demand for industrial space at time } t = f\ (\text{manufacturing output at } t-1),$$
$$\text{manufacturing output} = f\ (\text{employment, productivity}),$$
$$\text{productivity} = f\ (\text{investment, technology}).$$

Manufacturing output, in turn, is measured by the Federal Reserve Board Index of Manufacturing Output (FRB's IMO) for the USA, which is released monthly. AMB believed that this index was a good proxy for the entire supply chain in US industry. A supply chain is the flows of materials, intermediate products, information, and finance from suppliers to manufacturers (narrow definition) to wholesalers to retailers to consumers (broad definition). Since manufacturing is at the centre of this activity (importing from suppliers and exporting to resalers), AMB deemed a manufacturing index, like FRB's IMO, appropriate for capturing overall industrial activity.

Notice that their model did not reject the relationship of manufacturing employment to manufacturing output; what it rejected was using the US census classification of 'manufacturing employment' as a predictor of industrial RE demand, the way previous studies had done in imitation of office demand models, which, rather successfully, have associated 'raw' office employment with office RE demand. In the AMB (2002) model, on the other hand, it was felt that output was a better predictor of industrial RE demand because output rises stem from manufacturing employment growth and/or productivity improvements. (The model actually found an 88 per cent correlation between industrial RE demand and manufacturing output in the USA in the period under study.)

AMB further found that their IAI described the overall industrial RE market better than sub-parts of it (like warehousing, manufacturing, and R&D). Applied to the USA as a whole (rather than at a metropolitan level) over the 1990 Q1 to 2002 Q1 period with a six-month lag, the AMB IAI could explain 99 per cent of variations in an index of actual industrial net absorption (a proxy for industrial demand) over that period, and estimate it six months into the future. So, in essence, the AMB IAI model involves utilizing manufacturing output (as captured by FRB's IMO) as its main building block in order to forecast actual industrial net absorption six months ahead, on the assumption that industrial net absorption is a good proxy for industrial RE demand. (Recall, though, the Paisley model's caution about the difficulty of measuring 'latent' demand if the take-up rate happens to be equal to the actual vacancy rate.)

The NAIOP (2011) model

This was prepared by Anderson and Guirguis (2011) on account of NAIOP (the Commercial Real Estate Development Association of the USA, www.naiop.org/). Its stated purpose was 'to create a model that can forecast changes in demand for industrial real estate'. The authors ended up using two main variables that were found to lead changes in that demand:

1 The ISM PMI, which stands for the Institute for Supply Management (ISM)[16] Purchasing Managers' Index (PMI). It shows the economic health state of the manufacturing sector, and is made up of five elements: new orders, inventory levels, supply deliveries, production, and employment conditions. If it has a value of more than 50, the sector is expanding, if less than 50, the sector is contracting.
2 The FRB's IMO, which we have already met.

The authors used these variables with assorted time lags, along with past-period net absorption rates, in order to explain/estimate 'net absorption' at time *t*. Their study covered the period 1990 Q2 to 2003 Q3 time-wise, and the USA place-wise. Their ultimate choice of variables came after they had discarded other, seemingly relevant, variables, like 'manufacturing employment', in line with AMB's (2002) earlier work, which had found that total employment had an 80 per cent correlation with industrial RE demand, whereas manufacturing employment had a 75 per cent correlation. Anderson and Guirguis (2011) suggested that a reason for total employment's better correlation with industrial RE demand was simply that as total employment increases, more goods are produced and consumed, and as a result the usage of industrial space increases. And yet, they rejected using population as an explanatory variable because (i) much of industrial output is not meant for the population of a given country (or city) but is exported (Hughes, 1994) and (ii) corroborating this, the AMB (2002) study had found a correlation of only 6 per cent between the US population and industrial RE demand. Eventually, the authors found that the best predictors of this demand are the two variables mentioned (ISM's PMI and FRB's IMO), as in the context of their model they could predict 83 per cent of the variations in industrial property 'net absorption' in the period 2004 Q1 to 2010 Q1 (again, 'net absorption' was the proxy they used for industrial RE demand, like AMB (2002) had done).

Although the above models are very useful, the search for better demand-estimating models continues. The following are two promising areas of research:

1 'Downsizing' some of the above macro-models (like the AMB IAI, or the NAIOP model) to make them operative at the state, metropolitan, or city level – which requires analogous data, however, as, for example, the FRB's IMO is aggregated at the national level only.
2 While moving 'down' to this direction, it may be useful to incorporate firm-related variables, like profitability (the way it was attempted, e.g., in Tsolacos 2005), in order to combine the 'micro' side of things (i.e., firms treating industrial location choices as capital investment decisions) to the 'macro' side.

Summary of main points

1 Other than the level of rents, main determinants of demand for office, retail, and industrial space are as follows:

- For offices: office employment and amount of office space per employee; economic growth.
- For stores: geographical, economic, and demographic attributes of the trade area; economic growth.
- For factories: broadly, manufacturing output; at an individual level, site and building characteristics are important.

2 In commercial RE, particularly the office sector, a natural vacancy rate (NVR) can be identified. This is a specific proportion of vacant properties into all properties that tends to persist over time in the sense that deviations from it are temporary. Such deviations indicate that the particular RE commercial market is in disequilibrium; an actual vacancy rate that is less than the NVR marks a period of rising property rents, and vice versa.
3 It is possible that the NVR itself may change at some point in a particular market – if one or more of the factors that determine it change. It is just that such changes are infrequent because of the institutional and behavioural nature of those factors.
4 Demand for retail space is very much influenced by the method(s) used to identify and assess a retailing outlet's trade, or catchment, area.
5 Such methods range from the checklist and the analogue methods, to multiple regression analysis, gravity modelling, and the use of geographic information systems (GIS), and are often used in complementary ways. The retailing industry standard is the Huff model, increasingly assisted by GIS, while the checklist method is more appropriate for small businesses. The analogue method is also very popular.
6 Demand for industrial space is the most difficult to quantify. Even though, in the USA, manufacturing output has been found to be a good predictor of industrial 'net absorption' (the net decrease or increase in the 'take-up' of available vacant properties), and hence of industrial RE demand, the basic data are compiled at the national level. At a smaller geographical level, attempts to model the take-up of industrial space as a capital investment decision have looked promising.

Review questions and exercises

1 Show your understanding of the following concepts:

natural vacancy rate (NVR) versus actual vacancy rate
net absorption (as regards a property sector)
rent escalation
pre-letting
office class
break option
trade area
Reilly's model, break-point model, Huff's model

2 In our example to demonstrate Reilly's/Converse's gravity model, we found, first, that at a point X located 24 km from city A, and 6 km from city B, for every \$100 of trade that would be going to B, there would be \$25.83 of trade going to A. Yet when next we

calculated the break-point between the two cities, we found that it was located 20.11 from A and 9.89 from B. But since X is clearly inside B's trade area (which has a radius of 9.89 km), why should \$25.83 of trade from X go to A at all? Isn't there a contradiction or mistake here? Discuss.

3 Go around a couple of neighbourhoods or localities of your choice and find an appropriate site for a retail shop, using the checklist method. Which neighbourhood/site will you choose? Why? Remember to start by first coming up with a target customer profile and a target site profile. Do not forget, in the end, to incorporate actual rents in your analysis.

4 In the office market model presented in the text, what is the difference between the short-run and the long-run equilibrium? In other words, what is required for short-term, and what for long-term, equilibrium in the market?

5 Given the following demand and supply equations for office space,

$$R_d = 180 - 6Q,$$

$$R_s = -60 + 8Q,$$

$$\text{total space } S = 22,$$

find the equilibrium quantity of occupied space Q, the equilibrium rent R, the equilibrium cost of capital C, and the actual vacancy rate. Assume that the latter is equal to the NVR.

Now assume that R_d rises to $200 - 6Q$. Find the short-run equilibrium and the actual vacancy rate. Is it larger or smaller than the NVR?

Last, assume that R_s changes in response to the stated disturbance, so that $R_s = -80 + 8Q$. At what level of total space will (long-run) equilibrium be restored? At what level of rent? Of occupied space? What will be the cost of capital now?

Verify that the NVR at the restored equilibrium is equal to the NVR at the original equilibrium.

Using a spreadsheet program, prepare three diagrams illustrating the original equilibrium, the disturbance (i.e., the short-run equilibrium), and the re-established (long-run) equilibrium.

6 In an office property market, total stock is 4.8 million square metres. If, at a certain time, vacant space is 16 per cent of the stock, but the NVR characterizing this market is 6 per cent, how much is the 'overhang'? Assuming a net absorption of office space equal to 85,000 square metres per annum, in how many years will the overhang be absorbed? Name two crucial assumptions behind this calculation.

7 Explain why the industrial property sector is less cyclical than other property sectors. Can you find out whether the reasons offered hold in a country other than the USA? If not, how, in your opinion, would your specific findings affect the determination of industrial RE demand in that country? Even if empirical research does not shed light on this matter, you can still try to answer this question by means of a hypothetical, 'what if', scenario.

7 Housing demand and supply

Main sections

Having gone through this chapter, a student should be able to

1 Explain why, from an owner-occupier's viewpoint, house prices cannot be simple capitalizations of house rents.
2 List differences between demand for commercial property and housing demand.
3 Understand the basic architecture of housing demand and supply models.
4 List and explain the main steps involved in estimating future housing 'demand' in a particular jurisdiction.
5 Explain the differences between 'construction', 'changes in RE supply', and 'development'.
6 Discuss the profit-maximization problem of a construction firm involved in RE development, and why it is better to approach the developer's decision in terms of achieving at least a required rate of return.
7 Determine the top price a developer would in principle be prepared to pay for a site.
8 Describe and compare the 'Anglo-American' and 'Greek' modes of residential development.

In this chapter, we show, first, that the price of an owner-occupied dwelling cannot be the simple discounted value of any *imputed* rents the dwelling is supposed to generate, especially if the discount factor is limited to some version of the cost of capital. Second, we show that, as a result, it is perhaps better to focus on housing prices as *distinct* from rents (rather than on rents as the building blocks of prices) when constructing demand or supply models for owner-occupied housing. One demand model and a combined demand and supply model are provided by way of examples, along with a practical estimation of future housing 'demand' on a 'needs' basis. Turning to the construction sector, a housing developer's profit-maximization problem is investigated, focusing on use of the developer's required rate of return in order to calculate how much the developer would pay for a site. Finally, the 'Greek' and 'Anglo-American' modes of residential development are discussed and contrasted.

7.1 Dwelling price versus dwelling rent

On the basis of equation (5.11) in Chapter 5, a possible formulation for the value of a property, which is also renowned for its simplicity, is

$$P_t = \frac{R_t}{k}, \tag{7.1}$$

where P_t is price at time t, R_t is net rent at time t (assumed to be received in perpetuity), and k is the cap rate (cf. Chapter 5). In its simplest form, k is merely the cost of capital, for example the rate that the investor (buyer) would get if they placed their money in a financial instrument instead, usually a bank time deposit account. In the case of owner-occupied housing, however, both numerator and denominator in the above formulation are problematic.[1]

Regarding the numerator, there are three problems:

(I) The first problem is that rent in the case of owner-occupation can only be notional, i.e., imputed, rather than actual. Calculating an imputed rent on an owner-occupied home only makes sense if that rent were arbitrarily equated to what the particular property was thought to fetch if it were rented out, and in comparison with similar actually rented properties. But if the property were rented out, the level of actual rents would, *ceteris paribus*, drop in the area – maybe only a little if this home were the only additional property to be rented out, but substantially and visibly if all owner-occupied homes were turned into rented homes. Assuming, therefore, that the imputed rent on a given property is identical to the rent on a similar actually rented property is wrong.

(II) An alternative is to substitute the 'user-cost' (UC) of housing for rent. The former is equal to[2]

$$UC = (i + d + m + t - g)V \Rightarrow V = \frac{\text{UC}}{i + d + m + t - g}, \tag{7.2a}$$

where

i = after-tax nominal mortgage interest rate as a proxy for the cost of capital,
d = rate of property depreciation,
m = cost of property maintenance (proportional to the value of the property),
t = effective property tax rate, if applicable,
g = property price appreciation (which *reduces* the user-cost of housing),
V = property value (or market price),

Another version of the user-cost (adopted by Moody's Analytics, 2011) treats the latter as a percentage:

$$U_{tk} = (1 - \text{Tax}_{tk})(r_{tk} + \text{Ptax}_{tk}) + M_{tk} - P^{e}_{tk}, \tag{7.2b}$$

where

k	=	metropolitan area (in the USA),
t	=	time period,
U_{tk}	=	user-cost at time t in area k (i.e., the after-tax cost of homeownership),
Tax_{tk}	=	effective marginal income tax rate,
r_{tk}	=	effective mortgage rate,
Ptax_{tk}	=	effective property tax rate,
M_{tk}	=	percentage of house value representing maintenance costs and obsolescence,
P^{e}_{tk}	=	homeowners' expected house price growth over the horizon of their homeownership (estimated using long-run household income growth)

The difference between Equations (7.1) and (7.2a) is that in (7.1) both rent and the cap rate are determined exogenously, whereas in (7.2a) the UC is *originally* defined as a proportion of the (apparently known) value of the property. Equation (7.2a) is useful, however, because it focuses attention on the complicated nature of an appropriate cap rate for owner-occupied homes.

Now, knowing the user-cost on the basis of, say, (7.2a), it might be possible to employ it in the numerator of (7.1) in order to calculate the price of an owner-occupied home if it could be shown that it is really a rent equivalent. This would strengthen a view of the price of even owner-occupied housing as capitalized rents. In effect, formula (7.2a) might be fit for owner-occupied housing also.

Can the user-cost be considered equivalent to actual rent, though? Let us concede that in a purely (and more so in a perfectly) competitive market the user-cost should be the same as the rent or revenue from the property (Green and Malpezzi, 2000). But the real estate market is actually monopolistically competitive. As a result, there is bound to be a difference between user-cost and rent. Hence, user-cost cannot be a substitute for rent.

Let us explain this. In any competitive market, price tends to equal (minimum) average cost in the long run. Economic profit, viewed as a persistent difference between price and cost, tends to zero. In a monopolistically competitive market, the same thing could in principle happen (at a cost higher than the minimum, at a higher price, and at lower output), except *when* in such a market product differentiation is so pronounced and widespread that economic profits, i.e., persistent differences between price and cost, can be generated even over the long run – and in the property market this kind of product differentiation is certainly the norm if for no other reason (and there are plenty of those) than location.

(III) The third problem is that a prospective home-buyer would hardly base their decision *only* on a comparison between the rent they would be paying if they rented and the mortgage cost (if buying through credit) or the opportunity cost of their funds (if buying using their own accumulated savings). They would likely take into account at least five other things:

1 the possibility of capital gains;
2 the possibility of real estate offering a perceived inflation hedge;
3 the perceived association of an owned home with household safety and autonomy;

4 the prospect of leaving a seemingly secure asset to their children or partners; and
5 the possibility of using their future equity in the house in order to meet old-age exigencies.

It is perhaps not impossible to factor these things into the numerator, but clearly net (imputed) rents would not suffice. On the other hand, an investor into commercial property (including houses or flats meant for private renting) would limit the numerator to expected net (actual) rents from the property. This is a calculation that would be carried over to any future resale price of the property.

Turning to the denominator in Equation (7.1), using the mere cost of capital (whatever version of it) as a cap rate is also insufficient. *First*, even in the case of commercial property (CP), limiting oneself to using the cost of capital as a discount factor would ignore other elements, like expected inflation (which is not necessarily encapsulated in the rate offered on bank deposits, although it *is* usually incorporated in lending rates), a risk premium, a recapture premium, and a real return appropriate for the given industry sector (cf. Chapter 5). All of these transcend the rate associated with normal sources of capital (like own or bank funds). Indeed, if this were not so, a CP developer might as well be in the banking business if they could overcome the capital requirement hurdle. *Second*, in the case of owner-occupied housing the cost of capital does not capture the full user-cost (UC) of housing.

In conclusion, an imputed rent could not directly translate into property values – not by a long shot and not unless very complicated adjustments were made in the cap rate used. The problem is that 'the user-cost formula assumes rental and owner-occupied properties to be perfect substitutes, a very strong assumption if compared to the real world' (Bracke, 2011: 15). Having said this, it is also true that house prices and rents often tend to move together over time – it is just that their relationship is far from straightforward (cf. Guðnason, 2005: 8; Kashiwagi, 2011).

So, whereas an investor wishing to evaluate a property to let would be right in capitalizing the expected net rentals from the property (with the cap rate being relatively simple *in principle*), a prospective owner-occupier would primarily focus on price. He or she would still have to ask whether they could afford to buy the property, and a comparison with renting would of course be in order in many cases, but the connection between a possible rent for the property and its price is more complex when looked at from a user's rather than an investor's point of view. This is not a matter of personal preference or aesthetics only, as it affects the way housing demand is formed and should be measured.

7.2 Residential demand

There are some important differences between demand for commercial RE and demand for housing:

1 Generic housing is a necessity with strong social and political undertones and ramifications (cf. Ball, 1983); commercial property (CP), far less so.
2 In those developed countries where owner-occupation predominates, housing makes up most of most people's wealth. This further accentuates housing's role as a mechanism for inter-generational wealth transfer and/or as a hedge against any inadequacies of public or private pension systems. These aspects do not characterize CP, except in a very indirect way.

3 For most homeowners and many renters, housing is not only a means to an end but also an end in itself, i.e., it is associated with a strong utility aspect that typically transcends pecuniary considerations. Put differently, from the users' viewpoint, housing is more often than not a consumption rather than an investment good, even though the latter aspect is always there too. In the case of CP, the means-to-an-end dimension clearly predominates.

4 Owner-occupied housing is associated with strong capital-gain and inflation-hedge considerations. This implies an emphasis on the price of the asset rather than on income from the asset. On the other hand, owners of, or investors in, CP focus primarily on income, even though capital appreciation is still crucial, especially for financial institutions. This difference also raises issues (discussed above) as to the extent to which the price of owner-occupied housing can really be considered a discounted flow of future imputed rentals – whereas with CP things are much more clear-cut.

There are also two important similarities between housing and CP. Users of either calculate how much it will cost to have it, and whether they can afford it, given their current or prospective incomes. Conversely, users of CP and working-age users of residential property need to evaluate whether a particular piece of property will allow them to *achieve* a certain income, considering the way it affords them proximity to customers, or supplies, or simply work – only, in the case of housing users, proximity to work matters *along with* utility considerations, for example the amount of leisure time gained by being closer to work (because of less time spent on commuting) versus perceptions of better life quality in the suburbs. Additionally, leisure gains must be set against the higher price that housing usually has in or near employment hubs, compared to similar housing further away.

With these in mind, modelling residential demand will have to incorporate people's incomes (which in turn are affected by the business cycle phase), household preferences regarding leisure or other amenities, household spending choices between housing and non-housing, commuting time, demographics, the mortgage rate (relevant in buying a house rather than renting), even people's educational level. Naturally, the greater the number of variables, the greater, one hopes, the predictive power of such a model (assuming there are a lot of accurate data to feed into the model), but at the cost of less simplicity. (Simplicity can be a virtue both in decision-making and in facilitating data-gathering.)

7.3 Modelling residential demand: a (demanding!) example

Assuming that it *is* possible to talk about housing as a homogeneous good[3] (and therefore about a representative housing consumer), one way to model housing demand microeconomically is on the basis of a Cobb–Douglas utility function. In Chapter 2, we showed that such a demand model takes the form

$$H = \frac{Ba}{P_h},$$

with H = housing quantity demanded by the typical consumer, if $B = HP_h + XP_x$ (a budget constraint, where P_h and P_x are the prices of H and X, X being a vector, or basket, of non-housing goods) and $U(H, X) = H^a X^{1-a}$ (Cobb–Douglas utility).

In this form, housing demand incorporates income B (the budget constraint), the price of housing P_h, and consumers' preference for housing relative to non-housing (parameter a).

If this is the demand function for a typical consumer, extending this to the level of the market (N consumers) can be done by multiplying Ba/P_h by N.

The above formula can be adjusted to reflect demand in particular housing submarkets (e.g., for owner-occupation, rented accommodation, or 'good' or 'bad' areas), provided we know the utility preferences and incomes of households searching in these submarkets, and the prices of corresponding housing units. It can also be used to show consumer choice between, say, owner-occupation and renting.

In the context of a more advanced (but also fuller) analysis, the Cobb–Douglas utility function can take a form like

$$U = x_1^a x_2^b x_3^c x_4^d x_5^{1-a-b-c-d},$$

where

$$\begin{aligned} x_1 &= \text{owner-occupied housing in area A,} \\ x_2 &= \text{owner-occupied housing in area B,} \\ x_3 &= \text{rented housing in area A,} \\ x_4 &= \text{rented housing in area B,} \\ x_5 &= \text{all other goods,} \end{aligned}$$

whereas the budget constraint will be like

$$B = x_1 P_{x1} + x_2 P_{x2} + x_3 P_{x3} + x_4 P_{x4} + x_5 P_{x5},$$

And, more generally,

$$U = \prod_i x_i^{a_i} \left(\sum_i a_i = 1 \right),$$

$$B = \sum_i x_i P_{x_i}.$$

Cobb–Douglas demand is also characterized by unitary elasticity of substitution between, say, housing and non-housing. This means that the consumer's budget share going to housing stays the same if the price of housing increases (which means that the consumer buys a smaller quantity of housing instead).

7.3.1 The De Bruyne–Van Hove model

We shall now provide a specific example of how to model residential demand. The example is based on De Bruyne and Van Hove (2006),[4] and it focuses on (a) households' incomes and (b) households making two choices: one between more or less leisure time, with less leisure time resulting from a decision to spend more time on commuting, and one on allocating household income between housing and non-housing.

Consider an urban area made up of a central place (a 'Central Business District') and a periphery (maybe a ring of suburbs around the core). This is a typical situation in modern metropolitan areas and many other cities. Workers living in the core are assumed to work in the core, but workers living in the periphery have the choice of working in the core (thus having to commute to the core) or working in the periphery. If the total population of workers in the periphery is 1, the proportion of periphery workers working in the periphery is δ; hence, the proportion working in the core is $1-\delta$. Income is w (= the wage) times the number of hours worked, W, minus the cost of commuting, T.

Thus, income $= wW - T$. If W is the same in both areas, workers who commute to the core will necessarily have to give up some leisure time in order to work there.

Now, the income of a periphery resident working in the periphery is $w_p W_p$, but the income of a periphery resident working in the core is $w_c W_c - T$. Consequently, average income in the periphery is $\delta(w_p W_p) + (1-\delta)(w_c W_c - T)$. Moreover, W equals the total number of hours, M, available to a person (say, 24; more than that if the calendar unit is a month) minus leisure time L, minus commuting time C. Therefore,

$$\text{average income in periphery } = \delta w_p(M - L_p^p) + (1-\delta)[w_c(M - L_p^c - C) - T], \quad (7.3)$$

where L_p^p is the amount of leisure time if one lives and works in the periphery and L_p^c is the amount of leisure time if one lives in the periphery but works in the core. The two amounts differ by the commuting time, $C = L_p^p - L_p^c \Rightarrow L_p^p = C + L_p^c$. Hence, Equation (7.3) can be written as

$$\begin{aligned}\text{average income in periphery} &= \delta w_p(M - L_p^c - C) + (1-\delta)[w_c(M - L_p^c - C) - T] \\ &= (M - L_p^c - C)[\delta w_p + (1-\delta)w_c] - (1-\delta)T. \quad (7.4)\end{aligned}$$

This is now the budget, or income, constraint that will be used in solving the utility maximization problem of the average worker in the periphery – and, in so doing, we shall develop an expression for house price determination.

The average worker, or consumer, in the periphery has the following double problem: a choice between leisure and working, and one between spending on housing and spending on non-housing goods (and services). A number of utility functions can be used to describe this problem mathematically. De Bruyne and Van Hove (2006) opted for a Cobb–Douglas one as it overcomes the 'demand aggregation problem' (see Chapter 2).

Recall that such a utility function can involve a number of variables, as in $U(x,y,h) = x^{a_1}y^{a_2}h^{a_3}$, with $a_1 + a_2 + a_3 = 1$. In the case at hand, utility is a function of L_p^c, X, and H, where L_p^c = amount of leisure time if one lives in the periphery but works in the core, X = quantity of non-housing consumption, and H = quantity of housing consumption. Thus,

$$U(L_p^c, X, H) = (L_p^c)^{\alpha} X^{\beta(1-\alpha)} H^{(1-\beta)(1-\alpha)}.$$

Notice that $\alpha + \beta(1-\alpha) + (1-\beta)(1-\alpha) = 1$, i.e., as expected in a Cobb–Douglas function.

This utility function suggests that consumers in the periphery draw utility from leisure, housing, and non-housing. They will try to maximize their utility subject to their budget constraint:

$$\begin{aligned}\max U &= (L_p^c)^{\alpha} X^{\beta(1-\alpha)} H^{(1-\beta)(1-\alpha)} \\ &\quad + \lambda\left\{(M - L_p^c - C)\left[\delta w_p + (1-\delta)w_c\right] - (1-\delta)T - p_h H - p_x X\right\},\end{aligned}$$

where

p_h = average price of housing,
p_x = average price of non-housing.

The reader should recognize this as a Lagrangian function, where the term to the right of λ is equal to zero, as income received equals total spending. It will therefore give rise to the following four first-order conditions for optimization (see Chapter 2):

$$\frac{\partial U}{\partial L_p^c} = \alpha (L_p^c)^{a-1} X^{\beta(1-\alpha)} H^{(1-\beta)(1-\alpha)} - \lambda \left[\delta w_p + (1-\delta) w_c\right] = 0, \tag{7.5}$$

$$\frac{\partial U}{\partial X} = (1-\alpha)\beta \mathrm{X}^{\beta(1-\alpha)-1} (L_p^c)^{\alpha} H^{(1-\beta)(1-\alpha)} - \lambda p_x = 0, \tag{7.6}$$

$$\frac{\partial U}{\partial H} = (1-\beta)(1-\alpha) \mathrm{H}^{(1-\beta)(1-\alpha)-1} (L_p^c)^{\alpha} X^{\beta(1-\alpha)} - \lambda p_h = 0, \tag{7.7}$$

$$\frac{\partial U}{\partial \lambda} = (M - L_p^c - C)\left[\delta w_p + (1-\delta) w_c\right] - (1-\delta) T\alpha - p_h H - p_x X = 0. \tag{7.8}$$

Now dividing (7.5) by (7.7) will allow derivation of an expression for leisure:[5]

$$L_p^c = \frac{a p_h H}{(1-\alpha)(1-\beta)[\delta w_p + (1-\delta) w_c]}. \tag{7.9}$$

Equation (7.9) shows that there is a positive relationship between amount of leisure time and spending on housing (i.e., $p_h H$). Basically this is because the price of housing nearer the core incorporates the commuting expenses that otherwise people living further away would have to incur to travel to the core, so core housing is bound to be more expensive than peripheral housing (for similar housing units). Put differently, the smaller the distance between work place and living place, the more leisure one has – but at the cost of spending more on housing.

Then, dividing (7.7) by (7.6) leads to the following proportional relationship between the ratio of the price of housing to the price of non-housing and the ratio of the quantity of non-housing to the quantity of housing consumed:

$$\frac{1-\beta}{\beta} \frac{X}{H} = \frac{p_h}{p_x}. \tag{7.10}$$

It follows from (7.10) that

$$p_x X = \frac{p_h H \beta}{1-\beta}.$$

Plugging this into (7.8) results in an equation linking the price of housing, p_h, to the quantity of housing, H:

$$p_h = (1-\beta) \frac{(M - L_p^c - C)[\delta w_p + (1-\delta) w_c] - (1-\delta) T}{H}. \tag{7.11}$$

Recall that $M - L_p^c - C$ is equal to W, i.e., number of hours worked. The average wage is $\delta w_p + (1-\delta) w_c$, where δw_p is wage in the periphery times the proportion of periphery workers working in the periphery, and $(1-\delta)w_c$ is wage in the core times the proportion of periphery workers working in the core. Thus, the expression $W[\delta w_p + (1-\delta)w_c]$ is gross average income from work, which becomes net income if the cost of commuting, T, which is relevant to $1-\delta$ of all workers living in the periphery, is subtracted from gross income. Consequently, we have

$$p_h = (1-\beta)\frac{\text{Income} - (1-\delta)T}{H}. \tag{7.12}$$

Equation (7.12) suggests a negative relationship between price and quantity of housing (as expected in any demand model), a positive one between price of housing and income (again as expected for normal goods), and a negative one between price of housing and cost of commuting. The latter relationship mirrors a positive one between price of housing and amount of leisure time, as shown earlier. Notice, too, that a higher β (which is a positive exponent of X, the amount of non-housing consumption in the Cobb–Douglas utility function introduced earlier) would imply a smaller housing price, resulting from a stronger preference for non-housing over housing consumption.

Other factors could also be added in a housing demand model: demographics (e.g., Ermisch, 1996), tenure choice, mortgage interest rates, or expected house price appreciation (Dusansky et al., 2010). The last two can be taken care of through appropriate adjustments in (prospective) owner-occupiers' income. For example, a reduction in interest rates could be shown to be equivalent to a rise in the income of households who are in the process of buying their homes, or are contemplating to do so. An appropriate time horizon could then be factored in: i.e., loan maturity on one hand, and expected income over the same period on the other. And house price appreciation, although it *usually* translates into cash *when* a house is (re)sold, ('usually' because it is also possible to realize part of the increase in value through equity release schemes – see Chapter 4) could nevertheless be thought of as a capital gain equivalent to a series of smaller payments accruing to the household over a relevant time horizon. After all, according to Case et al. (2005), Benjamin et al. (2004), Campbell and Coco (2007), and Bajari et al. (2010a), house price appreciation seems to cause increases in non-housing consumption far more than increases in other kinds of wealth do – exactly as if the increases in house prices had amounted to rises in incomes.

Finally, there is some evidence (Lindenthal, 2007; Lindenthal and Eichholtz, 2010) that educational level exercises a positive influence on the demand for housing (i.e., better-educated people demand 'more', i.e., better, housing), although there remains a question mark over whether this factor works autonomously or through the higher income that better educated people usually command. In fact, education may even go some way towards counteracting what a number of researchers have identified as the damping effect of an ageing society on housing demand (Mankiw and Weil, 1989; Lindh and Malmberg, 2008; Malmberg, 2010).

7.4 Adding supply: an extended model[6]

A dwelling is supposed to generate (housing) services. Those 'services' (an unobservable, homogeneous, and divisible, commodity) are a theoretical construct proposed by R. F. Muth (1960). In practice, this implies that 'a grand house and a modest house differ only in the number of homogeneous service units they contain' (Epple et al., 2009: 2). Although the concept has been pivotal in generating a subsequent flood of high-quality housing research (because, among others, it facilitates the introduction of 'imputed rent' in studies of owner-occupied housing), it remains essentially problematic (cf. Section 7.1). Nevertheless, the very attributes of the concept allow one to assume, for example, that the sum of housing services is proportional to the housing stock (Egebo and Lienert, 1988). Looking at the latter, a possible demand equation for it (linking stock and price) is

$$S_t = a_1 P_t + V_t^d, \tag{7.13}$$

or, alternatively,

$$P_t = \frac{S_t - V_t^d}{a_1}, \tag{7.14}$$

where

S_t = stock (total quantity) of housing at time t,
P_t = price of a (standardized) unit of housing at time t,
V_t^d = a vector of other (exogenous) determinants of the demand for housing,[7] such as real per-capita income and demographics, at time t,
a_1 = slope of the demand line ($a_1 < 0$).

Turning to the supply of housing, a possible equation is

$$C_t = a_2 P_t - V_t^s, \tag{7.15}$$

where

C_t = total new construction[8] (which is also a proxy for housing investment) over period t,
P_t = price of housing at time t,
V_t^s = a vector of (exogenous) cost variables (e.g., opportunity cost of capital and cost of materials and labour),
a_2 = slope of the supply line ($a_2 > 0$).

But considering that this period's stock equals last period's stock plus this period's new construction minus this period's stock depreciation δ, new construction equals the change in the total stock from one period to the next plus stock depreciation δ during the current period. That is,

$$\text{if } S_t = S_{t-1} + C_t - \delta S_t, \text{ then } C_t = S_t - S_{t-1} + \delta S_t. \tag{7.16}$$

From (7.15) and (7.16), it is evident that

$$a_2 P_t - V_t^s = S_t - S_{t-1} + \delta S_t. \tag{7.17}$$

From (7.17), it follows that housing supply is described by

$$S_t = \frac{(S_{t-1} - V_t^s) + a_2 P_t}{1 + \delta}, \tag{7.18}$$

or, alternatively,

$$P_t = \frac{S_t(1+\delta) - (S_{t-1} - V_t^s)}{a_2}. \tag{7.19}$$

Then, from (7.13) and (7.18), or from (7.14) and (7.19), it is a simple matter to come up with expressions for equilibrium price and quantity (i.e., stock). (This is left as an exercise for the reader.)

7.5 Determinants of housing demand and supply

In the wake of the foregoing discussion, Table 7.1 sums up the most important factors that affect housing demand and supply. It is worth mentioning, in this connection, the seminal works of Muth (1960, 1969, 1971), and, regarding supply in particular, Poterba (1984), Malpezzi and Maclennan (2001), Glaeser et al. (2005), Epple et al. (2009), Levin and Pryce (2009), and Phang et al. (2010). For example, Poterba (1984: 748–9) introduced 'a residential investment equation based on an asset-market model of the housing sector, in which the principal driving force behind new construction is the real price of houses'. Earlier, Muth (1969) had expressed the price elasticity of housing supply (in the USA) as

$$e = \frac{\rho_K \varepsilon_s + e_L}{\rho_L},$$

where

ρ_K = share of capital (and, in general, non-land) costs in total development cost,
ε_s = elasticity of substitution (see Section 2.2.8) between land and non-land inputs,
e_L = supply elasticity of developable land,
ρ_L = share of land cost in total development cost.

This suggests that the elasticity of housing supply increases with ρ_K, ε_s, and e_L, but decreases if the share of land cost into total cost rises. As we will see later, this is because a higher share of land cost increases, *ceteris paribus*, the developer's uncertainty about their future return.

Levin and Pryce (2009) have also suggested a possible link between interest rates and housing supply that goes beyond the effect of rates on developers' borrowing costs: to the extent that house price rises are caused by declining real interest rates over the longer term, this may motivate developers to delay building in order to realize higher profits later on.

Different studies have come up with different estimates of the demand or supply elasticity of housing. This is not surprising since 'there are a large number of macro-economic, micro-economic and institutional factors that explain new housing supply which appear to vary in absolute and relative importance between countries' (Fortune et al., 2008) (cf. also, on the UK, Levin and Pryce, 2009). Thus, Malpezzi and Maclennan (2001) found that the long-run supply elasticity was smaller in the UK (between 1 and 4 in the pre-Second World War period, and between 0 and 1 in the post-Second World War period) than in the USA (4 and 10, and 6 and 13, respectively). And Sánchez and Johansson (2011) found that the long-run supply elasticity in 21 OECD countries from the 1980s to mid/late 2000s was

- >1 in the USA, Canada, Sweden and Denmark,
- 1 in Finland and Japan,

Table 7.1 Determinants (other than own-price) of housing demand and supply

Demand determinant	*Supply determinant*
1 Current income	1 Land availability (which depends on land ownership pattern and the laxity or otherwise of the planning function)
2 Expected (permanent) income	2 Expected price at time of completion (in practice, a function of past prices, as it typically takes one to two years to construct a house or apartment building).
3 Proximity to work	3 National or area-specific zoning and building regulations
4 Proximity to amenities (social and environmental)	4 Cost of construction (labour and materials; current borrowing cost; insurance and regulatory costs
5 Transport costs (monetary and time-related)	5 Cost of land (the developer-paid purchase price of land, which is roughly the difference between expected revenue from the development and the sum of construction cost and the developer's required return; also, the opportunity cost of keeping the land undeveloped)
6 Dwelling characteristics (other than location), e.g., house or flat; size; etc.	6 Developer's required rate of return
7 Tenure, expressed as a tenure-choice factor	7 Taxes (like VAT on newly constructed dwellings)
8 Mortgage interest rates, and other loan terms (relevant to those considering owner-occupation)	8 Building technology
9 Cost of dwelling maintenance	9 Long-term real interest rates (Levin and Pryce, 2009
10 Expected price appreciation (relevant to current or prospective owner-occupiers)	
11 Demographic factors (rate of population growth, rate of household formation, age distribution of population, dependency ratio*)	
12 Non-housing wealth of households	
13 Social characteristics of households, including educational level	
14 Saving interest rates, as they affect the speed with which households can save towards house purchase	
15 Capital-gains tax, to the extent that capital gains matter to home-owners	
16 Property taxes: if, e.g., owner-occupation is heavily taxed, then renting may be an alternative but only if there is enough rented accommodation in the area; otherwise, people may decide o stay put (i.e., share with relatives)	

* Dependency ratio = typically, the number of people younger than 15 and older than 64 divided by the number of people aged 15–64

- < 1 in 15 countries (among them Switzerland, the Netherlands, Austria, Italy, Germany, the UK, Australia, New Zealand, Israel, Ireland, Spain, France).

An important point in much of the academic literature on the topic is that housing supply is more responsive to *changes* in house prices than to their *levels*. Focusing on Britain, the USA, and Australia, Ball et al. (2011) showed this to be true. They calculated that, in *difference* form, the price elasticity of housing supply over the mid-1950s to 2007 was 4.5 in Britain, 5.5 in the USA, and 3.1 in Australia (Ball et al., 2011: 21). However, in terms of *levels*, the elasticities were weak in all three countries. This suggests that the choice of methodology can affect measurements. The same study argued that 'different spatial scales capture different aspects of the problem [of estimating the price elasticity of housing supply] and, therefore, there is merit from comparing results at international, national, regional, local and firm level' (Ball et al., 2011: 5).

Regarding demand, a crucial factor in determining the response of housing quantity 'consumed' to a change in house prices or to a change in consumers' incomes is the elasticity of substitution between housing and non-housing consumption (see Section 2.2.8). It has been suggested, however, that housing consumption responses to price changes depend 'not only upon the demand elasticity [...] but also upon the supply elasticity. [...] the response to a price reduction will be smaller with less elastic supply' (Hanushek and Quigley, 1980: 453).

An additional factor determining the price elasticity of housing demand is transaction costs, resulting, for example, in a −0.5 elasticity for owner-occupied housing in Brazil (Piza et al., 2011). Interestingly, the price elasticity of housing demand in the UK has been estimated at −0.5 also (Barker, 2003: 39). In addition, Piza et al. estimate that in Brazil, in line with other developing countries (cf. Malpezzi, 1999), price elasticity for renters is slightly higher than for owners, whereas the latter are more sensitive to income variation than renters (Piza et al., 2011: 22).

Finally, the income elasticity of demand for selected countries c. 2000 has been estimated as 1 for the UK, 0.6 for France, 0.4 for Italy, 1.9 for Spain, 1.1 for Ireland, 1.2 for the Netherlands, and 0.5 for Finland (Barker, 2003: 39, citing HM Treasury, 2003). Needless to say, such estimates are subject to variation over time and across space.

7.6 A practical example of housing 'demand' calculation[9]

Planning authorities and market practitioners often need to forecast housing 'demand' in a particular jurisdiction (country, state, county, city, or town) a number of years into the future. Such a forecast may, for example, support an estimate of how much land will have to be found to accommodate the number of additional housing units required (if the forecast identifies the need for more housing rather than less). The 'land' required does not have to be actual ground, i.e., suburban land. It may come about as a result of the planning function easing the zoning and building regulations in specific areas, so that high-rise apartment buildings can be erected instead, provided of course that high-rise does not conflict with other planning priorities, or with household preferences.

The steps involved in such a study may be as follows:[10]

1. Calculation of 'headship' rates (to be explained below), by age group, at the most recent census date (2001). The age groups used were from 0–14 to 70–74 and 75+.
2. Given population projections, by age group, calculation of future headship rates. In this case, the time horizon was 2021.
3. Calculation of 'household demand propensities' by age group (to identify dwelling-type preferences on the part of households), at the most recent census date.
4. Estimation of future household size and composition.
5. Data on current composition of housing stock.
6. Data on residential construction under way (on the basis of building permits).
7. Data on tenure types (because although type of tenure – e.g., owner-occupation or private renting – does not affect overall demand for generic housing, it is thought to provide 'some indication to builders as to the type of housing that may be more marketable' (Stantec, 2003: 3.9)).
8. Then, given population and household projections, and household demand propensities, the total number of different housing types for a number of years into the future can be forecast.

9 The difference between the forecast total and the current housing situation is the amount of new housing (broken down by type) required over the forecast period.
10 Once the quantity of required new housing is forecast, the corresponding land requirements can be estimated, and appropriate planning policies initiated.

Explanations

1 The 'headship' rate is the number of households in a given age group. For instance, in the City of Windsor in 2001 the number of households corresponding to the age group 15–19 was 350, and the number of people in that age group was 12,965. This does *not* mean that 350 households (where the breadwinner was between 15 and 19 years old) had, on average, 37 members each! It simply means that in that particular age group there could be found 350 households whose head was 15–19, while most people from that age group 'belonged' to households whose heads were of other ages. Thus, in this particular case, the headship rate was simply 350/12,965 = 0.027, meaning that 2.7 per cent of people in the given age group were household heads.
2 Now, given a population projection of 15,073 people in the 15–19 age group for the year 2021 (taken from statistical sources), applying the headship rate of 2.7 per cent to that projection gives a number of households in that age group by the year 2021 equal to 407.
3 In the context of this study 'household demand propensities' refer to demands for certain types of housing by people in different age groups. Thus, the 350 households identified as headed by 15–19-year olds in 2001 were found to be distributed into the following dwelling types:[11]

single detached	27.1%
semi-detached	2.9%
row	2.9%
duplex/apartment	15.7%
apartment <5 storeys	24.3%
apartment ≥5 storeys	27.1%
other single	0.0%

4 Data on future household size and composition is important in helping estimate the required size of housing units.
5 The current composition of the housing stock (i.e., categorization by dwelling type, and number of units in each category) will later be subtracted from total projections of number of dwellings by type in order to render the number of additional dwellings by type needed.
6 The number of dwellings under construction (or the number of dwellings for which building permits have been issued) will help estimate housing needs in later years of the forecast period.
7 Data on tenure types will help refine the projections, but such information is secondarily useful.
8 Thus, knowing that in, say, 2021 (or any other year during the forecast period) the number of people in, say, the 15–19 age group (or any other age group) will be 15,073, knowing the headship rate, which is 2.7 per cent, and therefore that the expected number of households will be 407, and knowing the distribution of household demand propensities (found in step 3), we can estimate the number of dwellings of different types demanded by those 407 households:

single detached	407 × 27.1% = 110
semi-detached	407 × 2.9% = 12
row	407 × 2.9% = 12
duplex/apartment	407 × 15.7% = 64
apartment <5 storeys	407 × 24.3% = 99
apartment ≥5 storeys	407 × 27.1% = 110
other single	0.0

Then, adding the number of dwellings under each dwelling type for each age group will give the total number of dwellings of a given type 'demanded' by the year 2021. Adding the numbers of dwellings under all dwelling types will give the total number of dwellings forecast to be 'demanded' in 2021. That number is of course equal to the total number of households projected for 2021 under the population projection scenario chosen, but the usefulness of this forecasting method is that it allows estimates of the numbers of different dwelling types 'demanded'.

9 For example, the total number of single-detached houses in the City of Windsor in 2021 was forecast to be 66,612 (Stantec, 2003: 3.10). The number of such houses in 2001 was known to have been 52,590 (Stantec, 2003: 3.10). The difference (14,022) is the number of single-detached houses forecast to be needed by 2021. The same analysis can be undertaken for other years all the way to 2021, thus breaking down the forecast period into tranches, each with its own requirement in terms of single-detached houses.

10 Estimation of the amount and kind of land required in order to satisfy the housing 'demand' projections is a technical planning matter and will not be pursued here.

The methodology presented above does provide insights into the number of housing units, and of what kind, that may be needed over the forecast period, but, on the other hand, it is more about implicit or pent up demand, and ultimately about 'needs', than about actual demand in an economic sense.[12] Still, considering the many problems involved in identifying market demand curves, the associated data collection problems, and the tall order of forecasting incomes and household preferences many years into the future, the 'needs-based' methodology is practicable, useful, reasonably accurate, and simple to apply.

Even so, disturbances that may push the forecast off course are always possible. One question, for example, is whether current house prices (and expected house prices based on current ones) are enough of an incentive to developers to build the extra quantity of housing apparently required. There may also be unexpected migration flows, or changes in the vacancy rate of either the owner-occupied or the rented sector. Or, easier credit terms may raise house prices *and* accelerate the rate of household formation. Higher house prices will induce developers to build more, and planning authorities may (or may not) yield to requests to release more land for development or introduce other accommodating arrangements. New house-building may overshoot the quantity of new housing demanded at existing prices, leading to market disequilibrium and subsequent adjustments. Such real estate market dynamics are investigated in Chapter 8.

7.7 Construction, development, and supply changes

There is some confusion surrounding the notion of (a) building construction versus development; (b) construction output and supply changes; and (c) new development versus redevelopment versus refurbishment.

The confusion between building construction and development exists for two reasons. First, in quite a few cases the roles of constructor and developer are carried out by the same entity. Second, official definitions do not draw a sufficiently clear distinction between the two.

For instance, the UK Town and Country Planning Act of 1990 defined 'development' as 'the carrying out of building, engineering, mining or other operations in, on, over or under land, or the making of any material change in the use of any buildings or other land', and 'building operations' to include 'demolition of buildings; rebuilding; structural alterations of or additions to buildings; and other operations normally undertaken by a person carrying on business as a builder'.[13]

Yet real estate *development* as an economic process is different from building or constructing: it typically involves the purchase and assembling of land,[14] the carrying of land-keeping costs,[15] getting planning permission, recognizing the opportune time to build, organizing the actual production (often through sub-contracting the job to builders), and selling the finished product to the market at large for profit (hence the term 'speculative development'). So development is mostly about financing and risk-taking rather than building, even though both functions can be executed by one entity.

There is also a difference between gross construction (of, say, new dwellings or offices) and changes in the supply of such space. Gross construction (including redevelopment and modification of existing structures) minus stock depreciation is of course a large part of a change in supply – but the latter may also include variations in vacant accommodation, whether for renting or for owner-occupation. Although we will not be examining the role of vacancies in housing market adjustment here, that role must not be underestimated (cf. Robinson, 1979: 25–6; Gabriel and Nothaft, 1988; Wheaton, 1990; Liang, 2006; Magnus, 2011), as, for example, approximately 14.3 per cent of housing units in the USA in 2011 Q2 were vacant.[16]

Last, whereas 'new development' refers to building on vacant plots (typically in the outskirts of cities), 'redevelopment' refers to substituting new for old structures (through demolition) and 'refurbishment' refers to satisfying existing occupiers' changing space requirements (e.g., through modifying the layout of a structure).

7.8 A developer's profit-maximization problem

As with any profit-maximizing firm, a developer-cum-constructor of dwelling units[17] wants to minimize his or her cost of production and maximize his or her revenue. We shall consider the rather typical case of a developer who builds on a given plot bought from a landowner, and treats land as a fixed resource, with capital and labour being loosely variable inputs, and ultimately determined by current building technology.

But the developer's profit-maximizing problem is something of a misnomer. First, because a large part of any potential 'economic profit' goes to the landowner in the form of land price rather than to the developer. Second, because 'maximization' of economic profit is constrained by planning authorities' restrictions regarding permissible output (in quantity as well as kind). Let us see how.

7.8.1 Profit maximization in the face of planning constraints

Let us for the moment ignore the suggestion we made above, namely that any potential profit from development is actually split between developer and landowner at the time the land is purchased. Instead, we shall consider development profit before such a split. It is unlikely that the developer will produce less floor space than the maximum permissible under planning and building regulations, even though the profit-maximizing output under an existing (or expected) market price may be less than the maximum permissible. The developer will try and produce the maximum amount of floor space allowed. To do otherwise would imply foregoing future profit potential.

This means that the developer will commence production when the expected market price at completion allows profit maximization at precisely the maximum permissible level of output and not a smaller one. It also means that the developer will time his acquisition of that particular plot so as to minimize his land-keeping costs, and decrease his uncertainty regarding future price movements. '[T]he decision to build or not build can thus be thought of as weighing the opportunity costs associated with keeping the land vacant against the expected gain from constructing a more appropriate building in the future' (Titman, 1985: 513).

In Figure 7.1, we show the situation described. Global cost minimization would occur if the developer built 6 thousand square metres of floor space. Bringing demand D_1 for floor space (and therefore price) into the picture would set the profit-maximizing output at about 7.5 thousand square metres of floor space (where marginal revenue MR_1 = marginal cost MC).[18] But if the maximum permissible amount of floor space is, say, 9.5 thousand square metres, demand would have to shift to D_2, so that profit will be maximized at that output (assuming no change in the cost function) since that's where MR_2 = MC.

Notice in Figure 7.1 that the volume of profit at the profit-maximizing level of output of 9.5 thousand square metres, i.e., (price – average cost) × quantity, is much larger than the volume of profit at the profit-maximizing level of output of 7.5 thousand square metres This difference, however, may well diminish, even substantially, if land-keeping costs are taken into account. Such costs (mainly interest foregone on capital tied up in land) are a function of (i) the price paid for land, (ii) the applicable interest rate, and (iii) the time elapsed between the current demand line D_1 and the shifted demand line D_2.

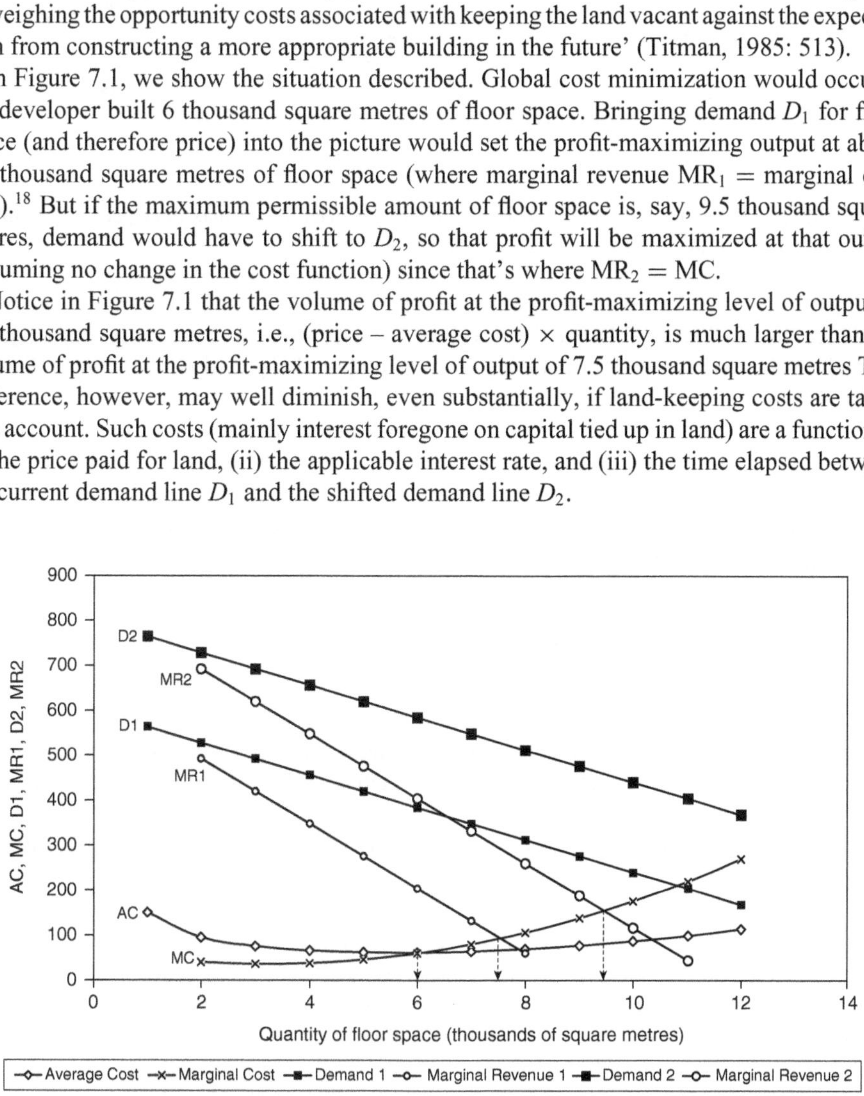

Figure 7.1 A developer's profit-maximization problem, given land and a maximum permissible amount of floor space: case of developer firm exceeding its capacity.

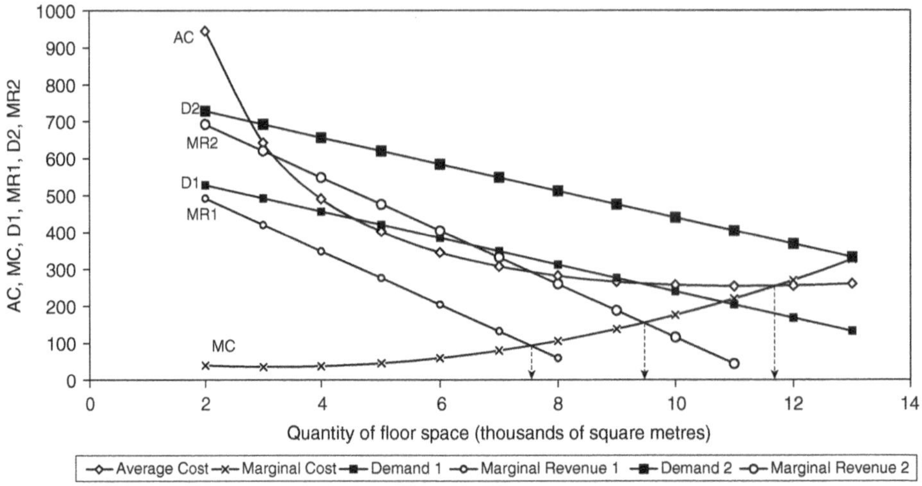

Figure 7.2 A developer's profit-maximization problem, given land and a maximum permissible amount of floor space: case of developer firm having excess capacity.

Notice also in Figure 7.1 that the developer-cum-constructor exceeds its capacity, i.e., it produces beyond the cost-minimizing level of output. This need not be always the case. Figure 7.2 shows another situation, where the firm operates under excess capacity (the typical case under monopolistic competition), as its average cost of production would be minimized at a level of output that exceeds the maximum permissible amount of floor space.

In Figure 7.2, the cost-minimizing output is about 11.7 units, but the maximum permissible amount of floor space is about 9.5 units. So even if, presently, demand conditions were such (i.e., D_1, MR_1) that profit would be maximized at about 7.5 units, the developer would probably wait until demand conditions changed to D_2, MR_2, so that the maximum permissible amount of floor space could be built with maximum profit.

7.8.2 The RRR approach to development

If standard profit maximization, centred on the MR = MC approach, is impracticable as it assumes that the developer freely chooses how much to build,[19] then another approach to the developer's problem might be in order.

The solution is to go for a required-rate-of-return (RRR) approach. This has the following advantages:

1 Calculations as to whether, and when, to develop are simplified. In particular, there is no need to specify demand and MR curves. What is basically needed, is (i) an estimate of expected sale price (itself a function of current and past prices), which will allow estimation of an expected return, (ii) an estimate of the cost of raising a given-size-and-type building, usually under given technology, and (iii) an appreciation of the RRR currently prevailing in the market for such projects.

2 Greater consistency with investment appraisal theory. After all, if maximum profit from a project is less than the return implied by the required *rate* of return, the project will

not be undertaken, even if the developer stands to earn his or her 'normal profit'. The latter is part of a firm's fixed cost, and is not necessarily the same as the return implied in a RRR (see Box 7.1).

3 Unlike the output of an agricultural or manufacturing concern, almost any type of RE, housing in particular, is not, in fact, a homogeneous commodity. As a result, if, for example, 'households have distinct preferences for lot size, supply decisions cannot be represented by the traditional cost-minimization model of the firm, in which firms alter land/nonland proportions in response to variations in land prices to produce housing at least cost' (Straszheim, 1975: 21). The RRR approach is not subject to such constraints.

4 Last, but not least, the RRR approach is very handy for dealing with the other problem mentioned: that 'economic profit' in development is typically the land price, a large part of which is paid by developer to landowner. That price needs to be factored into profit calculations, but it also depends on the estimated selling price of the units constructed. Hence, part of the developer's total cost (the land price part) depends on an implicit agreement between him and the landowner as to the expected revenue from developing the land, rather than being determined autonomously! By using the RRR approach, however, part of the land price goes to the developer in the form of a return that allows him to realize at least his RRR.

Box 7.1 'Normal profit' versus required rate of return (RRR)

'Normal profit' is the minimum return an entrepreneur must achieve on their capital in order to remain in their current line of business, or the return that an entrepreneur could have earned in the next best alternative business (Sloman, 1991: 186). Neither definition, however, renders 'normal profit' necessarily consistent with RRR as defined in Chapter 5, for RRR is determined at industry level and depends on actual rates of return achieved in the recent past, and the return implied by it may well be higher than normal profit.

Perhaps a way to distinguish between the two concepts is this: 'Normal profit' is an absolute amount (say, $\$X$), whereas RRR is a percentage. Thus an entrepreneur will undertake a project if they make at least \$20,000 out of it ('normal profit'); but if the current RRR for this type of project is, say, 6 per cent (a return of \$100,000), the entrepreneur will not undertake the project if the expected rate of return from the project is less than that (e.g., 5 per cent, a return of \$83,333). Obviously, in comparing a series of (equally risky) projects, the entrepreneur will choose the one offering the highest expected rate of return, over and above the 6 per cent RRR. An expected RR higher than the current RRR can be the case, for example, where a developer discerns an opportunity for profit others do not, or where the overall market outlook becomes particularly optimistic. The RRR will coincide with 'normal profit' if it drops enough (say, to 1.2 per cent) as to imply a return equal to \$20,000.

7.8.3 Profit maximization in the face of a land price

To ascertain how 'economic profit' would be determined in a development project, it might be useful if we contrasted two scenarios. In one, the developer's only reward is his or her

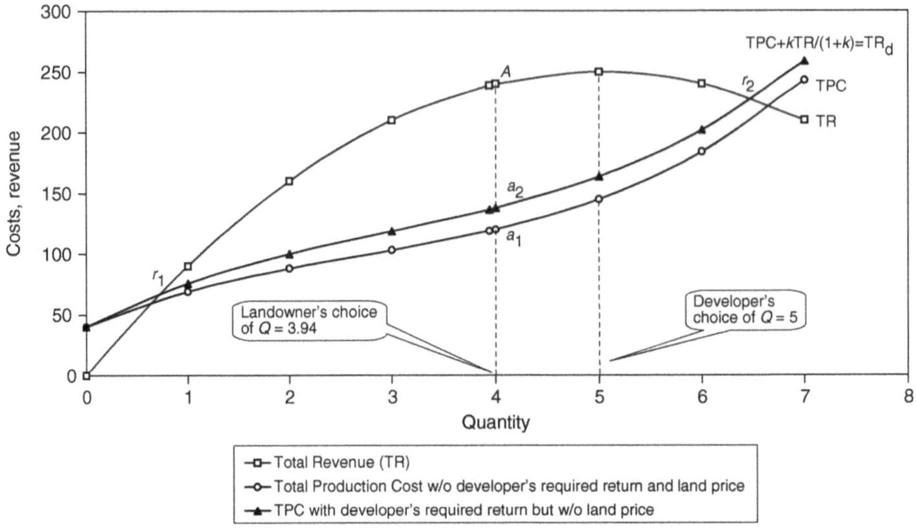

Figure 7.3 A RE development operation showing land price as the difference between sales revenue and production cost at different quantities, with and without developer's required return.

'normal profit'. In the other, 'normal profit' still exists, but the reward is additionally (and mainly) determined by application of a RRR.

Figure 7.3 shows (i) a total production cost (TPC) curve for an urban-land developer that includes only production costs but *no land price* and no required return; (ii) a total production cost curve shifted upwards by the inclusion of required return; and (iii) a total revenue (TR) curve, representing the sales value of the finished product.

Notice that TR and the developer's share of it are not necessarily equal; part of the TR goes to the landowner as land price. We call TR_d the developer's share of TR. (It is of course possible for developer and landowner to be the same entity.) We shall now show that only if the developer works on the basis of 'normal profit', rather than on the basis of a RRR, will 'economic profit' and thus land price, be maximized.

(A) The 'normal profit' scenario.

We assume that (i) 'normal profit' is part of fixed cost (cf. Box 7.1) and (ii) the developer is free to produce whatever Q he or she likes. That is, there is no planning constraint on Q. To develop our case, we shall first devise appropriate TR and TPC functions, then apply the optimization technique described in Section 2.1.3.

Assuming a linear demand curve, we have[20]

$$\text{TR} = \text{quantity} \times \text{price} = Q(d - eQ) = dQ - eQ^2 = \text{e.g.,} 100Q - 10Q^2,$$

and[21]

$$\text{TPC} = aQ^3 - bQ^2 + cQ + d = \text{e.g.,}\ Q^3 - 8Q^2 + 36Q + 40.$$

Therefore,

$$\pi = \text{profit} = \text{TR} - \text{TPC} = 100Q - 10Q^2 - Q^3 + 8Q^2 - 36Q - 40,$$

$$\frac{d\pi}{dQ} = 100 - 20Q - 3Q^2 + 16Q - 36 = -3Q^2 - 4Q + 64.$$

The Q that satisfies $d\pi/dQ = 0$ is given by

$$Q = \frac{-(-4) \pm \sqrt{(-4)^2 - 4(-3)(64)}}{2(-3)}$$

as either -5.3 or $+4$. At $Q = 4$, $d^2\pi/dQ^2 = -6Q - 4 < 0 \Rightarrow 4$ secures a maximum value for the π function.[22]

Consequently, the developer will produce a profit-maximizing output of 4 units at a TPC of 120 at a_1 and a TR of 240 at A (see Figure 7.3). Economic profit (over and above 'normal profit') will be TR – TPC = 240 – 120 = 120. This equals the price of land, which, unless the developer can negotiate a better deal, goes to the landowner for making the land available for development. An implication is that the developer's effective own revenue curve TR_d coincides with his TPC curve (since the developer's only reward is 'normal profit', included in fixed cost), as long as TR > TPC.

(B) The RRR scenario

If the developer's actual return is coterminous with his required return, and the latter is determined by a RRR = k, the given TPC curve shifts upwards by the addition of $k\text{TR}/(1+k)$, the developer's RRR-based reward.[23] This redefines the developer's own revenue curve TR_d as

$$\text{TR}_d = \text{TPC} + \frac{kTR}{1+k}.$$

Notice that if k = 0, the RRR scenario collapses back to the 'normal profit' one. The case of TR = 0 is of no particular concern in this *ex ante* calculation, where the project will be undertaken as long as TR > TPC. Thus, TR_d fluctuates while broadly following the contour of TPC (see Fig. 7.3), with $k\text{TR}/(1+k)$ reaching a maximum value at some level of Q (5, in this case).

The question now is – what does a given value of k imply for 'profit maximization', land price, and the developer's absolute return?

Optimizing, we find that the value of Q that maximizes 'profit' is 3.94 rather than 4. Once again, the 'profit' in question is just the price paid the landowner. Only now, it is 102.26 rather than 120 under the 'normal profit' scenario. The developer's return is 17.69. Interestingly, if production now takes place at 4 units of Q, as under the 'normal profit' scenario, land price and the developer's return become 102.22 and 17.8, respectively. Finally, if the developer builds 5 units of Q, he will maximize his return, at 18.52, whilst the landowner will get an even lower price, 86.48. These results are presented in Table 7.2a and contrasted in Table 7.2b.

Table 7.2a Land price calculation before and after introduction of developer's RRR = k = 0.08

Q	*TR*	*TPC*	*Land price LP_1 (before introduction of RRR) = TR – TPC*	*TR_d = TPC + (kTR)/(1 + k)*	*Land price LP_2 (after introduction of RRR) = TR – TR_d*	*Check: k = 0.08 = (TR – TPC – LP_2)/(TPC+LP_2)*	*Developer's RRR-based return = TR_d – TPC*
						0.08	
0.00	0.00	40.0	−40.00			#DIV/0	−40.00
1.00	90.0	69.0	21.0	75.6	14.3	0.08	6.67
2.00	160.00	88.0	72.0	99.8	60.1	0.08	11.85
3.00	210.00	103.00	107.00	118.56	91.4	0.08	15.56
3.94	238.76	118.81	119.95	136.50	**102.26**	0.08	17.69
4.00	240.00	120.00	**120.00**	137.78	102.22	0.08	17.78
5.00	250.00	145.00	105.00	163.52	86.4	0.08	**18.52**
6.00	240.00	184.00	56.0	201.78	38.2	0.08	17.78
7.00	210.00	243.00	−33.00				
8.00	160.00	328.00	−168.0				
9.00	90.0	445.00	−355.0				
10.0	0.00	600.00	−600.0				

Table 7.2b Profit maximization versus RRR, or how 'profit' becomes land price

	'Normal profit' scenario	*RRR scenario*		
		Case A	*Case B*	*Case C*
	Developer's return made of 'normal profit' only (as part of fixed cost); production takes place at a 'profit'-maximizing output	*Developer's return given by RRR; TCP curve shifts, but production takes place at a recalculated 'profit'-maximizing output*	*Developer's return given by RRR; TCP curve shifts, but production takes place at the output determined under the 'normal profit' scenario*	*Developer's return given by RRR; TCP curve shifts, but production takes place at the level of output at which developer's absolute return is maximized*
RRR		0.08	0.08	0.08
Output *Q*	4	3.94	4	5
TR	240	238.76	240	250
TCP	120	118.8	120	145
TR_d	120	136.5	137.78	163.52
Total economic profit created (= TR – TPC)	120	119.95	120	105
Of which:				
To developer:	Only 'normal profit'	17.69*	17.78*	18.52*
To landowner:	120	102.26	102.22	86.48

* Plus 'normal profit'

Remarks and conclusions

1. A developer is in business in order to maximize *his* profit, or return, not the landowner's.
2. Under the RRR approach, the *volume* of return may vary, but the *rate* of (required) return is preserved (e.g., at $k = 8$ per cent).
3. The landowner's maximum gain under the RRR approach (at $Q = 3.94$) differs from the developer's maximum return (at $Q = 5$), given the latter's RRR. Either kind of gain is achieved at a different output level.
4. This discrepancy suggests that there exists a relatively small range of quantities of potential output, associated with, and manifested in, a corresponding land price range, that enables determination of the purchase price of land through negotiations between developer and landowner. In the example above, the negotiation range involves land prices extending from 3.94 to 5 units of output. The reason why room for negotiation exists is that up to $Q = 3.94$ both parties have a common interest in maximizing output, and above $Q = 5$ both parties have a common interest in resisting further increases in output. Figure 7.4 shows why this is so: over the *bc* range – the negotiation range – the relationship between developer's RRR-based return and land price is inverse.
5. The developer's room for manoeuvre is actually more limited than indicated in Figure 7.4 because of indivisibilities in production. For example, room floor area, or storey height, cannot shrink too much.
6. Although over the entire range of positive returns (i.e., the range *ad* in Figure 7.4) a developer may in principle proceed with development since he will be securing his RRR, it must be noted that in practice not only would the developer reject operating over the *ab* and *cd* ranges (because he would not be maximizing return), but the landowner would too (because he would not be maximizing land price). This suggests that the landowner has a much more active role in development than is commonly thought: by trying to maximize land price, and resisting development at the 'wrong' range, he, no less than the developer, makes sure that land goes to its highest and best use (subject to the outcome of negotiations along the *bc* range).

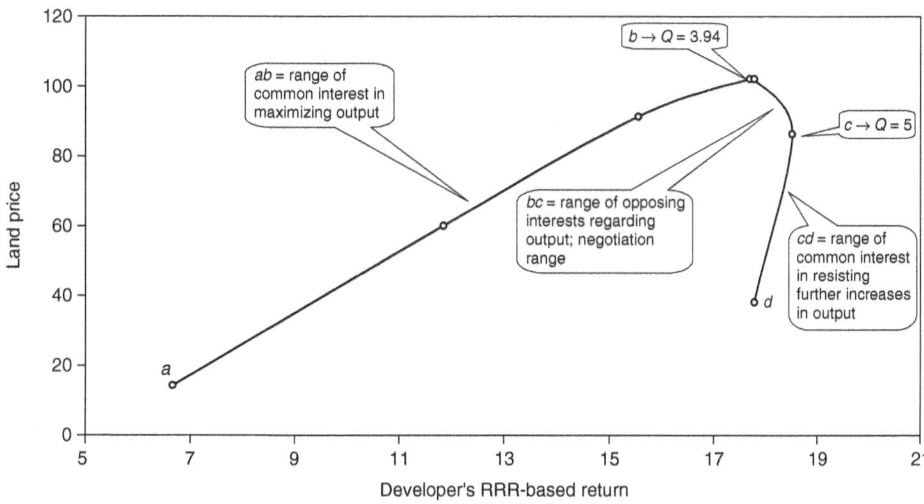

Figure 7.4 Developer's RRR-based return versus landowner's gain (i.e., land price).

7 It is of course always possible that production may take place over a range of output outside the negotiation range because, for example, a landowner may need to sell quickly. But this is unlikely since, in a competitive market with reasonable information flows, other developers should come in and bid up the land price.

8 The whole process of development is demand-driven. A market price per square metre (or square foot) is formed for each of various kinds of RE, which 'feeds' developers' estimates of future price. On that basis, and subject to (i) a developer's costs and RRR, (ii) indivisibilities in production, and (iii) negotiations between developer and landowner, a 'best' Q of output on a given plot is determined – somewhere along the *bc* range. A further constraint may be applied by planning authorities, which typically determine both the land use in a certain area, and the permissible amount of floor space, or building height, etc.

9 In the above analysis, the roles of developer and land owner were distinct. This need not be the case in real life – and often it is not. Nor does it matter, except as regards the negotiation bit. After all, the time at which the developer begins to own or hold the land may differ from the time at which construction starts. This makes bargaining between developer and land owner more complicated and opportunistic than otherwise, as the two parties may have different time horizons as well as different information as to a site's development potential.

Box 7.2 Proof that after a RRR is introduced, the developer's pre-RRR TPC shifts by the addition of $\frac{kTR}{1+k}$

Once we introduce an RRR $= k$, it is tempting to think that the original TPC curve shifts up by $1+k$, i.e., new TPC = old TPC *times* $1+k$.

In the example used, at $Q=4$, TR $=240$ and TPC $=120$. Then TPC$(1+k)=129.6$.

However, the developer will *not* pay $240-129.6=110.4$ for the land. This, because, in order for the developer to preserve an RRR $= k = 0.08$, the land price of 110.4 must be discounted by $1+k$. The developer is thus prepared to pay a maximum of $110.4/(1+0.08)=102.2$ for the land.

To see that this is so, consider the formula for the RRR:

$$\text{RRR} = k = \frac{\text{revenue} - \text{TPC} - \text{land price}}{\text{TPC} + \text{land price}} \Rightarrow$$

$$\Rightarrow \text{land price} = \frac{\text{revenue} - \text{TPC}(1+k)}{1+k} = \frac{240 - 120(1+0.08)}{1+0.08} = 102.2.$$

Therefore, the shifted TPC must be equal to

$$\text{TPC} + \text{developer's required return} = \text{TPC} + (\text{TR} - \text{TPC} - \text{land price})$$

$$= \text{TPC} + \text{TR} - \text{TPC} - \frac{TR - \text{TPC}(1+k)}{1+k} = TPC + \frac{kTR}{1+k}.$$

7.8.4 More on the negotiation dimension

A developer will try to maximize his profit, in the sense of securing, if possible, a return higher than the one implied in his RRR; but that would depend on bargaining between developer and landowner, on the one hand, and between developer and eventual buyer(s) of the finished product, on the other (cf. Wheaton, 1990), rather than on stylized calculations about producing that output (on a given land) at which MR = MC. In a purely, and especially perfectly, competitive market, just the RRR would be achieved; but the RE market is monopolistically competitive, and, moreover, asymmetric information between developers and landowners, or between developers themselves, is quite frequent.

Abstracting from taxes, the process of land price determination works like this. Different land uses compete for available space. Although more often than not it is the planning function that designates land uses in particular areas, even planning authorities have to respond, ultimately, to pent up demand for location in space. End-users of land who are prepared to pay more than others for locating themselves in an area or site win.[24] Obviously, the quantity of available space (i.e., of suitable lots) in an area is important, in addition to demand for locating oneself in the area. That is, given such demand, a greater quantity of available land will, *ceteris paribus*, result in lower land prices in the area, as shown in Figure 7.5.

From a developer's viewpoint, the price of land for a given use in a given area is incorporated in the price of the finished product (say, dwellings), which the highest-bidding end-users are willing and able to pay, and which a developer estimates on the basis of current prices and a related forecast. Subtracting from the price of the finished product the cost of construction plus the developer's return (as determined by his RRR) gives the maximum amount which a developer is prepared to pay for the site, tops.

In turn, competition between developers ensures that the land will sell at or near that maximum amount, with any (usually slight) deviations the result of the existence of a highest-bidding developer. A positive deviation will happen when the highest-bidding developer is either one whose estimate of the site's profit potential is higher than any other developer's, or one who accepts a lower rate of return than his or her RRR. This can happen occasionally – but if such instances become frequent, they will simply lead to a readjustment of RRRs among developers. A negative deviation, by contrast, will happen if the highest-bidding developer

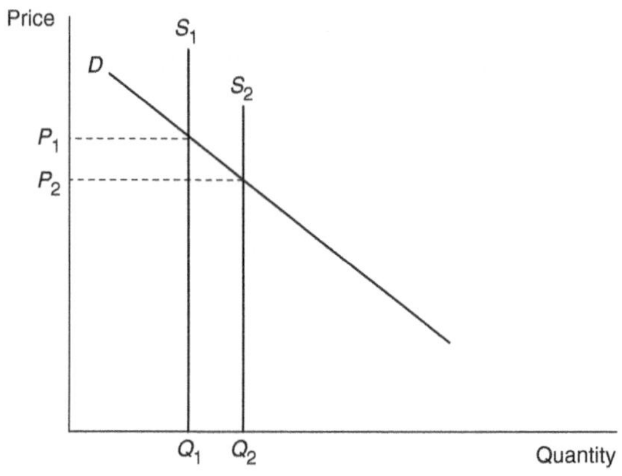

Figure 7.5 Given demand for land (i.e., location plus other characteristics of the land), it is land availability that will determine land price. If, for example, the total available quantity of land is fixed at Q_2 rather than Q_1 the land price will be P_2 rather than P_1.

faces no or only weak competition from other developers and also gets the upper hand in his bargaining with the landowner.

Thus owners of developable land are constrained in forming their ask prices by (a) current and expected demand for the finished product, (b) what other landowners (if any) in the area are doing, and (c) what developers are prepared to pay. Since a developer's estimate of the price of the finished product already incorporates the expected land price for the given use in the given area, it is the highest-bidding developer's offer price that ultimately determines how much a landowner will get for the land, rather than the landowner's whim. On her part, the landowner will not normally release the land unless the highest possible price is paid.

Consequently, if, in a certain area, planning authorities allow more land to be used for, say, housebuilding, developers will, *ceteris paribus*, calculate a lower selling price for the finished product, the average price of residential land in the area will decline (cf. Figure 7.3), and owners of pre-existing and additional developable plots will receive less for releasing their land. If, on the other hand, planning authorities, rather than extending a certain land use over more land, increase instead the permissible amount of floor space in an area, owners of pre-existing developable plots will receive more when they sell their land (since they will not be competing with additional plot owners), even though the price of each unit of the finished product will, *ceteris paribus*, decline.

7.9 What price for land?

We shall now contrast two quite prevalent modes of market-based residential development:[25] one typically associated with developed English-speaking countries (which was examined above), another found in Greece, Turkey, or other countries with a very wide distribution of landownership (which implies small plot sizes), where, moreover, bank funds for residential development have historically (i.e., for most of the post-Second World War period) been in short supply.

1 The 'Anglo-American', or 'AnAm', mode is shorthand for building on own land that has been assembled (often years before, in the form of land banks)[26] precisely for the purpose of development at the right time (i.e., when market prices are high enough).
2 The 'Greek' mode is shorthand for building on land owned by someone else: the output is then split between developer and plot-owner – which is how the latter is rewarded for making his or her land available for building.

An interesting variant of the 'AnAm' mode (which will not be examined here) is for a developer to buy from a landowner an option that gives the developer the right (but not the obligation) to buy (or lease) the land at an opportune time.[27] Like stock options, land options have value and are priced similarly (cf. Brown and Achour, 1984).

7.9.1 The 'Anglo-American' mode of residential development

Turning to this mode first, we shall ask how much a developer would pay for a site on which to build housing units. This calculation requires estimating:

1 The cost involved (including normal profit) in hiring the best combination of capital and labour to produce the maximum permissible amount of floor space in the given piece of

land (or the amount implied in the outcome of price negotiations between developer and land owner, as suggested in Section 7.8.2).

2 The rate of inflation applicable to that combination.
3 The rate of interest foregone on capital used to buy the land.
4 A Required Rate of Return (RRR) on the total capital outlay (cf. Ch. 5).
5 The developer's time horizon.
6 A price for the finished product at end of time horizon (which comprises building completion time plus any waiting time prior to that); alternatively, a rate of price inflation for the finished product, given the product's current price. ('Current' refers to the time the land is bought.)

Fundamentally, RRR is equal to

$$\text{RRR} = \text{k} = \frac{\text{revenue} - \text{cost}}{\text{cost}}, \tag{7.20}$$

where revenue = price × quantity

Quantity is the amount of permissible floor space (or the number and kind of, say, dwelling units produced), Price is expected price at time t, or current price times $(1+f)^t$, f being the annual expected price inflation of the dwelling units under consideration. Thus,

$$\text{revenue} = \left[P_0(1+f)^t\right]Q, \tag{7.21}$$

where

P_0 = current market price of (similar) dwellings,
Q = quantity of dwellings to be built on plot which the developer is thinking of buying,

and

$$\text{cost (or capital outlay)} = \left[(\text{LP}_L + \text{KP}_K)(1+e)^{t-m}\right](1+i)^m + P_T(1+r)^t, \tag{7.22}$$

where

LP_L = amount of labour × price of labour,
KP_K = amount of physical capital (equipment and building materials) × price of physical capital,
e = average price inflation rate of those inputs,
P_T = price of land when purchased by the developer, who is assumed to use his own funds for the purpose (P_T is not to be confused with the full value of the land, which is the difference between the price of the finished product and the cost of building, the latter including normal profit; the developer, however, would not pay the full land price, but less than that, as he would have to subtract an amount that would allow him to achieve his RRR),
r = interest rate foregone on funds tied up in land,
t = total amount of time (e.g., in years) between purchase of the land and completion of the project (when selling of the built units will take place)
m = construction time (e.g., in years),
i = developer's borrowing interest rate (assuming that the cost of K and L hired at time $t-m$ is loan-financed; typically $i > r$).

In this simple formulation,[28] the developer is supposed to buy the land using own funds, pay no taxes, and buy all required capital and labour at time $t - m$, i.e., m years before estimated project completion time, using borrowed funds, which the developer has to return with interest at completion time. But:

(a) If the developer uses own funds too in order to buy capital and labour, then $i = r$.
(b) If commencement of building occurs as soon as the land is bought, $m = t$ and $e = 0$.
(c) The longer the total project time t is, and in particular the longer it is in relation to m (in other words, the longer bought land will remain undeveloped), the more likely it is that the land has been bought with own, rather than borrowed, funds; for in such a case the developer will stay longer without cash from sales revenue with which to repay a possible loan towards land purchase.
(d) In reality, outlays for physical capital and labour would occur periodically (say, every month). Capital equipment, for example, could be leased for the duration of construction, with lease payments being made monthly. If capital equipment happened to be fully owned by the developer-cum-constructor, the cost of using it could be its annual depreciation. By the same token, disbursement of bank funds towards financing the cost of construction need not happen once and for all at the beginning of construction, but may well happen by means of a line of credit, allowing, say, quarterly disbursements as needed. Such considerations and possibilities would of course complicate cost calculations.
(e) Revenue calculations could also become quite complicated. For example, some or all of the dwelling units could be sold before completion. Or, not all of the units will be sold at completion, but, say, over the course of a year after that. It would be prudent to allow for the latter possibility (expressed as expected time of unit sales), since it raises project cost.

Of course L and K would make up a combination of inputs calculated to produce just the amount of permissible floor space, the particular combination chosen being at the point of tangency between an *isoquant* for the permissible floor space and an *isocost* line reflecting available capital for building (cf. Chapter 2). The proportions of L and K in that combination would in turn depend on building technology and the respective prices.

Going back to our simple formulation and plugging Equations (7.21) and (7.22) into (7.20), we have

$$k = \frac{[P_0(1+f)^t]Q - [(\mathrm{LP}_L + \mathrm{KP}_K)(1+e)^{t-m}](1+i)^m - P_T(1+r)^t}{[(\mathrm{LP}_L + \mathrm{KP}_K)(1+e)^{t-m}](1+i)^m + P_T(1+r)^t}. \tag{7.23}$$

Solving for P_T gives

$$P_T = \frac{[P_0(1+f)^t]Q - [(\mathrm{LP}_L + \mathrm{KP}_K)(1+e)^{t-m}(1+i)^m](1+k)}{(1+r)^t(1+k)}. \tag{7.24}$$

EXAMPLE 1

If the purchase of land, building on it, and selling the output are to take place instantaneously $(t = m = 0)$, Equation (7.24) collapses to

$$P_T = \frac{P_0 Q - (\mathrm{LP}_L + \mathrm{KP}_K)(1+k)}{1+k},$$

which means that if 'current' revenue from the finished product (if that product were available to be sold now) is, say, 600, the cost of construction is, say, 250, and k is 10 per cent, then the maximum amount that the developer can pay for the land is

$$P_T = \frac{600 - 250(1.1)}{1.1} = 295.5.$$

EXAMPLE 2

If, more realistically, the time horizon is 3 years, $m = 2$ years, and $f = 4$ per cent, $e = 3$ per cent, $r = 2.5$ per cent, and $i = 5$ per cent, then

$$P_T = \frac{600(1.04)^3 - 250(1.03)^{3-2}(1.05)^2(1.1)}{(1.025)^3(1.1)} = 306.1.$$

This is higher than in the $t = 0$ case because the rate of product price inflation is higher than the interest rate foregone on capital tied up in land.

EXAMPLE 3

With a higher r (land-keeping cost), say 5 per cent, and an implied still higher borrowing rate, say $i = 9$ per cent, $P_T = 265.8$.

EXAMPLE 4

Further extending the time horizon to, for example, 20 years (with $r = 5$ per cent and $i = 9$ per cent), $P_T = 259.9$, i.e., even less would be paid for the site now.

Notice that extending the time horizon for development from 3 to 20 years (with $r = 5$ per cent and $i = 9$ per cent) reduces P_T from 265.8 to 259.9, i.e., by about 2 per cent only. In reality, it would be very unlikely to use the same house price appreciation factor (i.e., 4 per cent) when the time horizon is 3 years and when it is 20 years. The factor (which is, after all, an estimate) would have to be reduced to reflect the greater uncertainty of cash inflows far into the future. If, for example, that factor were reduced to 3 per cent, P_T would become 180.7, a substantial discount from 265.8. Alternatively, greater uncertainty could be handled by increasing the developer's RRR, which would probably reduce building activity in the current period (cf. Titman, 1985: 513).

What would happen if there were no maximum permissible amount of floor space set by the planning authorities? A given site could be used more intensively (e.g., a taller structure could be built) – but only to the point where (expected) demand for accommodation in the particular location justified the extra building cost. As already mentioned, the price of the finished product (e.g., a dwelling) in a particular location or area is determined by users' demand for it, and by the supply of land in the given location or area (which is usually very inelastic,[29] and often simply fixed).

Put differently, because the supply of land in a particular location or area is inelastic, it is essentially users' demand that will determine the price of dwellings (or of units for other uses) and thus the maximum price of land, which is incorporated in the price of the finished product.[30] To a developer, that land price is the difference between finished product price and the sum of the cost of construction and the developer's required return.

Thus, the full value of the land (LV) is higher than what a developer is prepared to pay for a site. LV is (estimated) revenue (from the finished product) minus the cost of building (which includes normal profit), both calculated at time 0. The developer, however, is prepared to pay P_T only (given in Equation (7.24)), since he wants to secure a RRR by the end of time t. The difference between the two is[31]

$$\text{LV} - P_T = (\text{revenue at time } 0 - \text{building cost at time } 0) - P_T \text{at time } 0. \qquad (7.25)$$

EXAMPLE 5

If $t = 3$ years, $m = 2$ years, $P_0Q = 600$, construction cost at time 0 is 250, and $f = 4$ per cent, $e = 3$ per cent, $r = 2.5$ per cent, and $i = 5$ per cent, then P_T was found earlier to be 306.1. Then, according to (7.25), $LV - PT = (600 - 250) - 306.1 = 43.9$. In other words, P_T was 12.5 per cent smaller than LV at $t = 0$, as only this percentage difference (i.e., $-43.9/350$) could secure an overall RRR of 10 per cent for the developer at $t = 3$.

A corollary of this is that developers with shorter time horizons are more likely to obtain a desired piece of land than those with longer time horizons, since their offers will be closer to LV.

7.9.2 The 'Greek' mode of residential development

The basic idea is simple enough: a plot-owner agrees with a developer to allow the latter to build a block on the plot-owner's land, in exchange for a pre-determined number (and kind) of output units. Those units are usually residential apartments, but can also include small offices or ground-floor shops, mechanics' garages, cafés or eateries. What units do not go to the plot-owner, the developer keeps for himself to sell or rent as he sees fit. At the end of the project, the percentages of landownership between original plot-owner and developer have also changed to reflect the split in the ownership of the units produced. The deal between developer and plot-owner is referred to as an 'exchange arrangement' (in Greek, *antiparokhé*).

The plots involved are typically small. They may be vacant or contain an old structure, which has exhausted its economic value. In principle, the exchange arrangement could work in any plot, no matter what size, but the method developed historically as a way to overcome the absence of large-size plots, or of land banks, inside or on the (growing) periphery of cities and towns. Because of the small plot size, the buildings erected are medium- to high-rise (as high as planning law permits, that is, and sometimes a little more than that), and are typically made up of 5–50 apartments (depending on actual plot size and zoning regulations).[32] This way, the full value of the land is realized, for both plot-owner and developer (the respective shares determined by the splitting agreement between them).

The following conditions have been known to facilitate the rise of the 'exchange arrangement':

1 A private market over land and dwellings.
2 A wide distribution of landownership (hence small plots are the norm rather than the exception), which makes land banking impracticable or even impossible.
3 A planning function that is not averse to allowing high-rise building and therefore high building densities.

4 Lack of adequate bank financing of dwelling construction and, generally, of real estate development activity.

Formalizing the 'exchange arrangement' is not simply a matter of dividing the potential number of output units by two. There are two reasons for this:

(i) Given building costs, the number of output units going to the plot-owner and to the developer depends on the extent of the realizable land value, and ultimately the price per square metre that can be had for the output. So in 'good' times a typical distribution may be 50–50, but in 'bad' times the developer's cut may rise to, say, 55 or 60 per cent.
(ii) Different output parts have different values. So apartments on higher storeys typically are priced higher than apartments on lower storeys, and shops (usually located in the ground floor) may be priced in-between. A garage (in the ground floor or basement) will increase an apartment's value, and its absence will subtract from it. Thus, for example, instead of a plot-owner getting 8 apartments in a 16-flat high-rise, and the developer getting the other 8, it is possible that the plot-owner will get the 5 highest apartments, and the developer the other 11.

Notice that the only up-front explicit cost that the Greek developer has to meet is the building cost (along with sundry other costs). The Greek developer does not have to incur an up-front land cost (the difference between the discounted revenue from selling all the output units constructed on the land and the discounted cost of building them, minus the developer's profit as determined by his RRR). In the 'AnAm' way, though, the developer has to incur the full cost of the land up-front. Thus the exchange arrangement means an obvious accounting cost advantage for the Greek developer, but in addition the plot-owner finds himself with a number of flats for which he has paid nothing. This is especially true since in the vast majority of cases such plots were bought many years in the past or have been inherited.

On the other hand, the Greek developer faces a substantial opportunity, or economic, cost since he does not receive the full market value of the apartments constructed, but only the value corresponding to his pre-determined share of them! Thus the developer's RRR is

$$k = \frac{\alpha[P_0(1+f)^t]Q - [(\mathrm{LP}_L + \mathrm{KP}_K)(1+e)^{t-m}](1+i)^m}{[(\mathrm{LP}_L + \mathrm{KP}_K)(1+e)^{t-m}](1+i)^m}, \tag{7.26}$$

where

α = developer's percentage share of value of output,
t = time until completion, which in practice is about two years, coinciding with m,
m = construction time, usually two years for a typical apartment building,
f = annual dwelling price inflation,
e = annual price inflation of human and physical capital,
i = cost of borrowed funds; collapses to opportunity cost of developer's own funds if no bank funding is involved.

Notice in (7.26) that the developer's opportunity cost (the value share going to the plot-owner) is not included in costs; at the same time, the revenue going to the developer is limited to $\alpha[P_0(1+f)^t]Q$, α being less than 1. Further, considering that the developer is contractually obliged to start building immediately after the exchange arrangement is finalized, e is zero (i.e., the developer is assumed to procure the necessary inputs immediately).[33] As a result,

(7.26) becomes

$$k = \frac{\alpha[P_0(1+f)^t]Q - (\mathrm{LP}_L + \mathrm{KP}_K)(1+i)^m}{(\mathrm{LP}_L + \mathrm{KP}_K)(1+i)^m}. \tag{7.27}$$

Hence, α, the 'Greek' developer's value share, is

$$\alpha = \frac{(1+k)(\mathrm{LP}_L + \mathrm{KP}_K)(1+i)^m}{[P_0(1+f)^t]Q}. \tag{7.28}$$

The gross value amount (in the form of finished apartments) that the 'Greek' developer gets is

$$V_D = \alpha\left[P_0(1+f)^t\right]Q, \tag{7.29}$$

while the value amount (again in the form of finished apartments) that goes to the plot owner is

$$V_{PO} = (1-\alpha)\left[P_0(1+f)^t\right]Q. \tag{7.30}$$

VALUE SHARE EXAMPLES

If $k = 10$ per cent, the cost of physical inputs is 250, current revenue is 600, $f = 4$ per cent, $t = m = 2$ years, and $i = 5$ per cent, then

$$\alpha = \frac{(1+0.1)(250)(1+0.05)^2}{600(1+0.04)^2} = \frac{(1+0.1)(275.625)}{600(1+0.04)^2}$$
$$= 303.19/648.96 = 46.719 \text{ per cent.}$$

And if k is 30 per cent, then $\alpha = 358.31/648.96 = 55.21$ per cent. Notice that an increase in RRR by 200 per cent 'translates' to an 18 per cent increase in the developer's value share only.

THE VALUE OF LAND

What would be the value of land under the 'Greek' mode? It would be $600 - 250 = 350$ at time $t = 0$ (i.e., if the building could be erected instantaneously at time $t = 0$, so that the apartments could be sold at current prices, securing a revenue of 600), and $648.96 - 275.625 = 373.335$ at $t = 2$.

With $k = 10$ per cent, the developer's value share would be

$$V_D = \alpha\left[P_0(1+f)^t\right]Q = 0.46719(648.96) = 303.19,$$

and the plot-owner's value share (which appears as the value of land) would be

$$V_{PO} = (1-\alpha)\left[P_0(1+f)^t\right]Q = 0.53281(648.96) = 345.77$$

(or 53.3 per cent of the value of the finished building at $t = 2$). However, the true value of land was just shown to be 373.335, so why does the plot-owner only get 345.77? The difference is 27.6, which is the amount of return the developer requires in order to satisfy an RRR of

10 per cent over his building costs. In other words, the true cost of land is split between plot-owner and developer (just like in the 'AnAm' case), so that the latter will realize his 10 per cent RRR. Indeed, considering that the developer's building costs amount to 275.625, adding 27.6 to that yields 303.2, the developer's value share.

THE DEVELOPER'S RETURN

Would that also be the developer's return under the 'AnAm' mode and under roughly equivalent conditions? Well, under the 'AnAm' mode,

$$P_T = \frac{600(1.04)^2 - 250(1.03)^{2-2}(1.05)^2(1.1)}{(1.025)^2(1.1)} = 299.2,$$

$$k = \frac{600(1.04)^2 - 250(1.03)^{2-2}(1.05)^2 - 299.2(1.025)^2}{250(1.03)^{2-2}(1.05)^2 + 299.2(1.025)^2} = \frac{59}{590} = 10 \text{ per cent},$$

so the absolute return is 59. Under the 'Greek' mode,

$$k = \frac{0.46719(648.96) - 275.625}{275.625} = \frac{27.56}{275.625} = 10 \text{ per cent},$$

but the absolute return is 27.6. Thus, although under both modes the RRR is 10 per cent (as originally assumed), the absolute return amounts differ. This is due to the different capital outlays between the two modes: under the 'Greek' mode, only the cost of construction matters; under the 'AnAm' mode, the capital outlay has to include an up-front amount for the purchase of land, and then add land-keeping costs.

7.9.3 Concluding remarks

We can round up this discussion with the following remarks:

1 Assuming identical 'current' revenue, 'current' building cost, and k, i, r, f, t, and m under the 'Greek' and under the 'AnAm' mode (as in the example just cited), then, under the 'Greek' mode, the landowner receives *at building completion* a value of 345.77 at most (or 53.3 per cent of a total value for the finished product estimated at 648.96); by contrast, under the 'AnAm' mode, the landowner receives *at the moment he or she sells the land* a value of 299.2 at most (or 49.9 per cent of a 'current' revenue of 600 from the finished product). Notice that under both modes the landowner receives a land price based on the land's development potential (incorporated in $P_0(1+f)^t Q$), minus expected cost of construction, expected land-keeping costs (if any), and an amount corresponding to the developer's RRR. Of course bargaining between developer and landowner may result in a land price being paid that will allow the developer to strike an *ex-ante* rate of return higher than his or her RRR – and then, it will be this rate of return that the developer will later compare with his or her actually achieved *ex-post* rate of return.

2 Under the 'Greek' mode, the landowner seems to get a slightly better deal than his or her counterpart under the 'AnAm' mode (assuming roughly equivalent conditions between the two). The main reason is that under the 'Greek' mode, building starts right after the 'exchange arrangement' contract is signed, whereas under the 'AnAm' mode, building may start years later. This 'immediacy' allows 'Greek' landowners to price their land

using more or less the same current information about expected prices at completion that developers use. On the other hand, the 'Greek' landowner gets his or her 'reward' (i.e., completed apartments) *m* time later than the 'AnAm' landowner gets theirs. It is also likely that the RRR under the 'Greek' mode tends to be higher than under the 'AnAm' mode (see below). Taking these factors into account, the comparative value advantage of the landowner under the 'Greek' mode may easily evaporate.

3 Under both the 'AnAm' and the 'Greek' modes of residential development, the RRR is not immutable. A RRR of 10 per cent was assumed in most of the preceding examples for illustration purposes, but, whatever the RRR may be at a point in time in a country, it can change if *ex-post* rates of return are found by market practitioners to differ from *ex-ante* rates, as has already been suggested in Chapter 5, Section 5.5.4. Then current *ex-post* RRRs can easily become *ex-ante* RRRs for new deals. Higher RRRs in particular can be accommodated through generalized reductions in construction costs (building technology and input prices permitting), and through landowners accepting lower-value shares than otherwise.

In fact, starting from a relatively low level, developers' RRR may increase more easily in a 'Greek' context and/or be higher than in an 'AnAm' context since (i) historically, many small plot owners were/are unsophisticated people, who were/are only too happy to accept relatively low value shares (say, 45 rather than 50 per cent) for making their plots available for building in return for brand new apartments costing them nothing; (ii) the heyday of the 'exchange arrangement' in Greece was associated with rapid urbanization and rising incomes, which meant that *ex-post* rates of return often proved to be higher than *ex-ante* ones. As a result, developers would quickly increase their RRRs, with figures around 30 per cent prior to Greece's economic collapse in 2009 becoming typical.[34] By contrast, an internal rate of return of about 15 per cent has characterized much of UK residential development over a comparable period.[35]

4 The 'exchange arrangement' combined with other features of the Greek economy to create a consistently buoyant Greek housing and property market, largely protected from the cyclicality that has characterized the sector in developed market economies – something well documented in the literature (Wheaton and Nechayev, 2006; Ceron and Suarez, 2006; Cunningham and Kolet, 2007; Bracke, 2010). Since the 'Greek' mode involves many plot-owners getting apartments at practically nil opportunity cost, such people (helped by a tax regime that in the past did not tax the possession of property too heavily) were under no particular pressure to sell, even though many eventually did. The lag suited developers fine, since *they* realized a profit mainly by selling.

Plot-owners would either earmark unsold apartments for owner-occupation by close relatives or let them at rents that did not have to reflect a need to recover any explicit acquisition costs. This contributed to the relationship between dwelling prices and residential rents being anything but straightforward (a point already made in general terms in Section 7.1). In addition, the entry of new development-cum-construction firms into the industry was very easy, due to the absence of up-front land costs, minimal reliance on bank finance, and frequent presales.

So, construction activity would go on, encouraged by rising or high rates of return, urbanization, and economic growth (financed by gifts from Brussels and government borrowing after 1981, coupled with extensive tax evasion); owner-occupation and housing wealth would expand; and the very fact of a wide distribution of landownership that necessitated the 'exchange arrangement' also allowed many prospective buyers of residential apartments to increase their ability to buy by adding the proceeds from sales of rural assets to their rising incomes. This was quite important at a time when there was not much bank finance for house purchase.

Later (in the 1990s and 2000s), when housing credit became more widely available (probably elevated to the main means of financing house purchase), the housing market registered accelerated price growth, even though urbanization in Greece had drastically diminished by then, while owner-occupation was near 80 per cent. Overall, dwelling price growth in Greece was due to

(a) viewing property, and housing in particular, as a *permanent* family asset;
(b) a large part of housing wealth having been obtained without use of own funds or of mortgage credit;
(c) tax evasion on (rising) real incomes;
(d) persistent government budget deficits largely financed through raising foreign debt;
(e) low-cost housing credit since the mid-1990s, and especially after introduction of the euro in 2002; and
(f) a majority of developers having accumulated large profits in the past and having avoided exposure to outside financing.

These factors also explain the observed resistance of Greece's housing and property market to cyclicality.

In the end, it took the economic collapse of 2009–10 for property prices in Greece to drop noticeably, albeit slowly (see Table 7.3). The slow drop happened despite an estimated backlog of 150,000 newly constructed but unsold apartments (about 2.6 per cent of the housing stock) still owned by developers by end-2010. Importantly, and unlike the USA or Ireland, the Greek collapse did *not* originate with the property sector, but was caused by growing fiscal and trade imbalances and an unsustainable public debt (Manolopoulos, 2011).

A downside of the 'exchange arrangement', however, has been the very intensive utilization of urban space that it leads to, which has contributed to urban congestion and pollution, and to rather ugly and 'anarchic' cityscapes.

Summary of main points

1 Dwelling prices are not simple capitalizations of dwelling (imputed) rents, as owner-occupation is often valued in its own right, and it also confers advantages to the owner in excess of those associated with renting. Only if a dwelling is meant for letting, and is therefore clearly an income asset, may its price be equated to capitalized rent (after the cap rate has been properly defined).
2 Because of that, demand and supply models for owner occupied housing are likely to be more realistic if they focus on wholesale price rather than rent.
3 Another corollary is that residential demand differs from demand for commercial property.
4 Income, demographics, and household preferences (e.g., as regards the way households value commuting time versus leisure, or housing versus non-housing goods) are among the most important determinants of the demand for housing.
5 Housing demand and supply models have become quite powerful and sophisticated since 1980 or so, but have not yet overcome the problem of adequately identifying actual demand and supply, especially for forecasting purposes. 'Needs-based' approaches to

Table 7.3 Economic crisis and the RE sector in Greece

		Building permits issue	*Building permits for new dwellings*	*Number of bank-mediated dwelling transaction*	*Dwelling prices (1997=100)*
		(a)	*(b)*	*(c)*	*(d)*
1997		70,208	89,612		100.0
1998	ASE rise	73,351	97,306		114.4
1999	ASE bubble	67,410	88,516		124.5
2000	ASE bubble burst	69,587	89,389		137.7
2001	Adoption of €	76,693	108,021		157.5
2002	Introduction of € banknotes and coins	83,662	128,296		179.3
2003		83,677	127,051		189.0
2004	Olympic Games held in Athens.	82,236	122,163		193.4
2005	Expected introduction of VAT on new dwellings constructed with permits issued as of 1 January 2006.	98,569	195,207		214.5
2006	Introduction of VAT on new dwellings constructed.	84,536	125,387	108,253	242.3
2007	Burst of US house-price bubble begins.	79,407	103,865	148,125	257.3
2008	Minor recession in Greece. Global credit-crunch crisis. Serious riots in Athens in December.	66,740	79,601	116,034	261.1
2009	Onset of sovereign debt crisis in Greece; recession worsens.	57,001	61,490	74,586	249.8
2010	Facing bankruptcy, Greece seeks help from the 'troika'; recession deepens; property taxes escalate.	50,982	52,344	74,457	238.9
2011	Recession turns into depression; more and higher property taxes.	36,076	29,974	41,623	226.2

Sources: For (a) and (b), Hellenic Statistical Authority; for (c) and (d), Bank of Greece.
Troika = EC, ECB, IMF. ASE = Athens Stock Exchange.
The number of dwellings is greater than the number of buildings as some buildings are multi-apartment.

housing 'demand' estimation are much more practical and easy to apply, but, strictly speaking, are not about economic demand but about estimating housing needs.

6 Changes in housing supply may well be different from net construction (i.e., total construction minus depreciation), as such changes also include variations in the number of vacant dwellings on offer. Still, net construction is the most important determinant of changes in housing supply because it alone determines changes in the housing stock.
7 It is more effective and intuitive to approach residential development as an investment decision, involving achievement of *at least* a required rate of return (RRR), than as a textbook-style profit-maximization problem, involving the MR = MC condition.
8 Demand and cost conditions may circumscribe the potential level of land price paid a landowner for releasing land for development, but there is still room for negotiations between developer and land owner.
9 In accordance with the discussion in Chapter 5, the RRR is determined at industry level, with *ex-ante* RRRs on new deals being continuously corrected by actually achieved *ex-post* RRRs on old projects.

10 In the Anglo-American ('AnAm') mode of residential development, which involves building on own land and freely determining when construction will start, the developer will buy the land from the original landowner at a lower price than the full value of the land – the difference typically being the developer's return, as determined by his or her RRR.

11 The 'Greek' mode of residential development involves building on land shared between developer and original landowner, the latter being rewarded for making the land available for development by receiving a pre-determined number of finished apartments.

12 There is probably no substantial difference between the landowner under the 'AnAm' mode and the landowner under the 'Greek' mode as far as the land value received by each is concerned. However, the 'Greek' mode, in part because of additional features present in the countries in which it is practised, tends to shelter the national housing market from the internally generated cyclicality that characterizes it in developed, English-speaking, countries.

Review questions and exercises

1 Define 'development', 'new development, 'redevelopment', 'refurbishment', 'construction', and delineate their differences, if any.

2 Define the 'user-cost of housing'.

3 Define 'ripening' and 'waiting' costs in relation to development, 'land banking', and 'zoning'.

4 Offer arguments as to why the value of a dwelling may not be simply approached as a discounted stream of future imputed rents.

5 How is demand for commercial RE different from demand for housing?

6 Going to Section 7.3, divide Equation (7.5) by Equation (7.7) to come up with Equation (7.9); also, divide (7.7) by (7.6) to come up with (7.10).

7 Go to Section 7.4 and come up with an expression for equilibrium price, and another for equilibrium quantity, on the basis of Equations (7.13) and (7.18) or of (7.14) and (7.19).

8 The following is a Cobb–Douglas utility function for housing versus non-housing:

$$U(H,\ \mathrm{NH}) = H^{\alpha}\mathrm{NH}^{1-\alpha}.$$

If α is reduced, what will this mean, *ceteris paribus*, for the price of housing?

9 From Section 7.9 consider the example of a housing developer who has just bought a site to be developed within a time horizon of 15 years. Given that $m = 2$ years, and all other data are as set in Section 7.9 (i.e., revenue at time 0 = 600, outlay for labour and physical capital at time 0 is 250, $r = 5$ per cent, $i = 9$ per cent, $f = 4$ per cent, $e = 3$ per cent), if a developer makes a new forecast at the end of the 6th year, what should be the required revenue (taking account of building time, and assuming all output is expected to be sold at completion) in order for the developer to realize a 10 per cent return on total project cost from commencing building at the beginning of the 7th year? What is the effective, or *ex-post*, f (annual house price inflation) implied in your answer? That is, is it still 4 per cent (as forecast when the land was bought) or something else?

10 If, at the end of the 6th year, forecast revenue upon completion (if building starts at the beginning of the 7th year) is 950, and this revenue is in fact realized, what will be the developer's *ex-post* rate of return? A revenue of 950 implies what effective f (annual house price inflation) since the land was bought?

11 If, at the end of the 6th year, forecast revenue upon completion is 950 (if building starts at the beginning of the 7th year), but *ex-post* revenue (assuming all output is sold at completion) is in fact 755, what will be the developer's *ex-post* rate of return? What is the effective f (annual house price inflation) since the land was bought?

12 Go to www.vchr.vt.edu/pdfreports/Northampton%20Demand%20Analysis%20final.pdf. You will find there a Housing Demand Analysis for Northampton County, Virginia, published in June 2007. Compare this approach with Stantec Consulting Ltd's (2003) approach, found in www.citywindsor.ca/documents/D002114003Res.pdf, and mentioned in Section 7.6 of this book.

13 Go to Section 7.1. Compare Equations (7.2a) and (7.2b). In what ways are they similar/dissimilar?

14 Consider the following total revenue and total production cost functions faced by a developer:

$$\mathrm{TR} = 100Q - 10Q^2 \quad \text{and } \mathrm{TPC} = 2.5Q^2 + 40.$$

(a) Assuming RRR = 0, what is the profit-maximizing level of output Q?
(b) At that output, what are TR, TPC, and land price?
(c) Given a developer's RRR of 10 per cent, what would be TR, the effective TPC, land price, and the developer's absolute return?
(d) At what output would the developer maximize his or her absolute return?
(e) What would be the price of land in such a case?
(f) If planning authorities limited output on that particular plot to a value (of your own choosing) less than the profit-maximizing Q, how much would the developer pay for the land? Would the developer actually buy the land? Evaluate.
(g) Define the negotiation range.

15 How realistic would a straight-line TR be? If the TR line were straight, would there be a negotiation range? Explore both issues.

8 Construction flows and market equilibrium

Main sections

Having gone through this chapter, a student should be able to

1 Draw and explain a simple capital stock adjustment model (CSAM) for real estate (RE).
2 Draw and explain a more complex CSAM (proposed by DiPasquale and Wheaton), that integrates the capital market with the RE market.
3 Appreciate the significance of the model parameters for the behaviour of the model: for example, the slope of the construction function, a constant or changing amount of stock depreciation, the capitalization rate, and the time lag between the decision to build and completion.
4 Evaluate the role of price expectations ('rational' or 'myopic') for the behaviour of developers.
5 Explain the 'mean reversion' typically observed of RE prices.
6 Identify the conditions that, following an initial exogenous shock, will cause a RE market to return to equilibrium (if feasible at all) smoothly or through oscillations.
7 Understand the difference between endogenous and exogenous RE price dynamics.

8 Use both spreadsheet analysis and (first-order) difference equations in order to obtain numerical values for the state of a hypothetical RE market (stock, rents, prices, depreciation, construction output) at any point in time after an outside shock disturbs some assumed equilibrium.
9 Discuss the origins and behaviour of RE building cycles.

8.1 Capital stock adjustment models (CSAMs)

Built RE is a form of capital stock. As such, it changes over time through the addition of net flows of buildings. This means that the stock S at time t is equal to stock at a previous time $t-1$ plus whatever net flow (positive or negative) has happened in the meantime. If the changes are discrete (rather than continuous), one possible equation depicting the process is

$$S_t = S_{t-1} + (C_t - \delta S_t),$$

where

C = volume of new construction,
δ = a stock depreciation factor.

Changes in the stock of RE (particularly residential RE) have often been analysed by means of a capital stock adjustment model (CSAM). Pioneers in this regard, in the RE field,[1] have been Muth (1960) and Whitehead (1974). Based on their work, Robinson (1979) presented a diagrammatic CSAM, which is reproduced in Figure 8.1.

In Robinson's model the short-run supply curve of stock at the beginning is S_{sr1} (quite inelastic, but not fully so) and the initial demand is D_1. New (not net) additions to stock (the volume of construction) are q_1, in the right-hand diagram. Long-run equilibrium in this

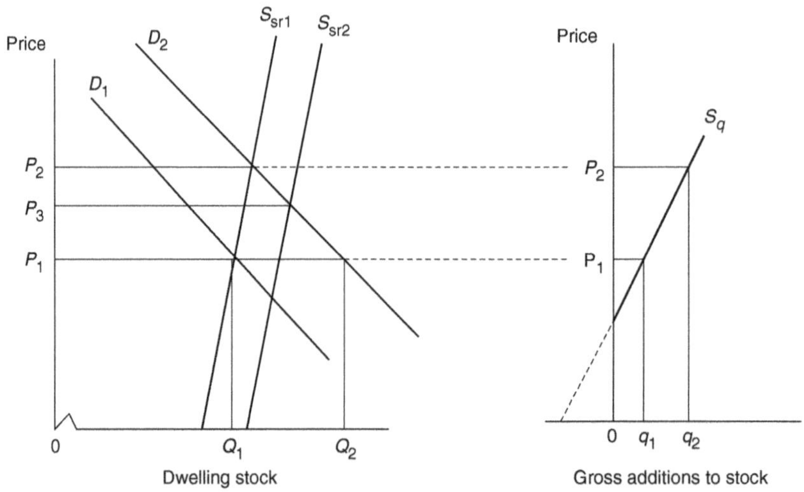

Figure 8.1 A capital stock adjustment model, based on Robinson (1979).

market is defined as that price P_1 at which new construction is equal to depreciation δ, thus maintaining a constant stock through time.

If, however, there is, say, an increase in demand to D_2, the model assumes that there will be a higher equilibrium price, P_2, which will cause developers (i.e., builders for an anonymous market) to build q_2 instead (more than the amount of depreciation). In turn the increased net construction will cause an increase in the short-run supply of stock to S_{sr2}. The market equilibrium price then drops to P_3, but this is still higher than the price P_1, which in this model is consistent with long-run equilibrium (zero net construction). More building will follow, until the stock has risen to Q_2 – and the equilibrium price has dropped back to P_1.

The reader must be careful to realize that the expression 'maintaining a constant stock through time' does not necessarily mean that over the long run the quantity of stock remains the same. It will increase of course (in a market economy), if there are demand-driven price rises – at which point net additions to the stock are shown to be again q_1, and, presumably, equal to stock depreciation; but once the equilibrium price has become such that new construction is just equal to stock depreciation, there is no further tendency for the quantity of stock to change – from whatever level it has reached in the meantime.

A problem with Robinson's (1979) model is that it seems to suggest that, following, say, an initial shift in demand, long-run equilibrium is, *ceteris paribus*, re-established at the original, pre-shock, price P_1 (although at an increased stock level). Connected to this is the question of why the long-run equilibrium towards which the market supposedly moves is one where the amount of new construction must be equal to the *original* amount of depreciation. (In Figure 8.1, for instance, the stock goes from Q_1, initially, to Q_2, finally – with depreciation returning to q_1.) More precisely, the model shows that after the initial increase in demand, and the concomitant increase in construction, the latter begins to drop until, at equilibrium, it is once again equal to the amount of stock depreciation that characterized the initial, pre-disturbance, stock level.[2] This is unlikely, for two reasons:

1 Re-establishment of equilibrium (even if possible in principle) takes time – we show this in Section 8.4.1, and it is also borne out by recent research (see Adams and Füss, 2010) – a long enough time that (i) the rate of physical depreciation itself may change[3] and (ii) the volume of depreciation, even at the initial rate, will materially increase, quite simply because the size of the stock will be expanding.

2 The main reason, however, for postulating an increasing amount (and/or rate) of depreciation is that the initial price 'jump' speeds up the economic depreciation of buildings – i.e., it makes redevelopment a lucrative option for more properties than was the case before (cf. Section 5.6). Economic depreciation is not the same thing as physical depreciation. The latter, however, seems to be the only kind implied in Robinson's (1979) model, since he accepts (p. 23) that in the model 'losses through obsolescence and demolitions [are] technically determined by the age distribution and the size of the stock'.

As a result, it makes sense to modify the model by assuming a *rate* of depreciation rather than a constant *amount* of it. Inevitably the rate, by being applied on an expanding stock, will also imply an *increasing* amount of stock depreciation. This is what we do in Section 8.2 below. The corollary is that, with a rising level of depreciation, re-attainment of the *original* long-run equilibrium becomes impossible, *ceteris paribus*: assuming that the original equilibrium was upset because of an increase in demand, the new equilibrium (construction = depreciation; also, demand price = supply price) is bound to be at a higher price than before.

In short, it is difficult to justify a return to a kind of (long-run) equilibrium at which new construction = original depreciation, as the increase in stock, which the model predicts on the wake of an increase in demand, would also imply more depreciation.

Further, actual achievement of equilibrium, whether at the old or at a new, different, price, is in practice problematic anyway, for the following reasons:

1 An initial outside shock may cause the system to experience a change in the parameters describing its behaviour (e.g., a change in the elasticity of construction).
2 Continuous changes in demand happen all the time in real life.
3 Changes in demand may, in the short run, not lead to price changes, but may be absorbed by changes in the *vacancy rate* (vacant properties as a percentage of all similar properties).
4 There are changes in the asset profile of real estate, and, in particular, changes in the current yield that investors demand in order to hold real estate assets.

This requires us to see if it is possible to integrate the real estate market and the capital market; and, moreover, do so without assuming that equilibrium requires going back to the original equilibrium price after a disturbance. This is attempted in subsequent sections.

The following points should be remembered:

1 If depreciation is a fixed amount, long-run equilibrium will, *ceteris paribus*, be re-established (if at all) at the original price but at a larger (smaller) quantity following an initial increase (decrease) in demand.
2 If depreciation is a constant rate, i.e., a fixed percentage of the stock and therefore linearly related to it, long-run equilibrium will, *ceteris paribus*, be re-established (if at all) at a different price from the original and at a larger (smaller) quantity following an increase (decrease) in demand.
3 The adjustment process will become more unstable and unpredictable if depreciation is nonlinearly related to the stock and is therefore a *variable* percentage of it. This is likely if older properties age faster, and rising prices speed up the economic devaluation of buildings.

8.2 The DiPasquale–Wheaton (DiPW) model

In 1992, Denise DiPasquale, then of Harvard University, and William C. Wheaton, then of MIT, published a seminal paper in the *Journal of the American Real Estate and Urban Economics Association*. It was entitled, 'The Markets for Real Estate Assets and Space: A Conceptual Framework'. The paper was important in that it presented a model of integration between the property market (or market for RE space), the capital market (or market for RE assets), and construction, which could help students and practitioners in the RE field gain a bird's-eye view of how the property market relates to 'the' interest rate and construction activity.[4] The model also broke down this relationship into constituent parts, which could be addressed and discussed separately. Indeed the pedagogical nature of DiPW's contribution has long been commended as its most significant characteristic (Achour-Fischer, 1999). It has also been constructively criticized (Viezer, 1999; Colwell, 2002) and applied (Viezer, 1999; Michelsen and Weiß, 2009).

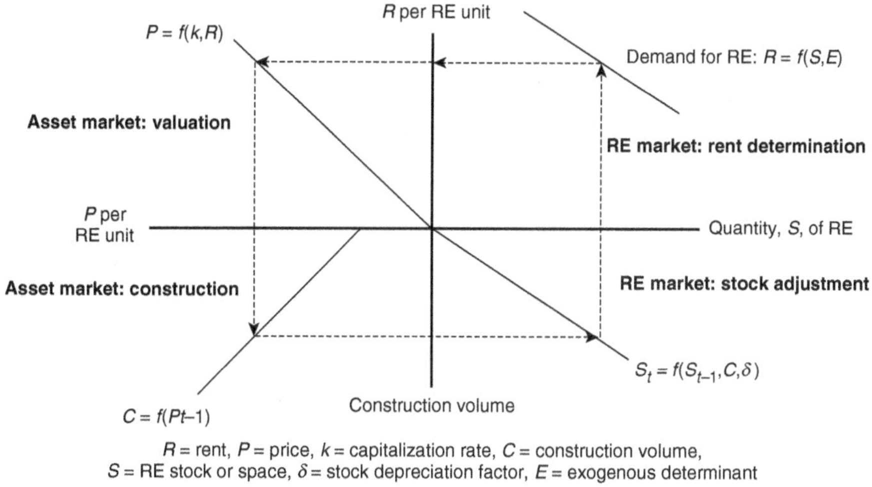

Figure 8.2 The DiPasquale–Wheaton (DiPW) model: links between RE market, capital market, construction, assuming equilibrium is maintained across periods, with $C = \delta S_t$, $P_{t-1} = P_t$, and $S_{t-1} = S_t$.

The DiPW model brings together four Cartesian diagrams to form a four-part super-diagram shown in Figure 8.2 (the first part is the top-right, or NE, quadrant, and it goes counter-clockwise from there).

- *NE quadrant:* Rent, the income yielded by (some kind of) RE in an area,[5] is a function of the quantity of RE[6] (also referred to as 'stock' or 'space') in that area, and of economy-wide influences (exogenously determined), for example persons in employment in the same area. Mathematically,

  $$R = f(S, E),$$

  where

  R = rent,
  S = stock,
  E = employment (or other relevant exogenous factor).

  S can be thought of as a particular type of RE, like residential or office. E can be, for example, persons employed in the area; it is the exogenous demand variable. Holding E constant (it is, after all, exogenous), R is then only a function of S, suggesting a simple demand line for real estate. Be that as it may, E is a simplification; in reality, incomes, interest rates, and/or other factors should be included in a demand expression for space (see the examples in Sections 7.3 and 7.4).
- *NW quadrant:* Given 'rent', the price of a unit of real estate can be arrived at as a function of that rent and of an appropriate 'capitalization rate' k (a discount factor: more on that in Section 8.7). In the simplest possible case, the price of a unit of real estate is taken to

be capitalized rent:

$$P = \frac{R}{k} = Rk^{-1}.$$

The assumption here is that at any point in time the given rent will last forever. This of course does not happen; hence the above model of price formation can be adjusted to take care of expectations as to the future course of rents (Wheaton, 1999; Davidoff, 2008). It is reasonable, for example, to assume that, *ceteris paribus*, rents will exhibit a downward trend as additional net construction (i.e., new construction greater than depreciated stock) comes into being (cf. Section 8.6 below). But that crucially depends on whether the characteristics that make a location desirable retain their value over time, and on whether new construction can imply access to the same characteristics without subtracting from the value of existing sites. (Such characteristics can be utility-related, for example in the sense of locational amenities, or revenue- and cost-related, for example in the sense of transport costs, or access to particular retail markets.)

In practice, because of the specificity of locations, new construction can very rarely imply access to the same utility and other characteristics of existing (good) locations (unless the landscape is rather homogeneous and transport costs insignificant). That means that such locations can retain their value (their high rent capacity) over a long enough term, such that $P = Rk^{-1}$ can make practical sense.

By the same token, new construction taking place in an inferior location will of course command lower rents – but it is still a kind of construction that represents the highest and best use of land for that inferior location. So, once again, this new construction will also command that particular level of rents for a relatively long time.

In the end, unless there are further increases in the demand for space, the increased net construction will exercise downward pressure on rents; but will do so slowly enough, to warrant use of the formula $P = Rk^{-1}$.

- *SW quadrant:* Once the price for a unit of space is given, developers decide whether they should undertake speculative development in response to that price. The rule is simple: as long as the price covers the cost of producing that unit of space, they will proceed with development. Development of course takes time: in what follows, we assume that starts in one period become completions in the next period – but, remember, a period is not necessarily equal to one calendar year. Thus, the volume of construction coming on the market is a function of a previous period price of a unit of space, when that price is over and above a given cost, c, per unit of space:[7]

$$C_t = f(P_{t-1}).$$

That cost has two dimensions, incidentally: (a) an area-wide cost, that is, the average level of construction labour costs in the given area, along with costs of raw materials, managerial expertise, capital equipment, obtaining regulatory permission, etc.; and (b) a project-specific cost, as, for example, taller buildings are costlier to construct.

- *SE quadrant:* The last part of DiPW's model links amount of additional net construction (which is forthcoming) to total quantity of real estate (stock or space) provided in the given area.

$$S_t = S_{t-1} + C_t - \delta S_t,$$

where

S_t	=	total quantity of real estate (stock or space) at (end of) period t,
C_t	=	construction during period t,
S_{t-1}	=	previous stock,
δ	=	rate of stock depreciation (notice that depreciation is a function of δ and of stock during period t); at equilibrium, of course, $C = \delta S$.

If we start from an equilibrium situation, additional net construction will be zero. There is new construction, but it is equal to amount of depreciated stock ($C = \delta S$). More than that will have to come about in response to rising real estate prices, themselves a result of rising rents (given the capitalization rate k), which in turn are a response to a shift of the original demand line linking rent to total amount of space in given area. Why would such a shift occur? Because, for example, of a rise in E (an exogenous factor depicting, say, increased population pressures, rising incomes, or a drop in the mortgage interest rate).

So now let the wheel roll: more construction leads to more total space, leads to lower rents, leads to lower prices, leads to less construction, and so on. Market equilibrium will be re-established when new construction is once again equal to amount of stock depreciation (which should be more than what it was at the initial equilibrium). In this formulation, the final level of rent (and, for a given k, the eventual equilibrium price) will be higher than the original (what it was before the exogenous shock to the real estate system), but lower than what it was just after the exogenous shock to system.

8.3 Summing up the DiPW model

The model makes use of the following equations:

$$R = f(S, E) \quad \rightarrow \text{NE quadrant,} \tag{8.1}$$

$$P = Rr^{-1} \quad \rightarrow \text{NW quadrant,} \tag{8.2}$$

$$C_t = f(P_{t-1}) \quad \rightarrow \text{SW quadrant,} \tag{8.3}$$

$$S_t = S_{t-1} + C_t - \delta S_t \quad \rightarrow \text{SE quadrant} \tag{8.4}$$

Notice that in the model the demand for space is not determined by the other quadrants but is exogenously determined. True, a net increase in construction will increase space and this will lead to a lower rent, but if we start from an equilibrium situation (given the cap rate and the construction function), there is no reason for construction to exceed depreciation unless there is an exogenous shift in the initial demand curve! So equilibrium will (probably) tend to be re-established in the NE quadrant of the DiPW model after an exogenous disturbance, but not along the given (the original) demand line – see Figure 8.3.

We will demonstrate the equilibrium adjustment process in Section 8.4. There are also three related questions to answer:

1 How will a given (demand) shock to the RE market 'ultimately' (i.e., at a re-established equilibrium) change the amount of space available and the level of rent? (See Section 8.4.)

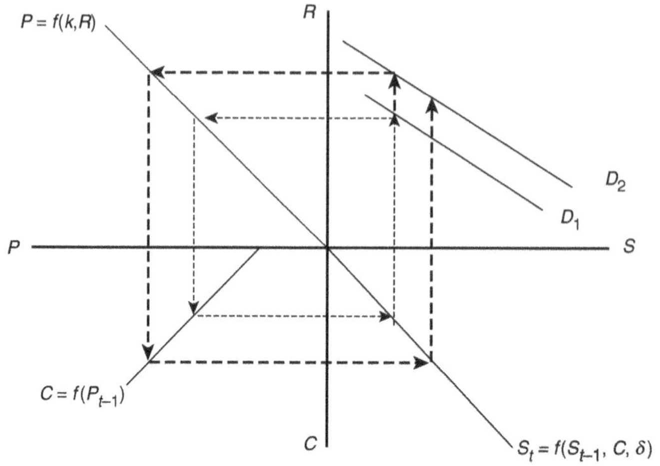

Figure 8.3 Dynamic interactions within the DiPW model: demand for RE increases, starting a spiral of rent, price, and construction changes. The thin broken line shows an initial equilibrium situation. The bold broken line shows (i) a rent rise after an increase in demand for RE from D_1 to D_2 and (ii) a rent drop one more period later as gross C exceeds depreciation.

2 Assuming we start from an equilibrium situation ($C = \delta S$), can equilibrium be re-established after a disturbance? Will it be the same as the original, or different? How soon, *ceteris paribus*? (See Section 8.8.)
3 Can we define a supply path that is consistent with both the original and the final equilibrium? (See Section 8.4.)

Let us now turn to these questions.

8.4 From the DiPW model to a modified CSAM

If re-establishment of market equilibrium is at all possible, this can happen only through a recursive process: a shift in demand causes rent to rise, causing price to rise, causing more net construction, causing a drop in rent. In turn, the reduced rent causes a volume of net construction that is less than before, but still above zero; eventually, a time may come when new construction = depreciated stock. At that point, equilibrium has been re-established, as there is no incentive for additional net construction. At that point, too, the quantity supplied of ‘space’ is equal to the quantity demanded, at a certain rent, which, assuming that depreciation has increased in the meantime, is higher than the rent associated with the original equilibrium. The broad process is presented in Figure 8.4.

In this model, the initial ‘jump’ in the demand for space causes a price (rent) increase to P_2, at the original equilibrium quantity of space, Q_{e1}. The higher price causes an increase in net additions to the stock, which shifts the short-run supply of space (S_{sr1}) rightwards, causing a drop in price, causing less net construction; as long as construction is greater than depreciation (which is also increasing), the increases in space will continue until, at P_{e2}, there is once again equilibrium (quantity of space demanded = quantity of space supplied), but (a)

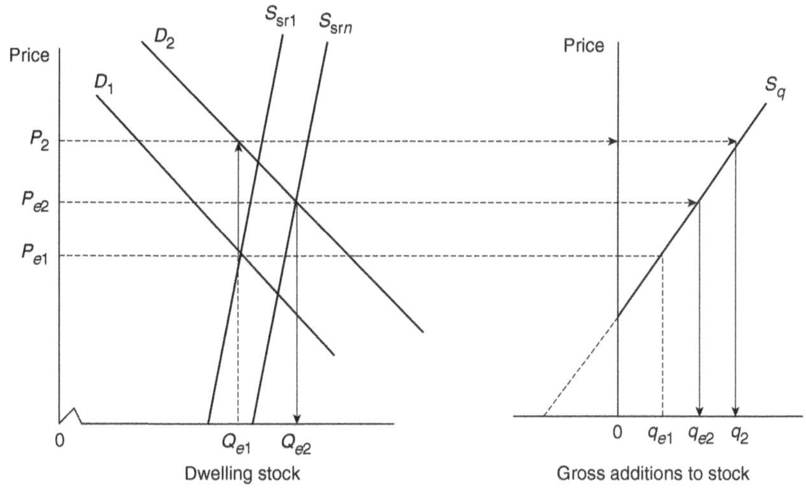

Figure 8.4 A capital stock adjustment model with shifted long-run equilibrium: the broad view.

at a higher equilibrium price than initially, (b) at an increased quantity of space, and (c) at a greater (equilibrium) volume of construction, which is equal to the (also greater) volume of depreciation.

In Figure 8.5, we examine the adjustment process in greater detail.

Explanation of Figure 8.5

As a result of some disturbance, demand shifts from D_1 to D_2. At the initial equilibrium stock Q_{e1}, demand price rises to $a(= P_2)$. At price a, the quantity supplied at the original supply line (S_{sr1}) is Q_2 (corresponding to a supply price b), but at that quantity, the demand price is c.

In the meantime, the higher demand price a has called forth more construction, q_2; which means that the quantity of space supplied is not Q_2, but larger: the supply line has shifted to S_{sr2}.

The demand price, though, has dropped to c. At price c, the quantity of stock supplied (on the basis of S_{sr2}) is given by supply price d. But because of yet more construction (although less than before, since the demand price has been dropping), the actual quantity of stock supplied is larger still, given by S_{sr3}.

The process goes on and on, associated with progressively lower demand prices, smaller increases in construction, and smaller increases in the stock. Eventually, equilibrium is reached at (approximately) P_{e2}, Q_{e2}, and supply S_{sr5}, with construction being simultaneously equal toq_{e2}(larger than initial construction q_{e1}, and equal to the larger volume of stock depreciation).

In this formulation, the process of adjustment does not involve jumping from one short-run equilibrium to another. This is problematic because it does not explain satisfactorily how each of those equilibria is arrived at. By contrast, any equilibria depicted in Figure 8.4 are notional (i.e., unrealized) rather than actual. The whole process of adjustment is dynamic and

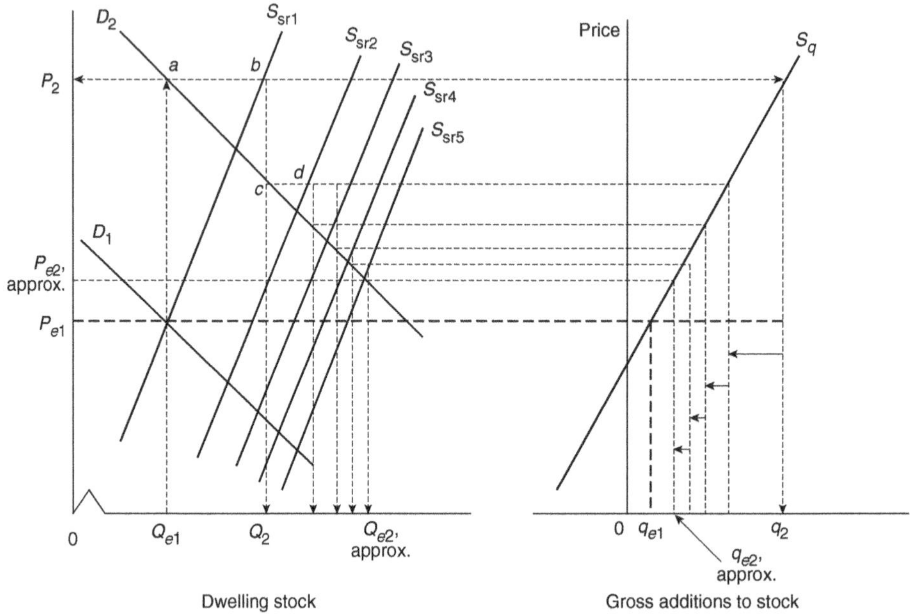

Figure 8.5 A capital stock adjustment model with shifted long-run equilibrium: the process in detail.

unstable until P_{e2} = demand price = supply price is reached, and construction = increased depreciation (assuming that the initial shock was a price rise).

To see the process of adjustment in action and with greater precision than is possible in Figure 8.5, we shall use the equations of the DiPW model, shown in Section 8.2 above – only we shall flesh them out by assigning parameter values.[8] We shall approach the recursive process twice: first by using a linear demand function, then by using a curvilinear one. The purpose is to find what will happen to rent, price, construction, and space once there is a disturbance to the initial equilibrium. The easiest way to do that is by means of a spreadsheet.

8.4.1 Example A: linear demand[9]

$R = f(S) = 110 - 0.08S$ (the demand line for space, with 'rent' as the price of space in the given period), (8.5)

$P = Rk^{-1}$ (price as capitalized rent), (8.6)

$C_t = f(P) = g + h(P_{t-1}) = g + h(110 - 0.08S_{t-1})k^{-1}$

(construction as a function of previous period price), (8.7)

starting quantity of space $= S_0 = 750$ units of floor space,

capitalization rate $= k = 10$ per cent,

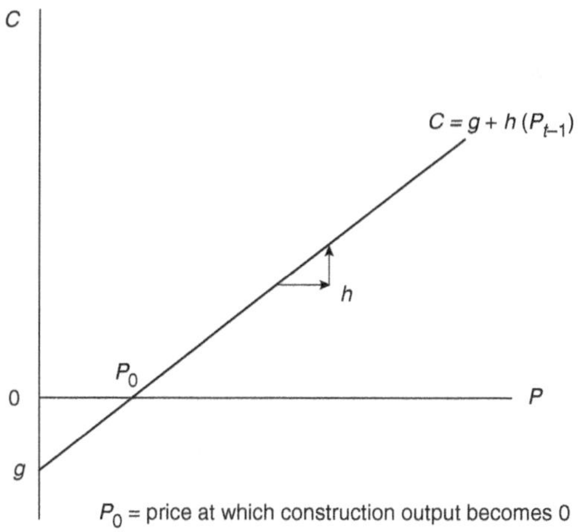

Figure 8.6 From Example A: construction C as a function of previous-period price.

$g = -5 =$ vertical intercept of the construction line, implying that at or below price P_0 there is no production (see Figure 8.6);

$h = 0.05 =$ slope of the construction line, i.e., the change in construction in response to a change in price,

$$S_t = S_{t-1} + C_t - \delta S_t, \tag{8.8}$$

where δ = rate of stock depreciation, set equal to 0.0267; thus, the extent of initial stock depreciation is $20(= 0.0267 \times 750)$.

Equations (8.5)–(8.7) give the following values for R, P, and C:

from (8.5), initial (equilibrium) $R = 110 - 0.08S = 110 - 0.08(750) = 50$,

from (8.6), initial (equilibrium) $P = Rk^{-1} = 50/0.1 = 500$,

from (8.7), initial (equilibrium) $C = g + hP = -5 + 0.05(500) = 20$.

It is important to notice that the fundamental condition for equilibrium is that initial $C =$ initial depreciation, or that $C = g + hP = \delta S = 20$. This requirement limits the values for g and h to those that satisfy it; put differently, if long-run equilibrium has indeed been achieved in this market, the values for g and h can be none other than those that satisfy $C = \delta S = 20$.[10]

Now let us assume a disturbance in the system. The disturbance is in the nature of a rise in demand, causing the latter to become $R_2 = 130 - 0.08S$. Since S has not had time to adjust to this increase in demand, $R_2 = 70$. Holding k, h, and g constant, constructors will now respond to the higher price P by contributing a positive net construction volume.

Making the rather reasonable assumption that developers' immediate response to current price signals leads to any additional output (decided by developers) being added to the stock one period after the period in which a price signal occurs, and following the recursive changes by means of a spreadsheet, we conclude that equilibrium will be re-established ($C = \delta S$) after approximately 115 time periods – see Table 8.1.

Table 8.1 Spreadsheet calculations for Example A

Period	*Construction C*	*Space S, in million square units*	*Price, or capitalized rent*	*Rent at which space is demanded*	*Depreciation (= δS)*	*Difference between construction and depreciation*	*Rent at which space is supplied*
0	**20**	**750**	**500**	**50**	**20**	**0.00**	50
1	20.00	750.00	700.00	70.00	20.0	0.00	50.00
2	30.00	759.74	692.21	69.22	20.26	9.74	50.52
3	29.61	768.85	684.92	68.49	20.50	9.11	51.01
4	29.25	777.36	678.11	67.81	20.73	8.52	51.46
5	28.91	785.33	671.74	67.17	20.94	7.96	51.89
114	24.00	899.92	580.06	58.01	24.0	0.01	58.01
115	24.00	899.93	580.06	58.01	24.0	0.00	58.01

Explanation of Table 8.1

Initially the market situation is as shown in row 0. As soon as the price becomes 700, construction starts rise to 30, i.e., 10 more than the level of depreciation. The extra 10 units are placed on the market in the next period, however. In that same period, depreciation rises to 20.26 units. That means that in period 2, space becomes 759.74(= 750 + 30 − 20.26). As a result, the rent at which space is demanded drops to 69.22. The lower rent causes construction to drop a little, to 29.61, while depreciation rises further, to 20.50. The recursions go on until, eventually, construction, at 24, is equal to the increased depreciation (24 also). At that point, total space in the given area has increased to 899.93 units, and rent has dropped to 58.01 (which is higher than the rent before the rise in demand, but lower than what it was before the quantity of space had begun to respond to the higher rent caused by the initial rise in demand).

Relaxing the assumption about the speed of response (assuming, that is, that additional output is added to the stock after *more* periods) is easily taken care of in the spreadsheet. The result is that the number of periods after which equilibrium is re-established becomes smaller. The economic rationale for this is that, with a delayed response, the price disturbance (a rise in this case), which was an incentive to developers to start new projects, tends to persist, period after period, until starts are translated into completions and put on the market. Before the additional completions hit the market, the persisting higher price level makes developers more confident, *ceteris paribus*, that the higher price is a good predictor of future prices – so they keep up the number of started projects, until, that is, the increased completions (relative to completions during initial equilibrium) begin to exercise a damping effect on the price level. Thus, construction activity becomes 'front-loaded': the longer the output response time (in terms of completions, not of starts!), the larger the front load, and the faster a new equilibrium, *ceteris paribus*, will be established.

The number of 115 periods that we found for re-establishment of equilibrium seems inordinately large. But (a) the periods do not have to be years; they can be semesters or quarters; (b) most of the recursions in Table 8.1 involve changes that in practice are very small: it is reasonable to assume that 'essentially' equilibrium will have been re-established when the difference between C and δS has not actually come down to zero but (say, because of indivisibilities in production) is around 1 unit of space (or 5 per cent of the initial volume of depreciation in the above example, which was 20 units).

Empirical evidence seems to corroborate that it takes a long time for RE equilibrium to be re-established: for example, Adams and Füss (2010) looked into the behaviour of house prices in 15 countries (11 Western European ones plus Australia, New Zealand, Canada, and the USA) from 1975 Q1 to 2007 Q2, and concluded that 'deviations from the long-term equilibrium result in a dynamic adjustment process that may take up to 14 years'. Wigren and Wilhelmsson (2007), too, looked into housing stock and price adjustments in 12 Western European countries from 1976 to 1999, and observed a low speed of adjustment on quantity (with demand and supply shocks taking 4 years before being fully incorporated into the housing stock), while the effect on housing prices was instantaneous. And Gounopoulos et al. (2012), studying house prices in Greece from 1985 Q1 to 2010 Q4, found that 'following an exogenous shock, reversion to the long-run equilibrium is a rather slow process'.

8.4.2 From example A: estimating supply

It seems, then, that equilibrium in this hypothetical RE market has been re-established at an $R =$ period price $= 58.01$ and at an $S =$ quantity $= 899.93$ (whereas initially $R = 50$ and $S = 750$). On that basis, it might be interesting to attempt a linear approximation of the path taken by the long-run supply of 'space' or 'stock' (as opposed to current construction) in this particular market. This is easily found as follows. The slope of a hypothetical long-run supply line is

$$\frac{\Delta P}{\Delta Q} = \frac{58.01 - 50}{899.93 - 750} = \frac{8.01}{149.93} = 0.053.$$

The vertical intercept is the price when quantity (i.e., RE stock) is zero. It is found by solving the following equation for a:

$$50 = a + 0.053(750),$$

which gives 9.95.[11] Thus, the long-run supply path we seek is given by $R = 9.95 + 0.053S$. (See Figure 8.7.)

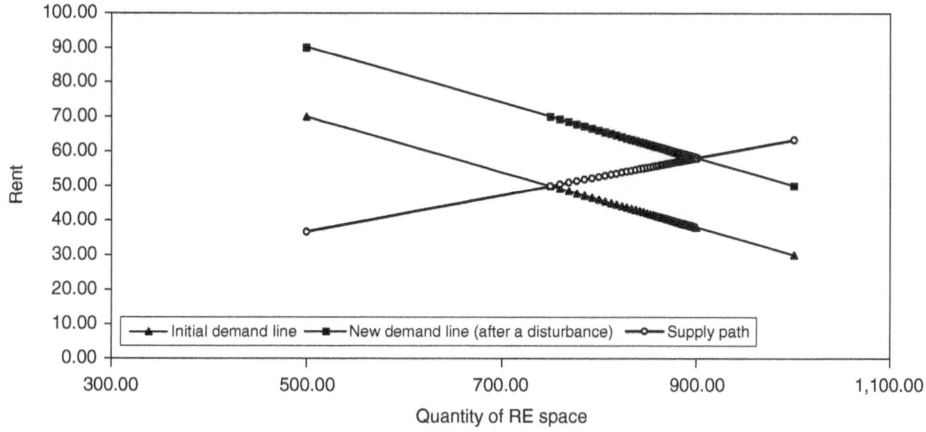

Figure 8.7 Linear demand: re-establishment of equilibrium and long-run supply.

Interestingly, the arc elasticity of the long-run supply that we found, over the segment linking the original to the final equilibrium, is

$$\varepsilon_s = \frac{1}{0.053}\frac{\text{Av}P}{\text{Av}Q} = \frac{1}{0.053}\frac{(58.01+50)/2}{(899.93+750)/2} = 1.235.$$

This hypothetical result seems large, considering that empirical estimates of housing supply in particular suggest that the latter is inelastic: for example, looking into the US housing market from 1975 to 1994, Mayer and Tsuriel Somerville (1996) noticed 'a fairly moderate response of supply to house price changes. A 10 percent rise in real house prices leads to a 0.8 percent increase in the housing stock, which is accomplished by a temporary 180 percent increase in the average number of quarterly starts, spread over four quarters.'

In other words, construction activity is (as expected, over the short term) more responsive to price changes than the total stock is. On the other hand, over the long term, the price responsiveness of the stock should increase. Thus, in Example A, re-establishment of equilibrium is completed after many periods (long-run, rather than short-run, supply): time enough for the supply of total stock to become elastic. But this does not mean that current construction is necessarily elastic: Vermuelen and Rouwendal (2007), studying the Dutch housing market, reported very low price elasticities (0.2–0.4) for newly constructed units (1970–2005) and for the quality of new construction (1970–98) combined.[12]

8.4.3 Example B: curvilinear demand[13]

In this example, we assume a curvilinear demand line linking rent and RE space; moreover, we introduce an exogenously determined variable (say, employment) explicitly.[14] Thus,

$$R = \frac{5000E}{S} \text{ (notice that this demand curve is iso-elastic, with elasticity} = -1), \quad (8.9)$$

$$P = Rk^{-1} \quad (8.10)$$

$$C = f(P) = g + hP_{t-1} = g + h\frac{5000E}{S_{t-1}}k^{-1}, \quad (8.11)$$

$$S_t = S_{t-1} + C_t - \delta S_t. \quad (8.12)$$

Here $g = -5$, $h = 0.05$, $k = 10$ per cent, $\delta = 2$ per cent, initial stock $= 250$, and $E = 1$. Assuming that E rises to 1.5, R rises from 20 to 30. With the help of a spreadsheet, successive recursions ultimately lead to a new equilibrium at a level of construction (and depreciation) equal to 6.51 (as opposed to 5, at the initial equilibrium), a stock of RE equal to 325.63, and a rent equal to 23.03.

On the basis of those results, estimating a long-run linear supply (like we did in Example A) gives $R = 9.976 + 0.04S$.

8.5 CSAMs and the role of expectations

If we compare Figures 8.1 and 8.5, i.e., Robinson's (1979) CSAM and the one proposed in Section 8.4, we conclude that the main difference is that in the former model, long-run equilibrium[15] is re-established at the original equilibrium price, implying a horizontal long-run supply path, and in the latter model, long-run equilibrium is established at a higher price (if the initial change in demand is an increase), implying an upward-sloping long-run supply path (see Figure 8.7). This happens because Robinson's CSAM assumes that, at re-established long-run equilibrium, construction = initial level of depreciation, whereas the second model assumes that, at the new equilibrium, construction = a risen level of depreciation. Because of that, the 'shifted long-run equilibrium' model is associated with faster re-adjustment than Robinson's CSAM.

Either model predicts some amount of initial over- (or under-) building in response to an outside shock. But how can such be? Do producers not know or realize that their collective response to, say, a rise in demand for space will create more of it, and thus change the price of space at the time any new stock is delivered (considering the time span involved between starts and completions)? And that, consequently, the new, immediately post-shock, price will not last?

8.5.1 'Excessive' response to a price shock

There are reasons why such an 'excessive' response is the likeliest, though. These are as follows:

1 *Herd behaviour*. The process whereby members of a group form expectations can be either individualistic or collaborative. Irrespective of the nature of the process, what matters is subsequent action. Kummerow and Quaddus (1998) describe a rational developer's thinking thus: 'If my project goes ahead and everybody else's does not, rents will be high and my project profitable. If everyone else also builds, market rents will fall and we will all lose money.' Quite so; but, herd behaviour is to go ahead with one's project, even though – or because – every other developer will be doing the same. Hence, individually rational behaviour (i.e., starting construction when there is a rise in RE prices due to, say, a rise in demand) may appear *ex-post* as irrational – but only *ex-post* and only with the benefit of hindsight regarding the collective – yet unintended – consequences of individual actions: in typical herd behaviour, all developers will build, causing ultimately a drop in price (see Baum, 2000; Cipriani and Guarino, 2008; Borgersen et al., 2010).

Things are hardly different if expectations have been formed collaboratively. In a controlled experimental environment, where subjects were asked to predict the next price of a risky asset, it was found that 'participants within a group tend to coordinate on a common prediction strategy' (Hommes et al., 2008). In real life, exchanges of information or commentary on market developments among members of a profession or industry are the norm rather than the exception. Such exchanges may amount to some kind of loose coordination among members, partly determining their understanding of market outlook. Even if there is no direct exchange, members are still, by and large, receivers of the same widely available information (e.g., on RE prices or returns), often coming from specialized vendors. Still, there is no guarantee that market actors will be using the same forecasting tools to predict the future, even in the face of identical information.

More importantly, there is no material difference between individualistic or collaborative expectation-formation, when the subsequent actions of group members are the same and have the same impact – like considerable price fluctuations (cf. Borgersen et al., 2010). If anything, 'collaboration' may reinforce any basic expectation-generating mechanism rather than correcting it. In the experiments mentioned, participants' predictions appeared to reflect trend-chasing behaviour or positive feedback expectations; their predictions deviated from realized market prices 'derived from an unknown market equilibrium equation with feedback from individual forecasts'; and price bubbles emerged endogenously, which were 'inconsistent with rational expectations' (Hommes et al., 2008; see more on 'rational expectations' below).

If herd behaviour, and price bubbles, are therefore the most likely outcomes of 'stakeholders' attempting to predict asset prices, and act accordingly, this explains, for example, why developers tend to overbuild in response to positive market signals. In the same vein, Baddeley (2005), studying the housing markets of England and Wales from 1981 to 2000, concluded that 'the housing market is more effectively modelled when [bubbles, herding and frenzies] are introduced into the analysis'.

2 *Uncertainty regarding the final market equilibrium, if attainable at all.* If we reject the idea that, following a disturbance, long-run equilibrium tends to be re-established at some initial, pre-disturbance, equilibrium price (which, in principle, is known), the actual price at which long-run equilibrium will be re-established becomes difficult to predict. The amount of information required in order to forecast some other equilibrium can be prohibitive.[16] Practically, this means that instead of developers (and other economic agents) adjusting their (price) expectations in response to a coming equilibrium, which is known in advance, they actually determine the nature of the coming equilibrium through their (price) expectations. Moreover, as we show below (Section 8.8) eventual re-establishment of an equilibrium is by no means assured, as it depends on the parameter values describing the particular RE market (e.g., the slope of the construction function). And it is far from likely that all developers use the same forecasting models and the same parameter values.
3 *Inadequacy of information.* Lack of full, certain, and reliable information on future market conditions (including future prices) tends to make market actors turn to proxies. The strongest – and cheapest! – proxies available are (i) current prices and (ii) rate of growth, and/or pattern, of past prices over a chosen time period. If such proxies create profit expectations, that is quite enough for many developers or investors to act upon that information (especially in the absence of other trustworthy information). The rest of market actors will probably follow suit, in typical herd behaviour.
4 *Relative land scarcity.* The scarcer, and the more desirable relative to other sites, land is, or is perceived to be, the greater the chance that the given land's rent-earning capacity, or its price, will persist; or, more to the point, the stronger the confidence of market actors that this will indeed be so. Prime urban-land uses in this respect are, e.g., office buildings, shopping centres, hotel complexes. Owners or developers of such sites are therefore likely to respond particularly quickly to appropriate price signals. Moreover, as soon as prime sites are committed to a use or built upon, it is other vacant sites' turn to become prime candidates for development. In a market upturn, this reinforces a 'bandwagon' development effect across the urban landscape,[17] but, in the first instance, the effect takes place in the context of particular land uses – and only later spills over to other uses. In the case of housing, significant land scarcity can exist either for physical reasons[18] or because of planning regulations.
5 *The capitalization rate k.* This includes a risk premium. But perceptions of risk are likely to become weaker, the more RE rents or prices rise, or are expected to rise. As a result herd behaviour will be reinforced. (There is more on k in Section 8.7.)

Taken together,

- herd behaviour
- uncertainty about a new equilibrium (value and attainability)
- inadequacy of information
- relative land scarcity
- the fluidity of the capitalization rate k.

imply that developers have a strong incentive to use current prices or rents, or the projected rate of growth of past prices or rents, as a guide to future prices or rents; to use, i.e., *myopic* (*naive* or *adaptive) expectations* rather than *rational expectations*.[19] This behaviour is almost certain to result in 'excessive' responses (i.e., over- or under-building) to current price signals. In fact, housing developers and investors are more likely to overreact simply because residential market participants are more numerous than in other RE markets, which makes herd behaviour more likely.

8.5.2 'Myopic' and 'rational' expectations[20]

The theory of rational expectations assumes that individuals take into account all available information in forming expectations – so that even if expectations turn out to be wrong, they will not *systematically* deviate from an expected value. This suggests that the theory is not about predicting when, say, a price shock (which by definition is unanticipated) will happen; rather, it is about economic actors predicating their behaviour on an understanding of what such a shock (like a sudden rise in demand for accommodation) will do to prices after taking into account all available information – like other actors' responses (Wheaton, 1992, pp. 210 and 215). After all, if the shock had been fully anticipated, it would have already been discounted into the current price of RE.

Rational predictions of future prices may well turn out to be wrong. The point is that if, for example, all builders expect prices to rise, but the result of their collective rush to build is a lower price than expected, this is one *unsystematic* deviation from an expected value. But builders will incorporate this incident into their estimates of what will happen to prices next time there is an initial RE price increase, so that a second (or maybe a third) deviation of expected from realized value will not happen (or will be smaller than before). In other words, systematic deviations under rational expectations are impossible. Yet, time after time, instances of herd behaviour are observed – and not just in RE.

Moreover, what could an expected value be in some RE market? It could be a re-established initial equilibrium, or, more probably, some other (whatever) equilibrium – but the first is very unlikely (cf. Section 8.6.3), and the precise value of the second (if attainable at all) is very difficult to forecast. The difficulty is compounded by the possibility that market participants may not all use the same 'fundamental' exogenous variables in their forecasts, they may not all attach the same probabilities of occurrence to different values of those variable(s), or they may not use the same equations, or the same cap or stock depreciation rates.

If market participants make even slightly different forecasts, their present *actions* will be slightly different from one another's. But even small differences may be enough to turn any future equilibrium into a flickering flame rather than a beacon.[21] Without a generally accepted expected value, the *ex-post* results of group behaviour will differ from the *ex-ante* rationale for individual behaviour, and adaptive expectations (i.e., using the past to predict the future; expectations driven by lagged price changes) are more likely to be the logical recourse open to market participants (cf. Brunes (2005), in regard to office building investment in Stockholm).

In turn 'myopic' expectations 'create herding behaviour in the market and initiate reinforcing effects' as well as 'inertia in price movements [which] thereby more easily tend to deviate from fundamentals' in the short run (Sorensen, 2006: 63, 86).

Of course, any rational forecaster of RE prices would use 'fundamentals', like population, employment, incomes, or interest rates. But no real-life forecast can accurately take into account the influence on prices of herd behaviour, of speculation (which by definition is not based on 'fundamentals'), or of the latter's extent and timing.

In fact, the existence of speculation suggests that for a considerable time prices in a market can deviate *systematically* from what they should have been – even though they are *mean-reverting*[22] in the long run (Sorensen, 2006; Glaeser and Gyourko, 2007; Gao et al., 2009; Borgersen, 2010). True, prices that are not based on 'fundamentals' eventually 'correct', but the point is that in the meantime real effects (like artificially high prices or overbuilding) have happened. The interesting thing is that such systematic deviations of prices from reasonably expected values have been known to recur throughout modern economic history. They are called 'bubbles', and the inevitable subsequent 'bursts' have not been known to become much of a lesson to future investors.

Possibly a weaker, but more realistic, form of rational expectations would involve developers forming price expectations not in relation to some specific equilibrium to be re-established in the future, but simply on the basis of an understanding that, given an initial increase in RE price due to a shock, subsequent prices will exhibit a declining trend. The trend will be towards an unknown equilibrium, but probably close to the pre-shock level: what is referred to as 'mean reversion'. It is unlikely, though, that even this 'understanding' will be enough to overcome the herd behaviour of builders, or other groups, in any reasonably competitive environment After all, the first to deliver completed properties when prices are rising will make the most money!

This analysis does not mean that people never act or form judgements based on rational expectations. For example, most of the time shocks like rises in incomes, changes in taxes, and planning announcements are quickly capitalized into RE prices, in whole or in part. But the existence of herd behaviour and speculation also indicates that to a very large extent people (a) use current prices or trends as proxies for forecasting the future and (b) imitate what others are doing in hopes of gain or of avoiding a loss. Usually this is very rational behaviour on the part of individuals – at the beginning. Too bad, then, it often ends in tears, and other unintended, yet in principle predictable, consequences.

8.5.3 Developers' responses to prices in the face of uncertainty

With all this uncertainty around, two questions emerge:

(a) Why do developers respond at all to a price rise?
(b) Why don't they respond by building an inordinately large number of RE units right after a price rise?

In answer to (a)

Developers respond because the higher price means more profit. If any one of them does not move quickly in order to produce more units of RE, then, in a competitive market, he will lose out to others – so they all move quickly (the herd behaviour hypothesis). The profit incentive would also make a monopolist constructor produce more output, but perhaps less quickly.

In answer to (b)

Developers do not build 'too much' right after a price rise for a number of reasons:

(i) Land scarcity. It would be a safe bet that the responsiveness of construction to increases in price (the elasticity) is greater where the landscape is relatively dull, obtaining planning permission is easy, and transportation to target-locations unproblematic, than where the opposite is the case.
(ii) Land-keeping costs. Building 'too much' presupposes the existence of massive land banks acquired by developers in the past: having done this presupposes, in turn, tying up huge amounts of funds to land, at an alarmingly high opportunity cost. It also presupposes that developers had correctly forecast the initial rise in the price of RE, as well as the timing of the rise. On the other hand, acquiring land for development after a shock had happened, and landowners had been apprised of the fact, would increase landowners' capital gains rather than developers' profits.
(iii) Another obstacle is the inevitable increase in costs subsequent to a large increase in the demand for construction resources.
(iv) Uncertainty about the future makes construction firms hesitant about committing too much financial capital to building (and, usually, borrowing to that effect) at any one time: as many have found to their consternation on the wake of a price bubble burst, overextending oneself implies significantly more risk.

Having suggested that developers do not build 'too much' does not mean that they build a quantity that is just right. With optimistic price expectations, overbuilding is virtually inevitable – and it does not take 'too much' of it to cause, say, the burst of a particularly large housing bubble (cf. Section 11.4). Further, construction starts become finished buildings with a time lag; by then, market conditions may well be different from when building decisions were taken.

8.6 The 'riddle' of mean reversion

Q: How, over the long run, can house prices revert to their mean if a post-shock equilibrium price differs from a pre-shock equilibrium price? This of course would be indicated by a tilting long-run supply, or price, path – cf. Figure 8.7.

A: A lot hinges on what we mean by 'mean' (cf. Section 2.3.4). There are two possibilities. One, that the mean in question is indeed the *same price* across equilibria, adjusted for inflation and house characteristics. Another, that it is really a long-run upward (or maybe downward) *trend line* rather than a single-value historic mean. Technically, the only difference between the two is that in the first case the mean graphs as a horizontal trend line, and in the second as a tilting trend line. Let us examine them both.

(A) The 'mean' as an actual historic value (i.e., a horizontal trend line)

Consider the following example. At the beginning of a year, the average house price is P_1. Over the course of the year, 1000 new households appear who demand houses. If there is no stock depreciation and builders supply 1000 new houses, identical to the average house, there should be no change in equilibrium price, which, *ceteris paribus*, will by year-end be equal to P_1, even though, during the year, there may have been price fluctuations in response to differences between the rate of buyers arriving on the market and the rate of sellers making deliveries. This situation is consistent with a horizontal long-run supply, or price, path.

But even a long-run supply, or price, path that initially tilts would not necessarily imply that reversion to an actual historic price cannot occur. This is how. The CSAM proposed in Figure 8.5, and the associated numerical example, showed what will happen in a market if a shock causes a price increase relative to an initial equilibrium price. If equilibrium is then re-established over the long run, it will be characterized by a *higher* price. Reversion to the historic (i.e., initial-equilibrium) price will not happen. If it were *nevertheless* observed, it would mean that a subsequent shock had negated the effect of the first shock, causing re-establishment of equilibrium at the *original* price. More generally, it would mean that *positive and negative shocks had cancelled one another*.

Yet over any particular time period, the balance of positive and negative shocks (in frequency as well as amplitude) may not be a zero-sum game: price gains may outweigh price losses, or vice versa. So reversion to an actual historic price (and therefore manifestation of a horizontal supply path) depends a lot on the choice of time period.

(B) The 'mean' as (a tilting) long-run trend

It is perhaps unrealistic to expect only chance or random shocks in a housing market (or others) and no repetitive and cumulative ones. Demographic changes and real per capita income growth are just two examples of the second type of shocks. A rising volume of stock depreciation (though not necessarily its proportion) is another (and it was assumed in Section 8.4). In such a case, long-run equilibrium will happen (if at all) at a price higher or lower than the original, depending on the direction and aggregate effect of the repetitive shocks. The related long-run price path will then be *systematically* either upward- or downward-sloping.

If so, reversion to a historic 'mean' (even if adjusted for inflation and house characteristics) will not happen. What is likely to happen, and be observed, is reversion to a 'mean' given by the long-term *trend* of house prices (adjusted for inflation etc.). That is, deviations from that trend line will represent the influence of non-repetitive, non-cumulative shocks, or, at any rate, shocks that tend to cancel one another against a backdrop of other shocks (like demographics or income growth) that may be exercising a consistent influence upon house prices. House prices would then be *trend-stationary* (cf. Section 2.3.4).

Hence, mean reversion exists when deviations from the long-run trend of prices (whether above or below the trend) collapse back to the trend. The implication is that reversion to a historic mean, for example to the same price, is really a special case of a trend-stationary time series, as that trend can be either horizontal or tilting.

Empirical evidence suggests that reversion of house prices to an *upward-tilting* long-run trend (which is the mean) is realistic. In confirmation, Table 8.2 shows median home values in the USA from 1940 to 2000, adjusted for inflation. The values are rising, reflecting the consistent influence of demographics, real incomes, and quality improvements.

Finally, Figure 8.8 demonstrates the relationship between trend and actual values by showing two well-known US real home price indices: the OFHEO Index, and the Case–Shiller Index. The way actual values fluctuate suggests that they tend to revert towards the trend line, i.e., towards their 'mean'.

Table 8.2 Long-term trend of home values in the USA, 1940–2000

Year	*Price*	*Year*	*Price*
1940	30,600	1980	93,400
1950	44,600	1990	101,100
1960	58,600	2000	119,600
1970	65,300		

Median home values, in $US (year 2000 = 100), referring to owner-occupied single-family housing units of less than 10 acres without a business or medical office on the property.

Source: www.census.gov/hhes/www/housing/census/historic/values.html.

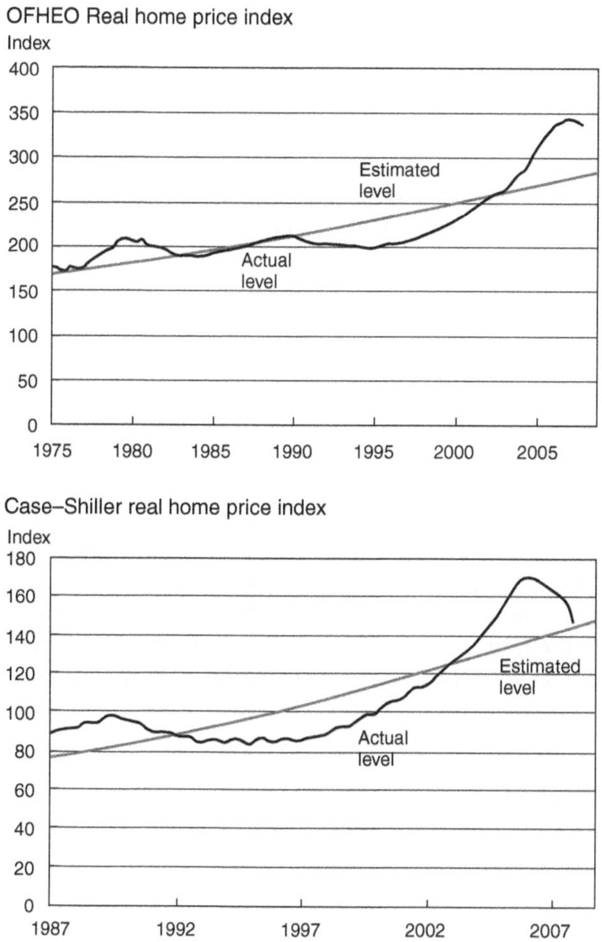

Figure 8.8 Evidence of mean reversion for US house prices. (Source: Shenk (2008).)

8.7 The capitalization factor *k* in the DiPW model

The hallmark of the DiPW CSAM is a postulated link between the physical RE market and the asset RE market. This draws attention to the nature and level of k, the capitalization factor. In turn, the need to incorporate k increases uncertainty as regards the timing or attainment of any future equilibrium. The reasons are diverse:

1. In the DiPW CSAM, k is used to discount future rents. If treated correctly, it includes a risk premium, which need not be the same for all developers. As a result, the construction industry's response to a change in rents may not be monolithic.
2. A change of k at some point, which may easily occur for reasons that go beyond the construction sector, will determine a different current price for RE, and therefore lead to another volume of construction. Consequently, any equilibrium the market was headed towards before the change in k will shift.[23]
3. A changed k will not only affect construction volume, but also stock depreciation volume. The reason is that k affects the time at which it is profitable to demolish and redevelop existing properties (cf. Section 5.6). But owners of such properties may well have different risk–return profiles from developers. This increases uncertainty as to any eventual equilibrium.

Bringing k into play (and, in general, linking the RE market and the capital market) is of course a major strength of the DiPW model. But the model has problems (some of which have been addressed in Viezer, 1999; Colwell, 2002; du Toit and Cloete, 2003). The main ones are as follows:

1. In its initial formulation, the DiPW model assumes that the cap rate k is exogenous. This is unlikely to be the case as, for example, higher expected prices of RE (themselves a function of current prices) tend to reduce the risk component of k and possibly k itself (cf. Section 11.6.1).
2. The model treats construction costs (see Figure 8.6) as exogenous too. In practice, the vertical intercept of the function, $C = f(P)$, may well *rise* if there is an influx of, say, manual labour into the relevant urban area (resulting simultaneously in higher RE prices and *lower* construction costs); or it may drop (i.e., construction costs will rise) as stronger demand for construction labour and materials will push up their prices.
3. The relationship between the interest-rate component of the cap rate and construction may be more complex than postulated in the model. For example, a long period of declining interest rates may, *ceteris paribus*, reduce developers' borrowing costs, but may also – through the augmenting effect of lower rates on RE prices – motivate them to keep land undeveloped longer (cf. Levin and Pryce, 2009).

Overall, the DiPW model offers itself up (arguably with appropriate modifications of the cap rate or the construction function) not merely as a pedagogical tool, but as a useful and conceptually appealing way of studying interconnections between RE and the wider economy. For example, Hua et al. (2001) modified the DiPW model to study the price–volume relationship between the pre-sales and the existing housing markets of Taiwan. Basically the pre-sales market involves the sale of houses that have not been built yet (but are on the planning or construction stage), and it exists in other Asian markets (and Greece) too. They concluded that both pre-sales and existing prices converge to long-run equilibrium.

Michelsen and Weiß (2009) used the DiPW model to study the East German housing market. They observed a disequilibrium that, to a large extent, they attributed to post-unification housing policy and the latter's strong fiscal incentives to invest into housing. du Toit and Cloete (2003) based their integrated property and asset market model (IPAMM) for South African property markets on the DiPW model. Their attempt was preceded by Viezer (1999), who presented a real estate econometric forecast model (REEFM), inspired by DiPW, for determining the change in the stock of space that links the space and capital markets in the short and long run. Vizier's REEFM was applied to 51 metropolitan office markets in the USA from 1985 to 1996. And Leung and Wang (2007) concluded that the DiPW model was capable of accounting for several developments in China's housing market.

8.8 RE shocks and cycles

It has long been observed that real estate activity (investment, construction) exhibits cyclical behaviour (Abramovitz, 1964; Gottlieb, 1976; Grebler and Burns, 1982; Barras, 1987, 1994, 2009; Barras and Ferguson, 1985, 1987a, b; Wheaton, 1999). Moreover, different types of RE exhibit different patterns of such behaviour (Grebler and Burns, 1982; Barras and Ferguson, 1985; Wheaton, 1999). For example, in Figures 8.9–8.11, a cyclical pattern (i.e., expansions and contractions that vary in amplitude) is obvious from data on housing completions in the UK (1949–2010) and the USA (1968–2010) and on investment on three other types of real estate in the UK (1955–2010).

In the wake of this chapter's preceding discussion, real estate cyclicality should come as no surprise: starting from an assumed equilibrium position, a demand shock causes a rise (or fall) in construction activity, which subsequently develops a corrective declining (rising) trend until some kind of equilibrium is reached. By itself, this is a one-cycle pattern. The pattern is helped (or caused, maintain some) by the durability of the product and the long lag

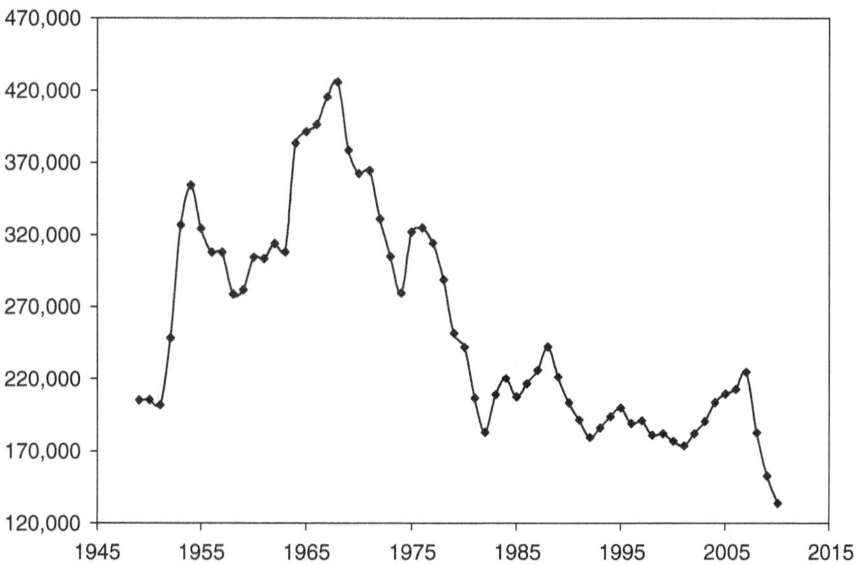

Figure 8.9 Building cycles in the UK, 1949–2010: all permanent dwellings completed. (Source: www.communities.gov.uk/housing/housingresearch/housing statistics/)

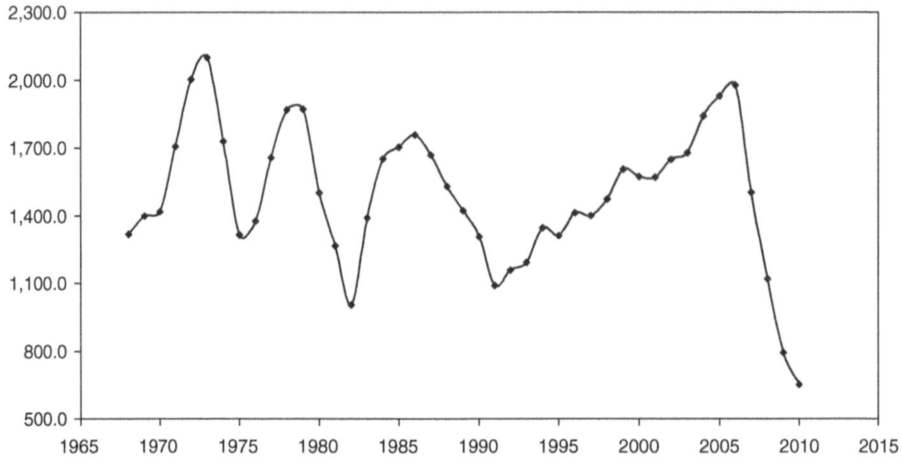

Figure 8.10 Building cycles in the USA, 1968–2010: new privately owned housing units completed (in thousands).

(Source: www.census.gov/const/www/newresconstindex.html)

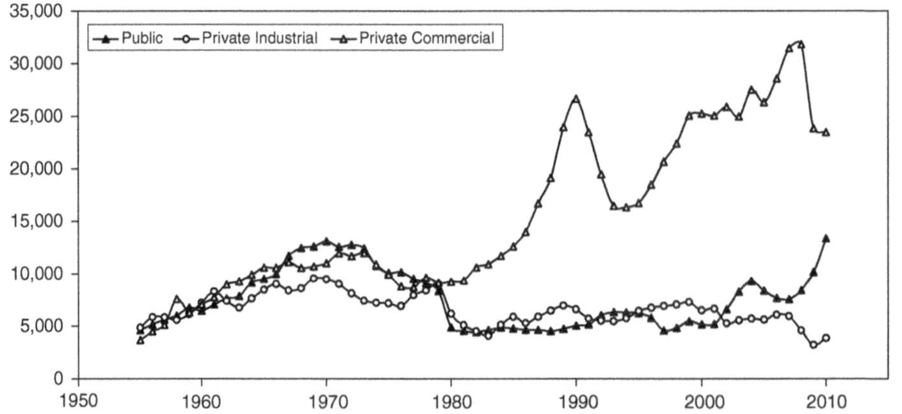

Figure 8.11 Volume of construction output in Great Britain, 1955–2010 (new work excluding infrastructure and housing): constant (2005) prices in £million.

(Source: www.ons.gov.uk/ons/rel/construction/output-in-the-construction-industry/november-2011/index.html.)

between the manifestation of demand for real estate and placing the product on the market for sale. Still, some questions remain:

(a) Is the one-cycle pattern the only one possible? For instance, if a spike is observed in construction activity, which then begins to drop, and then another spike, which also begins to drop, etc., is it safe to attribute such *repeated* oscillations to successive shocks to the system (like exogenously determined shifts in the demand for space)? Or could such oscillations be self-promulgating, giving rise to a multi-cycle pattern, following one initial shock?

(b) What is the origin of the initial shock? Three possibilities come to mind: (i) the influence of the trade cycle, which affects the wider economy; (ii) the influence of other macro-factors, like demographics; (iii) factors specific to particular RE sectors.

(c) If the oscillations are somehow linked to the trade cycle, is construction (and, in particular, residential construction) pro-cyclical – i.e., affected by the overall economic climate, moving up (down) in good (bad) times – or counter-cyclical? Is the pro- or counter-cyclical behaviour of different real estate sectors equally or unequally strong?

(d) Are such oscillations short- or long-term, and, if so, what are the causes for either? For example, could it be that short-term oscillations are linked to the trade cycle, but long-term ones are linked to long swings of urban development?

(e) Why do different real estate sectors (residential–industrial–office–retail) exhibit different cyclical patterns, i.e., contractions and expansions of different amplitudes?

(f) Is there a particular price-expectation requirement regarding the formation of cycles in RE? That is, can adaptive as well as rational expectations generate cycles, or only one or the other can do that?

In what follows, we shall try to answer these questions.

8.8.1 Question (a): one cycle or many?

(i) One-cycle case, or boring games with realistic parameters

In Section 8.4, we used Example A to demonstrate re-establishment of long-run equilibrium after a rise in demand. Because we had defined depreciation as a proportion of the (increasing) stock rather than as a fixed amount, final equilibrium happened at a level of construction higher than initially: construction = depreciation = 24 units of output (rather than 20).

The first 12 periods from this pattern of readjustment are shown in Figure 8.12.

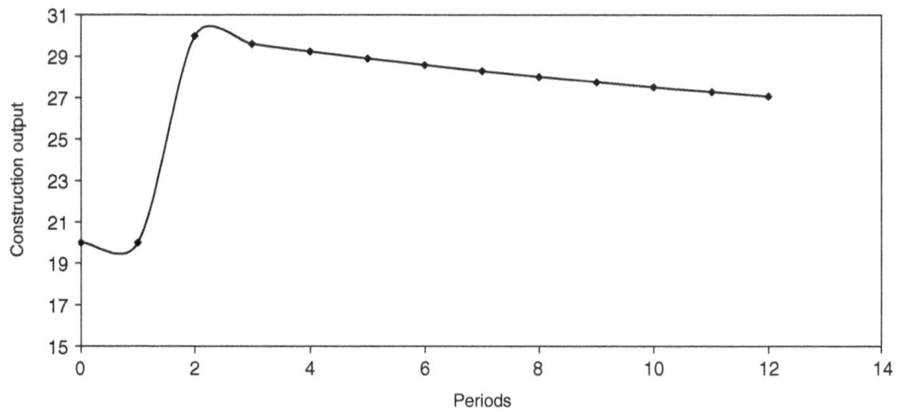

Figure 8.12 One-cycle case: smooth path towards equilibrium, with rising stock depreciation (first 12 periods shown).

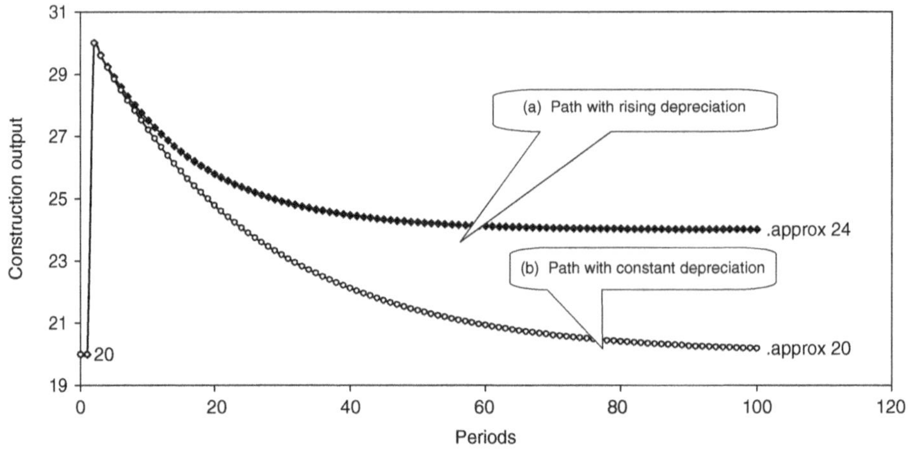

Figure 8.13 One-cycle case: smooth path towards equilibrium, with (a) rising depreciation and (b) constant depreciation (100 periods shown)

If we had assumed a constant amount of depreciation, we would still have the same pattern of readjustment, but the final equilibrium would have been the same as initially: construction = depreciation = 20. A comparison of the two patterns is shown in Figure 8.13, over 100 periods.

In both of the above diagrams, there is basically one cycle, initiated by a demand shock. Ultimately the cycle converges to some equilibrium set of values: either the initial one (case of constant amount of depreciation) or a higher one (increasing amount of depreciation). The readjustment pattern is smooth. At equilibrium, both the RE demand price = RE supply price *and* construction = depreciation.

(ii) Many-cycle case, or funny games with unrealistic parameters

One can imagine another scenario. There will still be convergence between the amount of construction and the amount of depreciation, but this will happen through repeated oscillations of construction rather than over a smooth path. This is shown in Figure 8.14.

The reasons for cases A (smooth readjustment) and B (readjustment through oscillations) relate to the parameter values used in Example A (cf. Wheaton, 1999). In the particular case of Figure 8.14, the change we introduced was a larger slope h for the construction line: 2 rather than 0.05. This was equivalent to assuming a larger elasticity of construction with respect to changes in price:

since $C = -5 + 0.05P \Rightarrow \varepsilon = 0.05P/Q$;

if $\quad C = -5 + 2P \Rightarrow \varepsilon = 2P/Q$.

As a result, the pattern of readjustment changed from smooth to an oscillating one. In other words, repeated cycles started occurring even though there was no further outside shock to the system, other than the initial shift in demand!

Still, some kind of equilibrium was reached eventually. In terms of equality between construction output and depreciation, equilibrium (a) was established at a higher level than

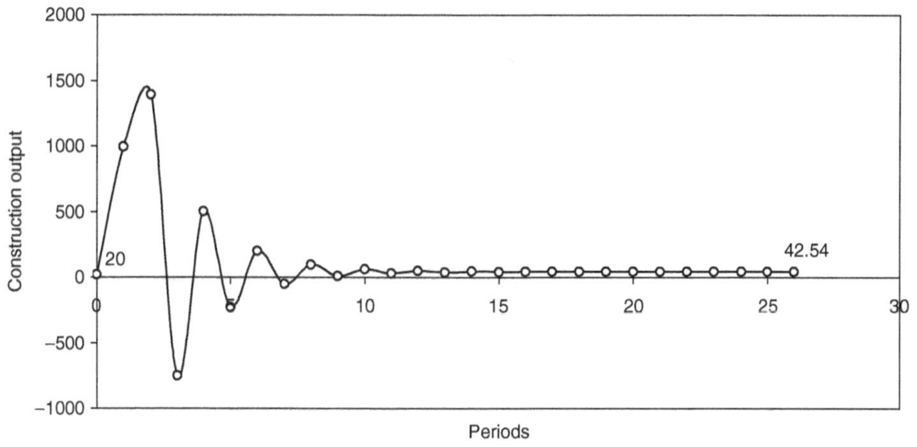

Figure 8.14 Many cycles: oscillating path towards new equilibrium. The reason for this is that elasticity of construction is higher than in the one-cycle case *and* higher than the elasticity of demand.

in the smooth cases (i.e., at 42.54 units of output, rather than 20 or 24) and (b) was reached must faster than in either of the smooth cases. Unfortunately, although at this equilibrium the rent at which RE space is demanded equals the rent at which RE space is supplied (as it should be), the level of the equilibrium rent is unrealistically low: 2.38, compared with a pre-shock rent of 50. In contrast, in the one-cycle case with rising depreciation the new (post-shock) equilibrium rent (58) had been between the pre-shock rent (50) and the immediately post-shock rent (70), which is a far more sensible outcome.

ECONOMIC INTERPRETATION OF FIGURE 8.14

Because the elasticity of construction has become larger than the elasticity of demand for space, the original price change causes a larger response from construction compared to the response of quantity demanded to the same price change. The initial response of construction in the particular case of Figure 8.14 is in fact so great that it causes price to drop not just below the original equilibrium level, but below zero! This is unrealistic; the only reason such a large increase in the elasticity of construction was envisaged (from 0.05 to 2) as to induce this result was to make Figure 8.14 more impressive and demonstrative.

The oscillating mechanism, however, should be easily interpreted: because of the drop in price, construction over-reacts, but this time in the opposite direction: so much so that it becomes negative. It is as if developers were demolishing buildings rather than erecting them! The excessive 'stock withdrawal' causes RE price to rise substantially, albeit less than after the initial price increase that had set the mechanism to motion. In turn, the rise in price causes developers to build a lot (although less than before). This goes on and on, with the oscillations becoming progressively less pronounced. Both the volume of construction and market price tend to converge to specific (equilibrium) values (see Figure 8.15).

On the other hand, if h increases even more, say to 3, then equilibrium cannot be re-established! The oscillations become explosive – see Figure 8.16.

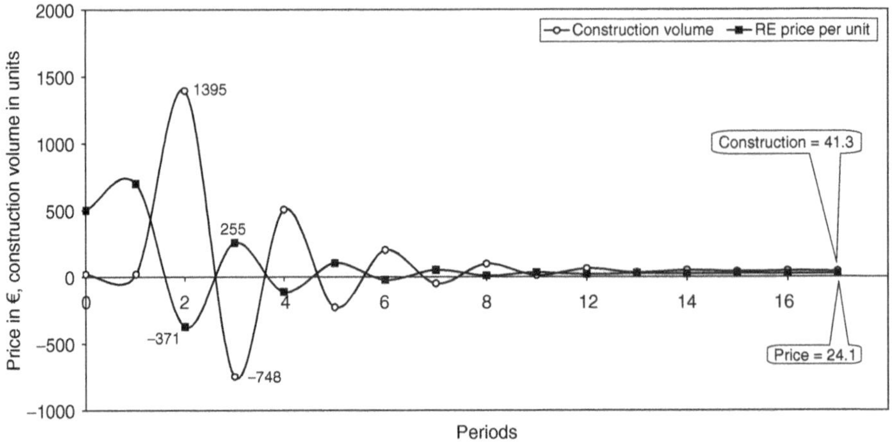

Figure 8.15 Oscillations of RE price and construction volume when construction is quite (but not 'excessively') sensitive to changes in price.

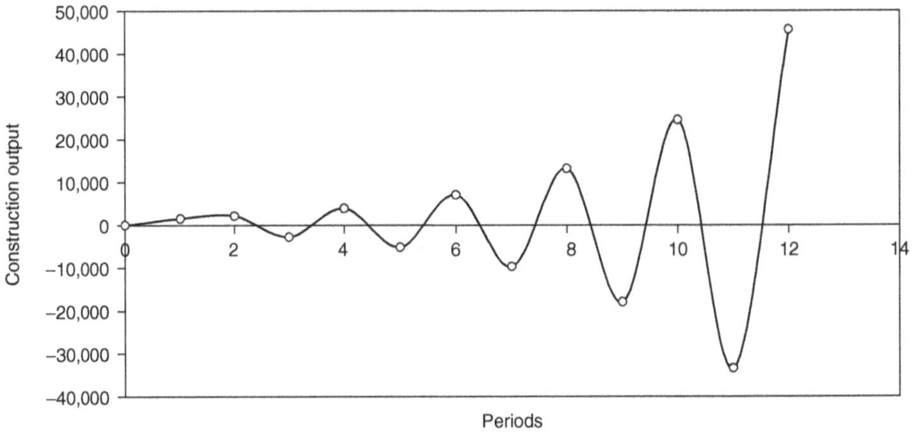

Figure 8.16 Oscillations of construction output become explosive: no equilibrium is possible. The reason for this is that the elasticity of construction is 'excessively' higher than the elasticity of demand.

It is perhaps apparent by now that the post-shock behaviour of a RE sector depends crucially on the values of the parameters that describe it. As a general rule, and holding other parameters constant, the larger the elasticity of construction, the stronger the chance that the system will become unstable, i.e., begin to oscillate. The existence of oscillations, however, does not mean that attainment of equilibrium is impossible. In fact, if initial oscillations are implosive (i.e., diminishing) a new equilibrium (even if unrealistic) will be attained faster! But, beyond a certain elasticity value, oscillations become explosive, causing divergence from any possible steady state.

Depending on a continuum of values for h (holding the elasticity of demand constant), the response of construction can vary from slow and smooth convergence to a possible equilibrium to divergence through increasing oscillations (in which case equilibrium is unattainable). So, although an initial shock to the system at equilibrium is required in order to jolt it into action, both a one-cycle smooth response and a multi-cycle oscillating pattern of construction are subsequently possible, without the need for additional exogenous shocks. The system can indeed feed upon itself.

8.8.2 Question (b): origin of the shock

Starting from an equilibrium position, any disturbance to the system must by definition come from outside. The disturbance may relate to the whole economy (the trade or business cycle), or be something that affects specifically the real estate sector (or a subsector of it), without the rest of the economy exhibiting a similar pattern. (But of course, in that case, what happens in the RE sector will affect the rest of the economy, reversing the arrow of causality.) Both sets of causes are possible. For instance, Wheaton (1999), studying completions and, in the case of apartments, permits issued from 1968 to 1996 in the 54 largest metropolitan areas of the USA, found that the industrial market and the multi-housing market correlated considerably with the wider economy, whereas the office market and the retail market did not.

However, whatever the nature of the disturbance that initiates the cycle in a property sector, the cycle can be modelled along the lines that have been presented above. It is just that if the disturbance relates to the wider economy, then the model must incorporate some economic growth factor – see Example B in Section 8.4.3.

Also, if that is the case, then the fluctuations in the wider economy will combine with fluctuations possibly generating from within the RE sector, creating additional complexity in the cyclicality pattern. And, of course, one way to find out empirically whether cycles in a RE sector correlate with the wider economy (possibly with a lag) is to compare the ups and downs of completions, permits, or investment levels (in constant prices) with some variable that expresses the trade cycle, like the unemployment rate.

Naturally this begs the question of why should some RE sectors appear to be relatively sensitive to the trade cycle, while others appear relatively autonomous. The answer has to do with the extent to which demand in certain subsectors (e.g., housing or industrial construction) is in turn particularly dependent on domestic economic conditions. Housing demand, for example, is predominantly local or domestic in nature, and depends strongly on household income and the mortgage rate: both of which relate strongly to the business cycle. Office demand, on the other hand, originates with activities that are managerial or clerical: the latter often transcend the time horizon involved in short-term trade cycles, as well as local or domestic market boundaries when their scope is wider (e.g., transnational corporations and export firms). Also, the institutional features of each RE sector (structure of property rights, sources and uses of capital, government and planning regulations, and taxation) have been shown to be important determinants of the specificity of its cycle (Barras, 1994; Wheaton, 1999; Kummerow and Quaddus, 1998; Baum, 2000; Cameron, 2003). Another such determinant is the extent to which investment in any particular RE subsector is included, or is considered for inclusion, in investors' portfolios of assets (Malpezzi and Wachter, 2004).

8.8.3 Question (c): pro- or counter-cyclical?

Again, this depends. If the cycle in a RE sector does not appear to relate to the trade cycle, its actual behaviour may well be counter-cyclical. But since its counter-cyclicality would not and could not be the result of a conscious decision on the part of market participants, but is merely a historic observation, it would be unsafe to expect that the next downturn or upturn in such a sector will be inevitably counter-cyclical. The specific features of the RE sector in question, and its (evolving) links to the wider economy and to investors' portfolios, would need to be taken into account before judging on the basis of past behaviour.

House-building, in particular, is undoubtedly pro-cyclical – if left on its own. It is positively influenced by the state of the wider economy, and it also tends to speed up recovery once house-building gets under way. With other RE sectors, the situation is less clear. But, at least in advanced countries, house-building has rarely been left on its own over the largest part of the post-Second World War period: it has often been used as a counter-cyclical tool by the government, typically in the context of Keynesian policies. A government's determination and effectiveness (or otherwise) in using the housing sector in this manner is therefore a key factor in assessing whether the sector is pro- or counter-cyclical. In the UK, for instance, the 'counter-cyclical collapse of social housing' has contributed to the sector's weak response to the late 1990s upswing in the wider economy (Cameron, 2003).

In the same vein, a distinction must be drawn between the intent to use a RE sector, chiefly housing, as a counter-cyclical tool, and any actual results achieved. Grebler and Burns (1982), in particular, have been quick to draw our attention to this issue, studying the US economy and construction sector. In a subsequent study (Burns and Grebler, 1984), they concluded that 'while public construction has often been advocated (and sometimes used) as a means of counter-cyclical intervention, this sector of the economy has in fact exhibited systematic pro-cyclical behaviour in relation to GNP fluctuations'. This they attributed to 'the positive response of state and local activity to variations in revenues which run with changes in business conditions' (Burns and Grebler, 1984: 375).

8.8.4 Question (d): short cycles, long swings?

Barras (1987) and Barras and Ferguson (1985, 1987a, b) used a method of time-series analysis called *spectral analysis*[24] in order to study building cycles in Britain, as manifested in five sectors: private industrial, private commercial, private housing, public housing, and other public building. They identified short (4- to 5-year) 'demand cycles' associated with business cycles, and long (up to 9-year) 'supply cycles'. Upon aggregation, the shorter cycles tended to be smoothed out, revealing a dominant post-war long swing in building activity. They compared this with previous long swings in the pre-1914 period, and in the inter-war years, and attributed them to successive waves of urbanization in Britain since the mid nineteenth century. Barras (1987) related the urbanization waves (each 20–30 years long) behind the identified long swings to long waves of technological development within the economy as a whole.

This insightful research ties in with the idea that urbanization and capitalism have evolved together, each feeding upon the other (cf. Lefebvre, 1972; Harvey, 1973; Dear and Scott, 1981). In fact, a very long wave of urban development can be superimposed on Barras' and Barras and Ferguson's urbanization waves, which is unfolding even now on a global scale.[25]

8.8.5 Question (e): different sectors, different cycles?

This should come as no surprise. The functions and function parameters determining the behaviour of any real estate sector are different. Such differences can range from the specification of the demand function for each sector to that of the construction function; to the depreciation factor δ affecting each subsector (as different sectors may well be characterized by different economic-cum-physical depreciation rates; to the time horizon involved in assessing future rents (an important factor in determining the prices of income properties; to the appropriate capitalization rate k to be used in discounting. A reason why k may be different across sectors is that the investors who are attracted to different sectors, depending on the latter's risk-return profiles, may have different attitudes to risk.

8.8.6 Question (f): cycles and expectations

The model whose behaviour was studied in Section 8.4.1 and Figures 8.12–8.16 was clearly based on 'myopic' expectations: construction completions in this period are a function of the last period's RE prices, in the sense that the latter provide an acceptable indicator of prices in the future: i.e., current prices 'translate' into expected prices, builders start building, and the output will appear next period (or two or three periods from now). So 'myopic' (or 'irrational') expectations can generate multiple cycles (oscillations), but the actual effect depends on parameter values (e.g., the slope of the construction function).

Rational expectations, on the other hand, imply that a decision to start building today is a function of expected price tomorrow, account being taken of the actions of other market participants. Normally, rational expectations are not compatible with cycles (Wheaton, 1999). To start generating a cyclical pattern, rational expectations would imply over-building today, in collective response to an expected RE price rise. But how can there be over-building if each builder takes into account the actions of other builders today?

In Section 8.5, we showed that 'irrational' price expectations are more likely in practice than rational ones. Still, if rational expectations were the case, could they generate cycles (oscillations) in RE output? Wheaton's (1999) answer to this question was cautiously affirmative – on two conditions:

1 That space under development is pre-leased, so the decision to invest can be based, partly, on current, rather than future, rents (and prices).
2 That there exists the possibility that a building project will be liquidated prior to full development. This is a risk that has to be taken into account in valuing the project. Now, at liquidation, and because of the specificity of the project, the only prospective buyers will most likely be owners of similar (existing, completed) assets. The liquidation value, as a result, will be closely linked to the value of such properties. From this point of view, current prices may well determine the decision to invest in the first place.

8.9 Appendix: a note on difference equations

Capital stock adjustment models (CSAMs), like those introduced above, can be solved using what are called difference equations: such an equation will link the value of a variable at time t to the value of the same variable at some previous time, $t - n$, where n can be 1, 2, or more. (If $n = 1$, it is a *first-order* difference equation.) The ways to find the value of the variable at a certain time vary: one way is to use a spreadsheet, which basically does the calculations for us; another is the tedious way of manually calculating successive values step-by-step, the value of a given period being fed into the equation for the value of next period; the third way (if $n = 1$), is to use an appropriate formula that will give us the value of the variable directly at whatever time we choose.

For instance, in Example A of Section 8.4, the quantity of space, S, that was eventually shown to be consistent with re-establishment of equilibrium was calculated by means of a spreadsheet. We shall now come up with the same result through (a) repeated manual calculations of S and (b) the application of a formula.

First method (tedious): manual calculations of total space , in order to arrive at a figure for S consistent with equilibrium (i.e., when $C = \delta S$)

The general formula for calculation of total space S at time t (i.e., S_t), assuming one-period steps, is

$$S_t = S_{t-1} + C_t - \delta S_t.$$

Given that $C_t = g + h(P_{t-1})$, $P = Rk^{-1}$, and $R_t = a - bS_t$ (remember that k is the capitalization rate and a is the vertical intercept of the demand line *after* it has shifted due to a disturbance), we have

$$S_t + \delta S_t = S_{t-1} + C_t,$$

$$S_t(1+\delta) = S_{t-1} + C_t = S_{t-1} + (g + hP_{t-1}) = S_{t-1} + \left[g + h\left(R_{t-1}k^{-1}\right)\right],$$

$$S_t = \frac{S_{t-1}(k - hb) + kg + ha}{k(1+\delta)} = S_{t-1}\frac{k - hb}{k(1+\delta)} + \frac{kg + ha}{k(1+\delta)}. \tag{8.13}$$

Thus, $S_2 = 759.74$, $S_3 = 768.85$; and $S_{115} = 899.93$. (S_2 is space supplied in the period after the initial shift in demand.)

At every step, the figure for total space arrived at should be used in order to compute the resulting difference between C and δS; the recursions go on until that difference has become insignificant (or zero, if precision is desired) – at which point a new equilibrium has been re-established.

The same results for S can be obtained if S_t is considered a function of previous period's rent, R_{t-1}, rather than of S_{t-1}. In fact, taking into account that if $R = a - bS$, then $S = a' - b'R$,

$$S_t = R_{t-1}\frac{h - b'k}{k(1+\delta)} + \frac{a'k - a'hb + kg + ha}{k(1+\delta)}. \tag{8.14}$$

Arriving at this formula and using it to find $S_2 = 759.74$ etc. is left as an exercise for the reader.

Second method (a shortcut): using a formula for solving one-period-lag difference equations, in order to calculate total space at whatever time period we choose; thereby, through a few trials and errors, quickly approximating total space at equilibrium (when $C = \delta S$)

Generally, if $y_n = a + by_{n-1}$, then the value of y at time t is given by

$$y_t = a\frac{1 - b^t}{1 - b} + b^t y_0,$$

where y_0 is the initial value of y. Therefore (following the notation of Example A and Equation (8.13)),

$$\text{if } S_t = S_{t-1}\frac{k-hb}{k(1+\delta)} + \frac{kg+ha}{k(1+\delta)} = S_{t-1}B + A,$$

then

$$S_{115} = A\frac{1-B^{115}}{1-B} + B^{115}(750) = 899.3, \text{ as per Table 8.1.}$$

Summary of main points

1 A capital stock adjustment model (CSAM) for RE shows how an equilibrium stock and price of RE can be re-established subsequent to a price shock through flows of new construction (minus stock depreciation) generated by RE price changes.

2 The DiPasquale–Wheaton CSAM has particular potential because it links the RE market with the capital market, showing how the two can interact. It does this by capitalizing rents (which, given supply, are demand-determined), and (usually after a one- or two-period lag) linking the resulting prices to construction, which then is added to the stock of RE (minus depreciation). However, the capitalization factor has attracted criticism, for example on the grounds that it is not necessarily exogenous.

3 Because of the inevitable time lag between the start and completion of building projects, expectations of RE prices at the time of delivery are particularly important.

4 Expectations can be future-based ('rational') or present-based ('myopic'). If they are the latter, over- or under-building in response to an initial price shock will result. If they are the former, over- or under-building is not 'normally' possible. In practice, price expectations tend to be present-based rather than future-based.

5 Elimination of over- or under-building (in response to a shock), and a return to a steady state (equilibrium) is not assured. It depends on the parameter values that describe the particular RE market.

6 Re-establishment of equilibrium, if feasible at all, can take place either smoothly or through oscillations in output. Again, the path taken depends on the model's parameter values.

7 RE cycles or oscillations are not only generated endogenously (following an *ad hoc* shock). They can also appear as responses to repeated outside shocks or trends that themselves follow a cyclical pattern (like the trade cycle or long waves or urban development).

8 Some types of RE, chiefly housing, have been ostensibly used by governments in order to counter the trade cycle. The actual counter-cyclicality of RE, in such cases, depends on a government's resources and determination.

Review questions and exercises

1 Draw and explain the standard DiPW model of capital market–RE market interaction.

2 Draw and explain in detail a CSAM with shifted long-run equilibrium.

3 Using a recursive approach and a spreadsheet, calculate equilibrium values for rent R, price P, construction C, and (stock of) space S after a rise in demand from

$R = 220 - 0.06S$ to $R = 240 - 0.06S$, given $C_t = -4 + 0.08P_{t-1}$, capitalization rate $k = 12$ per cent, and stock depreciation rate $\delta = 2.5$ per cent. Do your results make sense? Would they make more sense if you changed some of the parameters? Investigate.

4 Based on your (possibly adjusted) results in Question 3 above, determine long-run supply, and calculate its elasticity over the segment linking the original to the final equilibrium in this market.

5 How is price affected (between an original and a re-established equilibrium) if one assumes that, at a re-established equilibrium, (i) construction = original level of stock depreciation or (ii) construction = increased level of stock depreciation?

6 List and discuss reasons for an 'excessive' response by developers to a RE price shock.

7 Define myopic and rational price expectations. Are RE market participants likelier to be using myopic or rational expectations regarding future RE prices? Why?

8 Why would developers respond at all to a RE price shock? Why wouldn't they respond by building a very large number of RE units?

9 Why does (inclusion of) a capitalization rate k in a CSAM increase market uncertainty as regards any future equilibrium, following a price shock?

10 Generally, when is a RE market likelier to reach equilibrium after a price shock – when the elasticity of construction is large or when it is small, and in relation to what? What is the implication of either for the behaviour of construction output?

11 Do oscillations in construction output after a price shock imply that attainment of equilibrium in a RE market is impossible? Explain.

12 Which RE sector is, *ceteris paribus*, likelier to be affected most by an economy's trade cycle: residential or office? Why? Under what conditions?

13 Is housing construction pro- or counter-cyclical? Discuss.

9 RE taxation

Main sections

Having gone through this chapter, a student should be able to

1 Define and explain the main principles of taxation, and cite examples related to RE.
2 Analyse the problem of inability-to-pay RE taxes out of current income: consequences of such a situation, and how property value assessments may impact on the problem.
3 Evaluate whether it is 'better' to tax property or income from it.
4 Discuss whether property taxes affect economic growth less adversely than other taxes do.
5 Define and explain the property price capitalization effect of various RE taxes (municipal taxes, capital-gains taxes, property sales taxes), and express this effect formally in each case.
6 Explain the difference between actual and statutory *incidence* of a tax, and calculate the actual incidence of an *ad valorem* tax, given linear demand and supply equations.
7 Evaluate the pros and cons of taxing imputed rental income.
8 Determine how tax reform might help achieve neutrality between housing tenures.
9 Demonstrate graphically why there can be no single efficient allocation of resources between, say, owner-occupied housing and other goods without taking preferences into account.

9.1 An introduction to taxes and taxation

There is no perfect taxation system or perfect taxes. A tax system is in practice an ongoing compromise between various 'principles' of taxation (themselves potentially contradictory to one another) and government's need to finance its expenditure. Nor are the 'principles' value-free or agreed upon by all. For example, Foldvary (2006a: 3) writes: 'the "least bad" tax policy is one that does not violate a citizen's right to the fruits of his labor or his privacy; does not distort incentives to work and save; and minimizes the costs of compliance and administration.' If so, there can be no 'least bad' tax, since all taxes reduce people's income or wealth, while the argument that taxes finance public or quasi-public goods and services raises crucial issues as to whether such provision is enough compensation for the loss of welfare experienced by individuals because of taxation.[1]

Unfortunately a single chapter cannot do justice to the huge topic that is RE taxation. Proper treatment would take us deep into public finance and most other areas of economics; it would have to consider taxes on RE as well as subsidies to RE (like to owner-occupied or rented housing – see Quigley, 2007; Hoek-Smit, 2009; Oxley and Haffner, 2010); it would require evaluation of all, and specifically RE, taxes in the context of general taxation; and it would need to discuss the impact of RE taxation on RE investment strategies of financial institutions (cf. Coalition, 2009). It is to be hoped that what follows is a good starting point.

9.1.1 Kinds of taxes

1 Taxes on income, sometimes including tax on imputed rental income.
2 Taxes on capital.

(a) Inheritance tax.

(b) Wealth tax. In practice and in most countries, wealth taxes, if they exist at all, are levied on RE (like *council tax* in the UK, *taxe foncière* and *taxe d'habitation* in France, *Grundsteuer* in Germany, *municipal tax* or *mill* tax in Canada, and *property* or *millage tax* in the USA). Some jurisdictions, however, do levy more broadly defined wealth taxes. For example, in Greece, people must pay tax on swimming pools and boats owned, in addition to RE. In France, the *impôt sur la fortune* is levied on most of a taxpayer's non-professional assets (some things are excluded, in whole or in part, like works of art, collector's items, literary and artistic rights, and certain types of shares). And in the USA, depending on the state or even the county, 'personal property' (other than RE) is often taxed. For example, Pennsylvania and New York do not tax personal property, only RE; Washington State applies 'personal property tax' on household goods and personal effects if these items are used in a business (WSDR, 2010); and Greene County, Missouri, taxes a number of personal items (motor vehicles, mobile homes, watercraft, etc.) even if they are not used in business.

(c) Capital-gains tax, or CGT (levied on the difference between purchase price and sale price of a property). If it exists at all, this is usually applied on certain types of properties but not on others, the main exception being one's primary residence. Even then, however, different rules and qualifications apply. In some countries (e.g., France and Ireland), capital gains from the disposal of property are taxed autonomously; in others, they are deemed extraordinary income and taxed accordingly, i.e., at the taxpayer's marginal tax rate (see Box 9.1).

Box 9.1 Capital-gains taxes (CGT) on RE for individuals in selected countries

Australia: One's home is exempted (unless, and as long as, it has been rented out). On other RE, the amount of CG – minus a 50 per cent discount – is added to one's assessable income, and taxed at one's marginal tax rate.

Canada: Again, one's home is exempted, and 50 per cent of realized CG is taxed at one's marginal tax rate.

France: There is no CGT on one's principal residence. For other RE, there is no CGT if the property has been held for more than 30 years (according to rules coming into effect on 1 February 2012). The gross rate for French residents is 32.5 per cent, adjusted by a sliding allowance that depends on years of ownership (i.e., the rate will be 32.5 per cent in years 1–5, and nil in years 30+).

Germany: RE is not taxable if held longer than 10 years. Basic CGT is 25 per cent and effective CGT is approximately 28 per cent (with the inclusion of a 'solidarity' tax, initially used to finance the cost of reunification, and of a church tax).

Greece: There is no CGT on the sale of property yet. This may change. In October 2011, Greece's main opposition party published a set of tax reform proposals, including a 20 per cent CGT on the net-of-inflation value of 'disposed' properties above a certain threshold. This would be on top of standard transfer taxes on property, which would be lowered, however.

Ireland: A 25 per cent CGT applies, but there are various exclusions and deductions.

Portugal: CGT is not applied on the sale of one's home(s) if total profit is reinvested in another home or building plot. Otherwise, for residents, 50 per cent of CG (after deduction of proven costs over the last 5 years) is deemed income and taxed at a sliding scale of 12–40 per cent.

UK: One's primary residence is exempted from CGT. This extends to transferring the main residence to a husband, wife, or civil partner (provided the owner has lived with them for at least part of the given tax year) or to a child, but if any of those later sells the home, they may have to pay CGT. Transferring any other property to husband, wife, or civil partner (under the same provision) will not create a CGT liability, but, again, if any of those later sells the property, they may have to pay CGT. Transferring any other property to a child incurs a CGT liability. As of 23 June 2010, the CGT tax rate was 18 per cent for people subject to the basic income tax rate (i.e., 20 per cent), and 28 per cent for others (i.e., people subject to 40 and 50 per cent rates).

USA: An individual can exclude up to $250,000 of CG from the sale of their primary residence (or $500,000 for a married couple), if they have lived in the property for at least 2 out of the 5 years prior to the sale. As of 2013, there will be a 10 per cent CGT on CG from the sale of assets held long term (i.e., for more than a year) for people in the 15 per cent income bracket, and a 20 per cent CGT for people in higher brackets.

Sources:

(a) for France: www.french-property.com/guides/france/finance-taxation/taxation/capital-gains-tax/;

(b) for the UK: www.hmrc.gov.uk/cgt/property/basics.htm;

(c) for the USA: http://en.wikipedia.org/wiki/Capital_gains_tax_in_the_United_States;

(d) for Greece: www.nd.gr; (e) for others: http://en.wikipedia.org/wiki/Capital_gains_tax.

(d) Sales, or indirect, or expenditure, taxes, like VAT in Europe, or taxes on the transfer of RE property,[2] like the 'stamp duty' on RE transactions in the UK.[3] Sales taxes can be general, in which case they do not distort relative prices or incentives in the economy much, or selective (and are then usually called *excise* taxes), in which case they do. Property transfer taxes are selective because they usually involve different rates from those associated with general sales taxes. At the same time, because RE prices are typically higher than most incomes and higher than the prices of most other goods, even a low-rate transfer tax on RE *may* have a large effect on the quantity demanded of it, depending, among others, on the price and income elasticities of demand for RE (actually, for specific types of RE, since the latter is not a homogeneous good).

Table 9.1 shows more aspects of taxation of owner-occupied housing in selected countries.

9.1.2 Principles of taxation

A good taxation system is one that at least tries to comply with certain principles,[4] the 10 most important of which are as follows:

1 *Compatibility with government goals, both narrow and broad:*

(a) A narrow goal might be energy conservation (e.g., encouraging the use of solar water-heaters or home insulation). Another might be maximization of government revenue.

(b) A broad goal might be to strengthen the middle class by helping expand owner-occupation or by reducing the cost of inheritance or of wealth possession. To achieve such goals, taxation policy can employ a range of tools, from tax credits and deductions to subsidies (which are really negative taxes) to reduction (possibly

Table 9.1 Taxation of owner-occupied dwellings in selected countries, 2009

	Taxation of imputed rents	*Mortgage interest tax relief*	*Taxation of capital gains*
Belgium	Yes[1]	Tax deductibility with a limit	No
France	No	Tax credit for the first 5 years with a limit	No
Germany	No	No	No
Greece	Yes	Yes, on one's first home, with a limit	No
Netherlands	Yes[2]	Tax deductibility without limit	No
Ireland	No	Tax credit for the first 7 years with a limit	No
Italy	No	Tax credit with a limit	No
Spain	No	Tax credit with a limit on the amount of housing costs	No
UK	No	No	No
USA	No	Tax deductibility with a limit on the amount of mortgage principal ($1m)	No (if CG < $500,000)

Source: Ceriani et al. (2011), except for Greece (author's own information).

[1] Since 2005, 'cadastral' (i.e., imputed) rent on an owner's dwelling is no longer taxable, except if interest on a loan is deducted. Cadastral income on secondary residences is taxable, increased by 40%. (See Valenduc (2011).)

[2] In 2007, the imputed (net) rental income was calculated as 0.6% of the value of a home, up to a maximum of €8,750 (van der Hoek et al., 2007: 415).

elimination) of relevant tax rates. Another broad goal might be income and/or wealth redistribution for the purpose of maintaining social peace and cohesion as well as enhancing the population's purchasing power – but if redistribution is taken too far, it will destroy incentives to work, innovate, risk, invest, save (W-I-R-I-S for short).

2 *Ability-to-pay* (see Section 9.2 for a fuller discussion).
3 *Equity (horizontal and vertical)* (this is akin to notions of 'fairness'):

(a) Horizontal equity means that 'people in the *same circumstances* should be taxed equally' (Sloman, 1991: 335). This principle raises an interesting question: should two people realizing the same capital gain from the sale of property pay the same capital gains tax, or should their overall income and wealth situation – i.e., a broader view of their circumstances – be taken into account too?
(b) Vertical equity means that people with a greater ability to pay taxes should bear a greater tax burden, which can happen only in the context of either proportional or, more strongly and usually, progressive taxation. Vertical equity could imply, for example, that a CGT rate levied on the sale of property should increase with the amount of capital gain; or that a transfer tax levied on the value of property changing hands should increase with that value.

4 *Who benefits pays (the 'benefits-received' principle):*

(a) This principle would be illogical to apply in many cases. For example, you cannot ask the unemployed to finance their own unemployment benefits! A little redefinition could solve many such problems, however. For example, you can very well ask all employed workers to pay contributions towards the risk of becoming unemployed by naming them all 'potentially unemployed'. They would *all*, in effect, be buying *insurance* against unemployment rather than *some* (the unemployed) being forced in the untenable position of having to fund their own unemployment benefits.
(b) Because the link between taxes and benefits is often very tenuous (sometimes necessarily so), on many occasions benefits are diffused rather than focused, and the services that taxes finance may become increasingly irrelevant to any particular individual. This has an important consequence for RE taxation as in many countries local services are financed by local property taxes. The more the ostensible benefits from those services are removed from the experience of individuals or groups, the more direct and pronounced the (negative) effect of property taxes on property prices will become; and political resistance to those taxes will be all the greater. The two effects may be magnified if property taxes are imposed and collected centrally, and do not directly, obviously, and commensurately finance local services.

5 *Neutrality (i.e., minimal distortions, minimal disincentives):*

(a) A tax is neutral (or efficient)[5] if, in a competitive general equilibrium context, it does not distort *relative* market prices of goods and resources (and therefore – and more importantly – respective quantities), and also if it does not reduce *incentives* to W-I-R-I-S. Because complete avoidance of such distortions or reductions is virtually impossible, a tax policy goal would be to tax in ways that induce the least possible change in economic behaviour, and certainly the least economic loss to society.

(b) A tax on land is supposed to be neutral because its imposition will not make the land disappear.[6] Land will still be there after the tax, and, once the land's 'highest-and-best' use has been determined (which may be either the land's current use or some future use), the land will go to that use. However, this proposition is not as simple as it sounds, because if the tax is so high that it stops the after-tax return on the land from being at least as high as the after-tax return on the best alternative investment, the land in question will probably not be used, – so it *will*, in this sense, disappear. (See Chapter 10.)

6 *Efficiency (i.e., minimal 'deadweight loss').* This is really a special case of neutrality. DWL is economic loss to society due to a tax *on a particular* good or resource, such as land. (See Chapter 10.)

7 *Predictability* (taxes, tax rates, and tax scales must change as rarely as possible, and their legal or statutory incidence, i.e., who in law is liable for the tax, must be clear):

(a) *UK:* In 1976, a new 'development land tax' (DLT) was introduced for the purpose of siphoning off part of the increase in land values due to development; it was followed by 'planning gain' contribution in 1990, which was a benefit a developer would give a local authority (through negotiations) in return for planning consent. There was then a proposal in the Barker Report (2004) to turn this into a more straightforward tax called Planning Gain Supplement. The PGS did not come to pass (cf. Baron, 2006), but in 2010 the Community Infrastructure Levy (CIL) was implemented (in England and Wales), essentially for the same purpose as the other taxes mentioned: to extract contributions from developers. If nothing else, this historic account suggests a rather careful, if strained, process of tax introduction.

(b) *Greece:* Within two years (October 2009–September 2011), Greece's government steeply increased rates on pre-existing wealth, sales, and inheritance taxes on property; it arbitrarily associated imputed property values – which it also raised steeply – with higher imputed incomes, which it taxed more; and introduced *additional*, very high wealth taxes on property, to be paid through electricity bills. (All those taxes were on top of pre-existing local authority taxes, traditionally paid through electricity bills too.) In a recessionary context (both as cause and effect), the consequences were immediate: the numbers of RE transactions and of new building permits plummeted (see Box 9.2 and Table 7.3).

(c) An important proposition in RE taxation is that (wealth) taxes on RE are capitalized into RE values (see Section 9.4.4). The speed and extent of capitalization, however, depend on predictability: if economic actors' experience says that the amount of time between announcement of a change in property taxes and implementation of the change can be accurately predicted and verified, (nearly) full capitalization should occur upon announcement; if not, capitalization will be weak at first, increasing or decreasing with additional information.

8 *Simplicity* (taxes must be easy to understand, apply, and calculate).

9 *Collection efficiency* (i.e., the cost of collection must be small in relation to revenue).

(a) Although ability-to-pay and equity should be paramount considerations, tax collection problems must not be underestimated. The government that came to power in Greece in October 2009 decided to raise wealth taxes on property steeply. Two years later, it had failed to collect a penny, as the Tax Department had not managed to estimate the RE wealth of individual taxpayers, even though it relied on imputed values. In desperation, and facing national bankruptcy, the government hastily introduced a universal, even steeper, property tax, to be collected through electricity bills – on penalty of cutting power to non-paying households. Being in need of funds, and further breaching both the ability-to-pay and the equity principles, it also kept the previously imposed property taxes, hoping to collect those too eventually!

Box 9.2 Greece: World capital of crippling property taxation?

By the end of 2011, the Greek government had four main property taxes in place, applied simultaneously against a background of repeated increases in imputed property values as well as of deepening recession:

(a) Municipal tax paid through electricity bills.
(b) A steep 'regular' tax on 'high'-value RE assets (threshold €200,000).
(c) A steep *universal* 'extraordinary' (but to be repeatedly applied) property tax paid through electricity bills on penalty of cutting power to non-paying households.
(d) An 'extraordinary' tax on 'high'-value RE assets.

Taxes (b), (c), and (d) were introduced in 2010–11. The government's budgeted wealth tax revenue for 2012 was 6.7 per cent of total tax revenue, against 1.6 for 2010 and 1 for 2007.

The government had also steeply raised property sales and inheritance taxes, and had other *ad hoc* property taxes in place too – like the requirement for owners to pay government-approved engineers for a 'building energy certificate' every time they rented out a built property or upon selling one.

When in January 2012 Kapa-Research, a consultancy, conducted a related survey in Greece, it transpired that

- Only 21.1 per cent of those questioned said they had no RE property whatsoever.

From among RE property owners,

- 32.7 per cent said they would *probably not* be able to pay their property taxes in 2012;
- 18.1 per cent said they would *not* be able to pay their property taxes in 2012;
- 38.2 per cent said they would *probably* be able to pay their property taxes in 2012;
- 74.4 per cent of owner-respondents felt that owning property to rent today was not worthwhile.

Tax (c) alone, mentioned above, corresponded to

- one month's rent (34.2 per cent of landlord-respondents)
- two months' rent (31 per cent)
- three months' rent (11.2 per cent)
- four months' rent (14.5 per cent)

Source: www.kapa-research.com/.

10 *Minimal eschewal* (i.e., minimal room for tax-avoidance or tax-evasion). An unfortunate thing about RE is that it is a 'sitting duck' for governments that cannot or will not clamp down on income tax evasion. By the same token, such governments cannot be expected to comprehend the deleterious effects of taxing property that heavily on (a) ability to pay, (b) equity, (c) incentives to save for, or invest in, RE assets, and (d) economic growth (especially considering that construction has a low import content).

9.2 (In)ability to pay RE taxes

Such a problem may arise primarily with wealth or 'property possession' taxes. Usually these are recurrent taxes, payable every year, although at least one country – namely Greece in 2010–11 and beyond – has been known to introduce crippling extraordinary wealth taxes in a desperate fiscal situation (see Box 9.2). Other RE taxes that may involve an inability-to-pay problem are a tax on imputed rental income, some instances of CGT on RE, and inheritance tax on RE. (The latter often leads to forced sale of one's inherited RE to pay the tax – a situation that definitely stretches the definition of 'ability to pay' as it may cause a dramatic deterioration in a person's circumstances and way of life.) The inclusion of CGT may appear surprising since, by (standard) definition, a CGT is applied on the difference between sale value and purchase value (usually adjusted for inflation and repairs) – but there are subtleties to consider. For example, in the UK,

- if one makes a gift of one's second home to one's child, a CGT tax liability will be generated, even though there was no cash changing hands;
- in cases like this, it is not sale value that is important (which may, after all, be nil) but market value, which may be significant.

Turning to wealth or 'property possession' taxes, there are multiple issues to discuss, even though most people may be able to pay them ('most' being the operative word):

1 Since most instances of wealth today are derived from past incomes, a basic objection to wealth taxes is that they represent a way of taxing again incomes that are (supposed to) have been already taxed in the past! Additionally, because wealth taxes ignore current incomes, the latter may not be enough to enable payment of current wealth taxes, chief among which are RE taxes. The problem is that imposition of high property taxes rests on the highly questionable assumption that throughout the life of an individual, at all times and in all places, the value of RE owned correlates with current income. This assumption is only partially correct – and therefore capable of generating gross injustices. It was challenged by, among others, the California tax revolt of 1978 that led to the famous Proposition 13.[7] The latter reduced substantially the property tax burden on existing owners. At any rate, some of the consequences of inability to pay wealth or property taxes out of current income may call into question either the government's true intentions or its capacity to think clearly and with the long-term national or communal interest in mind. Such consequences include the following:

   (a) If this is a new tax, it will be a 'stab in the back' for people who, perhaps over generations (as in Greece), had built wealth portfolios on the basis of low or non-existent taxation of property ownership and on the assumption that this situation would go on indefinitely. Such portfolios would have been dominated by RE wealth[8] (rather than, say, gold, or bank savings, or mutual fund shares, or social or private insurance claims) and would therefore imply limited ability to pay out of current income or liquid assets any steep RE wealth taxes suddenly imposed. Shattering this assumption would create a mistrust of the state on the part of most citizens that would take a long time to heal; more importantly, it would negatively affect incentives to save for, or invest in, RE assets.

(b) People seriously hurt by this kind of tax may experience a loss in welfare (a change in their standard of living and way of life) far in excess of any 'social' (i.e., diffused) benefits from government spending of any revenue thus collected. Some may even be 'taxed out of their homes'. That's a dramatic reminder of the fact that there is no objective way to compare utilities across individuals.

(c) If such people are numerous (rather than, say, a private landowner owning large tracts of a country's land), thus forming a sizeable social group (typically, the 'middle' class), then, the abrupt restructuring or diminution of their wealth portfolios brought about by the tax will negatively affect the process of structuration of that class, almost certainly leading to its decline: inevitably social inequality will increase, and incentives to W-I-R-I-S will suffer.

(d) To pay a truly burdensome wealth tax on illiquid assets, many owners of such assets will have to liquidate at least some of them. Massive liquidations of this kind would depress the values of *all* similar assets, further enhancing the wealth losses of those owners as well as of others (including financial institutions with sizable RE holdings). The situation would become even more dire if the tax were introduced (and the liquidations happened) in a recessionary context (as was the case in Greece after the breakout, in 2009, of that country's sovereign debt crisis).

Interestingly, in the particular case of Proposition 13 mentioned above, one criticism levied against it (O'Sullivan et al., 1995) was that, by conferring property tax advantages to existing owners (or their kin), it reduced housing market liquidity and contributed to house price inflation in California. To the extent that this is an accurate appraisal (as, for example, overall population pressures and restrictive planning practices are likely to have contributed to house price inflation more than Proposition 13), one response may be to raise more revenue from income taxation rather than from property taxation as the latter is rather regressive – see Box 9.3.

Box 9.3 Property taxes relative to income

A regressive tax is one whose average rate (tax/income, i.e., the tax as a proportion of income) drops as income rises. A progressive tax has the opposite behaviour. Property taxes tend to be proportional to property values, but are regressive to the extent that property values show less than 100 per cent positive correlation with owners' incomes: the smaller the correlation, the greater the regressiveness.

For example, a 2005 Statistics Canada study found that in Canada '[p]roperty taxes are regressive relative to income in every municipality studied here [342 of them]. Even in municipalities with the least regressive taxes, the lowest-income homeowners paid at least twice the amount of tax per dollar of income in relation to the highest-income homeowners. In some municipalities, particularly those in large census metropolitan areas, lower-income homeowners had a tax burden four or five times greater than their higher-income counterparts. [...] because income inequality is far greater than inequality in property values, lower income homeowners end up spending a relatively large proportion of their income on property tax' (Palameta and Macredie, 2005: 18).

Also, in the UK, 'the poorest fifth of households pay five per cent of their household income in council tax; the middle fifth pay three per cent; and the richest fifth pay under two per cent' (Maxwell and Vigor, 2005: 4–5).

2 Another issue concerns a milder scenario: A government levies a wealth tax, but the tax is not as high as to necessitate liquidation of (illiquid) assets. It can be, and in effect is, paid out of income. (Put differently, it does not involve a serious restructuring or diminution of the taxpayer's wealth portfolio.) Is this a potentially problematic situation? Yes, for two reasons:

(a) If that is the case, why not tax higher incomes at higher rates, and be done with? At least this way government (e.g., local government taxing property) would almost certainly save itself significant administrative expenses involving assessment of property values. In the context of such a reform, income tax revenue would be collected by the central government (or federal and state governments in the USA), as it would almost certainly be inefficient for local governments to collect income taxes from residents.[9] The central government would subsequently apportion the appropriate amount to local authorities depending on (i) their population and (ii) the income tax revenue contributed by residents, so as to comply, at least in part, with the benefits-received principle of taxation. (Provided that institutional safeguards were put in place, a workable degree of local government autonomy could be preserved.) Any local authority services not funded this way would have to be funded by other means (e.g., user-fees or central government grants).

(b) To allow payment of wealth taxes out of income requires, first, some assessment of the value of taxable assets, second, application of suitable rates and assessment ratios, and, third, information on people's incomes and wealth. Questions emerge, however (particularly in relation to RE):

  (i) Is it imputed or market value we are talking about?

  (ii) If market value, is it market value in the current use of the (RE) asset, or 'highest-and-best' use market value? (Whose realization may presuppose demolition of an existing building and replacement by something else.)

  (iii) If 'current-use' market value, would that not ignore the development potential of many plots? True, given building and zoning regulations 'current-use' value and 'potential-use' value should coincide over the short- to medium-term, but not necessarily in all instances. Also, any calculation of current property values rests on the assumption that property transactions in the given area will continue at approximately an established or familiar level (see Box 9.4). If they do not, a tax authority will face the following problem: if the market slumps, it will lose revenue if it quickly re-assesses property values in its jurisdiction; if the market rises, a quick re-assessment may create or enlarge a wedge between taxpayers' incomes and ability to pay. A tax authority may of course respond to the latter

Box 9.4 How the New York State assesses properties

'A property's assessment is based on its market value. Market value is how much a property would sell for under normal conditions. [...] The assessor can estimate the market value of property based on the sale prices of similar properties. A property can also be valued based on the depreciated cost of materials and labor required to replace it. Commercial property may be valued on its potential to produce rental income for its owners. In other words, the assessor can use whatever approach provides the best estimate of a property's market value. Properties in suboptimal uses generally may not be assessed at market value; they must be assessed at their current-use value.'

Source: 'How the Property Tax Works', New York State Department of Taxation and Finance, January 2011, www.orps.state.ny.us/pamphlet/taxworks.htm, accessed 28 September 2011.

problem by lowering *rates* – or lowering *assessment ratios*[10] (a point made by Oates, 1969: 961). Either situation implies a wedge between property prices and tax revenue, challenging, once again, the wisdom of taxing RE rather than income directly.

(iv) Turning to 'highest-and-best' use market value (arrived at through some process of discounting expected net incomes from property), if a tax authority assessed RE prices on that basis, would that not sometimes lead to tax liabilities that would 'eat away' a very large portion of the standing property owner's income – often necessitating sale of the asset to pay the tax? That would be clearly unfair, and would take us back to inability-to-pay territory (inability, that is, unless forced sale of illiquid assets occurred or unless tax rates decreased substantially).

(v) There is also the problem of whether a government valuer or tax assessor can be as good a judge of a plot's 'highest-and-best' use as private agents operating in the reality of the marketplace. 'Heroic' assumptions would often be made, resulting in erroneous – hence unfair – assessments. Of course, private actors also make mistakes, but they do so in a politically non-coercive context of economic choice. A (democratic) government, on the other hand, has a moral obligation to be fair precisely because it coerces.

(vi) To remedy problems related to 'current-use' or 'potential-use' RE prices, a tax assessor will be tempted to resort to imputed prices (possibly close to 'current use' prices) for properties as a second-best solution. But imputed prices (as opposed to actual prices, which can only be market prices) have strong potential for arbitrariness and unfairness too. Moreover, the lower imputed prices were than actual prices, the more irrelevant taxation of RE would become; the closer/higher imputed prices were to/than actual prices, the greater the problems already mentioned in relation to calculating market prices or ability to pay would also be.

(vii) In some countries, ability-to-pay considerations have generated ways of reducing the burden of property taxation on eligible owners. For example, in the UK, there are means-tested *council tax rebates*. In the USA, there are *homestead exemptions* from property taxes and/or limits on property tax increases for owner-occupiers. Although such systems are by and large helpful, they are sometimes either underutilized by potential beneficiaries, or taken unfair advantage of by others. In other countries (e.g., Greece in 2011, due to extraordinary circumstances), there is no such help (nor databases that allow association of individuals' income and wealth), and property taxes are very unfair and regressive.

3 A third issue regarding 'ability-to-pay' taxes (and not just on RE) is whether this ability (even if calculated in relation to income alone) should involve a 'reasonable' *proportion* of income for all (i.e., a flat tax rate), or progressive taxation instead. True, people with higher incomes *appear* to have greater ability to pay progressively more tax. But such people may also have more commitments than less fortunate ones, or else they may be more sensitized to income incentives. Being made to pay progressively more tax may imply an inordinately high loss of welfare for them, or else 'disincentivize' them. Again, there is no objective way to measure and weigh their welfare loss compared with the welfare gains (presumably) experienced by other people on whom the government will spend the tax revenue. The problem is compounded if governments do not tax more in order to offer better public services, but in order to reward cronies, line the pockets of government members, or curry favour with groups of voters, Greece being a good example of this.

9.3 Is it better to tax property or income from it?

From an investor's point of view, there is no difference between facing a 'mild' wealth tax, which can and in effect *is* paid out of income, and facing the same tax levied directly on income. However, there may be a difference between the two taxes for the government as well as for the seller of the property. Let us explain:

Property A is expected to bring in £7200 p.a. forever. The discount rate an investor uses is 6 per cent, hence the market value of the property is, without taxation, £120,000. Now, assuming that the government applies a 50 per cent tax on property income, the net-of-tax income from the property drops to £3600 p.a. As a result (and assuming capitalization) the market value of the property becomes £60,000.

Conversely, if the government happens to value the property at £120,000 for tax purposes, and levies a 3 per cent tax on this value (rather than on property income), a tax obligation is created equal to £3600. The effective net-of-tax income from the property becomes £3600, and, once again, the market value of the property is £60,000.

We can then say that the two preceding cases are equivalent to one another in terms of tax revenue. They are also equivalent in terms of the investor's return, which in either case is £3600/£60,000 = 6 per cent. By extension, a tax rate of 3 per cent applied on the gross-of-tax assessed value of the property is equivalent to a 50 per cent tax rate applied on the gross-of-tax income from the property.

The investor's 6 per cent return will not change if the government applies a 3 per cent wealth or 'property possession' tax on the actual market value of the property, because the latter will then be

$$V = \frac{R - tV}{k} \Rightarrow V = \frac{R}{k+t}, \tag{9.1}$$

where

V = market value,
R = gross-of-tax net rental income from the property,
k = capitalization rate,
t = tax rate.

From Equation (9.1),

$$V = \frac{£7200}{0.06 + 0.03} = £80{,}000 \tag{9.2}$$

with the investor making a 6 per cent return, as before. This is because the tax would be £80,000 × 0.03 = £2400, the net-of-tax income would be £7200 – £2400 = £4800, and hence the return would be £4800/£80,000 = 6 per cent. But now tax revenue is less than before!

There is no mystery here: a government taxing property at what is in effect its after-tax market value will collect less tax than if it applies the same tax rate on the pre-tax value of the property, or an 'equivalent' tax rate on pre-tax income from the property. This result hinges on three assumptions: (i) property taxes are in fact capitalized into property values, (ii) the investor knows about the applicable tax and its rate, and (iii) the government levies the tax on the (known) market value of the property, as that value has been actualized through the buyer/seller transaction. Incidentally, the government does not even have to know the capitalization rate the investor has used; all that is required is for the government to accept the realized market value of the property.

However, because of the reduced tax revenue, any government will be tempted not to tax on the basis of the after-tax market value of the property, but on the basis of either pre-tax property income or of pre-tax property value. To the extent that income taxation entails lower administrative and assessment costs, a government will then be better off choosing this method over the taxation of wealth (especially since there would be no differential effect on the investor's rate of return). Another reason why income taxation should be preferred is that the only way for government to estimate a pre-tax value for the property that will bring in the same tax revenue as an 'equivalent' taxation of property income is to use the same capitalization factor the investor uses (i.e., 6 per cent). This is extremely unlikely.

But the most important reason is that income, rather than property, taxation is linked more accurately to ability to pay, and also distorts the land and housing markets much less.

On the other hand, if a government avoids taxing on the basis of the after-tax value of the property, it will, *ceteris paribus*, collect more revenue, but somebody else must end up worse off. That 'someone' cannot be the investor, who in all cases makes a 6 per cent return; this leaves the property owner, who under taxation of property income (or of 'equivalent', 'gross-of-rent', imputed property value) stands to get £60,000 rather than £80,000!

Of course this will happen if the tax in question is new and unexpected. Then existing owners will not have the opportunity to make compensatory adjustments, the way our investor did (through offering a lower price for the property he/she considered to buy) in the above example. In fact, existing owners will either have to bear the tax, or suffer a capital loss if they sell.

9.4 Property taxes, income taxes, and growth

In comparing property taxes with income taxes we must not neglect to examine how they are likely to affect economic growth. For example, Arnold (2008), studying the effect of different tax structures (involving taxes on personal income, corporate income, consumption, and property) on economic growth in 21 OECD countries from 1971 to 2004, found that property taxes, especially recurrent property taxes, were statistically associated with higher economic growth than taxes on consumption, personal income, and corporate income (in that order). In other words, corporate income taxes were associated with least growth, and property taxes with most growth.

However, this result cannot justify a blanket policy of increasing property taxes, because

1 A shift towards property taxes for the purpose of enhancing growth can only make sense in the context of a given, or lessened, overall tax revenue level (as a proportion of GDP), so that other taxes will be reduced commensurately. If property taxes increase in a way that pulls that level up (i.e., the overall tax burden), there will be less growth, not more (as the effect of all taxes on growth is negative).
2 It is very likely that in most of the OECD countries studied personal and corporate income taxes retarded growth more than property taxes did, mainly because of their progressivity (Arnold, 2008; Heady et al., 2009), or because they were too high. In contrast, property taxes are regressive; and while, in most countries at least, they are rarely high enough to 'tax people out of their homes', they are, in effect, paid out of income, resembling a regressive income tax. Regressive taxes of course tend to be good for growth because they burden higher incomes less than progressive taxes do. So the greater the proportion of (regressive) property taxes in the overall tax revenue (a proportion that in the sample countries was relatively small, anyway – see Table 9.2), and assuming that they do not become too high, the smaller the reductive effect of such taxes on growth.

Essentially the same result could be achieved by abolishing property taxes completely, at the same time holding overall tax revenue constant while increasing the regressivity of income taxation.

Table 9.2 OECD, 2008: taxes on property

In 2008, the share of taxes on property as a percentage of total taxation in the 33-country OECD was 5.4% (unweighted average) – down from 7.9% in 1965 (24 countries) and 5.7% in 2006. In selected countries, it was as follows:

USA	12.1	Greece	4.6
UK	11.6	Italy	4.3
Canada	10.5	Netherlands	4.2
Japan	9.4	Portugal	3.6
Australia	8.2	Turkey	3.6
France	7.8	Finland	2.6
Switzerland	7.5	Germany	2.3
Spain	6.8	Sweden	2.3
Ireland	6.4	Mexico	1.4
Chile	5.4	Austria	1.3

Source: www.oecd.org/dataoecd/13/41/43098778.xls, accessed 29 September 2011.

9.5 Are RE taxes capitalized in RE prices?

The short answer is 'yes, they are – but not fully'. Relevant taxes in the context of this question are wealth (or 'possession of property') taxes, usually applied by local authorities, capital-gains taxes applied on the difference between selling and purchase price (typically after account has been taken of inflation, and maybe after allowances for property repairs or improvements), sales (or excise) taxes applied on the selling price of a property (or, as in Greece, on an imputed value), and RE inheritance taxes.

9.5.1 Inheritance taxes

The impact of higher inheritance taxes on RE prices cannot be easily calculated, as it may take decades to unfold, and it also depends on prospective RE owners thinking (or not thinking) very long term, as well as on cultural characteristics. Nevertheless, Bellettini and Taddei (2011) have estimated that the 2001 abolition of bequest and donation taxes in Italy had by 2004 a substantial appreciating effect on Italian residential RE. The relationship between inheritance and RE (or any wealth asset) is better discussed in the 'non-economic' context of 'middle class' structuration: how desirable the latter is, what history tells us about the usefulness and economic role of the 'middle class' in particular national contexts, and to what extent the inter-generational transfer of RE wealth is pivotal in this regard.[11]

9.5.2 Tax capitalization and tax incidence

Recurrent property taxes, capital-gains taxes, property sales taxes, and tax subsidies all have *capitalization* effects. This means that property prices tend to be adjusted to reflect the charge on property owners' (or buyers') income or wealth that taxes represent. *Ceteris paribus*, if property taxes increase, property prices will drop – and vice versa.

Gyourko and Sinai (2003) looked into the spatial distribution of the 'tax subsidy to owner-occupied housing' in the USA c. 1989. They defined this subsidy as the non-taxation of imputed rental income plus the income-tax deductibility of mortgage interest and property taxes. They estimated that 'if there is full capitalization, the substitution effect [cf. Sections 2.2.7 and 2.2.8] arising from elimination of the subsidy will reduce house prices on the order of 20 percent [...]. If there is little or no capitalization, user costs of owning must increase [...] to between 4 and 6 percent of annual income for the typical owner' (Gyourko and Sinai, 2003: 24–5). Other evidence on the capitalization effect is in Capozza et al. (1998) for the USA, Berger et al. (1998),for Sweden, Charlot et al. (2008) for France,[12] Feldman (2010) for Michigan, Hilber and Turner (2010) for the USA, and Hilber et al. (2011) for England.

Or, the capitalization effect may, in the first instance, be upon quantities – see Capozza et al. (1998). In the same vein, Roy et al., studying the effect of mortgage interest and local property tax deductions upon single-family housing demand in the USA from 1994 to 2003, concluded that '[c]omplete elimination of the deductions could result in as much as a 12 per cent decline in the annual number of single-family housing units that are purchased' (Roy et al., 2006: 48).

A related issue is that of the real *incidence* of property, or of any other, taxes (i.e., how the tax burden is actually apportioned between buyer and seller, or between owner and renter, and in what proportions – see Section 9.7). The *real incidence* of a tax is likely to be different from its *statutory incidence* (i.e., who is legally liable for the tax).

The real incidence of any tax on a good or factor depends on the related demand and supply elasticities (see Section 9.7). Linking the incidence issue to the capitalization issue can complicate the analysis of either. For example, if a recurrent tax burdens possession of a property, buyers will capitalize this burden into their offer prices. If, as a result, sellers accept a lower price than their original ask prices, then part of the anticipated tax burden will fall on sellers. Generally the party (or side of the market) on whom the tax is statutorily levied will try and shift the tax burden by appropriately adjusting their ask price (if a seller) or their offer price (if a buyer). Who ultimately pays the tax is revealed in the market *ex post* (i.e., after transactions have taken place).

For example, someone wants to buy a €300,000 house. A transfer tax of 10 per cent is applicable. If the tax is statutorily levied on the seller, he or she will want to raise the ask price to €300,000/(1 – 0.1) = €333,333. If the tax is statutorily levied on the buyer, he or she will want to lower the offer price to €300,000/(1 + 0.1) = €272,727. In the end, and to the extent that there are other suitable properties on offer, but also other interested buyers, the tax will be shared between buyer and seller:

(a) Maybe the house will go for €285,000 – in which case the buyer pays €28,500 in tax, but the seller has received €15,000 less than his or her original asking price. So the seller has assumed $15/28.5 = 52.6$ per cent of the tax burden.
(b) Or maybe the house will go for €315,000 – in which case the seller pays €31,500 in tax, but the buyer has paid €15,000 more than his or her original offer price. So the buyer has assumed $15/31.5 = 47.6$ per cent of the tax burden.

In what follows, we shall deal with capitalization first, leaving a more detailed discussion of incidence for Section 9.7. Let us start with the simple proposition that, even if property tax capitalization is not fully reflected across RE prices, an investor into RE will certainly incorporate taxes in his or her appraisal of property investments.

9.5.3 Capital-gains taxes

Capital-gains taxes are essentially taxes on extraordinary income. Let us consider the capitalization problem they pose from the angle of an investor who is thinking of buying an urban property precisely in order to realize a capital gain. The investor is estimating the future price of the property to be F = €100,000, his RRR = k is 8 per cent, and his time horizon is one period. He is then prepared to pay

$$V = \frac{F}{1+k} = \frac{100{,}000}{1.08} = €92{,}593. \tag{9.3}$$

Suppose now that the investor is subjected to a 50 per cent capital-gains tax. The tax-affected amount he is now prepared to pay, V_t, becomes

$$V_t = \frac{F - t(F - V_t)}{1+k} = \frac{F(1-t)}{(1+k)-t} = \frac{100{,}000(1-0.5)}{(1+0.08)-0.5} = €86{,}207. \tag{9.4}$$

The implied rate of property price growth is $(F - V_t)/V_t = 0.16$. The investor's rate of return is confirmed as

$$R_e = \frac{F - V_t - t(F - V_t)}{V_t}$$
$$= \frac{V_t(1+h) - V_t - t[V_t(1+h) - V_t]}{V_t}$$
$$= h(1-t) = 0.16(1-0.5) = 0.08.$$

The tax paid is 0.5(100,000 – 86,207) = €6896.5

This is a formal result of course. The actual result may differ over a collection of properties, as different buyers are going to have different time horizons, RRRs, and estimates of property price growth.

9.5.4 Sales taxes

Sales taxes on the transfer of property are more properly considered excise taxes (on account of them usually being levied on the basis of different rates from those on most any product). Also, the incidence aspect of these taxes is perhaps stronger than with capital-gains or municipal taxes because they are applied on the current sale price rather than on the difference between purchase and subsequent sale price. Still, an investor, aiming to buy in order to realize a capital gain by selling, will have to consider what the future price is likely to be.

Again looking at things from an investor's (buyer's) point of view (and assuming she is the one liable for the tax), we can proceed along the lines followed in Section 9.5.3. The investor's time horizon is one year, the expected future price of the property (which she expects to 'take home') is €100,000, and her RRR is 8 per cent. The tax rate is 2 per cent. Then

$$V_t = \frac{F(1-t)}{1+k} = \frac{100{,}000(1-0.02)}{1+0.08} = €90{,}741. \tag{9.5}$$

Again, the introduction of the tax has reduced the investor's offer price from €92,593 (see Equation (9.3)) to a smaller amount due to the capitalization effect. The tax paid is €2000.

Question: What tax rate would equalize the tax to the one in Section 9.5.3? What would be V_t then?

9.5.5 (Recurrent) property taxes

Turning to annually paid property taxes (which are usually municipal taxes, but not necessarily so), we employ the idea that property values are capitalizations of future net rents. In the case of owner-occupation, those 'rents' can be thought of as the estimated annual value of 'housing services', or as the rents on similar properties actually rented. In Chapter 7, we suggested that this idea may not hold, as any link between house prices and notional rents on owner-occupied housing is rather tenuous. Still, this is no problem in the context of the present discussion, as what matters is the extent to which measurable variations in property prices can be statistically linked to measurable variations in property taxes rather than in rents – whether actual or notional. If such rents R are expected *ad infinitum* (or over a long enough period anyway), market value V becomes (given a capitalization factor k)

$$V = \frac{R}{k}. \tag{9.6}$$

If a tax τ is then imposed on rental income, value should become

$$V = \frac{R - \tau}{k}. \tag{9.7}$$

Assuming a finite investor horizon and a tax rate t imposed on the market value of the property, would not change the essence of the calculation (cf. Oates, 1969: 963):

$$V = \sum_{n=1}^{N} \frac{R - tV}{(1+k)^n} = \sum_{n=1}^{N} \frac{R}{(1+k)^n} - \sum_{n=1}^{N} \frac{tV}{(1+k)^n} \Rightarrow$$

$$\Rightarrow V + \sum_{n=1}^{N} \frac{tV}{(1+k)^n} = \sum_{n=1}^{N} \frac{R}{(1+k)^n} \Rightarrow V\left[1 + \sum_{n=1}^{N} \frac{t}{(1+k)^n}\right] = \sum_{n=1}^{N} \frac{R}{(1+k)^n} \Rightarrow$$

$$\Rightarrow V = \frac{\sum_{n=1}^{N} \frac{R}{(1+k)^n}}{1 + \sum_{n=1}^{N} \frac{t}{(1+k)^n}} = \frac{R \sum_{n=1}^{N} \frac{1}{(1+k)^n}}{1 + t \sum_{n=1}^{N} \frac{1}{(1+k)^n}}, \tag{9.8}$$

where N = number of years in investor's horizon.

EXAMPLE

Using a spreadsheet, and setting R = £7200, $N = 40$, $k = 6$ per cent, and $t = 3$ per cent, we get

$$V = \frac{7200(15.0463)}{1 + 0.03(15.0463)} \approx £74{,}641$$

(rather than the £80,000 found in Equation (9.2), as here the time horizon is finite). The tax is £2239.

One problem with Equation (9.8) is that the tax is applied only on the initial property value V. Another problem is that it considers only rental income, and not the possibility that at the end of the investor's horizon there may be a property value unrelated to the rental income earned until then. That value must be capitalized also. Let us see how.

An investor forecasts that a property she is thinking of buying now will be worth €F in N years (that is the 'take-home' price that the investor expects she will actually pocket if she sells). Assume, moreover, that the property tax is not applied every year on the initial value of the property, but on what that value is at the end of every year prior to the tax. Then the current value of the property from the investor's viewpoint would be[13]

$$V=\sum_{n=1}^{N}\frac{R-tV(1+h)^{n-1}}{(1+k)^n}+\frac{F}{(1+k)^n}=\sum_{n=1}^{N}\frac{R}{(1+k)^n}-\sum_{n=1}^{N}\frac{tV(1+h)^{n-1}}{(1+k)^n}+\frac{F}{(1+k)^N}$$

$$\Rightarrow V+\sum_{n=1}^{N}\frac{tV(1+h)^{n-1}}{(1+k)^n}=\sum_{n=1}^{N}\frac{R}{(1+k)^n}+\frac{F}{(1+k)^N}\Rightarrow$$

$$\Rightarrow V\left[1+\sum_{n=1}^{N}\frac{t(1+h)^{n-1}}{(1+k)^n}\right]=\sum_{n=1}^{N}\frac{R}{(1+k)^n}+\frac{F}{(1+k)^N}\Rightarrow$$

$$\Rightarrow V=\frac{\sum_{n=1}^{N}\frac{R}{(1+k)^n}}{1+\sum_{n=1}^{N}\frac{t(1+h)^{n-1}}{(1+k)^n}}=\frac{R\sum_{n=1}^{N}\frac{1}{(1+k)^n}+\frac{F}{(1+k)^N}}{1+t\sum_{n=1}^{N}\frac{(1+h)^{n-1}}{(1+k)^n}},\tag{9.9}$$

where h = annual growth rate of V.

This presents something of a conundrum. To solve (9.9), we need to know h, but to know h, we need to know both F and V (and the time between them) – and of the two we only 'know' F! However, the problem has a solution. The point is that the property value that is expected in N years is

$$F=V(1+h)^N\Rightarrow\tag{9.10}$$

$$\Rightarrow h=(F/V)^{1/N}-1.\tag{9.11}$$

Substituting (9.11) into (9.9), we get

$$V=\frac{R\sum_{n=1}^{N}\frac{1}{(1+k)^n}+\frac{F}{(1+k)^N}}{1+t\sum_{n=1}^{N}\frac{(1+h)^{n-1}}{(1+k)^n}}=\frac{R\sum_{n=1}^{N}\frac{1}{(1+k)^n}+\frac{F}{(1+k)^N}}{1+t\sum_{n=1}^{N}\frac{[1+(F/V)^{1/N}-1]^{n-1}}{(1+k)^n}}.\tag{9.12}$$

Setting

$$V\left\{1+t\sum_{n=1}^{N}\frac{[1+(F/V)^{1/N}-1]^{n-1}}{(1+k)^n}\right\}=R\sum_{n=1}^{N}\frac{1}{(1+k)^n}+\frac{F}{(1+k)^N},\tag{9.13}$$

the value of V (obtained by trial and error) that satisfies (9.13) is the maximum price the investor would be prepared to pay now in order to realize her RRR = k under the given assumptions.

EXAMPLE

Setting $R = 7200$, $N = 40$, $k = 6$ per cent, and $t = 3$ per cent, and an expected price F (to be realized at time N) equal to €2 million, we get

$$V\left\{1 + 0.03\sum_{n=1}^{40}\frac{[1+(2,000,000/V)^{1/40}-1]^{n-1}}{(1+0.06)^n}\right\}$$

$$= 7200\sum_{n=1}^{40}\frac{1}{(1+0.06)^n} + \frac{2,000,000}{(1.06)^{40}} = €302,778. \qquad (9.14)$$

With the help of a spreadsheet, the value of V that satisfies (9.14) is found to be €125,495. The implied annual growth rate for V is 7.17 per cent.

9.5.6 More on the capitalization issue

To find out whether, and to what extent, capitalization of municipal property taxes occurs in practice, one procedure is to correct for variables (other than tax) that also affect RE. If the focus is on dwellings, then house characteristics will be the variable(s) to correct for. The next step is to ascertain whether the average price difference between, say, houses in any two different jurisdictions (assuming that those apply different tax rates and/or assessment ratios) is equal to the difference between the discounted values of property taxes applied in either, and expected over a reasonable time horizon. Put simply, if we take two identical houses (subject to identical influences) in two different jurisdictions, the price of one is 100,000, the price of the other is 105,000, and the difference between discounted applied taxes on those is, say, $7000 - 2000 = 5000$, then the price difference must be due to the tax difference. (Proper discussion of this problem would take us to econometrics territory,[14] which is beyond the scope of this book.)

Some additional important points deserve mention:

1 Notice that the procedure suggested above does not require prices of owner-occupied houses to be capitalizations of notional rents (what an owner-occupier would perhaps be willing to pay per period in order to live in his or her house, rather than pay a lump-sum up-front). It simply takes house prices as given and then compares any differences between them (once other variables have been accounted for) with differences in property taxes.

2 A broad consensus so far is that property tax capitalization does exist, but is not perfect, i.e., property taxes by and large are capitalized into property prices, but not fully so (Sirmans and Stacy, 2008). Part of the reason is probably the fact that the Tiebout hypothesis (see below), which offers an explanation for property price capitalization, is not fully confirmed in practice.

3 Proper appraisal of the effect of differential property taxation[15] on property prices cannot happen unless the effect of public services funded by property tax revenue is also taken into account[16] (Oates, 1969). The idea here is that property taxes may depress property prices, but 'good' local public services boost them, and people will move around local authority jurisdictions in search of the 'package' of taxes and 'benefits' they like most (Tiebout, 1956).

> 'If this is true, the outputs of public services (as well as taxes) should influence the attraction of a community to potential residents and should thereby affect local property values'.
>
> (Oates, 1969: 957–8)

The Tiebout hypothesis, however, is perhaps best suited to situations where people work in a central business district, or CBD, and 'have a wide choice of suburban communities in which to reside' (Oates, 1969: 958). This results from its rather restrictive assumptions: residents of one jurisdiction are willing to move to another, face no moving costs, have perfect information, commuting is easy, etc.

4 Nevertheless, the Tiebout hypothesis (the benefit-tax view) is not the only possible mechanism behind property price capitalization. Another mechanism (the capital tax view – cf. Zodrow, 2006) involves adjustments in, say, housing consumption *within* a local authority jurisdiction, rather than *between* jurisdictions. According to this view, over the longer term, higher property taxes induce housing consumers to opt for smaller houses. This raises the price of land for small houses, and lowers it for large houses, but, more importantly, it reduces, *ceteris paribus*, demand for generic housing in the jurisdiction as well as housing investment, while it distorts the housing market. The interjurisdictional results (i.e., lower house prices in higher-tax areas) are much the same as under the Tiebout hypothesis. But because this adjustment in housing capital takes a long time to unfold, property tax capitalization from this source happens slowly.

5 A related mechanism simply involves rational investors, who, at the moment of buying a property, will capitalize any known deductions from gross property income – like property taxes. For example, McDonald and Yurova (2006) documented a property tax capitalization effect even in regard to industrial real estate. They examined the selling prices of 419 industrial properties that were sold in 2001–04 in two Chicago counties. They concluded that '[t]he property tax rate was higher in Cook County by 2.63 per cent of market value, and comparable properties sold for 16.2 per cent less in Cook County than in adjacent DuPage County'.

6 Property tax capitalization affects the *incidence* of property taxation (i.e., who actually bears the tax burden). There are various possibilities:

(a) *Landlord versus tenant:* If (i) the tax is known, (ii) the person legally liable for the tax is the landlord, (iii) tenant demand for the property is given, and (iv) a new tenancy agreement is about to be signed, then most of the tax will probably be borne by the landlord; if the tax is a surprise, landlords will bear the whole burden until existing contracts expire, and then some of the burden may be shifted on to tenants. For example, in a study of 259 buildings in downtown Chicago, McDonald (1993: 119) found that 'assessed value per square foot strongly influences a building's average gross rent per square foot. In 1991, 45 per cent of property tax differences across buildings were shifted forward to tenants. This result means, of course, that 55 per cent of property tax differentials were absorbed by the owners of the building and land.'

(b) *Current owner versus next owner:* If the tax has been in place for a long time, the current owner is likely to have bought the property at the tax-capitalized price, and will also sell at the tax-capitalized price. He paid less when he bought – he gets less when he sells. The net effect due to the tax is nil. Every owner bears the tax, but also pays a lower price to buy the property. If this is a new tax (or if there is an increase in a pre-existing tax), the current owner loses as, *ceteris paribus*, he or she will get less when they sell, so, in a way, they will be paying the next owner's property taxes or part thereof.

7 In most countries, property taxes are primarily used to finance local authority expenditure. Yet in January 2011 the mayor of Shanghai announced a move towards a trial property tax, 'aimed at curbing "speculative" investment' and at reining in surging housing prices (Bloomberg, 2011). Viewed this way, a property tax really becomes like a land value tax, one of whose touted merits is its 'anti-speculative' function (Foldvary, 2006a, b). But while it is true, on the basis of the preceding discussion, that property taxes tend to be (partially) capitalized into property prices, it is doubtful whether property, or land value, taxes are the best instrument to dampen house price inflation with (cf. Chapter 11).

8 Finally, the strongest capitalization effect should occur where the price elasticity of land, or housing, supply is smallest (Capozza et al., 1998; Sirmans et al., 2008; Hilber and Turner, 2010; Hilber et al., 2011). Because perfectly inelastic land, or housing, supply is unusual, herein perhaps lies a reason why capitalization of taxes (or of benefits) into property prices tends to be partial rather than complete (cf. Sirmans et al., 2008).

9.6 Taxation of imputed rental income

In some countries (e.g., the Netherlands, Belgium, Luxembourg, and Greece) imputed income from an owner-occupied home is taxed (a little). Elsewhere there is an ongoing discussion (mostly among academics) about the rationale for such a tax. Reasons in favour have been as follows:

1a By not renting instead, the owner saves the rent, which then presumably counts as extra income.[17]

1b In a similar vein, during any time period, a house-user receives a flow of housing services, just like the return provided by any capital asset, and therefore these must count as income.

2 Taxing imputed rental income would help the redistribution of income.

3 It would also help achieve neutrality between housing tenures.

4a A house is an investment asset; if the services it renders are not taxed, then this discriminates against other forms of investment.

4b As a result, not taxing imputed rental income makes the taxation system less 'efficient' or 'optimal'.

Let us have a closer look.

9.6.1 The 'imputed rent is income' argument

This can be so only by a rather idiosyncratic logic. Here are some reasons why 'not spending on rent because one doesn't rent' cannot be (taxable) income:

1 The argument about the 'flow of services' from housing is too *ad hoc*; by the same token, using one's own furniture, cutlery, DVDs, or car, one's free time, or any other consumption item should be taxed because they obviously generate such flows. Of course, one might point out that housing is also an investment asset, so the 'services' it generates

are the 'income' it provides, but this would amount to circular reasoning, as anything that generates services can be defined as an investment asset – or a consumption item, for that matter.

The way out of the conundrum is to assume that in a money-using market economy, an investment asset is anything that is used to generate an actual cash inflow – or at least a marketed output. Housing services consumed by an owner-occupier (or cutlery services consumed by an owner-user) are neither, whereas housing services sold a tenant are both. Thus, RE would realize its potential as an investment only at the moment it is sold for profit or rented out for income; and because housing is too substantial a transaction to ignore (unlike, for example, the sale of a second-hand car or camera), it is only the sale price of a house, actual rental income or the capital gain realized upon selling that could perhaps make sense to tax, just like transactions in company shares,[18] dividends or the capital gain on financial instruments in various countries.

2 The annual services an owner-occupied home provides are indeed being paid for, either through interest payments on a mortgage or through the opportunity cost of funds committed to the house rather than being allowed to earn interest or other income – or through both.
3 The value of all potential services from an item are supposed to be embodied in its purchase price. For example, whatever reasons one may have for becoming an owner-occupier affect demand for owner-occupation and hence its price; if bequest is one of those reasons or motives, then the price of owner-occupied homes will rise accordingly. In other words, one buys something precisely so that they (or their spouses or descendants) won't have to rent it.
4 Even an inherited owner-occupied home (or other property) has already been paid for (a) through the price paid by the original owner (on the assumption that the right to make an unencumbered bequest is at the heart of the 'natural' right to care for one's lineage), and (b) through inheritance tax. The latter of course is typically a fraction of the market value of the property; but even if it were nil, this would be beside the point. The point is that one of the most important reasons for becoming an owner-occupier is precisely to avoid being at the whim of a landlord – or of the state; another is to transfer this presumed advantage to one's spouse or children, in the context of familial strategies of inter-generational advancement.
5 In the Western world an increasing number of old homeowners are more likely to sell their home (or get a reverse mortgage on it – see Chapter 4) in order to finance retirement or nursing care than bequeath it to their children. The emerging picture is a bleak one, where most people will be burdened with mortgage payments for most of their lives. In effect, they will be renting from a bank rather than a traditional landlord. Then, a little after retirement, they will be divesting themselves of what had become fully theirs just a short time ago, because their pensions alone will not be enough to support a dignified way to death. It all means that an important reason for becoming owner-occupiers, the bequest motive, may be taken away from them anyway. This leaves another important reason, namely capital gain – but not for enjoyment: rather, it is for financing retirement, thereby relieving government budgets that are increasingly hard-pressed to support straining social security systems. This, alone, is enough of a reason not to tax imputed rental income, or, for that matter, capital gains on the sale of old people's homes.

This last argument against taxing imputed rental income must be weighed in the light of other considerations. Evans (2009) has pointed out that (in the UK, and, to a lesser extent, the USA) rising house prices may allow one generation to realize capital gains (e.g., in order to finance retirement), but at the expense of the next generation, who have to meet the higher prices and, to do that, have to save more towards paying for housing. Evans (2009: 2, 13) calls this untaxed capital gain[19] an 'implicit tax on housing' precisely because it has to be paid for by the next generation. Yet one may note that it is not old people selling their homes at high prices who burden the younger generation; if anything, massive sales of this kind are likely to depress house prices. Rather, high house prices must already exist for old people to be able to take advantage of.

Moreover, in older times, and still today in more traditional cultures, the young care(d) for the old directly, thereby repaying the care they received when they were *very* young; the pattern described by Evans (2009) can be seen as a more modern way of doing the same thing. In addition, if old homeowners did not have this option involving capital gains from RE, they would probably be saving more when young for their own retirement; but, in turn, that could mean less spending on the offspring's welfare, including, say, less money for tuition, or indeed less 'housing' to raise a family in.

9.6.2 The 'income redistribution' argument

In a society where only a few were owner-occupiers, taxing their imputed rental income might have been considered an income redistributive mechanism. But (a) the argument loses much of its force in a society where most are, or want to be, owner-occupiers, and (b) this is a very roundabout way of redistributing income; redistribution can be achieved much more easily and logically by taxing actual income instead – after all, a tax on imputed income would not be paid with notional euros or dollars, but with real money.

Thus, finding that 'the government [of Finland] loses significant amounts of tax revenue because imputed rental income is untaxed [...] [f]urthermore, the tax subsidy resulting from the non-taxation of imputed rental income is skewed toward high-income households who are more likely to be homeowners' (Saarimaa, 2008: 3) cannot justify introduction of imputed rental income taxation: first, because any tax not imposed results in some government revenue foregone anyway, but imposing taxes just for the sake of it seems a rather poor taxation strategy; second, because it is illogical not to directly tax higher incomes more (if that is desirable for, obviously, redistributive purposes), but go about it by first taxing imputed rental income. It is especially so when it is recognized that 'also some low-income households are homeowners and they may find it difficult to cope with tax payments if a tax on imputed rental income is implemented' (Saarimaa, 2008: 3).

9.6.3 The 'tenure-neutrality' argument

Let us consider a formal illustration of what is described as 'the tax subsidy resulting from non-taxation of imputed rental income and capital gain', 'by comparing the after-tax return a landlord and a homeowner receive from investing in a similar house' (Saarimaa, 2008: 5). The formulas below employ the user-cost of housing concept, first introduced in Section 7.1.

Given

I_L = the landlord's return,
I_O = the owner-occupier's return,
R_L = landlord's gross rent,
R_O = owner-occupier's gross rental income in housing services,

$R = R_L = R_O$ (a crucial assumption),
V = house value,
t = tax rate on income from capital,
d = depreciation, maintenance, operation, etc. costs,
τ = property tax rate,
M = value of loan taken for investment purposes,
g = capital gain or loss,

we set

$$I_L = (1-t)\left(\frac{R}{V} - d - \tau - i\frac{M}{V} + g\right)V, \tag{9.15}$$

$$I_O = \left[\frac{R}{V} - d - \tau - (1-t)i\frac{M}{V} + g\right]V. \tag{9.16}$$

Subtracting (9.15) from (9.16) gives

$$I_O - I_L = t[R - V(d+\tau)] + gtV = tV\left(\frac{R}{V} - d - \tau\right) + gtV. \tag{9.17}$$

Saarimaa (2008: 6) notes that 'under a tenure-neutral tax system', i.e., one that does not discriminate against either owner-occupation or renting in favour of one or the other, 'the difference $I_O - I_L$ should be zero'. He suggests that (9.17) can be made zero in three ways:

(a) by taxing the imputed rental income and capital gains of homeowners and allowing them to deduct mortgage interest and other expenses;
(b) by abolishing the tax on landlords' rental income and capital gains, and at the same time eliminating all deductions from landlords and homeowners;
(c) by abolishing the tax on landlords' rental income and capital gains, but allowing them to deduct interest expenses.

Question: How would (a), (b), or (c) result in (9.17) being zero? Hint: go back to (9.15) and (9.16), and work it out.

Useful as (9.17) may be as a definition of tenure-neutrality, it does not *prove* that imputed rental income is an entity that (i) exists and (ii) should be taxed. This has to be resolved at the level of first principles. Moreover, it is not at all certain that $R_L = R_O$, even for similar houses (cf. Section 7.1). And even if, coincidentally, they were, one may still question the desirability or otherwise of effecting tenure-neutrality on various grounds, for example labour mobility (this may support a case for favouring renting), middle-class structuration, or financing retirement (these may constitute cases for favouring owner-occupation).

9.6.4 The 'equal treatment of investments' argument

This can be the strongest argument in support of taxing imputed rents. In a nutshell, it says that '[i]f the imputed rent is untaxed while the return from investments is taxed the pattern of investment will clearly be distorted' (Evans, 2009: 7). Or, 'nontaxation [of net imputed rent] lowers the cost of investing in owner-occupied housing below the cost of investing in other forms of physical capital, causing the economy to invest too much in housing and not enough in other productive sectors, such as plant and equipment' (Bourassa and Grigsby, 2000: 527).

There is also a supposed 'fairness' aspect to the situation:

> 'A family that invests $10,000 in a savings bond [...] is taxed on the interest earned. An identical family that invests the same amount in a home is not taxed, even though the home also yields a return, albeit one that cannot be precisely measured'.
>
> (Bourassa and Grigsby, 2000: 527)

However:

1 Calling attention to a presumed danger of 'distorting the pattern of investment' smacks of a planning mentality (what the French call *dirigisme*) that sometimes verges on paternalism. In fairness, many supporters of the 'distortion' argument are indeed free-market proponents. Their point is that because owner-occupied housing is taxed differently from, and supposedly more favourably than, other investments, the investment pattern is not what it might have been otherwise. They do not explicitly express a preference for one pattern over another. Still, the argument does betray a certain dissatisfaction with national investment patterns, which, some think, tilt too much in favour of housebuilding in general, and owner-occupied housing in particular.

2 Such worries, however, are probably unwarranted in view of the fact that housebuilding has strong multiplier effects on the rest of the economy (see comments (3) and (4) below). Crucially housebuilding boasts a low import content, while it also makes a sizable contribution to employment. Far from crowding out 'other' investment, it enhances it in a dynamic market economy. It contributes to overall economic growth, or is affected by it, or both, as this (positive) relationship tends to be bi-directional (cf. Section 3.2.3). It was mostly in the context of post-Second World War discussions about growth (cf. Emmanuel, 1981: 197–248; Katsura, 1984), which were heavily influenced by the statist political climate of the times, that a government-directed 'optimal' investment mix was considered definable, feasible and desirable – cf. comment (3) below. Yet it was gradually realized that housebuilding's impact on economic growth is larger than many other industries' (see Box 9.5).

Box 9.5 Physical investment in housing and economic growth: the US and UK cases

'Despite being a relatively small share of the U.S. gross domestic product (typically 3–4 per cent of GDP), residential investment can have a more dramatic effect on GDP *growth*. This happens when residential investment *increases or decreases*. [...] In nine of the years between 1993 and 2005, it added over 0.4 percentage points annually to GDP growth as construction increased from 1.2 to 2.1 million units. [...] Since housing starts peaked at an annualized pace of over 2.1 million units in 2006 Q1, residential investment plunged [...] subtracting about 1 percent from GDP growth' (Wheaton and Nechayev, 2009).

Regenesis (2010), a UK consultancy, has calculated that in the UK the construction multiplier 'is higher than multipliers for chemicals (2.2), computers (2.2) and financial intermediation (2.1) [based on 1995 input–output tables]. In fact, construction [at 2.6] has the 4th highest gross output multiplier of any industry in the UK. Arguably, housing [which is not referred to separately in the National Accounts] may have an even higher multiplier [...] as it has a lower share of imported raw materials[.] Increased import propensities since 1995 mean that multipliers for all sectors will now be lower [and] actually lower than this because there are further linkages through taxation. On the other hand, housing productivity is thought to be lower than that for construction as a whole, meaning that jobs density for a given amount of spending is likely to be higher than for other forms of construction work.'

Table 9.3 Gross fixed capital formation by sector in selected countries, 2008: percentage shares

	Dwellings	*Other buildings and structures*	*Transport equipment*	*Other machinery and equipment*	*Cultivated assets*	*Intangible fixed assets**	*Residual item*
Ireland	38.0	34.7	11.1	9.2	0.0	6.9	
France	28.8	27.7	8.3	25.2	0.4	9.7	0.0
Finland	27.9	33.1	6.9	23.9	0.2	8.2	−0.1
Greece	26.6	18.2	17.3	34.9	0.1	4.5	−1.6
Germany	25.6	20.0	11.7	36.3		7.4	−1
Canada	25.0	31.2	8.8	28.4		7.7	−1.2
UK	20.3	36.8	6.0	30.1		6.8	0.0
USA	18.4	29.9	7.2	32.2		11.9	0.4
Sweden	13.7	20.9	10.6	40.9	0.3	14.4	−0.8
Japan	13.2	31.7	8.5	41.1		6.8	−1.2

* Intangible fixed assets are non-financial produced fixed assets that mainly consist of mineral exploration, computer software, entertainment, or literary or artistic originals intended to be used for more than one year.
Source: OECD Quarterly National Accounts, v. 2010/1.

3 Considered in an international context, national investment patterns are not by themselves exhaustively good or bad, but contribute to prosperity to the extent they enhance comparative advantages reflected in international competitiveness and trade flows. Table 9.3 shows a broad break-down of investment by sector in selected countries in 2008. A cursory look reveals that, although there is some similarity between countries (after all, with the exception of Greece and possibly of Ireland, the others are in the top development league), there is also enough disparity to suggest that there is no particular defining or 'optimal' investment pattern that could serve as a model for a country's economy (once the level of development has been accounted for). It would be surprising if such existed, as in a dynamic global economy countries with identical investment patterns would in the long run have little to offer each other by way of trade. Of course Table 9.3 is too aggregate; one would expect that at a finer level the disparities would be much more pronounced.

Table 9.3 also shows that in most of the countries mentioned dwelling investment is one of the largest categories (although a fuller analysis would have to look into this from a time-phase perspective too, as housing investment tends to move in cycles – see Section 8.8). On the other hand dwellings are not usually built for export! (This may be changing: in the same way tourism is an export industry, many older people from, say, Northern European countries may increasingly wish to – and in fact do – buy property in the sunny European South for retirement.) So the apparent strength of dwelling investment indicated in Table 9.3 may mean that either the pattern of investment is somehow 'distorted' in quite a few countries or that people in a country, very simply (and depending on the country's housebuilding phase), divert domestically generated incomes as well as gains from international trade to improving their standard of living – a very large part of which is inevitably epitomized in more/better housing.

4 Thus, a critical question is whether building owner-occupied homes in particular (rather than housebuilding in general), enhances the suggested positive multiplier, employment, and growth effects more than building for other tenures does; whether housebuilding would as a whole have been less than otherwise if private renting had been the dominant tenure; and then bring into the equation private preferences and utilities, as well as external benefits, widely felt to be associated with owner-occupied housing but not with renting. This calls for further research, of course; intuitively, though, this is almost certainly the case.

5 Indeed, a problem with a *dirigiste* mentality is precisely its tendency to belittle individual preferences and the huge utilities those may involve. Take rivets, for example: no matter how much a government may subsidize the production and/or consumption of rivets, it is highly unlikely that people will rush out to buy rivets. If people want (owner-occupied) housing, that is a choice that must be respected, if not encouraged for reasons (e.g., middle-class structuration) that may not be directly related to economics.

6 After all, housing is associated with sizable positive externalities, a point made by Kate Barker in her review of the UK housing supply: 'Housing has profound and often unappreciated impacts upon our lives. It directly affects our quality of life, our health and well-being; [...]. Housing also affects our national economic well-being: the rate of economic growth and our prosperity' (Barker, 2003: 1). Of course Barker does not refer in this passage specifically or explicitly to owner-occupied housing; but to the extent that the latter is 'more' of housing than rented housing is (because of its extra attributes, like autonomy, asset potential, and bequest potential), the positive sentiments contained in the passage quoted would certainly apply even more appropriately to owner-occupied housing.

7 Last but not least, any favourable tax treatment of owner-housing cannot possibly distort the pattern of investment in the economy as long as such treatment is capitalized into property prices! That is, the presumed benefit of favourable taxation is (quickly) reflected in (higher) house prices, thereby negating the benefit, at least in so far as such benefit is likely to distort investment patterns. Utilizing panel data from 63 metropolitan areas in the USA from 1970 to 1990, Capozza et al. (1998: 2) concluded that '[i]f changes in tax rates are completely absorbed by changes in land prices, leaving the user cost of capital unchanged, then these tax changes have no impact on the quantity of housing demanded or on the allocation of capital among uses'. They found that 'the dominant impact of the housing subsidy is on price, not quantity'.

Can the same, though, be said about any *unfavourable* tax treatment of owner-housing – namely that it would not distort investment patterns? Not really, because the response of consumption (or of investment) to tax incentives does not mirror the response to tax disincentives; *ceteris paribus*, there is an asymmetry there, depending on how (in)elastic supply of new housing is, and on whether the tax change is a decrease or increase. If a decrease, it will raise demand and most of the effect will tend to be on price because the rise in demand will generate an equilibrium closer to the inelastic range of new housing supply; if an increase, it will lower demand and most of the effect will tend to be on quantity because the drop in demand will generate an equilibrium closer to the elastic range of new housing supply (see Figure 9.1).

However, the total effect of a tax change on equilibrium price and quantity needs to take into account the response of existing supply too, in addition to that of new supply. That response depends on three things: (i) the extent to which the tax change impairs households' ability to pay; (ii) the extent to which households have secondary homes; and (iii) the extent to which households can move to cheaper houses, possibly in other jurisdictions. As a result of the influence of those three factors, the tax will make some households try to shed properties; this will increase the supply of existing houses in particular submarkets, and maybe throughout the market. Prices of existing houses will then drop. If new housing supply is affected by what happens to the price of old housing (cf. Section 3.3.2), it will decrease too (see Figure 9.2), exacerbating the adverse quantity effects depicted in Figure 9.1 (i.e., those that stem from a shift in demand from D_2 to D_1 to D_3).

9.6.5 The 'taxation efficiency' argument

If anything, optimal taxation would seem to require that capital income ought to be untaxed (Mankiw, 2009: 20) – and that would include housing, to the extent the latter is considered a capital good. The rationale is simple: 'a capital tax imposes an ever-increasing tax on consumption further in the future, so its violation of the principle of uniform commodity taxation is extreme' (Mankiw, 2009: 20). (That principle – which is filed under 'neutrality'

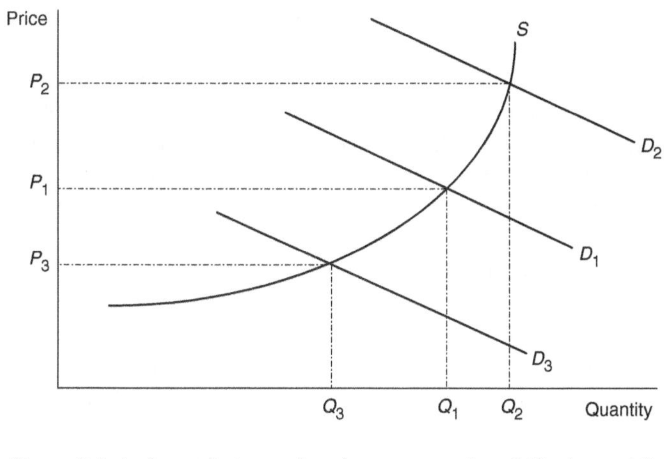

Figure 9.1 A change in tax on housing consumption shifts demand from D_1 to D_2 or to D_3, and has asymmetrical effects on equilibrium price and quantity, depending on the elasticity of new housing supply and on whether the tax increases or decreases.

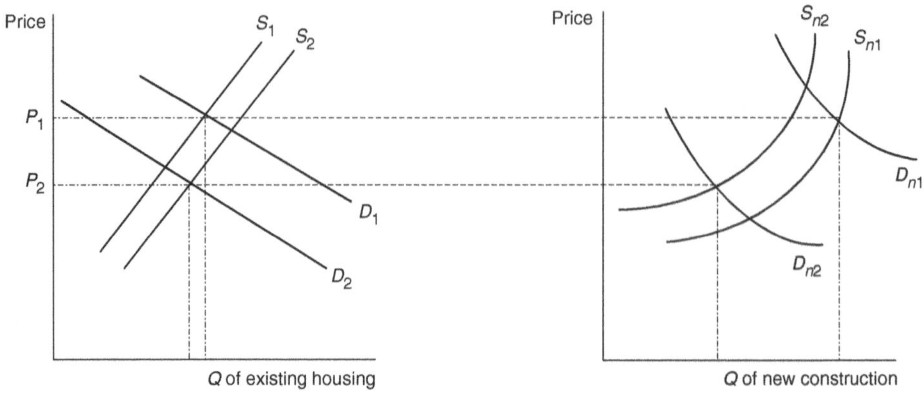

Figure 9.2 A new tax on housing consumption reduces demand, but also increases supply of existing housing as owners try to shed properties; this further reduces the equilibrium price. As a result developers downsize the expected, or future, sale price of new housing, and initiate fewer starts at the current price than suggested by the drop of demand only (from D_{n1} to D_{n2}).

in Section 9.1.2 – suggests that to minimize the distortionary effects of a tax on a commodity, all commodities should be taxed the same.)

Still, several studies have favoured taxing imputed rent along with business capital income on welfare or optimality grounds.[20] Eerola and Määttänen (2007), noticing that 'it need not be optimal to tax the imputed rent at the same rate as business capital income', set out to determine the optimal tax treatment of housing in what they called 'a dynamic general equilibrium setting'. They concluded that

1 The optimal tax treatment of housing depends on the tax treatment of *both* consumption and business capital income.[21]
2 If housing cannot be taxed, it may be optimal to tax labour income.
3 If it is optimal to tax labour income, the tax rate on business capital income should be zero in the long run.
4 When this is the case, housing should be taxed whenever consumption is taxed.
5 If it is not optimal to tax labour income, business capital income should be subsidized; the tax rate on imputed rent should be higher than the tax on business capital income, 'but it is not possible to determine whether the tax rate on imputed rent should be positive or not' (Eerola and Määttänen, 2007: 18–19).

If so, the case for taxing imputed rent on welfare or optimality grounds is not conclusive – to say the least. Studies of this nature are very sensitive to the initial assumptions used, including variables included – or not included – in the models. In fact, many researchers tend to underestimate the utilities involved in people's revealed preference for owner-occupied housing, or, worse, to suggest that there is some opportunity cost involved in this specific choice that people must be made to pay.[22] Yet such preferences may not be simply due to a favourable tax regime but may come 'from the heart'; if so, burdening owner-occupation with taxes (i.e., 'disincentivizing' its acquisition) will reduce people's welfare in ways that cannot be captured quantitatively. Herein lies an important reason for political resistance to imputed rent taxation, or to property taxes, at least in so far as the latter are not visibly associated with received benefits at the municipal level – and even then, such taxes are tolerated only if they do not strain households' ability to pay them. From this point of view, it is better to remove all direct subsidies to owner-occupation (like mortgage-interest tax relief)[23] than apply wealth taxes on it, or tax non-existent rents.

This prescription is in line with Bourassa and Grigsby's (2000: 541) conclusions about tax reform in the US owner-occupied sector: of the four main tax concessions for owner-occupied housing, namely 'nontaxation of imputed income, exemption of most capital gains, deductibility of mortgage interest, and deductibility of real estate taxes', they suggested that 'the first two concessions should remain and that the last two should be abolished', as 'both conceptual and administrative problems argue against taxing imputed rent and capital gains'. In the case of taxing imputed rent, they have spotted four difficulties: (a) the tax is really a levy on wealth rather than on (imputed) income; (b) the tax bears little relationship to ability to pay; (c) properties often experience declining values and high rental returns – and vice versa; and (d) there are administrative difficulties (in the USA) (Bourassa and Grigsby, 2000: 528–9).

9.6.6 Efficiency and preferences

A basic proposition in welfare economics (the so-called Pareto optimality criterion) is that, given perfect competition and no externalities, the optimum combination of goods will be at the point of tangency between the production-possibilities (p-p) curve and the highest possible indifference curve (Sloman, 1991: 371). At that point, the marginal rate of substitution between the two products will be the same as the marginal rate of transformation: MRS = MRT (cf. Sections 2.2.2 and 2.2.10). But this condition can be fulfilled on any point on the p-p curve (see Figure 9.3), depending on what the indifference curve (IC) map, which expresses people's preferences, is like. In short, different utility maps imply that different 'efficiencies' are possible.

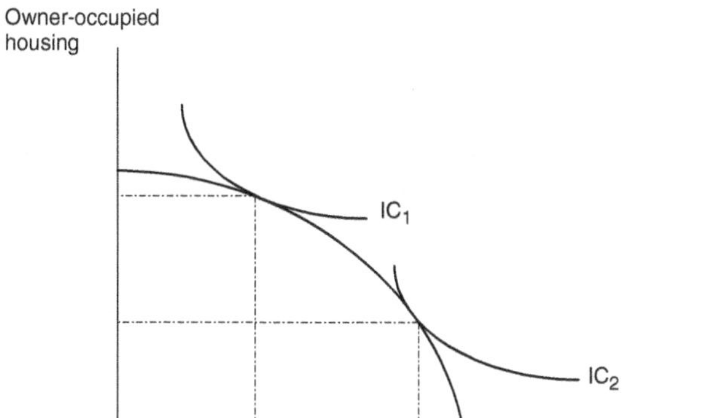

Figure 9.3 A production-possibilities frontier between housing and a composite good, with different consumer preferences: both tangency points are 'efficient'.

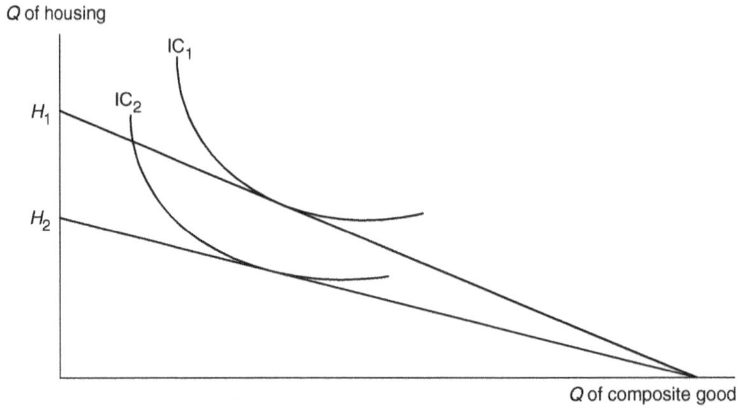

Figure 9.4 A rise in the cost of one good (e.g., own-housing) relative to the cost of another (e.g., a composite one) lowers households' budget line, and pushes them on a lower utility curve.

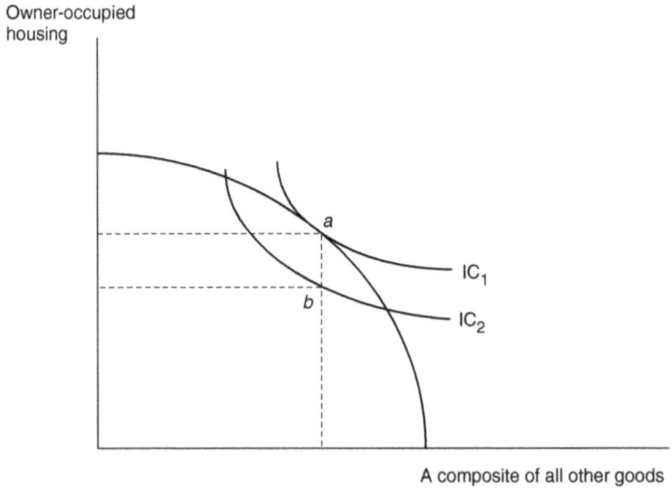

Figure 9.5 An attempt to change society's preferences by force (using, e.g., taxes as a weapon) may result in waste of resources and less output as shown by point *b* or any other point on IC_2.

Further, changing by force consumers' revealed preferences (as would happen if the effective cost of, say, house purchase and upkeep rose due to taxation), would result in them climbing down their indifference curve map (see Figure 9.4).

This would cause a waste of resources that would be reflected in society producing at a point inside its p-p frontier (see Figure 9.5). The reason is that households' preferences are derived from, and express, direct utilities as well as the utility impact of various externalities associated with the consumption of goods. Changing (revealed) preferences by force would thus impact on the structure of rewards and incentives, inevitably causing resource misallocation and waste. 'Force' of course would include the tax weapon, especially if it took the form of taxing property beyond one's ability to pay, or the form of taxing non-existent income, like imputed rent.

In fact, a case can be made about the positive efficiency effect of either directly subsidizing owner-occupation, or at least not burdening it, and generally not burdening the acquisition and possession of housing wealth with taxes (especially irrational or unfair ones). Let us, for example, take the (usual) case where people's preferences are strongly in favour of owner-occupied housing. Assume, moreover, that the currently produced (and consumed) combination of goods is inside the p-p frontier, due to market structure inefficiencies and other constraints affecting owner-occupied housing in particular. (Such a situation is a violation of the perfect competition assumption for Pareto optimality; on the other hand, it is more realistic.) If so, subsidies to owner-occupation (either direct ones or in the form of non-taxation), far from distorting the allocation of resources, might actually help raise efficiency if they enabled households to 'jump up' indifference curves, so that the combination of goods achieved was actually at the point of tangency between a higher IC and the p-p frontier (see Figure 9.6). The actual outcome of such a process would depend of course on various interactions between owner-occupied housing (on both the production and consumption side) and the rest of the economy.

9.7 Appendix: incidence calculation of an *ad valorem* tax

Consider the following linear demand and supply functions in a competitive market:

$$P_d = 16 - \tfrac{3}{5}Q,$$
$$P_s = 3 + \tfrac{4}{5}Q.$$

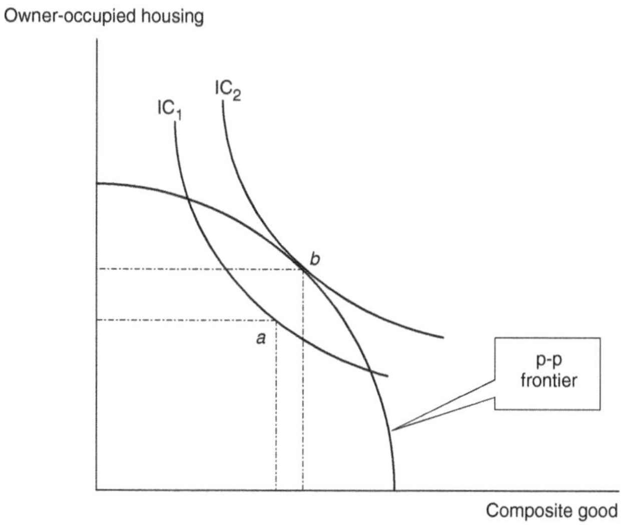

Figure 9.6 Initially society finds itself at point *a* due to various inefficiencies and constraints. In such a case discriminate (favourable) taxation or subsidization of the more constrained good (in this case, housing) *may* actually increase overall efficiency (depending on how owner-occupied housing and the composite good interact) by enabling achievement of point *b*.

It follows that at equilibrium E (see Figure 9.6), $P_e = P_1 = 10.4$ and $Q_e = Q_1 = 9.3$. Now assume that a tax rate t of 30 per cent is applied on the supply price. This changes the supply function to

$$P'_s = 3 + tP'_s + \tfrac{4}{5}Q = 3 + 0.3P'_s + \tfrac{4}{5}Q$$

$$\Rightarrow P'_s(1-t) = 3 + \tfrac{4}{5}Q \Rightarrow P'_s = \frac{3 + \frac{4}{5}Q}{1-t}.$$

Consequently, at equilibrium E_t, $P'_e = P_t = 11.97$ and $Q'_e = Q_t = 6.72$.

There has thus been a change in consumer-paid price due to the tax, equal to $P'_e - P_e = P_t - P_1 = 11.97 - 10.4 = 1.57$. At the same time, (a) the price received by suppliers *after the tax* for each unit of the new equilibrium quantity sold is $P_s = 3 + \frac{4}{5}Q = 3 + \frac{4}{5}(6.72) = 8.38$, and (b) the tax is equal to $11.97 - 8.38 = 3.59$, the so-called *tax wedge*. (This is also equal to $P'_e t = P_t t = 11.97(0.3) = 3.59$.) Hence,

$$\text{tax burden on the demand side} = \frac{\Delta P}{tP'_e} = \frac{1.57}{3.59} = 43.7\text{per cent},$$

the rest (i.e., 56.3 per cent) burdening the supply side (see Figure 9.7).

The apportionment of the tax burden between demand and supply sides depends on the respective own-price elasticities, as the side with the greater elasticity has a greater ability to shift the tax burden onto the other side. The average elasticity of demand between $P_e = P_1 = 10.4$ and $P'_e = P_t = 11.97$ is -2.3. The average elasticity of supply between $P_e = P_1 = 10.4$ and $P_s = 8.38$ is 1.5. Therefore, as a rough approximation,

$$\text{tax burden on demand side} \approx \frac{|\varepsilon_s|}{|\varepsilon_s| + |\varepsilon_d|} \approx \frac{1.5}{1.5 + 2.3} \approx 39.4\text{per cent},$$

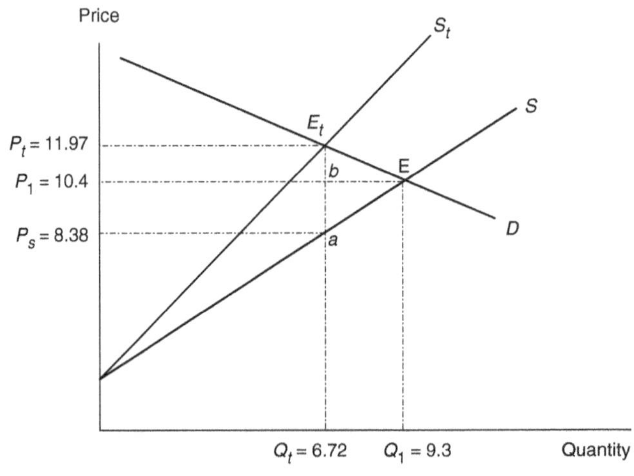

Figure 9.7 Tax incidence: case of an *ad valorem* tax applied on suppliers: supply decreases, market equilibrium changes from E to E_t tax revenue is $P_tP_saE_t$, consumers pay $P_tP_1bE_t$ of the tax, suppliers pay P_1P_sab of the tax, the equilibrium Q drops to Q_t, and there is a *deadweight loss* E_taE.

compared with 43.7 per cent found previously.[24] (Actually, the smaller the effect of the tax on price – i.e., the smaller the tax rate – the closer together the two results would come.)

The reason why in this example the tax burden is greater on the supply than on the demand side is simple: over the price range affected by the tax, supply is more inelastic than demand. If supply had been perfectly inelastic (meaning a supply line of infinite slope, as is often the case with land resources), then all of the tax would have been borne by the supplier(s).

Summary of main points

1 Main categories of taxes are on income, on capital, and on consumption.
2 Ten principles of taxation are introduced:
   - Compatibility with government goals
   - Ability to pay
   - Equity
   - Who benefits pays (the benefits-received principle)
   - Neutrality (minimal distortions, minimal disincentives)
   - Efficiency (minimal DWL)
   - Predictability
   - Simplicity
   - Collection efficiency
   - Minimal eschewal
3 Property taxes – especially recurrent and inheritance taxes – are in particular danger of being levied on people unable to pay them out of current income or out of liquid assets. On 'ability to pay' and 'equity' grounds (probably also on 'collection efficiency' and 'neutrality' grounds), therefore, income taxation is inherently better than property taxation; among property taxes, the one least problematic in this respect is capital-gains tax.
4 Property taxes are regressive to the extent that property values do not correlate 100 per cent with incomes. In fact, this tends to be the case.
5 Property taxes statistically appear to weigh less heavily on economic growth than other taxes precisely because they are regressive.
6 Property taxes tend to be capitalized into RE prices. The following formulas calculate the price V (or V_t) an investor is prepared to pay for a property in view of different taxes (where F = future value of property, R = net rent, t = tax rate, k = cap rate):

   (a) regarding capital-gains taxes,

   $$V_t = \frac{F(1-t)}{(1+k)-t} \quad \text{(one-period time horizon);}$$

   (b) regarding sales taxes,

   $$V_t = \frac{F(1-t)}{1+k} \quad \text{(one-period time horizon);}$$

(c) regarding municipal taxes,

$$V = \frac{R\sum_{n=1}^{N}\frac{1}{(1+k)^n} + \frac{F}{(1+k)^N}}{1+t\sum_{n=1}^{N}\frac{[1+(F/V)^{1/N}-1]^{n-1}}{(1+k)^n}}.$$

7 If local property taxes tend to be capitalized into RE prices, then any benefits from those taxes (in terms of public services) will also tend to be capitalized.

8 Taxation of imputed rental income from owner-occupation is highly problematic on various grounds: it is wrong in principle because imputed rent is not actual income; one buys the full ownership of something precisely so that they will not have to rent it; an owned item's purchase price encompasses and reflects any subsequent services the item may provide; if the government's goal is to discourage people from investing 'too much' in RE, this can be done more logically through other taxes that are at least levied on actual values or flows; if, on the other hand, the purpose is to treat all investments equally, the dual nature of housing as both consumption and investment suggests that it is again more logical to tax housing at the moment it functions as an investment, i.e., when capital gains are realized on it, rather than taxing non-existent income from it.

9 On the subject of 'distorted' investment patterns, policy-makers must always bear in mind that from society's point of view there is not one efficient combination of goods produced (e.g., housing versus all others). Different efficient combinations are possible, depending on people's preferences.

10 The real incidence of a tax (i.e., who bears the tax burden ultimately) is nearly always different from the statutory incidence (i.e., who is legally responsible to pay the tax). Real incidence is based on demand and supply elasticities. If, for example, supply is perfectly inelastic (as is often the case with land), suppliers will pay 100 per cent of a tax on land. Thus, an approximation of the percentage burden of a sales tax on buyers is given by

$$\frac{|\varepsilon_s|}{|\varepsilon_s| + |\varepsilon_d|}.$$

Review questions and exercises

1 On 24 September 2011, *The Economist* published a leader entitled 'Hunting the rich', whose main idea was that '[t]he wealthy will have to pay more tax. But there are good and bad ways to make them do so'. One of the suggestions made was that '[i]n Europe, where tax systems are more efficient [than in America], one option would be to shift more of the burden from income to property, which would collect more from the rich but have less impact on their willingness to take risks'. On the basis of the discussion in this chapter, do you agree? Debate this suggestion. (*Hint:* discuss it from the point of view of ability-to-pay/equity/compatibility with government goals/impact on economic behaviour/Arnold's (2008) study mentioned in Section 11.4.)

2 In France – and quite apart from a general wealth tax called *impôt sur la fortune* – there are two kinds of local property taxes: *taxe foncière* and *taxe d'habitation.* (Together, they are a bit like the UK *council tax*, which is based on the assessed value of a (residential) property and is applied fully if there are two adults living in it –

otherwise there are discounts.) The *taxe foncière* is a property tax (paid by the owner) and the *taxe d'habitation* a residence tax (paid by the occupier). An owner-occupier is liable for both taxes. Some discounts apply. (Source: www.france-property-and-information.com/taxes-in-france.htm.) Based *only* on this information, do you think that *in principle* the French local property tax system helps promote rented accommodation or not? (For more information – in case you want to expand your discussion, for example by considering how French tax law defines occupied properties – see www.french-property.com/guides/france/finance-taxation/taxation/local-property-taxes/.)

3 A regressive tax is one that 'eats away' a larger share of one's income the lower that income is. A progressive tax is the opposite. Are property taxes regressive or progressive then? Always or usually? On what could their regressivity or progressivity depend?

4 Go to the OECD table 'Taxes on property as percentage of total taxation' (www.oecd.org/dataoecd/13/41/43098778.xls). Go also to the OECD table 'Gross domestic product: GDP, volume – annual growth rates in percentage' (http://stats.oecd.org/Index.aspx). Without getting deep into econometrics, check to see if the declining trend in taxes on property as percentage of total taxation runs together with a declining, rising, or indeterminate trend in GDP growth rates. Interpret your result. In the light of Arnold's (2008) work, how would you tentatively explain a possible inverse relationship?

5 In 2010 an American citizen asked in Yahoo!Answers:

> 'A property tax is based on the value of your property. It is the same regardless of your income.
>
> If your income goes down, the tax becomes a bigger percentage of your income. If my house is already paid off (it is), I can't afford to move because of my low income. I can't pay rent, I can't make a mortgage payment. I can't sell my property because of the bad economy.
>
> Why am I being forced to pay such a regressive tax?'

Another American replied:

> 'Property taxes are collected and spent locally. If you hate living in a nice community with good streets, schools, parks, libraries, police, etc. then quit trying to sponge off others all your life and move to some dung pile community where taxes are lower. [...]
>
> They're the reason prosperous communities have nicer facilities than poorer ones.
>
> Usually property tax increases are voted on locally, so if you do not want to live in a nice community you can vote against them or move out.'

(Source: http://answers.yahoo.com/question/index?qid=20100803085833AAU42IM, @ 30.9.2011.)

Assess the pros and cons of those arguments. (Maybe you could have a class discussion about them.)

6 Go to Section 9.7. Now assume that the 30 per cent *ad valorem* tax is applied on the demand side. Find out whether the tax incidence stays the same as before. Use both the equilibrium comparison approach and the elasticities approach.

7 An investor whose RRR is 8 per cent is considering buying a property, to hold for 4 years. She estimates that the future value F of the property, which she will be able to pocket, will be €6 million.

(a) Suppose that municipal taxation over those 4 years is 2 per cent of the annual value of the property. The tax for any particular year is estimated on the basis of the value of the property at the end of the previous year. Rental income from the property over the 4-year period is expected to be €300,000 p.a. How much would the investor pay for the property now?

(b) Suppose that the only property taxation applicable is a 25 per cent capital-gains tax, which the investor would have to pay upon selling. How much would she pay now to buy the property?

(c) Suppose, finally, that there is just a 10 per cent sales tax levied on the buyer. How much would the investor pay now (including the tax) to buy the property? (Ignore the incidence issue.)

(d) In all cases, calculate the implicit rate of growth of the property price.

8 Argue against or in favour of taxation of imputed rental income.

10 Land uses, values, and taxation

Main sections

Having gone through this chapter, a student should be able to

1. Explain the concept of an urban hierarchy by reference to both central-place theory and the rank-size rule.
2. Define a bid-rent (or bid-price) curve, and a rent-gradient (or price-gradient).
3. Show how such a 'bid-curve' can be calculated in the case of a 'typical' firm, under different scenarios regarding the variability of revenue and/or product price.
4. Show how such a 'bid-curve' can be calculated in the case of a 'typical' household.
5. Explain how a pattern of land uses, and a pattern of land rents (or land prices) around a city core come into place.
6. Derive a total bid-rent, or bid-price, curve over all land uses in an urban area.
7. Evaluate arguments in favour of land value taxation (LVT).
8. Explain when LVT would involve no *deadweight loss* for society, nor would it reduce the quantity supplied of land.
9. Define *economic rent* from land, and discuss conditions under which it may or may not exist.
10. Explain when economic rent may be considered a windfall gain for a landowner.

10.1 The land-use pattern in a market economy

Back in Chapter 7, we worked out the price a housing developer would pay for land assuming that the price of the finished structure (which unavoidably includes the price of land) is determined by what the 'top' buyer would in turn be prepared to pay. This assumption reflected another, made in Chapter 1, namely that demand for land is (mostly) derived from either consumers' demand for the product of land (in case of agricultural, mineral, or 'amenity'-related land) or from users' demand for advantages afforded them by the land's location.

Whichever of the two reasons is the case, the end-result, in a market economy, is competition among users for land. Competition bids up the price of particular pieces of land, until the land realizes its 'highest and best value', and goes to the highest bidder. Of course, this is not always a particularly fast or unencumbered process; for the use of a given piece of land to change, other uses must prove more profitable or satisfactory than the current one. This takes time, especially since, in all likelihood, the given piece was devoted to its current use exactly because the latter had at some point in the past proven superior to other uses.

Moreover, not all landowners, including homeowners, respond easily or at all to market signals. There are those who like to stay put for non-economic reasons, and who can thus be said to enjoy priceless utility from their current relationship with their land, or at least a utility that no sane bidder would care to find and meet the price of. There is also the problem of indivisibilities, often compounded by imperfect information. For example, a homeowner who gets £200,000 from selling her house may not find another that, for that kind of money, will give her exactly the same level of utility. That is, those that might satisfy this requirement might cost more, and those that cost less might fail the requirement. This is because in real life housing is *not* a homogeneous good.[1]

Nevertheless, government action and competition among users (be they populations, groups of people or firms, or individual entities) broadly determine the pattern of land uses and therefore the pattern of land prices, across multiple cities or settlements, between city and country, and within cities. Let us see how this is so.

10.2 Land uses as expressions of urban hierarchies

A city is one big, unified yet varied land use. It has its own hinterland (i.e., surrounding settlements), it interconnects with other cities, and it is the best machine there is for effecting overall, diversified economic growth (cf. Jacobs, 1985). Those cities that are best at the growth game (cf. Storper, 2001; 2010) tend to incorporate other cities into their hinterland, forming city regions or even becoming world cities.

We thus have two related processes: one involving the patterned relationship between a city and its hinterland, and another involving the patterned relationship between a city and other cities. The latter process can be easily considered a larger-scale restatement of the former (cf. Anas et al., 1998).

The first process views a city, any city, as a hub of economic activity, a 'central place', an attractor of other settlements around it, while they, in turn, attract still smaller settlements around them. This is the gist of *central place theory*, developed by W. Christaller (1893–1969), a German geographer, and set out in his 1933 book *Die zentralen Orte in Süddeutschland*.[2] Such interconnections between settlements give rise to an *urban hierarchy*, which Christaller set down as a grid of hexagons – that is because circles would have left some spaces unaccounted for (see Figure 10.1).

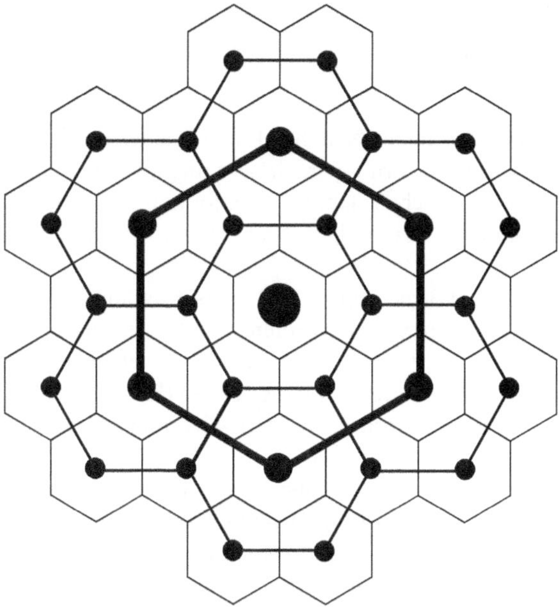

Figure 10.1 An urban hierarchy in the form of a grid of hexagons.
(Source: http://webhost.bridgew.edu/jhayesboh/dissert/chapter02/CHAPTERII.html.)

Christaller's main assumption was of an *isotropic* (i.e., identical in all directions) plane as the background for his urban hierarchy model. This is patently unrealistic. Actual urban hierarchies are not neatly structured, and occasionally the deviation from structure is quite pronounced, especially as regards the size of the biggest city in a country in relation to other city sizes. Yet his model raised the question of the extent to which all urban hierarchies tend to be structured in a similar way, irrespective of place or order of magnitude (i.e., to exhibit *scale invariance*)

It also raised the question of the extent to which larger 'central places', rather than extracting supplies from their hinterlands, supply instead (or as well) goods and services to smaller places around them, turning them into 'trading' or 'catchment' areas (i.e., a kind of export 'hinterland') for the bigger settlements. The possibility of this being the case is of course strengthened if urban settlements tend to fall into recurrent distinct patterns (or *a* distinct pattern) precisely because this is evidence of an organic relationship between settlements. If applied to particular countries or regions, Christaller's model may not replicate hexagonal urban hierarchies (which, after all, served mainly as a demonstration device in his model, even though the latter mirrored the Southern German urban landscape of his time), but its main proposition – that the nature of such hierarchies is canonical – has received remarkable empirical support through testing by means of the so-called *rank-size rule*.

This brings us to the second process mentioned, i.e., relations between cities. According to the rank-size rule for cities, the population of the *i*th city or town in an appropriate geographical unit (say, a country) is roughly equal to the ratio of the population of the biggest city to the population-size-rank of the *i*th city or town in the given unit. For example, if the third largest city in a country has a population of 100,000, the largest city will have a population of 3 (100,000) = 300,000; therefore, the product of any settlement's size and its rank in the urban hierarchy will tend to be constant, i.e., roughly equal to the population of the largest settlement.

The relationship shows better if one takes the logarithms of the variables involved. If the relationship exists, and if, while in logarithmic form, it graphs as a roughly straight line, it is said to follow a power law – and urban hierarchies appear to conform to this pattern. If the straight line that is generated by logarithmic scaling has a slope of -1, it is described as a Zipf curve (Kosmopoulou et al., 2007).[3]

In effect, a slope of -1 that persists over time implies that cities grow in parallel; if the slope becomes greater than $|1|$ over time, growth is divergent (the larger cities grow at a faster rate than smaller cities); and if the slope becomes less than $|1|$ over time, growth is convergent (the smaller cities grow at a faster rate than larger cities) (Kosmopoulou et al., 2007). Examples of urban hierarchies that conform to the rank-size rule are presented in Figure 10.2 (for Scotland) and Figure 10.3 (for Australia and New Zealand).

Some researchers have questioned the extent of applicability of Zipf's law for cities (e.g., Soo, 2005), but, studying US urban growth in the twentieth century, Kosmopoulou et al. (2007) have shown that in a changing urban landscape there is a need to redefine what is meant by a city (more accurately, to redefine cities' boundaries). If this is done correctly, then parallel city growth as per Zipf's law is confirmed. Similarly, Rossi-Hansberg and Wright (2007: 597) have developed a theory of urban structure and growth that 'produces a city size distribution that is well approximated by Zipf's law, but that also displays the observed systematic underrepresentation of both very small and very large cities'.

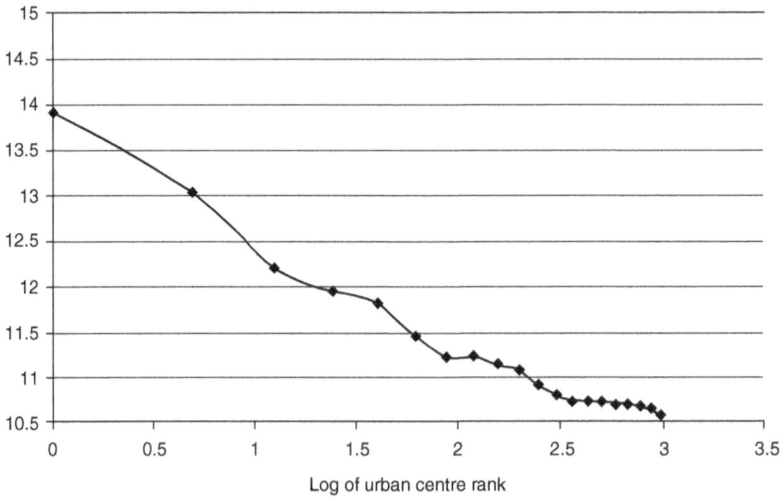

Figure 10.2 Application of the rank size rule: top 20 Scottish settlements, 2001.
(Source: *Economic Linkages Between Small Towns and Surrounding Rural Areas in Scotland: Final Report*, The Scottish Government, 2005, www.scotland.gov.uk/Publications/2005/03/20911/55374.)

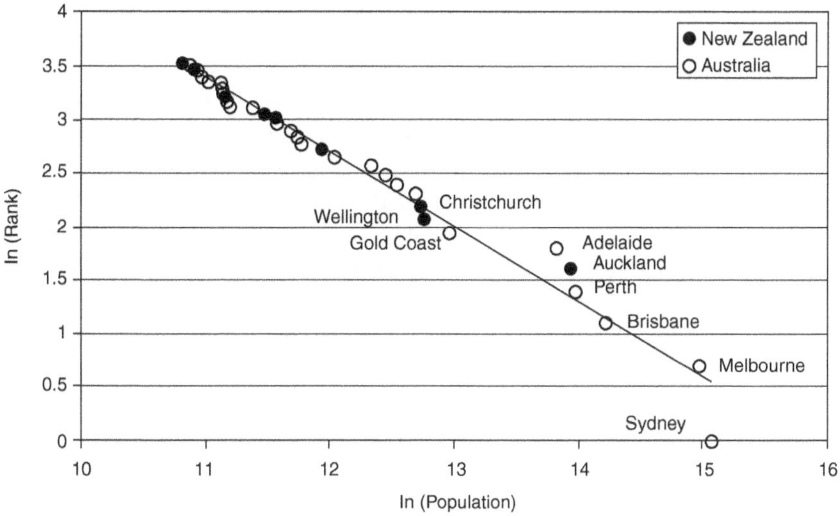

Figure 10.3 Zipf's Law for Australasian urban areas.

(Source: Maré, D. C., Labour Productivity in Auckland Firms, Motu Working Paper 08-12, June 2008, Appendix A: Auckland Urban Area in Context. Based on: World Population Rankings, available from www.demographia.com/db-worldua.pdf (NZ data verified against Statistics New Zealand (2005).)

10.3 Land uses outwards from a city's core

This theme was first investigated formally by J. H. von Thünen (1783–1850), a nineteenth-century German economist and landowner. In his 1826 book, *Der isolierte Staat* [*The Isolated State*], he linked the pattern of land rents at different distances from a city centre to the capacity of different land uses to meet transport costs to the city centre. It turned out that the further away an activity would be, the lower the land rent it would have to pay.

In more modern formulations, the city centre is described as the *point of maximum accessibility* – what has come to be known as the CBD (central business district) in a *monocentric* city. The description also applies to a city itself if it is the *central place* in a cluster of settlements (see Section 10.2). A CBD's, or a city's, advantage nowadays does not of course relate to being a market for agricultural produce, but, more generally, to being capable of offering the following:

1 Agglomeration economies. These are benefits to firms that result from a high spatial concentration of population and activities, like functional linkages (backward and forward) between firms carried out at low transport cost, easy exchange of information, and external economies (like proximity to a large labour pool). On the downside, agglomeration may also involve costs, like congestion, pollution, and criminality.
2 Access to political and business and media leaders and institutions, especially in the case of a country's, or state's, capital.
3 Increased chances of social interaction, extended shopping opportunities, greater diversity of entertainment, and easier and faster access to health care, financial and education services.

In von Thünen's time and place, access to land could be had by paying a rent rather than a purchase price; moreover, most land that mattered was agricultural land around or near cities. But in principle any form of payment, and any kind of land-based activity, can be modelled along those lines, with appropriate modifications. For instance, *polycentric* cities have multiple nuclei of administrative or commercial or amenity-related significance, and do so in no common order necessarily (even if there are perfectly reasonable explanations for the observed order in a given city).

Since von Thünen based his model on agricultural uses, he assumed that access to a market – and, in his time, that meant a nearby town and in particular the CBD – was all-important. This stems from the fact that agriculture relies mostly on *non-transferable inputs*, chiefly the land itself. In contrast, manufacturing relies on *transferable inputs* – like raw materials, many of which may be brought from overseas – so access to supply sources, if these are domestic, may matter more than access to markets, many of which may also be international rather than domestic anyway. If supply sources, or customers, are regional or international, a manufacturing firm's domestic location criterion may be access to a harbour or train station (and even that may not be crucial if the road network is good); or the criterion may be access to labour, which means that proximity to a city from a fringe location may matter more than nearness to its CBD, especially if the transport network between the firm's location and residential sectors or suburbs is good.

Essentially land-use-pattern theory attempts to explain how a *bid-rent* (or *bid-price*) *curve* is formed. The bid-rent (or bid-price) curve shows the *maximum* rents (or prices) that are paid at various distances from some focal point, such as the CBD. Strictly speaking, the *rent-gradient* (or *land-price-gradient*) is the slope of the bid-rent (or bid-price) curve (although sometimes the two terms are used interchangeably).

In traditional formulations, the rent-gradient is negative, reflecting decreasing rents with distance from CBD. However, if a CBD loses its advantage in terms of agglomeration economies, or if other nuclei of activity or interest arise in an urban area (like town-like suburbs along or near motorways), it is possible for a bid-curve from a city centre to become upward-sloping, or, more likely, to be broadly downward-sloping, but with significant humps here and there in the urban landscape. The specifics aside, it is always the case that the rent-gradient is downward-sloping outwards from any given point of maximum accessibility, appropriately defined.

As already suggested, land prices are typically determined by demand for either the products of the land or for location, in the sense of access to things that mean higher sales or lower costs to firms, and better income-earning prospects, along with amenities-related utility (including utility derived from landscape quality), to households.

But when a pattern of land prices – and uses – is thus determined, subsequent users may, for a time, take this pattern into account, or for granted, in order to select the right location for them. So land-price determination is a two-way process, with changes in business conditions, or in household preferences, employment opportunities or incomes, continuously redefining the land-use pattern.

Below, we shall develop a firm's and a household's bid-curves on the assumption that we are dealing with a *monocentric* city. Although research into the land-use pattern between city and country owes much to the pioneering work of von Thünen, Christaller, and Lösch, its subsequent application in an intra-urban context is immensely indebted to the insights of Alonso (1964), Mills (1967, 1972), and Muth (1969, 1971).

These three theorists are mostly linked to efforts to understand the spatial pattern of rents or land values in connection to land uses. Other theorists, earlier than the aforementioned, concentrated on describing existing land-use patterns mostly from a planner's or sociologist's perspective, for example E. Burgess (1886–1966), H. Hoyt (1895–1984), C. Harris (1914–2003), and E. Ullman (1912–76). Burgess developed his *zonal* or *concentric-ring model* in 1925, Hoyt developed his *sector model* in 1939, and the geographers Harris and Ullman developed their *multiple-nuclei model* in 1945. Although all three models were based on US cities of the times and thus tended to *describe what was* rather than *analyse its dynamics*, Burgess's model is particularly noteworthy in that it allowed for *zones of transition* between urban land uses.

10.4 A firm's bid-rent curve

Let us now see how a bid-rent curve and a rent-gradient for a firm are arrived at. Towards this end, we need to determine the maximum land rent that a local-market-oriented firm relying on non-transferable inputs would be prepared to pay in order to carry out production in a way that satisfies the firm's RRR. The idea here is that the output produced is not sold on the spot, where the land is, but elsewhere. This precludes, say, housebuilding from our consideration. Development-cum-building activity was discussed in Chapter 7. What we *will* discuss, further below, in this connection is how a residential bid-rent (or bid-price) curve is determined.

Regarding firms there are three possibilities:

1. A constant-revenue firm. This implies an iso-elastic demand curve with $\varepsilon = -1$. Total revenue would be $PQ = \mathrm{TR}^*$ (where the asterisk indicates constancy).
2. A variable-revenue, constant-price firm. This implies that Q varies, that demand is perfectly elastic with $\varepsilon = \infty$, and that there is pure competition. Total revenue would be $P^*Q = \mathrm{TR}$.
3. A variable-revenue, variable-price and variable-quantity, firm. This implies a down-sloping demand curve of varying elasticity. Since price $P = d - eQ$ (with d, e being vertical intercept and slope, respectively, of the demand function), total revenue would be $PQ = (d - eQ)Q = dQ - eQ^2$.

10.4.1 A constant-revenue firm

Let us start with an expression for the firm's RRR, or k:

$$k = \frac{\mathrm{TR} - \mathrm{TPC} - mDQ - R}{\mathrm{TPC} + mDQ + R}, \tag{10.1}$$

where

TR	=	total revenue (constant),
TPC	=	total production cost (but excluding rent or transport cost),
m	=	transport cost per unit per mile,
D	=	distance from relevant location (say, a CBD),
R	=	rent,
Q	=	quantity produced.

Then

$$R = \frac{\text{TR} - (1+k)(\text{TPC} + mDQ)}{1+k}. \tag{10.2}$$

If Q, and therefore P, are given (so as to maintain a constant TR), Equation (10.2) doubles as the firm's *bid-rent curve*. The reason is that in such a case each D would define the maximum rent that the firm can pay for location D miles from the city core, and still enjoy a RRR $= k$.

The change in R when D changes is measured by the derivative of R with respect to D, so

$$\frac{dR}{dD} = -\text{mQ} = \text{rent-gradient}, \tag{10.3}$$

which, if Q is standardized to 1, becomes

$$\frac{dR}{dD} = -m. \tag{10.4}$$

This simply suggests that as distance increases, rent decreases, and vice versa (see Table 10.1 and Figure 10.4).

To understand what a bid-rent curve means, consider the change in rent between, say, 4 and 5 miles from the CBD. It is, of course, $732 - 872 = -140$. At the same time, the change in the cost of transport is

$$\begin{aligned}
&\text{at 5 miles, cost of transport} &= (0.5)(280)(5) &= 700,\\
&\text{at 4 miles, cost of transport} &= (0.5)(280)(4) &= 560,\\
&\text{change in transport cost} &= &\quad +140,
\end{aligned}$$

In other words, what the firm gains by locating nearer the CBD, it loses by paying a higher rent!

Table 10.1 Relationship between rent R and distance D from a CBD, given a firm's TR, Q, TPC, RRR, and m

				Rent-gradient	
		Distance from CBD (in miles)	*Rent*	*slope of $R = f(D)$*	*$dR/dD = -mQ$*
TR	2500	0	1,432		–140
TPC	800	1	1,292	–140	–140
m	0.5	2	1,152	–140	–140
D		3	1,012	–140	–140
Q	280	4	872	–140	–140
R		5	732	–140	–140
k	0.12	6	592	–140	–140
		7	452	–140	–140
		8	312	–140	–140
		9	172	–140	–140
		10	32	–140	–140
		10.228	0.22	–140	–140

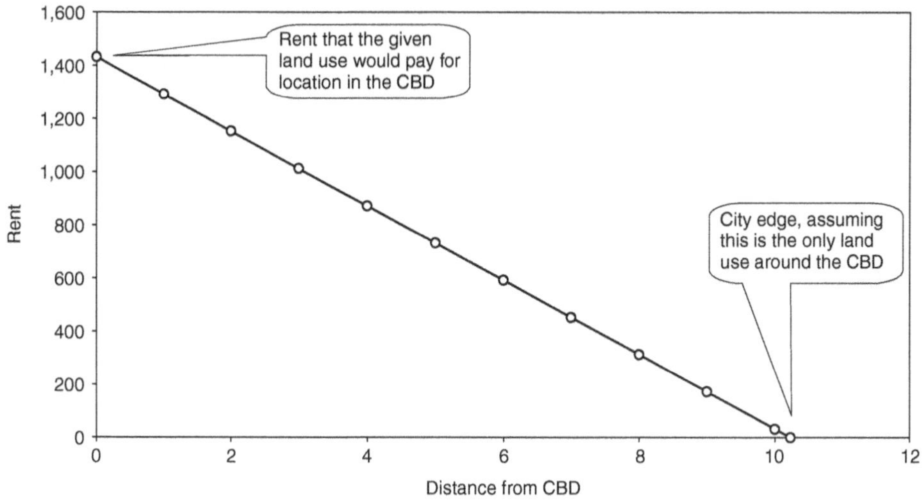

Figure 10.4 A typical bid-rent line, holding everything else constant.

Moreover, if we assume that this is the only land use around the CBD, and that it extends to the same radius to all directions, the total area of the city is found as

$$A = \pi D_m^2 = 3.14(10.2) = 326.7 \text{ square miles,} \tag{10.5}$$

where D_m = maximum distance from the CBD at which the given use can be found (as beyond 10.2 miles from the CBD land has no value, no use, and rent would turn negative).

10.4.2 A variable-revenue, constant-price firm

Given

RRR	=	k = required rate of return, $k \geq 0$,
P	=	product price,
Q	=	product quantity,
F	=	fixed cost per unit of land,
m	=	product transportation cost per quantity unit per mile,
D	=	distance from relevant location (e.g., a market),
R	=	rent per unit of land,
a, b	=	variable-cost parameters, $a > 0, b > 1$,
$F + aQ^b$	=	total production cost (TPC), not including transportation cost and R,

we have

$$R = \frac{PQ - (1+k)[F + aQ^b) + mDQ]}{1+k}. \tag{10.6}$$

Then the bid-rent curve and the rent-gradient are[4]

$$R = a(b-1)\left[\frac{P - mD(1+k)}{ab(1+k)}\right]^{b/(b-1)} - F \tag{10.7}$$

and

$$\frac{dR}{dD} = -m\left[\frac{P - mD(1+k)}{ab(1+k)}\right]^{1/(b-1)} < 0 \quad \text{as expected.} \tag{10.8}$$

Numerical example

Assume

$$P = 100,$$
$$k = 0.08,$$
$$a = 1.2,$$
$$b = 2.2,$$
$$m = 4,$$
$$D = 10,$$
$$F = 50.$$

Applying Equation (10.6), we find the rent that will be paid when the firm locates at a given D, say 10 miles, from the CBD, and, given price, produces different quantities. As Figure 10.5 shows, rent is maximized at 12.1 units of output, at a value of 297.1. The curve in Figure 10.5 is not the bid-rent curve, though, because it does not show the maximum rent that can be paid at different Ds from the CBD. It only shows the rent that is paid at a given D for each level of output.

Applying Equation (10.7), we find at last the maximum rent that can be paid at various distances from the CBD. Expectedly, when $D = 10$, maximum rent is 297.1 and $Q = 12.1$. The resulting curve is the bid-rent curve for the given firm (see Figure 10.6).

Thus, if this firm produces around 12 units of output, faces a price of approximately 100 and unit transport costs per mile of 4, and has an RRR of 8 per cent as well as the TPC function described above, it should locate at about 10 miles from the CBD. The reason is that on the basis of the information mentioned (12 units of output, etc.) the maximum rent that the firm can pay and still realize an 8 per cent RRR is just that which allows location at 10 miles form the CBD.

Of course, variations in price and hence in output happen all the time; in the farming sector, in particular, variations in industry output first, and then in price, are frequent due, for example, to weather conditions. While it is true that firms do not adjust their location due to chance or temporary price or cost variations because such moves are usually very costly, they will nevertheless move if substantial changes in product price, or transport costs, or in the RRR, persist – or if a firm's size changes.

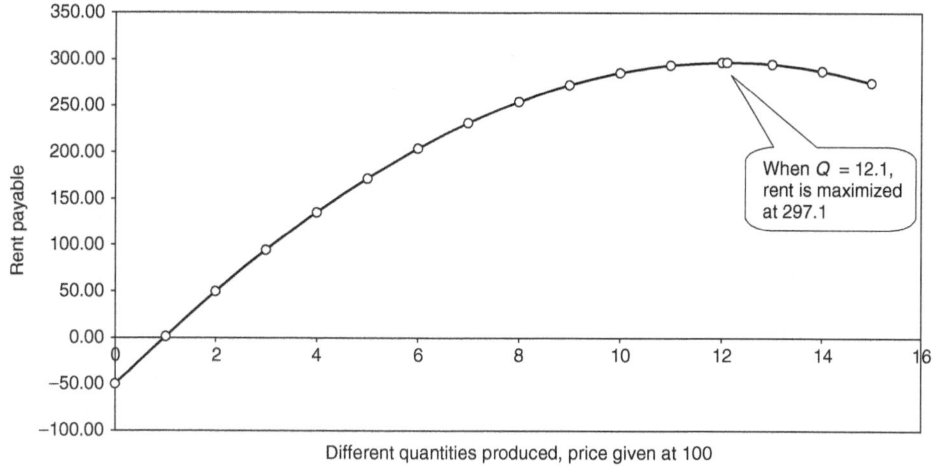

Figure 10.5 Rent payable at a distance of 10 miles from CBD when different quantities are produced.

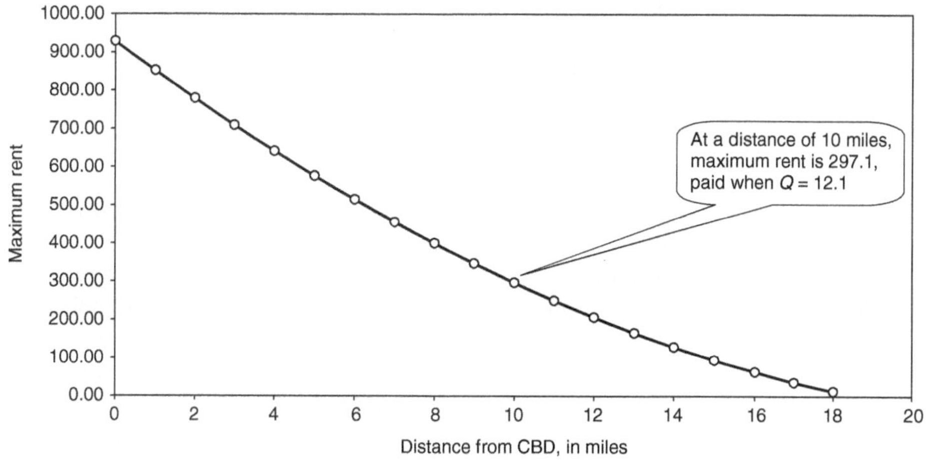

Figure 10.6 Bid-rent curve for given firm: maximum rent payable at different distances from CBD.

10.4.3 A variable-revenue, variable-price, and variable-quantity, firm

Deriving the bid-rent curve and rent-gradient for this case is left as an admittedly tedious exercise for the student. The treatment of case (b) above and the Appendix at the end of this chapter should be enough help. Just set TR equal to $dQ - eQ^2$.

10.5 A household's bid-price curve

There are various ways to go about this.[5] One way is to use De Bruyne and Van Hove's (2006) model of housing demand, presented in Section 7.3.1. Recall that, according to that model,

$$P_h = (1-\beta)\frac{\text{income} - (1-\delta)T}{H} = (1-\beta)\frac{\text{income} - (1-\delta)mD}{H}, \tag{10.9}$$

where

P_h	=	price of housing;
β	=	a positive exponent of the quantity of non-housing consumption, but excluding leisure, in the Cobb–Douglas household utility function adopted in the model; the higher β is, the smaller the housing price as households exhibit stronger preference for non-housing (i.e., amount of leisure time if one lives in the urban periphery but works in the core *plus* other non-housing consumption);
δ	=	proportion of people who, while living in the periphery, also work in the periphery; thus $1-\delta$ is the proportion of people who, while living in the periphery, work in the core;
T	=	cost of commuting to the core (which, with given commuting cost per travel unit, depends only on distance from the core; hence, $T = mD$, where m = unit cost of commuting, D = distance from city core);
H	=	quantity of housing consumed; it can be standardized to 1.

Taking the derivative of P_h with respect to D, we have

$$\frac{dP_h}{dD} = -\frac{(1-\beta)(1-\delta)m}{H}. \tag{10.10}$$

Because $(1-\beta)(1-\delta)$ is positive (since β and δ are percentages, and there will always be some periphery-living workers who also work there), (10.10) is negative.

In other words, (10.9) is not only a housing demand function but can also be interpreted as a bid-price function, and (10.10) is the price-gradient. Table 10.2 shows a numerical application of (10.9) and (10.10). Remember that a fundamental assumption of a Cobb–Douglas utility function is that houses and households are homogeneous, so what is valid for one is valid for all. It is this assumption that allows us to treat (10.9) as the households' bid-price function when we take income as given. As a result, we do not have to plug into (10.9) the number of houses in the area, or a figure for aggregate household income; the quantity of housing can be standardized to one, and the income of any household should be enough.

10.5.1 A more traditional approach

Just like De Bruyne and Van Hove's model, the classical approach to residential bid-curves assumes that houses and households are homogeneous. It then sets up household utility as a function of distance:

$$U_{(D)} = U_{(C,H)}, \tag{10.11}$$

where

C	=	non-housing consumption, represented by a composite (or 'numeraire') good,
H	=	housing quantity consumed.

Table 10.2 Households' bid-price curve, based on De Bruyne and Van Hove's (2006) model

		Distance from city core	*Price of housing*	*Price–gradient* = $-[(1-\beta)(1-\delta)m]/H$
β	0.6	0	8,560	
Annual income of single (typical) household	21,400	1	7,990	−570.24
H = quantity of housing, standardized to 1	1	2	7,420	−570.24
m = unit cost of commuting, i.e., annual cost of one-mile, two-way travel to the city core	1,620	3	6,849	−570.24
δ	0.12	4	6,279	−570.24
		5	5,709	−570.24
		6	5,139	−570.24
		7	4,568	−570.24
		8	3,998	−570.24
		9	3,428	−570.24
		10	2,858	−570.24
		11	2,287	−570.24
		12	1,717	−570.24
		13	1,147	−570.24
		14	577	−570.24
		15	6	−570.24

In turn,

$$C = Y - T_{(D)} - P_{h(D)}H, \tag{10.12a}$$

where

Y = income,
T = travel (i.e., commuting) cost as a function of distance D from city core,
P_h = price of housing as a function of distance D from city core.

We can also view $Y = C + T_{(D)} + P_{h(D)}H$ as the household's budget constraint.

Notice that Equation (10.12a) can be transformed into

$$P_h = \frac{Y - C - T}{H}, \tag{10.12b}$$

which can be interpreted as a household's bid-price function, just like Equation (10.9) above. Substituting (10.12a) into (10.11), we have,

$$U_{(D)} = U(Y - T_{(D)} - P_{h(D)}H, H). \tag{10.13}$$

The first-order condition for utility maximization demands that we set the derivative of $U_{(D)}$ equal to 0. Thus, by the chain rule of derivation (see Section 2.1.1),

$$\frac{\partial U}{\partial D} = \frac{\partial U}{\partial C}\frac{\partial C}{\partial D} = \frac{\partial U}{\partial C}\left(-\frac{dT}{dD} - \frac{dP_h}{dD}H\right) = 0. \tag{10.14}$$

Because $\partial U/\partial C > 0$ (as people have to consume some other goods and services in addition to commuting and housing), for (10.14) to be zero it must be true that

$$-\frac{dT}{dD} = \frac{dP_h}{dD}H, \tag{10.15a}$$

which is the only requirement for utility maximization in the context of the household's location problem. Put differently, the change in utility a housing consumer experiences as a result of a change in non-housing consumption will imply maximum utility if (10.15a) holds. For this to happen, an increase in commuting cost must be matched by an equal decrease in the price of housing (assuming that H is standardized to one), and vice versa. This is shown more clearly if (10.15a) is written as

$$dP_h = \frac{-dT}{H}. \tag{10.15b}$$

Further assuming that $T = mD$ (where m = unit commuting cost per mile),

$$-\frac{dT}{dD} = -m. \tag{10.16}$$

Hence,

$$\frac{dP_h}{dD} = -m, \tag{10.17}$$

again assuming that $H = 1$. So the price-gradient (the slope of price with respect to distance) is negative, as already shown in Equation (10.4).

10.6 How bid-curves help create a land-use pattern

It is now time we brought together our analyses of firms' and households' bid curves. To this end, let us put in the same diagram the bid curves from Tables 10.1 and 10.2. Notice that because Table 10.1 referred to a firm's bid-*rent* curve, we had to capitalize the (annual) rents into *prices* (i.e., land values) by dividing it by an appropriate capitalization rate, and thus make them comparable with the housing prices of Table 10.2. We took that rate to be 12 per cent, which may have been the banks' lending rate (as opposed to a savings deposits rate of, say, 8 per cent. Moreover, we assumed that the firm in question is representative of its industry. The results are shown in Table 10.3 and Figure 10.7.

The prices plotted on the vertical axis are basically land prices. Buildings may be assumed to be homogeneous in the context of each use, and subsumed under land prices, i.e., it is land prices rather than building prices that determine land uses. In the firms' case, both land prices (or rents) and building prices (or rents) are fixed costs (i.e., they do not depend on output once a firm's bid-curve and location have been determined), only a land price (or rent) is found here as a residual, after all other costs have been accounted for. In the households' case, the land-related part of housing price is likewise the residual part, the rest reflecting the construction cost of largely homogeneous buildings.

It is obvious from Figure 10.7 that from a land price of about 12,000 down to 'conversion point' C_1, land use by the given industry dominates residential use; firms can pay more

Table 10.3 Bid-curves from Tables 10.1 and 10.2

Distance from city core	*Firm's bid-rents from Table 10.1*	*Capitalized rent at*	*Household's bid-prices from Table 10.3*
		0.12	
0	1,432	11,935	8,560
1	1,292	10,768	7,990
2	1,152	9,601	7,420
3	1,012	8,435	6,849
4	872	7,268	6,279
5	732	6,101	5,709
6	592	4,935	5,139
7	452	3,768	4,568
8	312	2,601	3,998
9	172	1,435	3,428
10	32	268	2,858

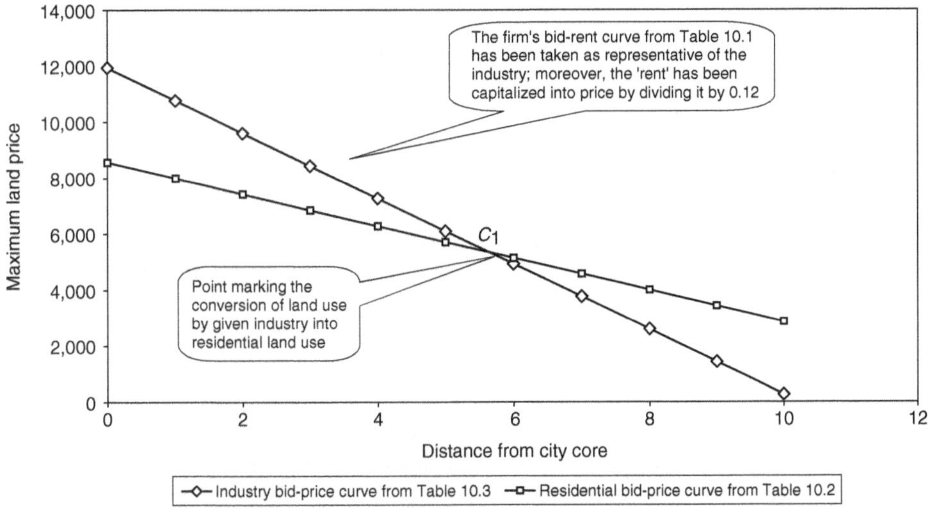

Figure 10.7 Putting together two bid-price curves.

than households for location near the city core. From conversion point C_1 downwards, residential use dominates; households can pay more than firms, so they'll take up the respective land.

How do we find the conversion point precisely? It is simple. From Table 10.3, we know (with some minute differences due to rounding) that the firm's bid-price equation is $P_f = 11{,}935 - 1167D$ and that the household's bid-price equation is $P_h = 8560 - 570D$. At the conversion point C_1, the prices must be equal, so solving this equation system for distance, we get $D = 5.65$.

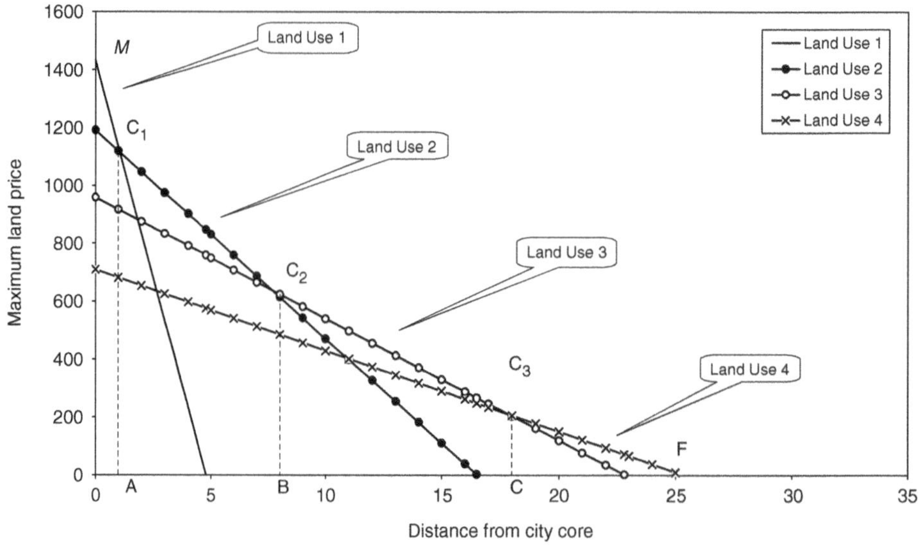

Figure 10.8 Four land uses giving rise to four different bid-price curves.

This pattern can be extended by the addition of quite a few land uses. This is shown in Figure 10.8.[6]

1 Land Use 1 dominates Land Use 2 from the globally highest land price *M* down to conversion point C_1. This corresponds to zone 0A around the city core.
2 Land Use 2 dominates Land Use 3 from conversion point C_1 down to conversion point C_2. This corresponds to zone AB around the city core.
3 Land Use 3 dominates Land Use 4 from conversion point C_2 down to conversion point C_3. This corresponds to zone BC around the city core.
4 Land Use 4 dominates from conversion point C_3 down to globally lowest land price F. This corresponds to zone CF around the city core.

Assuming that these zones truly encircle the city core, it is now possible to calculate the area of each. For that, we need to know the equations of the bid-price (or bid-rent) lines in Figure 10.8. In reduced form, these are as follows:

$$\text{for Land Use 1,} \quad R = 1432.1 - 300D;$$

$$\text{for Land Use 2,} \quad R = 1190.7 - 72D;$$

$$\text{for Land Use 3,} \quad R = 959.3 - 42D;$$

$$\text{for Land Use 4,} \quad R = 709.4 - 28D.$$

From these, it transpires that the coordinates of the various conversion points in Figure 10.8 are as follows:

$$\text{for } C_1, \quad (1.1, 1114.1);$$

$$\text{for } C_2, \quad (7.7, 636.3);$$

$$\text{for } C_3, \quad (17.8, 211.7).$$

Thus, the area covered by, say, Land Use 3 (between conversion points C_2 and C_3) is

$$A_{LU3} = \pi(17.8)^2 - \pi(7.7)^2 = 995 - 186 = 809 \quad \text{square miles,}$$

or 40.2 per cent of a total city area of $\pi(25.3)^2 = 2010$ square miles.

10.7 A bid-curve for all land uses in an urban area

It is often useful to create a total bid-price, or bid-rent, curve for an entire urban area, or for a cross-section of it. Such information enables planners or investors to have an idea of the related spread of land values over an area or decide where to locate, respectively. We could also say that, while the bid-curves in Figure 10.7 and 10.8 represent a bottom-up approach to location in space and land rent or land price formation (in which the rent or price are arrived at as residuals), a total bid-curve allows a top-down approach. For example, faced with an existing total bid-curve, i.e., an existing pattern of land values, a firm will decide where to locate by taking the rent or price in that location as given rather than as a residual.

Using the example of Figure 10.8, a quick way to go about creating such a curve is to take the maximum price (or rent) point, the minimum price (or rent) point, and the conversion points in-between. This exercise would yield the coordinates already found in the previous section plus (0, 1432.1) and (25.3, 0). Any good statistical package or MS Excel will fit a line to those data points, which will serve as the sought bid-price (or bid-rent) curve. Such a line may have the general form

$$P(\text{or } R) = b_1 e^{-b_2 D_i}, \tag{10.18}$$

where $e =$ the base of natural logarithms ≈ 2.71828, and D_i is the ith distance from a city's core. The line actually calculated here (defined as $P = 1366.8763e^{-0.110463352D_i}$) has been superimposed on the distinct bid-curves of Figure 10.8, and is shown in Figure 10.9.

The total bid-price (or bid-rent) curve is obviously nonlinear (cf. Brown, 2005: 7–8). The same is actually true of the bid-price (or bid-rent) curves for distinct land uses, as in real life there is heterogeneity between firms and between households or houses. Of course, a real-life bid-curve would need to be based on actual price or rent data as one goes outwards from a city core. A total bid-curve would have to be fitted on such data.

10.8 Land value taxation[7] (LVT)

We have explained how land values and a concomitant pattern of land uses, are created. It is only appropriate that we now discussed whether such land values ought to be taxed.

'Land value taxation is an annual tax on the market rental value of land' (Maxwell and Vigor, 2005: 5), and is not supposed to be applied on buildings or other improvements on the land (hence the split-rate property tax system in some US jurisdictions). The story of proposals to tax land goes back a long way (cf. Netzer, 2001), and stars very prestigious and influential proponents: Adam Smith (1776), Henry George (1879), Winston Churchill (1909, quoted in Barker, 2003: 116), Milton Friedman (Nobel laureate, 1976), William Vickrey (Nobel laureate, 1996),[8] and John Muellbauer (of Oxford University). Many local authorities in the USA actually use a two- or split-rate property tax (one on land, one on buildings,

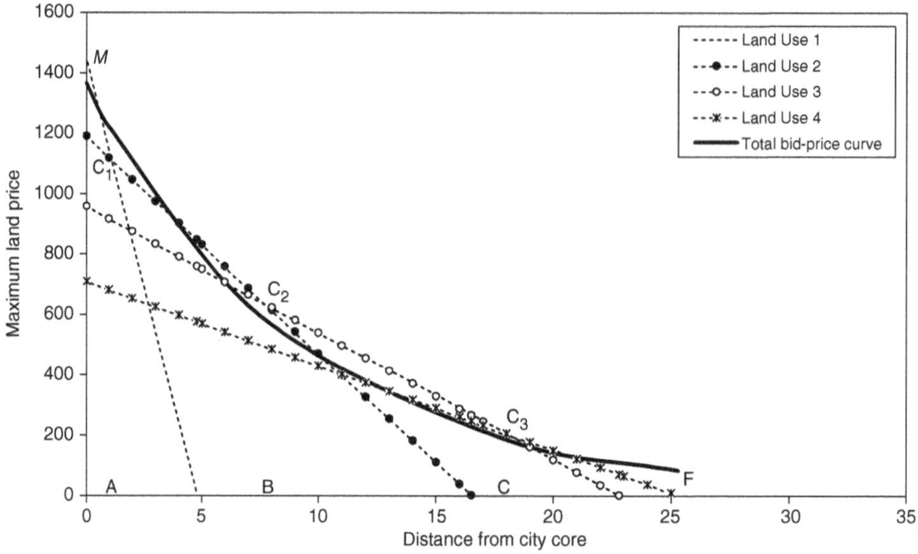

Figure 10.9 Bid-price curve for an entire city or a cross-section of it.

unequal to one another), and so do more than 700 cities worldwide.[9] In the UK, there have been weak forms of land value taxation (LVT), like development land tax and planning gain contribution, while parties like the Scottish Greens (Whitman, 2010) and some UK Labour politicians (under the Labour Land Campaign – Jones, 2008) also advocate LVT.

Some of the arguments advanced in favour of LVT rest on mostly ethical grounds, and rather flimsily at that;[10] others are intellectually robust (Muellbauer, 2005), forming part of careful and balanced approaches to overall taxation reform. For example, Muellbauer's proposals for the UK are (a) to scrap the Council Tax and replace it in part by a local income tax and in part by a 'reformed national property tax with uniform national rates indexed to local house prices' (Muellbauer, 2005: 111), and (b) to reform the Uniform Business Rate,[11] 'shifting half the basis for valuation away from business assets to land above some minimum value per hectare' (p. 112) and excluding farmland.

Five of the more robust arguments in favour of LVT are as follows:

1 Landowners contribute nothing to the value of land (which is determined exogenously), so land value should in fairness be taxed.
2 Public works paid by the public purse often create a windfall gain for private land owners in certain localities; an LVT is a good way to 'claw back' for the state some of the uplift in land values that this way private persons enjoy but have not created.
3 There will be no adverse economic consequences if land value is taxed, since land will still be there after the tax.
4 LVT will in fact encourage more efficient land use since it will make it costly to landowners not to make land available for its highest and best use.
5 An LVT will reduce or even eliminate land speculation and any concomitant RE price bubbles.

These are discussed in Section 10.9. But first let us explain a few things.

10.8.1 Preliminary remarks

To simplify the ensuing analysis, we shall be using the following two equations linking the value of RE (e.g., a land plot) to annual net rental income R from it and to the owner's, or a prospective user's/investor's, RRR (k for short):

$$V = \frac{R}{k} \quad \text{(value without taxation, rent received forever),}$$

$$V_t = \frac{R}{k+t} \quad \text{(from Equation (9.1) in Section 9.3; value with taxation, } t \text{ being a tax rate on the value of the property).}$$

Suppose $R = £7000$, $t = 2$ per cent, and $k = 6$ per cent. Then

$$V = \frac{7000}{0.06} = £116{,}667 \quad \text{and} \quad V_t = \frac{7000}{0.08} = £87{,}500,$$

where $V = £116{,}667$ is the pre-tax current value of the land but is also the PV of net incomes from the land received by the landowner in the land's current use.

A 2 per cent tax rate applied on the land will reduce its post-tax value to £87,500. But the tax rate is nominally applied on the pre-tax value of the land, so the tax is £2333. This means that, in relation to the PV of incomes before the tax, the annual after-tax income presently received implies a rate of return r equal to

$$r = \frac{7000 - 2333}{116{,}667} = 4 \text{ per cent}$$

(And even if the denominator is the post-tax value of the land, i.e., £87,500, then $r = 5.3$ per cent rather than 6 per cent.)

Because r is less than k, the landowner cannot/will not continue with the current use of the land or with the given plot. She will seek another investment alternative for her money and time, if for no other reason than that before the tax she was earning £7000 from the land (which was the minimum required), and after the tax she is earning £4667 only. If another use can be found that can yield a 6 per cent return or more (or maybe another user who can achieve 6 per cent or more), fine; otherwise, the land will be abandoned. In such a case, LVT will have reduced the quantity supplied of land; economically, the given land plot will have vanished!

Now suppose that the landowner sells the land, with no change in use, to another user, whose RRR is also 6 per cent. Because of the tax, the new user will only give $V_t = £87{,}500$ for the land. Assuming that the LVT is always applied on the current value of the land, the tax burden on the new user is $£87{,}500 \times 0.02 = £1750$. He will bear a tax, which reduces R, but has also paid less for the land. His RRR is preserved:

$$r = \frac{7000 - 1750}{87{,}500} = 6 \text{ per cent.}$$

We could present the landowner's problem in absolute terms too: before the tax, she is making £7000 – let us say it is the minimum required to keep her on the land. After the tax, she moves away – unless a buyer is found for whom a return equal to $£7000 - £1750 = £5250$ is just acceptable.

Notice that in this case LVT has not led to an improved land use. It has only led to a change of ownership. It is just that the landowner, instead of getting £116,667 for the land, has only got £87,500. She has in effect 'lost' £29,167, which, incidentally, is the capitalized value of the new user's tax burden: 29,167 = 1750/0.06. The landowner has merely absorbed the tax levied on the new user.

Changing tack a little, consider the following three cases involving a landowner who, overwhelmed by LVT, is thinking of selling his land to one of two interested users, each representing a different land use:

(A) Same pre-tax values, same tax rate (2 per cent), different RRRs, different *R*s:

$$\text{Land use X:}\quad V = \frac{10{,}000}{0.06} = 166{,}667,$$

$$V_t = \frac{10{,}000}{0.08} = 125{,}000;$$

$$\text{Land use Y:}\quad V = \frac{5000}{0.03} = 166{,}667,$$

$$V_t = \frac{5000}{0.05} = 100{,}000.$$

Here both uses have the same PV of expected pre-tax net incomes from the land, even though the annual net incomes differ; what makes the PVs equal to one another is the fact that the two users each has a different RRR, which doubles as a discount rate. Unsurprisingly the higher-income use is characterized by a higher RRR, probably due to the higher-income use being riskier.

Even though the two uses imply the same pre-tax land values, the after-tax values differ – and it is the after-tax value the landowner will pocket upon selling the land. A rational landowner will therefore choose to sell the plot to user X. Importantly, use X is also the 'highest' of the two since it attracts the highest income. So in this case LVT has favoured the land going to the 'better' use (which is also the riskier, though).

(B) Different pre-tax values, same tax rate (2 per cent), different RRRs, different *R*s – but the difference between the *R*s is now smaller than before:

$$\text{Land use X:}\quad V = \frac{10{,}000}{0.06} = 166{,}667,$$

$$V_t = \frac{10{,}000}{0.08} = 125{,}000;$$

$$\text{Land use Y:}\quad V = \frac{7000}{0.03} = 233{,}333,$$

$$V_t = \frac{7000}{0.05} = 140{,}000.$$

Here the landowner will sell the land to user Y, on account of the higher V as well as V_t the latter is prepared to pay. But use Y is inferior to use X since it creates a smaller annual net income! In this case, LVT has failed to favour the 'better' use.

(C) Same post-tax land values:

$$\text{Land use X:} \quad V = \frac{10{,}000}{0.06} = 166{,}667,$$

$$V_t = \frac{10{,}000}{0.08} = 125{,}000;$$

$$\text{Land use Y:} \quad V = \frac{5000}{0.02} = 250{,}000,$$

$$V_t = \frac{5000}{0.04} = 125{,}000.$$

Here the landowner is indifferent, *ceteris paribus*, between the two prospective users. LVT will favour one or the other of the two uses on a chance basis.

The above discussion allows us to make the following points:

1 A new LVT levied on a landowner who is just earning a RRR from the land will cause the post-tax rate of return on the land to drop below the RRR. The land will then be abandoned, or will undergo a change of use or ownership.
2 A change of ownership due to LVT does not necessarily imply a 'better' (i.e., higher-income yielding) use for the land.
3 In the act of selling the land, it is the previous owner – the seller – who absorbs the LVT in the form of a reduced land price received. (This point may have to be qualified if we look not just at a single plot, but at all plots suitable for a given use, and assume an upward-sloping land supply curve; in such a case an LVT may burden both seller and buyer – see Section 10.8.2.)
4 LVT will not/cannot automatically ensure that in all cases land will go to the best use from among available alternatives. The reason is that land values do not depend only on expected pre-tax net incomes from land (possibly associated with different uses), but also on different RRRs characterizing different uses and users – and, mostly due to the problem of risk, there is no clear-cut or linear connection between expected incomes and RRRs.

10.8.2 Tax incidence and deadweight loss (DWL)

In the absence of taxation, an equilibrium price means maximum *consumer surplus* and *producer surplus*, given market conditions. Consumer surplus is the benefit accruing to consumers as a group from the fact that when their behaviour is described by a downward-sloping demand function, they pay less for a good than what they would have been willing to pay. Producer surplus is the benefit accruing to producers as a group from the fact that when their behaviour is described by an upward-sloping supply function, they receive a higher price from the sale of a good than the price at which they would have been willing to sell the good. The sum of consumer and producer surplus is society's welfare gain from buying and selling at equilibrium. This is shown in Figure 10.10.

In Figure 10.10, equilibrium in a tax-free competitive market is at E_1, corresponding to price P_e and quantity Q_e. Consumer surplus is the area underneath the demand line and along the line P_eE_1.

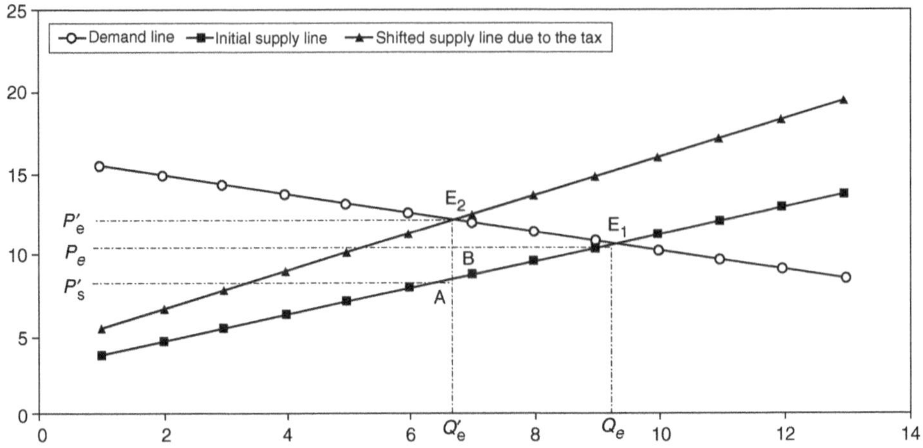

Figure 10.10 Tax wedge and deadweight loss due to an *ad valorem* tax applied on the supply side.

Suppose now that an *ad valorem* tax (i.e., a percentage of the value of the taxed item) is applied. In a competitive market, the effect of the tax is to raise the supply line, or lower the demand line; either will do. If the tax is statutorily applied on producers (sellers), the supply line will rise, as producers (sellers) will try to recoup their revenue by raising their ask price by the amount of the tax. Since, in this case, the tax is a percentage, the new supply line tilts in relation to the initial supply line. The result is a new equilibrium at E_2, with a new price P'_e and quantity Q'_e. In effect, suppliers will now be selling a smaller Q than before (which is no wonder, since they have raised P, trying to shift the tax burden onto consumers). By producing Q'_e, sellers will be selling at P'_e but receiving P'_s, the difference being the tax. This is the *tax wedge*. By selling less than before, sellers have managed to shift onto consumers part of their statutory tax burden. (See the Appendix to Chapter 9 for a numerical example.)

The post-tax consumer surplus is just the area under the demand line and along the line P'_eE_2; producer surplus is the area above the initial supply line and below the line P'_sA. Tax revenue is the rectangle$P'_eP'_sAE_2$. Assuming that taxes have provided services to society of commensurate value, society has nevertheless lost an amount of welfare equal to E_2AE_1. This is a *deadweight loss*, because it is welfare lost to consumers, lost to producers, and certainly lost to the government. Not surprisingly, the DWL corresponds to the reduction $Q_e - Q'_e$ in equilibrium quantity brought about by the tax.[12]

Part of the tax reduced consumer surplus by the rectangle $P'_eP_eBE_2$, and the other part reduced producer surplus by the rectangle $P_eP'_sAB$. In this case, the second rectangle is obviously larger than the first, so most of the tax burden must have fallen on the supply side of the market. In general (and excepting special situations),

- Taxes reduce consumers' and producers' welfare.
- Additionally, taxes create a net welfare loss for society (the DWL).
- The actual incidence of a tax is not necessarily the same (and usually is not) as its statutory incidence.

Actual incidence depends on a number of things, chiefly the kind of market in question, and the elasticities of demand and supply (see, again, the numerical example in the Appendix to Chapter 9).

Thus, if supply were perfectly inelastic, all of the tax burden would fall on sellers. More importantly, there would be no DWL for society. Why? Because in such a situation the fixed quantity could only be sold at whatever the demand-driven price happened to be – there would be no reduction in quantity. The prime example of perfectly inelastic supply is of course land – in the sense of a truly unique plot or site.

But if the supply of land can be viewed as an expanding collection of sites capable of satisfying demand for a given use, and potentially drawn from other land uses, then the supply line would be *upward-sloping*. This could happen in either a competitive land market (if potentially available plots are numerous and also reasonably homogeneous from the point of view of the intended use), or in a monopolistically competitive land market. The second alternative is more realistic, on account of the heterogeneity of land. This heterogeneity, however, is less than the one manifested in combinations of land and improvements, like buildings. The result of an LVT would then be some DWL, a sharing of the tax burden between land buyer and land owner/seller, and, crucially, some reduction in the quantity supplied of land.

10.9 Critical appraisal of arguments favouring LVT

10.9.1 Argument 1

> *'Landowners contribute nothing to the value of land (which is determined exogenously), so land value should in fairness be taxed.'*

Let us deal first with the correct suggestion that land values are determined 'exogenously'.

Changes in the value of land are determined by overall social and economic development processes. So does the value of labour and of capital, however – it is just that because land in specific areas or sites is in short supply (maybe even unique), and certainly is not mobile, it can be affected to a greater extent, more obviously, and in a more concentrated manner by such processes. Most categories of labour in the developed world are now earning higher real wages than they were earning 100 years ago. This is due both to the bigger quantities of a larger assortment of goods and services modern economies produce, and to higher productivity, both in specific sectors and overall. Some people of course are poor, and some workers are made redundant – but then some land too may and does lose value.

Thus, the value of *all* resources is determined 'exogenously'; land is not special in this regard.

More to the point, a buyer of land lends it value precisely because he commits funds to it. Equally, a young person lends value to her 'labour power' through paying for education (and sometimes it is the state – the taxpayer – that foots the bill); naturally in expectation of gain, but also in risk of not realizing that gain. An inheritor of land may not have committed funds; but she evaluates, weighs and compares opportunities for gain, committing the land to its 'highest and best' use (provided the return is satisfactory), exactly like an investor.[13] That is a useful, even critical, function, which cannot be undertaken very efficiently by government officials (which they would try to do if land were nationalized, as extreme proponents of LVT have in mind).

It is worth reiterating here conclusion (6) reached in Section 7.8.3 in connection with construction, namely that the landowner has a much more active role in development than is commonly thought: by trying to maximize land price, and resisting development at the 'wrong' land-price range (i.e., outside the 'negotiation range' between landowner and developer), she, no less than the developer, makes sure that land goes to its highest and best use (subject to the outcome of negotiations).

Notice the 'satisfactory return' factor mentioned above. To have any chance of realization, any prospective use of land needs to promise a higher return than the return from its current use. The latter may conceivably mean no use at all – an uncultivated piece of agricultural land owned by an absentee landlord, a brownfield site, or an abandoned downtown tenement. Even then, it is not assured that any odd return will be enough to bring that land into use. Things are not that simple, because any use of the land will require it to be combined with capital–labour–entrepreneurial ability. Yet any investor with command over such bundles of resources will almost certainly face many different investment options – so the prospective return on the given piece of land will need to be at least as high as the current acceptable return on equivalent resource bundles in order for investment in the given piece of land to be considered. If not, the given land will be 'lost' to the economy (at least for a while): economically, it will not exist.

We can link this observation to a more detailed account of the landowner's function. Investments involve potential combinations of resources: land–labour–capital–entrepreneurial ability. The cost of those resources – as well as their profit potential – must be signalled to investors. The *institution* of the private ownership of land (which is inevitably embodied into landowners themselves) serves precisely this function: to allow generation of accurate such signals (reflecting relative scarcity) on the basis of which

(a) investors will combine land parcels (representing *in toto* an array of locations with particular cost and profit profiles) with other resources in the most profitable way, and
(b) consumers and, in general, land users will make location choices.

Government allocation cannot do that very well (as it cannot do it in relation to any other resource when it is used for the creation and allocation of private goods), even though government can, must, and does intervene in the land market for other reasons (e.g., externalities). Without those private signals, efficient, or near-efficient, allocation of land resources cannot take place, and investments will probably be both fewer than otherwise and misallocated on the map. Not taking this into account is the hole in the proposal that with state ownership of land, '[p]eople and businesses could be charged rent for the land that they occupy based on its value' (Jones, 2008: 7): i.e., with state ownership of land, the value of land would be much, much lower – possibly even unknowable – than with private landownership as misallocation of land resources and waste would be much, much greater. And with lower land values, revenue from LVT would be lower also.

Thus, in executing their role as generators of appropriate land-price signals, landowners (whether as recent buyers of land or as stewards of inherited land) commit funds, take risks, bear opportunity costs, and facilitate the land allocation process. So they do contribute something after all – and naturally expect rewards.

For this reason, an LVT, if imposed at all, must not be as high as to discourage the 'best' use of land (in an opportunity cost sense) – and certainly not as high as to discourage *any* private use of the land. This would be the case if LVT were 100 per cent of all possible rental income from land, or of the land price, and would of course amount to nationalization.

If, on the other hand, land did not produce a rental income or utility for someone, an LVT would be a disincentive to holding land (whether this is a good or bad thing, is discussed further below), and might even be impossible to pay out of (other) current income. In short, if an LVT deters use of land resources – and to the extent it does – some land will be lost economically. Even if 'land loss' were not large, '[l]andowners would respond to the tax by devoting fewer resources to improving their land' (Mankiw, 1998: 164) – after all, a large part of the value of land comes from improvements, in addition to location.

The above analysis hinges on an important assumption: that land ownership is sufficiently distributed among the population. If there is too much concentration of land ownership (as in the case of *latifundia*[14] in South America or feudal remnants in some other countries), there will be no competition to generate sufficiently many or accurate signals about the true cost or profit potential of different sites, at least in socially beneficial ways. A wide distribution is much better, provided it does not hamper economies of scale, or production involving indivisibilities.

What the correct distribution is, one cannot easily tell: it is like asking what the correct size of the public sector should be. Barring extremes, there is no single correct size, as the answer depends on the nature of the economy and society in question, on the tasks and kinds of services a government is called upon to perform or offer, etc.

10.9.2 Argument 2

> *'Public works paid by the public purse often create a windfall gain for private land owners in certain localities; an LVT is a good way to "claw back" for the state some of the uplift in land values that this way private persons enjoy but have not created.'*

The following is a very apposite example: 'Costing £3.5 billion of public money to build, a [Transport for London]-commissioned report suggested that around Canary Wharf and Southwark tube stations alone, the up-lift in land value attributable to the [London's Jubilee Line Extension] was £2.8 billion[.] Other studies have put the overall up-lift figure along the whole extension nearer £10 billion' (Maxwell and Vigor, 2005: 2).

This of course is a special case of the 'exogenous' determination of land values already discussed. And, even though landowners in such localities pay taxes, they certainly pay far less than the money all taxpayers pay towards public projects. But is LVT the best instrument for capturing those *economic rents*?[15] One problem is that higher land values mean nothing unless they are turned into cash; which happens only at the moment a property is sold, i.e., precisely when the landowner has the doubtless ability to pay the tax, which then must be a capital-gains tax rather than an LVT! Otherwise, the latter would penalize people who may be 'enjoying' higher land values, but may not have asked for this benefit either – or have the ability to pay the tax.

10.9.3 Argument 3

> *'There will be no adverse economic consequences if land value is taxed, since land will still be there after the tax.'*

Already we have suggested that land can be 'lost', economically and at least temporarily. (The distinction between land's physical and economic presence should remind you of the one between a building's physical and economic life, discussed in Section 5.6.) Conversely, more land for a particular use can be found (by attracting it away from other uses) if the price is right.

Thus, if land for a certain use and in a certain area is characterized by an upward-sloping supply line, some land will be lost (economically) after imposition of an LVT, and probably after imposition of any property tax (since any property tax that is calculated on the basis of market prices includes a sizable LVT component). A loss will occur because the tax will interfere with current and expected rates of return on land. The extent of the loss (under imperfectly inelastic land supply) will clearly depend on actual land market conditions (elasticities and kind of market), and on the tax rates applied. Only if or when land supply becomes perfectly inelastic, will an LVT not reduce the quantity supplied of land. Paradoxically, the best way a government has to ensure such a reduction does not happen is by artificially stopping increases in the quantity supplied of land, for example by having a very restrictive planning function, so that sooner rather than later all land suitable for a certain use is taken up!

If there is perfect inelasticity of land supply (e.g., in downtown built and lived-in areas), then there may not be adverse economic consequences in the sense that the quantity supplied of land will not diminish. But what about the land that is *not* forthcoming exactly because of planning restrictions, or because of the LVT itself? In addition, there may well be human and social, i.e., welfare, consequences if there are owners who cannot pay the LVT. To avoid such consequences, an LVT may have to involve such low rates that it may be much ado about nothing. Once again – as suggested in Chapter 9 – income taxation would be better.

10.9.4 Argument 4

> *'LVT will in fact encourage more efficient land use since it will make it costly to landowners not to make land available for its highest-and-best use.'*

It is true that any LVT (or other recurrent property tax) represents an opportunity cost to the land owner: if she does not earn an income from the land, or sell it to someone who can (or whose utility from the land and/or their ability-to-pay is greater than that of the current owner), she will still have to pay LVT. The latter has the undoubted potential to change land uses – but will that be a good thing in all cases?

It is clearly good in cases of abandoned or brownfield land – provided better uses or more efficient users can be found. Otherwise, an existing owner will be burdened to no good effect, or the state will confiscate or purchase compulsorily the land if the owner will not or cannot pay the LVT.

Such cases must be balanced against possible broader effects or aspects of the LVT, for example the possibility of some land being lost economically, of LVT distorting land uses worse than a tax-free land market does, or of LVT being more difficult to pay, or collect, than other property, or indeed income, taxes.

Of course, LVT, in the sense of a disincentive to holding vacant or inferior land, would encourage more capital to be combined with land – but if the market offers opportunities, a developer or an owner would not need 'negative' encouragement in the form of LVT. And we have already shown in Section 10.8.1 that a change of use due to LVT is not necessarily for the better, as the following two contrasting cases demonstrate:

(A) *Harrisburg, capital of Pennsylvania.* In 2008, the UK's Labour Land Campaign touted Harrisburg as evidence that LVT works. Indeed it can, if one considers as evidence of working the inevitable fact that an LVT will burden vacant or derelict land with an obvious and very real opportunity cost.

> 'In 1982 [before the city more than doubled the tax rate on land in the context of its split-rate property tax system] Harrisburg, with a population of 52,000, was listed as the second more run-down city in the US. Since then, following the change, empty sites and buildings have been re-developed, with the number of vacant sites by 2004 down by 85 per cent. [...] More recently, the bias towards tax on land is now six to one [T]he heightened economic activity [...] has increased quite dramatically both the value of land and that of buildings'.
>
> (Jones, 2008: 9)

This is not bad. But was all that due to the land tax bias – especially if one takes into consideration the mentioned uplift in RE prices as well as the fact that Harrisburg's population between 1990 and 2010 stayed practically constant at around 50,000? Or the fact that Harrisburg had 4200 vacant structures in 1982, whose number was down to 500 by 1995?[16] Could the Harrisburg 'miracle' have been due to other factors? (Cf. Cohen and Coughlin (2005: 367–71).) Obviously, the LVT must have raised the cost of holding land vacant. But how could it create profitable alternatives? How could it do so when the local population stagnated? And how, moreover, could it lead to higher RE prices? There is a paradox here: without an increase in population, an LVT 'incentivized' development and created an uplift in land values. One then wonders what would have happened *without* the LVT! (Finding out what really may have caused the Harrisburg 'miracle' is left as an exercise for the student.)

(B) *Campos,an area to the north of Khios, capital of same-name Greek island.* Campos is practically located within the island capital. It comprises orchards and old houses and mansions, many of which – and the families living there – go back hundreds of years. It is a beautiful and historic place listed by the Ministry of Culture. Yet the Ministry of Public Finance applies recurrent and steep wealth taxes, as well as high inheritance taxes, on those properties, considering them urban (i.e., developable) rather than what they are: agrarian estates of special character and significance.

Naturally, their owners, since they do not exploit the estates financially, find it hard to continue paying the taxes, or secure the properties for their children. Yes, they could probably sell to wealthy Greeks or foreigners; or turn the estates into hotels – but at the cost of the destruction of a traditional community and their own way of life. Under the circumstances, who is going to tell whether a change of land use, or even a mere change of ownership, is somehow more socially beneficial than the utility loss those people are likely to experience – or than the external cost of a historic community forced to dissolve?

10.9.5 Argument 5

> *'AN LVT will reduce or even eliminate land speculation and any concomitant RE price bubbles.'*

This argument is part of a broader issue concerning the efficacy of using taxes as 'automatic stabilizers' in order to thwart RE price bubbles. The issue is addressed in detail in Sections 11.7.2 and 11.7.3. Although there the focus is on capital-gains, rather than land-value, taxation, the main conclusions should hold as follows. Fundamental demand and supply factors coupled with speculation are the main force pushing for rises in RE prices. Any tax intended to act as an 'automatic stabilizer' will tend to be either ineffective or likely to discourage healthy asset-price increases (because such increases are actually needed for growth-promoting investment), or require fiddling by the authorities (in which case the tax will be anything but an 'automatic stabilizer'), or increase turbulence in the RE market.

10.9.6 Concluding remarks

The Campos case (mentioned in Section 10.9.4) may be generalized by saying that an LVT 'would penalise the "asset-rich cash-poor", such as pensioners'. In response, it has been suggested that those people could be allowed 'to defer the tax liability until death'[17] and moreover 'should face the real opportunity cost of continuing to live in large houses' (Maxwell and Vigor, 2005: 8). This is disturbing. An abandoned and derelict downtown tenement is an obvious candidate for a change of use, usually involving redevelopment. But owner-occupied properties? Implying that somehow people should be punished for their (legal) utility choices through subjecting them to government-orchestrated actual and opportunity costs smacks of paternalism (to say the least). So does the other suggestion made above, namely that it is somehow alright to place extra burdens on the inter-generational transfer of wealth. Is it not better to let people, whether they have bought or inherited property, dispose of their own assets as they see fit rather than in reaction to government dicta made obligatory because they are cast in the form of taxes?

One might object to the tone of this question by pointing out that in a democracy, 'government dicta' reflect people's choices made through the voting process. This is simply untrue. In most elections, lesser issues are overshadowed by bigger ones; there is, moreover, an array of multiple issues supplying criteria for vote-casting. As a result, voters' preferences are not going to be consistent over different issues (cf. Arrow, 1951). More simply, if citizens vote for party or candidate A because they like their stance on an issue deemed terribly important, they will disregard A's stance on a 'minor' issue like, say, LVT – even though they may be against LVT.

A plebiscite (involving a 'yes' or 'no' answer to a single question) is of course much more straightforward a process. Going down this road, however, especially if a tax is portrayed as a 'fair' burden on the rich rather than on all, runs the risk of encouraging populism. The 'poor' will always be more than the 'rich'. Penalizing the latter, and in particular exposing them to the whims of fickle majorities, will play havoc with incentives to work–innovate–risk–invest–save (W-I-R-I-S).

That leaves 'dollar' votes as another way to express people's choices. It is not a failsafe process either – far from it! Its advantage is that it emphasizes the bottom-up creation of individual preferences rather than the top-down management of such. There are limits to either approach, usually involving serious externalities. In my view, however, forcing people out of their homes (including, yes, their second ones), or children out of their parents' homes, is just such a limit. This of course is a value-judgment.

In short, rather than imposing an LVT on all and sundry, it might be better to deal with cases like Harrisburg on an *ad hoc* basis. Such cases would predominantly be abandoned or derelict land, would have to be evaluated in view of a creditable and clear higher use, and would have to involve compulsory purchase (probably at pre-development value) and an auction process. In addition, if an LVT (or any other recurrent property tax) is to be imposed at all, special care should be exercised not to tax people out of their homes through the tax being too high in relation to income, and not to frustrate the process of inheritance. By default, then, income taxation, and capital-gains and sales taxation, appear much better options than recurrent property taxes, including LVT.

10.10 Economic rent from land

In everyday usage, rent is the periodic payment made to the owner of a property (a land plot or a building) for use by someone else.

Economic rent, however, is anything over and above *transfer earnings*, which are what a factor of production must earn to prevent it from moving to an alternative use (Sloman, 1991: 274).[18] Applying this distinction to land, and ignoring utility considerations, we could say that the landowner's transfer earnings (TE) are the minimum return he can secure from the land – which can mean either the return on the least profitable use of the land or the minimum return on a given use. If he can secure a higher return than that, the difference is considered economic rent (ER).

The practical import of the distinction between ER and TE is that, cast as an economic argument, it has been employed in politically motivated demands to introduce LVT. The argument is that if economic rent is more than what is necessary to keep the land in a given use, it may be possible to tax away the entire economic rent of land without affecting the quantity supplied of it (George;[19] Foldvary, 2006a).

This argument, however, rests on the assumption that the supply of land is perfectly inelastic. As such, it is problematic.

Let us take first an example (Sloman, 1991: 274) involving labour rather than land. If there is increased demand for, say, nurses (i.e., there is relative scarcity of nurses), new nurses will be attracted to the profession through higher wages; but wages will also rise for older nurses, who had joined the profession when the wage was lower – that wage was the TE of the older nurses. The additional wage older nurses will be now earning – a wage that was not necessary to keep them in the profession – is ER.

By the same token, a rise in demand for land will raise its value over the minimum that was necessary to keep the land in a certain use, thus creating ER for the landowners. Here is the purported difference between nurses and land. Nurses are a variable factor of production: more pay – more nurses; less pay – fewer nurses. Land, though, is supposed to be fixed. This assumption is a hole in the argument about LVT.

For if the supply of land is imperfectly inelastic (i.e., if the quantity supplied of land is variable rather than fixed), then a higher value, notwithstanding the fact that it creates ER for existing landowners, also attracts more (probably sub-standard) land to the given use, or transfers land to a higher use. Indeed, it is precisely the creation of ER for existing landowners that allows the 'generation' of more land. Take this away in the form, say, of taxation (whether of nurses' pay or of land values), and there will likely be less of the factor available, always depending on how scarce the latter is *in practice*. Reasons for this are (cf. Section 10.8.1) as follows:

- LVT on land whose owner is just earning a RRR will cause either abandonment of the land or a change of use or ownership.
- Abandonment or a change of use will mean less land for the given (the pre-existing) use.
- A new use – if such can be found – will not necessarily be a 'better' use – it may well be a riskier one, though.

- That leaves change of ownership as a factor that can possibly secure continuation of the given land use (if such is desirable).
- Yet a touted benefit of LVT is that it helps divert land to 'better' uses rather than effect merely a change of ownership. Moreover, an interesting implication of 'just' a change of ownership is that land for the given use is preserved, but there is less land for another, probably 'better', use!
- An LVT, by reducing post-tax returns on *all current* land uses, will probably make it more difficult to utilize sub-standard (i.e., low-quality) land, exacerbating any land scarcity problem there may be; on the other hand, it may act as an incentive to combine more capital with land, i.e., effect a more intensive use of land.

There is more. From a dynamic perspective, the minimum reward at which a factor of production will start becoming available will probably not stay fixed once a higher price is established and becomes the norm (remember, any price higher than the minimum involves creation of ER). Sooner or later, the minimum reward will rise, and the part of the supply line *below* the 'established' higher price will shift upwards and become more elastic. In Figure 10.11, this is shown as a shift of the supply line from P_{mr1}E to P_{mr2}E. As a result, if in the meantime there have been no increases in demand, TE will increase and ER will diminish.

The process holds for land too – with a twist. In the case of land, the process will continue until all land suitable for a given use has been utilized; at that 'saturation' point, the supply line *above* the 'established' higher price becomes vertical (see Figure 10.12), as no more land is presently forthcoming. Further increases in demand can then result in creation of ER only. This seems to justify LVT; but perfectly inelastic land supply is rather exceptional. Moreover, to the extent that LVT may interfere with land market efficiency on the way to 'saturation' (which is precisely what we have suggested in Section 10.9.1), it may cause more harm than good.

In Figure 10.12, P_{mr1} is the price consistent with the minimum required return on land initially; if that is not secured, the land is not utilized – economically, it vanishes. Land price is P_{e1}. Because of that difference, ER is created, equal to area *b*, with *a* being TE. The

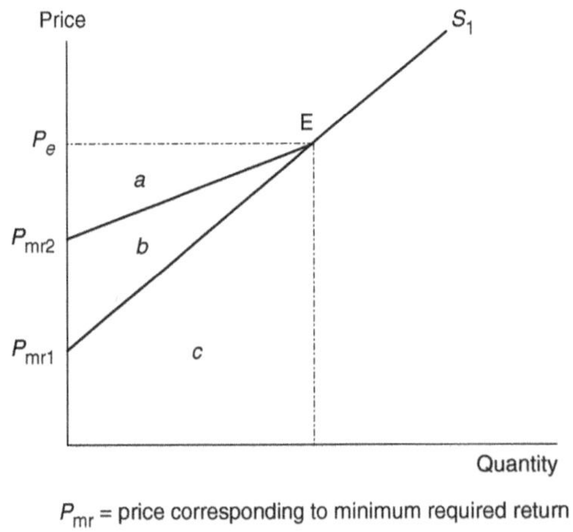

Figure 10.11 Economic rent (ER) and transfer earnings (TE). Initially, ER $= a+b$, TE $= c$. After P_{mr} rises, ER $= a$ and TE $= b+c$.

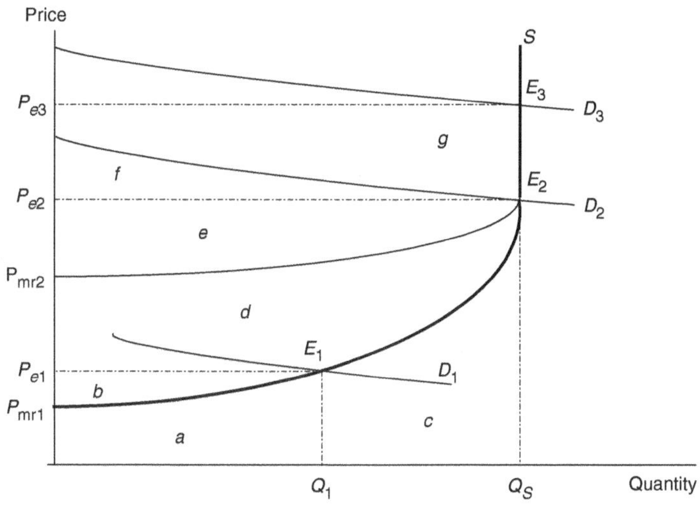

Figure 10.12 A dynamic view of economic rent (ER) from land. Only after all land suitable for a given use has been utilized will further increases in demand just create more ER, and the possibility of some of the additional revenue becoming transfer earnings (TE) vanishes.

equilibrium quantity of land is, at this point, Q_1. In time, increases in demand cause price to rise to P_{e2}, corresponding to quantity Q_s – beyond which no other suitable land is available. At that point, ER $= b+d+e$, and TE $= a+c$. In time, also, P_{e2} becomes the 'normal', or 'established' price. As a result, P_{mr1} rises to P_{mr2}, and ER $= e$, TE $= a+c+b+d$.

But above the 'saturation' point P_{e2}, corresponding to the 'saturation' quantity Q_s, further increases in the price of land (say, from P_{e2} to P_{e3}) cannot 'create' more land; assuming that landowners can secure their minimum return price (which by now has risen further and become equal to P_{e2}), they can ask whatever price the market will bear: all of the additional revenue (area $f+g$) will be ER. Below P_{e2}, on the other hand, all revenue becomes TE.

In essence, therefore, the amount of ER will appear as a windfall gain for the landowner to the extent that a difference between the minimum return price and the actual price for land is maintained; but (inevitable) rises in the minimum required return (RR) will make ER diminish, increasing at the same time the amount of TE. This diminution of ER is depicted in Figures 10.13(a) and (b), which show how land value is split between an investor's (e.g., developer's) minimum RR, the landowner's minimum RR, and ER, which also goes to the landowner in the form of a windfall gain (rather than in the form of TE) as long as the landowner's minimum RR does not rise.

It is very likely to rise, though, either because 'higher' uses are found for the given land or because, in time, the minimum return price tends to approximate the actual land price as the latter becomes the 'normal' or 'established' price. ('Higher' land uses are those that yield more net income, and may well be associated with more risk.) With a rising RR, ER will begin to lessen until possibly it becomes identical with the landowner's minimum requirement for making the land available for the given use. A couple of assumptions behind this result are (i) that the 'saturation' point has not been reached and (ii) that for the time being there have been no further increases in demand. When, or if, ER has become identical with the landowner's

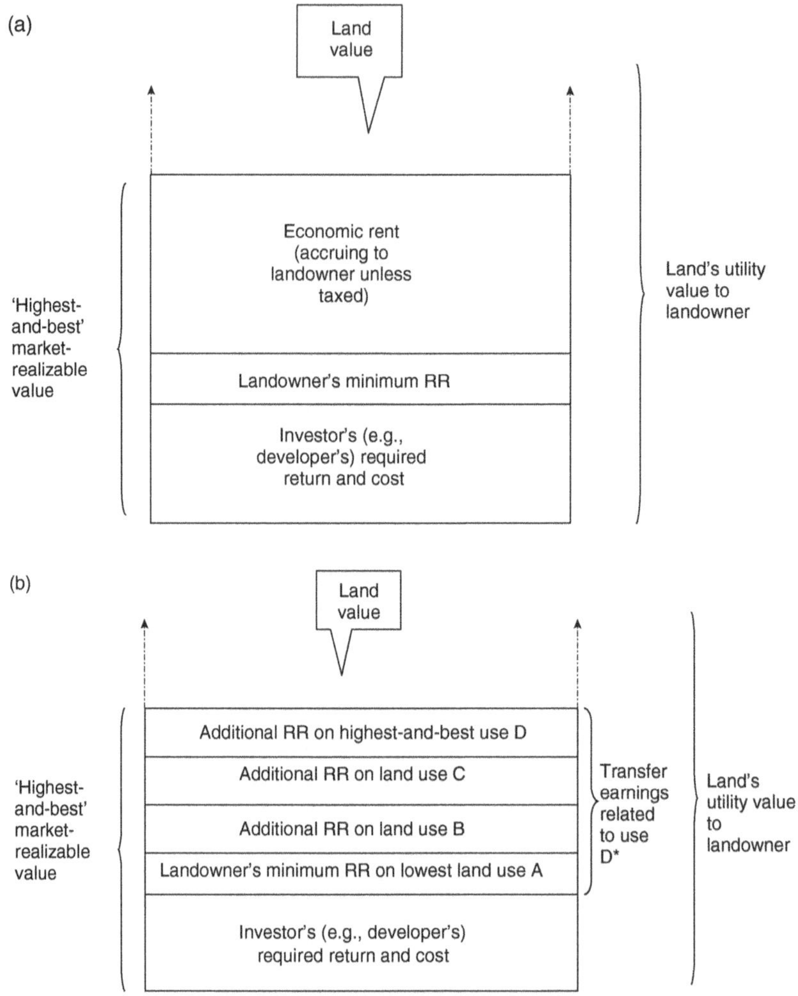

RR = required return. * If the price of land for use D has become the 'normal' or 'established' price, and therefore equals landowner's minimum RR.

Figure 10.13 Economic rent: (a) now it exists … (b) now it doesn't. (Figure inspired by Barker (2003: 116).)

minimum requirement, all of the landowner's return will be TE rather than ER. But if the two assumptions just mentioned do not hold, increases in revenue above the 'saturation' quantity Q_s will all amount to ER.

10.11 Appendix: derivation of bid-rent curve and rent-gradient when *Q* varies but *P* is given[20]

(This would be the case in pure competition – which suggests a perfectly elastic demand curve for the firm's output.)

Given

RRR	=	k = required rate of return, $k \geq 0$,
P	=	product price,
Q	=	product quantity,
F	=	fixed cost per unit of land,
m	=	product transportation cost per quantity unit per mile,
D	=	distance from relevant location (e.g., a market),
R	=	rent per unit of land,
a, b	=	variable-cost parameters, $a > 0$, $b > 1$,
$F + aQ^b$	=	total production cost (TPC), not including transportation cost and R,[21]

we have

$$\text{RRR} = k = \frac{PQ - (F + aQ^b) - mDQ - R}{(F + aQ^b) + mDQ + R}$$

$$= \frac{\text{revenue} - \text{TPC} - \text{transport cost} - \text{rent}}{\text{TPC} + \text{transport cost} + \text{rent}}.$$

If k is given, then the level of R that would satisfy the above equation is

$$R = \frac{PQ - (1+k)\left[(F + aQ^b) + mDQ\right]}{1+k}. \tag{10.19}$$

What is now required is to find the level of Q that would maximize R while preserving the firm's RRR. The reason is that the more R a firm can pay, the 'better' a location it can afford to bid for. 'Better' of course can have many meanings, especially – but not exclusively – as regards households' choices of residential location. In the case of firms, 'better' is usually taken to mean distance from a market, or, in classical formulations, from a CBD.

To find the rent-maximizing level of Q, we first need to find the first derivative of R with respect to Q. This is the so-called first-order condition for an extreme value of the function $R = f(Q)$. Then we need to find the second derivative of $R = f(Q)$. If the second derivative is negative, then setting the first derivative equal to zero and solving for Q will give us the value of Q that maximizes R:[22]

$$\frac{dR}{dQ} = \frac{P - (1+k)[abQ^{b-1} + mD]}{(1+k)}, \tag{10.20}$$

$$\frac{d^2R}{dQ^2} = ab(1-b)Q^{b-2}. \tag{10.21}$$

But $d^2R/dQ^2 < 0$, because $1 - b < 0$. This means that setting $dR/dQ = 0$ and solving for Q will indeed yield the value of Q that maximizes R:

$$\frac{dR}{dQ} = \frac{P - (1+k)[abQ^{b-1} + mD]}{1+k} = \frac{P - abQ^{b-1} - kabQ^{b-1} - mD - kmD}{1+k} = 0$$

$$\Rightarrow P - abQ^{b-1} - kabQ^{b-1} - mD - kmD = 0$$

$$\Rightarrow -abQ^{b-1} - kabQ^{b-1} = -P + mD + kmD$$

$$\Rightarrow abQ^{b-1} + kabQ^{b-1} = P - mD - kmD$$

$$\Rightarrow Q^{b-1} = \frac{P - mD(1+k)}{ab(1+k)}$$

$$\Rightarrow Q = \left[\frac{P - mD(1+k)}{ab(1+k)}\right]^{1/(b-1)}. \tag{10.22}$$

The equation for rent is given in (10.19):

$$R = \frac{PQ - (1+k)\left[(F + aQ^b) + mDQ\right]}{1+k}.$$

Substituting the expression for Q from (10.22) into the above right-hand term, and, for the moment, ignoring $(1+k)^{-1}$, gives[23]

$$\begin{aligned}
&PQ - (1+k)aQ^b - (1+k)mDQ - (1+k)F \\
&= P\left[\frac{P - mD(1+k)}{ab(1+k)}\right]^{1/(b-1)} - (1+k)a\left\{\left[\frac{P - mD(1+k)}{ab(1+k)}\right]^{1/(b-1)}\right\}^b \\
&\quad - (1+k)mD\left[\frac{P - mD(1+k)}{ab(1+k)}\right]^{1/(b-1)} - (1+k)F \\
&= \left[\frac{P - mD(1+k)}{ab(1+k)}\right]^{1/(b-1)}[P - (1+k)mD] \\
&\quad - (1+k)a\left[\frac{P - mD(1+k)}{ab(1+k)}\right]^{b/(b-1)} - (1+k)F \\
&= \frac{[P - mD(1+k)]^{1/(b-1)}}{[ab(1+k)]^{1/(b-1)}}[P - (1+k)mD] \\
&\quad - (1+k)a\left[\frac{P - mD(1+k)}{ab(1+k)}\right]^{b/(b-1)} - (1+k)F \\
&= \frac{[P - mD(1+k)]^{b/(b-1)}}{[ab(1+k)]^{1/(b-1)}} - (1+k)a\frac{[P - mD(1+k)]^{b/(b-1)}}{[ab(1+k)]^{b/(b-1)}} - (1+k)F \\
&= \frac{[P - mD(1+k)]^{b/(b-1)}}{[ab(1+k)]^{b/(b-1)}}\left\{\frac{1}{[ab(1+k)]^{-1}} - a(1+k)\right\} - (1+k)F \\
&= \left[\frac{P - mD(1+k)}{ab(1+k)}\right]^{b/(b-1)}[ab(1+k) - a(1+k)] - (1+k)F \\
&= a(b-1)(1+k)\left[\frac{P - mD(1+k)}{ab(1+k)}\right]^{b/(b-1)} - (1+k)F.
\end{aligned}$$

Therefore, and bringing $(1 + k)^{-1}$ back in, the *bid-rent curve* is

$$R = a(b-1)\left[\frac{P - mD(1+k)}{ab(1+k)}\right]^{b/(b-1)} - F. \tag{10.23}$$

The change in R with respect to a change in D (= distance from market), or, in other words, the *rent-gradient*, is then given by the chain rule of differentiation as

$$\begin{aligned}\frac{dR}{dD} &= a(b-1)\frac{b}{b-1}\left[\frac{P - mD(1+k)}{ab(1+k)}\right]^{1/(b-1)}\left[\frac{-m(1+k)}{ab(1+k)}\right] \\ &= -m\left[\frac{P - mD(1+k)}{ab(1+k)}\right]^{1/(b-1)}.\end{aligned} \tag{10.24}$$

This is negative, implying that rent rises as distance drops, and vice versa.

Let us take a moment to interpret a, b, k, m and F:

- The parameter a is a productivity factor. Remember, we first encountered it in the production function TPC $= F + aQ^b$. The smaller it is, the smaller the production cost will be for any given level of Q. Therefore, the smaller it is, the higher the rent a firm will be able to pay.
- The parameter b is an intensity factor, showing the extent to which a firm is subject to diminishing returns. If it is greater than 1, production cost rises faster than output. Therefore, the smaller it is, the higher the rent a firm will be able to pay.
- k is the RRR; the higher it is, the smaller the rent a firm will be prepared to pay.
- Finally, the smaller F (= fixed cost) or m (= unit transport cost per mile) are, the higher the rent a firm will be able to pay.

Together, a, b, k, m, and F determine the rent-paying abilities (or profiles) of different firms and industries. It is plausible that differences among firms in the same industry will be smaller in terms of those parameters than differences among industries. If so, differential land uses should emerge, at different distances from a presumed central location, each characterized by users of different rent-paying capacities. Set along a bid-rent curve (and actually creating it), such uses would then generate a city's land-use pattern (if we also include groups of residential land users, who, as is well known, are heterogeneous).

Summary of main points

1. The land-use pattern represented by different cities tends to be canonical, giving rise to *urban hierarchies*, either within a country or even across countries.
2. The land-use pattern within a city also tends to exhibit a certain order, which is generally indicated by a bid-rent, or bid-price, curve for land.
3. A bid-curve shows the maximum rent, or price, that different firms (or groups of firms) or households (or groups of households) are prepared to pay for location at different distances from a point of maximum accessibility in an urban area.
4. The rent-gradient, or land-price-gradient, is the slope of a bid-rent, or bid-price, curve, and is negative, implying that land rents or prices decrease with distance from the point of maximum accessibility.

5 Bid-curves for different land uses intersect with one another. If two bid-curves did not intersect, one would dominate the other completely, and the superior land use would completely 'evict' the inferior land use from the area. The intersections represent 'conversion points' marking changes in land use across the cityscape or landscape.
6 The sum of bid-curves in an urban area gives rise to a total bid-curve for the entire area, which is made up of the globally maximum rent or price, the globally minimum rent or price, and the 'conversion points'. This in turn informs the location decisions of firms and households.
7 An LVT is likely to have a negative impact on the supply of land available or forthcoming for different uses. The reason is that land for any specific use is only under relatively rare circumstances perfectly inelastic.
8 This implies that the price of land is not always identical with economic rent, going to landowners as a windfall gain, but may well include transfer earnings, depending on the speed with which 'established' land prices become equated to landowners' minimum required returns.
9 In addition, an LVT would interfere with the price signals – reflecting relative scarcity – that the institution of private ownership of land generates and sends to the economy as to the 'best' uses of the land.
10 Finally, because high land values only become an advantage to landowners if they sell their properties, a capital-gains tax would be a more appropriate instrument than LVT to capture economic rent from land with. It would certainly be much easier to pay, and would probably distort land market price signals less than LVT.

Review questions and exercises

1 Define the following terms:

bid-rent curve
rent-gradient
LVT
hope value
deadweight loss

2 Choose a country and test whether the hierarchy of its 10 largest cities conforms to the rank-size rule.
3 Derive the bid-rent curve and rent-gradient for a variable-revenue, variable-price, and variable quantity firm. Use any appropriate total production function you like. Check your answers with a numerical example, and show your results diagrammatically.
4 Explain and replicate the classical bid-rent curve model for a typical household.
5 Collect data on rents or prices of properties from a city's core outwards. Construct a total bid-rent, or bid-price, curve.
6 Going back to Question 5: If you have collected a sufficiently large number of data, can you identify bid-curves for distinct land uses, for example office, residential (possibly with subsectors), retailing, and industrial? Do these land uses fall into a distinct land-use pattern around the city core? To what extent?
7 Prepare a report on reasons for the so-called Harrisburg 'miracle' (see Section 10.9.4). Was it due to LVT or to other factors? Be objective.
8 Prepare a statement arguing *in favour* of LVT. Suggested sources: Maxwell and Vigor (2005), Foldvary (2006a, b, 2007, 2010, 2011), Jones (2008), Wightman (2010).

Contrast with Hartwich (2006). Do your arguments meet the counter-arguments presented in this book?

9 Winston Churchill once thundered in the House of Commons (4 May 1909): 'the land monopolist … renders no service to the community, he contributes nothing to the general welfare, he contributes nothing to the process from which his own enrichment is derived' (quoted in Barker, 2003: 116). Critically evaluate.

11 Housing market bubbles

Main sections

Having gone through this chapter, a student should be able to

1 Explain how the burst of the US housing market bubble of 2006 led to the financial sector and credit-crunch crisis of 2008–09.
2 Describe conventional ways of assessing whether house prices are 'too high' or 'too low'.
3 Advance reasons why house-price bubbles and bursts *may* matter more to the wider economy than equity price bubbles and bursts.
4 List possible consequences of the burst of a house-price bubble.
5 Explain in particular possible interactions between the owner-occupied and the rented sectors following the burst of a house-price bubble.
6 Evaluate the possibility of forestalling the formation of housing market bubbles.
7 Assess the rationale and efficacy of using taxes as 'automatic stabilizers' in the housing market.
8 Explain how the behaviour of various 'actors' in the housing market may bring about a house-price bubble, and how a burst might then follow.
9 In this connection, explain the possible role of developers' RRR in determining their behaviour.

11.1 Asset-price bubbles

When discussing asset-price bubbles, one is greatly tempted to talk at length about business cycle theory (-ies) in general, RE cycles in particular, or the relationship between business and RE cycles. The topic of cycles, of asset-price bubbles and bursts and their aftermath, is wonderful and exciting because it lies at the heart of the operation and history of capitalism.[1] Reasons of space, unfortunately, preclude such a course. Some very introductory remarks should therefore suffice, with most of the subsequent discussion being focused on the 2006 US housing market bubble, its burst in 2007–08, and a stylized model of housing market volatility informed by that experience as well as by the recent related experiences of Ireland and Spain. The UK also began to experience house-price deflation as of 2008, but that was much milder than in the USA, Ireland, or Spain, even though the UK market, as in most other countries, was still bearish by 2012 (Allen, 2011).

11.1.1 Causes of bubbles – and bursts

Three asset-price bubble bursts of global significance have occurred so far. All of them resulted in severe recessions that were deep and prolonged enough to deserve being called 'depressions'. The first happened in 1873, involving stock markets and industries like railways. It started in Austria, migrated to the USA in the same year, returned to Europe, and the ensuing Euro-American depression lasted up to 1896 (cf. Musson, 1959). Another happened in 1929, involving the US stock market. It caused a depression that ended about 10 years later. The third happened in 2007–08, involving the US housing market and a number of others. It quickly led to a financial-system, and then a sovereign-debt, international crisis. In between the last two, the burst of the Japanese stock- and RE-market bubbles, in 1991, has been notable for the lingering, drawn-out recession it caused in Japan (Kanaya and Woo, 2000) rather than for any severe damage it caused internationally (Nakaso, 2001). At least, this pattern gives academics a long time to study both the causes of bubbles and their bursts, and the effectiveness of pre-emptive measures as well as remedial ones subsequently applied.[2]

Asset-price growth typically happens because of increases in demand in excess of increases in supply,[3] due, in the first instance, to 'fundamental' forces operating. In the case of housing, such forces are, for example, population growth or rising real incomes. Now, if people bought or built houses using only their accumulated savings from incomes earned, there would be little danger of a house-price bubble forming in the owner-occupied sector, and even less danger of a price 'correction' in such a market damaging severely the wider economy. The reason is that ability to pay would then be coterminous with the owner's financial resources, and would not be artificially extended, and made more precarious, by credit.

The danger would increase significantly, however, if, even in the absence of credit, the spending capacity of households were augmented by flows of financial capital from overseas or from other sectors of the economy (e.g., the stock market). But if the spending capacity of households were indeed fuelled by credit, then any house-price bubble formed would be larger than otherwise, and especially so in the presence of other inflows of capital, while its inevitable burst would pose a serious threat to the wider economy.

Examples of the effect of such capital inflows on asset, or on specifically house, prices are as follows:

- The bubble that burst in 1873 in the Vienna Stock Exchange had been partly stimulated by the war reparations France made to Germany (following Germany's victory over France in 1871).

- The strong growth of house prices in Greece from 1981 to 2009 was largely caused by overseas loans to finance persistent government budget deficits as well as by 'gifts' from Brussels, following Greece's EEC/EU membership.
- Complementing this, over the period 1985 Q1–2010 Q4 in Greece, Gounopoulos et al. (2012) identified both an inverse relationship between the stock market index and the housing price index, and a positive correlation between equity market volatility and change in house prices. This, they interpreted as confirmation of 'the substitute nature of stock market investment versus housing market investment'.
- In the USA, there were significant capital flows into the RE sector following the collapse of the dot.com bubble in 2002 (Hemmelgarn et al., 2011).
- On top of that, there were net inflows of portfolio investment into the USA over 1995–2006 that contributed to the US housing market bubble of the mid-2000s (Hemmelgarn et al., 2011: 4–5).
- An improvement in the terms of trade between a country and the rest of the world may also cause a housing boom–bust cycle if (a) households are uncertain about the duration of the improvement and (b) changes in the terms of trade act as exogenous shocks upon the country's economy (see Tomura (2008) on Canada's experience from the late 1990s to 2007, and also Tumbarello and Wang (2010) on Australia, New Zealand, and Canada). What happens is that the improvement raises households' incomes, which fuel housing demand, but because of the fickleness of expectations, 'house prices will abruptly drop when the terms of trade stop improving' (Tomura, 2008: 2). In general, housing booms and busts get larger, the better access to international financial markets an economy has, as, among others, such access allows increases in the loan-to-value ratio in the domestic mortgage market (Tomura, 2008: iii).
- Something similar to the Canadian experience happened in Ireland after 1987 and in particular between 1995 and 2007 (with a slowdown from 2001 to mid-2003): the so-called 'Celtic Tiger' years, which were characterized by inflows of investment from overseas and export-led growth in the 1990s, and increases in domestic demand in the 2000s (Malzubris, 2008). Those developments contributed to rises in Ireland's real disposable income per capita between 1996 and 2006 at a rate of 9.1 per cent, compared with 4 per cent in EU-15, higher than in any other industrial country (Malzubris, 2008). Income growth, in turn, combined with low interest rates, mortgage market deregulation, easing of credit standards, the tax-deductibility of mortgage interest, and demographic pressures (mostly from immigration), to allow unprecedented levels of housing investment (Malzubris, 2008), against a backdrop of people's strong preference for it. The result was a housing market bubble from 2000 to 2006.[4]

Thus, necessary conditions for an asset-price bubble are as follows:

1 The operation of 'fundamental' drivers – like real incomes – causing rises in demand in excess of rises in supply.
2 Rises in buyers' spending capacity in excess of what is justified by recent or current real domestic production and accumulated savings, which can happen either as a result of financial flows into the country or as a result of easy, or easier, credit.
3 Widespread preference for investment in the particular asset class.

Sufficient conditions would then be one or more of the following:

(a) That such credit be given recklessly, i.e., in disregard of a sufficiently large number of borrowers' intrinsic ability or inability to service loans given.

(b) That beyond some point, (reckless) credit, or other capital inflows, rather than 'fundamental' drivers, be the main factor behind price rises.
(c) That there be rising positive expectations of capital gains, culminating in a speculative wave in the market.

For a bubble to burst, what would then be required is one or more of the following:

(i) A negative change in expectations.
(ii) A reduction in credit (or other inflows).
(iii) A reduction in many households' ability to service mortgage loans, especially if such reduction materially jeopardized banks' net worth.
(iv) A large increase, or sustained increases, in supply.

An example: The Spanish property bubble – and burst

'The [Spanish] real estate boom refers to the development craze in which thousands of Spaniards clamored to construct more and more homes and office buildings throughout the country over the last 30 years. The government encouraged the practice and the banks issued significant mortgages and long term loans for prospective buyers. Foreign investment also increased, with many natives of Northern Europe buying up land. This craze inflated the economy, and proved an unsustainable model. Spanish real estate prices rose over 200 per cent between 1995 and 2007, rendering many developments unaffordable and many Spaniards stuck with loans they could not shake off. Mirroring a similar housing boom in the United States, in 2008 the Spanish bubble also burst painfully. The [quantity supplied] of homes greatly exceeded the [quantity demanded] and thousands of building projects were abruptly abandoned. Today, one finds deserted foundations [...] all over the country, some 25 per cent of all projects constructed between 2000 and 2010.'

Shaheen (2011)

11.1.2 The significance of credit

In confirmation of credit's significance, Leamer (2007) stressed that '[T]his time [i.e., during the early to mid-2000s US house-price boom] it has been self-collateralizing loans [i.e., loans that were given on the assumption that house prices would go on rising] and relaxed underwriting standards that have allowed borrowers with weaker credit histories and lower ratios of income to qualify to buy homes at inflated prices late in a housing expansion' (Leamer, 2007: 31). And Sorensen (2006), studying house prices in Norway (1820–2005), the Netherlands (1630–2005), the UK (1931–2005), and the USA (1851–2005), concluded that 'the main reason for the creation of bubbles has been identified as liberalization of credit'.

If people financed house purchases with savings, the rate of house-price growth would in the long run depend mostly and directly on the rate of growth of private savings and this, in turn, on the rate of overall economic growth. This would reduce the chances of sudden or large increases in demand for owner-occupied housing, and would allow housebuilders to estimate future price growth more accurately, thus better matching their housebuilding activity to forecast demand. This is a self-evident truth if future homeowners are also those who finance or carry out the building of their own homes.

If, on the other hand, credit were involved, the danger of a bubble would increase, but if borrowers had proven ability to service their loans and did not lose that ability over the life of the loan (which implies the prior application of good credit standards), the chances of a bubble forming would again be insignificant. In a context of savings-financed housebuilding, or of maintained banking-system health, any adverse consequences of a housing market downturn would mainly affect the housebuilding industry – especially that part of it that builds for an anonymous market. The wider economy would still suffer to some extent, but the important thing is for the banking system to have retained its soundness through observing appropriate regulations and practices.

In the meantime, people without enough savings would be housed in the rented sector. Here, unlike what might happen in the case of mortgagers defaulting on loans, drops in incomes would lead to drops in rents, but – again unlike what might happen with banks – landlords' losses would mostly stop there and would not jeopardize other people's wealth (e.g., savings deposits with banks). On the other hand, population pressures and/or rising incomes would drive rents up. This would eventually induce current or prospective landlords to place orders with housebuilders. The latter – unlike what happens with building for an anonymous homeowner market – would be unlikely to build rented housing for an anonymous landlord market, so overbuilding could only or mainly occur because of too many building orders coming from landlords.

If such orders were 'excessive', there would eventually be a correction in the market, and reduced housebuilding. Just as with building for an anonymous homeowner market, the greater the extent to which building dwellings for rent had been financed by credit, the greater the danger of wider repercussions in the case of a market downturn. But it is unlikely that prospective housing landlords would credit-finance the building of dwellings for rent to such an extent as to cause too large an oversupply. There are two reasons for this. One is prudence, as future returns would come from rents over long periods of time, rather than from imminent capital gains. The other is that, in the absence of housing speculation fed by the prospect of quick capital gains, it is easier, by and large, to forecast 'fundamentals'-based demand for either rented or homeowner residential accommodation than for, say, office or retail space.

11.2 Why housing market bubbles matter a lot

There are two reasons:

1 There is evidence that fluctuations in housing investment are the single most important factor affecting the onset of recessions, as well as of recoveries, in a modern developed economy – to such an extent that Leamer (2007) gave the title 'Housing *is* the Business Cycle' to his paper on the contribution of housing to US business cycles. In fact, Leamer (2007: 10, 13) has suggested that '[f]or long-run growth, residential investment is pretty inconsequential, but for the wiggles we call recessions and recoveries, residential investment is very, very important. [...] *Eight of the ten recessions* [in the USA from 1947 to 2006] *were preceded by sustained and substantial problems in housing*'. It would seem that what happens in the residential sphere is a good predictor of subsequent developments in the rest of the economy.
2 House-price bubbles are more destructive than, say, equity-price bubbles (Helbling and Terrones, 2003; Posen, 2009: 11–12) – i.e., when they burst, as, sooner or later, they

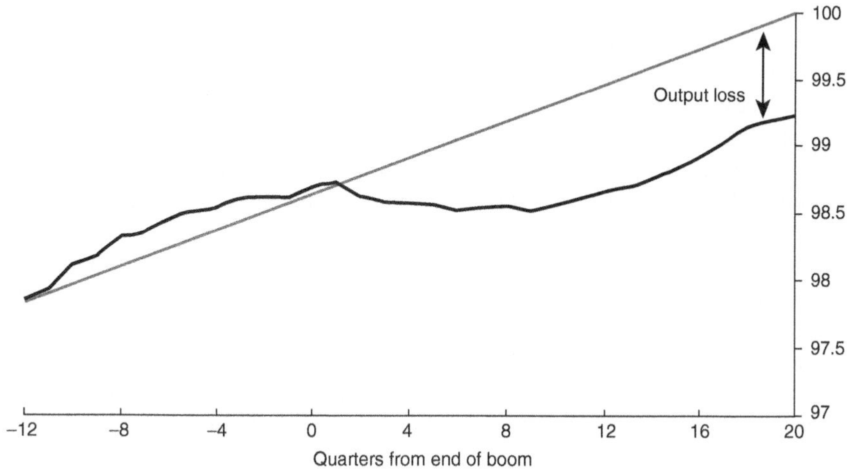

Figure 11.1 UK real GDP foregone due to end of a house-price boom, 1990 Q1. The pre-boom (straight-line) trend has been estimated up to quarter $t = -8$, and is extrapolated linearly thereafter.

(Source: Posen (2009: 25).)

must. A way to estimate the cost to the economy of the burst of an asset-price bubble is to compare output following the crest of the bubble to what it would have been if it had stuck to pre-crash trend (Posen, 2009: p. 11). Figure 11.1 shows this cost in regard to the UK house-price deflation that began in 1990 Q1, following a period of market expansion.[5]

Applying this method to a sample of 17 developed countries that experienced house-price booms after 1970, Posen (2009: 11, 25) concluded that '[T]he average output loss after real estate booms cumulates to over 5 per cent of GDP over five years [...]. If one performs the same exercise for equity price booms [...] there is no output loss on average over five years'.

On the other hand, the 1929 US stock market crash was pretty catastrophic too. Perhaps a reason why post-Second World War house-price booms and busts have been more damaging than equity-price booms and busts may be that equity-price booms are usually associated with the adoption of new technologies that have 'positive spillover effects on productivity' (Posen, 2009: 12). So when an equity-price bust comes, the technological effects are still there to push the economy forward – something that cannot be said of housing. Or, as is more likely, house-price busts are more damaging over the post-Second World War period because house-price booms tend to be fed by widespread credit to a greater extent than equity-price booms – just like the 1929 stock-price boom had been inordinately financed by credit (Galbraith, 1954; Kindleberger, 1978; but cf. White, 1990).

11.3 The US house-price bubble of 2006 – and its burst

By 2005, a worldwide house-price boom had been identified as history's biggest bubble (*The Economist*, 2005). At about the same time, Sorensen (2006) concluded that 'housing markets [in Norway, the Netherlands, the UK, and the USA] have become synchronized for the first time in history'. Such a concurrence could not have occurred without common factors at work, one of which, as already said, was credit liberalization internationally (Sorensen, 2006) Others were rising real incomes in most of the developed world, the rush to owner-occupy and government policies encouraging this, relatively low interest rates, perceptions of financial investment in houses as both safe and lucrative, and capital flows from abroad in many countries.

Yet for the burst of the US housing bubble to lead most of the international financial system to trouble, and to a credit-crunch crisis, something else was needed too: excessive interconnectivity between financial institutions (FIs) both domestically and across borders; extensive exposure of many FIs, both in the USA and abroad, to financial products largely and ultimately backed by US housing assets; and inability to price accurately such products or their individual risk, or evaluate the systemic risk they posed (Magnusson, 2008). These three factors, particularly the third, amounted to an increase in *asymmetric information*[6] between financial institutions and between the latter and other investors regarding trades in RE-based investment instruments, and became a major contributory factor to the crisis (cf. Mishkin, 2010: 199–221).

Increased asymmetric information meant that in the wake of the burst of the US housing bubble in 2007–08, many FIs, within and outside the USA, knowing that other FIs had been exposed to such products, whose (vaguely defined) values had just fallen dramatically, stopped trusting each other. This made them restrict lending, and a credit-crunch crisis ensued. Governments rushed in to prop up their faltering financial systems, thereby transforming national banking-system crises into sovereign-debt crises. The repercussions of this are still evolving, threatening the global economy and even the survival of the Eurozone.[7]

In essence, the story of the 2006 US housing market bubble is simple. Contextual or 'fundamental' factors (like rising incomes, employment patterns, desire to owner-occupy, and planning restrictions in certain jurisdictions) provided the backdrop. Not all of those factors worked the same way, or to the same extent, in all jurisdictions. For example, planning restrictions may have reinforced a bubble where other factors were present, as in California or Florida; or not, if they were not (see Section 11.4). Conversely, there were bubbles and subsequent crashes in cities (like Atlanta or Detroit) without significant planning restrictions.

Then came institutional or regulatory factors, the two most important of which were the following:

1 Relaxation of rules governing FI lending and other investment activities. For example, in 1999 the Gramm–Leach–Bliley Financial Services Modernization Act repealed the Glass–Steagall Banking Act of 1933 (which had been introduced in response to the 1929 crash and, among others, separated commercial banking from security investment activities): thereafter, banking and securities business could be pursued by the same institution. This increasingly exposed the deposit base of commercial banks to the risk represented by exotic investment products like MBSs (mortgage-backed securities), CDOs (collateralized debt obligations), and CDSs (credit-default swaps),[8] all of them fine examples of financial engineering.
2 Political support for expanding homeownership irrespective of potential problems. This was manifested, among others,[9] in government-sponsored enterprises extending (implicit) guarantees to buyers of MBSs, issued by the GSEs, which were backed by subprime mortgage loans. In a context of increased credit liberalization, this encouraged private lenders to extend mortgage loans to subprime borrowers, which led to a subprime

loan bubble, and in turn contributed to the overall housing market bubble.[10] As a result, '[s]ubprime mortgages rose from only 8 per cent of originations in 2003 to 20 per cent in 2005 and 2006' (Fernald, 2008: 2).

Those GSEs were the Federal National Mortgage Association (Fannie Mae, created in 1938) and the Federal Home Loan Mortgage Corporation (Freddie Mac, created in 1970), whose general remit was to buy mortgages on the secondary market, pool them, and sell them as MBSs – thereby increasing the funds available for mortgage lending in the US economy (cf. Tsounta, 2011). In 1992, the Housing and Community Development Act obliged them 'to facilitate the financing of affordable housing for low- and moderate-income families' and their consequent involvement with subprime mortgages began in 1995. The burst of the bubble in this market hit them hard, and early in September 2008 they were placed into *conservatorship* run by the Federal Housing Finance Agency.[11]

There were also *ad hoc* factors (cf. Hemmelgarn et al., 2011):

(a) Large net inflows of capital for portfolio investment into the USA after 1995.[12]
(b) Investors turning to RE in the wake of the dot.com bubble burst in 2002.
(c) The Fed gradually lowering the *Federal funds rate* from 6.54 per cent in July 2000 to 0.98 per cent in December 2003.[13]
(d) A rise in inflation from 1.55 per cent in December 2001 to 4.32 per cent in June 2006.

As the housing market bubble began to form, housing market speculation further inflated it, until the eventual pop was all the louder (cf. Ellis, 2008: iii). The burst came because

(i) The ratio of house prices to incomes had become too large: from 2000 to 2006, it rose to more than 4.5, way above its long-run historic average, which was a little less than 3.5 (see Figure 11.4).
(ii) The Fed gradually raised the *Federal funds rate* from 0.98 per cent in December 2003 to 5.25 per cent in August 2006.[14]
(iii) This contributed to a rise in foreclosures.
(iv) The subprime mortgage market was particularly (and expectedly) hit by the rise in interest rates, as by 2006 more than 90 per cent of subprime mortgages were carried at adjustable rates.[15]
(v) There was a surge in housing construction starts, for example from a total of 7,777.300 over 1996–2000 to a total of 9,179.400 over 2001–2005 (see Figure 11.2). In fact, the oversupply of vacant for-sale units at the end of 2007 in the USA was estimated by the JCHS of Harvard University at around 800,000, or 1 per cent of the housing stock (Fernald, 2008: 1).

Figure 11.3 sums up the formation of the US housing bubble of 2006, its subsequent burst, and how it led to a financial system crisis. The moral of the story, in line with the discussion in Section 11.1.1, is that the US house-price bubble happened mainly because of an imprudently conceived and badly executed combination of two kinds of ideologically fraught political interventions, the severity of whose unintended consequences was multiplied precisely because the two interventions reinforced one another: one intervention was inspired by a 'liberal' or 'free-market' ideology, the other by a 'populist' or 'socialist' one. The first was manifested in the advancing liberalization or deregulation of the financial sector that reached a peak in 1999, without even the minimal checks on FIs' excessive risk exposures that had

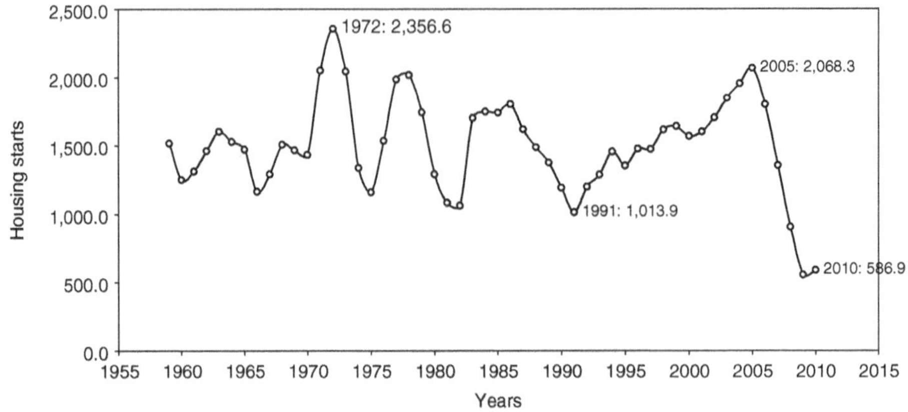

Figure 11.2 New privately owned housing units, in thousands, started in the USA, 1959–2010. (Source: www.census.gov/const/startsan.pdf.)

been put in place in 1933. The other was the decision to expand owner-occupation among high-credit-risk groups using credit, and to that end both extending implicit government guarantees (and burdening current and future generations of taxpayers) and encouraging or even 'persuading' private FIs to take part in the scheme. But for this catastrophic combination, US house prices would not have gone up as high as they had done by 2006. They would still have gone up due to other factors mentioned in Figure 11.3 – but not 'excessively'.

11.4 Planning restrictions and bubbles

An issue that has attracted some public and academic debate[16] in the USA is whether, and, if so, to what extent, planning restrictions (PRs) limiting the supply of land for housebuilding contributed to the housing market bubble of 2006. Such restrictions are also called 'prescriptive land use regulation', 'smart growth', etc.

In fact, it is interesting to note that whereas in the US there are those who accuse the planning function of restricting land supply and indirectly causing the house-price bubble of 2006 (cf., among others, O'Toole, 2009; Cox, 2011), in Ireland there are others (cf. Kitchin et al., 2010: especially 2–3) who accuse the planning function of having been too lax, thereby causing the *burst* of the Irish housing bubble in 2007–08 through the oversupply such permissiveness enabled!

A prudent answer to the issue seems to be that PRs contribute to a bubble where and when there are other forces already at work. On their own, PRs will not cause a bubble or a burst. PRs tend to reflect attempts towards a better environment, and the related interests of *existing* homeowners. Where that happens, cities tend to change 'from urban growth machines to homeowners' cooperatives' (Glaeser et al., 2005).

A word of caution is in order here, though: in places with elastic housing supply (which usually implies easier-to-find land for housebuilding), the supply response to rising prices is by definition larger than otherwise; this tends to restrain further rises in house prices in those places, but when the downturn comes, the overhang (i.e., new-built vacant homes for sale) will also be larger. This *may* actually cause faster price declines than in places with less elastic housing supply, but the decline *may* also be shorter since prices *may* not have risen

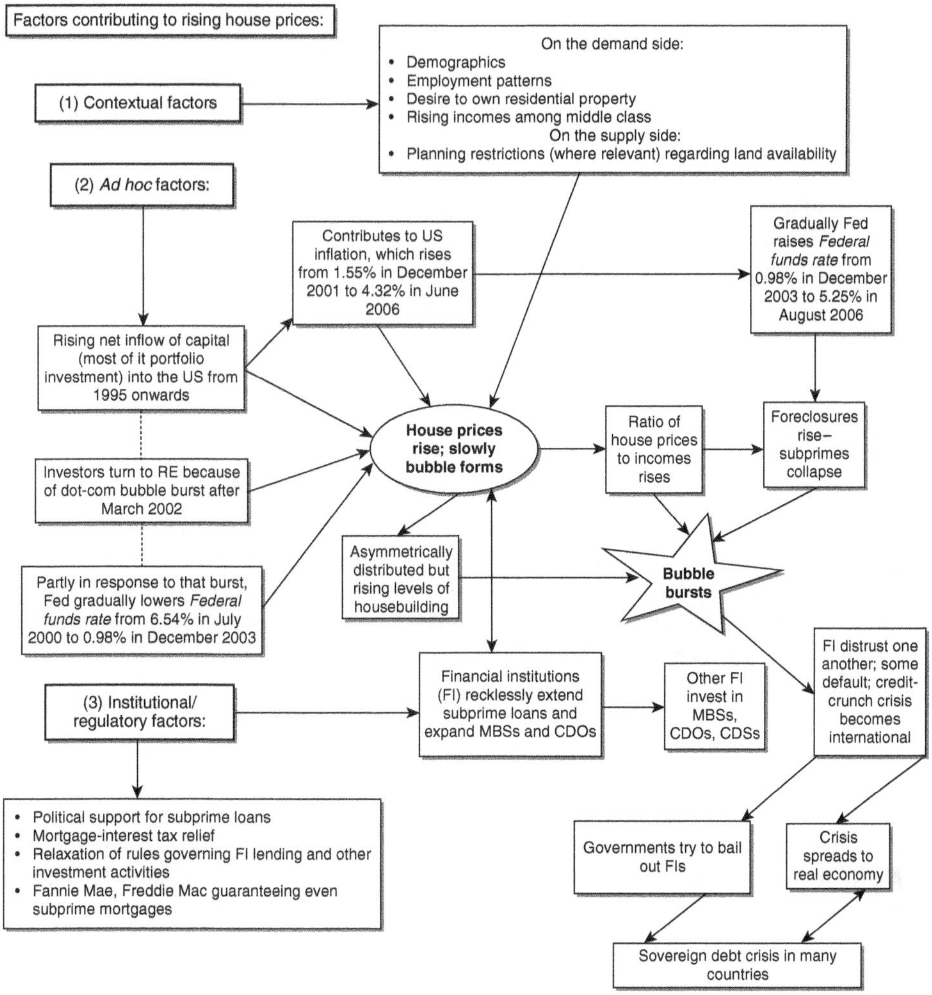

Figure 11.3 How the burst of the US house price bubble in 2007–08 led to the financial sector and credit crunch crisis of 2008–09.

up 'excessively' either. It all depends on combinations of factors affecting particular regions and cities.

More importantly, such overhangs, which are recognized *ex post* as instances of resource misallocation, have adverse welfare consequences in the affected places (cf. Glaeser et al., 2008). On the other hand, where the supply of land for housebuilding is inelastic, house-price volatility tends to be greater (cf. Huang and Tang, 2010), but welfare consequences are likely to be smaller.

Are they, though? In places with inelastic housing supply, when a bubble starts forming, the relatively high initial price rises will cause over-optimism among investors and developers (after all, 'adaptive' expectations are at work! – see Section 8.6.2). Unless, therefore, supply inelasticity is extreme, builders' response to expected higher prices will be stronger there than in places with more elastic housing supply. Because of that, 'the overall social costs of bubbles may well be larger in places where housing is more inelastically supplied' (Glaeser et al., 2008: 18).

What can a proper land policy response be to all that? In the USA (but much less so in the UK), there are large differences across jurisdictions regarding land use planning. But such inconsistency is unavoidable, even justifiable, because it reflects larger considerations and processes, such as the following:

1 The need to facilitate production of more housing as total population and the total number of households grow. This is a particularly strong argument in countries such as the UK, whose planning function is often accused of being overly restrictive (Barker, 2003, 2004; Robb, 2011), even if it is so with good 'green' reasons.
2 The need of expanding cities for more housing, a problem made more difficult in the presence of physical obstacles or environmental worries.
3 The need of countries to speed up economic growth, especially when facing recessions or indebtedness.
4 The need to strive for an optimum city size (if it can be defined – cf. Getz, 1979).
5 The need to deal with 'quality of life' or 'environmental quality' requests on the part of a city's population, or sub-groups thereof. Often such requests cannot or must not be ignored, even in view of potentially contrary objectives (like economic growth). Thus, restricting 'urban sprawl' or disallowing high-rise developments may make local house-price bubbles worse (if they happen for other reasons), but must always be weighed against residents' other concerns.

It helps, of course, when land supply restrictions can be overcome to a certain extent by the use of more capital (e.g., high-rise development) rather than land. Conversely, if there *is* urban sprawl, people may substitute land for capital, but may also employ more capital, i.e., go for larger houses. Then again, with greater sprawl, commuting time to the city centre increases (unless cities have multiple nuclei of employment or retailing), which makes locations nearer the centre more expensive anyway. So there are too many variables at work, which easily suggests that PRs are not the only, or even main, factor behind RE bubbles or bursts.

11.5 Conventional signs of a bubble

There are four ratios whose high values, if such is the case, may be indicative of a house-price bubble. The first two are affordability indices – since reduced affordability suggests that house prices have exceeded normal ability to pay for a house; it also suggests that a house-price correction is looming in the horizon. Affordability is determined, first, by the ratio of mortgage costs to incomes (the so-called debt-service, or *debt-to-income ratio*); mortgage costs are determined by interest rates, loan-to-value ratios, the tax treatment of interest expense (if applicable), other subsidies (if applicable), and of course house prices: *ergo*, and rather roughly, the *house-price-to-income ratio* is also important.

A third ratio that may serve as a bubble indicator is the *ratio of house prices to annual rents*, and a fourth is the *ratio of house-price to replacement cost* (i.e., the cost of building), which reflects Tobin's q ratio, introduced in Section 3.3.2. Recall that if this ratio is over 100 per cent, developers tend to produce more dwellings.

'Normal' values of those four ratios do not necessarily imply that a bubble is not forming. Conversely, but less safely, 'abnormally' high values do not necessarily imply that a bubble (a) exists or (b) is about to burst – which is the crucial issue after all. Of course what is 'normal' is not easy to define; one method is to compare the current value of a ratio with its long-term average or trend, which is not always a safe or satisfactory procedure as it depends on the number of years the analyst chooses to incorporate in his or her 'long-term' period of observations. The time-span issue is important because the longer the span, the greater the chance that there may have been a 'structural break' in the overall economic and social conditions between 'now' and 'then' that renders a historic average an unsafe indicator of today's threats and opportunities.

This point was at the heart of a debate that by the start of 2012 had not been resolved, namely whether house prices in Australia since the mid-2000s had been too high – and therefore represented a bubble-burst risk – or not.[17] Presumably such issues are resolved only when a bubble actually pops!

Nevertheless, an OECD study, covering the period 1970–2005, concluded that in 2005 (a still 'exuberant' year in America's housing market),

> '[I]n the countries with the largest house price increases (Ireland, the Netherlands, Spain and the United Kingdom) as well as in Australia and New Zealand, the ratio of nominal house prices to per capita disposable income (as well as the ratio of prices to rents [...]) exceed their long-term averages by 40 per cent or more. In Canada, Denmark, France and the United States, the run-up has been more moderate but these values still represent historical peaks.'
>
> (OECD, 2005: 127)

Moreover, IMF-originated academic research published in December 2010 had estimated that Australia's house prices were indeed overvalued by 5–10 per cent (Tumbarello and Wang, 2010).

After the burst of the US house-price bubble, things in the USA returned to 'normal', though: 'The ratio of house prices to household income [...] improved again in 2010 as the median[18] home price fell to about 3.4 times the median household income, the lowest level since 1995 and in line with the 1980–2000 average' (Fernald, 2011b: 19).

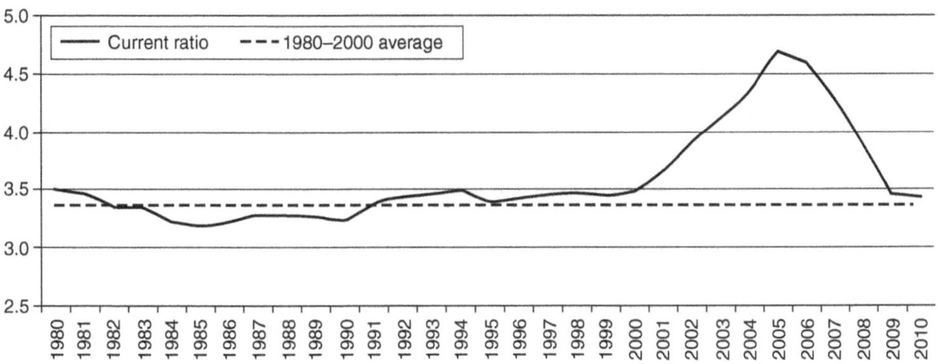

Figure 11.4 Following the burst of the housing market bubble, the US median price-to-income ratio returned to its long-run average.

(Source: JCHS tabulations of National Association of Realtors, Existing Home Sales Prices; and Moody's Economy.com, Median Household Income. Reprinted from *The State of the Nation's Housing* (2011) with permission from the Joint Center for Housing Studies of Harvard University. All rights reserved.)

In general, market practitioners feel the following:

1 A debt-service (or debt-to-income) ratio of 28 per cent (going up to 36 per cent if all of a household's debt-servicing costs, and not just those for mortgages, are included) seems to be lenders' basic guideline (see http://financialplan.about.com/od/realestatemortgages/a/howmuchhome.htm, accessed 29 October 2011; see also Schwartz and Wilson, 2008).
2 A house-price-to-income ratio of 2.5–3 is the rule of thumb (see www.doughroller.net/mortgages/how-much-house-can-i-afford/, accessed 29 October 2011).
3 A price-to-rent ratio of 5–6.7 suggests 'very undervalued housing', one of 40–50 suggests 'very overvalued housing', and one of 14.2–16.7 suggests 'fairly priced housing' (see www.globalpropertyguide.com/real-estate-school/How-to-avoid-buying-into-a-bubble, accessed 29 October 2011).

11.6 Consequences of a house-price bubble burst

The burst of a housing market bubble has a number of interconnected consequences, whose severity depends on the extent to which the rest of the economy (chiefly, the financial sector, but also household non-housing consumption) has in turn come to depend on the housing, particularly the owner-occupied, sector doing well. The immediate consequence – indeed, the manifestation of the burst – is a sizable drop in house prices. Another is a dramatic increase in the number of repossessions and foreclosures.[19] A third is developers revising downwards plans for construction starts. A fourth is a reduction in the wealth of most households. A fifth is recession in the national economy, which can become quite severe depending on how big the burst is and how exactly it affects the financial sector. A sixth is credit contraction, which can expand beyond the housing sector to affect other areas of credit, including inter-bank lending. A seventh is inter-tenure adjustment and changes in the vacancy rate. We shall examine the last one.

The number of housing market vacancies can vary, depending both on housing market cycle phase and on housing tenure (owner-occupation or renting), including linkages between tenures. For example, in the USA during 2008–09 (i.e., following the owner-occupied market downturn of 2007–08), the rental vacancy rate increased despite rising demand for rented accommodation and substantial drops in construction starts for rented accommodation from 2005 to 2009 – but that was due to too many formerly owner-occupied homes joining the rented sector (Fernald, 2011: 9). Eventually (i.e., after 2009), the rental vacancy rate began to drop (see Figure 11.5), as many households found it difficult to remain in, or join, the owner-occupied sector.

The process is depicted in Figure 11.6. (Notice that the process cannot be fully generalized, as it hinges on owner-occupation being the dominant as well as preferred tenure, on the 'Anglo-American' mode of residential development, and on credit being the dominant form of housing, as well as developers', finance.)

In Figure 11.6(a), initial market equilibrium is assumed to exist at price P_1, when Q_1 owner-occupied homes are demanded and supplied. Developers, however, begin to expect that house prices will rise to P_e. As a result, they start building projects, which eventually increase supply to Q_2. By that time demand has increased to D_2 *only* (as it must, sooner or later), suggesting a new equilibrium at Q_3. This implies a surplus of unsold dwellings equal to $Q_2 - Q_3$, which is added to any pre-existing number of vacant dwellings. Part of that surplus finds its way into the (private) rented sector.

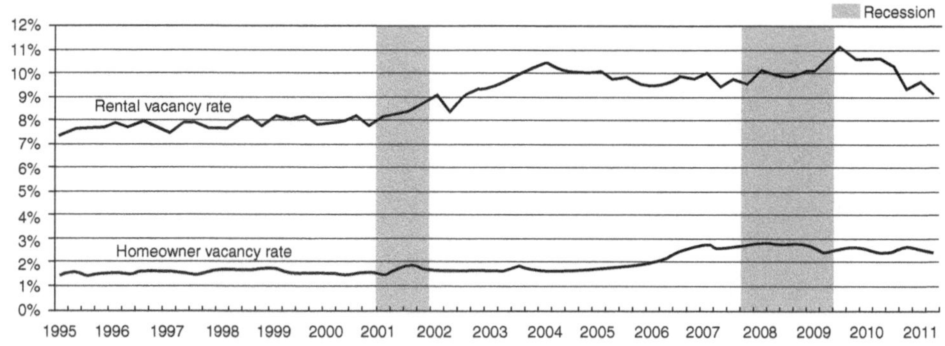

Figure 11.5 Quarterly rental and homeowner vacancy rates for the USA, 1995–2011.

At the same time, the fact that price expectations were not fulfilled causes a change in credit conditions: banks that are involved in the housing market become more careful as to whom they are prepared to lend, they restrain credit, re-evaluate the quality of their assets (such as housing loans or MBSs), and become uncertain of each other's trustworthiness. With less credit, housing demand drops to D_3 (maybe even below D_1), and equilibrium quantity to Q_4, suggesting that now price is less than P_1. The number of vacant homes further increases by $Q_3 - Q_4$, and some – probably most – of them also join the (private) rented sector.

In Figure 11.6(b), initial market equilibrium is assumed to exist at rental price R_1, when q_1 privately rented homes are demanded and supplied. Then supply increases to S_2 as some dwellings from the surplus of unsold dwellings defined as '$Q_2 - Q_3$' in Figure 11.6(a) join the rented sector. The quantity of rented homes supplied now increases to q_2, but equilibrium is at q_3, suggesting an increase in the number of vacant homes for rent equal to $q_2 - q_3$. When demand drops to D_3 in Figure 11.6(a), more dwellings from the '$Q_3 - Q_4$' surplus depicted in Figure 11.6(a) join the rented sector, causing supply to increase to S_3 and the quantity of rented homes supplied to rise to q_4. Equilibrium is now at q_5, suggesting an additional increase in the number of vacant homes for rent equal to $q_4 - q_5$.

Eventually, demand for rented accommodation shifts to D_2, as households who have lost their owner-occupied homes, and new households who, due to the changed credit conditions, cannot become owner-occupiers, come to the rented sector. The new equilibrium is now at q_6, implying a drop in vacancies (which are now equal to $q_4 - q_6$ plus, roughly, whatever the number of vacancies was during initial equilibrium, at q_1) as well as a rental price higher than the one associated with either q_3 or q_5 (and possibly higher than R_1, eventually).

11.7 Can asset-price bubbles be avoided?

Probably they can, on the basis of (a) correctly defining a bubble and (b) correctly diagnosing both the general and particular factors contributing to the formation of a bubble. Both requirements constitute a tall order – see the Australian debate mentioned in Section 11.5 – but not an impossible one: after all, truly catastrophic bubble bursts of global significance (as opposed to mild recessions or mere price 'corrections') do not happen often (see Section 11.1) – although they take longer to heal, which is why those periods are referred to as 'depressions'.

A related issue, which is actually more crucial than avoiding a bubble, is how to ensure that the burst of a bubble will have minimal effects on the wider economy, firms, and households

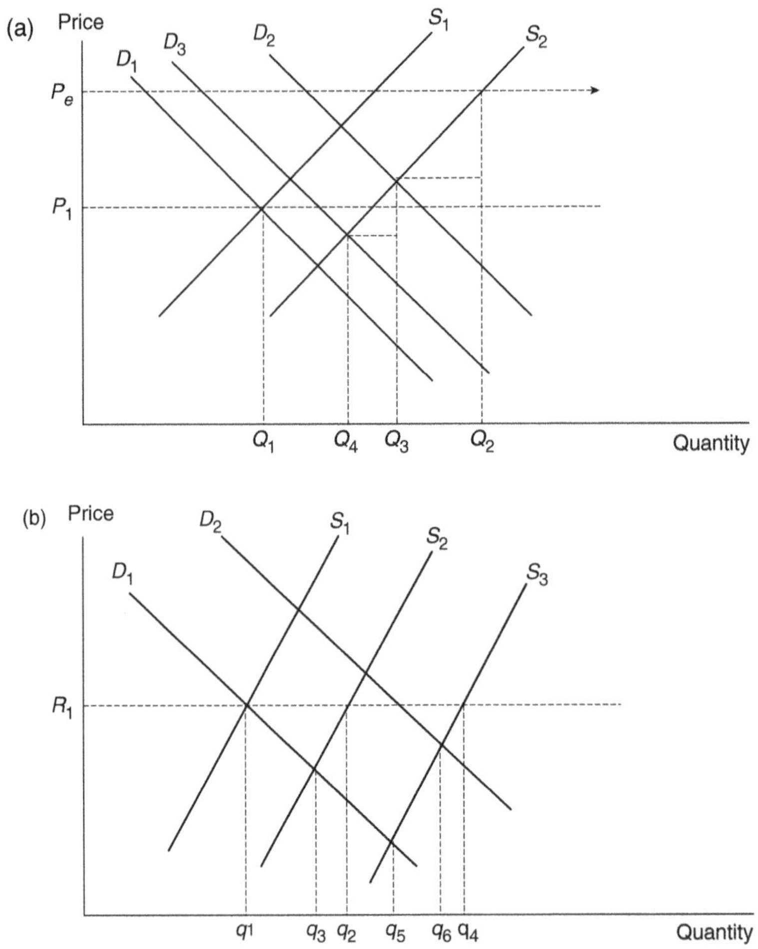

Figure 11.6 Effect of housing market overheating and subsequent collapse across tenures. (a) In the owner-occupied sector, there is overbuilding of owner-occupied homes due to high price expectations; eventually, demand rises lower than expected, then drops due to the onset of adverse credit conditions. (b) In the (private) rented sector, supply increases due to initial surplus of unsold dwellings in the owner-occupied sector and increases further due to a drop in demand in the owner-occupied sector; then demand increases due to an influx of households from owner-occupied sector and of new households who cannot owner-occupy.

even before policy-makers have run to mop things up. This is a different question from what the government or monetary authorities might have to do to mitigate such effects, including putting the economy back on track, after a bubble has burst.

11.7.1 Credit is key

International experience with the 2008–09 credit-crunch crisis (precipitated by the burst of the US housing market bubble) has shown that *ex-post* government or monetary action can be too abrupt, little, or late, and may even backfire (as evidenced by the transformation of the 2008–09 financial system crisis into a sovereign debt one in many countries). In fact having put a firewall around a potential bubble before it pops is the safest way to avoid having a bubble in the first place.

In Section 11.1, we stressed the potential role of credit in stimulating asset-price bubbles. The use of credit complicates matters because it subjects the formation of house (or other asset) prices to a force that enhances the power of fundamental demand or supply drivers in ways that (a) cannot be forecast accurately and (b) involve increased randomness (manifested in the possibility of default). It therefore amounts to greater risk, for lenders, other investors, and households. Above all, if the financial system is not subject to precautionary checks and balances, it will tend to spread and exacerbate those risks (e.g., through securitization) – not least because lack of, or improper, regulation will incentivize financial institutions to expand the volume of what is, essentially, a risky business. Initially, such risk-spreading may reduce the risk faced by any particular institution. Later, it will aggravate it as the risk may become systemic, and overall randomness will increase.[20]

In short, if asset purchases are financed by own funds, or by borrowed funds under strict and prudent regulations, the danger of a bubble forming is minimized. If asset purchases are credit-financed, especially if such credit is given recklessly, the danger increases, and will materialize unless dealt with in time. Notice that the level of interest rates *per se* is not as important in this respect as overall credit conditions and practices,[21] or as interconnections among financial institutions. Unfortunately, these are factors that even (or especially!) automated or normal-distribution-based risk-assessment models cannot quantify easily (Magnusson, 2008). Nor is control of monetary variables on the part of monetary authorities a substitute for appropriate risk-containment regulation of the financial system – the more so since monetary policy was not an important factor behind the 2006 house-price bubble in the USA or indeed in other countries (Posen, 2009).

A word of warning is in order here, though. The message so far is that the danger of house-, and other asset-, price bubbles can be minimized through appropriate regulation of the financial system, so as to make reckless or excessively risky credit impossible. But that presupposes that all credit can be effectively regulated – which is far from certain. Paul Krugman[22] (2011) had this to say about a Chinese RE bubble that was apparently emerging by the end of 2011, in comparison with the US experience of the mid-2000s:

> '[A]s credit boomed, much of it came not from banks but from an unsupervised, unprotected shadow banking system. There were huge differences in detail: shadow banking American style tended to involve prestigious Wall Street firms and complex financial instruments, while the Chinese version tends to run through underground banks and even pawnshops. Yet the consequences were similar: in China as in America a few years ago, the financial system may be much more vulnerable than data on conventional banking reveal.'

Nor is regulatory control of credit, or at least of the level of a FI's risk exposure, a process without danger: if taken too far, it may amount to price fixing, or rationing, and entail adverse effects upon resource allocation together with more political intervention in the economy. But it does not have to be taken too far: a set of pragmatic and prudent regulations governing risk-exposure and incentives towards risk-taking, readiness to impose severe penalties on transgressors, and periodic re-evaluation of the effectiveness of the regulatory framework by independent and transparently working bodies, may be the answer.

11.7.2 'Automatic stabilizers' as 'bubble-stoppers'

Even before the burst of the US house-price bubble in 2007–08, it was felt that something should be done about pre-empting asset, and in particular RE, price bubbles. Thus, in a seminal paper, Muellbauer (2005: 101) had stressed 'the need for stronger stabilisers of asset prices and hence the economy, such as property taxes', while van den Noord (2003: 5) had expressed a concern that generous tax breaks (i.e., tax changes) for house ownership in the euro area would result both in higher house prices (a capitalization effect) and their greater volatility. Following the burst of the US bubble, the call for some kind of 'automatic stabilizers' for house prices was repeated by Posen (2009), who specifically argued against monetary policy tools, hinting at taxes and regulations instead.

An 'automatic stabilizer' is any tool that automatically, i.e., without new explicit action on the part of policy-makers or the government, reduces the rate of asset price growth in an upturn, and reduces the rate of asset price decline in a downturn. A 'natural' and easy-to-implement 'automatic stabilizer' would be some kind of tax. The effectiveness of such a measure, however, is an open question. For example,

> 'The IMF and the OECD do not consider tax rules as the main reason for the housing bubble [in the USA in 2006]: housing prices increased in countries with different tax systems, and there were no tax breaks clear and big enough to explain the price dynamics that were observed.'
>
> (Hemmelgarn et al., 2011: 19)

Also, an IMF study conceded that '[t]axation does not explain the widespread house price boom – that occurred in countries with very different tax systems – and there are no obvious tax changes that might have triggered its collapse'. But it cautioned that '[h]ousing is commonly subject to special tax treatment that may have increased household leverage and house prices' (IMF, 2009: 17). Broadening the discussion, McDonald and Johnson (2010: 405) wrote that 'tax policies did not cause the recent global financial crisis', although 'they almost certainly contributed to key vulnerabilities in the international financial system'.

One tax and one subsidy (which is really a negative tax) have attracted particular attention regarding their role in the crisis: capital-gains tax (CGT), and mortgage interest deductibility (MID). Commentators' views are conflicting (Hemmelgarn, 2011: 20–5):

1. Some say that because CGT in the USA became lighter in 1997, it contributed to the subsequent house-price bubble. Others dispute this as, for example, house prices did not increase everywhere in the USA.
2. Turning to MID, some have causally linked it to rising house prices in, say, the Netherlands and Ireland. There, and also in the UK, average real house prices more than doubled in 2005–07 since 1985 (Hilbers et al., 2008). But although there was MID in the Netherlands and Ireland, there had been no MID in the UK on new loans since 6 April 2000. In the USA, (i) lower personal income taxation since the 1980s has reduced the benefit implied in MID, (ii) there was no break in MID that could explain the 2006 housing boom, and (iii) during the boom, house prices rose differentially across states and regions, although there were no interstate differences in MID (Hemmelgarn et al., 2011).

Once again, as in the role of planning restrictions in the US housing bubble, it seems that the role of either CGT or of MID has been, and probably is, auxiliary rather than central, as there were, or are, other forces at work.

Consequently, whether a tax, or other tool, may serve as an automatic stabilizer depends on a correct evaluation of the causes of asset-price bubbles (or declines – but really catastrophic declines tend to happen after the burst of a pre-existing bubble, so it is bubble-forming that worries economists and policy-makers). A problem is that bubbles do not all have the same causes. In Figure 11.3, for example, it is apparent that the US house-price bubble of 2006 was the result of both contextual and *ad hoc* factors. Even if contextual (i.e., long-term, broad-coverage) bubble-contributing factors are the same for an asset class (like housing) at all times and in all places, *ad hoc* factors may still be very important – enough so as to call to question the wisdom of applying 'automatic stabilizers' to the problem at hand.

The reason is that asset-price growth is not necessarily a bad thing; it may actually be required in order to stimulate general economic growth, and may also be a healthy *effect* of the latter. In such a situation, 'automatic stabilizers' (which by definition act counter-cyclically) might be counter-productive, arresting or even reversing a welcome trend before it had had time to bear fruit. They would actually be more counter-productive the larger they were – or else they would be so small as to be inconsequential. To get them 'just right' would, on the other hand, be a hit-and-miss affair.

'Automatic stabilizers' might be of greater help if they kicked off at the moment when asset prices were considered somehow 'too high' or 'near being too high' – but that would presuppose a non-automatic intervention on the part of policy-makers! It would also hinge on policy-makers correctly defining what 'too high' means, and correctly surmising that the point of danger or of action had been reached (again, compare the Australian debate on the matter, mentioned in Section 11.5). This is a very unsafe course to take, as 'actually recognizing an asset price bubble prior to a price crash is notoriously difficult' (Ambrose et al., 2011: 1).

Such a course would also involve another danger: that of a 'burst' as soon as policy-makers acted in order to stem the formation of a bubble!

An additional consideration is that, to the extent that a RE 'bubble' forms due to 'fundamental' forces operating (e.g., population pressures, rising incomes, maybe in conjunction with a restricted supply of land), it is doubtful whether 'automatic stabilizers' would be enough to counter the influence of those forces. At most, they would mask that influence for a time, distracting policy-makers from the need to attack the root of the problem: an imbalance between 'fundamental' changes in demand and the supply response; extraordinary financial inflows; reckless credit.

This suggests that one or more 'automatic stabilizers' might be useful only if they were employed together with measures aimed at addressing both 'fundamental' and *ad hoc* factors affecting demand for and supply of an asset, like housing.

In fact, focusing on fundamentals as well as on *ad hoc* factors, drawing a line between them, understanding what they are and how they operate, and the impact they are likely to have in the future, would probably allow policy-makers to part with the need to introduce 'automatic stabilizers' or take hasty and untimely action after a 'bubble' has already formed or prices are on their way there. As already suggested, a good example of an *ad hoc* price-spurring factor is mortgage-interest tax relief. Another is government guarantees of subprime loans. A third is a regulatory framework that enables, even encourages, financial institutions to take on more risk.

All three devices have a strong potential to contribute to house-price bubbles – so it is their abolition, rather than the introduction of 'automatic stabilizers', that should reduce the danger of a bubble. And of course 'bubble-stopping' must not neglect other concerns, like helping expand owner-occupation, protecting the environment, or taxing on the basis of ability-to-pay. If, for example, there is a need for government-guaranteed mortgages at all, it might be better to substitute public housing provision for those – or else ration the offer of such guarantees. After all, the US housing market crisis has shown that the systemic risk of extensive government guarantees in a context of reckless practices on the part of financial institutions is too great. Equally, the sovereign debt crisis has shown that government spending – for example on public housing provision, on other construction, on housing subsidies, on welfare, etc. – must be done in a context of fiscal prudence – or else systemic risk becomes great again.

The trick is to effect such reforms at an appropriate time during the business cycle – for example, not to tax property more, or remove or reduce mortgage-interest tax relief, during a recession but do so during a stabilized recovery (cf. Muellbauer, 2005: 107). The same holds for monetary policy: 'The best time to fight the housing cycle with tight monetary policy is when the wave is starting to rise, not when it is cresting. The worst time to stimulate the economy with loose monetary policy is when the wave is starting to rise. That is going to make the crest all the higher, and the crash all the more catastrophic' (Leamer, 2007: 3).

After such 'bubble-contributing' *ad hoc* factors have been dealt with, the next step is to address fundamentals. It is difficult to see what the state could do on the demand side in this respect. Can it, for example, affect demographics (e.g., the rate of population growth or the rate of household formation)? Other than checks on illegal immigration, this can happen only within narrow limits. Can the state affect economic growth? It does it all the time, but experience with bubbles has shown that governments tend to act retroactively more often than they do pre-emptively. And surely the need (and the challenge) is not for a government to discourage economic growth so that a bubble will not form, but to avert asset-price bubbles when there *is* economic growth.

In their desire to curry favour with electorates, incumbent parties tend towards fiscal profligacy; as a result, they burden future generations with taxes. Complementing this, they tend to be tolerant, if not outright encouraging, of the excesses and recklessness of financial institutions – i.e., of 'finance capital'.[23] Many governments also tend to stifle entrepreneurial creativity, or underestimate, even belittle, the capacity and responsibility of the private sector to produce real wealth. When, as a result of accumulated fiscal deficits, public debt gets out of control, governments inevitably burden the current generation with taxes in frantic efforts to salvage the economy. All this does not sound like sound demand or growth management.

On the supply side, though, a state can do much more to avoid housing bubbles, for example by smoothly and carefully releasing more land for housebuilding, allowing more high-rise development, but above all using the planning function to effect truly 'smart' growth. The latter's ostensible purpose is to combine economic growth and efficiency with people's 'quality-of-life' considerations. Meeting such challenges is certainly more difficult than relying on 'automatic stabilizers' to sort things out.

11.7.3 An example of an 'automatic-stabilizer' RE tax

Three taxes may do for this role: a sales tax, a capital-gains tax (CGT), or a recurrent property tax. All would burden the acquisition or possession of property; all could, in principle, serve to weaken a house-price spiral; all would be unlikely to stop it completely (unless the applied rates really became exorbitant – and then it would be a case of throwing out the baby – the housing market itself – along with the bathwater, i.e., the danger of a price bubble forming); all have pros and cons.

1 *Ex-ante*, a sales tax and a CGT can be made equivalent to one another through choosing appropriate rates to apply. *Ex-post*, equivalency may not be achievable precisely because a CGT presupposes existence of a CG to tax, whereas a sales tax will be applied anyway, no matter what the market conditions. Thus, a sales tax has the potential not only to reduce sellers' CG, but to 'eat away' a portion of the (inflation-adjusted) price a seller paid in the past to buy the property. This would be especially so during a housing market downturn, for then those selling may be under greater pressure to sell than buyers are keen to buy.

For example, a house bought at €100 may now be selling at €108. In 'normal' circumstances and in view of a 10 per cent sales tax levied on the buyer, the house might sell for €105 rather than €108; *ergo*, the seller would assume 28.6 per cent of the tax (i.e., 3/10.5).[24] In 'abnormal' ones, the buyer might be able to impose a price of $108/(1+0.1)=98.2$; *ergo*, the seller would assume $9.8/9.8=100$ per cent of the tax, and end up with a take-home revenue smaller than what he or she had paid for the house. Of course, in truly adverse circumstances, a buyer might be able to get the house at a very low price anyway; a sales tax would then make the seller's loss greater, thereby aggravating the housing market decline.

2 In contrast, a CGT would by definition target only CG, which might help to decelerate the drop in house prices. On the other hand, a sales tax might be more effective during an upward spiral, since it would burden the entire sales price rather than CG alone. But exactly because of this a sales tax *as an 'automatic stabilizer'* might easily bring more 'punch' to bear on the housing market than policy-makers had intended. And it is doubtful whether either a CGT or a sales tax would stop house prices from rising in the face of strong 'fundamental' demand drivers or of reckless credit (at least without the tax getting so high as to precipitate a housing market collapse). Between the two, a CGT would be a fairer and more logical tax to apply, since it would target the supposedly 'excessive' gains from selling rather than the sales price itself. It would also be easier to fine-tune (but perhaps more difficult actually to calculate, especially in the absence of registered or accurate past prices).

3 Recurrent property prices are particularly problematic because they may unduly burden people whose properties appreciate in value even though those people are neither sellers nor buyers – just homeowners. It is more reasonable, effective (from the point of view of 'automatic stabilization'), and fair to try and apply 'automatic stabilizers' at the moment it counts most (i.e., when buying or selling) rather than subject 'non-combatants' (i.e., standing homeowners) to them. Otherwise, policy-makers may be faced with unintended consequences (e.g., taxing people out of their homes or further decoupling local taxes from local benefits).

Let us therefore concentrate on CGT as a likely and possibly desirable candidate for an 'automatic stabilizer' tax, and work out an example. Nevertheless, we shall see that its exact effect as an 'automatic stabilizer' is difficult to quantify.

An example

A seller's ask price for a house she bought a year ago (i.e., period T_1) is \$300,000. She has arrived at this figure either by 'feeling' the market or by projecting a growth rate of, say, 6 per cent over her purchase price of \$283,019. Now a CGT rate of 20 per cent is announced. Other than CGT, there are no transaction costs.

If she sells the house at \$300,000, she will pay a CGT of \$3396.2, and pocket just \$296,603.8 – implying a 4.8 per cent rate of return. For the seller to secure pocketing \$300,000 after the CGT, she must sell the house at

$$P_S = \frac{P_H - P_P(t)}{1-t} = \frac{300{,}000 - 283{,}019(0.2)}{1-0.2} = 304{,}245.25,$$

where

P_S = sale price,
P_H = take-home price,
P_P = original purchase price,
t = CGT rate.

Before the tax was announced, a prospective buyer-cum-speculator (with a one-year time horizon T_2) would have counted on house prices rising further. Say that he expected the rate of growth to be 6 per cent as well; his target-price, therefore, would have been \$300,000(1 + 0.06) = \$318,000.

Then the CGT is introduced. To achieve a 6 per cent return, the investor must now pay less than \$300,000 to buy the house (cf. Equation (9.4) from Chapter 9):

$$V_t = \frac{F(1-t)}{(1+k)-t} = \frac{318{,}000(1-0.2)}{1.06-0.2} = 295{,}814.$$

So the transaction price will close between \$304,245.25 and \$295,814, depending on either side's bargaining power, with an expected value of \$300,030. However, things are more complex, because the buyer, after the CGT has been introduced, cannot know whether he will be able to sell the house at \$318,000. A future buyer will also calculate a lower price than that, the same way the current buyer has calculated a price lower than \$300,000. Moreover, it is not known what kind of discount the future buyer will effect; he or she may not have a one-year time horizon, or T_3; he or she may not be a speculator, but a long-term owner-occupier. It all amounts to a rise in uncertainty. As a result, the current buyer will have to discount his target sale price more, say, by 7 per cent. If so, then

$$V_t' = \frac{318{,}000(1-0.2)}{1.07-0.2} = 292{,}414$$

Hence, the expected value of the transaction price = (304,245.25 + 292,414)/2 = 298,330, i.e., less than 300,000. Then *ex-post* market experience over period T_1 will be of a house-price growth not of 6 per cent, but of 5.4 per cent. If this is realized, it also means that the original seller's rate of return cannot be 4.8 per cent, but 4.3 per cent.

A 5.4 per cent house-price growth will affect market estimates of future price growth, which will have to be down-sized, *ceteris paribus*. If they *are* downsized, then V_t may have to be recalculated, and so on. A way to speed up calculations is presented in Box 11.1. The method used is slightly different from what we have done above, mainly because no change in current buyer's cap rate is assumed.

Box 11.1 Stylized long-range calculation of what a buyer will pay now to buy a property subject to CGT

Without CGT,

$$V_0 = \frac{V_1}{1+k},$$

i.e., a current buyer A, whose cap rate is k, and who estimates that a period from now he stands to get V_1 from selling a property he is thinking of buying, is prepared to pay V_0 for the property.

With CGT $= t$, the buyer is prepared to pay

$$V_0 = \frac{V_1(1-t)}{(1+k)-t}.$$

But a future buyer B will make a similar calculation, so for her, V_1 will not necessarily be what the current buyer is estimating, but will be

$$V_1 = \frac{V_2(1-t)}{(1+k)-t}.$$

Expecting this, current buyer A will factor B's formula into his formula:

$$V_0 = \frac{V_2(1-t)^2}{[(1+k)-t]^2}.$$

Crucial assumptions A makes are that (a) the growth rate h for V_1 is known; (b) buyer B uses the same cap rate k as buyer A; (c) buyer B also has a one-period time horizon; (d) the same pattern holds for all subsequent buyers.

Further assuming that buyer A looks n periods into the future, buyer A is now prepared to pay

$$V_0 = \frac{V_1(1+h)^{n-1}(1-t)^n}{[(1+k)-t]^n}.$$

Going back to the example used in the main text (and assuming that $n = 8$), we have

$$V_0 = \frac{318{,}000(1+0.06)^{8-1}(1-0.2)^8}{[(1+0.06)-0.2]^8} = 268{,}102,$$

i.e., much less than what was calculated in the main text.

However, the assumptions used are so fluid and arbitrary that the result obtained is anything but certain. It would be safer to stick to the one-period horizon assumed in the text, and deal with uncertainty by increasing the cap rate buyer A would use.

A CGT may therefore dampen house-price growth. The effect should be greater if the CGT is calculated on the basis of a double-sliding scale: the shorter the holding period, or the higher the house price, the larger the tax. However, the exact effect cannot be known with certainty, as much will depend on negotiations between individual buyers and sellers, on market actors' own uncertainties, on future buyers' motives (speculative or for genuine owner-occupation), and on overall demand and supply elasticities. Thus, a CGT, despite being capable of acting as an 'automatic stabilizer' to a certain (or uncertain!) extent, also has the potential to exacerbate turbulence in the housing market. Yet, on grounds of ability to pay, and also because the alternatives (sales taxes or recurrent taxes) may be too heavy a tool to apply *if used as* 'automatic stabilizers', a CGT may be the least-bad choice (if an 'automatic stabilizer' tax is to be employed at all).

11.8 Expected return, RRR, and house-price volatility

Housing market processes (involving both exogenous and endogenous factors) affect housing prices in interactive ways that are likely (but not certain) to create house-price bubbles. On the other hand, if a bubble does form, it is certain that there will be a burst as *reversion* of house prices to (some definition of) their historic *mean*[25] will, sooner or later, take place (cf. Section 8.6.3; Sorensen, 2006; Glaeser and Gyourko, 2007). The problem is to understand what causes such reversion, given that most of the time, house (and other asset) prices exhibit *serial correlation*, i.e., a price in one period seems to be a relatively good predictor of price the next period.

11.8.1 'Fundamental' drivers and market 'actors'

One plausible proposition is that burst-causing factors are intrinsically related to bubble-causing ones, only they work in reverse. This approach, which looks into a possibly 'organic' connection between bubbles and bursts, should accompany statistical analyses of house-price changes, some of which try to tell whether asset prices are too high or too low, and others of which try to determine the expected length of an upturn or downturn (hence the concept of *duration dependence* – see Section 11.8.5).

Largely exogenous factors (cf. Belsky and McCue, 2007: 1–3) are 'fundamentals' like demographics, changes in employment patterns across cities and regions, commuting time to work (the longer the time, the lower the house price, *ceteris paribus*), location utility, a taste for owner-occupation, the size of the rented sector, real income growth,[26] social-security and health-care system generosity, interest rates and credit conditions (e.g., such that make sub-prime lending possible or even fuel it), various kinds of, mostly tax, subsidies, and land availability (which depends on geography and the planning function as well as on population pressures).

The critical endogenous factor is current and expected house prices as signals that affect subsequent behaviour on the part of the following:

1 'Flippers', i.e., people who act solely or mainly on the basis of a speculative motive – who, in other words, buy dwellings for the specific purpose of selling relatively quickly in order to realize capital gains. In so doing, they bid house prices up – but they are also the first to leave the market if things turn bad (and often are among those to suffer most if a bubble burst catches them between buying and selling).

2 'Patrons', i.e., people who support and value homeownership; who, consequently, buy or sell houses on the basis of, mostly, non-speculative motives (like getting into owner-occupation long-term, or financing retirement).
3 'Developers', whose decisions are based on both *expected return* (R_e) and *required rate of return* (RRR) from housebuilding (and also from building commercial properties, as the two interact).[27]

Some factors are partly endogenous and partly exogenous, like (i) credit, which increases with rising house prices (Posen, 2009: 6), exposing households (and financial institutions) to more risk; (ii) commuting time, in the sense that high house prices near one's place of work may force households to live further away; and (iii) the size of the rented sector, which depends a lot on the size of the owner-occupied one.

Patron activity (which depends on demand fundamentals) and flipping activity (which is the rogue element in the picture) affect demand for housing. Increases in demand initiate or sustain a house-price spiral that may generate a bubble; a subsequent reduction in the rate of demand increase or, more strongly, a drop in demand may then trigger a burst. Development activity, on the other hand, is mostly a response to demand rather than vice versa.[28] If smooth, it has the potential to dampen house-price growth and remove the prospect of a bubble forming. But it is susceptible to flares and 'overheating'. When that happens, it may precipitate the burst of a bubble, even if demand has kept on increasing; and it *will* precipitate a burst when 'overheating' coincides with a drop in demand.

In what follows, we shall focus on development activity, making use of the concepts of R_e and RRR. Flipping activity might also be approached on the basis of those tools, with adjustments, but it seems more sensible not to assign RRR-based behaviour to flippers – unless perhaps those are professional investors-cum-speculators. However, both flippers and developers largely base their next moves on past, current, or expected house prices, which they perceive as serially correlated. As buyers, flippers compare current prices with expected ones; as sellers, they compare current prices with past ones. Developers, moreover, compare expected prices with construction and land costs.

Beyond that, the immediate consequences of both groups' actions differ: with positive expectations, flippers push further up the prices of existing houses (thus giving developers an added stimulus to increase supply), either by rushing to buy or by postponing selling; developers initiate new housebuilding or renovations, thus *effecting* increases in supply.

The importance of developers' RRR, and of 'excessive' housebuilding as a factor likely to 'trigger' a bubble, has been often mentioned in the academic literature. For example, 'The price variable that I suggest drives builder behavior is the expected present value of receipts from selling a house' (Poterba, 1984: 749) – which of course begs the question of how the cap rate (i.e., the RRR) is determined; and Belsky and McCue (2007: 1), in their study of causes behind house-price declines in the USA, found that 'the presence and magnitude of job loss and the presence and magnitude of overbuilding [...] are the crucial determinants of both the probability that a place will experience a price decline and the magnitude of the decline. Interest rates appear to play a relatively minor direct role'.

Belsky and McCue (2007: 11) defined the number of excess housing units in a market at a point in time as the sum of 'unsold but uncompleted homes for-sale plus existing vacant homes for sale'; but as 'there are no good measures of either of these types of homes for sale at the metropolitan level', they resorted to a proxy that they felt was 'predictive of the probability of a price decline in a market. This measure is the *permit intensity*, defined as the short term average annual permits per capita relative to the long term median annual permits per capita of a particular metropolitan area over the long run.'

11.8.2 Market 'actors' behaviour

Fundamentals, price expectations, developers' RRR, and over/under-building combine together to determine private-housing market volatility. In broad terms, this is what happens:

1 Flippers' behaviour is determined by what in 1996 Alan Greenspan, then Fed Chairman, called 'irrational exuberance', a term that in 2000 re-appeared as the title of a seminal book by R. J. Shiller (2005). It means overly optimistic expectations (that are unsubstantiated by fundamentals) regarding the future course of prices of one or more asset classes.
2 Patrons continue buying first or even second homes as long as (i) they want access to owner-occupation for mostly consumption purposes and (ii) they can afford it (see Section 11.4 on affordability indices). Reduced affordability leads, sooner or later, to a decrease in demand for house purchase, even if other factors (e.g., demographics or employment patterns) might still be having a positive impact on demand. (And then the only palatable choices open to people who cannot afford access to the tenure in a given place are (i) staying with relatives,[29] (ii) moving elsewhere in the country, (iii) moving into the private rented sector, or (iv) moving into the public rented sector, if such exists.)

It is clear that flippers and patrons have overlapping motives for buying (and selling) houses, but only partially so. Their behaviour is affected by different forces and considerations. One way to model the behaviour of both groups is by means of a so-called excess-bid model, originally suggested by Smith et al. (1988), and applied to the US housing market by Ekins (2011). The model states that the average house-price change (as measured by an appropriate house-price index) from period $t-1$ to period t is a linear function of the number of bids to buy houses in $t-1$ minus the number of offers in $t-1$:

$$P_t - P_{t-1} = \Delta P = \alpha + \beta_1(B^F_{t-1} - O^F_{t-1}) + \beta_2(B^P_{t-1} - O^P_{t-1}), \tag{11.1}$$

where B^F and O^F are bids and offers by flippers and B^P and O^P are bids and offers by patrons. Equation (11.1) suggests that even if patrons' demand stagnates or weakens, house prices may still be rising (for a time) due to flippers' demand, and vice versa.

The difficulty of course is to operationalize Equation (11.1). Because actual data on bids and offers is impossible to come by, an alternative is to use proxies. Ekins (2011) suggests replacing patrons' (he calls them 'homeowners') bids and offers by a function for 'the shortage (surplus) of housing' (which is hard to determine in its own right), and flippers' (he calls them 'investors') bids and offers by a function for 'the rate of return' (which is also problematic when applied to non-professional flippers).

It must be noted that Equation (11.1) is not really a substitute for a mainstream housing demand function (which attempts to associate house prices to fundamental demand drivers, ranging from commuting time to demographics, incomes, or interest rates), because, after all, the number of patrons' bids (or offers) is determined precisely by such drivers. In the flippers' case, on the other hand, one must bear in mind that the most important behavioural driver is expected house-price change – which therefore cannot be determined by the number of flippers' bids or offers because they themselves are determined by that change.

Given demand (originating with flippers and patrons), development activity is particularly important, as it introduces new supply into the picture. It is also special because it is mainly and directly determined by developers' expected return R_e and RRR.

11.8.3 A model of housing market volatility

We can incorporate R_e and RRR into a model of owner-occupied housing market volatility by means of a number of steps:[30]

1 Initial situation: housing market is at equilibrium, with price $= P_1$.
2 Price P_1 is incorporated in house-price forecasts (which may make use of still older house prices, and in practice either reflect market practitioners' experience or common knowledge, or else are calculated by professional vendors – cf. Section 5.5.4). Say that the forecast price for the next relevant period is P_2.
3 P_2 and P_1 together determine a provisional expected rate of return R_e for market actors. This is given as $R_e = (P_2/P_1)^{1/n} - 1$, where $n =$ period number.
4 If $R_e > 0$, or if inflation-adjusted $R_e > 0$,

    (a) Flippers' demand for houses will increase as they will be expecting a positive capital gain (assuming that transaction costs have been accounted for).
    (a) Patrons' demand for housing may also be positively affected as some will fear that if they do not buy now they will be priced out of the market, and others will postpone selling to take advantage of expected higher prices. (Sooner or later, however, patrons' demand will begin to reflect affordability worries.)

    The opposite will happen if $R_e < 0$.
5 Simultaneously, and as a first approximation, reflecting market 'sentiment', if $P_2 > P_1$, or if inflation-adjusted $P_2 > P_1$, profit expectations rise; if $P_2 < P_1$, or if inflation-adjusted $P_2 < P_1$, profit expectations drop. (In practice, it is more likely that, at this stage, nominal P_2 rather than inflation-adjusted P_2 is used.) The usual (or at least welcome!) case is one of rising profit expectations; but this is not enough to determine what will happen to new housing supply because, in addition to inflation, a developer's RRR must also be taken into account.
6 Enter a given 'risk–expected-return' function, whose vertical intercept is some risk-free rate (assuming that such can exist), and which characterizes the 'average' developer. The function itself may graph as a straight line (in the case of risk neutrality), as an upward-sloping curve (in the case of risk aversion), or as a downward-sloping curve (in the case of risk-seeking).
7 The change in profit expectations causes the 'risk–expected-return' line to pivot around the risk-free rate. If the expectation is of a profit increase (decrease), the line will tilt upwards (downwards). (The risk-free rate, if it exists at all, may also change if, for example, the maturity of the instrument, with which the rate is associated, changes.) Such a movement means that, for a given R_e, the corresponding 'amount' of risk is now less (more) than before (see Figure 11.7). It can also mean that, following an upward shift, an R_e that is higher than previously can now be associated with less risk than before!
8 The R_e that was calculated in (3), together with its corresponding risk (after the shift of the 'risk – expected-return' line) will, over a period of time, affect developers' (or

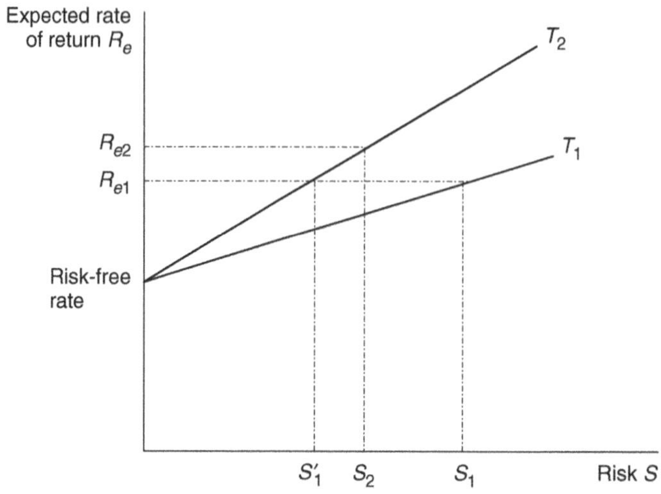

Figure 11.7 Risk–return trade-off: after the line has pivoted from T_1 to T_2, it is possible to have higher return and less risk than before.

professional flippers') RRR. The importance of the RRR is that it serves as a cap rate k for discounting future (gross or net) returns, e.g., future asset prices, in order for developers to ascertain what building and land costs to incur or what (house) price to pay now, while preserving k. If k = RRR = (revenue − costs)/costs, then costs payable = revenue/$(1+k)$. Or, in the case of professional flippers, current price payable = revenue/$(1+k)$. The difference of the present approach from that in Section 7.9 is that now RRR is not given, but needs to be estimated.

(In a more complete model, housing developers' RRR would also be determined by RRRs elsewhere in the economy, as already suggested in Section 5.5.4. Regarding flippers or similarly acting agents, in particular, the risk associated with house purchase may make more sense to estimate in the context of a portfolio approach. As is, the RRR is a function of R_e, the more so if the latter has become, or is thought to have become, 'established' in the given market – cf. Section 5.5.4.)

9 The RRR that will be eventually established may well be higher or lower than what it was before the R_e was itself re-adjusted as a result of forecasting a P_2.

10 It is even possible that the RRR that will be eventually established may be higher or lower than what it was before, irrespective of whether R_e itself has increased or decreased. The reason is that the RRR is assumed to be made up of a real-return component and a risk-premium component (in addition to an inflation component). So even if a new, higher R_e pulls up the real-return component of RRR, the overall value of RRR may actually drop if the risk-premium component declines sufficiently!

11 In the case of professional flippers, the RRR serves to discount real P_2, which we can denote by $P_2^{r,d}$. (Alternatively, if P_2 had not been already inflation-adjusted, RRR would definitely have to include an inflation component.)

12 If the discounted real price from the next period is more than the current price, (i.e., if $P_2^{r,d} > P_1$), then professional flippers will buy in order to sell.

13 In the case of developers, the RRR (possibly adjusted through the process described) will serve to determine either the price that a developer will pay for land or whether it

is profitable to commence housebuilding immediately anyway (i.e., either on land just bought or on land held for some time). The rule is simple: build if the RRR-discounted difference between the expected revenue from selling finished dwellings and the sum of construction and effective land costs is non-negative – cf. Section 7.9. This proposition is in line with Tobin's *q* ratio, introduced in Section 3.3.2.

14 We suggested above that the RRR does not change immediately. A higher R_e is consistent with a currently given RRR only if developers have reduced their estimates of risk commensurately. But as the 'risk–expected-return' line has shifted upwards due to risen profit expectations, this is precisely what has happened.

Summing up the key points, the above is a four-step process:

(i) Profit or loss expectations (based on forecast house prices) cause the 'risk–expected-return' function of investors to pivot.
(ii) Simultaneously, an expected rate of return (based on current and forecast house prices) is formed.
(iii) Then, the expected rate of return becomes associated with a new risk level on the basis of the tilted 'risk–expected-return' function.
(iv) Finally, there is an internal re-adjustment of the real return and risk components of the investors' RRR, with which they discount the forecast house prices in order to compare them to current prices. (In the developers' case, RRR is used to determine whether discounted revenue – costs $\geq$ 0).

Figure 11.8 illustrates the basic elements of the above model by showing a rather static housing market, where equilibrium (i) exists and (ii) consists of new construction equalling stock depreciation. The illustration is an adaptation of the DiPasquale–Wheaton diagram

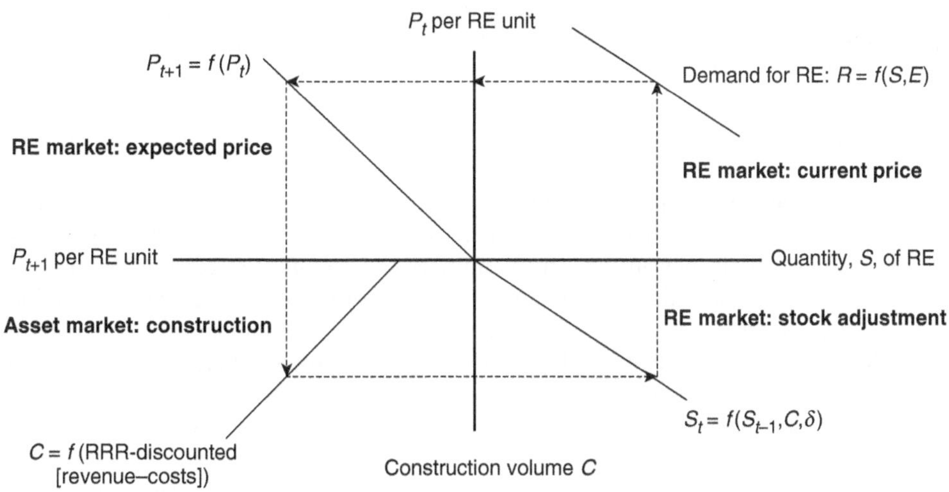

P_t = current price, P_{t+1} = future price, RRR = required rate of return, S = RE stock or space, δ = stock depreciation factor, E = exogenous determinant

Figure 11.8 A housing market where new construction = stock depreciation: developers use house price forecasts and RRRs to determine profitability.

introduced in Chapter 8; the main differences are (i) the use of house prices unmediated by rents and (ii) a more complex (i.e., partly endogenous) determination of the cap rate used, involving the RRR concept.

11.8.4 A model of housing market volatility (continued)

Given positive price expectations, there is a rise in demand for private housing, originating with both flippers and patrons. However, there may also be a rise in supply if older (and milder) positive price expectations on the part of developers had led them to initiate housing starts that are now coming to market. (In response to rises in demand, vacant privately owned houses may be put on the market too, perhaps after some renovation. If such quantity supplied is in reaction to current house prices, there is no shift of the supply curve of course; but if it is in expectation of still higher prices in the near future, there will be an increase in supply from that source also.)

More importantly, the current positive price expectations will motivate developers to increase building (assuming that land for housebuilding is or becomes available, or that more high-rise building is allowed). This agrees with research results:[31] on the basis of relevant data from 1969 Q1 to 1989 Q4, Poterba (1990) concluded that '[i]n the United States, a 10 per cent increase in real house prices would raise housing investment by between 0.1 per cent and 0.2 per cent of GNP [...]. For Canada, the elasticity is even larger; A similar-sized relative house-price move would lead to an increase of .3 per cent of GNP in single-family housing investment [...].' Thus:

15 Supply will also be increasing along with demand as past housing starts are finished and put on the market for sale. But since those starts were initiated when price expectations were less exuberant than they have subsequently become, their number was relatively small; therefore, the dampening effect on prices of those increases in supply are, *ceteris paribus*, quickly subsumed under further price rises due to renewed demand increases.

16 With demand increases larger than supply increases, the equilibrium price will actually rise. This will fuel profit expectations further, manifested mostly in flippers' behaviour.

17 The described cycle will then be repeated, forming an upward price spiral and increasing the probability of a bubble. Moreover, it is a cycle that is driven by essentially endogenous dynamics (i.e., price expectations rather than fundamentals).

18 If, in addition, demand increases due to exogenous factors (e.g., population pressures, income growth, cheaper mortgage credit, housing subsidies), profit expectations will rise even more, and the upward movement of prices will acquire stronger momentum.

19 But at some point in time, the 'rising wave' of construction will become just too big, causing a sizeable, noticeable, dampening effect on prices. A moment may thus come at which $P^{r,d}_{t+1} < P_t$. If a bubble has formed by then, it will probably burst (see Figure 11.9).

20 The ensuing 'correction' in the housing market will last either until renewed increases in demand happen for exogenous reasons or supply has decreased sufficiently. The latter can happen through (i) physical depreciation, (ii) a possible re-allocation of supply between housing tenures as seen from the viewpoint of any particular tenure, (iii) a sizable decrease in the vacancy rate, (iv) withdrawal of 'for sale' properties from the market, or (v) a combination of all four.

21 The above scenario is about the burst of a bubble with supply as trigger. But things are not one-sided. Beyond some point, further increases in demand cannot be sustained. A crucial factor is the ratio of incomes to mortgage costs, which in turn depend on both

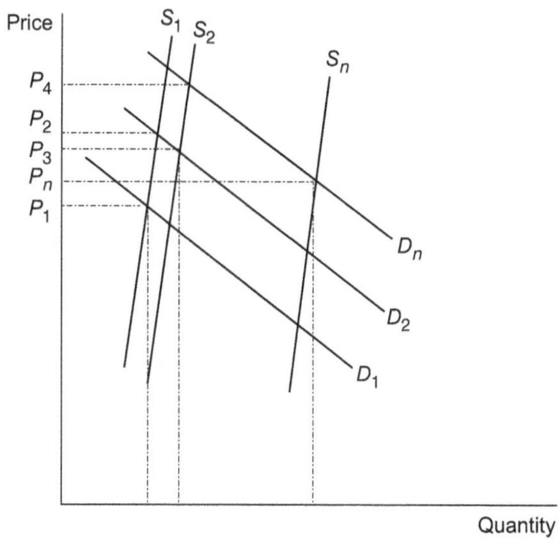

Figure 11.9 Housing market volatility: burst of a bubble. The scenario is of rising demand, with supply as trigger. Initially, rises in supply (in response to past housing starts becoming completed buildings) are moderate and overshadowed by demand rises; then supply increases accelerate as construction gathers momentum; when the 'rising wave' of construction crests, the bubble bursts as price drops from, for example, P_4 to P_n.

credit conditions and current house prices. This 'double-pronged' attack (overbuilding combined with an unsustainable ratio of incomes to mortgage costs) will check further price rises (depending on what happens to R_e as it affects the RRR), even if a massive increase in supply had not been enough, on its own, to do it.

22 Then a downward spiral will start operating, characterized by three kinds of surplus: (i) a surplus of unsold newly constructed dwellings; (ii) a surplus caused by flippers rushing to sell recently acquired properties; (iii) a surplus caused by patrons in debt-servicing difficulties abandoning the owner-occupied sector for the rented one.

One possible reason for such difficulties is of course the adverse effect on the national economy of declining levels of housebuilding activity. Eventually things will start to stabilize at a lower level (see Figure 11.10), after those who cannot repay their mortgages have abandoned the sector, flippers have counted their losses, and net increases in the housing stock have approached zero. But the journey from stabilization to recovery may be a long one.

23 A reason why recovery can be strained involves a certain asymmetry between the 'virtuous' cycle represented by an upward spiral and the 'vicious' one represented by a downward one. This asymmetry results from some of the possible consequences of shifts in the 'risk–expected-return' line (as a result of changes in profit expectations). For a constant R_e, an upward shift will result in less risk; but a downward shift (as would typically happen in a market downturn) will result in more risk. Also, a rising line can be associated with a higher return – less risk than before; but a dropping line can be associated with a lower return – more risk than before (see Figure 11.11).

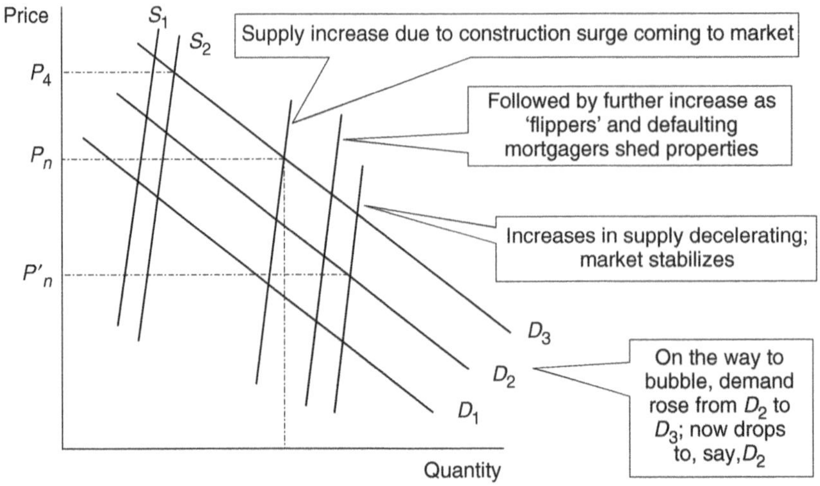

Figure 11.10 Market 'correction': there is a price bubble at P_4; the burst drops the price to P_n; there are more increases in supply, then deceleration; demand drops; there is market stabilization at, one hopes, price P'_n.

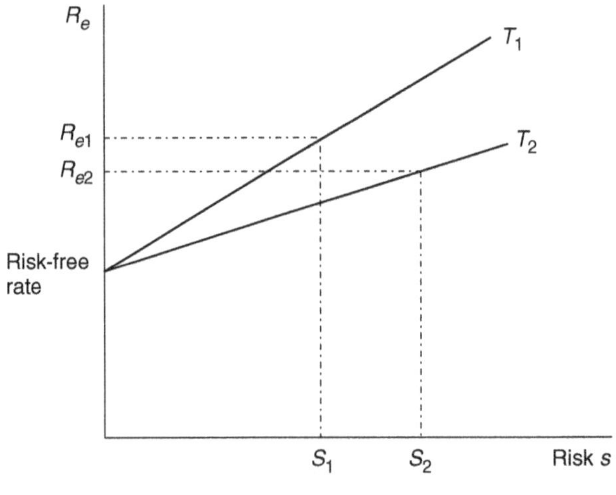

Figure 11.11 Risk–return trade-off: after the line has pivoted from T_1 to T_2, it is possible to have lower return and more risk than before.

And, because most developers, no less than most people, are risk-averse, the reduction in housing supply due to declining prices is likely to be faster and more persistent than the increase in supply due to rising prices usually is. That is, the response of supply to prices is characterized by *cyclical asymmetry* (cf., on the UK, Levin and Pryce, 2009; Ball et al., 2011).

24 Thus, whereas both an upturn and a downturn can be self-feeding, a downturn is more likely to need 'outside' help to be reversed, either in the form of autonomously stronger

demand related to 'fundamentals' or in the form of government-assisted demand boosts (cf. Bénétrix et al., 2011).

25 The rate of acceleration (deceleration) of demand shifts in relation to the rate of acceleration (deceleration) of supply shifts might be a good indicator of an upward spiral, or even a bubble, forming, or of a downward 'correction', or a burst, about to happen. (It is an open question whether it is safe to take the rate of acceleration or deceleration of house prices as a proxy for the relationship between the two previous rates mentioned.)

11.8.5 Concluding remarks

Theoretical and empirical research to date is consistent with the stylized model presented. For example, Malpezzi and Wachter (2005: 160) have suggested that 'even a simple model of lagged supply response to price changes and speculation is sufficient to generate real estate cycles. Second, the volatility of prices [...] is strongly related to supply conditions'. Sorensen (2006: 96–7) has found that in the short run house prices are momentum-driven, and can deviate substantially from equilibrium, while in the long run they are determined by 'fundamentals', the most important of which he identified as income (GDP), rent and construction costs. Cunningham and Kolet (2007) and Bracke (2011) have found *positive duration dependence* during housing market expansions but *not* during downturns. This means that upturns are more likely to end (i.e., have higher *exit probabilities*) the longer they last. The Cunningham and Kolet (2007) study covered 125 US cities from 1975 to 2005 as well as 12 Canadian ones from 1980 to 2005; the Bracke (2011) study covered 19 OECD countries from 1970 Q1 to 2010 Q1.

Cunningham and Kolet (2007) attributed their result to speculative activity, which drives house prices up during expansion phases, out of sync with the influence of fundamentals, and pointed out that speculation cannot occur during contraction phases because short selling (i.e., selling an asset one does not own) is not possible in housing markets. Hence, the end of a contraction phase depends largely on fundamentals, and 'to the extent that policy-makers influence real income growth and real interest rates they are likely to have a substantial effect on the duration of housing market contractions' (Cunningham and Kolet, 2007: 24). In the same vein, Bracke (2011: 19) concluded that 'booms represent departures from fundamentals that are increasingly difficult to sustain', while downturns are 'periods in which corrections need to take place'.

The above analysis pictures a housing market that has an inherent tendency to volatility (implying both the possibility of *mean reversion* in the long run, and of *serial correlation* in the short run – see Sorensen, 2006; Glaeser and Gyourko, 2007; Gao et al., 2009; Borgersen et al., 2010), but that can also register periods of relative calmness (implying price changes close to the trend) if (a) there is no speculation or herd behaviour and (b) the magnitudes of the changes associated with R_e, RRR, and demand- and supply-drivers are small and non-cumulative.

It also suggests uncertainty as to whether the market is, at any point in time, at a pre-bubble or a pre-burst stage. The uncertainty stems from many sources: on the supply side, one example is the extent to which a higher-real-return component in the RRR is possibly associated with a lower-risk component, because that extent is not really observable, especially beforehand. Econometric analysis can go a long way towards identifying bubbles before they burst (cf. Sorensen, 2006), even if it is cautious on occasion (cf. Case and Shiller, 2004), but this kind of research may not be accessible to non-specialists.

Various prestigious media sources did try to alert the public that by 2004–05 there was a housing bubble in quite a few countries (*The Economist*, 2003, 2005;[32] Krugman, 2005; McKibbin and Stoeckel, 2006; Hudson, 2006) but such warnings are more likely to precipitate a bubble burst once a bubble has formed than to provide any real remedy. This is why conventional or 'rule-of-thumb' ways of identifying bubbles – see Section 11.4 – will continue to be used. To those seeking a failsafe way to spot the crest of a bubble, or the trough of a burst, the uncertainty may appear disappointing; it is nevertheless inevitable.

Summary of main points

1 Asset-, including housing-, price bubbles happen when buoyant expectations of further price growth overshoot the influence of 'fundamental' factors determining demand and supply, and, at the same time, demand is 'excessively' enhanced, and speculative expectations begin to have material effects, with the help of 'outside' finance, particularly credit.

2 Bursts happen when market 'actors' realize, through an accumulation of signs, that the current level of prices is unsustainable.

3 In the housing sphere, the most potent of such signs are (a) a strong increase in the rate of house prices to incomes, relative to the ratio's long-run trend, and (b) an oversupply (or 'overhang') of dwellings.

4 The more a bubble has been financed by credit, and the greater and more varied the interconnections among financial institutions, or the complexity of their financial products, the more adverse the effects of the burst will be upon the wider economy.

5 Planning and land-use restrictions, and taxes, do not normally cause bubbles or bursts, but may contribute to them when other factors are also present and begin to work.

6 No single factor sparked the speculative wave that caused the US housing bubble of 2006. It was caused by a variety of demand-enhancing factors, the main ones being (a) lax and careless regulations governing the operation of financial institutions, assessments of their products, and credit conditions, and (b) overenthusiastic political support for expanding owner-occupation even among households with predictably poor ability to service their mortgage loans if even slightly adverse developments occurred (like rises in interest rates).

7 On the basis of historical experience, the danger of a bubble can be minimized mainly through more effective and prudent regulation of financial institutions, indeed of the entire financial system, and of the extension of credit.

8 'Automatic stabilizers' are supposed to be instruments, monetary or fiscal (i.e., taxes), that 'automatically' decelerate asset price rises or drops in a market upturn or downturn, respectively, thus contributing to market price stability.

9 It is doubtful whether any tax can serve as an effective 'automatic stabilizer' in the housing market, unless it becomes really steep during an upturn, in which case it will probably cause a market reversal, and will therefore tend to produce more price volatility, not less.

10 In addition, if relatively mild taxation is to be used as an 'automatic stabilizer', it is unlikely to have any significant effect (as bubbles and bursts are mainly caused by non-tax forces at work), unless it is applied at the beginning of a bubble. But bubbles are not known *ex ante*, and choosing when to apply the tax beats the very concept of an 'automatic stabilizer'.

11 Further, asset appreciation is not necessarily a bad thing. Often, it is just the inevitable effect of, as well as a stimulus towards, economic growth.

12 There are three kinds of 'actors' in an advanced owner-housing market: 'flippers', 'patrons', and 'developers'. Flippers are the speculators. Patrons are buyers with long-term prospective holding periods. Developers are builders of new homes. Developers' decisions are based on expected returns and their RRR. The latter is in turn influenced by market experience. Developers tend to oversupply in a housing market upturn, thus precipitating the eventual downturn. Downturns are made worse by flippers, mortgagers in difficulties, and foreclosing banks trying to sell properties.

Review questions and exercises

1 List and discuss possible causes of housing market bubbles and their bursts.

2 Why are housing market bubbles important? Are they more or less important than stock market bubbles? Why?

3 What is *duration dependence*? How does it relate to asset price bubbles? What is *permit intensity*? What is its purpose?

4 List conventional ways of checking for a housing market bubble.

5 What exactly are 'automatic stabilizers'? Do you think taxes could act as such in a housing market in order to avoid the formation of bubbles? What kind of taxes?

6 Do you think that housing market professional (or at least 'compulsive'!) flippers are likely to have the same RRR as housing developers? Why yes or why not?

7 How likely is it that planning restrictions (or 'prescriptive planning', 'smart growth', etc.) can be the main cause behind a housing market bubble? Discuss.

8 Go to Section 11.4 where the effects across tenures of the burst of the US housing market bubble of 2006 are summarized. Prepare a report with actual historic data – in addition to those already mentioned there – that substantiate or corroborate those effects. For example, house prices from 2001 and after; drops in construction starts for rented accommodation; vacancy rates in both owner-occupied and rented sectors; interest rates for house purchase; and annual number of notices of default, auction or repossession on properties. A good source is www.census.gov/hhes/www/housing.html; feel free to access more.

9 Go to Figures 11.6(a) and (b) Try to follow the process described in each by means of demand and supply equations. For parameters, use whatever sensible numbers you like. On the basis of your equations, calculate changes in the number of surplus homes or of vacancies at every step of the process.

10 By the end of 2011, two views were clashing regarding the proper way to deal with the Eurozone sovereign debt crisis:

- One view (policy A, which was the one applied when the crisis broke out in 2009–10, starting with Greece) stressed the need for severe fiscal austerity, efficiency-boosting domestic reforms, possibly some 'voluntary' debt-restructuring, and support loans from the 'troika' (IMF, EU, ECB).
- The other view (policy B) suggested that the only viable solution to the Eurozone crisis was for the ECB to print money (or create reserves) with which to buy back massive chunks of the public debt of those members who were most in trouble (cf. Paul Krugman's 'The Hole in Europe's Bucket', *The New York Times*, 23 October 2011). This one-off action would fuel inflation in the Eurozone (unemployment

notwithstanding), maybe up to 10 per cent in the first year, but thereafter the inflation rate would gradually drop; beneficiaries would be able to focus efforts on achieving growth (with help from much needed domestic reforms, which presumably would not stop), without being burdened by the seemingly vicious circle of austerity and recession that initial attempts at implementing policy A had brought about. Higher inflation would make Eurozone exports more expensive, but the drop in the euro exchange rate vis-à-vis other currencies would compensate for that.

(a) In theory, how could policy A/policy B impact on the housing markets of Eurozone members subjected to either A or B? What are your chosen assumptions? (*Hint:* Before you start building your scenarios, ascertain whether the sovereign debt crises of those members were or were not caused by prior developments in their housing markets.)
(b) Can you find some data to see what actually happened in the housing markets of, say, Greece, Portugal, Ireland, and Spain over the period 2009–12? (*Hint:* Focus on prices, sales volumes, and investment volumes as a percentage of GDP.)

12 RE performance and price measures

Main sections

Having gone through this chapter, a student should be able to

1. Tell the difference between 'value' and 'price'.
2. Tell the difference between RE 'valuation' and RE 'performance measurement'.
3. Define a money-weighted rate of return (MWRR), a time-weighted rate of return (TWRR), compare the two, and explain for whom – investor or investment manager – each is more appropriate.
4. Explain the difference between 'average price' and 'price index'.
5. Explain why a simple arithmetic house price average is not appropriate as a basis for a house-price index, why the median is comparably better, and why neither must be no. 1 choice for a house-price index.
6. List, define, compare, and generally, albeit briefly, discuss the main RE price indices in use today: hedonic, repeat-sales, mix-adjustment, and SPAR.
7. Perform calculations for constructing a simple price index under each of the four mainstream methods.
8. Give a basic account of hedonics theory as applied on housing.

12.1 Value versus price versus performance

To invest in a RE asset, an investor needs to know how much the asset is really (or 'intrinsically') worth, given estimates of future rental income from it, an appropriate discount rate, and maybe a resale or liquidation price.[1] This is valuation (or appraisal).

Price assessment is about finding out what the 'market' at large would be prepared to pay for the property – what is often referred to as 'fair value'.

The valuation figure needs to be compared with actual market price (or 'ask' price) to see whether the two match. If they do not, if, for example, 'ask' price is higher than estimated value, some adjustment (probably in the investor's offer price, or in the investor's expected return, or in the seller's ask price) will have to be made – or else the investor will walk away.

To assess whether the investment has been successful or not, and to what extent, one or more performance measures are required. In using such measures, the basic input is of course actual price paid to buy the asset, actual net income received since then, and actual price received from selling the asset, if this has been the case. If no sale has taken place, the (estimated) value of the asset at the time of performance measurement will have to do. In performance measurement, historic 'value', as opposed to actual purchase price, plays no role – whereas, in the absence of a realized sale price, current estimated value does. Put differently, valuation happens before investing or selling, performance measurement happens after investing or selling.

The construction of price indices involves a simpler issue: how realized prices, or at least recorded 'ask' prices, have evolved over time. No questions are asked as to what mathematical calculations took place in an investor's or seller's mind on the way to forming said prices. It is the end result – the formulated price – that matters. Naturally, once a reputable price index is up and running, market participants are almost certain to use it in order to find out what the current or future price for a particular property, or groups of such, is likely to be.

Asset performance measurement, including that for RE, does not have to involve an exogenous discount, or capitalization, rate – except as a benchmark for comparison. Past outlay and current value, and figures for net rental income in the interim period, are all the primary inputs needed. The purpose is to identify a rate of return that accurately portrays how well the investment under consideration has performed from the point of view of an interested party, say, an investment manager or an individual investor (who may be the manager's client).

Back in Chapter 5, we introduced the two main methods of investment appraisal: NPV and IRR. We went on to consider special cases (see Section 5.5.2), like 'rent growth only once, at time of next rent review' or 'constant rent growth, rent reviews every *m* years'. In so doing, we identified 'exotic' yield measures like 'equivalent yield' (EvY) or 'equated yield' (EtY). In this chapter, however, our focus is on methods of constructing RE price indices, and RE performance measures. Let us begin with the latter.

12.2 Main RE performance measures

There are two main methods of investment performance measurement. The first calculates a money-weighted rate of return (MWRR), which is in the nature of an internal rate of return (IRR), as defined in Section 5.5.1. The second calculates a time-weighted rate of return (TWRR), which is in the nature of an interest rate.

A MWRR considers all net inflows of cash from an investment undertaken at time t_0 up to and including time t_i. Time t_i may be the time when the investment was liquidated (sold), or a time deemed appropriate for calculating investment performance since t_0. Thus, the last 'inflow' considered may be either the proceeds from the sale of the asset or the estimated value of the asset at t_i. The discount rate that will equate the sum of the discounted inflows to the initial investment outlay is the investment's IRR, and doubles as the investment's MWRR.

The reason why this IRR is called MWRR is that, in addition to the value of the investment at t_i, it takes into account only actual cash inflows over the investment's holding period (or outflows, which are really negative inflows), disregarding intermediate changes in the 'paper' value of the investment. The TWRR, by contrast, takes into account both 'paper' variations in the investment's value (say, monthly ones) and cash inflows (or outflows).

An individual investor would prefer the money-weighted method of performance measurement because it focuses on any contributions to the investment (i.e., inflows of cash) the investor has made throughout the holding period, as well as any withdrawals from it (i.e., outflows of cash). After all, an investor's primary concern is a comparison between outlays (both positive and negative) towards the investment and the 'final' value of it.

Portfolio or mutual-fund accounts managed by investment managers on behalf of clients are a typical example of such an investment, as very frequently clients will contribute more money to their accounts (to be invested in underlying assets) or withdraw money from them (by liquidating underlying assets).

On the other hand, the MWRR is not very fair to the investment manager because the money-weighted method ignores intermediate changes in the value of the investment – which, however, are an indication of the 'goodness' of the manager's investment strategy and choices. For this reason the time-weighted method is the investment manager's preferred tool for assessing investment performance, as the method looks into cash inflows and outflows *as well as* intermediate changes in the value of the portfolio throughout the holding period.

12.2.1 Money-weighted versus time-weighted performance measures

To calculate a TWRR we need first to calculate holding-period rates of return (HPRR) for the investment. The general formula for a HPRR is

$$\text{HPRR} = \frac{V_1 - V_0 + \text{CF}_1}{V_0}, \tag{12.1}$$

where

V_0 = value of the investment at the beginning of the holding period,
V_1 = value of the investment at the end of the holding period,
CF_1 = sum of cash inflows (some positive, some negative) during the given period.

Table 12.1 compares MWRR with TWRR by means of an example.[2] The value of an investment on 31 December 2012 is £500,000. Its value at the end of every subsequent quarter during 2013 is shown in Table 12.1. In addition, the investor puts another £40,000 in the account on 31 August 2013, probably because by the same date the investment had gained £30,000 over its value on 30 June 2013 and prospects looked good. Finally, on 31 December 2013, the investor pays an annual fee of £3000 to the investment manager. What is the investor's rate of return (or MWRR)? What is the investment manager's rate of return (or TWRR)?

Table 12.1 Comparison of MWRR and TWRR

Money-weighted RR = IRR			*Time-weighted RR (chain-linked HPRRs)*		
Valuation and/or cash-inflow dates	*Valuations and/or cash inflows*		*Valuation and/or cash-inflow dates*	*Valuations and/or cash inflows*	*Holding-period RR (HPRR)*
31 December 2012	500,000		31 December 2012	500,000	
31 March 2013	460,000		31 March 2013	460,000	−8.00%
30 June 2013	480,000		30 June 2013	480,000	4.35%
30 September 2013	560,000		31 August 2013 plus appreciation but without contribution	510,000	6.25%
31 December 2013	550,000		31 August 2013 plus appreciation and contribution	550,000	
			30 September 2013	560,000	1.82%
By 31 August 2013, the investment appreciates by	30,000		31 December 2013 minus annual fee of $3,000	547,000	−2.32%
On 31 August 2013, the investor contributes to the account	40,000				
On 31 December 2013, the investor pays annual fee to investment manager	3,000		**Time-weighted RR =**		1.44%
IRR =		1.3636%			
PV of contribution		−39,640.5			
PV of annual fee		−2,959.6			
PV of value of investment on 31 December 2013		542,601.1			
Sum =		500,001.0			

(a) The investor's RR is simply the investment's IRR: the RR that equates the PVs of the two cash inflows plus the PV of the investment at the end of the entire holding period (EHP) under consideration to the investment's initial value of £500,000. The two cash inflows (a contribution of £40,000 and a fee of £3000) are negative since both sums represent investor outlays. Through trial and error using a spreadsheet, the IRR (= MWRR) is found to be 1.3636 per cent:[3]

$$PV = \frac{40,000}{[(1+i)^{(1/12)}]^8} + \frac{3000}{[(1+i)^{(1/12)}]^{12}} + \frac{550,000}{[(1+i)^{(1/12)}]^{12}} \approx 500,000 \tag{12.2}$$

(b) On the other hand, the investment manager needs to know how the client's account is performing over the EHP without the distorting effect of additional cash inflows. That requires chain-linking changes in the value of the client's account. Such changes must reflect the value of the account at different prescribed dates (say, every quarter or every month) as well as changes resulting from additional cash inflows (both positive and negative).

Thus, in Table 12.1, the change in the value of the account from 31 December 2012 to 31 March 2013 is -8 per cent. Then, by 31 August 2013, the account appreciates by $(510-480)/480 = 6.25$ per cent in relation to its value on 30 June 2013, i.e., by £30,000. Also, on 31 August 2013, the client contributes an additional £40,000, so that by 30 September 2013, the value of the account becomes

> 480,000 + 30,000 + 40,000 + 10,000 (which is an assumed further increase in the value of the account since 31 August 2013) = 560,000;

hence, between 31 August 2013 and 30 September 2013, the account appreciates by $(560-550)/550 = 1.82$ per cent.

Finally, by 31 December 2013, the account's value declines to £550,000 but the client has to pay £3000 towards the account's annual service fee, so the post-fee value drops to £547,000.

Chain-linking all those changes together we get

$$(1-0.08)(1+0.0435)(1+0.0625)(1+0.0182)(1-0.0232) - 1 = 0.0144,$$
$$\text{or } 1.44 \text{ per cent} \tag{12.3}$$

This is the investment manager's time-weighted RR, which may also serve as another way to measure the performance of the investment under consideration.

Generally,

$$\text{TWRR} = (1+\text{HPRR}_1)(1+\text{HPRR}_2)\cdots(1+\text{HPRR}_n) - 1. \tag{12.4}$$

Box 12.1 explains the rationale for the formula (12.4).

Box 12.1 Derivation of the TWRR formula

Consider a sum a_0 that earns interest at a rate i that may vary from one period to another. At the end of the first period,

$$a_0(1+i_1)=a_1 \Rightarrow \frac{a_1}{a_0}=1+i_1.$$

But any rate of return is given as

$$\frac{a_1-a_0}{a_0}=\frac{a_1}{a_0}-1,$$

which is also equal to $(1+i_1)-1$. At the end of the next period,

$$a_2=a_1(1+i_2)=a_0(1+i_1)(1+i_2)\Rightarrow \frac{a_2}{a_0}=(1+i_1)(1+i_2).$$

The rate of return is

$$\frac{a_2-a_0}{a_0}=\frac{a_2}{a_0}-1,$$

which is also equal to $(1+i_1)(1+i_2)-1$. Since the rate of return covers both periods, i.e., the time from a_0 to a_2, it is the TWRR.

The TWRR can also be found for two or more years by chain-linking the TWRR of each year. In the example used, the TWRR was 1.44 per cent. If the TWRR for 2014 is, say, 5.6 per cent, the TWRR for both years, i.e., for the entire two-year period, is of course

$$\text{TWRR}_{2y}=(1+0.0144)(1+0.056)-1=7.12 \text{ per cent.}$$

On the basis of TWRR_{2y}, the annualized average TWRR for each of the two years is found as the TWRR_{av} in the following formula:

$$1(1+\text{TWRR}_{av})^2=1+\text{TWRR}_{2y}.$$

Hence,

$$\text{TWRR}_{av}=(1+\text{TWRR}_{2y})^{1/2}-1=(1+0.0712)^{1/2}-1=3.5 \text{ per cent.}$$

And, generally, for t years,

$$\text{TWRR}_{av}=(1+\text{TWRR}_{ty})^{1/t}-1. \quad (12.5)$$

Let us return to Table 12.1 for a moment. If we take out the intermediate cash flows (i.e., the investor's contribution and the annual fee), it transpires that the TWRR and the IRR are one and the same: 10 per cent! (Verification is left as an exercise for the student.) This is inevitable as, in the absence of intermediate cash flows between the beginning and the end of the EHP, the very rate of return that makes the initial investment outlay grow to a given final value is also the one that makes the final value be discounted, i.e., collapse, back to the initial outlay.

12.2.2 A RE application

As of 2005, London-based IPD, one of the largest vendors of performance measures for commercial RE worldwide, has actually been calculating property rates of return using the time-weighted method. IPD turned towards TWRR for the following reasons (IPD, 2004):

1 To make their property performance indices compatible with performance indices for other assets (e.g., stocks and mutual fund shares), which for a long time had been based on the time-weighted method.
2 To meet client demand for more frequent reporting based on quarterly or half-year valuations.
3 To conform with international standards, such as those suggested in GIPS.[4]

An added reason for the turn towards TWRR was that the MWRR produced 'counter-intuitive' results (IPD, 2006). Let us see how. Table 12.2 shows a Price Index for a property class, on the basis of which the value of a property at end-December 2012 was £1,000,000, rising thereafter every month throughout 2013 by the rate(s) of growth of the Index. The property also yields a monthly rental income equal to £8333, or £100,000 annually. This information allows us to calculate a total rate of return, a capital gain rate of return, and a rental income rate of return as follows:

- $$\text{TRR for } i\text{th month} = \frac{\text{capital value}_i + \text{rental income}_i - \text{capital value}_{i-1}}{\text{capital value}_{i-1}}; \qquad (12.6)$$

  for example,

  $$\text{TRR for August} = \frac{1,165,859 + 8333 - 1,143,440}{1,143,440} = 2.69 \text{ per cent.}$$

- $$\text{CGRR for } i\text{th month} = \frac{\text{capital value}_i - \text{capital value}_{i-1}}{\text{capital value}_{i-1}}; \qquad (12.7)$$

  for example,

  $$\text{CGRR for August} = \frac{1,165,859 - 1,143,440}{1,143,440} = 1.96 \text{ per cent.}$$

- $$\text{RIRR for } i\text{th month} = \frac{\text{rental income}_i}{\text{capital value}_{i-1}}; \qquad (12.8)$$

  for example,

  $$\text{RIRR for August} = \frac{8,333}{1,143,440} = 0.73 \text{ per cent.}$$

Table 12.2 Calculation of 12-month rental income rate of return by the time-weighted method and the residual method (i.e., as difference between TRR and CGRR)

	Price index (Dec. 2000 = 100)	*Capital value (CV)*	*Income*	*Total rate of return (TRR)*	*Capital gain rate of return (CGRR)*	*Rental income rate of return (RIRR)*	
						As difference between TRR and CGRR	*As percentage of income into previous-period CV*
Dec.	224.50	1,000,000					
Jan.	228.79	1,019,129	8,333	2.75%	1.91%	0.83%	0.83%
Feb.	233.19	1,038,693	8,333	2.74%	1.92%	0.82%	0.82%
Mar.	237.68	1,058,703	8,333	2.73%	1.93%	0.80%	0.80%
Apr.	242.27	1,079,171	8,333	2.72%	1.93%	0.79%	0.79%
May	246.97	1,100,108	8,333	2.71%	1.94%	0.77%	0.77%
June	251.78	1,121,527	8,333	2.70%	1.95%	0.76%	0.76%
July	256.70	1,143,440	8,333	2.70%	1.95%	0.74%	0.74%
Aug.	261.74	1,165,859	8,333	2.69%	1.96%	0.73%	0.73%
Sept.	258.84	1,152,950	8,333	−0.39%	−1.11%	0.71%	0.71%
Oct.	255.98	1,140,209	8,333	−0.38%	−1.11%	0.72%	0.72%
Nov.	253.15	1,127,634	8,333	−0.37%	−1.10%	0.73%	0.73%
Dec.	250.37	1,115,222	8,333	−0.36%	−1.10%	0.74%	0.74%
12-month rates of return by the TWRR method:				22.06%	11.52%	9.54%	9.54%
12-month RIRR by the residual method, i.e., RIRR = TRR – CGRR =						10.54%	
12-month internal rate of return:				22.51%			
Price index rate of growth: from Jan. to Aug.,			1.0035	From Aug. to Dec.,		0.998	

For the whole of 2013 we then have, by means of the time-weighted method:

$$\text{TRR} = (1+0.0275)(1+0.0274)\cdots(1-0.0036)-1 = 22.06 \text{ per cent},$$

$$\text{CGRR} = (1+0.0191)(1+0.0192)\cdots(1-0.011)-1 = 11.52 \text{ per cent},$$

$$\text{RIRR} = (1+0.0083)(1+0.0082)\cdots(1+0.0074)-1 = 9.54 \text{ per cent}.$$

Notice that although, for any given month, RIRR = TRR – CGRR, this is not true for the whole year. For example, for August, RIRR = 0.0269 – 0.0196 = 0.0073; but for 2013, 0.2206 – 0.1152 = 0.1054 rather than 0.0954.

On the other hand, if we calculate RIRR by the residual method, i.e., as the difference between TRR and CGRR, the annual result (i.e., 0.1054) must be wrong because the figure found is even larger than the ratio of the entire annual rent (£100,000) to the initial CV (£1,000,000), which is obviously 10 per cent. But how can that be when, on a monthly basis, the same rental income is calculated over an increasing CV?

Instead, the time-weighted method takes this declining monthly RIRR into account, and gives a figure for the annual RIRR that is lower than 10 per cent, as intuitively it should be.

Not does it matter that under the time-weighted method, RIRR $\neq$ TRR – CGRR; for in reality the total return is not the simple sum of capital appreciation and rental income, considered independently, but also reflects the influence of rental income on capital appreciation.

Finally in Table 12.2, the IRR, i.e., the MWRR, is found to be 22.51 per cent, against 22.06 per cent for the time-weighted TRR. The difference is small of course, but the TWRR does reflect a certain degree of market adversity (i.e., negative capital growth from September to December 2013) that the money-weighted IRR fails to capture.

12.3 RE price indices: prologue

The vast majority of RE owners, brokers, agents, and investors the world over do not care much about the housing wealth effect, the impact of owner-occupation on labour mobility, the re-establishment of market equilibrium, the income multiplier of RE investment, or difference equations. They only care about knowing today's price of a piece of RE, and next year's, or the next ten years', price of the same. But even those who are more sophisticated, and wish to know the why's and the how's of property price determination, or of market developments, ultimately need to focus on prices as bottom-line figures.

Those, therefore, who provide such price figures offer an essential service. They also have to be more knowledgeable than the average investor. And they must use, as far as possible, robust techniques of price estimation, usually invented and tested by statisticians and econometricians.

We shall look into such techniques shortly. Technique, however, can only take one so far. At most, it can tell one what the price of a piece of RE currently is – within a certain error margin. But by the time this knowledge has been gained, prices have already changed; and the error margin will be getting larger the further into the future one gazes. Past prices alone are an insufficient guide in this regard. This is where technique needs to be assisted by analysis – the why's and the how's of things. This is the job of a RE economist.

Yet any RE economist walking unprepared into a residential neighbourhood cannot hope to beat the average local RE broker or agent (or home-buyer for that matter – cf. Bajari et al., 2010b: 2) in terms of correctly appraising local properties – particularly non-income ones – although with commercial properties the economist should fare much better. Conversely, the broker or agent is unlikely to be in a position to estimate the future state of the market, or assess the impact of forces acting upon it, better than an experienced economist.

This is the well-known idea that the road to knowledge is an interplay between data and analysis. We must bear this in mind simply because, despite owners' and investors' keen interest in prices as all that matters, and despite the robustness and sophistication of various RE price indices currently on offer world-wide, interpretation and a deep and wide view of things are still indispensable.

12.3.1 Price indices versus prices

RE price indices are constructed for both owner-occupied dwellings and commercial property (which may also be residential). In what follows, we shall focus on non-commercial residential RE, but two of the price-index techniques discussed – repeat-sales and hedonics – are by and large used for commercial property too (see Abraham, 1996; Booth and Marcato, 2003; Fisher, 2005; Haurin, 2005; Geltner and Pollakowski, 2007).

Generally a RE index has the following uses:

- It allows comparison of rates of return between the given property class and other property or asset classes (if, that is, they have price indices of their own).
- It provides essential investment information to buyers and sellers of particular properties in the given property class.
- It can serve as a rough proxy for approximating changes in prices of properties in other property classes if no relevant data exist.
- It facilitates studies of the factors that determine RE prices and of the way RE prices affect other economic magnitudes.
- It can be a primary input in RE price forecasting models, of both the time-series and the structural variety.[5]

A house-price index (HPI) in particular compares a current average or median price, usually weighted by various selected weights, with a corresponding past average or median price. Actually, the median is a better measure than the mean, because (a) it is much less influenced by 'abnormally' high or low prices in the data set, and (b) house prices are positively skewed. Whatever the measure of central tendency, construction of an index requires choosing a base period whose 'representative' house price will be compared with a subsequent house price. It is important to stress this point, because a period's, or a sample's, average or median price is not an index; a number becomes an index only when it is compared with a 'reference', or base-period, number which by assumption is equated to 100.

The equation used to calculate the average price may also offer an easy way to appraise similar properties in the space of time between two index calculation dates. For example, in the simplest possible case,

$$\text{average house price} = \frac{\text{sum of all house prices}}{\text{number of houses in sample}},$$

or

$$\overline{P} = \frac{1}{n}\sum_{p=1}^{n} P_i. \tag{12.9}$$

Hence, the price of a single house, outside the given sample, can be taken to be equal to the calculated average price plus or minus one standard deviation around this price. It is a very weak procedure because it assumes that all houses are identical, but is probably better than nothing.

Now, once we have two such average prices $\overline{P}_0$ and $\overline{P}_t$, where $\overline{P}_0$ = base-period price and $\overline{P}_t$ = period t's price, a price index showing how much, percentage-wise, the price in t has changed in relation to 0 would be

$$\mathrm{PI}_t = \frac{\overline{P}_t}{\overline{P}_0} \times 100. \tag{12.10}$$

This approach, however, is wrong for a number of good reasons:

1 We would not be comparing like with like. The period-t sample will almost certainly contain different dwellings from the period-0 sample, in terms of any of a number of

characteristics or attributes, like dwelling type, number of rooms, floor area, age, location, etc.

2 Consequently, the more the two samples differ from one another, the more misleading the measured price change will be.
3 The measured price change would be even more misleading if the change in sample composition between period t and period 0 coincided with the turning point in a house-price cycle. That is, if between the two periods, house prices began to decline, but the period-t sample contained more higher-priced properties than the period-0 sample, Equation (12.10) would give the false impression that the market was still on the rise.
4 The approach involves *systematic error*, or *bias*. This stems from two sources:

   (a) If the quality of the housing stock rises over the years, (12.10) will be reflecting the combined effect of house-price inflation and quality improvement. The latter typically commands a premium over the pre-improvement price quite apart from general house-price inflation. A good price index, though, is supposed to capture only the inflation effect.[6]
   (b) The *sample-selection problem*. It may be that certain dwelling types sell more frequently than others; also, the prices of those types may change faster than the prices of other types. As a result, the transaction prices of dwellings sold (those prices being the usual basis for forming period samples) will not accurately reflect the average price change for the entire dwelling stock (on account of those samples failing to represent the stock correctly).

Fortunately, there are methods, each with its own strengths and weaknesses, that allow us to compare like with like far more successfully than is possible with a price index like Equation (12.10), which is a ratio of simple (unweighted) arithmetic means (or medians) as defined in Equation (12.9). As for *bias*, the indices those methods produce are to various extents still susceptible to forms of it, but less so than Equation (12.10) is. These methods are the following:[7]

1 The *hedonic* (or *hedonic-regression*) method (Waugh, 1928; Court, 1939; *Griliches, 1961, 1967, 1971*; *Rosen, 1974; Muellbauer, 1974*; Halvorsen and Pollakowski, 1981; Cassel and Mendelsohn, 1985; Epple, 1987; Wallace, 1996; *Brachinger, 2002*; Janssen et al., 2001; Söderberg and Janssen, 2001; *Day, 2001*, 2003; Diewert, 2003; Murty, 2004; *Triplett, 2004*; Nesheim, 2006; Selim, 2008; *Bajari et al., 2010b*; *Eurostat RPPI, 2011; Fleming and Nellis, 2012*).
2 The *repeat-sales* (or *repeat-sales-regression, RSR*) method (Bailey et al., 1963; *Case and Shiller, 1987, 1989*; Conniffe and Duffy, 1999; Calnea, 2006a, b; *Geltner and Pollakowski, 2007*; *Standard and Poor's, 2009*; *Eurostat RPPI, 2011*).
3 The *mix-adjustment* or *stratification* method (Thwaites and Wood, 2003; *Meissner and Satchell, 2010*; Bank of Greece, 2011b; Nationwide, 2012; *Eurostat RPPI, 2011*).
4 The *Sale Price Appraisal Ratio* or *SPAR* method (*Bourassa et al., 2004*; Shi, 2008; Haan, 2009; Vries et al., 2009; *Eurostat RPPI, 2011*; Jónsdóttir and Jónasdóttir, 2011).
5 *Hybrid* methods, combining hedonics with repeat-sales or with mix-adjustment (Case and Quigley, 1991; Shiller, 1991; Quigley, 1995; Englund et al., 1998; Hwang and Quigley, 2004).

We shall now turn to a brief discussion of methods (1)–(4).

12.4 The hedonic method

This is perhaps the flagship of all mainstream methods. In addition to price index construction, the method can be and is used for valuing attributes that have significant welfare impact,[8] like environmental noise level, air quality (cf. Murty et al., 2004), means of commuting, or neighbourhood amenities; for identifying property submarkets (Day, 2003) or, combined with *geo-referencing*,[9] spatial variations in properties' location premium (Wu, 2002); or for complementing other price index construction methods, like mix-adjustment or RSR.

The word 'hedonic' comes from the Greek word for 'pleasure-giving', and was chosen because it suggests the idea that consumers value goods for the pleasure or utility that distinct attributes of the goods give them. This approach to consumer behaviour goes back to Lancaster's (1966) 'characteristics theory' (see Section 2.2.9), but the modern hedonic approach itself can be traced to Griliches' (1961) and Rosen's (1974) seminal papers, the latter being the first theory-rich extension of the method to housing. In this context, a good's, and particularly housing's, price is supposed to be a reflection of the implicit prices of the separate attributes 'making up' the good.

For this to hold, a crucial assumption is that a good is the sum of its attributes. This is questionable because, very probably, a good, like almost anything in life (including an animal's body, a human being, and society), is more than the sum of its parts. Another assumption is that those attributes are finite, identifiable and measurable – which is again far from certain.

An empirical problem with hedonics is that sometimes taking into account one more attribute may offer no additional appreciable measured effect on the price of a good. Including both (or all) such attributes will result in *over-specification* of the hedonic pricing model, causing erroneous statistical measurement. Alternatively, not all attributes, at least all the important ones, may be included in the model, resulting in *under-specification*, and erroneous conclusions about what determines price.

Below, we shall demonstrate construction of a hedonic price index for housing by means of a simple example. Remember, '[a] *hedonic price index is **any** price index that makes use of a hedonic function*' (Triplett, 2004: 41). The latter is a mathematical statement saying that the price of a good depends on the implicit prices of the characteristics or attributes of the good. We shall start with the simplest function possible, then introduce a more refined model that uses a semi-logarithmic functional form. We shall discuss what weights to use in a hedonic model, and finish by considering the model form and other problems.

12.4.1 A hedonics example

For ease of exposition, this example uses just 13 observations and six independent variables. The dependent variable is of course price per square metre of floor space. The six independent variables are as follows:

1 Floor area, in square metres.
2 Age of building. Ideally this should be in years or months. If no relevant data are available, the variable may be treated as a *dummy*, with 1 indicating a 'relatively new building' and 0 indicating a 'relatively old building'.
3 Type of dwelling: detached house (1 if the dwelling is a detached house, 0 if it is not).
4 Type of dwelling: apartment in an apartment (also-called multi-family) building (1 if the dwelling is an apartment, 0 if it is not).

In this example only a 'detached house' and an 'apartment' variable are explicitly shown; but the 'type of dwelling' set of variables has to include an additional case: e.g., a 'maisonette' type of apartment (which is made up of two apartments, say, one for the salon, kitchen, and a bathroom, and another for bedrooms and a bathroom, linked by an interior staircase). This case is not, of course, shown, since 'if not a detached dwelling' and 'if not an apartment', it must be a 'maisonette'; including the latter would have caused an indeterminacy problem.

5 Storey – i.e., the number of storeys in an apartment building where an apartment is located: 0 stands for 'ground floor', 1 for first floor, etc. A maisonette could have been indicated either by a 'halfway' number (say, 3.5 if it is partly on the third, and partly on the fourth, floor) or by the higher of the two (as done here). With detached houses, the storey number may be set at 0 in all cases; alternatively, at 1 (if a 2-storey house), at 1.5 (if a 3-storey house), etc.

6 Garage: 1 if it exists, 0 if it does not.

Many other variables could or should have been included too: variables relating to a greater number of dwelling types, to tenure, to kind of heating, other dwelling characteristics, and to location (quality of housing in the neighbourhood, distance from employment or shopping centres, socio-economic and environmental features, etc.). If so, the number of observations should have risen, so as always to exceed the number of variables used. Generally, for this type of work, and depending on the total number of dwellings in any reasonably large area (e.g., a country) or of housing transactions therein, a good sample should run into thousands of observations.

The purpose now is to find out how those six independent variables 'determine' the price of housing. Each variable contributes something towards the price, with any unexplained variations in price being the result of randomness (i.e., of not-included, perhaps unknown, variables). The data used are shown in Table 12.3(a). The simplest possible functional form for the regression of dwelling prices on the dwelling characteristics given in Table 12.3(a) is linear:

$$P = a_0 + a_1(x_1) + \ldots + a_n(x_n) + \varepsilon, \tag{12.11}$$

where

P	=	price,
a_i	=	regression coefficient,
x_i	=	mean value of xth variable,
ε	=	error term, indicating deviations from the trend.[10]

Using any good statistical package (like DataDesk, EViews, SPSS or Stata), the above regression yields the following values for the coefficients. The latter are the implicit prices of the dwelling characteristics represented by the independent variables:[11]

constant		1367.91
floor area	a_1	3.55164
age	a_2	41.1921
detached house	a_3	522.805
apartment	a_4	–408.009
storey	a_5	93.2252
garage	a_6	1274.58

Table 12.3a A simple example of the hedonic method for constructing a house price index

First period	*Sample data*						
	Dependent variable	*Independent variables*					
				Type of dwelling			
	Price per square metre (in €)	*Floor area (in square metres)*	*Age*	*Detached house*	*Apartment*	*Storey (in case of apartment)*	*Garage*
			(1 = new)	(1 = yes)	(1 = yes)		(1 = yes)
	2,800	120	0	0	1	3	1
	3,500	90	1	1	0	0	1
	1,800	110	0	0	1	2	0
	1,950	60	0	0	1	5	0
	2,200	250	1	0	1	4	0
	2,150	140	0	0	0	4	0
	4,500	200	1	0	0	3	1
	1,200	85	0	0	1	1	0
	800	45	0	0	1	0	0
	5,500	650	0	1	0	0	1
	3,200	222	1	0	0	5	1
	1,650	75	0	0	1	4	0
	2,800	92	0	0	1	2	1
Arithmetic mean	2,619	164.5385	0.307692	0.1538462	0.6153846	2.5384615	0.461538
Price mean given by regressing prices on dwelling characteristics	**2,619**						

Therefore, the regression equation is

$$P_1 = 1367.91 + 3.55164(164.5385) + \ldots + 1274.58(0.461538) = 2619, \qquad (12.12)$$

which, as it happens, 'explains' 85 per cent of the variations in price.[12] Notice that in this regression equation, all coefficients have positive signs, meaning that price varies directly with changes in them, except for 'apartment', which has a negative sign. This means that when the dwelling type is an apartment, price drops, and when it is not an apartment, price rises.

In a subsequent period, the above procedure is repeated, inevitably on the basis of another sample of properties sold, as shown in Table 12.3(b). This time, the regression coefficients are as follows:

constant		1834.63
floor area	a_1	1.27448
age	a_2	799.385
detached house	a_3	1162.26
apartment	a_4	–350.231
storey	a_5	235.556
garage	a_6	66.0673

Table 12.3b A simple example of the hedonic method for constructing a house price index

Second period	*Sample data*						
	Dependent variable	*Independent variables*					
	Price per square metre (in €)	*Floor area (in square metres)*	*Age*	*Detached house*	*Apartment*	*Storey (in case of apartment)*	*Garage*
			(1 = new)	(1 = yes)	(1 = yes)		(1 = yes)
	3,500	180	0	1	0	0	1
	4,200	76	1	0	0	4	1
	2,400	120	0	1	0	0	1
	2,200	65	0	0	1	2	0
	2,300	240	1	0	1	1	1
	2,000	150	0	0	0	2	0
	4,700	180	1	1	0	0	1
	3,100	90	1	0	1	3	0
	1,900	59	0	0	1	0	0
	5,300	648	1	0	0	6	1
	3,700	300	1	0	0	4	1
	2,500	87	0	0	1	1	1
	3,000	170	1	0	1	4	1
Arithmetic mean	3,138	181.9231	0.538462	0.230769	0.46153846	2.0769231	0.692308
Price mean given by regressing prices on dwelling characteristics	**3,138**						

Therefore the regression equation is

$$P_2 = 1834.63 + 1.27448(181.9231) + \ldots + 66.0673(0.692308) = 3138, \tag{12.13}$$

which in this case 'explains' 59 per cent of the variations in price.

We thus have two dwelling-price periods to compare: the first from Table 12.3(a) and the second from Table 12.3(b). If we define the first period to be our base period, the corresponding price index will be equal to 100. An *unweighted* comparison between the first and the second period average prices will then yield a second period price index equal to

$$\mathrm{PI}_2 = \frac{3138}{2619} \times 100 = 119.8,$$

suggesting a 19.8 per cent rate of dwelling-price growth. This, however, is wrong! The reason is that between the two periods, the prices that are being compared refer to different 'quantities' or 'weights', i.e., to different average values for the dwelling characteristics. For a correct price comparison, we need to use the second-period implicit prices, or regression coefficients (each referring to a different dwelling characteristic), weighted by the first period 'quantities', which are the average values of the independent variables reported in

Table 12.3(a). We should then calculate

$$P_2 = 1834.63 + 1.27448(164.5385) + \ldots + 66.0673(0.461538) = 2882. \qquad (12.14)$$

Hence, the 'correct' PI for the second period is

$$\text{PI}_2 = \frac{2882}{2619} \times 100 = 110.0,$$

suggesting a 10 per cent rate of 'true' dwelling-price growth.

In general, the price index formula would be

$$\text{PI} = \frac{\sum P_t Q_b}{\sum P_b Q_b} \times 100, \qquad (12.15)$$

where

P_t = given period (implicit) prices,
Q_b = base period quantities (i.e., weights),
P_b = base period (implicit) prices.

Incidentally, an equation like (12.11) or (12.12) has the added usefulness of allowing estimation of the price of any particular dwelling in the space between two index calculations. Suppose, for example, that after the second-period regression calculation has been done, we want to estimate the price of a dwelling with the following characteristics:

floor area	300
age	1
detached house	0
apartment	1
storey	4
garage	1

The price of this dwelling would then be estimated as

$$P = 1834.63 + 1.27449(300) + \ldots + 66.0673(1) = 3674.$$

12.4.2 A semi-logarithmic functional form

In the previous section, both the dependent variable (price) and the independent variables were taken as they are, i.e., no transformations were effected. Although there is no definitive theoretical justification for choosing between different possible functional forms in applied hedonic analysis, a procedure that is widely used is the Box–Cox test (Box and Cox, 1964; Fleming and Nellis, 2011: 10). On the basis of this methodology, and without getting into details, it would appear that for house-price work, the semi-logarithmic functional form is more appropriate than the linear one.

Adoption of this recommendation means that the dependent variable (price) will be expressed in natural-log form (see Section 2.1.1). For the two periods of the example in Section 12.4.1, the transformations are shown in Table 12.3(c).

Table 12.3c Transformation of price data into natural logarithms

First-period data		*Second-period data*	
Actual price	*Natural log*	*Actual price*	*Natural log*
2800	7.937374696	3500	8.160518247
3500	8.160518247	4200	8.342839804
1800	7.495541944	2400	7.783224016
1950	7.575584652	2200	7.696212639
2200	7.696212639	2300	7.740664402
2150	7.673223121	2000	7.60090246
4500	8.411832676	4700	8.455317788
1200	7.090076836	3100	8.03915739
800	6.684611728	1900	7.549609165
5500	8.612503371	5300	8.5754621
3200	8.070906089	3700	8.216088099
1650	7.408530567	2500	7.824046011
2800	7.937374696	3000	8.006367568

Then regressions of the natural logs on the (untransformed) independent variables are run. (This is an exercise for the student.) The results are as follows:[13]

For the first period,

$$\ln(\text{price}) = 7.75033243.$$

Hence,

$$\text{price} = \text{antilog}(7.75033243) = \text{EXP}(7.75033243) = 2322,$$

$$\text{adjusted } R^2 = 79.5 \text{ per cent.}$$

For the second period,

$$\ln(\text{price}) = 7.99926087.$$

Hence,

$$\text{price} = \text{antilog}(7.99926087) = \text{EXP}(7.99926087) = 2979,$$

$$\text{adjusted } R^2 = 63.4 \text{ per cent.}$$

Now, applying the coefficients of the second-period regression to the quantity weights of the first period gives

$$\ln(\text{price}) = 7.921820523.$$

Hence,

$$\text{price} = \text{antilog}(7.921820523) = EXP(7.921820523) = 2757.$$

Consequently, the price index of the second period, using the price of the first period as base, will be

$$\mathrm{PI}_2 = \frac{2757}{2322} \times 100 = 118.7,$$

suggesting an 18.7 per cent rate of dwelling-price growth.

Generally,[14]

$$\mathrm{PI} = \frac{\operatorname{antilog} \sum P_t Q_b}{\operatorname{antilog} \sum P_b Q_b} \times 100. \tag{12.16}$$

12.4.3 Varying the weights

One problem with both price index formulas (12.14) and (12.15) is that when the weights used (i.e., the quantities of dwelling attributes) are from just a single past period (Q_b) they will eventually become dated. For example, in the case of Halifax, the base period is 1983. But even if the base period is more recent (as, for example, in the case of Nationwide), additional problems remain. One is the presence of an upward or downward bias in the index (see Box 12.2). Another is that the sample of dwellings transacted in any given period almost certainly does not represent, attribute-wise, the sum-total of the dwelling stock. This is the sample-selection problem mentioned above.

Rephrasing this, we can say that there is no way of knowing the extent to which the base-period quantities of dwelling attributes represent the assortment of attributes typically and on average demanded by the population of housing consumers. In contrast, the basket of commodities, on which a CPI is based, is constructed as a result of a survey that is supposed to capture the (lump, unbundled, or discrete) preferences of all, or at least most, consumers – in so far as those preferences are revealed by consumers' budget allocations. But the dwellings bought in any (base) period only represent the preferences of a generally small subset of all possible buyers of dwellings.

This means that when the characteristics of those dwellings are used in subsequent periods in order to construct the PI of those periods, the PI necessarily shows the price appreciation of that particular set of characteristics – rather than the (unknown) set of attributes typically and on average demanded by consumers.

Since, however, the latter set is unknown, what is the solution? Taking the quantities of attributes characterizing the entire dwelling stock, i.e., the 'typical' or 'average' dwelling, cannot be the answer, because most dwellings do not change hands in any given year, and many do not do so for very long periods of time. A possible solution is to take into account not the entire stock, but rather the stock that is being sold from the base period to whatever the most recent subsequent period for index calculation happens to be.

In the example of Section 12.4.1, this can be achieved by combining the independent variable data from the first and second periods, taking the mean values of the variables (i.e., finding Av Q_{bt}), plugging those mean values into Equations (12.12) and (12.14), recalculating, and then using either formula (12.15) or (12.16) to calculate the PI for the second period. Thus,

(a) The mean values (Av Q_{bt}) of the combined independent variable data are as follows:

floor area	173.2308
age	0.423077
detached house	0.192308
apartment	0.538462
storey	2.307692
garage	0.576923

(b) From Equation (12.11),

$$P_1 = 1367.91 + 3.55164(173.2308) + \ldots + 1274.58(0.576923) = 2832. \quad (12.17)$$

(c) From Equation (12.13),

$$P_2 = 1834.63 + 1.27448(173.2308) + \ldots + 66.0673(0.576923) = 3138. \quad (12.18)$$

(d) From Equation (12.15),

$$\mathrm{PI} = \frac{\sum P_t \,\mathrm{Av}\, Q_{bt}}{\sum P_b \,\mathrm{Av}\, Q_{bt}} \times 100 = \frac{3138}{2832} \times 100 = 110.8. \quad (12.19)$$

The natural logs for the prices of the two periods (using the combined mean quantities as weights) are

for the first period, 7.82495592,

for the second period, 7.9605407.

Hence,

$$\mathrm{PI} = \frac{\text{antilog} \sum P_t \,\mathrm{Av}\, Q_{bt}}{\text{antilog} \sum P_b \,\mathrm{Av}\, Q_{bt}} \times 100$$

$$= \frac{\text{antilog}(7.9605407)}{\text{antilog}(7.82495592)} \times 100 = \frac{2866}{2502} \times 100 = 114.5. \quad (12.20)$$

This procedure is likely to have a smoothing effect on the rate of price change. The drawback is that with every new period price-index calculation, the price indices of all previous periods may have to be recalculated, since there will be one more set of new data available for inclusion in the Av Q_{bt} calculation. This could be cumbersome, but nothing that modern computers cannot handle. More serious is the lack of consistency over time that such an index will display (see Box 12.2). Unfortunately, there is no perfect index; any index represents a trade-off between various properties that a good index must have. In this particular case, the trade-off is between correcting for the sample-selection bias and index consistency.

Box 12.2 Laspeyres, Paasche, Fisher indices

A student familiar with price index statistics will have recognized the price indices calculated in Sections 12.4.1–12.4.3 as of the Laspeyres type because they use past-period weights. An alternative would have been to use current-period weights, in which case the indices would have been of the Paasche type. A problem with the Laspeyres index is that it tends to create an upward bias to the price, while the Paasche index tends to do the opposite.

The reason for the Laspeyres index's upward bias is that it ignores the consumer's tendency to substitute a new combination, or bundle, of goods (or of attributes, in case of a generic or heterogeneous good like housing) for the old one, in response to the inter-period change in price(s). The consumer would do that in order to hold his or her level of utility, or standard of living, constant. By assuming bundle-maintenance, though, the substitution effect is not accounted for: because the consumer has altered the bundle of attributes he or she buys in the new period (in response to changed prices), the true cost to him or her of, say, a rise in the price of housing is less than if he or she had actually gone on to buy the same bundle as in the base period. Hence the new-period index overstates the true price of housing.

In contrast, the Paasche index, by moving back towards the base period the bundle of goods, or of attributes, bought in the current period, increases the price of, say, housing in the base period – and for this reason understates the true housing price growth in the current period.

A tentative solution to the problem is to use Fisher's ideal index, which is the geometric average of the Laspeyres and Paasche indices:

$$\mathrm{PI_F} = \sqrt{(\mathrm{PI_L})(\mathrm{PI_P})} = \left[(\mathrm{PI_L})(\mathrm{PI_P})\right]^{1/2}. \tag{12.21}$$

Another may be to use the approach suggested in Section 12.4.3. Both solutions, however, and also Paasche-based indices, reduce the consistency of the index over time; i.e., the historic index numbers are altered as data from every new period become available and are used in the index (re)construction.

12.4.4 The functional form problem in hedonics

Many forms of the hedonic pricing model are possible. The four most common are the following (Brachinger, 2002):

(a) The *linear approach*, employed above in Equations (12.11)–(12.14):

$$P = a_0 + \sum_{n=1}^{n} a_n x_n, \tag{12.22}$$

where a_n are regression coefficients (i.e., implicit prices) and x_n are quantity weights of the independent variables used.

(b) The *exponential* or *semi-logarithmic* approach:

$$P = a_0 \prod_{n=1}^{n} \exp(a_n x_n), \tag{12.23a}$$

or

$$\ln P = \ln a_0 + \sum_{n=1}^{n} a_n x_n, \tag{12.23b}$$

which is the one employed in Section 12.4.2.

(c) The *power-function* or *double-log* approach:

$$P = a_0 \prod_{n=1}^{n} x_n^{a_n}, \tag{12.24a}$$

or

$$\ln P = \ln a_0 + \sum_{n=1}^{n} a_n \ln x_n. \tag{12.24b}$$

(d) The *logarithmic* approach:

$$P = a_0 + \sum_{n=1}^{n} a_n \ln x_n. \tag{12.25}$$

Unfortunately, there is no established theoretical framework that definitively proves that one functional form is 'better' than another (Rosen, 1974; Halvorsen and Pollakowski, 1981; Wallace, 1996; Murty et al., 2004; Selim,2008; Bajari et al., 2010b; Fleming and Nellis, 2011). Thus, the choice of functional (or model) form is largely an empirical question. In 1964, Box and Cox devised a statistical test for the functional form that, subsequent to Griliches' (1967) suggestion, has become the standard for use in hedonics work (Fleming and Nellis, 2012), although even this approach is not free of certainly constructive criticism (see Cassel and Mendelsohn, 1985). In 1981, Halvorsen and Pollakowski proposed a statistical procedure, which employs a highly general functional form (a quadratic Box–Cox functional form) that yields all other relevant functional forms as special cases (but, again, cf. Cassel and Mendelsohn, 1985). Nevertheless, much promising work is being done to the direction of providing theoretical underpinnings to hedonic functional form specification, as in Bajari et al. (2010b).

A clarification is in order here: that there is (yet) no theory-based way to indicate a 'best' functional form for hedonics (other than that the appropriate form must ideally be non-linear) does *not* mean that there is no theory of hedonics *per se*. Rosen's (1974) contribution was pivotal in this regard, and the interested student should also consult Triplett (2004), Day (2001), and the Appendix to this chapter. In fact, Rosen built on earlier work by, among others, Muth (1960), who first viewed housing as a bundle of housing services, an approach that commends itself for hedonic analysis.

12.5 The repeat-sales method

Most well-known RE price indices in the USA are of the repeat-sales variety. The method was originally proposed by Bailey et al. (1963), was brought to the mainstream by Case and Shiller (1987, 1989), and is now finding imitators in other countries. For example, the Land Registry in the UK uses this method to calculate its house-price index (Calnea, 2006a, b).

The essence of the method is to compare prices of properties sold in one period with prices of the *same* properties sold in a previous period. The assumption of 'sameness' is crucial: possible sources of change may be improvements to a property in the meantime, or depreciation. At any rate, to the extent that the 'old' and 'new' prices refer to the same property, the problem of quality change (which the hedonic method specifically addresses and struggles with) is automatically taken care of.

This is all well and good, but there is another problem. The time distance or difference between original sales and resales may not be – and typically is not – the same for all properties. Property A may be resold two years from its original sale, which gave the property's 'base-period' price; property B may be resold three or four or ten years from its original sale. Moreover, its original sale may have happened at a later time period than property A's original-sale time period. Adding the two resale prices and dividing by the sum of the two original prices will not, then, be a proper procedure: we will not be comparing like with like.

The way to deal with this problem[15] is by relating the price change for each individual property to the times the first and second sales happened (and therefore to the time distance between the two sales). This requires running a regression using time-dummy variables – which means that we need to

1 Acquire enough data: mainly, see that our 'observations' (i.e., properties in the sample) are more than the number of time periods over which we will calculate the index. The more, in fact, the better.
2 Select our base period as well as the time span of interest (i.e., the total number of periods over which we shall calculate an index). Presumably, the time span will start from the base period and end with the current period.
3 Calculate price ratios: second sale/first sale.
4 Take the *natural logarithm* of each ratio. This now will be our dependent variable, since our purpose is to measure a property price change over the whole span.
5 Assign appropriate time-dummy variables. Every original sale (and its attendant price) takes the value -1. Every resale takes the value $+1$. Everything else takes the value 0. Every time period (e.g., a year) will now be characterized by a column of ± 1s and 0s.
6 Calculate an average value for each dummy-variable column (i.e., for each year).
7 Run the regression, remembering not to include the base period.
8 Use the coefficients that the regression throws up, and the dummies' average values, in order to estimate the average property-price change between the beginning and the end of the whole time span of interest.
9 Take the antilog of the estimated result (since the dependent variable was cast in the form of natural logs). This will be the index sought, and its percentage difference from the base-year price (which is 1 of course) will be the percentage change in the average property price between the base period and the current period.

Thus, the repeat-sales equation would formally be (cf. Conniffe and Duffy, 1999: 406–7; Eurostat RPPI, 2011: 98)

$$\ln\left(\frac{P_{n,t+\tau}}{P_{n,t}}\right) = a_0 + \sum_{t=1}^{T} a_t D_t + \varepsilon_n^t, \tag{12.26}$$

where

$P_{n,t}$	=	price of property *n* originally sold at time *t*,
$P_{n,t+\tau}$	=	price of property *n* resold at time $t+\tau$,
a_0	=	regression constant,
a_t	=	coefficients of time-dummies,
D_t	=	time-dummy variables,
ε_n^t	=	error term, showing how price changes for individual properties deviate from expected values.

A numerical example of a repeat-sales regression[16] (RSR) follows in Tables 12.4a–12.4d.

On the basis of Tables 12.4c and 12.4d the value of the repeat-sales price index at end of 2017 is

$HPI_{2017} = -0.242265 + 0.0183491(-0.0833) + \ldots + 0.646042(0.5) = 0.145113$, which is the natural logarithm of the number we seek. Exponentiating (i.e., taking the antilog of) 0.145113 gives 1.15617 (or 115.6, which is the value of the index in 2017, with 2011 = base year). In other words, between 2011 (= base year) and 2017, house prices in the given sample appreciated by 15.6 per cent, on average. This contrasts with 17.66 per cent, which is the percentage change – in relation to the base year – in the average of all the second-sale to first-sale price *ratios* in the given sample (i.e., 1.1766) – but without accounting for the fact that the time distance between second-sale and first-sale is not the same for all properties

Table 12.4a An example of repeat-sales regression. 1st part: raw sales-price data (in £, €, or $)

	2011	*2012*	*2013*	*2014*	*2015*	*2016*	*2017*	*Sum of 1st sales*	*Sum of 2nd sales*
Property									
1	75,000						140,000	75,000	140,000
2	88,000				94,000			88,000	94,000
3		150,000				162,000		150,000	162,000
4	180,000						240,000	180,000	240,000
5				210,000			260,000	210,000	260,000
6	122,000				134,000			122,000	134,000
7	160,000					176,000		160,000	176,000
8			145,000				155,000	145,000	155,000
9					120,000		100,000	120,000	100,000
10			65,000		70,000			65,000	70,000
11	130,000			160,000				130,000	160,000
12				160,000			180,000	160,000	180,000
								133,750	155,917

Note: Property 11 has been resold twice in the price-index period (2011–17). It is therefore treated as two separate properties, 11 and 12.

Table 12.4b An example of repeat-sales regression. 2nd part: calculation of natural logarithms (ln) of ratios of 2nd-sale prices to 1st-sale prices

Property	*Ratio of 2nd to 1st sale*	*ln of ratio*	*2011* *Base period*	*2012*	*2013*	*2014*	*2015*	*2016*	*2017*
1	1.8667	0.6242	75,000						140,000
2	1.0682	0.0660	88,000				94,000		
3	1.0800	0.0770		150,000				162,000	
4	1.3333	0.2877	180,000						240,000
5	1.2381	0.2136				210,000			260,000
6	1.0984	0.0938	122,000				134,000		
7	1.1000	0.0953	160,000					176,000	
8	1.0690	0.0667			145,000				155,000
9	0.8333	−0.1823					120,000		100,000
10	1.0769	0.0741			65,000		70,000		
11	1.2308	0.2076	130,000			160,000			
12	1.1250	0.1178				160,000			180,000
Average =	1.1766								

Table 12.4c An example of repeat-sales regression. 3rd part: assignment of time-dummy variables

Property	*Ratio of 2nd to 1st sale*	*ln of ratio*	*2011* *Base period*	*2012*	*2013*	*2014*	*2015*	*2016*	*2017*
1	1.8667	0.6242	75,000	0	0	0	0	0	1
2	1.0682	0.0660	88,000	0	0	0	1	0	0
3	1.0800	0.0770		−1	0	0	0	1	0
4	1.3333	0.2877	180,000	0	0	0	0	0	1
5	1.2381	0.2136		0	0	−1	0	0	1
6	1.0984	0.0938	122,000	0	0	0	1	0	0
7	1.1000	0.0953	160,000	0	0	0	0	1	0
8	1.0690	0.0667		0	−1	0	0	0	1
9	0.8333	−0.1823		0	0	0	−1	0	1
10	1.0769	0.0741		0	−1	0	1	0	0
11	1.2308	0.2076	130,000	0	0	1	0	0	0
12	1.1250	0.1178	0	0	0	−1	0	0	1
Averages =				−0.0833	−0.1667	−0.0833	0.1667	0.1667	0.5000

in the sample. (The ratio of *all* second sales to *all* first sales gives (155,917) / (133,750) = 1.1657, and, for the same reason, cannot be accepted as the 'true' index.)

Notice that 'the repeat sales method suffers from revision of previously computed figures: when additional repeat sales information becomes available, re-estimation will result in changes in the coefficients estimated and thus in the price indexes inferred' (Eurostat RPPI, 2011: 102). On the other hand, 'when the sample period is extended and the coefficients re-estimated, sample selection bias might be getting smaller as more and more repeat sales are observed' (ibid., 102).

Table 12.4d An example of repeat-sales regression. 4th part: results of regression of natural logarithms of ratios to time-dummy variables

Variable	*Coefficient*
Constant	−0.242265
2012	0.018349
2013	0.232804
2014	0.308701
2015	0.444896
2016	0.337575
2017	0.646042

12.6 The mix-adjustment method

The mix-adjustment, or *stratification*, method for constructing house-price indices works by placing dwellings into cells, or strata, each comprising properties of specific attributes that set any given cell apart from any other. In increasing order of cell complexity (but also of precision), the following are just some examples:

- large dwellings in area A
- large dwellings with a floor area smaller than 201 square metres and larger than 150 square metres in area A
- large dwellings etc., less than 5 years old in area A
- large dwellings etc., etc., of single-house type in area A.

This way, the composition or 'quality mix' of the properties sold is controlled for – hence the name 'mix-adjustment'. Each cell, or stratum, is then able to yield a mean (or median) price, which makes sense since all the properties in the cell have the same attributes. This is handy for comparison with the corresponding cell from a chosen base period. Dividing the current period mean (or median) price of a cell by the one from the base period produces then a price index for the given cell.

In turn, each cell is weighted by its relative importance in the quality mix. This can be the proportion of the total transaction value of the properties in a base-period cell into the total transaction value of all the base-period cells; or it can be the proportion of dwellings in the entire housing stock (as per census data) with the same combination of attributes as any given cell.

Subsequently, all the weighted price indices from the individual cells are added together, which renders the overall house-price index for the current period.

Table 12.5 shows an example of stratification. In this case, the purpose is to find the probability of any randomly chosen dwelling being sold in the given period. This can be useful as it can show which properties sell most, i.e., which combination of attributes is the most actively traded. It can also help identify the representative dwelling, which in this case is 'new apartment in area C'. This is not necessarily obvious from the absolute number of properties in the same cell (584), as, for example, the cell 'new apartment in area A' includes 616 properties, yet the probability of a house being in that cell is lower (15.58 per cent) than that for the representative cell (16.34 per cent). The reason of course is that a house has a higher probability of being in area C (36.36 per cent) than in A (34.69 per cent).

Table 12.5 Mix-adjustment: identifying and working with the cells

Examples of variables:		*Area*		*Type of dwelling*		*Age*
Sub-categories under each variable:						
For area:		A, B, or C				
For type:		Single house or apartment				
For age:		Old or new				
	Number of properties		*Number of properties*		*Number of properties*	*% distribution*
Old	720	Single	1258	Old single	297	9.72%
New	2333	Apartment	1795	New single	423	13.87%
				Old apartment	961	31.49%
				New apartment	1372	44.93%
Sums:	3053		3053		3053	100.00%

	Properties per area per type per age group			
	A	B	C	Sums:
Old single	104	112	81	297
New single	212	96	115	423
Old apartment	127	504	330	961
New apartment	616	172	584	1372
	1059	884	1110	3053
% distribution	34.69%	28.96%	36.36%	100.00%

	% distribution per cell				
	A	B	C		
Old single	3.37%	2.81%	3.53%	→	9.72%
New single	4.81%	4.01%	5.04%	→	13.87%
Old apartment	10.92%	9.12%	11.45%	→	31.49%
New apartment	15.58%	13.01%	16.34%	→	44.93%
	34.69%	28.96%	36.36%	→	100.00%

Cell index calculation:

$$P_m^{0t} = \frac{\text{median price of cell } m \text{ in period } t}{\text{median price of cell } m \text{ in base period } 0}. \tag{12.27}$$

Weight calculation:

$$w_m^0 = \frac{\text{value of all properties in cell } m \text{ in base period } 0}{\text{value of all properties in all cells in base period } 0} \tag{12.28}$$

Bear in mind that the choice of value weights depends on the purpose of estimation. If the goal is to estimate the price change of the whole housing stock, then the stock value shares of the cells should be used. For example, if there are 10 apartments in the housing stock, and there are 80 dwelling units in the total housing stock, the weight of the 'apartment' cell in the sample data (if such a single cell exists) will be 12.5 per cent. If, however, the goal is to estimate the price change of sold properties, then the expenditure shares of the cells should be used. For example, if the total expenditure on all properties sold in the base year is £300, and the expenditure on 'apartments' is £120, the weight of the 'apartment' cell will be 40 per cent.

Sample index calculation:

$$P^{0t} = \sum_{m=1}^{M} w_m^0 P_m^{0t}, \tag{12.29}$$

with M = number of all cells, or strata (cf. Eurostat RPPI, 2011: 53).

12.7 The SPAR method

SPAR stands for sale price appraisal ratio. It is an arithmetic repeat index (Bourassa et al., 2004: 7). It comes in two forms: equal-weighted and value-weighted. It is used in New Zealand (Bourassa et al., 2004), the Netherlands (Vries et al., 2009; Haan, 2009), and also Sweden and Denmark.

Equal-weighted SPAR index I_{Et}

This is

$$I_{Et} = \frac{\frac{1}{n_t}\sum_{i=1}^{n_t}\frac{S_{it}}{A_{i0}}}{\frac{1}{n_{t-1}}\sum_{i=1}^{n_{t-1}}\frac{S_{it-1}}{A_{i0}}} I_{Et-1}, \tag{12.30}$$

where

S_{it}	=	sale price of dwelling i in period t,
S_{it-1}	=	sale price of dwelling i in the previous period $t-1$,
A_{i0}	=	appraised value of dwelling i in the appraisal or base period,
n	=	number of sales,
I_{Et-1}	=	100 (= value of index in base period).

INTUITIVE INTERPRETATION

In repeat-sales the task is to find a 'matched pair' between an original and a subsequent sale of the same dwelling in order to keep quality largely constant. This necessarily limits the sample size, as one is forced to ignore dwellings that, for example, have been sold in this period but have not been sold in any previous period during the index's time horizon. But with Equation (12.31), the problem of matching is solved, as most, if not all, dwellings that have been sold in this period come with appraisal values obtained simultaneously in the recent past.

INDEX CONSTRUCTION

First, there must exist appraisal values for properties formed in period 0. The provider of such values is usually some government agency.

Alternatively, the appraisal values may come from the databases of banks that extend housing loans – but in such a case the values may be biased upwards or downwards, depending on a bank's policy and circumstances, the structure of valuers' fees, or even on the valuers' appraisal method(s). Of course, the last factor may constitute a problem that will be present in government appraisals also, to the extent that valuers' appraisals tend to rely on historic prices or to imitate *grosso modo* other concurrent prices.[17]

Subsequently, in period $t-1$, a set of properties is sold. For each property, a ratio of its selling price to its appraisal value is calculated (that's the SPAR). The average of those ratios is then extracted. This shows how much the average price of the properties has changed in relation to the average appraisal value. Further ahead, in period t, another set of properties (maybe including some from the $t-1$ set) is sold. The procedure is repeated.

Finally, taking the ratio of the two average ratios shows the deviation of prices in t from their corresponding appraisal values in relation to the deviation of prices in $t-1$ from their own corresponding appraisal values. If the two deviations are equal, there has been no change in property prices between $t-1$ and t. If the t deviation is greater than the $t-1$ deviation, prices have increased, and if it is less, the opposite. In the special case when $t=1$, and hence period $0=$ period $t-1$, no deviation would of course mean no price change between period 0 and period 1.

This way, there is little need to take property characteristics explicitly into account, because those are already accounted for in the initial SPARs as, by and large, sale price and appraisal value concern the same property every time. (In practice, there may still be changes in a property's qualities between any two periods.)

Value-weighted SPAR index I_{Vt}

This is

$$I_{Vt}=\frac{\sum_{i=1}^{n_t} S_{it}\Big/\sum_{i=1}^{n_t} A_{i0}}{\sum_{i=1}^{n_{t-1}} S_{it-1}\Big/\sum_{i=1}^{n_{t-1}} A_{i0}}I_{Vt-1}. \tag{12.31}$$

The difference from I_{Et} is that, instead of extracting the average SPAR for all properties, I_{Vt} takes the SPAR of the sums of sale prices and appraisal values. Generally, I_{Vt} is more appropriate for use in portfolio valuation (Shiller, 1991), whereas I_{Et} is more appropriate for yielding property-price growth rates (Bourassa et al., 2004).

Table 12.6 presents an example of the SPAR index calculation.

12.8 Who uses what HPI?

See Table 12.7.

12.8.1 Automated Valuation Models

Many mortgage lenders (and some specialized service companies) use in-house AVMs to estimate the value of a property without appraiser subjectivity or bias. According to Downie and Robson (2007), AVMs are software systems that use one or more proprietary algorithms to estimate the market value of a given property at a specified date. They do that speedily and at low cost.

Table 12.6 Example of SPAR index calculation

Property →	*1*	*2*	*3*	*4*	*5*	*Average SPAR ratio*	*Sums*	*SPAR ratio of sums*
Current-period sales:								
Sale price	340,000	175,000	520,000	340,000	115,000		1,490,000	
Appraisal	300,000	160,000	480,000	380,000	130,000		1,450,000	
SPAR ratio	1.133	1.094	1.083	0.895	0.885	1.018		1.028
Previous-period sales:								
Sale price	300,000	150,000	450,000	360,000			1,260,000	
Appraisal	260,000	115,000	460,000	370,000			1,205,000	
SPAR ratio	1.133	1.094	1.083	0.895		1.051		1.046
Index numbers:						Equal-weighted	Value-weighted	
Base period						100		100
Current period						96.83		98.27

Note: Example based on Bourassa et al. (2004: Table 1).

Basic inputs required by an AVM are the street address and a description of the subject property. Subsequently, the AVM searches its database for comparable transactions or indices to generate the subject's value. At its simplest, an AVM will take a past transaction price or valuation for the subject property and update it by means of a house-price index, or a more sophisticated repeat-sales method may be used. Alternatively, an AVM will utilize hedonic regression to identify dwellings with similar characteristics in the locality of the subject property.

The accuracy of an AVM result relates to how homogeneous property types are, and to the number of comparable transactions in a given subject area. Sometimes, it may not be possible to value a property by means of an AVM – hence the concept of the 'hit rate', i.e., the ratio of returned model results to the number of addresses submitted by the user of the AVM.

12.9 HPI comparison

There is no perfect HPI. Each has strengths and weaknesses. Some of those are presented below (cf. Bourassa et al., 2004; Hansen, 2006; Rappaport, 2007; Haan, 2009; Eurostat, 2011; Fleming and Nellis, 2012; HomeCo, 2012).

12.9.1 Hedonic indices

Since empirical hedonics-based price estimates utilize the multiple regression technique, it is useful to remind ourselves of two problems almost always encountered in regression work (cf. Fleming and Nellis, 2012; see Section 2.3.2 of this book):[18]

1 *Multicollinearity* happens when two or more independent variables provide no or very little *additional* explanation of variations in the dependent variable, compared with what one of the independent variables alone can offer. For example, it may be that in a certain country or region the independent variable 'detached house over size *X*' correlates very highly with the independent variable 'upper-class household'. One of them should then probably be omitted; other solutions to the problem are also possible.

Table 12.7 Some house price indices (HPI)

	Provider	*Name*	*Comments*
Australia	Australian Bureau of Statistics (ABS)	ABS HPI	Stratification approach according to (a) the long-term level of prices for the suburb in which the house is located, (b) the neighbourhood characteristics of the suburb. Quarterly. Coverage: eight capital cities. See ABS (2009).
Canada	Teranet–National Bank of Canada	Teranet–National Bank HPI	Repeat-sales index. Monthly. Coverage: six Metropolitan Areas. See Teranet–National Bank (2007).
Cyprus	BuySell Cyprus Real Estate	Transaction PI, Asking PI	Hedonic indices, based on work by Platis and Nerouppos (2005).
France	France's notaries and INSEE, France's statistical agency	Notaires–INSEE indices	Hedonic indices, resulting from collaboration between notaries, who collect the data, and INSEE. Quarterly. Coverage: the whole of France. See Laferrère (2006).
Greece	Bank of Greece	RE PI (REPI)	Mix-adjustment, using 50 geographical cells, 2 age cells, 3 'floor area' cells. In addition, apartment prices are all converted to 'first-storey' apartment value equivalents. Data provided by financial institutions. Monthly.
Ireland	Central Statistics Office Ireland	Residential Property PI (RPPI)	Mix-adjustment, using data on mortgage drawdowns provided on a monthly basis by eight of the main mortgage lending institutions. Cash transactions are excluded. Coverage: all of Ireland.
Netherlands	Dutch Land Registry Office (Kadaster)	HPI Kadaster	Weighted repeat-sales index, tracking price changes in the owner-occupied stock in the Netherlands. Monthly (see Jansen et al., 2008). Since January 2008, the Dutch Land Registry and Statistics Netherlands have published SPAR-based indices (see de Vries at al., 2009).
New Zealand	Quotable Value Ltd and Reserve Bank of NZ	QV Quarterly HPI	SPAR
	RE Institute of NZ and Reserve Bank of NZ	REINZ HPI	Median Sale HPI and Stratified Median HPI. Monthly.
Spain	Kyero.com	Kyero.com Spanish HPI	Median calculation excluding 'unusually high or low prices'. Quarterly.
Turkey	REIDIN.com	Turkey RPPI (TRPPI)	Stratified median index for 7 major cities, 71 districts, 481 sub-districts. Monthly. The national TRPPI is a weighted average of the city indices. Data obtained from RE agents, newspapers, magazines, websites, asset management companies.
UK	Department of Communities and Local Government (formerly Office of the Deputy Prime Minister)	DCLG HPI	Mix-adjustment and hedonics. Monthly. Data based on a sample of mortgage completions data from the Regulated Mortgage Survey (RMS) as collected by the UK's Council of Mortgage Lenders (CML) and Matrix Solutions, a UK consultancy. The RMS sample provided to DCLC covered around 60 per cent of UK mortgage completions for house purchase in the first half of 2011.

	Financial Times/Acadametrics Ltd	Acadametrics HPI (formerly known as FT HPI)	Index comprises the published Land Registry house price data (including cash purchases), smoothed and seasonally and mix-adjusted by Acadametrics, combined with an 'Index of Indices' model in order to account for transactions not yet reported to the Land Registry (see Acadametrics, 2011).
	FindaProperty.com	FindaProperty.com HPI	Mix-adjustment based on asking prices of more than 780,000 properties from around 10,500 estate agents. Monthly. Index developed in association with Calnea Analytics Ltd.
	Halifax (a division of Bank of Scotland plc)	Halifax HPI	Hedonic regression, based on work by M. C. Fleming and J. G. Nellis (see Halifax, 2012). Index utilizes Halifax's own database. Base year = 1983.
	HM Land Registry	Land Registry HPI	Repeat-sales regression. Monthly. Largest database on housing transactions (whether for cash or with a mortgage) in England and Wales; contains details on over 15 million sales, of which over 5 million are identifiable matched pairs. See Calnea (2006a, b).
	Home.co.uk	HomeCo Asking PI (API)	Mix-adjustment based on asking prices for more than 750,000 properties from Home.co.uk Property Search Engine. Monthly. Properties above £1 million and below £20,000 are excluded. Index developed in association with Calnea Analytics Ltd.
	Nationwide Building Society	Nationwide HPI	Mix-adjustment, using four property types, two buyer types, three property ages. Index utilizes Nationwide's own database. See Nationwide (2012).
	Rightmove plc	Rightmove HPI	Mix-adjustment based on sellers' asking prices as posted on the Rightmove website, which, Rightmove claims, accounts for about 90 per cent of all properties on sale. Monthly.
USA	Federal Housing Finance Agency (formerly Office of Federal Housing Enterprise Oversight)	FHFA HPI	Repeat-sales index. Monthly. Obtained by reviewing repeat mortgage transactions on single-family properties whose mortgages have been purchased or securitized by Fannie Mae or Freddie Mac since January 1975. It includes house price figures for the nine US Census divisions. Index based on work by K. E. Case and R. J. Shiller. See Calhoun (1996).
	Radar Logic Inc.	Radar Logic Daily*TM* Index	Median-based residential price index, following manipulation of data under the claim that the frequency of transactions is proportional to price per square foot raised to a power. See Kagarlis et al. (2007).
	Standard & Poor's	S&P Case–Shiller US National Home PI	A composite of quarterly single-family home price 'repeat-sales' indices for the nine US Census divisions. Index based on work by K. E. Case and R. J. Shiller. See Standard & Poor's (2009).

In the case of hedonic regression, multicollinearity might result if, for example, 'detached house' correlated highly with 'garage'; or 'number of rooms' with 'floor area'. It is probably fair to say that multicollinearity can never be completely avoided, only minimized.

2 *Heteroscedasticity* happens when the deviations of the actual values of a dependent variable from the values predicted by a regression tend to increase or decrease systematically at higher values of the (or *an*) independent variable. Technically, heteroscedasticity means that the variance of the error term is not constant. For example, low-income households can typically afford *only* smaller dwellings than high-income ones. But the latter can afford larger as well as smaller dwellings. In fact, some of them might opt for smaller houses for reasons of their own, even though they could buy larger ones if they so wished. So higher incomes might be systematically associated with increasing deviations of actual from predicted values for dwelling size, the higher those incomes became. That is heteroscedasticity.

In the case of hedonic regression, heteroscedasticity would result if, for example, the older a house got, the larger the deviations of actual from predicted values for price became. This might happen if some older houses were associated with lower prices because of depreciation, and some other older houses were associated with higher prices because of their 'traditional' character.

In the cases of both hedonic and repeat-sales regression, heteroscedasticity also manifests itself in that house prices tend to increase over time (or over considerable periods of time).

To understand why the above constitute problems, and for properly dealing with them, the student is advised to consult any good statistics or econometrics textbook.

The great strength of hedonics-based HPIs is that they account for quality change in the compared samples between base and current period more thoroughly than other methods. Moreover, they do so without limiting the data sets to properties that have actually been sold at least twice over the entire time frame between base and current period, the way repeat-sales-based HPIs do. In principle, hedonics-based HPIs also avoid the problem of quality change (due to depreciation on the one hand and improvements on the other) that is inevitably present in repeat-sales-based HPIs and to a certain extent distorts them.

However, hedonics-based HPIs have other problems:

1 The functional form problem has already been mentioned.
2 There are statistical dangers, like multicollinearity.
3 They have tremendous data requirements.
4 There is a danger of omitting important variables from the hedonic model, like the socio-economic profile of the neighbourhood where a house is located, proximity to a metro station, air quality, or the pull of an employment centre relevant to the neighbourhood. In relation to the latter example, another danger is that the 'correct' employment centre (if there are more than one) may be misdiagnosed.
5 There is also the problem of continuous revisions of the HPI as more data becoming available may necessitate re-estimation of the index. In truth, this is a problem with any index. There is some evidence, however, that hedonic measures are 'substantially' more stable, in this respect, than, say, repeat-sales measures (Clapham et al., 2007).

12.9.2 Repeat-sales indices

The great advantage of repeat-sales indices is that they seem to solve the problem of quality change with much fewer data than hedonic indices. More importantly, they seem to solve it decisively since the indices are based on 'matched pairs' of properties, without worries about omitting explanatory variables or using too many of those. However,

1 Repeat-sales indices largely ignore the problem of property depreciation between two dates, or of improvements made to the property. The problem may be mitigated, though, by including some hedonic characteristics in the standard repeat-sales model (Shiller, 1991).
2 Repeat-sales indices may also exhibit heteroscedasticity since house prices tend to increase over long time periods. To deal with this problem, Case and Shiller (1987, 1989) have advanced the *weighted repeat-sales method.* This involves running a RSR the standard way, then taking the residuals (i.e., the deviations of actual from predicted values) and using them as weights in a new RSR to correct for heteroscedasticity.
3 Another danger is that between two dates, depreciation and improvements may not be the only factors that will affect the quality of a (resold) property. Changes in the locale may also occur, and will be more pronounced the greater the distance between the two dates. Perhaps including even more hedonic characteristics in the repeat-sales model may be the solution here too, but then the model begins to look suspiciously like a hedonic one!
4 A repeat-sales index may need to be revised more often than a hedonic one.
5 The gravest problem in a repeat-sales index, however, is that it uses only properties that have been sold at least twice. This limits the size of the sample, perhaps unnecessarily. More importantly, it creates sample-selection bias. This is how:

> 'If there is a systematic difference between price changes in houses that have been sold only once and those which have been sold more than once, then repeat-sales will provide biased estimates of overall house price changes. Similarly, if there are systematic differences between different types of repeat-sales houses and their rate of turnover (that is, houses sold two, three, four times and so forth), then it is possible for houses with high turnover rates to become over-represented in the sample, again resulting in measurement bias.'
>
> (Hansen, 2006: 9)

12.9.3 Mix-adjustment, or stratification, indices

The advantages of the mix-adjustment method is that it helps construct indices that take into *some* account various characteristics of properties (so there is *some* control for quality change), do not bother with functional form for the way the characteristics relate to one another, and make use of all observed transactions (so they do not rely on 'matched pairs'), and for which the data requirements can be as many or as few (depending on number of characteristics used, two being the low limit) as available information allows and the analyst wants.

The disadvantages are as follows (Eurostat RPPI, 2011):

1 A mix-adjusted index is sensitive to changes in the mix of property types sold that fall into the distinct cells associated with a given characteristic. For example, if the characteristic

is 'location', and the sub-categories, or cells, are Location A, Location B, etc., the index will reflect changes in the number of properties falling into those locations. But the index will not be able to account for changes in the mix of property types sold that are not related to location. The problem may be dealt with by including another characteristic in the model – but only to some extent, as the problem will reappear again further down the line. In a way, the problem is similar to the 'attribute-omission' problem faced by hedonics.

2 Indeed, trying to deal with the first disadvantage by making the stratification very detailed will necessarily reduce the number of observed property transactions in each cell. This will increase the *standard deviation* around the sample index itself, and make it less accurate. The hedonic method, on the other hand, is generally not subject to this particular problem.
3 Anyway, making the stratification more detailed requires that the emerging characteristics, at cell level, are available for all observed data (so that the right property can be allocated to the right cell). This may easily not be the case, considering that the mix-adjustment method is often used precisely in order to circumvent a data availability problem.
4 In the particular case where housing stock weights are used in the index, creating too many cells (each expressing a different property characteristic and sub-category) will necessitate finding equivalent stock values to use as weights. Such data may not be available.

12.9.4 SPAR indices

SPAR indices are easy to construct, require much fewer data than hedonic indices, and deal with the quality adjustment problem satisfactorily (since they rely on comparing a recorded transaction value with an appraisal value on a 'matched pair' basis). Importantly, a SPAR index is consistent, i.e., is not prone to revisions, as it is 'independently related to the base period's price index. Late sales only affect their own period's index but do not affect other periods as the repeat sales method does' (Shi, 2008).[19] Nor does a SPAR index suffer from sample-selection bias (see Section 12.3.1), which, for example, characterizes repeat-sales indices too.

The disadvantages of SPAR indices are as follows:

1 They presuppose accurate appraisals of property values (Vries et al., 2009). Typically, these range from mildly erroneous to very inaccurate depictions of market reality.
   (a) In many countries, like the USA, the UK, or New Zealand, local authorities have experience in assessing property values for tax purposes, but the methods employed, or the frequency of assessments, vary greatly across countries. For example, in New Zealand, assessments are carried out by local authorities every three years (usually), on the basis of government statistical guidelines and of the sales comparison approach (see Section 5.5), but still errors, both systematic and random, happen (Shi, 2008).
   (b) In other countries, governments produce 'objective' or imputed property values for tax purposes, with results that leave a lot to be desired. For example, Greece's governments in the past produced 'objective' appraisals that underestimated true property values; since 2010, they have been doing the opposite.

2 The SPAR method, unlike the hedonic method *in principle*, cannot decompose a property price into its land and structure components (Eurostat RPPI, 2011).

3 Like the repeat-sales method, the SPAR method cannot deal adequately with depreciation and improvements of the dwellings between appraisal date and transaction date (Eurostat RPPI, 2011).

12.10 Appendix: hedonics theory

The seminal paper for hedonics theory as applied to RE is Rosen (1974). Nevertheless, Day (2001) has provided an excellent – and highly accessible – exposition of the theory, which is consequently recommended to readers wishing to move further into the subject.[20] Hedonics theory as it pertains to the housing market is about the pricing of goods (dwellings) that are made up of bundles of separable characteristics or attributes, each with its own implicit (because invisible) price. Very briefly, it goes like this:

(A) On the demand side (Figure 12.1)

In Figure 12.1, the following notation is used on the graph axes:

x	=	composite good (or equivalent in money),
θ	=	the consumer's bid for attribute z_1, after he has spent part of his income to buy x, while keeping his utility constant,
P_{z_1}	=	price of attribute z_1,
z_1	=	dwelling attribute z_1, out of z attributes.

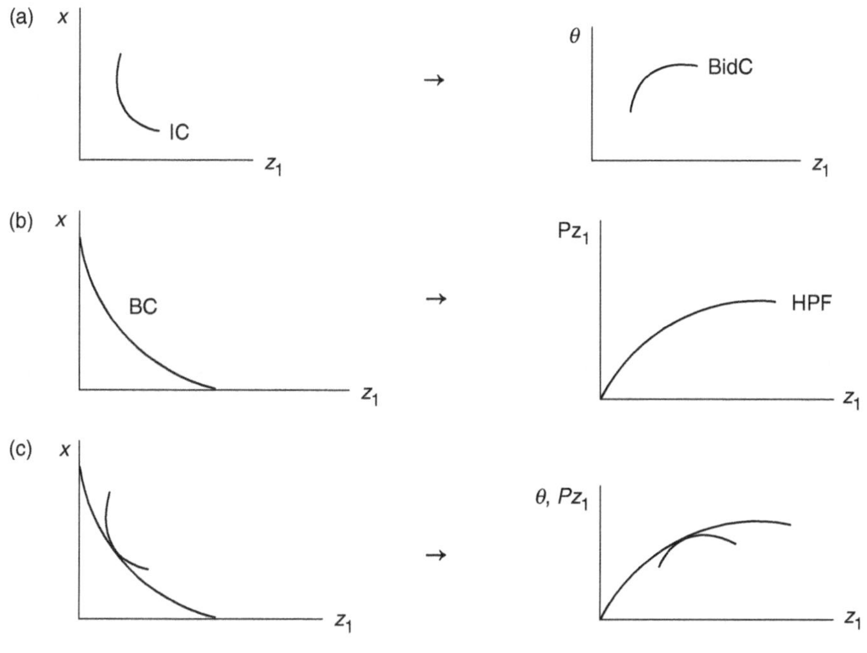

Figure 12.1 Household residential choice in a hedonics framework (a) from an indifference curve (IC) to a bid-curve (BidC), (b) from a budget constraint (BC) to the hedonic price function (HPF), and (c) optimal choice: tangency points.

An individual's indifference curve (IC) – see Section 2.2.2 – between a given housing attribute (like location, floor area, or dwelling type) and all other goods is transformed through inversion into a *bid-curve* (BidC) for the attribute (see (e) below). This is a curve showing combinations of spending on the attribute (which implies commensurately opposite changes in spending on all other goods, out of a given budget) and quantities of the attribute, all such combinations providing the same utility to the individual.

There is of course a constraint on spending. In standard (i.e., non-hedonic) consumer choice theory, the income or budget constraint (BC) is linear, but in the case of a heterogeneous good like housing (i.e., a good made up of many attributes), it becomes nonlinear (see (d) below). The nonlinear constraint is then transformed through inversion into a hedonic price function (HPF) for the given attribute (see (f) below). That function represents the market-given (but implicit) price for the attribute, and the individual takes it for granted in a competitive market. (It is in this sense that the HPF acts like a constraint on spending.)

The individual's optimal (i.e., utility-maximizing) residential choice would then be at the point of tangency between the HPF and the individual's highest possible bid-curve. (The analysis can of course be extended to any number of attributes simultaneously, only it would then be cast in terms of surfaces rather than lines.) Other housing consumers would define their own optimal choices in a similar way along the given HPF.

(B) On the supply side

In Figure 12.2, the following notation is used on the graph axes:

P_z = the price of a property made up of z attributes,
ϕ = the sale price that the supplier needs for offering attribute z_1 in order to secure a given level of profit π.

As a housing consumer wants to maximize utility, a housing supplier wants to maximize profit. The latter is the difference between his revenue from selling a dwelling of z attributes

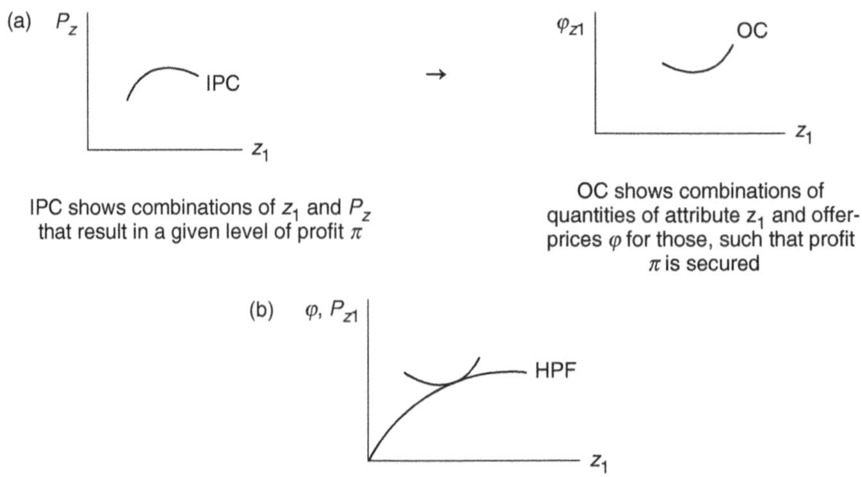

Figure 12.2 Housing supplier's supply choice in a hedonics framework (a) from an isoprofit curve (IPC) to an offer-curve (OC) and (b) optimal choice: at point of tangency between OC and market price curve HPF for attribute z_1.

at a certain price (the property price) and the cost of providing those attributes over which the supplier has some measure of control. The paramount cost element is of course the purchase (or construction) price of the dwelling – a sunk cost, but one that nevertheless involves a current opportunity cost for the supplier's capital.

Different bundles of attributes are possible. For a given cost, all such bundles that yield the same profit to the supplier form an inverse-bowl-shaped isoprofit curve. Bundles that yield higher profit would then fall on *higher-placed* isoprofit curves.

Inversion of an isoprofit curve would then describe an *offer-curve* (OC), to show the price of any given attribute that a supplier would need to receive (in reward for offering the attribute) in order to secure the given level of profit.

Enter the hedonic price function (HPF), which shows the market price of the given attribute. Assuming that, as in the consumer's case, the supplier has no control over the market price of the attribute, his optimal (i.e., profit-maximizing) position in regard to the given attribute would then be at the point of tangency between his highest possible offer-curve and the HPF curve. Other suppliers would define their own optimal positions in a similar manner along the HPF curve.

(C) Demand and supply together (Figure 12.3)

Equilibrium in the housing market, from the point of view of considering dwellings as bundles of attributes, each with its own implicit price, would then occur along the market's HPF curve (for any given attribute; or for all possible attributes if we treat the HPF not as a curved line but as a curved surface, and similarly so for bid- and offer-curves). At each point on the HPF curve, a consumer's optimal bid-curve and a supplier's optimal offer-curve would become tangent to each other.

(D) Why is the budget constraint (BC) nonlinear in hedonic analysis?

In most goods cases, the BC is linear because additional units of those goods can be had at the same price. In other words, their marginal prices are constant. In the property market, the BC is typically (but not always) nonlinear, for the following reasons:

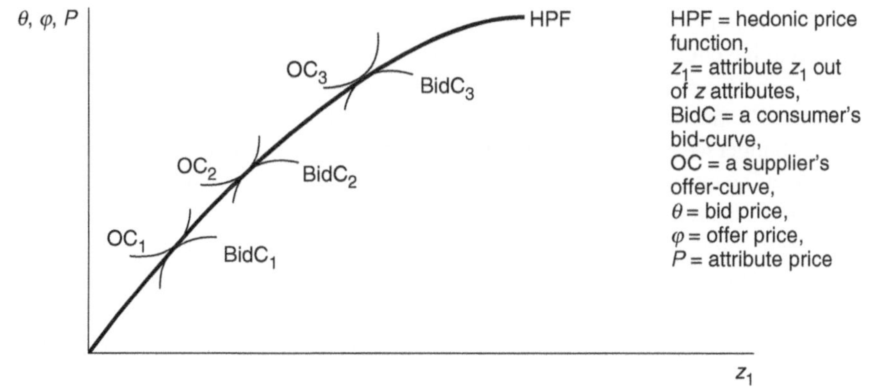

Figure 12.3 Equilibrium in a hedonic market for housing.

1 Dwellings (and other RE too)are heterogeneous goods (i.e., they are made up of bundles of attributes).
2 They can have their attributes 'repackaged' only within very narrow limits (location and, almost certainly, basic structure being the main, yet very important, attributes that cannot change).
3 They are priced as collections of attributes, but often the price of any one attribute depends on the quantity present of one or more other attributes. For example, a garden that also provides parking space may be more desirable, and therefore command a higher price, than an equal-sized garden that does not.

Consequently, households' willingness to pay for more units of most any distinct attribute will usually decline, causing the attribute price to decline, the greater the quantity present of a given attribute. This implies a variable marginal price for the attribute. In turn, a variable price implies that buying more units of the given attribute does not result in sacrificing a constant quantity of some other good(s) as with a linear BC. Hence, the BC applicable to dwelling attributes will, in most cases at least, be non-linear.

(E) How is the consumer's bid-curve derived?

The basic input is the indifference curve (IC) model of consumer choice. Given a budget constraint, a household will maximize their utility by choosing that bundle of goods which corresponds to the point of tangency between their highest possible IC and their budget constraint (BC).

In a typical IC graph we have good A on one axis, and good B on the other. Let us now imagine that on the horizontal axis we have the quantity of a given dwelling attribute z_1 and on the vertical axis the quantity of all other goods a consumer buys (together, these goods are called a *composite*, or *numeraire*, good).

How much money would the housing consumer be willing to spend to buy the given dwelling attribute? That depends on the consumer's given level of utility. For any given utility level (represented by a distinct IC), the consumer, by going down their IC, sacrifices some of the composite good to get one more unit of the dwelling attribute, keeping her utility constant. Her willingness to pay (i.e., to sacrifice) declines, therefore, the more of the attribute she presently has. What she can pay, however, depends on how much of a budget she has.

If we represent the amount of the composite good x by money, then, for a given budget, the consumer will have less money to spend on x the more of z_1 she buys. We can thus imagine combinations of quantities of z_1 and of money *not* spent on x between which the consumer would be indifferent. Why? Because money *not* spent on x is money left after part of the consumer's budget has been actually spent on x, so that the consumer has availed herself of a combination of quantities of z_1 and x that allow her the same utility as any other combination on her given IC. But money *not* spent on x is really what the consumer can use to bid for her desired quantity of z_1! So combinations of different quantities of z_1 and their respective bids are really our familiar IC, only the latter is inverted: on the horizontal axis we still have the quantity of attribute z_1, but on the vertical axis we have the amount of money θ the consumer would bid for varying quantities of z_1, given her budget, so that her utility is constant.

For example, one combination might be 2 units of z_1 and a \$50 bid (i.e., 2 units of z_1 for which the consumer would bid \$50) if, out of a \$150 budget, she spent \$100 on x, so that her utility from x and z_1 bought remained constant. Another combination might be 6 units of z_1

and a \$120 bid (implying \$30 to spend on x). The consumer would be indifferent between the two combinations because they would both give her the same utility.

Notice, in the above example, that the first combination would suggest a consumer's implicit valuation of z_1 (i.e., z_1's implicit price from this consumer's point of view) equal to $\$50/2 = \$25$. The second combination, however, would throw up an implicit price equal to $\$120/6 = \$20$, in line with the idea of a bid-*curve* rather than a straight line.

(F) What, then, about the form of the HPF?

It is difficult to specify a particular form for the HPF on the basis of the above theoretical analysis. There are two reasons for this:

1 The characteristics and preferences of households (and of suppliers, too) in the housing market would need to be known in advance. This is a very tall order.
2 The price of any one attribute is not constant but, very often, depends on the quantity (-ies) of other attributes in the bundle. The way attributes interact cannot be known *a priori* either.

As a result, hedonic price estimation tends to be an empirical endeavour. It is also often the case that, rather than going from (unknown) household characteristics and preferences to specifying a HPF, researchers will use market data to try and estimate such characteristics and preferences from various empirically tested HPFs (cf. Day, 2001).

Summary of main points

1 Valuation differs from market price. The former is about what a property is worth, given various assumptions regarding the value of future incomes from the property, of an appropriate discount rate, and/or of comparable properties. Price reflects what an actual seller and one or more actual prospective buyers think the property is worth, especially at the moment of an actual transaction.
2 Property performance measurement is about estimating how a commercial property in particular has performed financially when viewed as an investment. It takes into account the purchase price of the property, changes in the value of the property during the holding period, net incomes from the property, and, if applicable, the resale price of the property.
3 The main methods for property performance measurement involve calculating either a money-weighted rate of return (MWRR), or a time-weighted rate of return (TWRR). The first is appropriate for investors, the second for investment managers.
4 The MWRR method calculates an investment's IRR. The TWRR method is similar, only it takes into account changes in the value of the investment during the holding period too. Otherwise, both take into account cash inflows and outflows during the holding period.
5 An HPI is not an average or median house price; it is, rather, the result of a comparison between two 'representative' house prices from two different periods: a base-period and a subsequent one. It shows how the 'representative' house price (an average or median price, appropriately weighted) has changed over time.
6 Although an unweighted median price is a better choice than an unweighted average price, neither is really appropriate to base a HPI on, because neither accounts for the heterogeneous nature of housing or for the quality 'drift' between periods.

7 Four HPI construction methods that, to differing degrees, solve the above two problems are (a) the hedonic method, (b) the repeat-sales method, (c) the mix-adjustment, or stratification, method, and (d) the SPAR method.
8 Between the four, the most robust is the hedonic method, but it requires a lot of data and specification of an appropriate functional form; the easiest to use is the SPAR method, but it hinges on there being reliable property appraisals to start with. Repeat-sales and mix-adjustment are good compromises. Between the two, mix-adjustment is the easiest to use, and particularly appropriate where there are not many 'matched pairs' of sales to use.

Review questions and exercises

1 Invent a data set like the one in Table 12.1, and derive an MWRR and a TWRR.
2 Is the mean or the median a better choice as a measure of central tendency for house prices? Why?
3 Why are neither the mean nor the median good choices for inclusion in a HPI? Give four reasons.
4 What are two sources of systematic error, or bias, in a HPI?
5 You want to run a hedonic regression. You are considering four house types: apartment, detached, semi-detached, and terraced. How many dummy variables will you use for those? Why?
6 Give brief descriptions of each of the four main HPI methodologies that exist, as well as of the advantages and disadvantages of each.
7 Give the profile of the user for whom each of the four main HPI methodologies that exist might be most appropriate.
8 Following the tabular examples in the text, invent or collect data sets for each of the four main HPI methodologies mentioned, and derive the corresponding indices.
9 Think of an example of 'multicollinearity' and another of 'heteroscedasticity'. Both must be relevant to HPI construction.
10 How would you explain the possibility that, despite your reading this book, and particularly Chapter 12, almost all RE agents might still outsmart you in more accurately estimating the market price of a house than you could? Would that render your going through this book a waste of time?

Epilogue

This is not a happy time to write about real estate (RE) economics. The developed world is in the midst of an economic crisis, with no signs of abating. The crisis is manifested in, or caused by, unsustainable levels of sovereign and/or private debt, too precarious exposure of financial institutions to those, asset-price drops, deteriorating international competitiveness, increasing income inequality, widening gap between finance and real (i.e., productive) capital, and worsening demographics – all against a backdrop of adverse climate change.

Regarding RE, there are three reasons for pessimism. The first has to do with the depressive effect of the crisis on the real estate sector; in fact, the crisis was triggered by the burst of a housing market bubble in a number of countries – the USA, Spain, and Ireland being prime examples. Presently, China seems likely to follow suit.

The second reason has to do with governments in a rising number of hit countries turning to more and increasingly steep and indiscriminate taxation of RE in order to achieve fiscal goals – or so they think. The trend started in late 2009 with Greece, whose government's pretence was that property ownership and prices are highly correlated with income – an assertion that is largely untrue, and manifestly so in a recession. By 2012, it had spread to Portugal, Ireland, Spain, and Italy, with France close behind, and vocal proponents in the UK too. Even a sober, and certainly non-tax-loving, newspaper like *The Economist* suggested in a 24 September 2011 leader that perhaps more tax revenue should be shifted from income to property.

The consequences should be anticipated by almost anyone who has studied this book: a further decline (that is, in addition to the general-recession-induced decline) in building activity and employment, and in property prices, the latter hitting both financial institutions' and households' balance sheets. This should contribute significantly to recession evolving into depression, thereby defeating the goal of collecting more tax revenue, especially where excessive overall and real estate taxation are in the process of becoming permanent, as in Greece.

In that country, newly introduced RE taxes have fallen like a hurricane on a complacent and, by now, demoralized population. The toll so far: four different kinds of *main* property wealth taxes applied simultaneously plus assorted others, much increased transfer and inheritance taxes, much increased imputed property prices, and virtual abolition of income taxation, as presently the government does not tax declared incomes but imputed incomes, which it calculates arbitrarily on the basis of (imputed) value of personal wealth owned, chiefly property. Proponents of land value taxation might approve in principle; but one doubts whether this picture of human misery and expropriation is what most of them really had in mind.

People in other countries have perhaps no conception of the injustice and terror presently experienced by a majority of Greek households who over decades had invested most of their incomes and savings into property, or had inherited such, taking advantage of a traditionally very wide distribution of land ownership. Many of those households are suddenly facing the prospect of losing everything; not because they have fallen behind with mortgage payments or because they have evaded income taxes, but because the government of Greece as of 2010 has applied exorbitant taxes on property, in total disregard of households' ability to pay, or even of whether there is a single breadwinner in a household. And it is all the more galling because those who tax people out of their homes are part of the same bunch of politicians, irrespective of party, most of whom are responsible for Greece's sovereign debt mess; who have been lining their own pockets; who since the crisis began have been resisting government budget cuts, and the downsizing of the country's totally inefficient and bloated public sector, simply because most of its employees have been appointed not in response to real needs but in exchange for votes given over many elections.

By taxing RE so much, not only has the Greek political system dealt a severe blow to the RE sector, worsening the Greek economy's recession, but, more importantly, is undermining much of Greece's middle class – whose material basis had always been possession of property (but which never enjoyed true social hegemony). In effect, Greece's political class – Left, Right, and Centre – has 'pulled the rug' from underneath a large fraction of Greece's 3.7 million households, for whom a tax-free roof over their heads, and generally the tax-free possession of property, would or could have been one certainty, one anchor, in the face of dwindling, even vanishing, incomes. The government's rationale is of course chillingly cynical: if you cannot pay the crippling property taxes, sell; someone else will buy, even at 90 per cent discount, who, precisely because of that, will then be able to pay those taxes. If the Greek experience portends similar fiscal practices in other countries hit by the sovereign debt crisis, then advanced societies' future looks bleak.

This brings us to the third reason for being pessimistic. The tax-attack on property, especially if it is anything near the Greek scale, is bound to halt, then reverse, the process of the formation – or 'structuration' – of a middle class in advanced societies. For the middle class has historically been linked to property possession, of one form or another, to feelings of pride and security, and to stakes in the 'system', stemming from such possession. The attack on property, therefore, poses a threat greater than the recession itself. Without a strong middle class, democracy, national consciousness, meritocracy, and long-term economic performance will suffer. History – from ancient Athens and republican Rome to modern-day capitalist society – tells us that much. In contrast, the Dark Ages were a period of history with little by way of a middle class, mostly noblemen and serfs.

Some economists might beg to differ. They might argue, for example, that forcing Greeks away from their culture of property possession might make them turn to 'productive' investment instead. But to what purpose? In all countries, most people, given the opportunity, opt for owner-occupation, sooner or later. Higher incomes are nothing unless they enable 'the good life', including a better life for one's children. People want their countries to be internationally competitive, and enjoy higher incomes, in order to 'build lives' rather than sustain body and soul together for just one more 'productive' day at a factory or office. The ultimate importance of RE, particularly residential RE, is that it supplies people with the material basis for achieving 'the good life' – and for this reason RE investment is indeed of a fundamentally 'productive' kind.

RE economics is a wonderful subject. Properly studied and practised it can help the smooth and efficient functioning of the main process whereby a modern middle class comes into being and grows. Education, culture, and income are also important, even indispensable, but the key is property possession, both as cause and as incentive for effort. This is the framework that lends RE economics a sense of moral purpose and a measure of social usefulness. Divorced from such a framework of individual rights to property, inheritance, and freedom from state oppression (including exorbitant taxation), RE economics can only end up being irrelevant to an increasing majority of people. Let us hope that modern societies will not go down that road.

1 January 2012

Notes

1 Real estate (RE)

1 A wonderful treatise on the general concept of 'property' is Reeve (1986).
2 A 1997 United Nations study on urban land policies in developing countries made the same point: 'Once land is traded as a commodity, a land market is considered to exist' (UN ESCAP, 1997).
3 The terms 'subsector' and 'submarket' are often used interchangeably. The term 'subsector', however, should be used where the land or buildings in question are not actually marketed, but made available through other means, such as public housing.
4 Like *jonsei* housing in South Korea (see Chapter 4).
5 See Robinson (1979) and Maclennan (1982) for excellent introductions to housing economics.
6 Pryce and Evans (2007: 9–11) in particular offer a very illuminating discussion on the problem of defining housing submarkets.
7 'Utility' means satisfaction, or, more precisely, 'want-satisfying power'.
8 Strictly speaking, financial investment means investment in financial instruments. Here the term refers to purchase of existing physical assets as opposed to fixed capital formation.
9 For example Basle II rules (for banks) and Solvency II rules (for insurance companies).
10 It's also not possible to buy half a bar of chocolate at a sweet shop. But to all intents and purposes, the small amounts of money involved in all such cases imply near-perfect divisibility in practice.
11 *Ceteris paribus* (Latin) means 'other things held equal' (i.e., all other factors that may also affect the variable under consideration do not change from their given values, whatever the latter may be). In the example cited, we are suggesting that increasing lending rates for the finance of RE will cause lending rates for industrial or retail finance to increase also. Adding '*ceteris paribus*', we are cautioning that this effect will work as suggested only if other factors that also tend to influence lending rates for industrial or retail finance do not actually change.
12 REIT = real estate investment trust = a mutual-fund-like company that uses investors' pooled capital to buy, manage, or sell income properties or mortgage loans.

2 RE: tools of analysis

1 Readers should notice that in this case $h = 10 - x$, so we might as well substitute $10 - x$ for h in the primitive function and optimize for x. But the purpose here is merely to demonstrate the Lagrangian technique, as there may well be cases where substitution of this kind is not possible, as, for example, in $x^2 + xh = 10$.
2 They do not have to be parallel to one another; they must simply not intersect in the context of a given frame of reference, which in practice means a given diagram.
3 See Section 2.2.5 for more on the income and substitution effects.
4 This analysis of the income and substitution effects is based on Slutsky's approach. Eugene Slutsky (1880–1948) was a Russian mathematician and economist.
5 In other words, we are talking about intra-temporal substitution here, rather than inter-temporal. The former is across goods (e.g., housing versus non-housing), the latter is across time. ε_S also measures the curvature of an indifference curve.
6 Relevant contributions pre-dating Lancaster (1966) were Court (1941) and Houthakker (1952). Muth's (1966) paper also deserves mention.

7 *T* stands for *terra*, the Latin word for land.
8 The regression technique implied here is OLS (ordinary least squares).
9 Autocorrelation is usually detected by means of the *Durbin–Watson statistic.*
10 Endogeneity exists when one or more explanatory or independent variables in a regression correlate with the error term. The situation implies that the variables that are supposed to affect the dependent variable also depend on it. For example, changes in income affect housing demand, hence housing prices; the latter affect housing investment (and maybe general consumption), so income is affected too.
11 In case of variables cast as time series, the time series must be co-integrated for the researcher to surmise causality – cf. Section 2.3.3.
12 The two most common tests involve (i) the Granger–Engle two-step process and (ii) the Johansen procedure.
13 That is not a time series; the purpose here is to explain what we mean by 'constant mean'.
14 Through appropriate tests (like a so-called *unit-root* test), one can usually tell whether a time series is stationary or not.

3 RE in the wider economy

1 An exception may occur where increases in incomes as a result of, say, a government deficit-financing a large public sector are spent on imports and, moreover, induce households to adjust upwards their expected incomes. They therefore feel comfortable drawing on their savings in order to finance current consumption of imported goods and services, which causes a sizable trade deficit.
2 Found in OECD → Statistics → OECD.Stat → National Accounts, at www.oecd.org (accessed in January 2011). Over time, there may be changes in the OECD database, resulting in differences between Table 3.1 and information available on the OECD site.
3 Imputed rents are the notional rents that owner-occupiers are supposed to pay to themselves for their properties. They are calculated by comparison with actually rented similar properties (or properties generating flows of comparable services). There is a problem with this approach, though: if all properties were actually rented (i.e., if there were no owner-occupation at all in a country), would actual rents be the same as they are now?
4 An additional difference is in the nature of a statistical discrepancy. In the Australian example, the transition from GDP to GVA goes like this: 1,253,121 − 88,581 − 7,640 = 1,156,900.
5 Regarding factors (2) and (3), the source is J. Annabel, National Income and Production, National Accounts Branch, Australian Bureau of Statistics, e-mail posted on 17 January 2012.
6 The standard formula is $M = \frac{1}{1-c(1-t)+m}$.
7 *Ex post* = after the event. The opposite expression is *ex ante* = before the event.
8 For a discussion, see Rama and Lawrence (2009).
9 Source of definitions: www.scotland.gov.uk/Topics/Statistics/Browse/Economy/Input-Output/Multipliers.
10 Fitting an S-curve on a set of data points between variables x and y whose relationship can indeed be described by such a curve is done by means of the formula
$Y = b_1 + \exp\left(b_2 + \frac{b_3}{x}\right)$, where b_1, b_2, and b_3 are parameters supplied by a statistical software package like DataDesk.
11 The parameters for the two S-curves are as follows: in Figure 3.2, $b_1 = 0.035293325$, $b_2 = -3.5074119$, and $b_3 = -431.78633$; in Figure 3.3, $b_1 = -7.7139173$, $b_2 = 2.0807419$, and $b_3 = 8.1998789$.
12 Tobin, J. (1918–2002): an American economist and Nobel Prize laureate (1981).
13 A hedonic price index takes into account the particular characteristics of dwellings (see Chapter 12).
14 A replacement cost index measures the cost of building a structure in replacement of an existing one.
15 An agency within the US Department of Housing and Urban Development, founded in 1992, and succeeded in 2008 by the Federal Housing Finance Agency.
16 www.communities.gov.uk/documents/housing/xls/table-101.xls (accessed 9 December 2010).
17 www.communities.gov.uk/documents/housing/xls/1473575.xls (accessed 9 December 2010).
18 www.nationwide.co.uk/hpi/historical/Sep_2009.pdf (accessed 9 December 2010).

19 Source: National Statistical Service of Greece. (a) On number of transferred properties: 'Table: Number, value, and tax collected by category of transferred property, Jan.–Dec. 1998'. (b) On housing stock and construction figures: www.statistics.gr/portal/page/portal/ESYE.
20 See Catte et al. (2004), Case et al. (2005), FRBSF (2007), Muellbauer (2007), Attanasio et al. (2010), Smith and Searle (2008), Bostic et al. (2009), Calomiris et al. (2009), Miller et al. (2009), Slacalek (2009), Sousa (2009), and Carroll et al. (2010).
21 The standard mathematical presentation implies that consumption is a linear function of asset holdings and the present value of future incomes, and assumes liquid assets, perfect capital markets, no uncertainty and CRRA (= constant relative risk-aversion) utility. See Slacalek (2009: 9) and Wakker (2008).
22 These are two complementary and very important hypotheses developed in the late 1950s and early 1960s by the economists F. Modigliani, R. Brumberg, M. Friedman, and A. Ando. For concise introductions, see Deaton (2005) on the life-cycle hypothesis and Meghir (2004) on the permanent-income hypothesis.
23 For example, like those set out in the Basle II Accord (for banks) and the Solvency II Framework (for insurance companies).
24 Li and Yao (2007) note that a change in housing wealth will affect not only households' non-housing consumption (the effect varying with age) – which is what interests us here – but also households' welfare (= difference between lifetime housing costs and housing wealth).
25 Because borrowing in this case presupposes mortgaging (i.e., collateralizing) one's property.
26 Because if the changes were anticipated, they would have been factored into most households' PI adjustments.
27 This is a bit simply put. More precisely, changes in house prices tend to redistribute wealth between those who 'long' housing (i.e., those for whom the value of their home exceeds the present discounted value of the housing services they plan to consume over their remaining lifetime) and those who 'short' housing (i.e., for whom the opposite holds) (Buiter, 2010: 1). Also, Bajari et al. (2005: 483–5) focus on the effect of changes in house prices on households' welfare rather than directly on consumption. The difference is a subtle one as '[t]he welfare adjustment is defined as the amount of the consumption good necessary to keep a household's value function constant after a change in house prices.'
28 The R^2, or coefficient of determination, in regression analysis shows the proportion of changes in the dependent variable 'explained' by changes in the independent variable. It takes values from 0 to 100.
29 N. Kondratiev (or Kondratieff): Russian economist (1892–1938), famous for his theory of long waves of capitalist development.
30 Associated with William of Occam (or Ockham): English philosopher, c. 1288–c. 1348.
31 PSID = Panel Study of Income Dynamics (Survey Research Centre of the University of Michigan).
32 This is the sum of frictional ('wait-and-seek') and structural (related to changes in the structure of production) unemployment. If homeownership has an effect on unemployment at all, this must be through the frictional unemployment channel (due to transaction costs and to cultural–behavioural factors).

4 RE finance: loans, equity withdrawal, and MBSs

1 Lien = a lender's legal right to keep something that belongs to a borrower until the debt has been paid.
2 There are differences between *repossession* and *foreclosure*, depending on whether one is in the UK or the USA. In the UK, *repossession* means that the lender will take back the mortgaged property, sell it, subtract from the proceeds the outstanding loan balance (plus expenses) due the lender, and give any remainder to the borrower who has defaulted. *Foreclosure* means that the lender will take back the mortgaged property, sell it, and keep everything. Repossession does not require a court order (although it is customary for lenders to seek one), foreclosure does so. In the USA, on the other hand, foreclosure is basically repossession as applied on real estate property. It may or may not require a court order (that depends on State law), but does require a written notice of intent by the lender, and (usually) a 30-day waiting period.

3 For example, Mortgage Interest Relief At Source (MIRAS), which British housebuyers enjoyed from 1969 to April 2000, when (then) Chancellor of the Exchequer Gordon Brown abolished it, reportedly calling it a 'middle class perk' (MIRAS, 2011).
4 'Bank', as used here, is shorthand for any mortgage-loan-granting financial institution.
5 An example was/is Life Assurance Premium Relief (LAPR), a UK tax break applied on certain life assurance policies that started on or before 13 March 1984. Also, in both the USA and the UK, the value gains of certain long-term annuity schemes with insurance companies are not taxed.
6 The 12 banks of the FHLB system are owned by thousands of regulated financial institutions. Their purpose is to fund other banks to enable them to make residential mortgage loans.
7 A basis point = 1/100 of a percentage point, i.e., 0.01 per cent, or 0.0001.
8 The word 'may' is used deliberately, as a 'loss' would depend on the bank's time horizon and the maturity structure of loans and deposits. A fuller discussion of interest rate risk would require (Macaulay) duration gap analysis, and not simply a comparison of the weighted averages of asset and liability interest rates – but going down that road would add quite a few pages to this book. F. Macaulay (1882–1970) was an American economist who fathered the concept of duration, which is the weighted average time (in years) to receive all cash flows from a financial instrument.
9 We pointed out in our discussion of an interest-and-capital repayment loan that the interest part varies from one instalment to the next. In a prepayment penalty, the usual procedure is to calculate the interest simply as a percentage of the original principal. In the example of Table 4.1, a 3-month prepayment penalty would have therefore been [200,000(4%)/12](3) = 2000.
10 A loan-to-value (LTV) ratio is the value of a loan for house purchase divided by the value of the property. As much as competition and business volume considerations permit, financial institutions insist on relatively low LTVs in order to safeguard themselves in cases of borrowers' default in a potential house price depreciation.
11 For this to happen, short-term interest rates must have dropped and be expected to stay at this lower level, or even fall moderately, in the future, i.e., the yield curve must be either mildly upward-sloping or flat.
12 Source: www.mortgagesorter.co.uk/costs_buying_home.html (accessed 13 January 2011), www.ukcitymedia.co.uk/mortgages/mortgage_costs.php (accessed 13 January 2011).
13 A first-time buyer would also have to pay Stamp Duty Land Tax (on residential properties worth more than £125,000) and building insurance. A borrower who remortgages will not, generally, have to pay stamp duty, unless a second name is added to the title deeds. For more on stamp duty in the UK, see www.hmrc.gov.uk/sdlt/intro/rates-thresholds.htm#1 (accessed 29 January 2011).
14 In the UK valuation fees result from three types of valuation survey: a basic property valuation, a homebuyer's property report, and a full structural property survey.
15 See 'Home Equity Line of Credit'. www.thetruthaboutmortgage.com/home-equity-line-of-credit-heloc (accessed 16 January 2011).
16 'Basics of reverse mortgages', in www.bankrate.com/finance/retirement/basics-of-reverse-mortgages-1.aspx (accessed 12 January 2011).
17 'Reverse Mortgages – Growing Market in India'. http://hubpages.com/hub/Reverse-Mortgages-Growing-Market-in-India (accessed 15 January 2011).
18 Holmans (2008) has cautioned against too much optimism in this regard: 'That a substantial minority of older households will have no homes at all because they will be tenants is not the only limitation to the validity of a model that sees the value stored in older owner-occupiers' houses as a source that can be drawn on for financing their care or providing them with incomes. Some of the dwellings in the owner-occupied stock have low values and so would not last long as a funding source for care or other purposes' (p. 42).
19 See http://seniorjournal.com/NEWS/ReverseMortgage/2007/7-07-09-RevMortMarket.htm (accessed 15 January 2011).
20 See http://reversemortgagedaily.com/2010/01/27/reverse-mortgage-industry-reaches-2-market-penetration/ (accessed 15 January 2011).
21 Vass (2008: 1).
22 See www.ship-ltd.org/.
23 In housing economics, one's home is supposed to generate an imputed income, in the sense of a continuous flow of housing services enjoyed by the homeowner. Income real estate is an investment term describing properties that generate actual income for the owner.

24 This is a point well established in the literature. See UN ESCAP (1997), Erbas and Nothaft (2002), and Everhart et al. (2006), with further evidence from Uganda (Deininger and Daniel Ayalew, 2007), China (Deininger and Songqing, 2007), and Ethiopia (Deininger et al., 2008).
25 Informal housing: dwellings not in compliance with current regulations and those that occupy land illegally (Erbas and Nothaft, 2002: 14).
26 Erbas and Nothaft (2002: 14).
27 This is a rather optimistic view of history: countries and societies can decline as well as progress. In Greece, for example, huge numbers of illegal immigrants since the early 1990s, and especially after 2004 (a time marked by a preponderance of newcomers too culturally different to assimilate), have been changing Greek urban life, and the physiognomy of Greek cities, for the worse, making Athens in particular 'third-world'-like. Greece's post-2009 sovereign debt crisis and inefficient, unproductive, statism-ridden economy have not helped matters either.
28 Broadly, the larger the size of the mortgage market and the range of mortgage products available, the 'deeper' the housing finance system.
29 Bourassa and Hoesli (2010) comment on the Swiss situation thus: 'Swiss-style house prices and home ownership rates can certainly be found in the more costly parts of other countries, including the U.S. To use one of that country's most expensive cities as an example, the 2000 U.S. census reports that median house prices in the City of San Francisco were $396,400, or about SFr. 574,500 (using the 1998 exchange rate), which is comparable to our standard price for Geneva. San Francisco's home ownership rate in 2000 was 35%, while the national rate was about 66%.'
30 See www.firstrungnow.com/mortgage-guides/shared-equity-mortgages.aspx and www.natwest.com/personal/mortgages/g3/shared-equity.ashx.
31 Source: Wikipedia, 'Securitization', http://en.wikipedia.org/wiki/Securitization (accessed 30 January 2011).
32 The interested reader is referred to Hartzell et al. (1987), *The Economist* (1987), Boleat (1988), Hess and Smith (1988), Books and Najafi (1989), Peston (1991), TEGoVA (2002), Rajapakse (2005), Xiangguo (2005), Haffner (2008), and NERA (2009).
33 See Wikipedia, 'Credit rating agencies and the subprime crisis', http://en.wikipedia.org/wiki/Credit_rating_agencies_and_the_subprime_crisis (accessed 30 January 2011).
34 The choice of the earlier year was dictated by the availability of data in the source.

5 RE as an investment decision

1 Very useful introductions to the subject are IPF (2007), Briddell (2010), GMAC (2005), RREEF (2010a and 2010b), Chen and Mills (2004), and Roberts and Sobolik (2010).
2 Taken from RREEF (2007: 2).
3 Cited from NAREIT at www.reit.com/AboutREITs/AllAboutREITs.aspx (accessed 21 January 2012).
4 See also Lindberg (2002), Briddell (2010), WFA (2010), and www.aref.org.uk (the UK Association of Real Estate Funds).
5 For a definition of correlation, see Chapter 2.
6 Foreign exchange (FX) risk, which accompanies investment in international RE stocks (assuming different currency areas of course) has been found to reduce the gains from diversification often (Worzala and Sirmans, 2003).
7 FTA = Financial Times Actuaries.
8 'Cash' returns in Table 5.5 are measured by the 7-day sterling LIBOR (BBS, 2008: 6).
9 To be found at www.cushwake.com.
10 For example, IPD's UK Annual All Property RTR for 2009 was 3.5 per cent; the 3-, 5- and 10-year RTRs were −8.0, 1.8 and 6.4 per cent, respectively. The 3.5 per cent figure came from an income return of 7.4 per cent and a capital growth of −3.6 per cent. Source: IPD UK Annual Property Index – results for the year to 31 December 2009. A more detailed description of IPD's performance methodology is in Chapter 12 of this book.
11 A thorough and advanced treatment of property appraisal (from a UK perspective) is in Baum and Crosby (2007). See also Pagourtzi et al. (1999), Oregon (2003), and Hungria-Garcia (2004).
12 After Myron J. Gordon, American economist, 1920–2010. His model dates from 1959.

13 Proof:

$$\mathrm{PV} = \sum_{t=1}^{N+1} \frac{a(1+g)^{t-1}}{(1+i)^t} = a\left[\frac{(1+g)^0}{(1+i)^1} + \frac{(1+g)^1}{(1+i)^2} + \ldots + \frac{(1+g)^N}{(1+i)^{N+1}}\right]. \qquad \text{(A)}$$

Multiplying both sides of (A) by

$$\frac{1+i}{1+g},$$

we get

$$\mathrm{PV}\frac{1+i}{1+g} = a\left[\frac{1}{1+g} + \frac{1}{1+i} + \frac{1+g}{(1+i)^2} + \ldots + \frac{(1+g)^{N-1}}{(1+i)^N}\right]. \qquad \text{(B)}$$

Now subtract (A) from (B):

$$\mathrm{PV}\left(\frac{1+i}{1+g} - 1\right) = a\left[\frac{1}{1+g} - \frac{(1+g)^N}{(1+i)^{N+1}}\right].$$

Assuming that $i > g$,

$$\frac{(1+g)^N}{(1+i)^{N+1}} \text{ tends to zero as } N \text{ gets very large,}$$

so we have

$$\mathrm{PV}\left(\frac{1+i}{1+g} - 1\right) = a\frac{1}{1+g} \Rightarrow \mathrm{PV} = \frac{a}{i-g}.$$

It is reasonable to assume that $i > g$ because g is in the nature of a promised rate of interest (expected to occur autonomously in the rental market), whereas i, the investor's required rate of return, has to incorporate a risk premium to account for the uncertainty inherent in that promise.

14 This is a simplification that assumes that rents are received annually in arrears. The UK reality is that they are received quarterly in advance. A discussion of the required adjustment is in French (1997).

15 A way out of this illogical situation is presented in McNamara (2009).

16 The cost of development is not just the cost of the actual construction. In some countries (e.g., the UK and the USA), development land has often been acquired years before commencement of construction. This means that developer's capital has been tied in land for an equal amount of time. The implied (opportunity) cost must also be taken into account.

17 Adapted from Sivitanides (2011). See also Sivitanides et al. (2001).

6 Demand for office–retail–industrial space

1 The interested reader can consult Sivitanidou and Sivitanides (1999).

2 Let us contrast the figures for Dublin to some large-scale estimates (Sanderson et al., 2006). In 2004, the office NVR for the Asia–Pacific region was 5.6 per cent, for Europe 6.7 per cent, for North America 11.6 per cent, and for the world 8.1 per cent. The relatively high figure for North America as opposed to Europe is attributed to the fact that American cities are more 'spread out' than European ones, implying weaker location preferences, and thus a more elastic demand for office space. In turn, more elastic demand for location-centred office space means prospective occupiers are more willing to extend their search for office space over a wider area, resulting in more vacant space (a high NVR) at any one time.

3 Net absorption is the increase or decrease of space occupied by tenants in the market place (Shorett et al., 2007: 10). Obviously, historical net absorption is a guide for the future only if past patterns of economic growth persist.
4 For mathematical search models in RE markets, including references, see McDonald (2000).
5 Reminder: the capitalization rate r is the number (a percentage) that 'translates' the net operating income NOI from a property into its value V, as in $V = \text{NOI}/r \Rightarrow r = \text{NOI}/V$. In this form, r is simply the standard yield on a real estate investment, and therefore comparable to other yields in the economy.
6 This section has been based on an analysis of the Seattle office market by Shorett et al. (2007).
7 Full treatment of this topic is way beyond the scope of this book. The interested reader can consult Reilly (1931), Converse (1949), Huff (1964, 2003, 2008), Nakanishi and Cooper (1974, 1982), Koontz (1994), Yrigoyen and Otero (1998), Segal (1998), Dramowicz (2005), Bruno and Improta (2006), ESRI (2007), Rogers (2007), Anderson et al. (2010), and Gattis (2010).
8 The break-point model is easily derived from Reilly's original model. Just recognize that at the break-point, T_A/T_B must be 1.
9 Orris C. Herfindahl, US economist (1918–72).
10 Alfred H. Thiessen (1872–1956): American meteorologist.
11 G. F. Voronoi or Voronoy (1868–1980): Russian mathematician.
12 Actual construction of Thiessen/Voronoi polygons is usually – and accurately – done by means of GIS software, like ArcGIS (made by the GIS industry leader ESRI, a Californian company), MapInfo (currently owned by Pitney Bowes Business Insight, a New York company), or GRASS GIS, a free, open-source GIS. For a manual method, see http://docs.bentley.com/en/HMSewerCAD/SewerCAD_Help-08-34.html.
13 Source: Access Commercial, a UK brokerage firm. www.accesscommercialmortgages.com/ (accessed 6 March 2011).
14 Recall that 'net absorption' is the increase or decrease of space occupied by tenants.
15 Brown et al. (2000) also contains a useful review of previous related work.
16 Founded in 1915, the ISM is the largest supply management association in the world (www.ism.ws/). Its headquarters are in Tempe, Arizona.

7 Housing demand and supply

1 Even though a direct link between (imputed) rents on owner-occupied dwellings and prices is often assumed in the literature, for example, 'the equilibrium market value of a house is equal to the future stream of rents that house purchase enables the buyer to avoid' (Levin and Pryce, 2009: 7).
2 Adapted from Green and Malpezzi (2000: 54–5) and Cournède (2005: 8). Proposed by Poterba (1984).
3 This is a strong assumption to make. It may, in fact, 'be seriously misleading in describing the owner-occupied housing markets' in particular. A reason is that 'households regard housing services as multidimensional, with some of their attributes directly associated with particular characteristics of the capital stock', like lot size or stock age (see Straszheim, 1975: 19–22). In the context of 'hedonic' analysis in particular, which is used for constructing 'hedonic' house-price indices (discussed in Chapter 12), housing is definitely treated as a heterogeneous good. Back in Chapter 1, however, we suggested that *generic* housing can be a proper object for analyses conducted at a high level of generality.
4 With thanks for permission granted. Any errors in this presentation are of course my responsibility. The mathematical groundwork is introduced in Chapter 2 of this book.
5 Hint: Set $\alpha(L_p^c)^{a-1}X^{\beta(1-\alpha)}H^{(1-\beta)(1-\alpha)} = \lambda\left[\delta w_p + (1-\delta)w_c\right]$ and $(1-\beta)(1-\alpha)$ $\text{H}^{(1-\beta)(1-\alpha)-1}$ $(L_p^c)^{\alpha}X^{\beta(1-\alpha)} = \lambda p_h$. Then utilize the following law of exponents: $X^m/X^n = X^{m-n}$.
6 Based on Egebo and Lienert (1988). Another interesting, but more modern and sophisticated, housing market model is that due to Bhattacharjee and Jensen-Butler (2005), which incorporates 'both the macroeconomic relationship between prices, demand and supply and a microeconomic model of search, matching and price formation', applied to England and Wales. Yet another is that of Bajari et al. (2010a), which, in the wake of the recession that started in December 2007 in the USA, simulates how US housing 'consumer behaviour responds to house price and income declines

as well as tightening credit'. And, not to ignore the case of social or public housing, Gibb (2000) has modelled housing choice and demand in the social housing system of Glasgow.

7 The vector of exogenous variables may be in additive or multiplicative form; if in multiplicative form, it may be transformed into logarithms, so that it can subsequently be used in a regression equation to estimate the dependent variable.

8 Actually, new housing construction is hardly ever completed within one period; completions within a given period are usually the result of construction projects that were initiated at least two periods ago (more in the case of big office or industrial projects). In Chapter 8, this realistic twist is adopted in the discussion of how equilibrium is achieved in a dynamic RE market.

9 The study this example draws upon was made by Stantec Consulting Ltd in 2003, and refers to the City of Windsor in Ontario, Canada. The City had 209,218 inhabitants in 2001, and 216,473 in 2006.

10 Figures mentioned are from the Stantec (2003) study, and serve merely as educational illustrations.

11 In other countries, the categorization of dwelling types may differ of course.

12 An informative discussion of the difference between demand-based and needs-based housing forecasts is in Robinson (1979: 54–9).

13 www.legislation.gov.uk/ukpga/1990/8/section/55.

14 'Assembling of land' may mean buying the different property rights pertaining to a given plot, like the freehold and the leasehold in the UK, and/or buying adjacent pieces of land to create a bigger plot.

15 Referred to as 'ripening' and 'waiting' costs: the former is mostly the interest foregone on funds tied up in the land while the developer is waiting for a good time to start building; the latter is the same thing, only it covers the period of construction (assuming planning permission has been given) and the period until revenue from the project starts coming in.

16 Source: US Census Bureau, www.census.gov/hhes/www/housing/hvs/qtr211/files/q211press.pdf (accessed 5 August 2011).

17 The following analysis applies essentially to office space too, the main difference from dwelling space being that in the former the decision to develop or build depends mostly on forecast actual net rental income from the development (or on that income's capitalized value), whereas in the latter it is based mostly on the forecast selling price of the finished dwelling units. We have already pointed out that the price of a dwelling is not necessarily equal to capitalized income from it, as, in the case of owner-occupation, that income is typically imputed and therefore not directly comparable to the rental income that could be achieved from actually letting the property.

18 This is the standard condition for profit maximization: that profit is maximized at the level of output at which MR = MC (or at which the difference between total revenue and total cost is greatest).

19 Another frequent assumption is that inputs (capital, labour) are interchangeable. This is not very realistic because of (a) indivisibilities and (b) the way available technology dictates the production process.

20 If P were a datum rather than a function of output (as is often the case from the point of view of a housebuilding firm over a production cycle), TR would graph as a straight line upsloping from the origin.

21 The proposed functional form is quite realistic as it implies that initially MC drops with output (probably due to synergism and economies of scale), then rises as diminishing returns set in. Another possibility could have been $\text{TPC} = F + aQ^b$ (where F = fixed cost), used in Chapter 10. A third could have been $\text{TPC} = f(K, L) = K^a L^{1-a}$, a typical Cobb–Douglas function (see Section 2.2.3) where K = capital and L = labour. Such a function suggests constant returns to scale.

22 Notice that at 4 units of output, the slope of the TC curve at point a_1 is equal to the slope of the TR curve at point A. These slopes represent MC and MR, respectively. If they are equal, it means that at 4 units of output the firm is maximizing its profit.

23 See Box 7.2 at the end of this section for an explanation.

24 How a pattern of land uses emerges, dependent on end-users' demand for location, is discussed in more detail in Chapter 10.

25 These are not the only possible modes of residential development, nor are these modes confined to, or the only ones in, the countries mentioned. In Israel, for example, most land is owned by the Israel Land Authority (Minhal). Parcels are leased to developers through closed-bid auctions, who have an obligation to build within three years (usually). See www.natam.co.il/en/madrih.asp?category=038_. Vaguely echoing this practice, 'the thrust of

urban planning [in Syria] is to use expropriation as a principal tool of planning. Expansion areas are acquired at agricultural use prices [...]. The public sector then sells the land off for individual private development with certain restrictions [...]: i.e., no transactions until the land is developed' (McAuslan, 2008: 8).

26 Land banking is 'the acquisition of unimproved land or improved vacant lots for the purpose of development or disposition at a future date' (RREEF, 2008: 3).

27 See www.residentiallandlord.co.uk/propertyoptions.html.

28 For a more advanced analysis from a US perspective, see Buttimer et al. (2008).

29 This was one of the main points of the famous Barker Review of Housing Supply in the UK (2004): 'it is clear that more greenfield and brownfield land will be needed if an adequate supply of houses is to be delivered' (Barker, 2004: 11).

30 In other words, demand for land is a derived demand, depending on land use (cf. Muth, 1971; Kau and Sirmans, 1981).

31 That there must be a difference is made evident if we consider a landowner who developed the land himself: his profit would be the difference between revenue from the finished product and the cost of building (including normal profit). In other words, he would pocket the entire land value as it would appreciate. An outside developer, however, would not pay all of that difference (i.e., the land value, which is a cost to him), for then he would not be able to achieve an RRR. Consequently, he would pay less than the full LV.

32 'Zoning', as practised by planning authorities, involves assigning permitted land uses, or building height, or lot coverage to different geographical areas.

33 This is a simplification, the same as the one mentioned in the previous section. In reality, such inputs are bought or rented throughout the construction period.

34 According to Greek market practitioners.

35 Source: www.sustainability.vic.gov.au/resources/documents/Business_Models_For_Enabling_Sustainable_Precincts_Case_Study_OneBrighton.pdf, p. 2 (accessed 4 August 2011).

8 Construction flows and market equilibrium

1 In the broader field of economics, the first to use CSAMs were Kaldor (1940) and Kalecki (1935). For a concise but demanding introduction to their work, see Szydlowski and Krawiec (2001).

2 A way out of the difficulties encountered when one assumes that, at re-establishment of equilibrium, construction = initial depreciation is to define long-term equilibrium as that price at which the *rate* of new construction (as percentage of the stock) is equal to the *rate* of depreciation (as percentage of the stock). But this is not what Figure 8.1 shows, and, anyway, using rates rather than absolute amounts conflicts with Robinson's (1979) treatment of depreciation as fixed.

3 Through at least two avenues: (i) net additions to the stock, period-after-period, which will affect the age distribution of the latter; and (ii) the possibility that, with time, older buildings age faster.

4 The model is sometimes referred to as the Fisher–DiPasquale–Wheaton model, on account of the fact that J. D. Fisher (1992) published a related article in the same medium at the same time. We choose to focus on the DiPW model, though, due to its intuitiveness, simplicity, and sheer pedagogical power.

5 In an alternative model formulation, which deviates from the DiPW model, current and expected prices rather than current rent and current price are used – see Section 11.8.3

6 Fisher (1992) has cautioned against using the term 'RE' too freely as users of at least certain kinds of properties (like hotels or regional malls) often pay for more than the tangible real property. He wrote (p. 163): 'Whether that portion of rent attributed to these other services should be capitalised into what we call "real estate" is a debatable issue.' See also Fisher and Kinnard (1990).

7 DiPasquale and Wheaton (1992) call the construction curve in the SW quadrant of their diagram a 'replacement cost curve for RE', which slopes upward because the cost of construction rises with greater building activity. It is better, though, to view this as a curve showing how much new construction is forthcoming given RE price rises (once a certain cost of construction – given by the vertical intercept of the construction function – is covered by the market price of the property to be built). A higher price will then call forth more construction simply because it will mean more profit. A rise in the cost of construction can be depicted by a rise in the vertical intercept (a shift of the construction line). A more sophisticated version of the model should perhaps also look into the possibility that the stock depreciation rate δ will rise with RE price because RE

price rises are likely to bring redevelopment time for an increasing number of properties nearer the present.

8 This strategy has the advantage of showing clearly and easily the model's dynamic behaviour (cf. Wheaton, 1999: 212).

9 Based on Wheaton (1999) and Davidoff (2008).

10 The importance of the actual values of the equation parameters in a recursive model has been stressed and shown by Wheaton (1999).

11 Intuitively, the 'jump' from $S = 750$ to $S = 899.93$ is 149.93 – which means that to let 750 go down to zero, we must make 5.0 times a backward 'jump' of 149.93 (as $5.0 = 750/149.93$). The corresponding change in P is therefore $5.0(8.01) = 40.05$, which gives a vertical intercept of $9.95(= 50 - 40.05)$.

12 They attributed their results to the existence of a large social rental sector in Netherlands and to government interventions in the land and housing markets – which makes sense, as such interventions may act as impediments to the price adjustment mechanism of a competitive economy.

13 Based on Wheaton (1999) and Davidoff (2008).

14 In a more complex formulation, the exogenous variable can be linked to economic growth rate d, as in $R = 5000E_tS^{-1}$, where $E_t = (1 + d)E_{t-1}$. So E may well jump up or down, but thereafter will continue growing by d. Cf. Wheaton (1999: 214).

15 Remember that long-run equilibrium means two conditions: (a) demand price = supply price and (b) construction = depreciation.

16 Kummerow and Quaddus (1998), studying office market cycles, observed that the unstable dynamics of office market systems result from, among others, 'poor forecasting, market research, and valuation techniques'.

17 Cf. von Böventer (1978: 263): 'the existence of a bandwagon implies that [...] households buy the more of a commodity, the more *other* households buy.'

18 'Physical reasons' refer to the geology or aesthetics of a site, its associated amenities, and its relative distance from desirable locations.

19 In *naive expectations*, tomorrow's expected price is today's price; in *adaptive expectations* (a more refined form of naïve expectations, really), expected price is a weighted average of the previous price and the previous expected price; and in *rational expectations*, the expected price is a function of today's and future prices. Naive or adaptive expectations are also referred too as 'myopic'.

20 For a critique of both, see Gertchev (2007).

21 Cf. the paper by Ambrose et al.(2011: 16) on house prices in Amsterdam from 1650 to 2005: 'While prices do revert back to fundamentals, this reversion may take decades with the move towards equilibrium more a fading out than a crash.'

22 This is the idea, based on observations of sample behaviour, that deviations from an estimated average (i.e., mean) value (of, say, prices) tend to revert to that average.

23 Michelsen and Weiß (2009), in their study of the East German housing market, also spotted this problem (while making use of the DiPW framework): 'How quickly the housing stock derives its new equilibrium depends on additionally constructed space [...] and the rate of physical depreciation.'

24 Time-series analyses may be divided into frequency-domain methods and time-domain methods. Spectral analysis, along with wavelet analysis, belong to the first set; auto-correlation and cross-correlation belong to the second set. Spectral analysis, in particular, decomposes a time series into a spectrum of cycles of different lengths. See Barras (1985) and Iacobucci (2003).

25 'In 1900, only 14% of humanity lived in cities. By the century's close, 47% of us did so.' From 'Half of humanity set to go urban', by D. Whitehouse, Science Editor, BBC News (http://news.bbc.co.uk/2/hi/science/nature/4561183.stm).

9 RE taxation

1 Taken in isolation, that loss is of course a sign of Pareto-inefficiency.

2 A transfer tax, as opposed to a common sales tax, is a tax on the transfer of title to property, and as such is levied not only on property sales transactions but on bequests too.

3 As of 1 December 2003, the formal name of this tax is Stamp Duty Land Tax: it is a self-assessed transfer tax on land transactions. Unlike old-style 'stamp duty', HM Revenue and Customs is able to raise assessments to recover unpaid SDLT. (Source: http://en.wikipedia.org/wiki/Stamp_duty_in_the_United_Kingdom; accessed 31 October 2011.)

4 An excellent concise introduction to the theory and practice of optimal taxation is in Mankiw et al. (2009).
5 The concept of an efficient tax as used here differs from the concept of a 'tax-efficient' instrument, which is one that achieves the same pre-tax return as another, only it is taxed at a lower rate.
6 'Tax something, there will be less of it – except land' (C. L. Harriss, quoted in Cohen and Coughlin, 2005: 364).
7 See http://en.wikipedia.org/wiki/California_Proposition_13_(1978).
8 In 2001, in Greece, 1538 regular dwellings corresponded to 1000 households (of whom 20.3 per cent rented). (Source: www.statistics.gr.) The corresponding ratio in England was 1033: 1000, while 30 per cent of the stock was rented. (Source: *Housing and Planning Statistics 2010*. www.communities.gov.uk/documents/statistics/pdf/1785484.pdf.)
9 An additional point was made by Muellbauer (2005: 109): 'Property taxes linked to market prices are necessarily more volatile than income or sales taxes[.] This suggests that they are not ideal as the main source of local revenue.'
10 In the USA, an *assessment ratio*, applied on a property's current market value, determines the *assessed value* of a property, on which subsequently a *property tax rate* will be applied to determine the *property tax payable* (after some adjustments, like deducting *homeowner exemption*).
11 Here is an interesting analogy: Kuran (2010) has suggested that the egalitarianism implicit in the Islamic law of inheritance inhibited capital accumulation in the Islamic world at a time when the West was rising economically.
12 The French study is interesting in that, over the period 1994–2004 (in urban France), 'the local property tax rate has no impact on property prices, while the amount of taxes paid appears to have a negative effect on property price'.
13 To simplify calculations, R is assumed to be constant, even though V is assumed to increase. This could be justified as a case (improbable though it is) where V is affected by rising demand for alternative uses for the site as time goes by, with no effect on the rent set down on an existing lease.
14 Relevant papers are Oates (1969), Quang Do and Sirmans (1994), Yinger (2005), McDonald and Yurova (2006), Tsoodle and Turner (2008), and Sirmans and Stacy (2008).
15 That is, property taxation at different rates across jurisdictions.
16 This holds for all taxes. For example, in Greece the level of public services (national and local) has for ages and with few exceptions been so unsatisfactory (even though the public sector is huge and terribly expensive), that pervasive tax evasion is a rational, even ethical, response to this waste. Of course, tax evasion runs counter to equity; this only shows that an act or behaviour can be both ethical and unethical, depending on context.
17 A good example is in Evans (2009: 7).
18 This, Sweden did from 1984 to 1991, the UK does even now on certain transactions (via the Stamp Duty Reserve Tax), and the EU may do in the near future. See http://en.wikipedia.org/wiki/Tobin_tax (accessed 31 October 2011).
19 At least where people's primary residences are concerned.
20 For references, see Eerola and Määttänen (2007: 1).
21 The addition of consumption was a welcome contribution to the literature on the subject.
22 For example, 'people should face the real opportunity cost of continuing to live in large houses' (Maxwell and Vigor, 2005: 8). Also: 'with higher taxes induced by higher house prices, households with spare rooms will be more inclined to rent out the space, increasing the effective supply of housing' (Muellbauer, 2005: 108), as if it is perfectly natural or ethical to force people to share their homes with complete strangers.
23 A good review of arguments against such relief is in Tsounta (2011: 18–21).
24 On the supply side, the tax burden would be approximated by $\frac{|\varepsilon_d|}{|\varepsilon_s|+|\varepsilon_d|}$.

10 Land uses, values, and taxation

1 This observation is not meant to negate the value of an impressive corpus of housing and urban economics research, which since the 1960s has treated housing only or largely as a homogeneous commodity (cf. Muth, 1969; Straszheim, 1975; Maclennan, 1982). Housing may not be a homogeneous good, but if, to all intents and purposes, a majority of housing consumers behave as if it is, then many of the results of that research should broadly hold.

2 Translated into English by C. W. Baskin under the title *Central Places in Southern Germany*, and published by Prentice Hall in 1966. Christaller's theory was later modified by August Lösch, German economist and location theorist, in his 1940 book *The Spatial Organization of the Economy*, published in English as *The Economics of Location* (1954) by Yale University Press.
3 G. K. Zipf was a linguist who suggested (1935, 1949) that the frequency of a word in any natural language corpus (i.e., an extended body of written or spoken material) is inversely proportional to its rank in the word frequency table for the corpus. Thus the most frequent word will occur approximately two times as often as the second most frequent word, three times as often as the third most frequent word, etc. Source: http://en.wikipedia.org/wiki/Zipf's_law.
4 How this bid-rent curve is derived is shown in the Appendix to this chapter.
5 For the classical approach, see Alonso (1964), Mills (1967, 1972), and Muth (1969, 1971). For later expositions, see Straszheim (1975), Brueckner (1987), Gin and Sonstelie (1992), Briassoulis (2000: 4.5.4), and Sieg (2011).
6 The lines in Figure 10.8 have been drawn on the basis of hypothetical land-price equations like those used in Tables 10.1 and 10.2.
7 Not to be confused with taxing income from land, the transfer of land, or capital gains from such a transfer. LVT is just a wealth tax on the possession of land, calculated as a percentage of the estimated value of land, and paid annually.
8 Quoted in Cohen and Coughlin (2005: 359).
9 E. D. Craig, quoted in Cohen and Coughlin (2005: 359).
10 Consider this phrase from Labour Land Campaign's site: 'a tax on land values is a fair tax, because the person who owns land derives benefit from something which he or she has not made' (www.labourland.org/lvt/what_is_lvt.php, accessed 28 September 2011). Accordingly, by the same logic, a movie DVD one owns (or a seamstress's sewing machine) should be taxed because one derives benefit from it (and in fact the seamstress derives *financial* benefit from her machine) although they have not made those items …
11 That is, the percentage of the rateable value of a business property in the UK paid as tax.
12 Generally, the less competitive a market is, the greater the DWL even in the absence of taxation, and the greater, in particular, the reduction in consumer surplus.
13 There is another thing to be said about the role of inheritance (rather than of any particular inheritor) in regard to the issue discussed: that the right to bequeath and inherit acts as an additional, sometimes very strong, incentive to invest in property – so that the life chances of one's children are enhanced.
14 Large landed estates. In relation to *latifundia*, Conning (2003: 27–8) has concluded that although in some cases 'estate production in fact responded very flexibly to […] new opportunities […], where landlords could not price-discriminate 'an inverse farm size-productivity relationship [emerged]; where they could do so, this happened 'at the expense of peasant welfare'. In general, 'landlords who withhold land from the market raise the price of land access to levels well above the social marginal product of land […] compared to a competitive factor market where no agent would ever be willing to pay more than [the equilibrium market price] for access to an additional unit of land.'
15 On the topic of economic rent, see Section 10.10.
16 Source: http://en.wikipedia.org/wiki/Harrisburg,_Pennsylvania.
17 In a similar vein, Wightman (2010), in a report on LVT commissioned by the Scottish Green Party, concedes that 'hope value' (the uplift in the value of land purchased, due to a 'hoped for' change of use) may not be taken into account for LVT purposes, in regard to land owners who have owned their property for a long time, chiefly farmers.
18 Economic rent is used mostly in relation to land resources; in relation to entrepreneurial activity, it is referred to as supra-normal profit.
19 Henry George, 1839–1897: American political economist, famous for his book *Progress and Poverty*, published in 1879.
20 The interested reader could consult Hoover and Giarratani (1999: Chapter 6 on Land Use) for a more extensive treatment of this topic, although they do not make explicit use of an RRR.
21 This is not the only TPC function possible, of course. The one used here was suggested by Hoover and Giarratani (1999). One of its advantages is that it conforms to the *law of diminishing returns*, as TPC rises faster than output, so it is particularly apposite for agricultural uses. Given technology, a firm's marketing orientation, and perhaps appropriate definitions of 'output', this functional form may also do for some industrial, retailing, and office uses.

22 For rules of differentiation, see Section 2.1.1.
23 The following calculation makes heavy use of the laws of exponents.

11 Housing market bubbles

1 See Schumpeter (1939), Galbraith (1954), Kindleberger (1978), Helbling and Terrones (2003), Perez, (2003), Reinhart and Rogoff (2008), and *The Economist* (2011e).
2 Regarding RE bubbles see Baddeley (2005), Malpezzi and Wachter (2005), Shiller (2005), Foldvary (2006b), Glaeser (2006), Sorensen (2006), Leamer (2007), Case and Quigley (2008), Roberts (2008), Posen (2009), Glaeser and Gottlieb (2010), Schulmerich (2010), Amrine (2011), Bénétrix et al. (2011), Ceriani et al. (2011), and Hemmelgarn et al. (2011).
3 It may also happen because of drops in supply, but this is less common.
4 The dramatic expansion of the Irish property sector was manifested in (i) construction accounting for 10 per cent of GDP by 2006, compared with 5 per cent a decade earlier, (ii) residential construction accounting for over 80 per cent of the increase in the value of total construction investment between 2000 and 2005, (iii) new house prices rising by a cumulative 300 per cent in real terms and 340 per cent in nominal terms between 1992 and 2006, with the housing stock rising by 150 per cent, and (iv) by 2006 real new house prices being overvalued by 20–40 per cent (Malzubris, 2008).
5 That was the last expansion before the one that ended in 2008 Q1 (see www.nationwide.co.uk/hpi/downloads/UK_house_price_since_1952.xls).
6 *Asymmetric information* exists between two parties involved in a transaction when one party has fuller, or more accurate, knowledge than the other about the risks and benefits associated with the transacted item or asset. It comes in two forms: *adverse selection* and *moral hazard* (see Mishkin, 2010).
7 FIs that made headlines at that time were the UK's Northern Rock bank (nationalized on 22 February 2008), Bear Stearns of New York (sold to JP Morgan Chase in March 2008), Lehman Brothers (which went bankrupt on 15 September 2008), AIG (the insurance giant, which was just saved by the Fed on 16 September 2008), Iceland's banks (in September 2008). Among countries, the first that got into trouble were Iceland, Greece, Portugal, and Ireland, subsequently followed by Spain and Italy.
8 For MBSs, see Section 4.7. CDOs are bond instruments, just like MBSs, but unlike them they are 'backed' by more varied pools of underlying assets (including MBSs). In the run-up to the US housing market bubble burst, they became notorious for including large amounts of *subprime* MBSs in those pools. CDSs are instruments that oblige the seller to compensate the buyer in case of loan default. Unlike an insurance policy, the buyer does not need to have an insurable interest in the loan.
9 For example, the American Dream Downpayment Act, signed on 16 December 2003 (Hemmelgarn et al., 2011).
10 See http://en.wikipedia.org/wiki/Government_policies_and_the_subprime_mortgage_crisis and http://en.wikipedia.org/wiki/US_subprime_mortgage_crisis.
11 When referring to government control of private corporations such as Freddie Mac or Fannie Mae, *conservatorship* implies a more temporary control than does nationalization (see http://en.wikipedia.org).
12 Between 1995 and 2000, the US Capital and Financial Account 'increased from 1.54 per cent to 4.25 per cent of GDP [...] to peak at 6.10 per cent of GDP in 2006' (Hemmelgarn et al., 2011: 4).
13 See www.federalreserve.gov/releases/h15/data.htm#fn2. The *Federal funds rate* is the rate of interest that banks charge one another on overnight loans made from temporary excess reserves. It is the interest rate the Fed can best control (McConnell et al., 2009: 670).
14 See www.federalreserve.gov/releases/h15/data.htm#fn2.
15 See http://en.wikipedia.org/wiki/US_subprime_mortgage_crisis, accessed 17 November 2011.
16 See O'Toole (2009) and K. Philipsen's response in http://archplanbaltimore.blogspot.com/2009/11/how-urban-planners-caused-housing.html; D. Merriam's blog at www.planetizen.com/node/41867; Glaeser et al. (2005); Glaeser et al. (2008); Huang and Tang (2010); Cox (2011); Demographia (2011).
17 See *The Economist* (2011a, d); Bloxham (2011); Joye (2011a, b); Soos (2011); McMahon (2011).
18 The 'median' is the value below which 50 per cent of the observed values in a sample fall.

19 In the USA, 'A record 2.87 million properties got notices of default, auction or repossession in 2010'. See www.bloomberg.com/news/2011-01-13/u-s-foreclosure-filings-may-jump-20-this-year-as-crisis-peaks.html (accessed 13 August 2011).

20 Referring to the credit-crunch crisis that began in 2008, Magnusson (2008:1) concluded that '[S]ecuritization made it possible to avoid two basic principles in the banking system: the possibility to value financial instruments on a realistic basis ("marked to market"); and transparency.'

21 '[L]ower real [interest] rates can explain only one-fifth of the rise in [US house prices] from 1996 to 2006' (Glaeser and Gottlieb, 2010: 1).

22 Paul R. Krugman (born 1953) is an American economist and Nobel laureate (2008).

23 Term coined by R. Hilferding, 1877–1941, Austrian-born Marxist economist, in his book *Das Finanzkapital* [*Financial Capital*], published in Vienna in 1910.

24 See Section 9.5.2 on tax incidence.

25 'Mean reversion implies that in the long run, housing markets move toward equilibrium values based on fundamental supply and demand factors' (Moody's Analytics, 2011). The mean in question is typically a long-term trend rather than a specific (real) price.

26 Higher-income households typically tend to owner-occupy more frequently than lower-income ones. In 2010 Q4 in the USA, 81.7 per cent of households with family income greater than or equal to the median family income were homeowners; the corresponding figure for households with family income less than the median was 51.4 per cent. See www.census.gov/hhes/www/housing/hvs/qtr211/files/q211press.pdf (accessed 31 October 2011).

27 The extent of such interaction in the US 2006 RE bubble is disputed. See the Mulligan–Krugman debate in Amrine (2010: 10–12).

28 In some places in the USA during the 1996–2006 house-price cycle, 'the boom [described as the biggest house-price bubble in history] was big enough and irrational enough to suppress price signals from lots of new supply. Instead, availability of land simply fed speculative activity, which has made the popping of the bubble much more painful' (Palmer, 2011: 7).

29 In 2008, approximately 46 per cent of young adults aged 18–34 in the European Union still lived with at least one of their parents (Choroszewicz and Wolff, 2010: 1). The figure is only indicative of the 'popularity' of this alternative; it does not mean that none of those people could afford owner-occupation, and is certainly affected by culture.

30 The main differences from the model depicted in Section 5.5.4 (and Figure 5.8) is that (i) owner-occupied house prices are not in fact capitalizations of (non-existent) actual rents but are determined as lump-sums, and (ii) in the owner-occupied housing market, the role of vacancies is less important than in the rental market.

31 That the quantity supplied should increase with price is basic economics. What is less clear is the extent of supply's response to price changes, i.e., the price elasticity of supply (PES). It would appear that this varies from > 1 to < 1 across countries, depending on a variety of factors (Sánchez and Johansson, 2011). For an explanation of construction's relatively low PES in the UK, see Levin and Pryce (2009).

32 *The Economist*'s (2005) leading comment was: 'The worldwide rise in house prices is the biggest bubble in history. Prepare for the economic pain when it pops.'

12 RE performance and price measures

1 See Abraham (1996), Pagourtzi et al. (1999), and Booth and Marcato (2003) for more extensive discussions of RE valuation and performance-measurement methods.

2 This example was inspired by an article in *Investopedia* (www.investopedia.com/exam-guide/cfa-level-1/quantitative-methods) entitled 'Money vs Time-Weighted Return'.

3 When interest is calculated for sub-periods within a year, the usual procedure is to adjust the denominator to $(1+i/m)^{mt}$, where i = annual interest rate, $m = 4$ if interest is calculated quarterly, or $m = 12$ if interest is calculated monthly, etc., and t = number of years. But dividing i by m is not very precise. A better procedure, if, for example, interest is calculated monthly for n months in a year, is to adjust the denominator into $[(1+i)^{1/12}]^n$. This is because the i is really the chain-linked product of $(1+j)^{12} - 1$, where j = implicit monthly interest rate, hence $j = (1+i)^{1/12} - 1$. Consequently, if interest is calculated monthly, $1 + i$ needs to be adjusted to $[(1+i)^{1/12}]^n = (1+i)^{n/12}$.

4 GIPS stands for Global Investment Performance Standards (www.gipsstandards.org), published by the CFA Institute, a global association of investment professionals. See GIPS (2008).

5 Time-series models look into history, chiefly past prices. Structural models look into market fundamentals and how they affect prices in order to forecast the latter. Of course, in that case the forecasts of structural models are only as good as the forecasts of fundamentals. An example of a structural model for house-price forecasting is the one developed by Moody's Analytics (2011).

6 This is not as simple as it sounds. If the purpose of a price index is to measure, say, the burden on consumers' income or budget of a good's rising price, the price premium for a generalized quality improvement may not need to be distinguished from the rest of the price rise that reflects 'pure' inflation. Of course, a quality improvement also reflects a rise in welfare, but that is not what a typical price index is supposed to measure.

7 The sources shown in italics are those deemed particularly important or educational.

8 However, the proper way of doing that goes beyond hedonics alone, as it requires estimation of a household demand curve for the attribute in question that presupposes knowledge of household characteristics and preferences (cf. Day, 2001).

9 Geo-referencing, i.e., geo-coding with the help of a GIS, was also used in Bourassa et al. (2004) to calculate distance to the CBD in their New Zealand study.

10 We will ignore the error term in the rest of this simple analysis.

11 Strictly speaking, the coefficients can be interpreted as implicit or shadow prices only if the MRSs between characteristics are the same across housing consumers.

12 The measure employed is the (adjusted) coefficient of determination R^2 – see Section 2.3.1. An 'adjusted' R^2 takes into account the number of independent variables in the regression model; it increases only if each new variable improves the explanatory power of the model more than would be expected by chance. It is always less than or equal to R^2. Additional tests for the 'goodness of fit' of the regression exist but are ignored here.

13 In what follows, 'antilog' is the inverse function of a logarithm. The natural log, ln, is the logarithm of a number to the base $e(\approx 2.7182818)$; its antilog is the number itself. For example, $\ln 2800 = 7.937374696$ because $2.7182818^{7.937374696} = 2800$; therefore, 2800 is the antilog of 7.937374696. In Microsoft Excel notation, 'antilog' is rendered by EXP, meaning 'exponent'.

14 This is the PI formula used by Halifax, and, in a very similar manner, by Nationwide.

15 An excellent intuitive explanation of the repeat-sales method, with numerical examples that in fact do *not* involve regression, is in Geltner and Pollakowski (2007).

16 Again, the error term will be ignored.

17 Hence'[t]he [SPAR] method can [...] only be used in countries where accurate assessed values of the properties are available' (Eurostat RPPI, 2011: 32).

18 Another problem, common in time-series data, is *autocorrelation* (or serial correlation).

19 'However reassessments tend to disturb the index's consistency over time since the new assessed values will form a new relevant reference point for the SPAR index's construction until the next reassessment period' (Shi, 2008).

20 Before attempting this, however, a student should perhaps go over Sections 2.1.1–2.1.5 and 2.2.2 of this book, and generally be sure that he or she understands both the use of Lagrange multipliers as in constrained optimization, and indifference-curve theory.

References

AARP (American Association of Retired Persons) (2008) *Reverse Mortgage Loans: Borrowing Against Your Home*, Washington, DC: AARP Foundation.

Abraham, J. M. (1996) 'On the Use of a Cash Flow Time-Series to Measure Property Performance', *The Journal of Real Estate Research*, 11 (3): 291–308.

Abramovitz, M. (1964): *Construction Cycles and Long Swings in Economic Growth*, NBER Books, No. abra64-1.

ABS (2002) *The Construction Industry's Linkages with the Economy*, Australian Bureau of Statistics, 1301.0-Yearbook Australia 2002.

ABS (2009) *House Price Indexes: Concepts, Sources and Methods, Australia 2009.* www.abs.gov.au/ausstats/abs@.nsf/mf/6464.0 (accessed 3 February 2012).

Acadametrics (2011) *Index Monitor*, 8 March. www.acadametricstest.com/Index%20Monitor.pdf (accessed 4 February 2012).

Achour-Fischer, D. (1999): 'An Integrated Property Market Model: A Pedagogical ToolM, *Journal of Real Estate Practice and Education*, 2 (1): 33–43.

Adams, Z. and Füss, R. (2010): 'Macroeconomic Determinants of International Housing Markets. *Journal of Housing Economics*, 19: 38–50.

ADMB (Association of Danish Mortgage Banks) (1998) *Danish Mortgage Bonds.* www.housingfinance.org/uploads/Publicationsmanager/Europe_danishmortgagebonds.pdf (accessed 30 January 2011).

Alhashimi, H. and Dwyer, W. (2004) 'Is There Such an Entity as a Housing Market?', Presented at the 10th Annual Pacific Rim Real Estate Conference, Bangkok, January.

Ali Khan, R. (2008) 'Role of Construction Sector in Economic Growth: Empirical Evidence from Pakistan', Paper presented at First International Conference on Construction in Developing Countries, August 4–5, Karachi, Pakistan.

Allen, K. (2011) 'Will UK Property Prices Weather a New Recession?', *The Observer*, 9 October 2011.

Alles, L. and Murray, L. (2009) 'Investment Performance and Holding Periods: An Investigation of the Major UK Asset Classes', *Journal of Asset Management*, 10: 280–92.

Alonso, W. (1964) *Location and Land Use*, Cambridge, MA: Harvard University Press.

Altoon, R. A. (2010) 'Repositioning Distressed Retail Real Estate Assets', *Retail Property Insights*, 17 (3): 14–8.

AMB (2002) 'Determinants of Industrial Real Estate Demand', AMB Property Corporation, July. www.amb.com/assets/amb_iai_07–03–02.pdf (accessed 24 February 2011).

AMB (2009) 'The Long-Term Prospects for Global Trade and Industrial Real Estate Demand', AMB Property Corporation, June. www.amb.com/assets/trade_and_industrial_real_estate.pdf (accessed 5 March 2011).

Ambrose, B. W., Eichholtz, P., and Lindenthal, T. (2011) 'House Prices and Fundamentals: 355 Years of Evidence'. http://nilskok.typepad.com/EPRI/AEL_JMCB_2011.pdf (accessed 21 November 2011).

Amrine, B. S. (2011) 'Origins and Characteristics of Recent Residential Real Estate Bubbles', *Undergraduate Economic Review*, 7 (1): Article 7.

Anas, A., Arnott, R., Small, K. (1998) 'Urban Spatial Structure', *Journal of Economic Literature*, 36 (3): 1426–64.

Anderson, R. I. and Guirguis, H. (2011) *Industrial Space Demand*, Prepared for and funded by the NAIOP Research Foundation, January. www.naiop.org/foundation/2011reports/IndustrialSpaceDemand.pdf (accessed 24 February 2011).

Anderson, S., Volker, J., and Phillips, M. (2010) 'Converse's Breaking-Point Model Revised', *Journal of Management and Marketing Research*, 3, January. www.aabri.com/manuscripts/09219.pdf (accessed 21 February 2011).

Ang, A. and Chen, J. (2002) 'Asymmetric Correlations of Equity Portfolios', *Journal of Financial Economics*, 63 (3): 443–94.

Arnold, J. (2008) 'Do Tax Structures Affect Aggregate Economic Growth? Empirical Evidence from a Panel of OECD Countries', OECD Economics Department WP 643, OECD Publishing.

Arnott, R. (1987) 'Economic Theory and Housing', ch. 24 of *Handbook of Regional and Urban Economics*, edited by E. S. Mills, v. 2: 959–88.

Arrow, K. (1951) *Social Choice and Individual Values*, New Haven, CT: Yale University Press (2nd edn, 1977).

Attanasio, O., Leicester, A., and Wakefield, M. (2010) 'Do House Prices Drive Consumption Growth? The Coincident Cycles of House Prices and Consumption in the UK'. www.homepages.ucl.ac.uk/~uctpjrt/Files/AttLeicWake_Jan17.pdf (accessed 26 December 2011).

Babin, B. J., Boles, J. S., and Babin, L. (1994) 'The Development of Spatial Theory in Retailing and its Contribution to Marketing Thought and Marketing Science', in Fullerton, R. A., ed., *Research in Marketing: Explorations in the History of Marketing*, Greenwich: JAI Press, pp. 103–16.

Baddeley, M. (2005) 'Housing Bubbles, Herds and Frenzies: Evidence from British Housing Markets', University of Cambridge Centre for Economic and Public Policy Brief 02/05. www.landecon.cam.ac.uk/research/reuag/ccepp/publications/PB02–05.pdf (accessed 11 November 2011).

Bailey, M. J., Muth, R. F., and Nourse, H. O. (1963) 'A Regression Method for Real Estate Price Index Construction', *Journal of the American Statistical Association*, 58: 933–42.

Bajari, P., Benkard, C. L., and Krainer, J. (2005) 'House Prices and Consumer Welfare', *Journal of Urban Economics*, 58: 474–87.

Bajari, P., Chan, Ph., Krueger, D., and Miller, D. (2010a) 'A Dynamic Model of Housing Demand: Estimation and Policy Implications', NBER WP 15955.

Bajari, P., Cooley, J., Kyoo il Kim, and Timmins, C. (2010b) 'A Theory–Based Approach to Hedonic Price Regressions with Time-Varying Unobserved Product Attributes: The Price of Pollution', NBER WP 15724. www.nber.org/papers/w15724 (accessed 28 December 2011).

Ball, M. (1983) *Housing Policy and Economic Power: The Political Economy of Owner-Occupation*, London: Methuen.

Ball, M., Goody, J., Meen, G., and Nygaard, A. (2011) *Housing Supply Revisited*, School of Economics, University of Reading. www.communities.gov.uk/documents/corporate/pdf/1854907.pdf (accessed 25 October 2011).

Ball, M. and Wood, A. (1999) 'Housing Investment: Long Run International Trends and Volatility', *Housing Studies*, 14 (2): 185–209.

Bank of Greece (2011a) *Annual Report for 2010*, Athens, Greece.

Bank of Greece (2011b) 'Bank of Greece Compilation Methodology of Real Estate Price Indices', Economic Research Department, Real Estate Market Analysis Section. www.bankofgreece.gr/BoGDocuments/EN_Method_of_RRPI_of%20_BG.pdf (accessed 9 January 2012).

Barker, K. (2003) *Review of Housing Supply – Securing Our Future Housing Needs – Interim Report – Analysis*, HMSO, December.

Barker, K. (2004) *Review of Housing Supply – Delivering Stability: Securing Our Future Housing Needs – Final Report – Recommendations,* HMSO, March.

Barker, K. (2005) 'The Housing Market and the Wider Economy', Speech at the Institute of Economic Affairs, State of the Economy Conference, 24 January.

Baron, R. (2006) 'Planning Gain Supplement', Institute of Directors Tax Policy Comment. www.iod.com/MainWebsite/Resources/Document/policy_paper_planning_gain_supplement.pdf (accessed 25 September 2011).

Barras, R. (1987): 'Technical Change and the Urban Development Cycle', *Urban Studies*, 24 (1): 5–30.

Barras, R. (1994): 'Property and the Economic Cycle: Building Cycles Revisited', *Journal of Property Research*, 11 (3): 183–97.

Barras, R. (2009): *Building Cycles: Growth and Instability*, Wiley-Blackwell.

Barras, R. and Ferguson, D (1985): 'A Spectral Analysis of Building Cycles in Britain', *Environment and Planning A*, 17 (10): 1369–91.

Barras, R. and Ferguson, D (1987a): 'Dynamic Modelling Of The Building Cycle: 1. Theoretical Framework', *Environment and Planning A*, 19 (3): 353–67.

Barras, R. and Ferguson, D (1987b): 'Dynamic Modelling of the Building Cycle: 2. Empirical Results', *Environment and Planning A*, 19 (4): 493–520.

Baum, A. (2000): *Evidence of Cycles in European Commercial Real Estate Markets n and Some Hypotheses*, University of Reading, UK. www.reading.ac.uk/LM/LM/fulltxt/0500.pdf (accessed 26 December 2011).

Baum, A. E. and Crosby, N. (2007) *Property Investment Appraisal*, 3rd edn, Oxford: Wiley-Blackwell.

BBS (2008) 'An Introduction to Risk and Return, Correlation and Diversification', June. www.bbs–actuaries.co.uk/publications/factsheets (accessed 28 March 2011).

Belsky, E. S. and McCue, D. (2007) 'Why Do House Prices Fall? Perspectives on the Historical Drivers of Large Nominal House Price Declines', Harvard University Joint Center for Housing Studies, W07-3. www.jchs.harvard.edu/publications/markets/w07-3.pdf (accessed 25 October 2011).

Bellettini, G. and Taddei, F. (2011) 'Real Estate Prices and the Importance of Bequest Taxation', Collegio Carlo Alberto Notebooks, WP 107. http://carloalberto.org/assets/working-papers/no.107.pdf (accessed 24 October 2011).

Bénétrix, A. S., Eichengreen, B., O'Rourke, K. H. (2011) 'How Housing Slumps End', 54th Economic Policy Panel Meeting hosted by the National Bank of Poland, Warsaw, 27–28 October 2011. www.cepr.org/meets/wkcn/9/981/papers/benetrix_etal.pdf (accessed 8 November 2011).

Benjamin, J. D., Chinloy, P., and Jud, G. D. (2004) 'Real Estate Versus Financial Wealth in Consumption', *Journal of Real Estate Finance and Economics*, 29 (3): 341–54.

Berger, T., Englund, P., Hendershott, P. H., and Turner, B. (1998) 'Another Look at the Capitalization of Interest Subsidies: Evidence from Sweden', NBER WP 6365, January.

Bhattacharjee, A. and Jensen–Butler, C. (2005) 'A Model of Regional Housing Markets in England and Wales', CRIEFF Discussion Papers 0508, Centre for Research into Industry, Enterprise, Finance and the Firm.

Bloomberg (2011) 'Shanghai Prepares for Trials of Property Tax to Curb "Speculative" Buying'. www.bloomberg.com/news/2011-01-16/shanghai-prepares-for-property-tax-program-this-year-update1-.html (accessed 28 September 2011).

Bloxham, P. (2011) 'The Australian Housing Bubble Furphy', *Business Spectator*, 18 March.

Boleat, M. (1988) *New Lenders and the Secondary Mortgage Market*, London: The Building Societies Association.

Books, R. P. and Najafi, J. J. (1989) 'Elements of Design for a Commercial Mortgage Security: An Issuer's Primer', *Housing Finance Review*, 8: 3–29.

Booth, P. M. and Marcato, G. (2004) 'The Measurement and Modelling of Commercial Real Estate Performance', *British Actuarial Journal*, 10 (1): 5–61. www.jstor.org/pss/41141629 (accessed 9 January 2012).

Borgersen, T-A, Sommervoll, D. E., Wennemo, T. (2010): 'Endogenous Housing Market Cycles', *Journal of Banking and Finance*, 34 (2): 557–67.

Bostic, R., Gabriel, S. and Painter, G. (2009) 'Housing Wealth, Financial Wealth, and Consumption: New Evidence from MicroData', *Regional Science and Urban Economics*, 39 (1): 79–89.

Bourassa, S. C. and Grigsby, W. G. (2000) 'Income Tax Concessions for Owner-Occupied Housing', *Housing Policy Debate*, 11 (3): 521–46.

Bourassa, S. C. and Hoesli, M. (2010) 'Why Do the Swiss Rent?', *Journal of Real Estate Finance and Economics*, 40: 286–309.

Bourassa, S. C., Hoesli, M., and Sun, J. (2006) 'A Simple Alternative House Price Index Method', *Journal of Housing Economics*, 15: 80–97.

Böventer, E. von (1978) 'Bandwagon Effects and Product Cycles in Urban Dynamics', *Urban Studies*, 15 (3): 261–72.

Brachinger, H. W. (2002) 'Statistical Theory of Hedonic Price Indices', DQE WP 1, Department of Quantitative Economics, Freiburg University. www.unifr.ch/dqe/papers/files/wp0001.pdf (accessed 28 December 2011).

Bracke, P. (2010) 'Housing Cycles: A Survival Analysis'. www.bgse.uni-bonn.de/graduate-program-1/exchange-program/edp-papers/bracke (accessed 5 August 2011).

Bracke, P. (2011) 'How Long Do Housing Cycles Last? A Duration Analysis for 19 OECD Countries', IMF WP/11/231.

Briassoulis, H. (2000) 'Analysis of Land Use Change: Theoretical and Modeling Approaches', in *The Web Book of Regional Science*, published by the Regional Research Institute, http://rri.wvu.edu/WebBook/Briassoulis/contents.htm, accessed 22 Nov. 2011.

Briddell, E. Todd (2010) *A Guide to Global Real Estate Investment Options*, Urdang Capital Management Inc. (a subsidiary of BNY Mellon Corporation), June.

Brown, G. and Matysiak, G. (2000) *Real Estate Investment*, Harlow, UK: Financial Times/Prentice Hall.

Brown, J. A., Fraser, W. D., MacMillan, N., and Asquith–Charlton, J. (2000) 'An Investigation of the Relationships Between Demand, Take-Up, Supply And Rents in the Scottish Industrial Property Market', RICS Research Foundation, September, London. www.rics.org/site/download_feed.aspx?fileID=1920andfileExtension=PDF (accessed 24 February 2011).

Brown, M. (2005) *Country Note: Housing Finance in Switzerland*. www.bis.org/publ/wgpapers/cgfs26brown.pdf (accessed 30 January 2011).

Brown, R. L. and Achour, D. (1984) 'The Pricing of Land Options', *Urban Studies*, 21: 317–23.

Brown, R. J. (2005) *Private Real Estate Investment – Data Analysis and Decision Making*, Real Estate and Land Use Institute, San Diego State University, California.

Brueckner, J. K. (1987) 'The structure of urban equilibria: A unified treatment of the Muth – Mills model', ch. 20 of *Handbook of Regional and Urban Economics*, edited by E. S. Mills, v. 2: 821–45.

Brunes, F. (2005) 'Do Investors Behave Myopically when Deciding to Invest in Office Buildings? An Empirical Study Using Tobin's *q*', Report 5:69, Royal Institute of Technology (KTH), Stockholm. www.infra.kth.se/se/byfa/publikationer/meddelandenOchAvhandlingar/69_4.pdf (accessed 20 February 2011).

Brunnermeier, M. K. (2009) 'Deciphering the Liquidity and Credit Crunch 2007–2008', *Journal of Economic Perspectives*, 23(1): 77–100.

Bruno, G. and Improta, G. (2008) 'Using Gravity Models for the Evaluation of New University Site Locations: A Case Study', *Computers and Operations Research*, 35 (2): 436–44.

Buiter, W. H. (2010) 'Housing Wealth Isn't Wealth', *Economics*, 3: 2010–22, August 5. www.economics-ejournal.org/economics/journalarticles/2010-22 (accessed 8 February 2011).

Burns, L. S. and Grebler, L. (1984) 'Is Public Construction Countercyclical?', *Land Economics*, 60(4): 367–377.

Busch-Geertsema, V. (2000) *Housing Policy in Germany*. Response to questionnaire provided by A. Kofler, ICCR, Vienna. Working Paper for EuroHome-Impact project, Bremen. www.iccr-international.org/impact/docs/housing-policies-de.pdf (accessed 30 January 2011).

Buttimer, R., Clark, S., and Ott, S. (2008) 'Land Development: Risk, Return and Risk Management', *The Journal of Real Estate Finance and Economics*, 36 (1): 81–102.

Calhoun, C. A. (1996) *OFHEO House Price Indexes: HPI Technical Description*, March. www.fhfa.gov/webfiles/896/hpi_tech.pdf (accessed 3 February 2012).

Calnea (2006a) *Land Registry House Price Index Methodology*, Calnea Analytics Ltd. www.calnea.net/LandRegistryIndex.pdf (accessed 9 January 2012).

Calnea (2006b) 'An Improved National Price Index Using Land Registry Data', Calnea Analytics Ltd, 11 December www.mouseprice.com/articles/public/Upload/house_price_index_study.pdf (accessed 9 January 2012).

Calomiris, C., Longhofer, S. D., and Miles, W. (2009) 'The (Mythical?) Housing Wealth Effect', *NBER WP* 15075, June.

Cameron, D. (2003): *The Barker Review of Housing Supply: Some Analytical Comments*, Department of Economics, Oxford University. http://hicks.nuff.ox.ac.uk/users/cameron/papers/barker0803.pdf (accessed 26 December 2011).

Campbell, J. Y. and Cocco, J. F. (2005) 'How Do House Prices Affect Consumption? Evidence from Micro Data', http://kuznets.fas.harvard.edu/~campbell/papers/campbellcocco09082005.pdf (accessed 11 February 2011).

Capozza, D. R., Green, R., and Hendershott, P. H. (1998) 'Taxes and House Prices', www.umich.edu/~reecon/restate/faculty/Capozza/tax1097b.pdf (accessed 7 November 2011).

Carroll, C. D., Otsuka, M., and Slacalek, J. (2010) 'How Large Are Housing and Financial Wealth Effects? A New Approach', European Central Bank, WP 1283, December.

Case, B. and Quigley, J. M. (1991) 'The Dynamics of Real Estate Prices', *Review of Economics and Statistics*, 73 (1): 50–8.

Case, B. and Shiller, R. J. (1987) 'Prices of Single-Family Homes since 1970: New Indexes for Four Cities', *New England Economic Review*, September/October, 45–56.

Case, B. and Shiller, R. J. (1989) 'The Efficiency of the Market for Single-Family Homes', *American Economic Review*, 79 (1): 125–37.

Case, K. E. and Quigley, J. M. (2008) 'How Housing Booms Unwind: Income Effects, Wealth Effects, and Feedbacks through Financial Markets', *European Journal of Housing Policy*, 8 (2): 161–80.

Case, K. E., Quigley, J. M., and Shiller, R. J. (2005) 'Comparing Wealth Effects: The Stock Market vs the Housing Market', *Advances in Macroeconomics*, 5 (1): 1–34.

Case, K. E. and Shiller, R. J. (2004) 'Is There a Bubble in the Housing Market?', Cowles Foundation Paper 1089.

Cashell, B. W. (2009) 'The Fall and Rise of Household Saving', Congressional Research Service Report for Congress, 1 September.

Cassel, E. and Mendelsohn, R. (1985) 'The Choice of Functional Forms for Hedonic Price Equations: Comment', *Journal of Urban Economics*, 18 (2): 135–42.

Catte, P., Girouard, N., Price, R., and Andre, C. (2004) 'Housing Markets, Wealth and the Business Cycle', OECD, Economics Department WP 394.

CB Richard Ellis (2005) *Real Estate Market Characteristics 2006.* www.cbre.eu/emea_en/research/special_topic_reports/temp%20reports/Real_Estate_Market_Characteristics_2006.pdf (accessed 17 February 2011).

CB Richard Ellis (2009) *Global Office Occupier Guide 2010.* www.fsurealestate.com/downloads/GlobalOfficeOccupiersGuide2010_online.pdf (accessed 18 February 2011).

CB Richard Ellis (2010Q3) *Global Market Review: Office Rental Cycle Q3 2010.* www.cbre.com/EN/Research/Documents/GRC_Q3%202010_final.pdf (accessed 23 February 2011).

Ceriani, V., Manestra, S., Ricotti, G., Sanelli, A., and Zangari, E. (2011) 'The Tax System and the Financial Crisis', Banca d'Italia *Questioni di Economia e Finanza*, Occasional Papers 85, January.

Ceron, J. and Suarez, J. (2006) 'Hot and Cold Housing Markets: International Evidence', WP 2006_0603, CEMFI.

Chen, J. (2006) 'Housing Wealth and Aggregate Consumption in Sweden', Uppsala University, Department of Economics, WP 16.

Chen, L. and Mills, T. I. (2004) *Global Real Estate Investment Going Mainstream*, UBS Real Estate Research.

Chen, J. and Zhu, A. (2008) 'The Relationship Between Housing Investment and Economic Growth in China: A Panel Analysis Using Quarterly Provincial Data', Uppsala Universitet, Department of Economics, WP 17.

Chichernea, D., Miller, N., Fisher, J., Sklarz, M., and White, B. (2008) 'A Cross Sectional Analysis of Cap Rates by MSA', *Journal of Real Estate Research*, 30 (3): 249–92.

Choroszewicz, M. and Wolff, P. (2010) '51 Million Young EU Adults Lived with their Parent(s) in 2008', *Eurostat: Statistics in Focus*, 50.

Cigdem, A. (2008) 'Stock Market Fluctuations, Housing Wealth and Consumption Behavior in Turkey', in *Essays in Global Linkages and Business Cycles*, PhD Dissertation, Department of Economics, The George Washington University.

Ciochetti, B. A. and Fisher, J. D. (2002) 'The Characteristics of Commercial Real Estate Holding Period Returns (IRRS)', Real Estate Research Institute (RERI). www.reri.org/research/article_pdf/wp104.pdf (accessed 10 April 2011).

Cipriani, M. and Guarino, A. (2008): 'Herd Behaviour and Contagion in Financial Markets, *The B.E. Journal of Theoretical Economics*, 8 (1): Article 24.

Clapham, E., Englund, P., Quigley, J. M., and Redfearn, C. L. (2007) 'Revisiting the Past and Settling the Score: Index Revision for House Price Derivatives', Berkeley Program on Housing and Urban Policy, WP 81489.

CML (2004) 'The FT House Price Index', Council of Mortgage Lenders, 10, June 7.

Coaker, W. J. (2007) 'Emphasizing Low-Correlated Assets: The Volatility of Correlation', *Journal of Financial Planning*, September, pp. 52–70.

Coalition (2009) 'REITs and Cross-Border Property Investment: Opening up the Internal Market for Real Estate and Promoting Market Safety and Security', Proposal to the European Commission prepared by ELO, EPF, RICS, TEGoVA, 7 April. www.rics.org/site/download_feed.aspx?fileID=2933andfileExtension=PDF (accessed 23 October 2011).

Cochrane, W. and Poot, J. (2007) 'Homeownership and New Zealand Labour Market Flexibility: A Spatial Perspective', www.melbourneinstitute.com/forums/workshop/Papers/Cochrane,%20Bill_paper_050207.pdf (accessed 15.3.2011).

Cohen, J. P. and Coughlin, C. C. (2005) 'An Introduction to Two-Rate Taxation of Land and Buildings', *Federal Reserve Bank of St Louis Review*, May/June, 359–74.

Colwell, P. F. (2002): 'Tweaking the DiPasquale–Wheaton Model', *Journal of Housing Economics*, 11 (1): 24–39.

Conniffe, D. and Duffy, D. (1999) 'Irish House Price Indices – Methodological Issues', *The Economic and Social Review*, 30 (4): 403–23

Conning, J. (2003) 'Latifundia Economics', Hunter College Department of Economics WP 02/1. http://arrow.hunter.cuny.edu/research/papers/HunterEconWP02-1.pdf (accessed 2 October 2011).

Converse, P. D. (1949) 'New Laws of Retail Gravitation', *Journal of Marketing*, 14: 379–84, January.

Cournède, B. (2005) 'House Prices and Inflation in the Euro Area', Economics Department WP 450, OECD.

Court, A. T. (1939) 'Hedonic Price Indexes with Automotive Examples', in *The Dynamics of Automobile Demand*, General Motors Corporation, New York, pp. 99–117.

Court, L. M. (1941) 'Entrepreneurial and Consumer Demand Theories for Commodity Spectra', *Econometrica*, 9, No. 1 (April): 135–62; No. 2 (July–October): 241–97.

Cox, W. (2011) 'The Housing Crash and Smart Growth', NCPA Policy Report 335, June.

CRE (2011) *Compendium of Statistics*, January 14th, Published by Commercial Real Estate Finance Council. www.crefc.org/uploadedFiles/CMSA_Site_Home/Industry_Resources/Research/Industry_Statistics/CMSA_Compendium.pdf (accessed 31 January 2011).

Cremer, H. and Gahvari, F. (1998) 'On Optimal Taxation of Housing', *Journal of Urban Economics*, 43 (3): 315–55.

Crone, T. M. (1989) 'Office Vacancy Rates: How Should We Interpret Them?', FRB of Philadelphia *Business Review*, May, pp. 3–12.

Cunningham, R. and Kolet, I. (2007) 'Housing Market Cycles and Duration Dependence in the United States and Canada', Bank of Canada WP 2007-2. www.iearesearch.com/papers/wp07-2.pdf (accessed 8 November 2011).

Cussen, M. P. (2008) 'The Basics of REIT Taxation', Posted in *Investopedia* (www.investopedia.com), 21 February (accessed 21 January 2012).

Danske Research (2008) *Danish Mortgage Bonds*. www.danskebank.com/da-dk/ir/Documents/Other/DanishMortgageBondMarket2008.pdf (accessed 30 January 2011).

Davidoff, T. (2008) 'Lecture Notes for MBA 280 (Real Estate Investment and Market Analysis)', University of California, Berkeley, Walter A. Haas School of Business, Department of Finance. www.docstoc.com/docs/13303569/Lecture-Notes-for-MBA-280 (accessed 26 December 2011).

Davies, J. B., Sandstrom, S., Shorrocks, A., and Wolff, E. N. (2006) 'The World Distribution of Household Wealth', UNU-WIDER Paper, www.iariw.org/papers/2006/davies.pdf (accessed 10 March 2011).

Davis, M. A. and Heathcote, J. (2007) 'The Price and Quantity of Residential Land in the United States', *Journal of Monetary Economics*, 54 (8): 2595–620.

Davis, M. A. and Ortalo-Magné, F. (2011) 'Household Expenditures, Wages, Rents', *Review of Economic Dynamics*, 14 (2): 248–61.

Day, B. H. (2001) *The Theory of Hedonic Markets: Obtaining Welfare Measures for Changes in Environmental Quality Using Hedonic Market Data*, Economics for the Environment Consultancy (eftec), 12 March. www.cserge.ucl.ac.uk/publications.html (accessed 7 January 2012).

Day, B. H. (2003) 'Submarket Identification in Property Markets: A Hedonic Housing Price Model for Glasgow', CSERGE WP 2003–09.

de Roos, J. A.and Rushmore, S. (2003) 'Hotel Valuation Techniques', in Raleigh, L.E. and Roginsky, R.J. (eds), *Hotel Investments*, 3rd edn, East Lansing, MI: Educational Institute of the American Hotel and Motel Association.

De Bruyne, K. and Van Hove, J. (2006) 'Explaining the Spatial Variation in Housing Prices: An Economic Geography Approach', Paper provided by Katholieke Universiteit Leuven in its Open Access Publications series. www.econ.kuleuven.be/ces/discussionpapers/Dps06/Dps0615.pdf (accessed 7 February 2011).

Dear, M. and Scott, A. J., eds (1981) *Urbanisation and Urban Planning in Capitalist Society*, London: Methuen.

Deaton, A. (2005) 'Franco Modigliani and the Life Cycle Theory of Consumption', Paper presented at the Convegno Internazionale Franco Modgliani, Accademia Nazionale dei Lincei, Rome, 17–18 February.

Deichmann Haagerup, C. (2009) 'Tobin's *q* for Danish Single-Family Houses', Paper presented at ISA International Housing Conference, Glasgow. www.gla.ac.uk/media/media_129775_en.pdf (accessed 6 February 2011).

Deininger, K. and Daniel Ayalew, A. (2007) 'Do Overlapping Property Rights Reduce Agricultural Investment? Evidence from Uganda', World Bank Policy Research WP 4310.

Deininger, K., Daniel Ayalew, A., and Tekie, A. (2008) 'Impacts of Land Certification on Tenure Security, Investment, and Land Markets: Evidence from Ethiopia', World Bank Policy Research WP 4764.

Deininger, K. and Songqing, J. (2007) 'Securing Property Rights in transition: Lessons from Implementation of China's Rural Land Contracting Law', World Bank Policy Research WP 4447.

Degner, J. (1987) 'Reform of Subsidies for Owner-Occupied Housing in Germany', *Housing Finance International*, February, pp. 31–2.

Demary, M. (2009) 'The Link between Output, Inflation, Monetary Policy and Housing Price Dynamics', MPRA Paper 15978, University Library of Munich.

DEMHOW (Demographic Change and Housing Wealth) (2010) *Releasing Housing Equity*, February. www.demhow.bham.ac.uk/reports/C3.pdf (accessed 29 January 2011).

Demographia (2011) 'The Association Between Prescriptive Land Use Regulation and Higher House Prices'. www.demographia.com/db-dhi-econ.pdf (accessed 19 November 2011).

DiPasquale, D. and Wheaton, W. C. (1992) 'The Markets for Real Estate Assets and Space: A Conceptual Framework', *Journal of the American Real Estate and Urban Economics Association*, 20 (1): 181–197.

DiPasquale, D. and Wheaton, W. C. (1995) *Urban Economics and Real Estate Markets*, Englewood Cliffs, NJ: Prentice Hall.

Disney, R., Gathergood, J., and Henley, A. (2010) 'House Price Shocks, Negative Equity, and Household Consumption in the United Kingdom', *Journal of the European Economic Association*, 8(6): 1179–207.

Diewert, E. (2003) 'Hedonic Regressions: A Consumer Theory Approach', in R. C. Feenstra and M. D. Shapiro, eds, *Scanner Data and Price Indexes*, Chicago: University of Chicago Press, pp. 317–48.

Dokko, Y., Edelstein, R. H., Lacayo, A. J., and Lee, D. C. (1999) 'Real Estate Income and Value Cycles: A Model of Market Dynamics', *Journal of Real Estate Research*, 18 (1): 69–95.

Donald Jud, G. and Winkler, D. T. (2003) 'The Q Theory of Housing Investment', *Journal of Real Estate Finance and Economics*, 27 (3): 379–92.

Dornbusch, R., Fischer, S., Startz, R. (2004): *Macroeconomics*, 9th edn, New York: McGraw-Hill.

Downie, M. L. and Robson, G. (2007) *Automated Valuation Models: An International Perspective*, The School of the Built Environment, Northumbria University, October, Part of research programme commissioned by the Council of Mortgage Lenders, London.

Dramowicz, E. (2005) 'Retail Trade Area Analysis Using the Huff Model', www.directionsmag.com/articles/retail-trade-area-analysis-using-the-huff-model/123411 (accessed 24 February 2011).

Dvornak, N. and Kohler, M. (2003) 'Housing Wealth, Stock Market Wealth and Consumption: A Panel Analysis for Australia', Economic Research Department, Reserve Bank of Australia, Research Discussion Paper 7.

Dumaua, M. B. (2010) 'Input–Output Multiplier Analysis for Major Industries in the Philippines', Paper presented at the 11th National Convention on Statistics, EDSA Shangri-La Hotel, 4–5 October.

Dunse, N., Jones, C., Brown, J., and Fraser, W. (2002) 'The Spatial Pattern of Industrial Rents and the Role of Distance', Paper presented at the 8th Annual Meeting of the Pacific Rim Real Estate Society, Christchurch, New Zealand.

Duranton, G. & Storper, M. (2008) 'Rising trade costs? Agglomeration and trade with endogenous transaction costs', *Canadian Journal of Economics*, 41 (1): 292–319.

Dusansky, R., Koç, Ç., and Onur, I. (2010) 'Household Housing Demand: Empirical Analysis and Theoretical Reconciliation', *The Journal of Real Estate Finance and Economics*, Online First, 31 March.

du Toit, H. and Cloete, C. E. (2003) 'Appraisal of the Fisher–DiPasquale–Wheaton (FDW) Real Estate Model and Development of an Integrated Property and Asset Market Model', Paper delivered at the Pacific Rim Real Estate Society 9th Annual Conference, 19–22 January, Brisbane, Australia.

EDHEC (2007) *Property Derivatives: A Primer*, an EDHEC Risk and Asset Management Research Centre Publication, November.

Eerola, E. and Määttänen, N. (2007) 'The Optimal Tax Treatment of Housing Capital in the Neoclassical Growth Model', Helsinki Center of Economic Research, DP 178, August.

Egebo, Th. and Lienert, I. (1988) 'Modelling Housing Investment for Seven Major OECD Countries', OECD, Department of Economics and Statistics, WP 63, December.

Ekins, W. G.(2011) 'The Role of Capital Gains Taxes in the Housing Bubble'. http://ssrn.com/abstract=1945273 (accessed 29 October 2011).

Ellis, L. (2008) 'The Housing Meltdown: Why Did it Happen in the United States?', BIS WP 259, September

EMF HypoStat (2009) *A Review of Europe's Mortgage and Housing Markets – 2008*. November.

EMF HypoStat (2010) *A Review of Europe's Mortgage and Housing Markets – 2009*. November.

Emmanuel, D. (1981) *The Growth of Speculative Building in Greece: Modes of Housing Production and Socioeconomic Change 1950–1974*, PhD Thesis, London School of Economics.

Englund, P., Quigley, J. M., and Redfearn, C. L. (1998) 'Improved Price Indexes for Real Estate: Measuring the Course of Swedish Housing Prices', *Journal of Urban Economics*, 44 (2): 171–96.

Englund, P., Quigley, J. M., and Redfearn, C. L. (1999) 'The Choice of Methodology for Computing Housing Price Indexes: Comparisons of Temporal Aggregation and Sample Definition', *Journal of Real Estate Finance and Economics*, 19 (2): 91–112.

Epple, D. (1987) 'Hedonic Prices and Implicit Markets: Estimating Demand and Supply Functions for Differentiated Products', *Journal of Political Economy*, 95 (1): 59–80.

Epple, D., Gordon, B., and Sieg, H. (2009) 'A New Approach to Estimating the Production Function for Housing', Carnegie Mellon University, Tepper School of Business, Paper 443. http://repository.cmu.edu/tepper/443 (accessed 23 October 2011).

Erbas, S. N. and Nothaft, F. E. (2002) 'The Role of Affordable Mortgages in Improving Living Standards and Stimulating Growth: A Survey of Selected MENA Countries', IMF WP 02/17, January.

Ermisch, J. (1996) 'The Demand for Housing in Britain and Population Ageing: Microeconometric Evidence', *Economica*, 63 (251): 383–404.

ERWP (Equity Release Working Party) (2005) *Equity Release Report 2005*, UK: The Actuarial Profession. www.actuaries.org.uk/research-and-resources/documents/equity-release-report-2005-volume-1-main-report (accessed 26 December 2011).

ESRI (2007) *GIS for Retail Business*, Environmental Systems Research Institute, Inc., California, February.

Eurostat RPPI (2011) *Handbook on Residential Property Price Indices*, Draft Version 3.0, January. http://epp.eurostat.ec.europa.eu/portal/page/portal/hicp/documents/Tab/Tab/RPPI_Handbook%20_combined_V3_0.pdf (accessed 7 January 2012).

Evans, A. W. (2009) 'Optimal Taxation Theory and the Taxation of Housing', Report to the Department of Communities and Local Government, Centre for Spatial and Real Estate Research, University of Reading. www.henley.reading.ac.uk/web/FILES/REP/Optimal_Taxation_Theory.pdf (accessed 16 October 2011).

Everhart, S., Heybey, B., and Carleton, P. (2006) 'Egypt: Overview of the Housing Sector', *Housing Finance International*, June.

Ewijk, C. van and Leuvensteijn, M. van (2010) 'Reduce Tax on Residential Mobility'. www.voxeu.org/index.php?q=node/4817 (accessed 15 March 2011).

Feldman, N. E. (2010) 'A Reevaluation of Property Tax Capitalization: The Case of Michigan's Proposal A', www.bus.umich.edu/ConferenceFiles/MTAXI/Feldman.pdf (accessed 7 November 2011).

Fernald, M., ed. (2008) 'The State of the Nation's Housing', Report prepared by the Joint Center for Housing Studies of Harvard University. www.jchs.harvard.edu/publications/markets/son2008/son2008.pdf (accessed 17 November 2011).

Fernald, M., ed. (2011a) 'America's Rental Housing: Meeting Challenges, Building on Opportunities', Report prepared by the Joint Center for Housing Studies of Harvard University. www.jchs.harvard.edu/publications/rental/rh11_americas_rental_housing/AmericasRentalHousing–2011–bw.pdf (accessed 6 August 2011).

Fernald, M., ed. (2011b) 'The State of the Nation's Housing', Report prepared by the Joint Center for Housing Studies of Harvard University. www.jchs.harvard.edu/publications/markets/son2011/son2011.pdf (accessed 29 October 2011).

Fisher, J. D. (1992) 'Integrating Research on Markets for Space and Capital', *Journal of the American Real Estate and Urban Economics Association*, 20 (1): 161–80.

Fisher, J. D. (2005) 'US Commercial Real Estate Indices: the NCREIF Property Index', in Bank for International Settlements (ed.), *Real Estate Indicators and Financial Stability*, 21: 359–67.

Fisher, J. D. and W. N. Kinnard (1990) The Business Enterprise Component of Operating Properties', *Journal of Property Tax Management*, 2 (1): 19–27.

Flatau, P., Forbes, M. Wood, G., Hendershott, P. H., and O'Dwyer, L. (2002) 'Home Ownership and Unemployment: Does the Oswald Thesis Hold for Australian Regions?'. www.mbs.murdoch.edu.au/workingpapers/189.pdf (accessed 15 March 2011).

Fleming, M. C. and Nellis, J. G. (2012) *The Halifax House Price Index – Technical Details*. www.lloydsbankinggroup.com/media/word/HPI/13.08.09TechDetails.doc (accessed 9 January 2012).

Foldvary, F. E. (2006a) 'The Ultimate Tax Reform: Public Revenue from Land Rent', A Civil Society Institute Policy Study, January. www.foldvary.net/works/policystudy.pdf (accessed 23 March 2011).

Foldvary, F. E. (2006b) 'An Austrian Analysis of Real Estate'. www.foldvary.net/works/aare1.html (accessed 28 September 2011).

Foldvary, F. E. (2007) 'Answering the Questions on LVT', *Economic Affairs*, 27 (2): 88–9.

Foldvary, F. E. (2010) 'Arguments Against Land Value Taxation'. www.progress.org/2010/fold687.htm (accessed 7 December 2011).

Foldvary, F. E. (2011) 'Rebuttal to Arguments Against Land Value Taxation'. www.progress.org/2011/fold706.htm (accessed 7 December 2011).

Fortune, C.C., Anthony, J., Moohan, J. (2008) 'International Variations in New Housing Supply', *International Journal of Housing Markets and Analysis*, 1 (4): 379–92.

Fraser, W. D. (1993) *Principles of Property Investment and Pricing*, 2nd edn, Basingstoke, UK: Macmillan.

FRBSF (2007) 'Disentangling the Wealth Effect: Some International Evidence', *FRBSF Economic Letter*, 2, 19 January

Freeman, T. (1995) 'The Sale and Purchase of Mortgage Portfolios', in *The UK Secondary Mortgage Market – Securitisation and Portfolio Sales*, London: Council of Mortgage Lenders, October.

French, N. (1997) 'Commercial Valuation Models: Annual Data in Quarterly Cash Flows', RICS Research, London, Cutting Edge 1997.

FSA (2005) *Raising Money from Your Home*, May.

FSA (2010) *Mortgage Brokers*, October.

FTSE (2007) 'FTSE UK Commercial Property Index Series'. www.ftse.com.

FTSE (2008) *FTSE Indices for Property Derivatives*, FTSE Group.

Fuerst, F. (2006) 'Predictable or Not? Forecasting Office Markets with a Simultaneous Equation Approach', MPRA Paper 5262. http://mpra.ub.uni–muenchen.de/5262/1/MPRA_paper_5262.pdf (accessed 20 February 2011).

Gao, A., Lin, Z., and Na, C. F. (2009) 'Market Dynamics: Evidence of Mean Reversion and Downward Rigidity', *Journal of Housing Economics*, 18 (3): 256–66.

Gabriel, S. A. and Nothaft, F. E. (1988) 'Rental Housing Markets and the Natural Vacancy Rate', *AREUEA Journal*, 16 (4): 419–29.

Galbraith, J. K. (1954) *The Great Crash 1929*, London: Penguin (reprinted 2009).

Gardner, A. and Matysiak, G. (2005) 'Holding Periods and Investment Performance: Analysing UK Office Returns 1983–2003', Henley Business School, University of Reading, Real Estate and Planning WP 31.

Gattis, C. (2010) 'Retail Site Selection for Small Business', February. http://bluepointstrategies.com/uploads/Retail_Site_Selection_for_Small_Business.pdf (accessed 28 February 2011).

Geltner, D. and Pollakowski, H. (2007) 'A Set of Indexes for Trading Commercial Real Estate Based on the Real Capital Analytics Transaction Prices Database', MIT Center for Real Estate, Release 2, 26 September. http://mit.edu/cre/research/credl/rca/MIT-wp-r2.pdf (accessed 27 December 2011).

Gertchev, N. (2007) esearch/credl/rca/MIT-wp-r2.pdfl *Quarterly Journal of Austrian Economics*, 10 (4): 313–29.

Getz, M. (1979) 'Optimum City Size: Fact or Fancy?', *Law and Contemporary Problems*, 43 (2): 197–210.

Gibb, K. (2000) 'Modelling Housing Choice and Demand in a Social Housing System: The Case of Glasgow', Seminar Paper Series SOO-OO1, January, Program on Housing and Urban Policy, Institute of Business and Economic Research, Fisher Center for Real Estate and Urban Economics, University of California, Berkeley.

GIPS (2008) GIPS Guidance Statement on Calculation Methodology, www.gipsstandards.org/standards/guidance/archive/pdf/GSCalcMethRevised.pdf, accessed 18 December 2011.

Gin, A. & Sonstelie, J. (1992) 'The Streecar and Residential Location in Nineteenth Century Philadelphia', *Journal of Urban Economics*, 32: 92–107.

Glaeser, E. L. (2006) 'The Economic Impact of Restricting Housing Supply', Rappaport Institute for Greater Boston, PB-2006-3, May.

Glaeser, E. L. and Gottlieb, J. D. (2010) 'Can Cheap Credit Explain the Housing Boom?'. www.economics.harvard.edu/files/faculty/25_Glaeser_Cheap_Credit.pdf (accessed 5 November 2011).

Glaeser, E. L. and Gyourko, J. (2007) 'Housing Dynamics', Harvard Institute of Economic Research, DP 2137.

Glaeser, E. L., Gyourko, J., and Saiz, A. (2008) 'Housing Supply and Housing Bubbles', *Journal of Urban Economics*, 64 (2): 198–217.

Glaeser, E. L, Gyourko, J., and Saks, R. E. (2005) 'Urban Growth and Housing Supply', NBER WP 11097, January.

Glaeser, E. L., Gyourko, J., and Saks, R. E. (2005) 'Why Have Housing Prices Gone Up?', *The American Economic Review*, 95 (2): 329–33.

Glass, L. D. and Clayton, J. (2009) 'Cap Rates and Real Estate Value Cycles: A Historical Perspective with a Look to the Future', Babson Capital Research Note, June.

GMAC (2005) *Defining and Determining Core and Non-Core Real Estate Investment Strategies*, GMAC Institutional Advisors LLC, January.

Goodhart, C. and Hofmann, B. (2008) 'House Prices, Money, Credit, and the Macroeconomy', *Oxford Review of Economic Policy*, 24 (1): 180–205.

Gottlieb, M. (1976): *Long Swings in Urban Development*. NBER Books, gott76-1.

Gounopoulos, D., Merikas, A. G., Merika, A. A., and Triantafyllou, A. (2012) 'Explaining House Price Changes in Greece', *Applied Financial Economics*, 22 (7): 549–61.

Graaf, T. de and Leuvensteijn, M. van (2007) 'The Impact of housing Market Institutions on Labour Mobility: A European Cross-Country Comparison', European Network of Economic Policy Research Institutes, WP 54/July.

Granger, C. W. J. (2003) *Time Series Analysis, Cointegration, and Applications (The Nobel Lecture)*, Stockholm, Sweden, December. http://nobelprize.org/nobel_prizes/economics/laureates/2003/granger–lecture.pdf (accessed 30 November 2010).

Grebler, L. and Burns, L. (1982) 'Construction cycles in the US since WWII', *Real Estate Economics*, 10 (2): 123–51.

Green, R. K. and Hendershott, P. H. (1999) 'Home Ownership and Unemployment in the US'. www.nmhc.org/Content/ServeFile.cfm?FileID=165 (accessed 15 March 2011).

Green, R. K. and Hendershott, P. H. (2001) 'Home Ownership and the Duration of Unemployment: A Test of the Oswald Hypothesis'. http://cura.osu.edu/research/roundtables/data/hendershott1.pdf (accessed 15 March 2011).

Griliches, Z. (1961) 'Hedonic Price Indexes for Automobiles: An Econometric Analysis of Quality Change', in Stigler, G. (chairman): *The Price Statistics of the Federal Government*, New York: Columbia University Press.

Griliches, Z. (1967) 'Hedonic Price Index Revisited: Some Notes on the State of the Art', *1967 Proceedings of the Business and Economic Statistics Section, American Statistical Association*, pp. 324–32.

Griliches, Z., ed. (1971) *Price Indexes and Quality Change: Studies in New Methods of Measurement*, Cambridge, MA: Harvard University Press.

Grimes, A. and Young, C. (2010) 'A Simple Repeat Sales House Price Index: Comparative Properties Under Alternative Data Generation Processes', Motu WP 10-10, September http://motu-www.motu.org.nz/wpapers/10_10.pdf (accessed 14 January 2012).

Guðnason, R. (2005) 'Market Price and User Cost', Paper presented at OECD Seminar: Inflation Measures: Too High – Too Low – Internationally Comparable?, Paris, 21–22 June. www.oecd.org/dataoecd/54/39/35013825.pdf (accessed 18 July 2011).

Gujarati, D. N. (2003) *Basic Econometrics*, 4th edn, New York: McGraw–Hill.

Gyourko, J. and Sinai, T. (2003) 'The Spatial Distribution of Housing-Related Ordinary Income Tax Benefits', *Real Estate Economics*, 31 (4): 527–75.

Haan, J. de (2009) 'House Price Indexes: Hedonic, Repeat Sales and SPAR Methods', Statistics Netherlands, 15 December.

Haffner, M. E. A. (2008) 'Subsidization as Motor to Residential Mortgage Securitization in the US', *Journal of Housing and the Built Environment*, 23: 337–51.

Halifax (2012) *The Halifax House Price Index*. www.lloydsbankinggroup.com/media/word/HPI/Methodologyfromweb130809.doc (accessed 9 January 2012).

Halvorsen, R. and Pollakowski, H. O. (1981) 'Choice of Functional Form for Hedonic Price Equations', *Journal of Urban Economics*, 10 (1): 37–49.

Hansen, J. (2006) 'Australian House Prices: A Comparison of Hedonic and Repeat-Sales Measures', Reserve Bank of Australia, RDP 2006-03.

Hartwich, O. M. (2006) 'Taxing Land Value is Just Another Questionable Tax', *Economic Affairs*, 26 (4): 61–3.

Hartzell, D. J., Lepcio, A., Fernald, J. D., and Jordan, S. (1987) 'Commercial Mortgage-Backed Securities: An Investor's Primer', *Housing Finance Review*, 6: 169–91.

Harvey, D. (1973): *Social Justice and the City*, London: Hodder & Stoughton.

Haurin, D. R. (2005) 'US Commercial Real Estate Indices: Transaction-Based and Constant-Liquidity Indices', in Bank for International Settlements (ed.), *Real Estate Indicators and Financial Stability*, 21: 232–42.

Head, A. and Lloyd-Ellis, H. (2010) 'Housing Liquidity, Mobility, and the Labour Market', Queen's University, Kingston, Ontario, Economics Department WP 1197.

Heady, C., Johansson, A., Arnold, J., Brys, B., and Vartia, L. (2009) 'Tax Policy for Economic Recovery and Growth', University of Kent, School of Economics Discussion Papers, December. ftp.ukc.ac.uk/pub/ejr/RePEc/ukc/ukcedp/0925.pdf (accessed 29 September 2011).

Helbling, T. and Terrones, M. (2003) 'When Bubbles Burst', Chapter 2 (pp. 61–94) in *World Economic Outlook: Growth and Institutions*, IMF, April.

Hemmelgarn, T., Nicodeme, G., and Zangari, E. (2011) 'The Role of Housing Tax Provisions in the 2008 Financial Crisis', European Commission's Directorate-General for Taxation and Customs Union, WP 27, March.

Hendershott, P. H., Lizieri, C. M., and MacGregor, B. D. (2008) 'Asymmetric Adjustment in the London Office Market', WP in Real Estate and Planning 7, Henley Business School, School of Real Estate and Planning, University of Reading.

Hess, A. C. and Smith, C. W. (1988) 'Elements of Mortgage Securitization', *Journal of Real Estate Finance and Economics*, 1: 331–46.

HFN (Housing Finance Network). www.housing–finance–network.org/.

Hilber, C. A. L., Lyytikäinen, T., and Vermeulen, W. (2011) 'Capitalization of Central Government Grants into Local House Prices: Panel Data Evidence from England', CPB Netherlands Bureau for Economic Policy Analysis, DP 167.

Hilbers, P., Hoffmaister, A. W., and Shi, H. (2008) 'House Price Developments in Europe: A Comparison', IMF WP/08/211, October.

Hildenbrand, W. (2008) 'Aggregation Theory', in Durlauf, S. N. and Blume, L. E., eds, *The New Palgrave Dictionary of Economics*, 2nd edn, Basingstoke, UK: Palgrave Macmillan.

HKMA (Hong Kong Monetary Authority) (2001) 'The property market and the macroeconomy', *HKMA Quarterly Bulletin*, May, pp. 40–9. http://www.info.gov.hk/hkma/eng/public/qb200105/fa02.pdf (accessed 3 February 2011).

Hoek, M. P. van der and Radloff, S. E. (2007) 'Taxing Owner-Occupied Housing: Comparing the Netherlands to Other European Union countries', *Public Finance and Management*, 7 (4): 393–421.

Hoek-Smit, M. C. (2009) 'Housing Subsidies: Who Gets What and Why it Matters', Urban Forum Presentation, The World Bank, March 12.

Hoffmann, M. and Nitschka, T. (2010) 'Securitization of Mortgage Debt, Asset Prices and International Risk Sharing'. www.cepr.org/meets/wkcn/1/1744/papers/Hoffmann.pdf (accessed 31 January 2011).

Holmans, A. (2008) *Prospects for UK Housing Wealth and Inheritance*, Cambridge Centre for Housing and Planning Research, Study commissioned by the CML.

HomeCo (2012) *A Guide to House Price Indices*. www.home.co.uk/guides/house_prices_indices/toc.htm (accessed 4 February 2012).

Hommes, C., Sonnemans, J., Tuinstra, J., and van de Velden, H. (2008) 'Expectations and Bubbles in Asset Pricing Experiments', *Journal of Economic Behavior and Organization*, 67 (1): 116–133.

Hongyu, L., Park, Y. W., and Siqi, Z. (2002) 'The Interaction between Housing Investment and Economic Growth in China', *International Real Estate Review*, 5 (1): 40–60.

Hoover, E. M. & Giarratani, F. (1999) 'An Introduction to Regional Economics', in *The Web Book of Regional Science*, published by the Regional Research Institute, http://rri.wvu.edu/WebBook/Giarratani/contents.htm, accessed 1 Dec. 2011.

Houthakker, H. S. (1952) 'Compensated Changes in Quantities and Qualities Consumed', *The Review of Economic Studies*, 19 (3): 155–64

Hua, C-C, Chang, C-O, Hsieh, C. (2001) The Price–Volume Relationships Between the Existing and the Pre-Sales Housing Markets in Taiwan', *International Real Estate Review*, 4 (1): 80–04.

Huang, H. and Tang, Y. (2010) 'Residential Land Use Regulation and the US Housing Price Cycle Between 2000 and 2009', University of Alberta, Department of Economics, WP 2010–11.

Hudson, M. (2006) 'The New Road to Serfdom: An Illustrated Guide to the Coming Real Estate Collapse', *Harper's Magazine*, May, pp. 39–46.

Hughes, W. T. (1994) 'Determinants of Demand for Industrial Property', *The Appraisal Journal*, 62(2): 303–9.

Huff, D. L. (1964) 'Defining and Estimating a Trade Area', *Journal of Marketing*, 28: 34–8.

Huff, D. L. (2003) 'Parameter Estimation in the Huff Model', *ArcUser*, October–December: 34–6.

Huff, D. L. (2008) 'Calibrating the Huff Model Using ArcGIS Business Analyst', An ESRI White Paper, September.

Hungria–Garcia, R. (2004) 'Property Yields as Tools for Valuation and Analysis', Report 52, Building and Real Estate Economics, Department of Infrastructure, KTH (Swedish Royal Institute of Technology).

Hypostat (2005) *A Review of Europe's Mortgage and Housing Markets*, European Mortgage Federation, November 2006.

Hypostat (2008) *A Review of Europe's Mortgage and Housing Markets*, European Mortgage Federation, November 2009.

Hypostat (2009) *A Review of Europe's Mortgage and Housing Markets*, European Mortgage Federation, November 2010.

Iacobucci, A. (2003) *Spectral Analysis for Economic Time Series*. OFCE, 2003–07, November. www.ofce.sciences-po.fr/pdf/dtravail/wp2003-07.pdf (accessed 27 December 2011).

Ibbotson, R. G. and Siegel, L. B. (1984) 'Real Estate Returns: A Comparison with Other Investments', *Real Estate Economics*, 12 (3): 219–42.

IBRD/World Bank (2008) *Financing Homes*, Washington, DC: World Bank and International Finance Corporation.

IMF (2009) 'Debt Bias and Other Distortions: Crisis-Related Issues in Tax Policy', prepared by the Fiscal Affairs Department, approved by C. Cottarelli, 12 June.

IPD (2004) 'IPD Technical Note: Understanding the Time-Weighted Method of Calculating Investment Performance', Investment Property Databank, August, www.propertynz.co.nz/files/Research/IPD%20Methodology.pdf, accessed 18 December 2011.

IPD (2006) 'Calculating Income Return in the Time-Weighted Methodology', Investment Property Databank, www.ipd.com/LinkClick.aspx?fileticket=s3moBlMT6Qg%3Dandtabid=935andmid=11123, accessed 19 December 2011.

IPD (2009) *The IPD Index Guide Edition Five – September 2009*, Investment Property Databank.

IPD (2011) *IPD Index Guide Edition Seven – December 2011*, Investment Property Databank, www.ipd.com/Portals/1/downloads/indices/index%20guide/index_guide_Edition%207_2011_web.pdf, accessed 19 December 2011.

IPF (2007) *Understanding Commercial Property Investment – A Guide for Financial Advisers*, Investment Property Forum, www.ipf.org.uk/mainwebsite/Resources/Document/ifa_guide_June%2007.pdf (accessed 3 April 2011).

IVG (2003) *International Valuation Guidance Note* No. 2. www.ivsc.org/ (accessed 6 February 2011).

Jacobs, J. (1985) *Cities and the Wealth of Nations: Principles of Economic Life*, Vintage Books.

Jansen, S., De Vries, P., Coolen, H., Lamain, C., and Boelhouwer, P. (2008) 'Developing a House Price Index for the Netherlands: A Practical Application of Weighted Repeat Sales', *Journal of Real Estate Finance and Economics*, 37: 163–86.

Janssen, C., Söderberg, B., and Zhou, J. (2001) 'Robust Estimation of Hedonic Models of Price and Income for Investment Property', *Journal of Property Investment and Finance*, 19 (4): 342–60.

JLL (2010) 'Half Time on the Property Clock as Modest Rental Growth Continues', *Pulse: The Jones Lang LaSalle Property Clock Q4 2010*. www.joneslanglasalle.eu/MediaResources/EU/Research/Property%20Clock%20Q4%202010_FINAL_a.pdf (accessed 23 February 2011).

Jones, C., Leishman, C., and Watkins, C. (2002) 'Examining the Persistence of Housing Submarket Price Differences', Paper presented at the Pacific Rim Real Estate Society Conference, Christchurch, NZ, January.

Jones, J. (2008) 'Land Value … for Public Benefit', Labour Land Campaign. www.labourland.org/downloads/papers/land_value_for_public_benefit.pdf (accessed 28 September 2011).

Jónsdóttir, G. R. and Jónasdóttir, L. G. (2011) 'A Comparison of the SPAR and a Stratified-Model House Price Indices', Paper presented at the 12th Meeting of the International Working Group on the Price Indices (The Ottawa Group), Wellington, New Zealand, 4–6 May.

Joye, C. (2011a) 'A Property Bubble Long Shot', *Business Spectator*, 25 March.

Joye, C. (2011b) 'Disposable House Price Myths', *Business Spectator*, 20 December.

Jud, G. D. and Winkler, D. T. (2003) 'The *Q* Theory of Housing Investment', *Journal of Real Estate Finance and Economics*, 27 (3): 379–92.

Kagarlis, M., Peterson, D., Eberlein, R., Fiddaman, T. (2007) *The Radar Logic Daily^{TM} Index*, 28 March, Ventana Systems Inc. and Radar Logic Inc. www.radarlogic.com (accessed 3 February 2012).

Kahn, J. A. (2008) 'What Drives Housing Prices?' *FRB of New York Staff Papers*, 345, September.

Kain, J. F. and Quigley, J. M. (1970) 'Measuring the Value of Housing Quality', *Journal of the American Statistical Association*, 65: 532–48.

Kaldor, N. (1940) 'A Model of the Trade Cycle', *Economic Journal*, 50: 78–92.

Kalecki, M. (1935) 'A Macroeconomic Theory of Business Cycles', *Econometrica*, 3: 327–344.

Kanaya, A. and Woo, D. (2000) 'The Japanese Banking Crisis of the 1990s: Sources and Lessons', *IMF* WP/00/7.

Kashiwagi, M. (2011) 'Self-Fulfilling Beliefs and Bounded Bubbles in the US Housing Market', European University Institute – Max Weber Programme, Series/Report 2011/08. http://cadmus/eui.eu/handle/1814/17955 (accessed 4 August 2011).

Katsura, H. M. (1984) *Economic Effects of Housing Investment*, Report prepared for the Office of Housing and Urban Programs, US Agency for International Development. http://pdf.usaid.gov/pdf_docs/PNAAU426.pdf (accessed 20 October 2011).

Kau, J. B. and Sirmans, C. F. (1981) 'The Demand for Urban Residential Land' *Journal of Regional Science* 21 (4): 519–28.

Kim, K.-H. and Renaud, B. (2009) 'The Global House Price Boom and its Unwinding: An Analysis and a Commentary', *Housing Studies*, 24 (1): 7–24.

Kindleberger, C. P. (1978) *Manias, Panics and Crashes: A History of Financial Crises*, New York: Wiley, 2000.

Kitchin, R., Gleeson, J., Keaveney, K., and O'Callaghan, C. (2010) 'A Haunted Landscape: Housing and Ghost Estates in Post-Celtic Tiger Ireland', NIRSA WP 59, July.

Klyuev, V. and Mills, P. (2006) 'Is Housing Wealth an "ATM"? The Relationship Between Household Wealth, Home Equity Withdrawal, and Saving Rates', IMF WP 06/162.

Koontz, C. M. (1994) 'Retail Location Theory: Can It Help Solve the Public Library Location Dilemma?', in Greiner, J. M., ed., *Research Issues in Public Librarianship*, Westport, CT: Greenwood Press, pp. 171–81.

Korgel, J. (1997) 'Real Estate and Tobin's *Q* theory', Cutting Edge, RICS.

Kosmopoulou, G., Buttry, N., Johnson, J., and Kallsnick, A. (2007) 'Suburbanization and the Rank-Size Rule', *Applied Economics Letters*, 14 (1): 1–4.

Krishnan, C. N. V., Petkova, R., and Ritchken, P. (2009) 'Correlation Risk', *Journal of Empirical Finance*, 16 (3): 353–67.

Krugman, P. (2005) 'Greenspan and the Bubble', *The New York Times*, 29 August.

Krugman, P. (2011) 'Will China Break?', *The New York Times*, 19 December.

Kummerow, M. and Quaddus, M. (1998): *Office Market Cycles: A System Dynamics Approach to Improve Allocative Efficiency*, Curtin University of Technology, Perth, Western Australia. www.systemdynamics.org/conferences/1998/PROCEED/00062.PDF (accessed 27 December 2011).

Kuran, T. (2010) *The Long Divergence: How Islamic Law Held Back the Middle East*, Princeton, NJ: Princeton University Press.

Laferrère, A. (2005) 'Hedonic Housing Price Indexes: The French Experience', in BIS, ed., *Real Estate Indicators and Financial Stability*, 21: 271–87.

Lancaster, K. J. 1966. 'A New Approach to Consumer Theory', Journal of Political Economy, 74: 132–57.

Leamer, E. E. (2007) 'Housing *is* the Business Cycle', Proceedings, Federal Reserve Bank of Kansas City, pp. 149–233. www.kc.frb.org/publicat/sympos/2007/pdf/leamer_0415.pdf (accessed 15 November 2011).

Lee, S. L. (2003) 'When Does Direct Real Estate Improve Portfolio Performance?', Henley Business School, University of Reading, Real Estate and Planning WP 17.

Lefebvre, H. (1972): *La pensée marxiste et la ville*, Paris: Casterman.

LEK Consulting (2009): *Construction in the UK economy. The Benefits of Investment*, Study commissioned by the UK Contractors Group, October.

Leontief, W. (1986) *Input–Output Economics*, 2nd edn, New York: Oxford University Press.

Lerbs, O. (2010) 'Does Home Ownership Really Cause Unemployment? Evidence from German Regional Data'. http://www.infer-research.net/upload/Does%20home%20ownership%20really%20cause%20unemployment.pdf (accessed 15 March 2011).

Leung, C. K. Y. and Wang, W. (2007): 'An Examination of the Chinese Housing Market through the Lens of the DiPasquale–Wheaton Model: A Graphical Attempt', *International Real Estate Review*, 10 (2): 131–165.

Leuvensteijn, M. van (2000) 'Is Home-Ownership an Impediment to the Labour Market?', A CPB Netherlands Bureau for Economic Policy Report, 2000/4.

Levin, E. J. & Pryce, G. (2009) 'What determines the price elasticity of house supply? Real interest rate effects and cyclical asymmetries', *Housing Studies*, 24 (6): 713–36.

Li, W., Liu, H., and Yao, R. (2009) 'Housing over Time and over the Life Cycle: A Structural Estimation', *FRB of Philadelphia WP,* 09-7, March.

Li, W. and Yao, R. (2007) 'The Life-Cycle Effects of House Price Changes', *Journal of Money, Credit and Banking*, 39 (6): 1375–1409.

Liang, Y. (2006) 'The Anatomy of Vacancy Behavior in the Real Estate Market'. www.reri.org/research/article_pdf/wp145.pdf (accessed 6 August 2011).

Lindberg, L. (2002) 'Property Investment Vehicles: An International Comparison', Division of Building and Real Estate Economics, Department of Infrastructure, Royal Institute of Technology, Stockholm, No. 172.

Lindenthal, Th. (2007) 'Demographic Change and the Demand for Housing; British evidence'. http://arno.unimaas.nl/show.cgi?fid=11469 (accessed 17 July 2011).

Lindenthal, Th. and Eichholtz, P. (2010) 'Demographics, Human Capital, and the Demand for Housing'. http://nilskok.typepad.com/EPRI/EL_WP_2010.pdf (accessed 17 July 2011).

Lindh, Th. and Malmberg, B. (2008) 'Demography and Housing Demand – What Can We Learn from Residential Construction Data?' *Journal of Population Economics*, 21 (3): 521–39.

Lopes, J., Ruddock, L., Ribeiro, F. L. (2002) 'Investment in Construction and Economic Growth in Developing Countries', *Building Research and Information*, 30 (3): 152–9.

Lunde, J. (1997) 'Fifteen Years with Index-Linked Mortgages: Successes and failures', *Journal of Housing and the Built Environment*, 12 (4): 401–22.

McAuslan, P. (2008) Positive Planning: A New Approach to Urban Planning Law in Syria. www.mam-sy.org/userfiles/file/AP9/Urban%20Planning%20a%20New%20Way%20Forward.pdf (accessed 3 August 2011).

McCartney, J. (2010) 'Predicting Turning Points in the Rent Cycle Using the Natural Vacancy Rate – An Applied Study of the Dublin Office Market', Paper read before the Statistical and Social Inquiry Society of Ireland, 2 November www.ssisi.ie/McCartney_SSISI_2–11–10.pdf (accessed 15 February 2011).

McCluskey, W. J., K'akumu, O. A., and Olima, W. H. A. (2005) 'Theoretical Basis of Land Value Taxation', Chapter 1 of W. J. McCluskey and R. C. D. Franzsen, *Land Value Taxation: An Applied Analysis*, Aldershot, UK: Ashgate Publishing. www.ashgate.com/pdf/SamplePages/Land_Value_Taxation_Ch1.pdf (accessed 7 December 2011).

McConnell, C. R., Brue, S. L., and Flynn, S. M. (2009) *Economics*, 18th edn, New York: McGraw-Hill.

McDonald, J. F. (2000) 'Rent, Vacancy and Equilibrium in Real Estate Markets', *Journal of Real Estate Practice and Education*, 3 (1): 55–69.

McDonald, J. F. (1993) 'Incidence of the Property Tax on Commercial Real Estate: The Case of Downtown Chicago', *National Tax Journal*, 46 (2): 109–20.

McDonald, J. and Johnson, S. (2010)' Tax Policies to Improve the Stability of Financial Markets'. www.bancaditalia.it/studiricerche/convegni/atti/FiscalPolicy/Session2/McDonald_Johnson.pdf (accessed 19 November 2011).

McDonald, J. F. and Yurova, Y. (2007) 'Property Taxation and Selling Prices of Industrial Real Estate', *Review of Accounting and Finance*, 6 (3): 273–84.

McGough, T. and Tsolacos, S. (1999) 'Interactions within the Office Market Cycle in Great Britain', *Journal of Real Estate Research*, 18(1): 219–232.

McGough, T. and Tsolacos, S. (2001) 'Do Yields Reflect Property Market Fundamentals?', London, City University Business School, Real Estate Finance and Investment Group, Research Paper 1.

McKibbin, W. and Stoeckel, A. (2006) 'Bursting of the US Housing Bubble'. www.economicscenarios.com/public/pdfredir_sample.asp?issueNo=14 (accessed 13 November 2011).

Maclennan, D. (1982) *Housing Economics*, Harlow, UK: Longman .

Maclennan, D. and Tu, Y. (1996) 'Economic Perspectives on the Structure of Local Housing Systems', *Housing Studies*, 11(3): 387–406.

McMahon, S. (2011) 'Australian House Prices Not Sustainable, says Moody's', *Herald Sun*, 14 December.

McNamara, M. (2009) 'Solving *k*', *Australia and New Zealand Property Journal*, 2 (3): 193–6. www.bates.net.nz/userfiles/file/SOLVING%20K.pdf (accessed 28 March 2011).

Magnus, G. (2011) 'The Dynamics of Prices, Liquidity, and vacancies in the Housing Market', 18 March, http://home.uchicago.edu/gfmagnus/page3/assets/Magnus%20JMP.pdf (accessed 6 August 2011).

Magnusson, C. (2008) 'At Risk – From Credit Crunch to Information Systems', Confederation of Swedish Enterprise, 29 September. http://www.svensktnaringsliv.se/multimedia/archive/00014/At_Risk_From_Credi_14597a.pdf (accessed 6 November 2011).

Mallick, H. and Mahalik, M. K. (2010) Constructing the Economy: The Role of Construction Sector in India's Growth, *Journal of Real Estate Finance and Economics*, 40: 368–84.

Malmberg, B. (2010) 'Low Fertility and the Housing Market: Evidence from Swedish Regional Data' *European Journal of Population*, 26 (2): 229–44.

Malpezzi, S. and Maclennan, D. (2001) 'The Long-Run Price Elasticity of Supply of New Residential Construction in the United States and the United Kingdom', *Journal of Housing Economics*, 10 (3): 278–306.

Malpezzi, S. and Wachter, S. M. (2005) 'The Role of Speculation in Real Estate Cycles', *Journal of Real Estate Literature*, 13 (2): 141–64.

Malzubris, J. (2008) 'Ireland's housing market: bubble trouble', ECFIN Country Focus, 5 (9), 26 September. http://ec.europa.eu/economy_finance/publications/publication13187_en.pdf (accessed 20 December 2011).

Mankiw, N. and Weil, D. (1989) 'The Baby Boom, the Baby Bust, and the Housing Market', *Regional Science and Urban Economics*, 19(2): 235–58.

Mankiw, N. G. (1998) *Principles of Economics*, Oak Brook, IL: The Dryden Press.

Mankiw, N. G., Weinzierl, M., and Yagan, D. (2009) 'Optimal Taxation in Theory and Practice', NBER, WP 15071, June.

Manolopoulos, J. (2011) *Greece's 'Odious' Debt*, London: Anthem Press.

Maré, D. C. (2008) 'Labour Productivity in Auckland Firms', Motu WP 08–12, June.

Mason, B. J. and Mayer, M. L. (1990) Modern Retailing: Theory and Practice, 5th edn, Homewood, IL: BPI-Irwin.

Mauboussin, M. J. (1999) 'Get Real: Using Real Options in Security Analysis', in *Frontiers of Finance*, Vol. 10, Credit Suisse First Boston Corporation, 23 June.

Maxwell, D. and Vigor, A., eds (2005) 'Land Value Tax: worth the Transition?', Institute for Public Policy Research, University of Oxford.

Mayer, C. J. and Tsuriel Somerville, C. (1996): *Unifying Empirical and Theoretical Models of Housing Supply*, WP Series 96, Federal Reserve Bank of Boston.

Meghir, C. (2004) *A Retrospective on Friedman's Theory of Permanent Income*, University College London and The Institute for Fiscal Studies, IFS WP 1.

Meissner, C. and Satchell, S. (2010) 'A Comparison of the Case–Shiller House Price Index Methodology With the Acadametrics House Price Index Methodology', Acadametrics Ltd, London, 8 March. www.acadametricstest.com/Meissner%20Satchell.pdf (accessed 7 January 2012).

Michelsen, C. and Weiß, D. (2009): *What Happened to the East German housing Market? – A Historical Perspective on the Role of Public Funding*, DP 20, Halle Institute for Economic Research.

Miles, D. and Pillonca, V. (2008) 'Financial Innovation and European Housing and Mortgage Markets', *Oxford Review of Economic Policy*, 24 (1): 145–75.

Miller, E. (2008) 'An Assessment of CES and Cobb–Douglas Production Functions', Congressional Budget Office. http://www.cbo.gov/ftpdocs/94xx/doc9497/2008-05.pdf (accessed 26 March 2011).

Miller, N., Peng, L., and Sklarz, M. (2009) 'House Prices and Economic Growth', *Journal of Real Estate Finance and Economics*, DOI 10.1007/s11146-009-9197-8, Published online by Springer Science and Business Media, 11 July 2009.

Mills, E. S. (1967) 'An Aggregative Model of Resource Allocation in a Metropolitan Area', *The American Economic Review*, 57 (2): 197–210.

Mills, E. S. (1972) *Studies in the Structure of the Urban Economy*, The Johns Hopkins Press, Baltimore, Maryland.

Minnesota Housing Finance Agency (2009): *The Economic Impact of Minnesota's Housing Investment*, January. www.mnhousing.gov/idc/groups/secure/documents/admin/mhfa_007814.pdf (accessed 6 February 2011).

MIRAS (2011) Mortgage Interest Relief at Source. en.wikipedia.org/wiki/Mortgage_Interest_Relief_At_Source (accessed 29 January 2011).

Mishkin, F. S. (2010) *The Economics of Money, Banking, and Financial Markets*, 9th edn, Boston: Pearson/Addison-Wesley.

MIT CRE (2011) Moody's/REAL Commercial Property Price Index, 7 November http://mit.edu/cre/research/credl/rca.html (accessed 9 January 2012).

Monk, S., Tang, C. and Whitehead, C. (2010): *What Does the Literature Tell Us About the Social and Economic Impact of Housing?*, Report to the Scottish Government: Communities Analytical Services. Scottish Government, Social Research. www.scotland.gov.uk/Resource/Doc/313646/0099448.pdf (accessed 6 February 2011).

Moody's Analytics (2011) *The Moody's Analytics Case–Shiller Home Price Index Forecast Methodology*. www.economy.com/home/products/samples/case-shiller-methodology.pdf (accessed 23 October 2011).

Morley, S., Fisher, P., and Cooke, H. (2007) 'Pre-Letting of Office Developments: A Guide for Occupiers', London: GVA Grimley.

Mueller, G. R. (1999) 'Real Estate Rental Growth Rates at Different Points in the Physical Market Cycle', *Journal of Real Estate Research*, 18 (1): 131–50.

Muellbauer, J. (1974) 'Household Production Theory, Quality, and the "Hedonic Technique"', *The American Economic Review*, 64 (6): 977–94.

Muellbauer, J. (2005) 'Property Taxation and the Economy After the Barker Review' *The Economic Journal*, 115 (March): 99–117.

Muellbauer, J. (2008) 'Housing, Credit and Consumer Expenditure', CEPR DP 6782, London.

Munro, M. and Karley, N. (2005): *Housing, Financial Services and the Scottish Economy*, CML Research, October

Munro, M. and Maclennan, D. (1987) 'Intra-Urban Changes in Housing Prices: Glasgow 1972–83', *Housing Studies*, 2 (2): 65–81.

Murty, M. N., Gulati, S. C., and Banerjee, A. (2004) 'Measuring Benefits from Reduced Air Pollution in the Cities of Delhi and Kolkata in India Using Hedonic Property Prices Model', Institute of Economic Growth, Delhi University Enclave. http://iegindia.org/workpap/wp249.pdf (accessed 28 December 2011).

Musole, M. (2000): '*Probing the Existence of Building Cycles in Developing Countries: The Zambian Case*', paper presented at the RICS' Cutting Edge Research Conference, London, 6–8 September.

Musson, A. E. (1959) 'The Great Depression in Britain, 1873–1896: A Reappraisal', *The Journal of Economic History*, 19 (2): 199–228.

Muth, R. F. (1960) 'The Demand for Non-Farm Housing', in A. C. Harberger, ed., *The Demand for Durable Goods*, Chicago: University of Chicago Press.

Muth, R. F. (1966) 'Household Production and Consumer Demand Functions', *Econometrica*, 34, July: 699–708.

Muth, R. F. (1969) *Cities and Housing: The Spatial Pattern of Urban Residential Land Use*, Chicago: University of Chicago Press.

Muth, R. F. (1971) 'The Derived Demand for Urban Residential Land', *Urban Studies* 8 (3): 243–54.

Nakanishi, M. and Cooper, L. G. (1982) 'Simplified Estimation Procedures for MCI Models', *Marketing Science*, 1 (3): 314–22.

Nakaso, H. (2001) 'The Financial Crisis in Japan during the 1990s: How the Bank of Japan Responded and the Lessons Learnt', BIS Papers 6, October.

National Statistician (2010) *National Statistician's Review of House Price Statistics*, UK Government Statistical Service, December.

Nationwide (2012) *Nationwide House Price Index Methodology*. www.nationwide.co.uk/hpi/Nationwide_HPI_Methodology.pdf (accessed 9 January 2012).

NERA (2009) 'Study of the Impact of Securitization on Consumers, Investors, Financial Institutions and the Capital Markets', commissioned by the American Securitization Forum, June 17. www.americansecuritization.com/uploadedFiles/ASF_NERA_Report.pdf (accessed 30 January 2011).

Nesheim, L. (2006) 'Hedonic Price Functions', Institute for Fiscal Studies, Department of Economics, UCL, cemmap (Centre for Microdata Methods and Practice) WP CWP 18/06.

Netzer, D. (2001) 'What Do We Need to Know About Land Value Taxation?', *American Journal of Economics and Sociology*, 60 (5): 97–118.

O'Sullivan, A., Sexton, T. A., Sheffrin, S. M. (1995) *Property Taxes and Tax Revolts: The Legacy of Proposition 13*, Cambridge: Cambridge University Press.

O'Toole, R. (2009) 'How Urban Planners Caused the Housing Bubble', *Policy Analysis* No. 646, Cato Institute, October.

Oates, W. E. (1969) 'The Effects of Property Taxes and Local Public Spending on Property Values: An Empirical Study of Tax Capitalization and the Tiebout Hypothesis', *Journal of Political Economy*, 77 (6): 957–71.

OECD (2005) Recent House Price Developments: The Role of Fundamentals, OECD Economic Outlook 78. www.oecd.org/dataoecd/41/56/35756053.pdf (accessed 29 October 2011).

OECD (2011) 'Housing and the Economy: Policies for Renovation', Chapter 4 in *Economic Policy Reforms 2001 – Going for Growth*, OECD, Paris.

Oregon (2003) *Appraisal Methods*. www.oregon.gov/DOR/PTD/docs/303-415/303-415-03.pdf?ga=t (accessed 12 January 2012).

Oswald, A. J. (1997) 'The Missing Piece of the Unemployment Puzzle: An Inaugural Lecture'. www2.warwick.ac.uk/fac/soc/economics/staff/academic/oswald/inaugura.pdf (accessed 15 March 2011).

Oswald, A. J. (1999) 'The Housing Market and Europe's Unemployment: A Non-Technical Paper', www2.warwick.ac.uk/fac/soc/economics/staff/academic/oswald/homesnt.pdf (accessed 15 March 2011).

Ottensmann, J. R., Payton, S., Man, J. (2008) 'Urban Location and Housing Prices within a Hedonic Model', *The Journal of Regional Analysis & Policy*, 38 (1): 19–35.

Oxley, M. and Haffner, M. (2010) 'Housing taxation and subsidies: international comparisons and the options for reform', Joseph Rowntree Foundation programme paper: Housing Market Taskforce. http://www.jrf.org.uk/sites/files/jrf/housing-taxation-systems-full.pdf (accessed 22 October 2011).

Pacheco, L. M. and Barata, J. M. (2005) 'Residential and Stock Market Effects on Consumption across Europe', *European Journal of Housing Policy*, 5 (3): 255–78.

Pagourtzi, E., Assimakopoulos, V., Hatzichristos, T., and French, N. (1999) 'Real Estate Appraisal: a Review of Valuation Methods', *Journal of Property Investment and Finance*, 21 (4): 383–401.

Palameta, B. and Macredie, I. (2005) 'Property Taxes Relative to Income', *Perspectives on Labour and Income*, Statistics Canada, 22 March, pp. 14–24, www.statcan.gc.ca/pub/75-001-x/10305/7796-eng.pdf (accessed 27 December 2011).

Pearson, J. (2007) 'A Comparative Business Site-Location Feasibility Analysis Using Geographic Information Systems and the Gravity Model', *Papers in Resource Analysis*, Vol. 9, St Mary's University of Minnesota Central Services Press. www.gis.smumn.edu/gradprojects/pearsonj.pdf (accessed 27 February 2011).

Perez, C. (2003) *Technological Revolutions and Financial Capital: The Dynamics of Bubbles and Golden Ages*, Cheltenham, UK: Edward Elgar Publishing.

Peston, R. (1991) 'Cosmetic Change May Have Harmful Side Effects', *Financial Times*, 4 October.

Phang, S.-Y, Kim, K.H., and Wachter, S. (2010) 'Supply Elasticity of Housing', Singapore Management University, Research Collection School of Economics, paper 1253. http://ink.library.smu.edu.sg/soe_research/1253 (accessed 23 October 2011).

Philip Davis, E. and Zhu, H. (2004): 'Bank Lending and Commercial Property Cycles: Some Cross-Country Evidence', BIS WP 150.

PIA (Property Industry Alliance) (2010) *Property Data Report 2010*, Prepared by Paul Mitchell Real Estate Consultancy Ltd, July. www.bpf.org.uk/en/files/reita/reita_org_documents/BPF_PIA_property_data_web.pdf (accessed 7 April 2011).

Piazzesi, M., Schneider, M., and Tuzel, S. (2007) 'Housing, consumption and asset pricing', *Journal of Financial Economics,* 83: 531–69.

Platis, S. and Nerouppos, M. (2005) 'Asking Price and Transaction–Based Indices for the Cyprus Housing Market'. www.buysellcyprus.com or www.splatisecon.com (accessed 9 January 2012).

Posen, A. (2009) 'Finding the Right Tool for Dealing with Asset Price Booms', speech to the MPR Monetary Policy and the Economy Conference, London, 1 December. www.iie.com/publications/papers/posen1209.pdf (accessed 28 September 2011).

Poterba, J. (1984) 'Tax Subsidies to Owner–Occupied Housing: An Asset–Market Approach', *Quarterly Journal of Economics*, 99 (4): 729–52.

Poterba, J. M. (1992) 'Taxation and Housing Markets', in Shoven, J. B. and Whalley, J., eds, *Canada–US Tax Comparisons*, Chicago: University of Chicago Press, pp. 275–94. www.nber.org/chapters/c7486.pdf (accessed 7 November 2011).

Poterba, J. and Sinai, T. (2008) 'Income Tax Provisions Affecting Owner–Occupied Housing: Revenue, Costs and Incentive Effects', NBER WP 14253.

PREA (2011) *Compendium of Statistics*, Pension Real Estate Association, 1 April.

PRUPIM Research (2010) *Natural Vacancy Rates*. London: Prudential Property Investment Managers Ltd. www.prupim.com/site/media/documents/3230_Natural_Vacancy_Rates.pdf (accessed 20 February 2011).

Pryce, G. and Evans, G. (2007) *Identifying Submarkets at the Sub-Regional Level in England*, University of Glasgow. www.communities.gov.uk/documents/planningandbuilding/pdf/identifyingsubmarkets.pdf (accessed 27 December 2011).

Pyhrr, S.A., Roulac, S. E., and Born, W. L (1999) 'Real Estate Cycles and Their Strategic Implications for Investors and Portfolio Managers in the Global Economy', *Journal of Real Estate Research*, 18 (1): 7–68.

Quang Do, A. and Sirmans, C. F. (1994) 'Residential Property Tax Capitalization: Discount Rate Evidence from California', *National Tax Journal*, 47 (2): 341–8.

Quigley, J. M. (1995) 'A Simple Hybrid Model for Estimating Real Estate Price Indexes', *Journal of Housing Economics*, 4 (1): 1–12

Quigley, J. M. (2002) 'Transaction Costs and Housing Markets', WP WO2-005, February, Program on Housing and Urban Policy, Institute of Business and Economic Research, Fisher Center for Real Estate and Urban Economics, University of California, Berkeley.

Quigley, J. M. (2007) 'Just Suppose: Housing Subsidies for Low-Income Renters', Report prepared for Revisiting Rental Housing: A National Policy Summit, November 2006.

Quigley, J. M. (2008): *Urbanisation, Agglomeration, and Economic Development*, International Bank for Reconstruction and Development/The World Bank, on behalf of the Commission on Growth and Development, WP 19.

Raa, T. ten (2006) *The Economics of Input–Output Analysis*, Cambridge: Cambridge University Press.

Rabianski, J. S. and Black, R. T. (1997) 'Why Analysts Often Make Wrong Estimates about the Demand for Industrial Space', *Real Estate Review*, 27 (1): 68–72.

Rajapakse, P. J. (2005) 'Residential Mortgage Securitisation: The Australian Perspective', *Global Jurist Topics*, 5 (3): Art. 1, The Berkeley Electronic Press.

Rama, I. and Lawrence, P. (2009): *Partial Multipliers: When More Is Less*. Economics and Policy Research Branch, Policy and Strategy Group, Victorian Department of Primary Industries. www.agrifood.info/connections/2009/Rama_Lawrence.html (accessed 6 February 2011).

Rappaport, J. (2007) 'A Guide to Aggregate House Price Measures', *Economic Review*, Q II: 41–71, FRB of Kansas City.

Reeve, A. (1986) *Property*, Basingstoke, UK: Macmillan.

Regenesis Consulting and Oxford Economics (2010) *The Role of Housing in the Economy*, A report commissioned by the Homes and Communities Agency. http://hcaadmin.com/public/documents/Housing_Investment_and_the_Economy.pdf (accessed 20 October 2011).

Reilly, W. J. (1931) *The Laws of Retail Gravitation*, New York: Knickerbocker Press.

Reinhart, C. M. and Rogoff, K. S. (2008) 'This Time is Different: A Panoramic View of Eight Centuries of Financial Crises'. www.nber.org/~wbuiter/cr1.pdf (accessed 17 November 2011).

Renaud, B. (1997) 'The 1985 to 1994 Global Real Estate Cycle: An Overview', *Journal of Real Estate Literature*, 5 (1): 13–44.

Robb, C. (2011) 'Don't Let Nimbys Pull Up the Housing Ladder', *The Guardian*, 15 September. www.guardian.co.uk/commentisfree/2011/sep/15/nimbys-housing-ladder-crisis-homeowners (accessed 20 November 2011).

Roberts, L. (2008) *The Great Housing Bubble: Why Did House Prices Fall?*, Monterey, CA: Cypress Publishing.

Roberts, M. and Sobolik, M. (2010) 'Why US Core Real Estate?', *Investment Perspective*, Invesco Real Estate, August. www.institutional.invesco.com/portal/file/invescoinst/pdf/II-RECRE-IVP-1-E%5B1%5D.pdf (accessed 5 April 2011).

Robinson, R. (1979) *Housing Economics and Public Policy*, Basingstoke, UK: Macmillan.

Romer, C. and Bernstein, J. (2009): *The Job Impact of the American Recovery and Reinvestment Plan*. otrans.3cdn.net/ee40602f9a7d8172b8_ozm6bt5oi.pdf (accessed 6 February 2011).

Ronald, R. (2006) 'Characterizing East Asian Home Ownership: Examining the Significance of Diversity in Housing Systems', *Housing Finance International*, March: 3–11.

Rosen, S. (1974) 'Hedonic Prices and Implicit Markets: Product Differentiation in Pure Competition', *Journal of Political Economy*, 82: 34–55.

Rossi-Hansberg, E. & Wright, M. L. J. (2007) 'Urban Structure and Growth', *Review of Economic Studies*, 74: 597–624.

Rouwendal, J. and Nijkamp, P. (2007) 'Homeownership and Labour Market Behaviour: Interpreting the Evidence', Tinbergen Institute DP TI 2007 – 047/3.

Roy, A. G., Anderson, J. E., Schmidt, J. R. (2006) 'Housing Tax Deductions and Single-Family Housing Demand', *International Journal of Applied Economics*, 3 (2): 48–64.

RREEF (2007) 'The Future Size of the Global Real Estate Market', RREEF Research, July.

RREEF (2008) *A Perspective on Residential Land Invest*ment, RREEF Research, 65, May.

RREEF (2010a) 'Global Real Estate Insights 2010', RREEF Research, February.

RREEF (2010b) 'The Return to Core: Back to Basics', RREEF Research, April.

Russell, B. (1946) *History of Western Philosophy*, 4th impression, London: George Allen & Unwin.

Saarimaa, T. (2008) 'Imputed Rental Income, Taxation and Income Distribution in Finland', VATT DP 446, Government Institute for Economic Research, Finland.

Sanderson, B., Farrelly, K., and Thoday, C. (2006) 'Natural Vacancy Rates in Global Office Markets', *Journal of Property Investment and Finance*, 24 (6): 490–520.

Sarioglu, G. P., Pellenbarg, P. H., Terpstra, P. R. A., and Balamir, M. (2007) 'Rented and Owner-Occupied Housing: A Descriptive Study for Two Countries – Turkey and the Netherlands', Paper presented at the ENHR International Conference, 25–28 June, Rotterdam.

Scanlon, K. and Lunde, J. (2007) 'Product Development in European mortgage Markets: More Choice, More Risk', Paper presented at the ENHR International Conference, 25–28 June, Rotterdam.

Scanlon, K. and Whitehead, C. (2004) *International Trends in Housing Tenure and Mortgage Finance*, London: Council of Mortgage Lenders.

Schlatterer, M. and Linsin, J. (2008) *Residential Market Germany*, CB Richard Ellis Special Report.

Schulmerich, M. (2010) 'Stock Market Crashes and Financial Bubbles: What History Tells Us', SSgA Capital Insights.

Schumpeter, J. A. (1939) *Business Cycles: A Theoretical, Historical, and Statistical Analysis of the Capitalist Process*, Eastford, CT: Martino Publishing (reprinted 2005).

Schulz, R. and Werwatz, A. (2005) 'Real Estate Valuation and Tobin's *Q*: An Empirical Analysis'. www.socialpolitik.de/tagungshps/2005/Papers/Werwatz.pdf (accessed 6 February 2011).

Schwartz, M. and Wilson, E. (2008) 'Who Can Afford to Live in a Home? A Look at Data from the 2006 American Community Survey'. www.census.gov/hhes/www/housing/special-topics/files/who-can-afford.pdf (accessed 29 October 2011).

Segal, D. B. (1999) 'Retail Trade Area Analysis', *Journal of Database Marketing*, 6 (3): 267–77.

Shaheen, T. (2011) 'The Burst of Spain's Property Bubble', *The Olive Press*, 21 January 2011. www.theolivepress.es/spain-news/2011/01/21/the-burst-of-spains-property-bubble/accessed 18 January 2012.

Shenk, M. (2008) 'Home Price Indexes', *Economic Trends*, FRB of Cleveland, March, pp. 18–9.

Shi, S. (2008) 'Evaluating a House Price Index Based on the Sale Price Appraisal Ratio (SPAR) Method', Department of Economics and Finance, Massey University, New Zealand.

Shiller, R. J. (1991) 'Arithmetic Repeat Sales Price Estimators', *Journal of Housing Economics*, 1 (1): 110–26.

Shiller, R. J. (2005) *Irrational Exuberance*, 2nd edn, Princeton, NJ: Princeton University Press.

Shimizu, C., Nishimura, K. G., and Watanabe, T. (2010) 'Housing Prices in Tokyo: A Comparison of Hedonic and Repeat Sales Measures', JSPS Grants-in-Aid for Creative Scientific Research, Understanding Inflation Dynamics of the Japanese Economy, WP Series 62.

Shorett, P. K., Briscoe, R. J., and Andrews, J. (2007) *Seattle Office Market Analysis*, Seattle: GVA Kidder Mathews. www.bomaseattle.org/files/GVA%20Seattle%20Office%20Market%20Analysis%20_2007%20May_.pdf (accessed 19 February 2011).

Sieg, H. (2011) 'Land Prices, Transportation Technologies, and the Spatial Distribution of Workers in a City', http://www.sas.upenn.edu/~holgers/urban/muth_mills.pdf, accessed 6 Dec. 2011.

Sierminska, E., Brandolini, A., and Smeeding, T. M. (2006) 'Comparing Wealth Distribution Across Rich Countries: First Results From the Luxembourg Wealth Study', *Luxembourg Wealth Study WP Series* 1. http://ssrn.com/abstract=927402.

Sierminska, E. and Takhtamanova, Y. (2007) 'Wealth Effects out of Financial and Housing Wealth: Cross Country and Age Group Comparisons' *FRB of San Francisco WP Series* 1.

Silos, P. (2005) 'Housing Tenure and Wealth Distribution in Life-Cycle Economies', Federal Reserve Bank of Atlanta, WP 25.

Sinclair, S. (2010) 'FSA Decides Against All-Advised Mortgage Market'. www.ifaonline.co.uk/ifaonline/news/1898272/fsa–decides–advised–mortgage–market (accessed 31 January 2011).

Sirmans, S. G., Gatzlaff, D. H., and Macpherson, D. A. (2008) 'The History of Property Tax Capitalization in Real Estate', *Journal of Real Estate Literature*, 16 (3): 327–44.

Sivitanides, P. S. (2011) 'Cap Rates and Interest Rates'. www.property-investing.org/cap-rates.html (accessed 6 April 2011).

Sivitanides, P., Southard, J., Torto, R. G., and Wheaton, W. C. (2001) 'The Determinants of Appraisal-Based Capitalization Rates', *Real Estate Finance* 18 (2), 27–37.

Sivitanides, P. S., Torto, R. G., and Wheaton, W. C. (2003) 'Real Estate Market Fundamentals and Asset Pricing', *The Journal of Portfolio Management*, Special Issue, pp. 45–53.

Sivitanidou, R. and Sivitanides, P. (1999) 'Office Capitalization Rates: Real Estate and Capital Market Influences', *Journal of Real Estate Finance and Economics*, 18 (3): 297–322.

Skinner, J. (1993) 'Is Housing Wealth a Sideshow?', *NBER WP* 4552, NBER.

Slacalek, J. (2009) 'What Drives Personal Consumption? The Role of Housing and Financial Wealth', European Central Bank, WP Series 1117, November.

Sloman, J. (1991) *Economics*, Hemel Hempstead, UK: Harvester Wheatsheaf/Prentice Hall.

Smith, V. L., Suchanek, G. L., and Williams, A. W. (1988) 'Bubbles, Crashes, and Endogenous Expectations in Experimental Spot Asset Markets', *Econometrica*, 56 (5): 1119–51.

Söderberg, B. and Janssen, C. (2001) 'Estimating Distance Gradients for Apartment Properties', *Urban Studies*, 38 (1): 61–79

Soo, K. T. (2005) 'Zipf's Law for Cities: A Cross Country Investigation', *Regional Science and Urban Economics*, 35 (3): 239–63.

Soos, P. (2011) 'Blowing away the bubble deniers', *Business Spectator*, 16 December.

Sorensen, J. K. (2006) 'The Dynamics of House Prices: International Evidence', MPRA Paper 10253, University Library of Munich, Germany.

Sousa, R. M. (2009) 'Wealth Effects on Consumption. Evidence from the Euro Area', European Central Bank, WP Series 1050, May.

Standard & Poor's (2009) *S&P/Case–Shiller Home Price Indices – Index Methodology*, November. www.standardandpoors.com (accessed 7 January 2012).

Stantec Consulting Ltd (2003) *City of Windsor Annexed Area Master Plan Study: Housing Demand Analysis*, Prepared for the Corporation of the City of Windsor, Windsor, ON, Canada. www.citywindsor.ca/documents/D002114003Res.pdf (accessed 19 June 2011).

Statman, M. (1982) 'Fixed Rate or Index-Linked Mortgages from the Borrower's Point of View: A Note', *Journal of Financial and Quantitative Analysis*, 17: 451–7.

Storper, M. (2010) 'Why Does a City Grow? Specialization, Human Capital, or Institutions?', *Urban Studies*, 47 (10): 2027–50.

Storper, M., Agnew, J., Scott, A. J., Soja, E. W. (2001) 'Global City Regions: An Overview', in A. Scott, (ed.), *Global City-Regions: Trends, Theory, Policy*, Oxford Univesity Press, Oxford, pp. 11–30.

Straszheim, M. R. (1975) *An Econometric Analysis of the Urban Housing Market*, NBER, Urban and Regional Studies No. 2.

Swiss Re (2008) 'Innovative Ways of Financing Retirement', *Sigma*, 4.

Syz, J., Vanini, P., and Salvi, M. (2006) 'Property Derivatives and Index-Linked Mortgages'. www.landecon.cam.ac.uk/research/reuag/maastricht/pdf/8_Vanini-Salvi.pdf (accessed 29 January 2011).

Szydlowski, M. and Krawiec, A. (2001) 'The Kaldor–Kalecki Model of Business Cycle as a Two-Dimensional Dynamic System', *Journal of Nonlinear Mathematical Physics*, 8 (Suppl.): 266–71.

TEGoVA (2002) *European Mortgage Securitisation: A Valuer's Guide*, Published by TEGoVA (The European Group of Valuers' Associations) with the assistance of the Verband Deutscher Hypothekenbanken (Association of German Mortgage Banks), Brussels, November.

Teranet–National Bank (2007) *The Teranet–National Bank House Price Index™*. www.housepriceindex.ca/documents/MethodologyEN.pdf (accessed 3 February 2012).

The Economist (1978) 'The New Leviathans – Property and the Financial Institutions: A Survey', 10 June.

The Economist (1987) 'Does Britain Need Mortgage-Backed Securities?', 10 October, p. 85.

The Economist (2003) 'Close to Bursting: A Survey of Property', 31 May.

The Economist (2005) 'In Come the Waves: The Global Housing Boom', Special Report, 18 June, pp. 52–4.

The Economist (2010) 'Repent at Leisure: A Special Report on Debt', 26 June.

The Economist (2011a) 'Hong Kong Phew-Whee', 3 March.

The Economist (2011b) 'Bricks and Slaughter: A Special Report on Property', 5 March.

The Economist (2011c) 'Hunting the Rich', 24 September.

The Economist (2011d) 'House of Horrors, Part 2', 26 November.

The Economist (2011e) 'Lessons of the 1930s: There Could Be Trouble Ahead', 10 December, pp. 68–70.

Thwaites, G. and Wood, R. (2003) 'The Measurement of House Prices', *Bank of England Quarterly Bulletin*, Spring, pp. 38–46.

Tiebout, C. (1956): 'A Pure Theory of Local Expenditures', *Journal of Political Economy* 64 (5): 416–24.

Titman, S. (1985) 'Urban Land Prices Under Uncertainty', *American Economic Review,* 75 (3): 505–514.

Tobin, J. and Brainard, W. C. (1976) 'Asset Markets and the Cost of Capital', Cowles Foundation Paper 440, Reprinted from *Private Values and Public Policy, Essays in Honor of William Fellner*, Amsterdam: North-Holland, 1977.

Tomura, H. (2008) 'A Model of Housing Boom and Bust in a Small Open Economy', WP 9, Monetary and Financial Analysis Department, Bank of Canada.

Triplett, J. E. (2004) 'Handbook on Hedonic Indexes and Quality Adjustments in Price Indexes: Special Application to Information Technology Products', OECD DSTI WP 9, 8 October, OECD Publishing.

Tse, R. Y. C. and Ganesan, S. (1997) 'Causal Relations Between Construction Flows and GDP: Evidence from Hong Kong', *Construction Management and Economics*, 15: 371–6.

Tsolacos, S., McGough, T., Thompson, B. (1999) 'Affordability and Performance in the Industrial Property Market', *Journal of Property Investment and Finance*, 23 (4): 311–28.

Tsolacos, S. and Thompson, B. (2001) 'Industrial Land Values – A Guide to Future Markets?', *Journal of Real Estate Research*, 21 (1/2): 55–76.

Tsoodle, L. J. and Turner, T. M. (2008) 'Property Taxes and Residential Rents', *Journal of Real Estate Economics*, 36 (1): 63–80.

Tsounta, E. (2011) 'Home Sweet Home: Government's Role in Reaching the American Dream', IMF WP/11/191.

UN ESCAP (1997) *Urban Land Policies for the Uninitiated.* www.unescap.org/huset/land_policies/index.htm (accessed 8 May 2011).

van den Noord, P. (2003) 'Tax Incentives and House Price Volatility in the Euro Area: Theory and Evidence', OECD Economics Department WP 356, OECD Publishing. doi.org/10.1787/410243688730 (accessed 27 December 2011).

van der Hoek, M. P. and Radloff, S. E. (2007) 'Taxing Owner-Occupied Housing: Comparing the Netherlands to Other European Union Countries', MPRA Paper 5876. http://mpra.ub.uni-muenchen.de/5876/ (accessed 7 October 2011).

Valenduc, Ch., Haulotte, S., and Deloderre, E. (2011) *Tax Survey 23*, Research and Information Department, Federal Public Service Finance, Belgium.

Vass, J. (2008) *Equity Release*, Booklet sponsored by FSA, May.

Viezer, T. W. (1999): 'Econometric Integration of Real Estate's Space and Capital Markets', *Journal of Real Estate Research*, 18 (3): 503–519.

Vries, P. de, Haan, J. de, Wal, E. van der, and Mariën, G. (2009) 'A House Price Index Based on the SPAR Method', *Journal of Housing Economics*, 18 (3): 214–23.

Wakker, P. P. (2008) 'Explaining the Characteristics of the Power (CRRA) Utility family', *Health Economics* 17: 1329–44.

Wallace, N. E. (1996) 'Hedonic-Based Price Indexes for Housing: Theory, Estimation, and Index Construction', *Economic Review*, 3 (3): 34–48,

Walsh, P. (1995) 'Recent Development in the Sterling Mortgage-Backed Securities Market', in *The UK Secondary Mortgage Market – Securitisation and Portfolio Sales*, London: Council of Mortgage Lenders, October.

Warnock, V. C. and Warnock F. E. (2008) 'Markets and Housing Finance', *Journal of Housing Economics*, doi:10.1016/j.jhe.2008.03.001.

Waugh, F. V. (1928) 'Quality Factors Influencing Vegetable Prices', *Journal of Farm Economics*, 10 (2): 185–96.

WFA (2010) 'A guide to investing in private equity and private real estate funds', Wells Fargo Advisors. https://saf.wellsfargoadvisors.com/emx/dctm/Marketing/Marketing_Materials/Equities/e6549.pdf (accessed 6 April 2011).

Wheaton, W. C. (1977) 'Income and Urban Residence: An Analysis of the Consumer Demand for Location', *American Economic Review*, 67 (4): 620–31.

Wheaton, W. C. (1987) 'The Cyclic Behavior of the National Office Market', *AREUEA Journal*, 15: 281–99.

Wheaton, W. C. (1990) 'Vacancy, Search, and Prices in a Housing Market Matching Model', *The Journal of Political Economy*, 98 (6): 1270–92.

Wheaton, W. C. (1999) 'Real Estate "Cycles": Some Fundamentals', *Real Estate Economics*, 27 (2): 209–30.

Wheaton, W. C. and Nechayev, G. (2006) 'Past Housing "Cycles" and the Current Housing "Boom": What's Different This Time?', March 14. http://econ-www.mit.edu/files/1760 (accessed 5 August 2011).

Wheaton, W. C. and Nechayev, G. (2009) 'US Residential Investment: A Sleeping Giant'. http://web.mit.edu/cre/research/pdf/wheaton-nechayev_sleeping-giant_12-29-09.pdf (accessed 19 October 2011).

Wheaton, W. C. and Torto, R. G. (1990) 'An Investment Model of the Demand and Supply For Industrial Real Estate', *Real Estate Economics*, 18(4): 530–47.

Wheaton, W. C., Torto, R. G., and Evans, P. (1997) 'The Cyclic Behavior of the Greater London Office Market', *Journal of Real Estate Finance and Economics*, 15 (1): 77–92.

White, E. N. (1990) 'The Stock Market Boom and Crash of 1929 Revisited', *Journal of Economic Perspectives*, 4 (2): 67–83.

White, L. J. (2004) 'Mortgage-Backed Securities: Another Way to Finance Housing', paper prepared for the Joint Congress of UN–HABITAT and the European Federation of Building Societies, Berlin, 22–24 September. www.stern.nyu.edu/eco/wkpapers/mortgagebacked.pdf (accessed 30 January 2011).

Whitehead, C. M. E. (1974): *The UK Housing Market: An Econometric Model*, Farnborough, UK: Saxon House.

Wightman, A. (2010) 'A Land Value Tax for Scotland: Fair, Efficient, Sustainable', Report commissioned by the Scottish Green Party, October.

Wigren, R. and Wilhelmsson, M. (2007): 'Housing Stock and Price Adjustments in 12 West European Countries Between 1976 and 1999', *Housing, Theory and Society*, 24 (2): 133–54.

Wolswijk, G. (2006) 'Determinants of Mortgage Debt Growth in EU Countries', *European Journal of Housing Policy*, 6 (2): 131–49.

Worzala, E. and Sirmans, C. F. (2003) 'Investing in International Real Estate Stocks: A Review of the Literature', *Urban Studies*, 40 (5–6): 1115–49.

WSDR (2010) 'Personal Property Tax', Washington State Department of Revenue. October. http://dor.wa.gov/docs/pubs/prop_tax/persprop.pdf (accessed 25 September 2011).

Wu, F. (2002) 'Georeferencing Social Spatial Data and Intra-Urban Property Price Modelling in a Data-Poor Context: The Case Study for Shanghai', in Kidner, D., Higgs, G., and White, S., eds, *Socio–Economic Applications of Geographic Information Science*, London: Taylor & Francis, pp. 163–70.

Wulff, M. and Low, N. (2004) 'Did the Houses Save the World? International Perspectives', *Urban Policy and Research*, 22 (1): 5–11, March.

Xiangguo, Li (2005) 'On the Securitization of Housing Mortgage Loans', *Canadian Social Science*, 1 (1): 34–8.

Yang, J., Zhou Y., and Leung, W. K. (2011) 'Asymmetric Correlation and Volatility Dynamics Among Stock, Bond, and Securitized Real Estate Markets', *Journal of Real Estate Finance and Economics*. www.springerlink.com/content/p2tl82545254u250/ (accessed 6 April 2011).

Yinger, J. (2005) 'Property Tax Capitalization', Chapter 5.4 of *Housing and Commuting: The Theory of Urban Residential Structure*, Version 1.4 of an e-book published in December 2006. http://faculty.maxwell.syr.edu/jyinger/ebooks/housing_commuting/ch_5.4.pdf (accessed 27 September 2011).

Yrigoyen, C. C. and Otero, J. V. (1998) 'Spatial Interaction Models Applied to the Design of Retail Trade Areas'. http://econpapers.repec.org/paper/wiwwiwrsa/ersa98p81.htm (accessed 28 February 2011).

Zhu, H. (2002) 'The Case of the Missing Commercial Real Estate Cycle', *BIS Quarterly Review*, September.

Zodrow, G. (2006) 'Who Pays the Property Tax?', *Land Lines*, 18 (2).

Index